FIFTH · EDITION

EDUCATING EXCEPTIONAL CHILDREN

Samuel A. Kirk
University of Arizona

James J. Gallagher
University of North Carolina

HOUGHTON MIFFLIN COMPANY · BOSTON
Dallas   Geneva, Illinois   Lawrenceville, New Jersey   Palo Alto

The authors would like to dedicate this edition to the many, often anonymous, colleagues who pioneered the education of exceptional children in the nineteenth and early twentieth centuries.

Cover photograph by James Scherer.
Sailboat: Courtesy of The Toy Store of Concord, Concord, MA

Chapter-opening photo credits: Chapter 1, p. 3, Don Ivers/Jeroboam; Chapter 2, p. 35, Terry McKoy/The Picture Cube; Chapter 3, p. 69, Elizabeth Crews/Stock, Boston; Chapter 4, p. 115, Jerry Howard/Positive Images; Chapter 5, p. 165, Andrea Helms; Chapter 6, p. 211, George Bellerose/Stock, Boston; Chapter 7, p. 263, Juilie O'Neil; Chapter 8, p. 311, Meri Houtchens-Kitchens; Chapter 9, p. 357, Alan Carey/The Image Works; Chapter 10, p. 415, Gale Zucker; Chapter 11, p. 457, Alan Carey/The Image Works; Epilogue, p. 493, James Scherer.

Excerpt on pp. 9–11 from F. Warren, "Call Them Liars Who Would Say All Is Well," in H. Turnbull and A. Turnbull (eds.), *Parents Speak Out: Then and Now*, 1985, Columbus, OH: Charles E. Merrill. Copyright 1985 by Charles E. Merrill. Reprinted by permission of the publisher.

Excerpt on pp. 23–24 from A. Turnbull, B. Strickland, and J. Brantley, *Developing and Implementing Individualized Education Programs*, Second Edition, Columbus, OH: Charles E. Merrill. Copyright 1982 by Charles E. Merrill. Reprinted by permission of the publisher.

Excerpt on pp. 73–76 from James J. Gallagher, *Teaching the Gifted Child*, Third Edition. Copyright 1985 by Allyn & Bacon, Inc. Reprinted by permission.

Excerpt on pp. 187–189 Michael D. Orlansky, *Encouraging Successful Mainstreaming of the Visually Impaired Child*, MAVIS Sourcebook 2, 1980. Reprinted with permission of the Social Science Education Consortium, Inc., Boulder, Colorado, 80302.

Excerpt on p. 189 from A. L. Corn and I. Martinez, *When You Have A Visually Handicapped Child in Your Classroom ...*, ©1977, is reproduced with kind permission from American Foundation for the Blind, 15 West 16th Street, New York, NY 10011.

Excerpt on p. 205 from Irving Dickman, *Sex Education and Family Life*, ©1974, is reproduced with kind permission from American Foundation for the Blind, 15 West 16th Street, New York, NY 10011.

Excerpt on pp. 229–231 from T. Stephens, A. Blackhurst, and L. Magliocca, *Teaching Mainstreamed Students*. Copyright 1982 by John Wiley & Sons, Inc. Reprinted by permission of the publisher.

Excerpt on pp. 305–306 from M. Behrmann, *Handbook of Microcomputers in Special Education*, 1984, San Diego, CA: College Hill Press. Reprinted by permission of the publisher.

Excerpt on p. 336 from M. Kerr and C. Nelson, *Strategies for Managing Behavior Problems in the Classroom*, 1983, Columbus, OH: Charles E. Merrill. Reprinted by permission of the publisher.

Excerpt on p. 396 from S. A. Kirk and J. C. Chalfant, *Academic and Developmental Learning Disabilities*, 1984, Denver, CO: Love Publishing Co. Reprinted by permission of the publisher.

Excerpts on pp. 406–407 and 410 from Janet Lerner, *Learning Disabilities: Theories, Diagnosis, and Teaching Strategies*. Copyright ©1985 by Houghton Mifflin Company. Used by permission.

CONTENTS

Three

Four

Five

CHILDREN WITH VISUAL IMPAIRMENTS 164

Six

Seven

CHILDREN WITH COMMUNICATION DISORDERS

Eight

CHILDREN WITH BEHAVIOR PROBLEMS

Nine

Ten

Eleven

Epilogue

PREFACE

AUDIENCE AND PURPOSE

Educating Exceptional Children, fifth edition, is an introductory text for those who will work with exceptional children: prospective special and regular elementary and secondary school teachers, counselors, psychologists, inservice educators, paraprofessionals, other professionals such as rehabilitation personnel, and parents.

The most important development in special education during the past twenty-five years has been the movement to integrate exceptional children into the regular education program to the greatest degree possible. Federal and state laws have mandated a free, appropriate education for all children in a setting that is as close as possible to the regular classroom—the least restrictive environment. Special education is no longer the exclusive province of special educators. Practically all elementary and secondary school teachers can expect to encounter exceptional children in their classrooms. And with this implementation of mainstreaming and the marked decrease in institutionalization of exceptional individuals, we are all—as a society—becoming increasingly aware that these individuals are, like ourselves, an important part of the human community.

The special needs of these children have become the shared responsibility of regular education teachers, counselors, psychologists, and other members of the educational team including parents of exceptional children. This text is intended to assist in the preparation of those individuals for their roles in meeting the needs of exceptional children in modern society.

ORGANIZATION

We have chosen to focus this text on the exceptional child as a learner. Throughout the book we consider two dimensions that impinge on the educational program developed for an exceptional learner: individual differences and modifications of educational practices.

Exceptional children differ in some important aspects from others in their age group; they also differ within themselves in their patterns of development. Thus, we discuss both interindividual and intraindividual differences. By emphasizing intraindividual differences and applying this concept to the varying groups of exceptional children, we attempt to supply an integrating element that gives meaning to both the differences and similarities among children. Adaptations of educational practices are presented for each exceptionality within a common framework of curriculum content, skills, and learning environment modifications. The first chapter in the text, "The Exceptional Child in Modern Society," offers historical background on the field of special education and an overview of issues and trends that have affected the development of programs for the exceptional learner. Coverage is devoted to the three dimensions of the environment that influence the exceptional child—the family, the school, and the society at large. In addition, we discuss the role of the courts, state and federal legislation, and the methods for determining the prevalence of exceptional children. These topics are also addressed throughout the text within the context of specific areas of exceptionality.

The second chapter, "Individual Differences and Special Education," explains in detail the organizing principles for this fifth edition, emphasizing the significance of intraindividual differences and the educational modifications that are necessary to meet the special needs of the exceptional learner. In addition, the chapter covers the various steps in the process of assessing and identifying the exceptional learner and in the planning of an individualized education program (IEP) for this child. We also discuss the controversy surrounding the use of labels. Finally, a full treatment of the recent interest in and implementation of early childhood education programs is included.

The fifth edition of EDUCATING EXCEPTIONAL CHILDREN continues to provide basic information about the characteristics and distinctive problems of exceptional learners, using the categorical terminology necessary for purposes of communication. Chapters 3 through 11 focus on the various clusters of exceptional children and cover the topics of definition, classification, identification, prevalence, causes, and characteristics as well as the special educational adaptations that might be made for children in each cluster.

REVISIONS IN THIS EDITION

The text has undergone a thorough revision that highlights new emphases in special education and that provides a more complete portrait of the field as it stands now. Central among the new emphases in the field is an increasing awareness of the exceptional child first and foremost as a human individual who is influenced by and must cope with the larger environments of family, school, and society. We address this ecological theme in several ways in the fifth edition. Lifespan discussions are now included in most chapters: these sections allow us to view the individual throughout the entire lifespan and focus on such issues as work and higher education opportunities, social adjustments in adulthood, and integration into the community. We have also included *Of Special Interest* boxed articles in each chapter that highlight either the personal experiences of an exceptional individual or that speak in greater depth to issues that go beyond the classroom.

The coverage included in each specific categorical chapter has also been completely analyzed for currency and reworked wherever necessary. Three chapters deserve particular mention. We are now including a separate chapter on children with physical handicaps. The new chapter, written by Dr. Beverly Rainforth of the University of Connecticut, contains much timely material pertinent to the educational adaptations and complete scope of treatments appropriate for these children. Chapter 6, "Children with Hearing Impairments," was extensively revised by Dr. Robert Rittenhouse of Illinois State University and discusses in a forthright manner the critical new discoveries and ongoing controversies in the education of deaf children. For Chapter 7 on children with communication disorders, Dr. Patricia McAnally of the University of Minnesota, reworked and updated discussions of language development.

The fifth edition of *Educating Exceptional Children* includes in every chapter a discussion of the uses of new technology—and especially of microcomputers—for the purposes of more effective instruction in special education. And, finally, a completely new Epilogue in the form of an interview with a dynamic practitioner (Ms. Carol Long, a consultant teacher in a school district in Massachusetts) addresses the critical issue of communication between regular teachers and specialists and provides a real-life situation to better ground and illustrate text discussions.

FEATURES IN THE FIFTH EDITION

In order to make this text easy to study and more appealing to use, the following features have been included:

Focusing Questions for each chapter help readers set goals and establish purposes for their reading of each important topic.

Introductions to each chapter offer an overview of the chapter's contents and give students a framework into which they can fit new ideas.

Summaries of Major Ideas conclude each chapter and highlight, in a clear, point-by-point format, the major concepts presented in the chapter.

Unresolved Issues encourage students to discuss and propose solutions for problems that are still at issue in the field of special education.

References of Special Interest provide, on a chapter-by-chapter basis, a selected list with descriptive annotations of appropriate bibliographic references.

A **Glossary** at the end of the book offers readers definitions of all key terms.

STUDY GUIDE

A Study Guide for the text is also available and, like the basic text, has undergone extensive revision to make it more compatible with students' needs.

The new Study Guide for the fifth edition is intended to complement the student's use of the text and class experiences through four types of learning approaches: organizing knowledge, reinforcing knowledge, evaluating knowledge, and expanding knowledge. The *Study Guide* is in three parts. Part I consists of a chapter-by-chapter learning guide that incorporates focusing questions, a complete chapter outline of headings, a full presentation of key terminology, numerous questions that include both objective items and short-answer essays that go beyond the checking of facts, and mini-cases offering illustrative vignettes. Answer keys appear at the end of the guide so that students may have immediate feedback on their responses to review questions. Part II contains full case studies that focus on different areas of exceptionality, and Part III features a list of commonly available publications related to exceptional children and guidelines for critical reading of periodical literature.

ACKNOWLEDGMENTS

We are grateful to a large group of our colleagues and specialists in various exceptionalities for their criticisms and suggestions during the revision of the text. Those who have provided useful, and in some cases invaluable, assistance include:

Frank Wood
University of Minnesota
Patricia Connard
The Ohio State University
Jennifer York
University of Wisconsin

H. D. Fredericks
Western Oregon State
  College
Jay Melrose
University of Massachusetts,
  Amherst

Stephen Quigley
University of Illinois, Champaign-
  Urbana
Sharon Freagon
Northern Illinois University
Janet Lerner
Northeastern Illinois
  University
Oliver Hurley
Georgia State University
Joanne Whitmore
Kent State University
Samuel Ashcroft
Vanderbilt University
Natalie Barraga
University of Texas at Austin

Barbara Keogh
University of California,
  Los Angeles
Tom Lovitt
University of Washington
John Umbreit
The University of Arizona
William Durden
Johns Hopkins University
Michael Guralnick
The Ohio State University
Kathryn Meadow-Orlans
Gallaudet College
C. Milton Blue
The University of Georgia

Their critical comments and ideas have helped shape and improve our presentation of material.

We also wish to acknowledge the help provided by Phyllis Pressley whose daily assistance was instrumental in bringing this volume to its present condition.

Our families deserve thanks for their tolerance of the necessary time and energy that this text required.

As a final note, we would expect the reader to understand that while our society has come a long way from the placement of handicapped individuals in distant and isolated institutions, we still have a great deal to learn about the best ways to help exceptional children and adults become truly integrated into modern American society. Judges and legislators can force the exceptional child into physical conjunction and association with children who are not exceptional, but they cannot force understanding, or acceptance, or an effective educational program. That job belongs to all who work with exceptional children. This text tries to faithfully present what is currently known about exceptional children and also what remains to be solved by this and future generations.

Samuel A. Kirk
James J. Gallagher

EDUCATING
EXCEPTIONAL
CHILDREN

C·H·A·P·T·E·R
One

THE
EXCEPTIONAL CHILD
IN
MODERN SOCIETY

Focusing Questions

How have perspectives on treating exceptional individuals changed over time?

What are the major forces that affect an exceptional person's development?

How have families been instrumental in obtaining services for exceptional children?

What trends show that exceptional individuals are becoming more integrated into society?

What roles have the courts and the federal government played in affirming the rights of exceptional individuals?

*E*xceptional children are different in some significant way from others of the same age. For these children to develop to their full adult potential, their education must be adapted to those differences. This book focuses on the nature of those differences for special subgroups of children and the range of special educational programs designed for them.

Although we focus on the needs of exceptional children, we find ourselves describing their environment as well. Even as the lead actor on the stage captures our attention, we are aware of the importance of the supporting players and the sets to the play itself. Both the family and the society in which exceptional children live are often the key to their growth and development. And it is in the public schools that we find the full expression of society's understanding—the knowledge, hopes, fears, and myths that are passed on to the next generation.

Education in any society is a mirror of that society. In that mirror we can see the strengths, the weaknesses, the hopes, the biases, the central values of the culture itself. The great interest in exceptional children shown in public education over the past three decades indicates the strong feeling in our society that all citizens, whatever their special conditions, deserve the opportunity to fully develop their capabilities.

"All men are created equal." We've heard it many times, but it still has important meaning for education in a democratic society. Although the phrase was used by this country's founders to denote equality before the law, it has also been interpreted to mean equality of opportunity. That concept implies educational opportunity for all children—the right of each child to receive help in learning to the limits of his or her capacity, whether that capacity be small or great. Recent court decisions have confirmed the right of all children—handicapped or not—to an appropriate education, and have mandated that public schools take the necessary steps to provide that education. In response, schools are modifying their programs, adapting instruction to children who are exceptional, to those who cannot profit substantially from regular programs.

WHO IS THE EXCEPTIONAL CHILD?

There have been many attempts to define the term *exceptional child*. Some use it when referring to the particularly bright child or the child with unusual talent. Others use it when describing any atypical child. The term generally has been accepted, however, to include both the child who is handicapped and the child who is gifted. Here, we define the **exceptional child** as a child who differs from the average or normal child in (1) mental characteristics, (2) sensory abilities, (3) communication abilities, (4) social behavior, or (5) physical characteristics. These differences must be to such an extent that the child requires a modification of school practices, or special educational services, to develop to maximum capacity.

Of course, this is a very general definition, one that raises several questions. What is average or normal? How extensive must the difference be to require special education? What role does the child's environment play in the definition? What is special education? All of these questions are asked in different forms throughout this text as we discuss each group of exceptional children.

If we define an exceptional child as one who differs from the group norm, then we have many kinds of exceptionalities. A redhead would be an exceptional child if all the other children in the class had brown or blond hair. But that difference, though interesting to a pediatrician or geneticist, is of little concern to the teacher. A redhead is not an exceptional child educationally speaking because the educational program of the class does not have to be modified to serve the child's needs.

Children are considered educationally exceptional only when it is necessary to alter the educational program to meet their needs: if their exceptionality leaves them unable to read or to master learning in the traditional fashion, or places them so far ahead that they are bored by what is being taught. The term *exceptional children*, then, may mean very different things in education, in biology, in psychology, or in other disciplines.

In education, we group children of like characteristics for instructional purposes. For example, we put six-year-olds in the first grade. In the same way, and for the same reasons, we group exceptional children. The following groupings are typical:

- Intellectual differences, including children who are intellectually superior and children who are slow to learn
- Sensory differences, including children with auditory or visual impairments
- Communication differences, including children with learning disabilities or speech and language impairments
- Behavioral differences, including children who are emotionally disturbed or socially maladjusted
- Physical differences, including children with nonsensory handicaps that impede mobility and physical vitality
- Multiple and severe problems, including children with combinations of impairments (cerebral palsy and mental retardation, deafness and blindness).

CHANGING PERSPECTIVES
ON EXCEPTIONAL CHILDREN

The first profession that paid significant attention to exceptional children was the medical profession in the nineteenth and early twentieth centuries. That group focused its attention on the unique characteristics of the children, the characteristics that could help diagnose their condition and treatment. Very little attention was paid the surrounding environment, the family or the culture, and its influences on those children. If a child were deaf or blind or mentally retarded, it was accepted that the condition existed entirely within the child, and that the basic problem was to find some means to remove the condition or to help the child adapt to the surrounding world.

As programs for exceptional children gradually expanded and included more children with mild handicaps—communication disorders, learning disabilities, behavior disorders, or mild mental retardation—it became clear that *exceptional child* was not just a description of personal characteristics; it involved a mix of the individual's characteristics and the special demands the environment made on that individual. With this recognition of the role of the environment in defining exceptionality, the field has moved from a **medical model**, which implies a physical condition or disease within the patient, to an **ecological model**, in which we see the exceptional child in complex interaction with environmental forces.

Think about *juvenile delinquency*. Even the term implies that the problem of deviant behavior exists within the child, and that the responsibility for solving the problem rests with the child. Many sociologists are outraged by the concept, which they claim blames the victim for his or her problems (Ryan, 1971). In order to understand the impact of the environment as a contributing factor to exceptional conditions, we can draw an analogy between treating disease and dealing with juvenile delinquency. In certain urban neighborhoods, the prevalence of childhood illness is far above average. Two alternative strategies can be used to handle the situation: (1) We could individually treat every child who becomes sick, or (2) we could try to correct the environment that causes the illness. In cases of juvenile delinquency, we could try to treat or punish each child who creates a disturbance in a delinquency-prone area, or we could try to clean up the dimensions of that environment that seem to predispose youngsters to deviant behavior.

The recent accumulation of evidence from psychologists, sociologists, and educators emphasizes the importance of the forces surrounding and interacting with the child. The questions posed by the various professions, however, are different, and lead to different emphases. For example, the physician wants to diagnose the condition and give biomedical treatment; the psychologist wants to know how the condition affects the cognitive and social development of the child; the

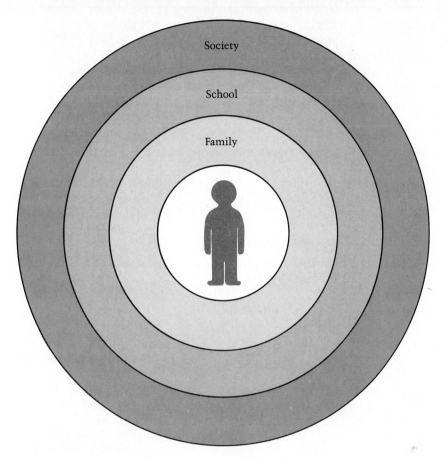

FIGURE 1.1
Ecological influ-
ences on the
developing child

educator wants to know how the condition affects the child's learning particular content and skills.

ENVIRONMENTAL INFLUENCES ON EXCEPTIONAL INDIVIDUALS

In order to fully understand exceptional children, we have to understand the environment in which those children exist. As Figure 1.1 indicates, the child is at the center of a complex network of forces: the family, the school and associated treatment programs, and, finally, the larger society. The impact of each of these forces can change as the child develops. The family may be more important in early years; society, more important in later years.

Educators and psychologists have long recognized the powerful influence that mothers and fathers have on their children. But it is also clear that children have a powerful influence on their parents (Bell, 1979). A child who is hyperactive or has difficulty paying attention can irritate other members of the family, who in turn may react negatively to the child. That angry response can increase the child's problem. It is often the effect of family and peer forces on the child that we are interested in, as much as the personal characteristics of the child.

In addition, the school—an environment in which the child will spend about one thousand hours a year, over a twelve-year period—exerts a powerful influence on the developing individual. This topic will be explored fully in Chapter 2. Social forces and values can also influence exceptional children. It may well be the reaction of nonhandicapped individuals to the deaf child's inability to speak, not the deafness itself, that causes some of that child's social problems. Similarly, it may be the acceptance or nonacceptance on the part of the larger society that has a great deal to do with whether the family is comfortable with children who are handicapped, or whether the schools see it as part of their responsibility to provide special educational programs for those children. Will the exceptional child, young adult, or mature adult be able to cope with his or her exceptionality? The answer to this question may lie more with family, school, and society than with the individual or the nature of the exceptionality itself.

Occasionally, the societal factors become so important that a category of exceptionality literally disappears. Robinson (1978) reported that predominantly agricultural countries such as China do not recognize the concept of *mild* mental retardation at all. The ability to read is not of great importance when a person's major life task is planting and harvesting rice. Only when the society becomes increasingly technologically complex, do some children reveal individual academic problems that require attention. In a society such as ours that is committed to advanced technology, the ability to read has become a critical aspect of social adaptability; the child who cannot read or learn quickly is in substantial trouble in both academic and social settings.

Families of Exceptional Children

One of the critical elements in the ecological setting of any child is the family. For the exceptional child, the importance of the family environment is heightened.

People who are not handicapped have difficulty understanding what it's like to have a handicapping condition. Blindness, deafness, or a physical handicap can be simulated, but there remains for the nonhandicapped person a rich storehouse of visual, auditory, and motor memories not available to those who have been handicapped from birth. It is even harder to imagine what it's like to be mentally retarded. Everyone knows how failure feels, but how many have experienced chronic, inevitable failure at almost every task, compounded by the inability to even recognize that failure? Imagine what that does to an individual. Similarly, it is hard to grasp the problems of the gifted child, puzzled by those who can't see what is so obvious to him or her.

It is easier to project ourselves as parents of children who are handicapped or gifted. That is an experience that can happen to anyone who has children, regardless of educational background, family status, or financial condition. Over the last couple of decades, we have begun to appreciate more fully the pain and stress that are part of having a child who is handicapped, and to realize the degree of courage and external support necessary for parents to maintain their equilibrium under those circumstances.

Most parents who must cope with a severely handicapped child face two major crises. The first is the symbolic death of the child who was to be. Expectant parents inevitably think about the future of their unborn child. They set goals for that child—for success, for education, for financial security. The mother and father who are ushered into a pediatrician's office and told that their child is severely handicapped suffer the symbolic death of that child-to-be, the loss of their dreams and hopes; and some parents react with severe depression (Farber, 1976).

There is a second, quite different crisis faced by these parents: the problem of providing daily care for their exceptional child. The child who is cerebral palsied or autistic is often difficult to feed, to dress, to put to bed, and the thought that the child will not go through the normal developmental process to adult independence weighs heavily on the parents.

The special problems of siblings also have to be considered. What happens when a younger sibling begins to surpass an older brother or sister who is handicapped, or begins to be ashamed of the deviant behavior? One sister describes the guilt and love like this:

> I have a short story to tell. It is one of many stories of happiness and sorrow. It is a story of which I am not very proud, and one I have never told my parents. I will tell it now because it is time, and I have learned from my mistakes, as all people can.
>
> George is twenty-one years old today. He is a frequently happy, often troubled young man who has grown up in a society reluctant to accept and care for him even though he cannot fare for himself.
>
> I am very lucky. My crime was easily forgiven by someone who loved me very much, without reservation. George and I were very young. I was his frequent babysitter. As an older sister more interested in ponies and playing outdoors, I felt a great deal of resentment toward George and, of course, toward

Parents of children with handicaps, realizing that external supports were necessary to help them help their children, stirred and prodded society and the schools to recognize their responsibilities.
(Copyright © Betty Medsger 1979)

my persecutors, my mother and father. It was a day like any other day when I had been told to take care of George. They always seemed the same, those days, because I had no choice in the matter, and if I had had one, I would have refused. It was that simple for me. I had better things to do.

We were waiting in the car for our mother to come with the groceries. The recurring memory breaks my heart every time I think of it. He was antagonizing me again. Those unbearable, unreal sounds that haunted and humiliated me. They were the nonsense noises that made the neighborhood children speculate he was from Mars. I could hear their taunts, and rage welled up in me. How could I have a brother like this? He was not right at all. He was a curse. I screamed at him to "Shut up!" He kept on. He wouldn't stop. My suppressed anger exploded. I raised my hand and slapped him again and again across his soft, round baby face. George began to cry, low, mournful whimpers. He never once raised a hand to protect himself. Shaking with fear and anger, [unable to think clearly,] I just looked at him. In that swift instance I felt more shame and revulsion for myself than I have ever felt toward anyone. The rude ugliness of it will never leave me. I hugged him to me, begging for forgiveness. And he gave it to me unconditionally. I shall never forget his sweet, sad face as he accepted my hugs.

In that instance I learned something of human nature and the nature of those who would reject people like George. I had been one of them; sullen, uncaring, unwilling to care for someone who came into the world with fewer advantages than I myself had. Today, I am a better person for having lived through both the good times and the bad times that our family experienced as a result of my brother's autism. I have a sense of understanding and compassion that I learned from growing up with George. Best of all, I have my brother, who loves me with all the goodness in his heart.

My message is simple. Look into your hearts and into the hearts of all people to see what is real, what makes them real people. For we are all the same. Accept people for what they are and work to make the world a receptive place—not just for those who are perceived as normal. (Warren, 1985, p. 227)

In the 1940s and 1950s parents were often identified as a cause of the problems of the exceptional child, and in many cases became the scapegoat for most of the attendant problems revealed by the child, particularly in cases of behavioral disturbance. This scapegoating has diminished with the realization that parents of exceptional children are victims too, and that they need help more than censure.

Parents as Advocates

The recognition that society and schools have a responsibility for exceptional children stemmed in large measure from the activities of those children's parents. Parents who found themselves unable to get help for their children from local authorities created their own programs in church basements, vacant stores, or any place that would house them. These informal groups, loosely formed around the common needs of the children, often provided important information to new parents struggling to find aid for their children with handicaps. They were also a source of emotional support for those parents, a means of sharing and solving the problems of accepting and living with exceptional children.

These local groups quickly realized that fundamental changes were needed in the allocation of educational resources at local, state, and federal levels. No casual, haphazard approach was going to provide the kind of help needed by parents or their exceptional children. Accordingly, in the 1940s and 1950s, they began to form large parents' groups, like the National Association of Retarded Citizens, the United Cerebral Palsy Association, and, in the 1960s, the Association for Children with Learning Disabilities.

These parents' organizations have successfully stimulated legislation providing for additional trained personnel, research, and a variety of other programs that have brought children with handicapping conditions to the attention of the general public and have attracted more qualified people into the field (Cain, 1976).

Organized parents' groups for gifted children have only recently been formed, and have not yet had the same political influence as the national organizations for handicapped children. Still, these groups are helping the parents of gifted children to cope with the problems of precocious development (Gallagher, 1985).

The Exceptional Child and the School

After the family there is probably no single entity that has such a pervasive influence upon the developing child as the school, public or private. Not only is it a center for learning, providing opportunities for the child to develop those skills and knowledges that will allow him or her to adapt to the society as an adult, but it is also a social training ground. In this latter respect, school provides the child with opportunities to learn how to respond to adult requirements; to interact with his or her peers; to form friendships; and to learn how to work cooperatively with others.

The school is particularly important for exceptional children—who may need very special kinds of assistance to become productive adults. The public schools have not always welcomed the presence of the exceptional child and have had to be reminded by parents, the courts, and legislatures of their responsibilities to provide a free public education for *all* of the children in our society. Handicapped children have been excluded in the past for a wide variety of reasons, all of which can be translated into the perception that these children did not fit into the established program. Even gifted children, while rarely excluded, were forced to fit into programs that truly did not meet their special needs. However, in recent decades the schools have accepted their role more positively and have often been innovative in seeking ways to carry out these responsibilities.

Chapter 2 will provide an overview of how the schools have tried to organize themselves and their resources to meet the challenges of accepting and educating exceptional children. The remaining chapters of this book will be devoted to the specific adaptations for children with specific exceptionalities.

The Exceptional Individual in Society

Although there have been dramatic changes in the roles played by families and schools, the truly revolutionary changes over the last few decades have occurred in society's view of exceptional individuals. We

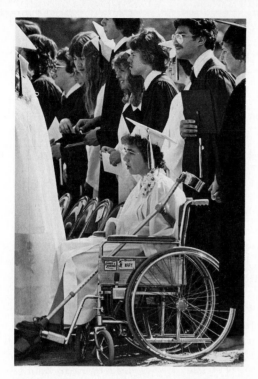

In recent decades the school has accepted its role—as the provider of a free public education for all children—more positively and often quite innovatively.
(Alan Carey/The Image Works)

have moved from a social posture of rejection and the charitable isolation of children with handicaps to the acceptance of them as contributing members of society.

History of Educating Exceptional Children

As we look back in history, we find that the concept of educating every child to the highest performance possible is a relatively new idea. The current use of the term *exceptional* is itself a reflection of radical change in society's view of those who differ from the norm. We have come a long way from the Spartan practice of killing malformed infants, but the journey has been a slow one.

We can identify four stages in the development of social attitudes toward children and adults with handicaps:

1. During the pre-Christian era, children with handicaps were neglected or mistreated.
2. During the spread of Christianity, those children were protected and pitied.

3. In the eighteenth and nineteenth centuries, institutions were established to provide separate education for exceptional children.
4. In the latter part of the twentieth century, there has been a movement toward accepting people with handicaps and integrating them into society to the fullest extent possible.

In the United States, our attitudes toward individuals with handicaps have followed a similar pattern of development. In early years, there were no public provisions for children or adults with special needs. They were "stored away" in poorhouses and other charitable centers, or left at home with no educational provisions. It was estimated that, as late as 1850, 60 percent of the inmates of this country's poorhouses were people who were deaf, blind, "insane," or "idiots" (National Advisory Committee on the Handicapped, 1976).

Nineteenth-century reformers—people like Horace Mann, Samuel Gridley Howe, and Dorothea Dix—gave impetus to the second stage, the establishment of residential schools. During the period from 1817 to the beginning of the Civil War, a span of nearly fifty years, many states established residential schools for children who were deaf, blind, mentally retarded, or orphaned, patterning them after similar schools in Europe. In 1817, a residential institution for the deaf was created in Hartford, Connecticut, and called the American Asylum for the Education and Instruction of the Deaf. It is now the American School for the Deaf. In 1829, the New England Asylum for the Blind was founded in Watertown, Massachusetts. It was later named the Perkins School for the Blind. Thirty years later, a residential school for the mentally retarded, Massachusetts School for Idiotic and Feebleminded Youth, was established in South Boston. These schools offered training, but equally important provided an environment that often protected the individual throughout life.

The third stage in the development of provisions for children with handicaps in America was the establishment of special classes in public schools. The first day class created for deaf children was in Boston in 1869. It was not until 1896 that the first special class for children who were mentally retarded was organized, in Providence, Rhode Island. It was followed, in 1899, by a class for children with physical impairments, and, in 1900, in Chicago, by a class for children who were blind. Since 1900, special classes have been organized in many public schools throughout the nation.

In the fourth stage, which started in the mid-1960s, there has been an attempt to bring children with handicaps as close to the normal classroom as possible. Using the philosophy of the **least-restrictive environment**, children leave the classroom only as long as necessary to meet their educational needs.

Significant Contributions. In the political arena we honor the founders of our country: Washington, Jefferson, Madison, Adams, and others. Although they are long dead, we recognize that their ideas, their perseverance, their values have shaped our society in many ways. Similarly, in special education, there have been a number of people whose pioneering work with exceptional children still influences the field today. The present is hard to understand without a sense of those whose contributions changed the face of education in their time and ours.

Table 1.1 is a list of some of those people together with a description of their major contributions. The concepts of intelligence developed by Alfred Binet are still in modified use today, as are Braille's system of communication and Seguin's and Montessori's educational exercises. The work of Bell and Gallaudet still have impact on deaf children today. Above all, Howe's belief that children need more than custodial care, that all children, whatever their circumstances, deserve an education, continues to guide current thinking.

Recent Trends

Recent changes in societal attitudes are marked by legislation that supports exceptional children and adults in society, by court decisions that establish their rights as citizens, and by integration in that mirror of society, the public schools. The thrust to greater social and educational integration has brought many exceptional children and adults back into the normal community and regular educational system from more segregated settings.

The changing social environment of exceptional children has spawned a new and different vocabulary. Three terms that are in common usage today are **normalization, deinstitutionalization**, and **mainstreaming**. All reflect the interest of society in trying to integrate exceptional children and adults more effectively into the community at large.

Normalization. The creation of as normal as possible a learning and social environment for the exceptional child and adult (Bank-Mikkelsen, 1969).

Deinstitutionalization. The process of releasing as many exceptional children and adults as possible from the confinement of residential institutions into their local community.

Mainstreaming. The process of bringing exceptional children into daily contact with nonexceptional children in an educational setting.

One of the arguments for normalization and deinstitutionalization is that placement in an institution aggravates rather than helps the exceptional condition. Wolfensberger (1972) believed that part of the bizarre or unusual behavior often seen in adults with handicapping conditions who have lived for a long time in institutions is caused by the restrictive nature of those institutions, not their diagnosed condition. An institution that forces the individual to conform to a rigid

Table 1.1
Significant Ideas Influencing American Special Education

Initiator	Dates	Nationality	Major Idea
Jean Marc Gaspard Itard	1775–1838	French	Single-subject research can be used to develop training methods for those who are mentally retarded.
Samuel Gridley Howe	1801–1876	American	Children who are handicapped can learn and should have an organized education, not just compassionate care.
Edward Seguin	1812–1880	French	Children who are mentally retarded can learn if taught through specific sensory-motor exercises.
Francis Galton	1822–1911	English	Genius tends to run in families, and its origin can be determined.
Alfred Binet	1857–1911	French	Intelligence can be measured, and can be improved through education.
Louis Braille	1809–1852	French	Children who are blind can learn through an alternative system of communication based on a code of raised dots.
Thomas Hopkins Gallaudet	1787–1851	American	Children who are deaf can learn to communicate by spelling and gesturing with their fingers.
Alexander Graham Bell	1847–1922	American	Children who are hearing handicapped can learn to speak, and can use their limited hearing if it is amplified.
Maria Montessori	1870–1952	Italian	Children can learn at very early ages, using concrete experiences designed around special instructional materials.
Anna Freud	1895–1982	Austrian	The techniques of psychoanalysis can be applied to children to help their emotional problems.
Lewis Terman	1877–1956	American	Intelligence tests can be used to identify gifted children, who tend to maintain superiority throughout life.
Alfred Strauss	1897–1957	German	Some children show unique patterns of learning disabilities, probably due to brain injury, that require special training.

THE BEST CAMP EVER

On a sunny day recently, Valerie Katkan, 27, of Brockton, [Mass.,] frowns in apprehension as she mounts a patient horse named Pasha.

Katkan's black velvet riding cap bobs uncertainly as she grimaces and grasps the horse's reins in a nervous, shaky fist. This is Katkan's first time on a horse.

"You look great," Carole LeBlanc, her instructor, assures her.

Katkan ignores LeBlanc's comments and concentrates instead on keeping her balance atop Pasha.

Safe and back on the ground, Katkan calls her first horseride excellent. "I loved it the whole time," she asserts.

Katkan is one of 30 Massachusetts residents enjoying summer day camp. After horseback riding, she and others will go swimming, try their hands at archery, paddleboating, and arts and crafts in activities typical of most summer camps across the country.

It's all common enough except for one factor. These kids and young adults, ranging between the ages 5 and 27, [are mentally retarded]. Despite the appearances—the whirling mass of kids playing soccer, the excited shouts of children splashing in the pool or gulping down their peanut butter and jelly sandwiches and granola bars—this camp, the Handi-Kids Camp here, is dedicated to therapy. In four 2-week sessions (each session dedicated to a specific disability), the children learn skills that will help them cope in society.

In this first session of the summer, mentally retarded children learn acceptable ways of interacting with others. In upcoming sessions, physically handicapped children will learn exercises to strengthen their underdeveloped or seldom-used muscles. Blind and autistic children will gain a better self-image and better concentration. Children . . . with muscular dystrophy, multiple sclerosis or cerebral palsy will leave with better coordination. The experiences these kids take home with them will linger in mind and body much longer than the usual summer camp experience lingers in the minds of most children.

"My goals are to expose these kids to as many unrestricted opportunities as possible, to get them to cooperate, socialize and play with each other. And to have fun," says Patti Phillips, program coordinator at Handi-Kids.

"A lot of times when children first come they don't know how to interact with people," Phillips says. "They might hit each other instead of saying hello, or they might give someone a handshake every five minutes." After a two-week day camp session at Handi-Kids, the same child who engaged in incessant handshaking might learn a more acceptable way of greeting others.

Activities are specially devised to emphasize the individual successes of the children rather than competition and winning. For example, horseback riding is designed to help strengthen weak muscles through the rhythmic motion of the horse's gait, and archery aids in developing concentration, coordination, and a steady hand. Activities such as body tracings (in which the kids outline

continued

continued

the shape of each other's bodies on a piece of paper) have been formulated to boost the self-esteem of the children who may have been ridiculed because of their handicap.

"There are more realistic goals that they can reach," says Phillips.

Beth Silvestri-O'Neal, a counselor at the camp who specializes in expressive therapy and has worked at the camp for six years, says she has seen the confidence and self-esteem of the campers burgeon while at the camp.

"The most rewarding thing is to see kids with a limited physical realm try different activities and succeed at them," she says. "Lots of kids come year after year and are really withdrawn, and year after year I can see the progression."

She recalls a boy who was fearful of water at the beginning of a summer camp session but who within two weeks was swimming.

The camp was built in 1975 by the Knights of Pythias, a nonprofit humanitarian foundation dedicated to helping the needy and sick. The Handi-Kids program originated in 1963 with its main function to provide wheelchairs, crutches and other aids to those who couldn't afford them. By 1968 the organization had broadened its scope to include sending physical therapists into the homes of handicapped children.

"We found we could only do two or three kids at a time that way," says Aba Alperin, assistant center director at Handi-Kids. "We talked to doctors who conveyed the idea to us that what the kids really needed was a summer camp. The children never got out of the house and they needed to learn how to play with other kids."

. . . The annual budget has [now] reached $191,000 ($60,000 for the summer camp program alone) and the King Solomon Lodge of the Pythians is seeking the funds to expand the camp and allow more children to take advantage. There are special afterschool programs available in the winter. The camp is free for all those who participate. Children are referred by physicians, schools, parents, friends and community service organizations. Everyone who applies cannot be accepted, however, and there is a growing waiting list.

"When I look at the grounds I think, 'I remember when this was a swamp.' How'd we do it?," says Alperin.

As for the 120 children who will attend the camp during the summer months, they know nothing about swamps. Just that they enjoy archery, the horses, the pool, and the camp in general.

"The first time I came I could feel it," says Katkan, after she gives a hug to one of the counselors she has proclaimed her "favorite."

"This is the best camp I've ever been to."

SOURCE: "The Best Camp Ever," by Pamela Reynolds, *The Boston Globe,* Friday, July 12, 1985, pp. 13–14. Reprinted with courtesy of *The Boston Globe.*

With the coming of normalization and deinstitutionali-
zation, many exceptional individuals are no longer re-
stricted to a residential institution but instead are
integrated into the community at large.
(Paul Conklin)

schedule in eating, in sleeping, or in social behavior is not the ideal
environment for building social independence.

We can see in these concerns the realization that the social envelope,
the environment in which the exceptional individual exists, can play
an important role in the definition of a problem, as well as in the
behavioral outcomes for the individual.

State and Federal Legislation

One of the ways we express society's wants in a democracy is through
legislation. Until the late 1950s, efforts to establish special education
programs at the local level were often fragmentary and haphazard. In
one town, a special education program would begin at age 9 or 10 and
stop when the student reached age 14. In another, there would be a
special vocational program for exceptional high school students but
no program for younger students. Many educators and parents felt that

By pressuring their representatives and speaking out themselves, exceptional individuals have been instrumental in getting new laws passed and new programs established.
(Rose Skytta/Jeroboam, Inc.)

if children had problems, it was better to treat them as soon as possible. And that if special attention were provided early, it ought to be continued, as needed, throughout junior and senior high school. But, often the additional resources to support these programs were not available in local school systems.

Since the turn of the century, individual states have been involved in a limited way in subsidizing programs in public schools for children with sensory handicaps (blindness, deafness) and physical impairments. And some states have helped organize and support classes for children who were mentally retarded or had behavioral problems.

After World War II, many states expanded their involvement, providing financial support for special classes and services in local schools for children with all types of handicaps. These new and larger programs created a personnel emergency in the late 1940s and early 1950s. Professional special educators were in short supply, and the field of special education was not firmly established.

It was obvious that federal legislation was needed, both to equalize educational opportunities across the country and to bring qualified people into special education. But that legislation was not easy to obtain. It violated a strong tradition in the United States that education is a state and local responsibility. Still, organized parents' groups with the support of other interested citizens convinced Congress that they needed help. Their arguments were compelling, as were their intense feelings.

Why should handicapped children and their parents be penalized through the accident of birth in a particular state or a particular region of a state? Were not American citizens (in this case the parents of children who are handicapped) entitled to equal treatment anywhere in the United States? Should they, in addition to the burdens of having children with special needs, be forced to move their family to another community where special education resources were available, or to send their children to some institution far away from home and family because no local resources existed? The blatant unfairness of the situation called out for attention.

After much debate, in the late 1950s, Congress began to pass limited measures directed toward research and personnel training in the fields of mental retardation and deafness. In 1963, Public Law 88–164 authorized funds for training professional personnel and for research and demonstration. The law represented a strong initiative by President Kennedy, whose interest was heightened by his sister's mental retardation. Those first efforts were followed by many others, as shown in Table 1.2. From that small beginning stemmed twenty years of legislation to ensure that all children with handicaps have access to an appropriate education.

By the end of the 1960s, federal initiatives included

- special grants to states to encourage new programs for children with handicaps.
- support of research and demonstration projects to find better ways to educate children with handicaps.
- establishment of regional resource centers to help teachers develop specific educational programs and strategies.
- extension of provisions for training leadership personnel to head training programs and administer programs for exceptional children.
- establishment of a nationwide set of centers for deaf-blind children to aid children with multiple handicaps.
- a requirement that some funds for innovative programs in general education be reserved for special projects for children with handicaps.
- establishment of a Bureau of Education for the Handicapped within the Office of Education, to administer these and other provisions for children with handicaps.

Table 1.2

Highlights of Federal Education Policy for Handicapped Children

Title	Purpose
PL 85–926 (1958)	Provided grants for teaching in the education of handicapped children, related to education of children who are mentally retarded.
PL 88–164 (1963) (Title III)	Authorized funds for research and demonstration projects in the education of the handicapped.
PL 89–10 (1965)	Elementary and Secondary Education Act. Title III authorized Assistance to handicapped children in state-operated and state-supported private day and residential schools.
PL 89–313	Amendments to PL 89–10. Provided grants to state educational agencies for the education of handicapped children in state-supported institutions.
PL 90–170 (1967)	Amendments to PL 88–164. Provided funds for personnel training to care for individuals who are mentally retarded, and the inclusion of individuals with neurologic conditions related to mental retardation.
PL 90–247 (1968)	Amendments to PL 89–10. Provided regional resource centers for the improvement of education of children with handicaps.
PL 90–538 (1968)	Handicapped Children's Early Education Assistance Act. Provided grants for the development and implementation of experimental programs in early education for children with handicaps, from birth to age 6.
PL 91–230 (1969)	Amendments to PL 89–10. Title VI consolidated into one act—Education of the Handicapped—the previous enactments relating to handicapped children.
PL 92–424 (1972)	Economic Opportunity Amendments. Required that not less than 10% of Head Start enrollment opportunities be available to children with handicaps.
PL 93–380 (1974)	Amended and expanded Education of the Handicapped Act in response to right-to-education mandates. Required states to establish goal of providing full educational opportunity for all children with handicaps, from birth to age 21.

Table 1.2 *continued*
Highlights of Federal Education Policy for Handicapped Children

Title	Purpose
PL 94–142 (1975)	Education for All Handicapped Children Act. Required states to provide by September 1, 1978, a free appropriate education for all handicapped children between the ages of 3 and 18.
PL 94–142, Section 619	Amendment to PL 94–142. Expanded services to preschool handicapped children (ages 3 to 5) through provision of preschool incentive grants.

SOURCE: Adapted from "Alternative Administrative Strategies for Young Handicapped Children" by S. Behr and J. Gallagher, 1981, *Journal of the Division of Early Childhood 2*, pp. 113–122.

This flood of provisions served notice that the federal government had accepted responsibility for providing support resources for children with handicaps and for encouraging the states to carry out their basic responsibilities.

By 1973, special education programs had increased dramatically across the country. States began putting a much greater share of their educational dollars into educating children with handicaps, increasing their contributions by almost 300 percent (Gallagher, Forsythe, Ringelhein, & Weintraub, 1975). Still, programs and resources were not consistent from state to state. To deal with that inconsistency, and to help the states handle the costs of court-mandated programs, Congress passed Public Law 94–142, the Education for All Handicapped Children Act. The measure, which took effect in 1977, was

> to assure that all handicapped children have available to them . . . special education and related services designed to meet their unique needs, . . . to assure that the rights of handicapped children, and their parents or guardians, are protected, to assist states and localities to provide for the education of all handicapped children, and to assess and assure the effectiveness of efforts to educate handicapped children. (House of Representatives Report 94–332, June 26, 1975, p. 35)

Six key principles lay at the heart of PL 94–142, principles that have shaped special education over the last decade:

1. *Zero reject.* All children with handicaps are to be provided a free and appropriate public education. This means local school systems do not have an option to decide not to provide needed services.

During the planning of an individualized education program (IEP), which is mandated by PL 94–142, team members including classroom teachers and specialists determine the best course of action for a particular child. (Ulrike Welsch)

2. *Nondiscriminatory evaluation.* Each student must receive a full individual examination before being placed in a special education program, with tests appropriate to the child's cultural and linguistic background. A reevaluation is required every three years.

3. *Individualized education programs.* An individualized education program (IEP) must be written for every handicapped student who is receiving special education. The IEP must describe the child's current performance and goals for the school year, the particular special education services to be delivered, and the procedures by which the outcome will be evaluated.

4. *Least-restrictive environment.* As much as possible, children who are handicapped must be educated with children who are not handicapped. The philosophy is to move as close to the normal setting (regular classroom) as feasible for each child.

5. *Due process.* Due process is a set of procedures to ensure the fairness of educational decisions and the accountability of both professionals and parents in making those decisions. These procedures allow parents to call a hearing when they do not agree with the school's plans for their child, to obtain an individual evaluation from a qualified examiner outside the school system, or to take other actions to ensure that both family and child have channels through which to voice their interests and concerns.

6. *Parental participation.* Parents of children who are handicapped are to participate in planning for their child, to be involved in the development of the individual plan, and to have access to their child's educational records (Turnbull, Strickland, & Brantley, 1982).

To carry out the provisions of the law, the federal government authorized the spending of up to $3 billion by 1982, promising much larger sums of money to aid the states than had previously been provided. By 1985, the government had actually spent about $1 billion a year. In return for that aid, states are required to show evidence that they are doing their best to help children with handicaps receive needed services.

Specific provisions in the law placed substantial pressure on public school systems, demanding a good deal more in the way of assessment, parent contact, and evaluation than most school systems had been accustomed to providing. Not surprisingly, many educators have protested the burden that these requirements place on them. Consequently, the law and its regulations are currently under review.

Abeson and Zettel (1977) explain that the legislation was never intended to mandate that all children with handicaps be educated in regular classrooms. For many children with moderate to severe handicapping conditions, the regular classroom might be inappropriate. But the law has brought many of these youngsters back into the orbit of the public schools from state institutions or their homes, offering attention that was previously denied them.

In less than three decades, the federal government has moved from little involvement in special education to become a major partner in local and state programs for those who are handicapped. Only gifted children are not partaking of this cornucopia of federal legislation. They are not included in the government's definition of exceptional children, and remain without meaningful assistance at the national level. Although an Office of Gifted and Talented and some small training and research funds were established in 1976, they were wiped out in a governmental reorganization five years later.

Role of the Courts

Since World War II, individuals and groups interested in the education of children with handicaps have appealed to local, state, and federal governments for help. Only since the early 1970s, however, has there been a sustained effort to use the courts to bring additional resources to these children and their families.

The movement toward judicial action was a recognition of the success minority groups had had using the courts to establish their rights. Beginning in 1954 with the classic school desegregation case, *Brown* v. *Board of Education*, the courts had reaffirmed the rights of minority citizens in a wide variety of settings. If court decisions could protect the rights of one group of citizens, they should do the same for those who are handicapped. Soon, supporters of people with handicaps were working to translate abstract legal rights into tangible social action through the judicial system.

One of the most vigorous actions focused on judicial support of the rights of children with handicaps to an appropriate education. Most state constitutions guarantee the right of every child to a free public education. For example, Article X, Section 1, of the Wisconsin constitution, adopted March 13, 1848, reads: "The legislature shall provide by law for the establishment of district schools which shall be free to all children between the ages of four and twenty years" (Melcher, 1976). Seizing on the principle that all children have a right to education, various interest groups have brought legal suits against the states to compel them to provide special education services.

Class action suits have been influential in changing the status of handicapped children in the United States. A **class action suit** provides that legal action taken as part of a suit applies not only to the individual who brings the particular case to court but to all members of the class to which that individual belongs. This means the rights of all people with handicaps can be reaffirmed by a case involving just one handicapped child.

The rulings in several recent court cases have reaffirmed the rights of those who are handicapped (Smith & Barresi, 1982):

- A handicapped child cannot be excluded from school without careful due process, and it is the responsibility of the schools to provide appropriate programs for children who are different (*Pennsylvania Association for Retarded Children* v. *Commonwealth of Pennsylvania*, 1972; *Goso* v. *Lopez*, 1974; *Hairston* v. *Drosick*, 1974).
- The presumed absence of funds is not an excuse for failing to provide educational services to exceptional children. If there are not sufficient funds, then all programs should be cut back (*Mills* v. *Board of Education*, 1972).
- Children with handicaps who are committed to state institutions must be provided a meaningful education in that setting, or their incarceration is considered unlawful detention (*Wyatt* v. *Stickney*, 1972).
- Children should not be labeled "handicapped" or placed into special education without adequate diagnosis that takes into account different cultural and linguistic backgrounds (*Larry P.* v. *Riles*, 1979).
- Bilingual exceptional children need identification, evaluation, and educational procedures that reflect and respect their dual-language background (*José P.* v. *Ambrach*, 1979).

These court decisions created the expectation that something would be done, but did not guarantee it. Just as laws have to be enforced and money promised has to be appropriated, so court decisions have to be executed. Closing down state institutions, reorganizing public schools, providing special services to all children with handicaps—these were substantial and costly changes. And they raised a serious problem for program administrators. Where would the money for implementation come from? Ultimately, state and local leaders turned to Washington, pressuring Congress to pass the Education for All Handicapped Children Act. That act compelled the federal government to help pay for the changes the courts were demanding.

Even with federal assistance, though, implementation has come slowly. The outcome of the burst of judicial activity is yet to be determined. And, in the process, we can expect ongoing adjustment to both laws and educational procedures.

PREVALENCE OF EXCEPTIONAL CHILDREN

Defining Prevalence

How many children are exceptional? This is one of the fundamental questions in the field of special education. We must know numbers to determine our personnel and other resource needs.

Epidemiologists used two different indexes to determine the frequency of a condition in the general population: the incidence rate and the prevalence rate. **Incidence** refers to the number of new cases occurring in a population during a specific interval of time. The incidence rate answers the question "How many youngsters were born with cerebral palsy in the United States in 1980?" **Prevalence** refers to the number of people in a given category in a population group during a specified interval of time (for example, the number of learning disabled children who are of school age this year). The prevalence rate is determined by finding the number of individuals with a certain condition, and dividing that figure by the total population for the age range. Throughout the text we report only prevalence figures. They are most relevant to educational planning because they tell us how many exceptional children are actually present in a given age group at a given time.

Determining Prevalence

It seems that determining the prevalence of exceptional children would be a relatively easy task. But it is not, and it is worth noting why it is not. Suppose you had to find out the number of children in this country who are mentally retarded, learning disabled, gifted, or emotionally disturbed. How would you go about it? You could put an item in the national census, asking people to check a box if they have children with these exceptional conditions. But this procedure could produce errors. Some parents might not want to say they have an exceptional child; others might not even know.

Suppose you asked teachers to provide a list of all exceptional students within their current experience. Here again you'd have problems. Some teachers might not know that a child is exceptional if the condition is mild.

The identification of a child with handicaps is by no means a clear-cut process; many factors must be taken into account and many careful judgments made before a classification is determined.
(Meri Houtchens-Kitchens)

Suppose you contacted existing special education programs and counted the number of exceptional students enrolled in them. Yes, you'd know the number of children currently being served, but what about those who are not receiving service, or those who have not been identified, or those who are not even in school?

Obviously, our easy question is actually a difficult one. Instead of precise figures, the prevalence rates we are able to obtain are based on small samples of children identified at local or regional levels and projected to a national level.

Determining the prevalence of exceptional children is further complicated by disagreement among professionals on issues of identification. What is the dividing point between a child who is emotionally disturbed and one who is having temporary adjustment problems? At what point of developmental delay do we classify a child as mentally retarded? Identification is not always a clear-cut process.

These factors make us cautious about the actual number of exceptional children in the various classifications in the United States. Although here and in each chapter of this book we discuss the issue of prevalence, remember we are using general estimates for communi-

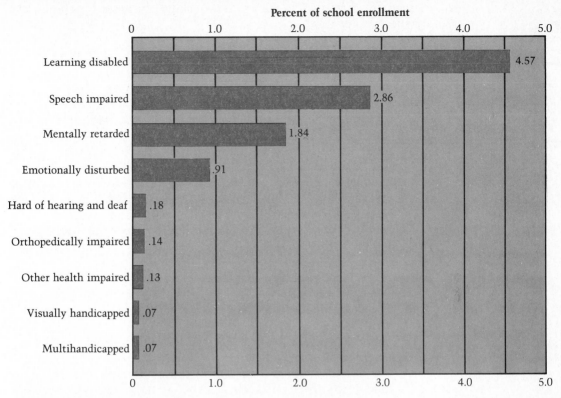

Percent of school enrollment

Learning disabled	4.57
Speech impaired	2.86
Mentally retarded	1.84
Emotionally disturbed	.91
Hard of hearing and deaf	.18
Orthopedically impaired	.14
Other health impaired	.13
Visually handicapped	.07
Multihandicapped	.07

SOURCE: Seventh Annual Report to Congress on the Implementation of Public Law 94–142: The Education for All Handicapped Children Act, 1985. Washington, DC: U.S. Department of Education.

FIGURE 1.2
School enrollment by handicapping conditions, 1983–1984

cation purposes. We are not trying to, nor can we, defend them at this point.

Figure 1.2 shows the school enrollment of children by handicapping condition in school year 1983–1984. Because all children with handicaps supposedly are being served by federal law, these figures should represent the true prevalence of exceptional children in the society of school-age youngsters. Almost 4.6 percent of the school enrollment is made up of children with learning disabilities, an interesting figure when we consider that the category did not exist before 1963. Almost 3 percent of children have reported speech and communication problems, while almost 2 percent are identified as mentally retarded. Fewer than 1 percent are classified emotionally disturbed.

The rest of the categories in the figure comprise about 0.6 percent of the school population. Gifted children, whose numbers are reported by state directors of programs for them, make up between 4 and 6 percent of the student population (Gallagher, Weiss, Oglesby, & Thomas, 1983). All together, the population of exceptional children falls between 10 and 15 percent of the overall school population—4 to 6 million children in the United States who should be receiving some form of special education.

SUMMARY OF MAJOR IDEAS

1. The exceptional child is different from the average child in ways that require changes in school practices for the child to reach full potential.
2. Educational programs usually reflect the attitude of the larger society toward a particular group of children.
3. The major categories of exceptionality within the field of special education include children with mental differences (unusually rapid or slow mental development); visual and auditory handicaps; communication disorders; learning disabilities; behavioral and emotional disorders; multiple and severe handicaps; and physical handicaps.
4. The special education field has moved from a medical model, which focuses on the diagnosis of individual conditions, to an ecological model, which focuses on the individual's interaction with the environment.
5. Families play a critical role in the life of children who are handicapped.
6. The parents of exceptional children must first adjust to the symbolic death of the child who was to be, then cope with the constant pressure of caring for the child who is.
7. Parents of exceptional children have organized to become a potent political force, influencing legislatures to provide resources to educate their children and petitioning the courts to reaffirm their rights to equity.
8. The school and the larger society also play major roles in the development of the exceptional child.
9. Attitudes toward exceptional children have moved from rejection and isolation to integration as much as possible into society and public schools.
10. The Education for All Handicapped Children Act contained six key principles that now shape special education programs: zero reject, nondiscriminatory evaluation, individualized education programs, least-restrictive environment, due process, and parental participation.
11. During the post–World War II era, substantial gains in support have been achieved through the actions of state and federal legislatures, confirming society's determination to provide equity to exceptional children and their families.
12. The courts have taken a series of actions to guarantee free public education for all children with handicaps, but implementation of those rulings has been slow.

UNRESOLVED ISSUES

Every generation leaves as its special legacy to the next certain problems for which solutions have not been found. There are many issues in the field of special education that today's professionals have been either unable or unwilling to resolve. The end-of-chapter sections entitled Unresolved Issues briefly describe several widely debated topics as a beginning agenda for the current generation of students who will face these problems in their professional or private lives.

1. *The search for exceptional children.*   The boundary line separating exceptional children from nonexceptional children has become blurred where children with mild handicaps are concerned. Yet legislation and the courts call for eligibility standards to clearly separate those who should receive special help from those who should not. How do we distinguish, for example, between the child who is emotionally disturbed and the child who is suffering a temporary behavior problem?

2. *Deinstitutionalization–normalization.*   With some years of experience behind us now with releasing mentally retarded or behaviorally disturbed children and adults from large residential institutions, we can see a shift of problems from the institution to the community. Unless the community provides supportive services, group homes, and occupational opportunities, the anticipated normalization of exceptional people is not likely to occur. In fact, we run the risk of substituting one form of misery for another.

3. *Gifted and exceptional children.*   Many people have difficulty integrating the special needs of gifted children with the needs of other exceptional children, a difficulty compounded by the exclusion of gifted children from federal legislation for exceptional children. Although gifted children do not have the major learning problems of many children with handicaps, the issue of unfulfilled potential is as critical for them. We agree with over half of the states in this country that include gifted children in their definition of exceptional children. Certainly their unmet needs in regular school programs, and the demands on schools to provide special learning environments, curriculums, and trained personnel for children with special gifts parallel the needs of other exceptional children.

4. *How much special education is enough?*   Recent court decisions have declared that the requirement in PL 94–142, Education for All Handicapped Children, for a "free appropriate public education" is satisfied as long as the state provides personalized instruction with support services that permit the child to benefit educationally and to move from grade to grade with passing marks (*Board of Education* v. *Rawley,* 1982). It does not require the state

to *maximize* the potential of each handicapped child. Such a legal opinion is bound to raise questions with educators as to how much is "enough." In addition, it will act as a signal to advocates for the handicapped that the courts are not necessarily going to be on their side on future issues. It is likely that within the next decade we will continue to see a struggle to determine just how much additional support will be "sufficient" to satisfy the law.

REFERENCES OF SPECIAL INTEREST

Ballard, J., Ramirez, B., & Weintraub, F. (1982). *Special education in America: Its legal and governmental foundation*. Reston, VA: Council for Exceptional Children.

> An excellent review of the major legislative and judicial actions that have affected exceptional children over the last two decades. The individual chapters explore the consequences of those actions for public school programs. A separate chapter focuses on gifted children, who are often ignored in this context.

Blatt, B., & Morris, R. (Eds.). (1984). *Perspectives in special education: Personal orientations*. Glenview, IL: Scott Foresman & Co.

> This unusual book describes ten pioneers in special education and presents personal reminiscences about their careers. As they tell how they developed their own ideas, they also give a personal history of special education. This book is especially useful for those who wish insight into how we, in special education, got to where we are today.

Gliedman, J., & Roth, W. (1980). *The unexpected minority: Handicapped children in America*. New York: Harcourt Brace Jovanovich.

> A report from the Carnegie Council on Children, which views the problems of handicapped children as a civil rights issue. The authors point out that those who are handicapped are a hidden minority group in our society, sharing many of the characteristics of other minority groups. They urge parents to greater activism in controlling services, both educational and vocational, for their exceptional children.

Powell, T., & Ogle, P. (1985). *Brothers and sisters—A special part of exceptional families*. Baltimore: Paul H. Brookes.

> A comprehensive review of the role played by nonhandicapped siblings in families with a handicapped child. The book examines sibling relationships from early childhood into adulthood. A special feature is an appendix that cites literature to help brothers and sisters understand the nature of their siblings' problems and why they behave the way they do. A second appendix lists sources of information for siblings and parents, including major parent and professional organizations.

Turnbull, H., & Turnbull, A. (Eds.). (1985). *Parents speak out: Then and now* (2d ed.). Columbus, OH: Charles E. Merrill.

A series of personal experiences told by professional families, each of whom has had a child who is handicapped. The parents discuss the frustrations of coping with their child, and the conflicts and difficulties they have had as parents dealing with other professionals. The book gives a good sense of the anger and despair felt by many of these parents.

C·H·A·P·T·E·R TWO

INDIVIDUAL DIFFERENCES AND SPECIAL EDUCATION

Focusing Questions

How do we define and measure interindividual and intraindividual differences?

What steps do we follow in the assessment process?

What elements are part of the individualized education program?

What alternative learning environments are being used today for exceptional children?

How are special educators using technology in the instruction of exceptional children?

What role does the family play in early intervention programs for young children with handicapping conditions?

How do alterable variables affect the special education program?

*W*e are all aware of how children of the same age vary physically. Some are tall and thin, others are short and chubby, with lots of variations in between. We find this same variation in other areas of development—intelligence, emotional maturity, and social development.

These individual differences can create a serious problem for the classroom teacher. If a third-grade lesson is directed at the average 8-year-olds, what happens to the child in the class whose intellectual development is at a 5-year-old level? Or to the child with the social maturity and cognitive abilities of an 11-year-old? Or to the youngster with the emotional maturity of a 4-year-old? The teacher has a problem. The lesson is going to be too difficult for one child and too easy for the other, while the third is creating a behavioral control problem for good measure.

INDIVIDUAL DIFFERENCES

When youngsters in the same classroom are remarkably different it is difficult for the teacher to help them reach their educational potential without some kind of assistance. The help that the schools devise for children who differ significantly from the norm is called special education.

What sometimes goes unnoticed is that some students not only differ substantially from others along key dimensions of development (interindividual differences) but also differ widely within their own abilities (intraindividual differences). A child may have the intelligence of an eleven-year-old but the social behavior of a six-year-old. Both interindividual and intraindividual differences are the concern of special educators.

Interindividual Differences

The development and extensive use of tests and measurements by American educators are designed to document various levels of development and in specific cases to determine why a particular student is not progressing satisfactorily. When these tests are administered to a population, they reveal the extent of interindividual differences in a school system, a state, or a nation.

Academic Performance

In any grade level there is a range of academic performance. Figure 2.1 shows the performance in 1980 of all sixth-grade students in North Carolina on the reading section of the California Achievement Test.

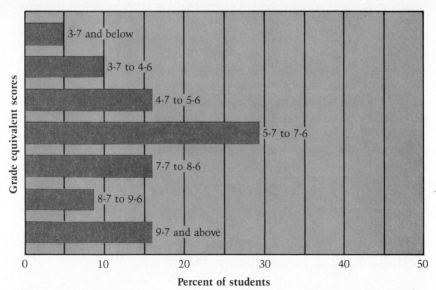

SOURCE: Data adapted from *Annual Testing Program* by the North Carolina Department of Public Instruction, Division of Research, 1981. Raleigh, NC: Author. Copyright 1981 by the Department of Public Instruction.

FIGURE 2.1
California Achievement Test results in reading for sixth-grade students in North Carolina, 1980.

(North Carolina requires all students to take the same achievement test in grades 3, 6, and 9 as a means of charting overall performance in the state.) Because the mean or average performance here closely matches national norms for the test, we would expect similar findings in student populations in most states.

Figure 2.1 gives the grade equivalent scores obtained by the students in reading.[1]

Approximately 29 percent of the youngsters scored within 1 grade level, plus or minus, of their grade status at the time of the examination. Another 16 percent scored 1 to 2 grade levels below the norm, and the same percentage scored 1 to 2 grade levels above the norm.

A small group—5 percent of the students—showed reading skills 3 grades or more below the norm, indicating a serious need for special education services. Another 10 percent scored between 2 and 3 grades below the norm. For these children, teachers would have to modify the programs, lessons, and assignments intended for youngsters at the sixth-grade level.

It's also interesting that almost 1 out of every 4 sixth-grade students was performing significantly above grade level, indicating a readiness

---

1. A grade equivalent score means that the student has obtained a raw score equal to the average performance of that grade. Although these scores have some serious statistical problems, they communicate useful information to teachers. We used them descriptively here.

Children vary greatly within their own abilities and capabilities; for example, a child with a physical handicap may have above-average intelligence. Such intraindividual differences are a prime concern of special educators.
(Alan Carey/The Image Works)

for more challenging material than the typical sixth-grade curriculum. But what is most striking about the data in the figure is how far away from the norm so many students were. Almost 4 out of every 10 students—39 percent—were either 2 or more grade equivalent scores below the norm or above it.

Without introducing the other dimensions in which students differ (motivation, social abilities), the teacher has three very different groups of students to deal with: those who are performing at grade level, those who are well below grade level and need major remediation, and those who are well above grade level and need greater challenge. It's not surprising, then, that teachers and principals reach out to special education to meet the varied educational needs of their students.

Academic Aptitude

Interindividual differences show up, not only in academic performance, but also in academic aptitude. The measure of that aptitude can tell teachers and schools a great deal about their student population and about how many students are performing below their potential.

For decades the standard measure of academic aptitude has been intelligence tests. These tests measure the development of memory, association, reasoning, and classification—the mental operations so important to school performance. In fact, these tests are accurate predictors of academic performance: Those who score high on intelligence tests generally do well in school; those who score low generally do poorly. You probably recognize these sample items from tests you've taken:

Mental operations	*Sample items*
Memory	Who was the first president of the United States?
Association	Glove is to hand as shoe is to _____.
Reasoning	If Paul is taller than Sam and Sam is taller than Tom, then Tom is _____ than Paul.
Classification	Which of the following does not belong? CHAIR SOFA TABLE RED

The mental operations they test are crucial to academic performance. Any serious problem with or delay in the development of these skills can create significant problems in school.

Intelligence tests assume a common experience base for most children, and are clearly inappropriate for youngsters for whom English is a second language or who have had atypical early childhood experiences.

The results of intelligence tests are usually reported in IQ scores that compare the child's performance with that of other children the same age. For the vast majority of American children tested, the results arrange themselves in a Gaussian curve—the normal distribution shown in Figure 2.2. This means that when a large sample of the population is examined, we find most members of the group clustered near average, with fewer and fewer members spread out to the extremes.

Figure 2.2 shows the normal dispersion of IQ scores on the Wechsler Intelligence Scale for Children (WISC). Over 68 percent of children score between 85 and 115 on the Wechsler scale. About 14 percent of children score between 70 and 85, with a similar percentage scoring between 115 and 130. A much smaller number (about 2 percent at either end) scores below 70 or above 130. At these extremes we find the children whose developmental differences require special attention.

These distributions represent a theoretical curve of the range of intelligence among children based on an intelligence test. When we measure reading, writing, spelling, height, weight, or even the length of the little finger, we find that the distribution follows this same theoretical curve. For example, notice how similar the distributions are in Figure 2.1 and Figure 2.2.

FIGURE 2.2
The theoretical distribution of IQ scores

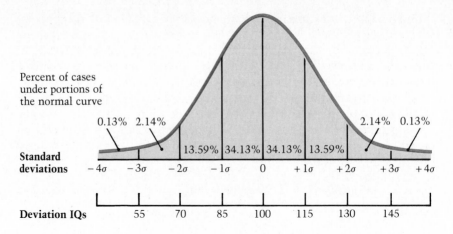

Intelligence tests have come under severe attack in recent years. One reason is the strong disagreement over the meaning of IQ scores. In the past, those scores have been used to indicate innate intellectual potential, to predict future academic performance, and to indicate a child's present rate of mental development compared to others of the same age. The sharpest criticism has been raised over the use of IQ scores to indicate intellectual potential. Extensive discussion leaves little doubt that intelligence tests should never be used to try to demonstrate the innate superiority of one sex or one ethnic or racial group (Sternberg, 1982). These tests are not pure measures of genetic potential. But they are valuable predictors and indicators of academic ability, and can and should be used professionally for these purposes.

Intraindividual Differences

Intraindividual differences—the differences in abilities within the child—give us the information we need to develop individualized programs of instruction. These programs adapt to the strengths and weaknesses of the individual child. They do not consider how that child compares with other children.

Intraindividual differences can show up in any area: intellectual, psychological, physical, or social. A child may be very bright but unable to or hear. Or a child may be developing normally physically but be unable to relate socially to peers. For teachers it is just as important to know the child's unique pattern of abilities and disabilities as it is to know how that child compares with other children.

Are there discrepancies in development? What can the child do? What is difficult for the child to do? Are there discrepancies in achievement? Is the child reading at a first-grade level and doing arithmetic at a third-grade level? All of these questions are part of the diagnosis and remediation process.

Social adaptation greatly influences how the exceptional child responds to remediation. Many failures to respond to special programs reflect behavioral and social problems, not academic ones. It is difficult to remediate a reading disability if a child has a severe attention problem or becomes aggressive when frustrated. For this reason special educators often focus on behavioral and social problems before they tackle academic difficulties.

Most of our information about the adaptive behavior of the exceptional child comes from direct observation or from interviews with family members and teachers—people who have known the child over an extended period of time. Also tests of adaptive behavior—like the AAMD Adaptive Behavior Scale, the Vineland Social Maturity Scale, and the System of Multicultural Pluralistic Assessment (SOMPA)— are available (Mercer & Lewis, 1977). Figure 2.3 shows sample items that measure degree of socialization and the extent to which a psychological disturbance is present. These instruments also explore histories of violent or antisocial behavior and of eccentric or unacceptable

FIGURE 2.3
Sample items assessing adaptive behavior

X. Socialization

[60] Cooperation (Circle only *ONE*)

Offers assistance to others	2
Is willing to help if asked	1
Never helps others	0

[61] Consideration for Others
(Check *ALL* statements which apply)

Shows interest in the affairs of others	—
Takes care of others' belongings	—
Directs or manages the affairs of others when needed	—
Shows consideration for others' feelings	—
_____ **None of the above**	

XIII. Psychological Disturbances

	Occasionally	Frequently
[37] Tends to Overestimate Own Abilities		
Does not recognize own limitations	1	2
Has too high an opinion of self	1	2
Talks about future plans that are unrealistic	1	2
Other (specify _____)	1	2
None of the above _____	Total	
[38] Reacts Poorly to Criticism		
Does not talk when corrected	1	2
Withdraws or pouts when criticized	1	2
Becomes upset when criticized	1	2
Screams and cries when corrected	1	2
Other (specify _____)	1	2
None of the above _____	Total	

SOURCE: From *AAMD Adaptive Behavior Scale for Children and Adults* by the American Association on Mental Deficiency, 1974. Washington, DC: Author.

habits, and measure both self-direction and responsibility. From the ratings, educators are able to tell how a child is adapting in terms of social and cooperative behaviors, and they are thus aided in creating an individualized program to meet the child's needs.

DEVELOPMENTAL PROFILES

Figure 2.3 shows the developmental profiles of two children. Joan is an intellectually gifted ten-year-old. Her mental ability tests at age 14; her achievement in reading and arithmetic, at 3 to 4 grades beyond her fifth-grade classmates. These are the interindividual differences between Joan and her classmates. But notice that Joan's performance shows many intraindividual differences. Although mentally she has

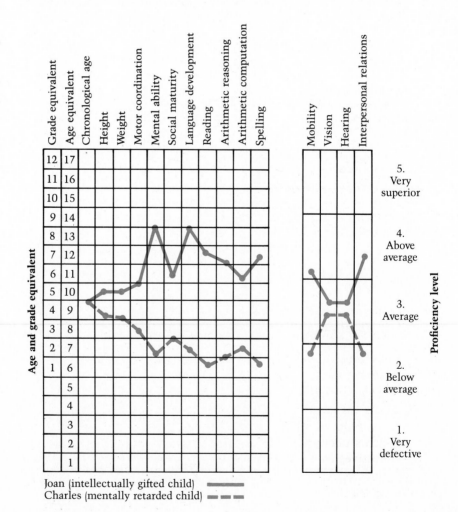

FIGURE 2.4
Profiles of an intellectually gifted child and a mentally retarded child

Joan (intellectually gifted child) ━━━━
Charles (mentally retarded child) ▬ ▬ ▬

the ability of a fourteen-year-old, her physical development is about average for a girl her age and her social maturity only slightly higher. If her parents or teachers expect her to behave like a fourteen-year-old in every dimension of development because her mental development is at that level they are going to be disappointed.

The second profile in Figure 2.4 is of Charles, a child who is mentally retarded. His profile shows him to be behind in development and performance in almost every dimension. Although he is 10 years old, his mental ability and academic performance are at first- and second-grade levels. These interindividual differences separate Charles from his classmates. In addition, Charles shows substantial intraindividual differences, ranging from the 6-year level in academic achievement to the 9- and 10-year levels in physical development and life age.

Joan and Charles have very different exceptionalities. Yet both present the same problem for their teachers and schools: Their interindividual and intraindividual differences set them apart from their classmates and require special attention.

ASSESSING EXCEPTIONAL STUDENTS

In the field of special education is a vast array of trained personnel whose objective is to provide an effective education for exceptional children. We find, not only teachers with special training in various areas of exceptionality, but also a large number of supplementary personnel (psychologists, social workers, communication specialists) and consultants (audiologists, opthalmologists, psychiatrists, neurologists). How do we trigger this complex network of special educators into action?

These educators and specialists use extensive testing and ratings to determine the child's interindividual and intraindividual differences. Their analysis of those differences allows them to make better educational decisions about the child. The assessment process involves five steps:

1. *Screening.* Quickly and economically finding those children who need more thorough (and costly) examination.
2. *Diagnosis, classification, and placement.* Collecting additional information to determine which special program the child needs or is eligible for.
3. *Instructional planning.* Using diagnostic information to design an individualized education program based on the child's needs.
4. *Pupil evaluation.* Administering tests to determine whether a particular student is indeed making expected progress and meeting the objectives that were originally established.
5. *Program evaluation.* Determining the effectiveness of a special program through tests and observation (Ysseldyke & Shinn, 1981).

Before an individual child's specific learning needs can be determined, both informal and formal evaluation must be conducted by classroom teachers and specialists. (Alan Carey/The Image Works)

Much of the misuse of tests comes from using an instrument that functions in one of these dimensions to answer questions about another. It is wrong, for example, to use a screening instrument to design an instructional plan.

A comprehensive assessment includes measurements or data collected across a number of developmental domains, including intelligence, academic achievement, social behavior, self-image, perceptual-motor abilities, vision, hearing, and other areas appropriate to the particular child.

We can see how the process works in the case of Diane, a seven-year-old. Diane was a slim child, somewhat small for her age. She was promoted to second grade mainly on the hopes of her first-grade teacher; her actual performance was not good. In the second grade, Diane was having trouble with the basic skills, reading and arithmetic. She was an unhappy child who did not talk a lot and who did not have many friends in the classroom.

In some school systems, Diane's problems might have been picked up by a screening before kindergarten or at the beginning or end of first grade. In this kind of screening, every child is quickly examined for major problems in vision, hearing, and learning ability. If a difficulty shows up, the child is referred for an intensive evaluation.

In Diane's school system, academic performance takes the place of the screening process. In fact this is how most students find their way into special education—through academic failure or through the perceptive observation of school personnel. As Bailey and Harbin (1980) pointed out:

> Children are not usually referred for evaluation on a teacher's whim. A referral indicates a significant educational problem that is unlikely to be remedied without some form of additional intervention with the teacher or child. (p. 595)

Diane's second-grade teacher recognized a problem and referred the child for diagnostic evaluation. She was given a series of tests and interviews to determine whether she did have a problem and to identify that problem. In the process the diagnostic team eliminated a number of factors that might have caused Diane difficulty. They looked for signs of physical disabilities, of serious emotional disturbance, of mental retardation, of environmental disadvantage.

The whole process of identification and diagnosis is designed to place the child with appropriate specialists. If Diane had had a hearing problem, for example, she would have been sent to an audiologist and given training in the use of a hearing aid. If she were mentally retarded, she would have received instruction appropriate to her mental level. If she had had a visual memory disability, her special education program would have focused on that problem.

After the initial diagnosis and classification a more thorough analysis of specific learning problems or difficulties was carried out. This was done to create a long-range individualized education program (IEP) for Diane, not simply to determine her placement in the school system or in the special education program. Earlier examinations had defined Diane's abilities and disabilities; now the educational team analyzed those abilities and disabilities to design a specialized program and teaching strategies for the child. Once the program goals were set and the individual program implemented, a plan would be set up to measure Diane's progress at subsequent points to see if these objectives had been achieved.

Pros and Cons of Classification and Labeling

The laws that were passed to increase funding for local schools to educate children with handicaps have created a problem. Because the laws state that special resources are only for handicapped children, it's become necessary to see to it that the children who are receiving help *are* handicapped. A legislator who wants to help children who are mentally retarded wants to be sure the money goes to help those children, not someone else.

The second step in the assessment process—the diagnosis that leads to classification and labeling—is the basis of a major controversy in special education. Is Diane deaf? Is she mentally retarded? Is she emotionally disturbed? There is no question that classification is an important part of the process: We have to identify the problem in order to remediate it. But many people question the end product of the classification, the label that attaches to the child.

Gallagher (1976) described several of the problems involved in labeling children by their exceptionalities:

- *The label becomes the person.* When we use the term *mentally retarded child* we're referring to just one characteristic of the child (like height or weight or personality). By using instead *a child who is mentally retarded,* we are not simply playing with words; we are making ourselves aware that mental retardation is only one facet of the child.

- *The label affects self-image.* If someone calls you crazy or stupid, it bothers you. But if enough people do it, you may begin to believe it yourself. One study found that high school boys who attended a class for retarded students would deny that they were enrolled in the special class (Jones, 1972). Former residents of institutions for the mentally retarded go to great lengths to deny that they ever lived in an institution or were "mentally retarded" (Edgerton, 1967). Labels, then, play a part in our self-image.

- *Labels can increase subgroup discrimination.* Many studies have shown a disproportionate number of minority group children in special education programs. This has raised the question of whether schools are using these programs as a form of segregation (Heller, Holtzman, & Messick, 1982). Certainly the incorrect labeling of some of these minority children as mentally retarded follows them through the school system (Mercer, 1975).

If labeling has these negative effects, why do we continue the practice? First, there are those who are not convinced that official labels create a problem. Children can be devastatingly cruel to those they perceive as different whether the school officially labels them different or not. This peer reaction can be more affecting then anything the school does.

And there are reasons that labeling is effective:

- *Differential treatments.* One of the standard uses of labeling is to provide the basis for some type of differentiated treatment. A child who is unresponsive to verbal communication and who seems chronically unhappy may be deaf or mentally retarded or emotionally disturbed. The label we place on the child creates a very different type of treatment program. And the earlier that differentiation is made, the more effective the program.

- *Search for etiology.* Epidemiologists must classify conditions as a preliminary step in identifying the factors that cause them (Kramer, 1975). Without these distinctions, scientists lose one of their most powerful weapons in the prevention of various disorders.

- *Obtaining needed resources for treatment.* Many special educators believe that needed resources for training and research and services would disappear if we no longer identified conditions. Are people more likely to give money to a general cause ("improving children") than to help children who are deaf or blind or mentally retarded?

INDIVIDUALIZED EDUCATION PROGRAM

One of the many innovations brought forth by the Education for All Handicapped Children Act is the requirement that every handicapped child have an individualized education program (IEP). That program defines the instructional plan:

- The nature of the child's problem
- The program's long-term objectives
- The program's short-term goals
- The special education services
- The criteria for gauging the effectiveness of those services

Table 2.1 is part of a comprehensive education plan for Joe, a fifth-grade student who is reading at a second-grade level. Because Joe's problems extend into other academic and developmental areas, his actual IEP would include plans to remediate his handwriting and arithmetic skills and behavior, as well as his reading skills.

Joe's IQ score (68 on the Wechsler scale) places him in the mild mentally retarded range. This makes him eligible for special educaton services in a resource room, a special classroom where he will work for an hour a day with a teacher trained in special education. And, because part of Joe's reading problem stems from poor vision—he does not wear his glasses regularly—the plan addresses that problem too.

Joe is typical in the sense that he has a variety of difficulties that are preventing him from performing his best. He needs a broad individualized education program.

SPECIAL EDUCATION ADAPTATIONS

The nature of special education is to provide exceptional students with services not available to them in the regular education program. Special education programs are different from regular programs because

Table 2.1
A Portion of Sample IEP (Joe, Grade 5)

Components of Plan	Data Included in IEP

1. Documentation of student's current level of educational performance	1. Woodcock Reading Mastery Test
	   Letter identification: 3–0 grade equivalent
	   Word identification: 1–8 grade equivalent
	   Word attack: 2–0 grade equivalent
	   Word comprehension: 4–3 grade equivalent

2. Annual objectives (the attainments expected by the end of the school year)	2. Student's oral reading rate at his reading level will increase from 30 words per minute to 36 words per minute. Student will apply context clue to decode difficult words.
3. Short-term goals, stated in instructional terms, leading to mastery of annual objectives	3. When presented with a list of 40 words and phrases frequently seen on signs, listed in order of difficulty, the student will correctly pronounce 30 of them.
4. Documentation of special education and related services to be provided to the child	4. Joe will be placed in a special resource room for children who are mildly mentally retarded. School psycholoIgist will work with parents to get Joe to wear his glasses. A complete medical and neurological examination is needed.
5. Appropriate evaluation procedures for determining mastery of short-term goals, to be applied on at least an annual basis	5. Brigance Diagnostic Inventory of Basic Skills administered after 4 and 9 months (for all reading objectives). Daily teacher observation.

SOURCE: Adapted from *Developing and Implementing Individualized Education Programs* (2d ed.) by A. Turnbull, B. Strickland, and J. Brantley (Eds.), 1982. Columbus, OH: Charles E. Merrill. Copyright 1982 by Charles E. Merrill. Adapted by permission.

they try to take into account the child's interindividual and intraindividual differences. It's important to realize that special education does not exist because regular education has failed. Classroom teachers simply cannot respond fully to the special needs of exceptional children. They have neither the time nor the resources.

There are three ways to adapt instruction to the interindividual and intraindividual differences found in exceptional children. We can change the actual content of lessons, the specific knowledge being taught; we can modify the skills being taught; or we can vary the environment to create an appropriate setting in which to learn.

Content

Some exceptional children require modifications in the content of the curriculum originally intended for students their age. For children who are gifted, we can accelerate content or provide different kinds of learn-

The instruction of special skills that enable exceptional individuals to cope better with their impairments is one of the important purposes of special education.
(Anorea Helms)

ing experiences. For students who are mentally retarded, we can relate lessons to their immediate experiences, to their homes, families, and neighborhoods. Instead of teaching about civilizations of the past or countries in Asia or South America, we can talk about their own towns and cities. For children with hearing problems, we may make linguistic changes in the curriculum; for children with visual problems, we can minimize visual-channel information. The point is we can adapt the content of the curriculum to the special needs of the students.

Skills

One educational objective is the mastery of skills, of reading, of arithmetic, of writing. Most students spend their first three years in school mastering basic skills. These skills are often taught in ways that encourage students to practice other skills—punctuality, attentiveness, persistence—skills that can lead to better social adaptation. Exceptional children often are taught the skills that average students master without special instruction. In addition, they sometimes must learn special skills to cope with their handicap. A blind student may learn braille; a deaf student, sign language. These are critical communication skills. In fact almost all exceptional children require some kind of skill training appropriate to their special needs.

Learning Environment

Often a special learning environment is necessary to help exceptional children master particular content and skills. Unlike modifications in content and skills, which in most instances can be made without affecting anyone outside the immediate group or classroom, changes in the learning environment are felt throughout the entire educational system. This may be one reason environmental modifications are the subject of greater controversy than are changes in either content or skills. When we move youngsters from the regular classroom to a resource room for an hour a day, we generate a series of activities. First, we have to allot space in the school for the resource room. Then, the classroom teacher must modify instruction to accommodate the students who are out of the class for part of the day. And, of course, a whole battery of special personnel must be brought into the system to identify eligible children and to deliver special services.

Figure 2.5 shows some of the most common learning environment modifications. The width of each section indicates the proportional number of exceptional children likely to be found in the particular setting. Starting at the bottom, the number grows as the settings move closer to the regular classroom, at the top of the diagram. The philosophy of least restrictive environment advocates special instruction for children that enables them to master necessary content and skills in a setting that is as close to normal as possible. That is, children who can be served effectively in a resource room should not be assigned to a special class; children who can learn with an itinerant teacher do not need a resource room. One objective of special education is to move exceptional children in the direction of the least restrictive environment, and eventually into the regular classroom.

Teacher Consultants and Itinerant Teachers

Whenever possible, we try to mainstream exceptional children, to keep them in regular classrooms. To help the classroom teachers understand these children's problems and ways to remediate them, many school systems provide trained teacher consultants. These consultants are available to regular teachers to answer questions about a child, materials, or methods of instruction, and to provide supplementary teaching aids and materials.

Speech-language pathologists, social workers, school psychologists, remedial reading teachers, and learning disability specialists may deal with exceptional children and classroom teachers on an itinerant basis. They usually serve several schools, visiting exceptional children and their teachers at regular intervals or whenever necessary. This means youngsters spend most of their time in the regular classroom, and are taken out of the classroom only for short periods of tutorial or remedial help.

FIGURE 2.5
Special learning environments for exceptional children

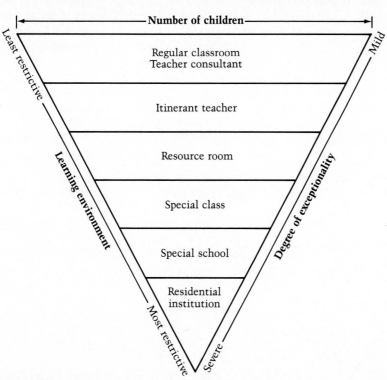

NOTE: Hospital and homebound services provided for handicapped children who may be confined for long periods of time fall within the realm of the residential institution setting on the scale of special education learning environments.

SOURCE: "Special Education as Developmental Capital" by E. Deno, 1970. *Exceptional Children*, 37, pp. 229–237. Copyright 1970 by the Council for Exceptional Children. Reprinted with permission.

Resource Rooms

Wiederholt, Hammill, and Brown (1978) defined a *resource room* as "any instructional setting to which a child comes for specific periods of time, usually on a regularly scheduled basis" (p. 13). The usual setting for a resource room is a small classroom, where a special teacher works with children for brief periods during the day. Resource room teachers consult with classroom teachers to develop programs that are intended to eventually eliminate the need for resource room help.

Part-time Special Classes

Part-time special classes accept children who require more time for special instruction than the short period in the resource room. The programs for the children in these classes are the responsibility of the special class teacher. Children in part-time special classes may spend half a day in the special class and the other half in the regular classrooms, in subjects in which they can compete. In junior and senior high schools, part-time special classes are used for exceptional children who are unable to meet standard class requirements and need sustained remedial or developmental lessons apart from the regular curriculum.

Self-contained Special Classes

At times moderately and severely handicapped children learn more effectively in self-contained special classes, where the special education teacher assumes primary responsibility for their programs. In the past this kind of class was the most common for all exceptional children. Today it's been substantially replaced, especially for mildly handicapped students, by itinerant teachers, resource rooms, and part-time special classes. Still, the self-contained special class continues to play a role in the total program for exceptional children.

Special Day Schools

Some school systems have organized day schools for different kinds of exceptional children, especially those who are behaviorally disturbed, orthopedically handicapped, moderately mentally retarded, and multiply handicapped. In line with the philosophy of the least restrictive environment, we see fewer special schools today. Children with mild handicaps can adapt to regular classrooms. And contact with other children prepares exceptional children for a life in which they have to make adjustments to others without handicapping conditions.

Residential Schools

Every state in this country has residential schools or institutions for children with handicapping conditions (mental retardation, blindness, deafness, orthopedic handicaps, behavioral disturbances). Some of these institutions are privately administered; most, however, are administered by public agencies. Historically, residential schools are the oldest educational provision for exceptional children. Most have been built away from population centers and too often have become segregated, sheltered asylums with little community contact.

Hospital and Homebound Services

Sometimes children with physical handicaps are confined to hospitals or their homes for long periods of time. To avoid educational retardation, specially trained itinerant teachers travel to the students and

Some hospitals provide full-time teachers to instruct children with physical handicaps who may require long periods of hospitalization.
(© Christopher Morrow/Stock, Boston)

tutor them during their convalescence. Usually local school systems assign teachers to help homebound children for an hour or more a day assuming their condition permits.

Technology and Microcomputers

Special education has often led the way in the acceptance and use of technology in education. This may well be due to the problems special educators face. Because they are educating children with such special difficulties, they have been willing to try any new device that promises help: special typewriters, hearing aids, print magnifiers, machines that trace eye movements as the student reads. The latest and perhaps the most significant of these technological devices is the microcomputer. The microcomputer allows the child to learn at his or her own rate and provides immediate feedback and reinforcement. It makes the process of learning more active and self-directed.

The microcomputer has become particularly important in special education because it offers specific advantages to exceptional children. First, there are a number of microcomputer programs available to teach basic reading and arithmetic skills—two important problem areas for exceptional children. Second, the microcomputer works well in resource rooms, providing specialized remedial lessons that allow exceptional children to remain in the regular classroom for most of their instruction. Third, many microcomputer activities use a gamelike format that special educators have found effective for teaching visual motor skills and specific academic skills. Fourth, youngsters who learn to operate the equipment have the satisfaction of being independent and controlling their own program, not an everyday experience for most exceptional children. Finally, the microcomputer makes record keeping much easier. Its tracking system allows the school to keep updated records on the tests students have taken, their progress in individualized programs, and a host of evaluative reports.

Yin and White (1984) conducted case study interviews on the uses of microcomputers in twelve school systems, each of which had been using the machines for at least a year and a half. They found heavy use in special education, particularly for basic skills instruction. One teacher remarked that it "was like having an extra aide in the classroom" (p. C–5). They also found that the computers seemed to enhance cooperation between special education teachers and classroom teachers in planning lessons for exceptional children. These teachers were working together, choosing lessons on the microcomputer that met joint needs.

The microcomputer is a relatively new tool, and we are finding new uses for it on a regular basis. Still, there is already an impressive list of applications for exceptional children (Nave, Browning, & Carter, 1983):

- Deaf children are learning language skills with computers and video discs (Galbraith, 1978).
- Computers are providing special learning sequences for mentally retarded children who have short-term memory deficits and are impulsive learners (Grimes, 1981).
- Their data storage capability (for instance, their ability to list thousands of teacher objectives) makes computers a resource for teachers working on specific target skills (Brown, 1982).
- Computerized communication boards are helping children who cannot speak to communicate with others (Rahimi, 1981).
- Computers are translating braille into print and print into braille for children with severe vision problems (McConnell, 1982).

Vanderheiden (1982) pointed out that there are a number of very special uses that can be made of the microcomputer for exceptional children who have lost or have never had the use of their hands, who

FOR DISABLED, COMPUTERS ARE CREATING NEW LIVES

Once forced to rely on others to read, write or speak for them, about 20,000 people across the country are now using specially adapted personal computers to help make up for their disabilities.

The technology has the potential to allow about four million Americans to compete in mainstream employment and education, according to experts in the field.

For the visually impaired, a voice synthesizer can be attached to a computer to read words that appear on a video display terminal. A similar device can be programmed to speak for people who cannot talk.

Software can translate the text appearing on a computer screen into printed Braille. The same text can be displayed on a VersaBraille, which has plastic pins that can be raised and lowered to form a line of Braille.

People with limited mobility can use keyboards with oversize keys or devices that can replace keyboards altogether. These include plastic tubes that can be operated by what is known as "sip and puff," a system for translating inhaled and exhaled air into text. For the deaf, computer mail, printed information that can be transmitted instantly to and from other computers, can replace office telephones. . . .

"This technology is going to change lives as nothing has before," said Dr. Frank G. Bowe, director of research for the Federal Architectural and Transportation Barriers Compliance Board in Washington. . . . "You may be handicapped, but for the first time in history you and the computer can do almost anything anyone else can do. If you can't see, don't worry, the machine does. If you can't get to and from work, the machine can by getting orders from the boss to you and your work to the boss."

Scott Luber is a 25-year-old accountant with muscular dystrophy who works for Nankin, Schnoll & Company, an accounting firm in Milwaukee. He is one of hundreds of men and women who are employed because of their proficiency with adapted computers. "They told me if I could adapt a computer to my needs, I'd be hired," Mr. Luber said.

Atop a special mechanized desk, he uses an I.B.M. PC with a miniature keyboard, actually a Sharp pocket computer. Resting his hands on the desk, he manipulates two pencils to strike the computer's keys.

Computers can also help children with disabilities in school. "A deaf child can participate in class, can answer a teacher's questions, can even joke with other students in the classroom," Dr. Bowe said.

Shoshana Brand, 10, is blind and has cerebral palsy. She attends . . . a public school in El Cerrito, Calif. Before she got her computer three years ago, she needed other people to read and write for her. "She learned that if she waited long enough, someone would tell her what to write, and she didn't learn," said her mother, Jacquelyn Brand. "Now she is actually going through the

continued

continued

process of writing and developing her own thoughts." Mrs. Brand added that her daughter is advancing two academic years for every year spent in school. Shoshana uses an Apple IIe computer equipped with an Echo II voice synthesizer and a keyboard with keys twice the usual size. She types with her thumbs.

Some of these computer adaptations have been available since 1979, but the majority of people with disabilities—an estimated 25 million in the United States—still do not have computers. Of these, about four million, those who are mentally alert and in relatively good health, could likely use a computer to best advantage on the job or in school.

However, only 20,000 are doing so. . . . The cost and a lack of awareness on the part of many rehabilitation counselors and teachers are the main reasons more people with disabilities are not using computers. . . .

An adapted computer, with software, often costs between $2,000 and $10,000. Some equipment is available for as little as $200, but the Kurzweil reader, which reads printed pages aloud in a synthesized voice, costs $30,000. . . .

Medicare and Medicaid rarely pay for adapted computers, and Federal laws enacting programs that provide aid for people with disabilities—the Education for All Handicapped Children's Act and the Rehabilitation Act of 1973, for example—do not specifically list computers as "appropriate purchases." The available money is far more likely to be used for basics such as wheelchairs or special-education teachers.

"The laws are vague and applied unevenly by people who have a stake in keeping their budgets down and by people who don't know that the technologies are available," said Clyde J. Behney, health program manager for the Office of Technology Assessment. . . .

Some state departments of education and rehabilitation have purchased computers for a few individuals with disabilities. "But even in states that are meeting this area, only a small portion of individuals who could truly benefit are able to get computer-based devices," said Dr. Gregg C. Vanderheiden, director of the Trace Center, which works with people with disabilities at the University of Wisconsin at Madison. . . .

Dr. Vanderheiden said that computers are a good buy for government medical and rehabilitation programs. "They can make individuals more independent and allow them to live more productive lives," he said. "That would save money in the long run."

According to the National Institute of Handicapped Research, Federal and state governments spend some $60 billion annually to support people with disabilities; about $25 to $30 million goes to researching rehabilitation technology. Of that, about $2 million goes toward research on adapted computers. . . .

Technology that can be used by people with disabilities lags behind the general computer market. Each new computer model requires new accessories and software before it can be used by people with disabilities.

continued

continued

Dr. Vanderheiden . . . met with computer manufacturers at the White House last February in an effort to create a standard system for interconnecting devices to all new personal computers. . . .

That sort of cooperation, along with increasing numbers of special-education teachers and rehabilitation counselors who are taking computer training classes, are hopeful signs, said Dr. Martha Redden, director of the Project on the Handicapped at the American Association for the Advancement of Science in Washington.

"It's still new, but there is no question that attitudes are changing," she said. "People are learning that a computer could be put alongside a wheelchair or a hearing aid in opening new worlds for the disabled."

SOURCE: From "For Disabled, Computers Are Creating New Lives" by Sherry Sontag, August 24, 1985, pp. 1, 48. Copyright © 1985 by The New York Times Company. Reprinted by permission.

have never been able to explore their world through physical manipulation:

> Learning that involves manipulation, such as might be found in chemistry, physics, and other sciences, presents another problem area. Here, microcomputers and computer-aided instruction can allow an individual to manipulate and explore ideas, concepts, figures, etc., in structured but flexible ways. Such programs can allow severely physically disabled individuals to handle "flasks" and "chemicals" on the TV screen and carry out experiments and manipulations that would otherwise be beyond their direct control. (p. 142)

Vanderheiden also described vocational applications for students who are disabled:

> Because of the many ways in which microcomputers can aid individuals with disabilities, and because of the direction in which many aspects of the employment world are heading, it is quite clear that microcomputers hold future vocational potential for disabled individuals. (p. 142)

Advocates like Papert (1980) believe that the microcomputer is going to revolutionize the educational process, that "schools as we know them today will have no place in the future" (p. 9). Whether this is true or not, it's clear that the microcomputer is a valuable tool to help teachers in special and regular education.

EARLY CHILDHOOD PROGRAMS FOR CHILDREN WITH HANDICAPS

In the chapters that follow we talk about what the public and private schools are doing for exceptional children once they reach school age. But what about the five or six years before that? What is being done for exceptional children during the crucial period of early development?

Fortunately, many exceptional children receive services from birth on, services that allow these children to respond more readily to later programs in school.

In fact, the number of medical, social, and educational services available to young children is growing. But most of these programs are geared for moderately and severely handicapped youngsters. They tend to ignore both mildly handicapped and gifted children. Why? Often mildly handicapped youngsters go unnoticed. Only when demands for academic competence and social conformity are made on them in school do their developmental limitations become obvious. Gifted children rarely receive systematic attention before school because few people see any necessity for being concerned about children who are progressing faster than normal.

Screening for Handicapping Conditions

The fact that all children in our society are expected to be in school by the age of 6 makes screening these children for possible handicapping conditions in early school years feasible. The children are where we can find them and can concentrate our professional services to identify those who need special help.

But how do we find preschoolers who need professional attention? One effort to identify these children is called Child Find. Obstetricians, pediatricians, social workers, and others who come into contact with handicapped children and their families provide their names so that services can be made available to them. Also, some neighborhoods, church groups, and day care centers are screened by teams of professionals checking vision, hearing, learning ability, and language development to identify children in need. And several states (Nebraska, Minnesota, North Carolina) have established telephone hot lines for parents looking for help in or near their community (Thompson, 1985).

Obviously it's impossible to screen all children for all conditions. It's important, then, to know what conditions we are screening for and why. Frankenburg (1977) described five criteria for using screening as a technique:

• The condition should be treatable or controllable.
• Early treatment should help more than later treatment.

Many exceptional children of preschool age, who are diagnosed very early in life, receive services from birth on, services that allow these children to respond more readily to later programs in school.
(Bohdan Hrynewych/Southern Light)

- A firm diagnosis should be possible.
- The condition should be relatively prevalent.
- The condition should be serious or potentially so.

The Family

The discovery that their child has a handicapping condition is clearly a crisis for the family. Although certain families seem to cope well with the situation, there is evidence that the pressures of having a handicapped child take their toll. Gallagher and Bristol (in press) found that there were approximately twice as many divorces in families with young handicapped children as in families with children of similar age with no handicaps. Embry (1980) found an increase in child abuse in families with handicapped children. Many of these parents also feel guilty, as though they had done something to cause the handicap (hardly likely in most cases). To add to these difficulties, a handicapped child can be a serious financial drain on the family because of necessary medical, social, and special educational services (McAndrew, 1976).

Family intervention services treat, not only the child with the handicap, but parents and siblings as well. Wolery and Bailey (1985) noted several reasons family intervention services are important:

- Families with handicapped children experience high levels of stress and may need professional support.
- Families may not know how to interact appropriately with their children.
- Families may not perceive themselves as having control over their future and need information regarding rights and service options. (pp. 120–121)

In addition, family members often play a key role in the treatment program. Using a parent (almost always the mother) as a teacher offers the child the presence of a caring adult who can spend a great deal of time working with the child to develop self-help skills and appropriate social behaviors. Effective parent training shows the parent precisely how to proceed on the task and provides instruction in necessary teaching skills (Zangwell, 1983; Blacher, 1985).

Some feel that parents should not be forced into being a part of the treatment team, that sometimes the most important help we can offer parents is *respite care*. This program provides child care services for the handicapped youngster while parents take time for themselves or share a weekend vacation away from the constant responsibilities of having a handicapped child (Joyce & Singer, 1983).

Although relatively few parents seem to need serious counseling or psychotherapy, having a counselor to talk over problems managing the child can be important. Many parents report that the most satisfying help they receive comes from other parents of handicapped children, often through an organized group like the National Association for Retarded Citizens. These other parents have been "there" and can provide understanding and sympathy when they are sorely needed (Turnbull & Turnbull, 1985).

The Importance of Multidisciplinary Teams

The many different services needed by young handicapped children can cut across the skills of various professions. No one person—no pediatrician, no special educator, no language specialist—can diagnose and treat a moderately or severely handicapped child. For example, some children born with cerebral palsy also have vision impairments. Those children may need

- physical therapy to help develop remaining muscles.
- speech and language therapy to help them talk and use language.

- developmental education training to help prepare them for later schooling.
- family counseling to prepare their families for the problems of coping with their handicaps.
- opthalmological examinations to treat the vision impairment.

Obviously we need a team of professionals to put these services together and coordinate them. To meet the multiple needs of handicapped children and their families, many clinics and centers house all different kinds of professionals.

Handicapped Children's Early Education Program

An awareness of the importance of the early development of children with handicaps led the Office of Special Education Programs in 1968 to initiate the Handicapped Children's Early Education Program (HCEEP). The purpose of the program was to demonstrate practices for preschool handicapped children and to encourage communities and states to begin preschool programs of their own.

In 1984 there were over eighty demonstration centers across the United States illustrating a wide variety of practices for children with varying handicapping conditions. The programs listed below show the diversity of the demonstration programs:

- The Language and Cognitive Development Center in Jamaica Plain, Massachusetts, deals with severely emotionally disturbed children who manifest compulsive repetitive behavior. The program's novel theoretical base focuses on Hispanic children living in a low-income area.
- The University of Washington has designed a correspondence course that matches up parents in similar circumstances so that more experienced parents can help "newer" parents. The project was designed after letters received by the university described a lack of services and a need for specific information.
- The Children's Hospital Center in Oakland, California, is serving high-risk infants in double jeopardy because of dysfunctional parent-child relationships. The project demonstrates the cooperation of health, mental health, and developmental and educational agencies at the local level (DeWeerd, 1984).

The centers are just one part of a coordinated network of programs. There are over fifty outreach projects nationwide demonstrating other programs for handicapped preschoolers. Figure 2.6 describes one of these programs. And the HCEEP funds studies of issues like the early development of social behaviors, the facilitation of parenting handicapped children, and program evaluation. Also a technical assistance program provides help to local projects and to state departments of education that want to establish a state program for preschool children with handicaps.

ALTERABLE VARIABLES: OUR LIMITATIONS

We've talked about how we identify exceptional students, how we develop individualized education programs to help them, and how we adapt content, skills, and environment to make their learning easier.

FIGURE 2.6
Sample Outreach Program: Precise Early Education for Children with Handicaps (PEECH)

Address	University of Illinois Colonel Wolfe School 403 East Healey Champaign, Illinois 61820	Phone: (217) 333–4894
Fiscal Agency	University of Illinois	
Director	Merle B. Karnes	
Coordinator	Wendy Boyce Sercombe	
Other Staff Titles	replication specialist, evaluator, materials developer	

Source of Continuation Funding for Service Delivery Program:

Joint agreement between Rural Champaign County Education Cooperative and the University of Illinois

Description of Demonstration Model:

PEECH is a center-based program serving handicapped children age 3 to 5 years and their families. Although the mildly to moderately handicapped are the project's primary population, procedures have been adapted for lower-functioning, sensory-impaired children. The project obtains pre- and posttest data on all children. Teachers assess each child's abilities using the Systematic Child Observation and Assessment for Programming (SCOAP) instrument, set individual goals and objectives, and continually evaluate child progress.

Major Outreach Goals:

- To train personnel to develop, implement, and demonstrate a model early education program for preschool handicapped children.
- To prepare and disseminate materials to help early childhood personnel educate handicapped children.

Major Outreach Services:

PEECH provides intensive training to each year's replication site and presents component workshops on topics relevant to early childhood special education. The project mails materials to interested professionals throughout the United States.

Features and Products:

The project developed the SCOAP child assessment instrument and provides the instrument to replication sites. PEECH has also developed classroom and parent activity manuals and numerous handouts on relevant topics in early childhood special education.

SOURCE: From *Directory—1983–84 Edition Handicapped Children's Early Education Programs* (p. 93) by D. Assael (Ed.), 1984. Chapel Hill, NC: University of North Carolina at Chapel Hill, Technical Assistance Development System.

These are special education methods, effective ways to educate children with special needs. But these are not infallible or all-powerful. They do not work for every child and every handicapping condition. There are problems beyond the reach of special education—variables that limit effective remediation.

Scientists look for all the factors that have an impact on the developing child; special educators, recognizing that there are factors beyond their control, are more interested in the elements that can be changed or modified in some significant way to help the child. They search for what Bloom (1982) called "alterable variables."

Not all of the elements that relate to student performance can be changed. Student aptitude, family income, ethnic background, home environment, neurological damage—all have an important effect on student performance but as educators we are powerless to manipulate or change them significantly. These are factors that set limits on what we can achieve in special education programs.

This means we have to focus these programs on factors we can change, on the alterable variables. The first step in determining those variables is to look at the factors that seem to influence school performance for all children, exceptional or not. Walberg (1984) synthesized the results from several generations of research on school achievement. He found nine factors, falling into three categories, that contribute significantly to student learning in the affective, behavioral, and cognitive domains:

Student aptitude

1. Ability or prior achievement as measured by the usual standardized tests.
2. Development, as indexed by chronological age or stage of maturation.
3. Motivation or self concept, as indicated by personality tests or the student's willingness to proceed- intensively on learning tasks.

Instruction

4. The amount of time students engage in learning.
5. The quality of the instructional experience, including psychological and curricular aspects.

Environmental factors

6. The home.
7. The classroom social group.
8. The peer group outside the school.
9. Use of out-of-school time (i.e., the amount of leisure-time television viewing). (p. 20)

Which of these elements can be altered through special education? Instructional strategies—the amount of time students spend in learning and the quality of instruction—come under the direct influence of educators, as does the classroom social group. By working with parents and community, we can have an indirect influence on motivation, the home, the peer group outside school, and free time use. But there is nothing we can do about prior achievement or maturation.

How do these variables—alterable and inalterable—affect special education? First, they help us define our involvement. For example, a student whose home environment is causing an academic problem would probably not be eligible for learning disability programs. These programs focus on developmental problems that impede learning, not environmental ones. We would help this student, then, in other ways. Second, these factors help us define our methods. Special education programs are developed around the child, the child's current abilities and needs. They are geared to the child's own pace. We don't emphasize what the child has done in the past or where the child is in relationship to classmates; we concentrate on what the child is able to do now and build the program from that point—moving slowly, step by step, to our objectives. Those objectives, of course, are the third effect these alterable variables have on special education. By knowing what we can change and what we can't change, we're able to set realistic goals for each child, to allow each child to achieve to the best of his or her abilities.

ORGANIZING PRINCIPLE: THE CHILD

Any book on education must focus on one of the three major dimensions of the education process: (1) the learner, (2) teacher-learner interaction (instruction), or (3) the learning environment.

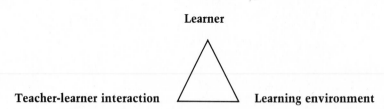

When we focus on the learner, we talk about individual children or clusters of children. When we focus on teacher-learner interaction, we organize material around teaching techniques (the stimulation of language development or social skills). When we focus on the environment, we organize the text around various environmental modifications (special classes, resource rooms, itinerant teacher programs).

We've used the first of the approaches—the exceptional child as a learner—to organize this book. We believe it's important to paint a

Starting from the vantage point of the exceptional child as a learner, it is easier to select the most appropriate learning environment and to develop the most suitable instructional strategies for that learner.
(© Meri Houtchens-Kitchens 1982)

portrait of the exceptional child as a human being. Once we recognize the individuality of each child, it's easier to choose the most objective instructional strategies and the most suitable learning environment.

SUMMARY OF MAJOR IDEAS

1. Measures of academic performance (achievement tests) and cognitive ability (intelligence scales) indicate an impressive range of interindividual differences among children. Planning instruction to accommodate these differences is a major problem for classroom teachers.
2. Intelligence tests should never be used to indicate genetic potential; they are effective, however, for predicting academic performance and determining a child's current rate of mental development in relation to agemates.
3. Intraindividual differences are major variations in the abilities or

development of a particular child. They are an important factor in planning the child's individualized education program.

4. The assessment of exceptional children involves discovery (screening or referral), diagnosis for placement purposes, and an individualized education program, as well as ongoing evaluation to assess pupil progress and program effectiveness.

5. Labeling exceptional children is an essential step in obtaining resources to help them, but it can affect their self-image and the attitudes of their peers toward them.

6. An individualized education program defines (a) the nature of the child's problem, (b) the program's long-term objectives, (c) the program's short-term goals, (d) the special education services, and (e) the criteria for gauging the effectiveness of those services.

7. There are three ways to adapt instruction to the needs of exceptional children: by changing curriculum content, by modifying the skills we teach them, and by altering the learning environment.

8. Alternative learning environments range from the use of teacher consultants in the regular classroom to placement in special residential schools. The purpose of modifying the learning setting is to provide the child with the best learning setting.

9. Microcomputers are an effective educational tool for exceptional children because they allow students to progress at their own rate and provide immediate feedback on performance.

10. Many attempts have been made to provide comprehensive, multidisciplinary services for preschool children with handicaps. The availability of these services varies markedly from one community to another.

11. Services for the preschool child with handicaps focus on the family, helping family members adapt to the presence of a handicapped child, as well as helping the child.

12. Alterable variables are those factors that influence student learning that can be modified by educational programming. The knowledge that certain variables are not affected by instructional programs helps us define our involvement, our methods, and our objectives for special education.

UNRESOLVED ISSUES

1. *Special education and regular education.* Special education assumes competent educational programs in regular schools. Children who are not able to respond to these programs are identified as exceptional students and given special help.

But what if a regular program falls short of basic competence? What if it is not providing a stimulating or appropriate educational environment for all students? What is the role of special education here? Too often, poor educational programs flood special education programs with borderline students. We cannot protect the rights of children in need if we use special education programs for those who are not exceptional.

2. *Malleability of children.* We in education are in the business of trying to improve the status of children. How much change can we expect from educational programs? We know that children are pliable, but what are the limits of their malleability?

A quiet child is not going to be transformed into an extrovert by our efforts. A child who is mentally retarded is not going to become a gifted child by our efforts. We must know the limits of our expectations in order to judge the success of what we do.

3. *Microcomputers and personal instruction.* Microcomputers present us with some tempting possibilities. They interact with children in ways that teachers cannot. In a typical classroom, the teacher can't respond instantly to every student, offering reinforcement and encouragement. Yet it's hard for us to believe that the human relationships that are formed between teacher and student can be replaced by a computer, however comprehensively it's programmed. The teacher is still the most influential element in the educational process—a source of thoughtful, flexible responses. And our classrooms in the future must learn to mix that humanity with technology.

REFERENCES OF SPECIAL INTEREST

Kauffman, J., & Hallahan, D. (Eds.). (1981). *Handbook of special education.* Englewood Cliffs, NJ: Prentice-Hall.
A valuable reference for special educators. The thirty-four chapters expertly cover current issues in conceptual foundations, service delivery systems, curriculums and methods, and child and environmental management. This is a book to keep on the library shelf for some time to come.

McLoughlin, J., & Lewis, R. (1981). *Assessing special students: Strategies and procedures.* Columbus, OH: Charles E. Merrill.
This book successfully combines clinical observations and testing procedures in developing a model of assessment for special students. The authors discuss the nature of assessment and its technical aspects. Much of the book focuses on the application of assessment to school problems and the ways tests are used in team decision making.

Nave, G., Browning, P., & Carter, J. (1983). *Computer technology for the handicapped in special education and rehabilitation: A resource guide.* Eugene, OR: International Council for Computers in Education.
A comprehensive collection of abstracts from articles, books, monographs, and reports that apply computer technology to the special education problems of those who are handicapped. The book has separate indexes by author, handicapping condition, periodicals, and so forth.

C·H·A·P·T·E·R Three

CHILDREN WHO ARE GIFTED AND TALENTED

Focusing Questions

What are the special problems of girls who are gifted?

How can we modify the behavior of gifted underachievers?

What roles do heredity and the environment play in the development of intellectual giftedness?

In what ways are gifted children identified?

How are productive-thinking skills integrated into special education programs for gifted youngsters?

How are content acceleration, enrichment, sophistication, and novelty different?

*E*ver since a senior member of the tribe brought a few children into the cave to teach them about survival in prehistoric times, it's been evident that some youngsters learn faster than others, remember more easily than others, and are able to solve problems more efficiently and creatively than others. It's also been obvious that these youngsters are often bored with the pace of instruction, a pace geared to average children, and that they pose a challenge to their teachers, occasionally an embarrassing one. Picture a bright child in the prehistoric cave innocently asking, "What happens if the spear misses the saber-toothed tiger?"

Society has a special interest in gifted children, both as individuals and as potential contributors to society's well-being. As individuals, they have the same right to full development as do all children. In addition, many of the leaders, scientists, and poets of the next generation will come from the current group of gifted and talented children. Few societies can afford to ignore or scorn that potential.

All other *exceptional* children have deficits in one or more areas of development. Gifted children are the only group of exceptional youngsters with surplus ability or talent. As this chapter shows, that very surplus creates unique educational challenges for these children, their families, and the typical school system.

DEFINITIONS

The term *gifted* has been used traditionally to refer to people with intellectual gifts, and we use it here the same way. Each culture defines *giftedness* in its own image, conferring on the gifted individual abilities it prizes. Ancient Greece honored the orator; Rome valued the engineer and the soldier. From that definition we learn something about the values and lifestyles of the culture. We also learn that the exceptional person is often a blend of individual ability and societal need or reaction.

In the United States, an early definition of giftedness was tied to performance on the Stanford-Binet Intelligence Scale, which was developed by Lewis Terman shortly after World War I. Children who scored above a certain point—an intelligence quotient score of 130 or 140 or whatever was agreed on—were called gifted. They would represent 2 to 3 percent of the age-group population.

Essentially, a high score on the Stanford-Binet or other intelligence tests meant that children were developing more rapidly than their agemates. It was not so much the uniqueness of what they were doing as the time developmentally at which they were doing it. A child

Individuals capable of high performance on a musical instrument are included in the definition of gifted and talented.
(George Bellerose/Stock, Boston)

playing chess is not a phenomenon; but a child playing chess seriously at age 5 is. Lots of children write poetry, but not at age 6, when most are just learning to read. Early rapid development is one of the clear indicators of high intellectual ability, and that is what is picked up by intelligence tests.

Over the past two decades, attempts have been made to broaden our concept of giftedness by including other dimensions of ability. One popular definition was proposed by former U.S. Commissioner of Education Sidney Marland (1972). His description has been used in federal legislation, and although subsequent efforts have modified it, it still covers the territory well.

> Gifted and talented children are those identified by professionally qualified persons who, by virtue of outstanding abilities, are capable of high performance. These are children who require differentiated educational programs and services beyond those normally provided by the regular program in order to

realize their contribution to self and society. Children capable of high performance include those with demonstrated achievement and/or potential ability in any of the following areas:

1. General intellectual ability
2. Specific academic aptitude
3. Creative or productive thinking
4. Leadership ability
5. Visual and performing arts (p. 10)

This definition does not restrict giftedness to linguistically facile children; instead, it recognizes youngsters with a diversity of talents. Despite this effort to go beyond the cognitive domain, strong emphasis is still placed on intelligence tests for identifying gifted children because (1) they are well-developed, proven instruments, and (2) they tap those intellectual operations so crucial to high performance in school-related activities.

Table 3.1 shows several of the intellectual operations expected of schoolchildren. Gifted students perform much better than their age-mates in all of these dimensions. Some operations seem more dependent on experience than others, and IQ scores clearly depend, not only on native ability, but also on the opportunity to experience ideas. You cannot remember what a giraffe is if you've never seen or heard of one. IQ tests in general have been criticized for focusing too much on memory, association, and convergent reasoning, and too little on divergent reasoning and evaluation, which would seem to be important in creativity. Questions that test divergent reasoning ("What would happen if oil was suddenly not available?") are rarely found in intelligence tests, or in the classroom for that matter.

Children who are highly creative consistently generate innovative solutions to problems or create unique products on their own initiative. When this creation is verbal, we expect students to perform well in the intellectual operations of divergent reasoning and evaluation. When creativity is in a nonverbal area (art, music), we expect similar excellence in divergent reasoning and evaluation but within the symbol system (musical notes, scales) of the concept field.

Students who excel in leadership are consistently looked to by peers and adults to take charge of group activities and they receive the support and admiration of peers for their efforts. Often a student who is high in one of these areas of ability is high in them all. We will see an example of that in Cranshaw, a boy we describe in the next section.

Not everyone agrees on the usefulness of distinguishing between *gifted* and *talented*. **Talented** generally refers to a specific dimension of skill (musical, artistic) that may not be matched by a child's more general abilities. In most children, however, there is a substantial positive relationship between intellectual giftedness and talent.

Table 3.1
Intellectual Operations

Intellectual Operations		Questions or Test Items	Presumed Cultural Influence
Memory	Short-term	Repeat what I say: 3–7–2–9–6	Only requires paying attention to task.
	Long-term	What is a giraffe?	Must have had prior experience with the concept as well as remembering.
Relations		Foot is to shoe as hand is to _____.	Relies partly on experience and partly on basic thinking processes.
Classification		Name the one that doesn't belong: Horse/Whale/Cow/Flounder	Concepts are most often taught. Ability to understand clusters or groupings appears fundamental.
Reasoning	Convergent	If Sam is taller than Pete and Sam is shorter than Joe, then Pete is _____ than Joe.	Little cultural influence. Basically an internal intellectual process.
	Divergent	What would happen if oil was suddenly not available?	Number and kinds of answers depend on past experience—also self-confidence and freedom from inhibitions.
Evaluation		Who is the stronger president, Washington or Lincoln?	The criterion "stronger" is learned, but the ability to match or compare seems to be a basic thinking process.

The direction in which gifts and talents emerge depends on several factors: experience, motivation, interest, emotional stability, hero worship, parental urging, even chance. Many intellectually gifted individuals might also have been successful in another area if their interests and training had been focused on that direction.

DEVELOPMENTAL PROFILES

We would like you to meet two children, Cranshaw and Zelda. Both are 10 years old and in the fifth grade. Cranshaw probably meets the criteria of intellectual, creative, and leadership giftedness; Zelda, the intellectual criteria. Their developmental profiles (Figure 3.1) show some of the issues teachers of gifted students must face (Gallagher, 1985). In particular, the profiles indicate the strong intraindividual differences we often find in gifted children, with their mental abilities outstepping their physical and social development.

Cranshaw is a big, athletic, happy-go-lucky youngster who impresses the casual observer as the "all-American boy" type of youngster. He seems to be a natural leader and to be enthu-

FIGURE 3.1
Profiles of two
gifted students

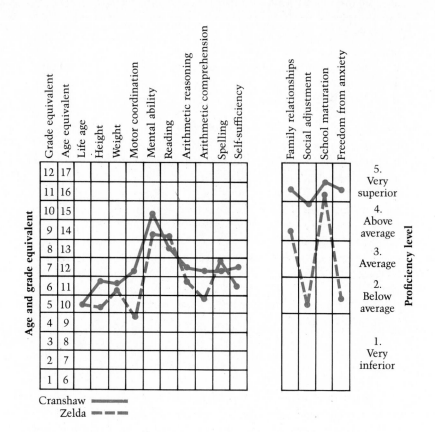

SOURCE: From *Teaching the Gifted Child* (3d ed.) by J. Gallagher, 1985, p. 23. Boston: Allyn & Bacon.

siastic over a wide range of interests. These interests have not yet solidified. One week he can be fascinated with astronomy, the next week with football formations, and the following week with the study of Africa.

His past history in school has suggested that teachers have two very distinct reactions to Cranshaw. One is that he is a joy to have in the classroom. He is a cooperative and responsible boy who can not only perform his own tasks well but be a good influence in helping the other youngsters to perform effectively. On the other hand, Cranshaw's mere presence in the class also stimulates in teachers some hints of personal inferiority and frustration, since he always seems to be exceeding the bounds of the teachers' knowledge and abilities. The teachers secretly wonder how much they really are teaching Cranshaw and how much he is learning on his own.

Cranshaw's family is a well-knit, reasonably happy one. His father is a businessman, his mother has had some college education, and the family is somewhat active in the community. Their attitude toward Cranshaw is that he is a fine boy, and they hope that he does well. They anticipate his going on to higher education but, in effect, say that it is pretty much up to him what he is going to do when the time comes. They do not seem to be future-oriented and are perfectly happy to have him as the enthusiastic and well-adjusted youngster that he appears to be today.

Zelda shares similar high scores on intelligence tests to those manifested by Cranshaw. Zelda is a rather unattractive girl who is chubby and wears rather thick glasses that give her a "bookish" appearance. Her clothes, while reasonably neat and clean, are not stylish and give the impression that neither her mother nor Zelda have given a great deal of thought to how they look on this particular child. Socially, she has one or two reasonably close girl friends, but she is not a member of the wider social circle in the classroom and, indeed, seems to reject it.

Teachers respond to Zelda with two generally different feelings. They are pleased with the enthusiasm with which Zelda attacks her schoolwork and the good grades that she gets. At the same time, they are vaguely annoyed or irritated with Zelda's undisguised feeling of superiority toward youngsters who are not as bright as she is; they tend to repel Zelda when she tries to act like an assistant teacher or to gain favors that are more reserved for the teacher.

Zelda and her family seem to get along very well with each other. The main source of conflict is that the family has values that Zelda has accepted wholeheartedly but that are getting her into difficulty with her classmates. Her father is a college professor and her mother has an advanced degree in English literature. They seem to value achievement and intellectual performance almost to the exclusion of all other things.

Their social evenings are made up of intellectual discussions of politics, religion, or the current burning issue on the campus. These discussions are definitely adult-oriented, and Zelda is intelligent enough to be able to enter occasionally into such conversations. This type of behavior is rewarded much more by the parents than is the behavior that would seem more appropriate to her age level.

Figure 3.1 shows the range of abilities in different developmental areas for Cranshaw and Zelda. If all the points on the scale were at the same height as their mental ability, there would be little trouble in placing them educationally. Cranshaw shows a wide variation from the physical development of an average eleven-year-old to the mental abilities of an average fifteen-year-old. This means that any standard placement at any [grade] level will displace Cranshaw physically, academically, or socially.

Zelda has an intellectual and academic profile similar to Cranshaw's. Both are doing as well as might be expected on the basis of these measurements. Zelda is slightly inferior to Cranshaw in arithmetic. However, it is in the personal-social area where real differences are apparent. While Cranshaw's adjustment here has the same superior rating as his academic record, Zelda has social difficulties. She is not accepted by her peers and worries about it. . . . Her inability to understand how her own behavior causes antagonism is also apparent—and quite important. (Gallagher, 1985, pp. 22–24)

The teachers of students like Cranshaw and Zelda face several basic challenges: How do we interest Cranshaw in reading-related subjects when his mental ability is four years ahead of his age level? How do we encourage Zelda to work in arithmetic and other areas of less interest to her? And what do we do about her attitudes and unhappiness?

CHARACTERISTICS

What is it that sets gifted students apart from their peers? How do those characteristics affect their educational planning?

To answer these questions, we look for general patterns among gifted youngsters and for deviations from those patterns (the variance of characteristics within the group). Our objective, then, is to identify and study groups of gifted students, ideally over time, to see the form their development takes. One reason why the monumental longitudinal study, begun in 1920 by Lewis Terman, is of particular interest to us is because it gives us a chance to follow a very large set of intellectually gifted individuals for more than a half century as they matured into adulthood and old age.

The Terman Longitudinal Study

After his revision and the publication of the Binet-Simon Tests of Intelligence in 1916, Lewis Terman, a professor of psychology at Stanford University, turned his attention to gifted children. In 1920 he began a study of 1,528 gifted children, which was to continue for over fifty years, following them into maturity and old age. During that period, Terman was instrumental in designing and supervising the research that led to a set of five volumes entitled *Genetic Studies of Genius* (1925–1959).

Terman conducted his search for gifted children in California's public schools. He used teacher nominations and group intelligence tests as screening procedures. (Those procedures are now considered to limit the findings because they tend to eliminate gifted children who underachieve or whose behavior irritates teachers.) He based the final selection of subjects on their performance on the Stanford-Binet Intelligence Scale. Most showed an IQ score of 140 or higher; the average for the group was 151.

Table 3.2 summarizes Terman's findings. The results, on average, were favorable in practically every dimension. The group did well, not only in school and career, but also in areas like marriage, character, and mental health. This study more than any other put an end to the stereotype of the gifted child as puny, sickly, and socially immature. In individual children, of course, all these conditions could be present; but as a group, these children were generally healthy and well adjusted.

Table 3.2
Characteristics of Intellectually Gifted Students
(Terman Longitudinal Study)

Characteristics	Findings
Physical	Above average in physique and health; mortality rate 80 percent that of average.
Interests	Very interested in abstract subjects (literature, history, mathematics); broad range of interests.
Education	Rates of college attendance eight times that of general population; achieved several grades beyond age level throughout school career.
Mental health	Slightly lower rates for maladjustment and delinquency; prevalence of suicide somewhat lower.
Marriage–family	Marriage rate average; divorce rate lower than average. The group's children obtained an average IQ score of 133.
Vocational choice	Men chose professions (medicine, law) eight times more frequently than did the general population.
Character tests	Less prone to overstatement or cheating; appeared superior on tests of emotional stability.

SOURCE: Adapted from *Genetic Studies of Genius* (Vols. 1, 4, 5) by L. Terman (Ed.), 1925, 1947, 1959. Stanford, CA: Stanford University Press.

Oden (1968) concluded her comments on the group as follows:

> All of the evidence indicates with few exceptions the superior child becomes the superior adult. . . . Two-thirds of the men and almost as large a proportion of the women consider that they have lived up to their intellectual abilities fully or reasonably well. (pp. 50–51)

Special Groups of Gifted Children

There are many subgroups within the category of gifted and talented children beyond the intellectually gifted individuals described by Terman. How well these groups are adapting depends to a significant degree on how their families raise them, how their schools utilize their special gifts, and how society sees them.

Children of Extraordinary Ability

It is generally accepted today that superior intellectual ability predicts high academic performance and personal adjustment. But doubts linger about those youngsters of extraordinary ability—the 1 in 100,000 at the level of a von Braun or Einstein. It is easy to think about coping with students who are two or three years ahead of their age group in development. But what happens to the students who are seven or eight years advanced?

There have been many American prodigies. The stories of two, William Sidis and Charles Fefferman, have had very different endings. Sidis was a mathematical prodigy who knew algebra, trigonometry, geometry, and calculus by age 10, was admitted to Harvard University at age 11, and graduated cum laude at age 16. Despite his scholastic success, Sidis's emotional adjustment was always a problem. He retreated into social isolation, strenuously avoiding all academic life and publicity. He died in his middle forties, penniless and alone (Montour, 1977).

Many believe that this is what happens to prodigies: "The faster the rocket goes up, the faster it comes down." "Early ripe, early rot." However, much more typical is the story of Charles Fefferman. Fefferman is the youngest person in recent history to be appointed to a full professorship at a major university. He received that appointment at the University of Chicago at age 22. Encouraged by his father, a Ph.D. in economics, he was taking courses in mathematics at the University of Maryland by the age of 12 and had entered college as a full-time student at age 14. He combined his studies with a normal social life, socializing with his friends who were in junior high at the time. He has won a number of prizes for his work in mathematics, and at age 27 was the first recipient of the $150,000 Allan Waterman Award of the National Science Foundation (Montour, 1978).

It is unrealistic to think that any educational system is going to reorganize its program to fit children like these, who may appear once in a lifetime. Still, the potential impact of these children on society is so great that some degree of attention—individualized tutoring, apprenticeship to other talented individuals—is called for.

These extraordinarily precocious students represent one of our greatest and rarest of natural resources. We must learn more about them to understand both the origin of the condition and the ways to help these children adapt to an often difficult social environment. To date, however, we have only fragmentary case studies and retrospective views of their lives (Feldman, 1979).

Gifted Girls

There is a growing belief that gifted girls represent one of the largest groups of untapped intellectual potential in this country. The recent emergence of the women's movement has brought the issue to a higher level of social consciousness. Although we can see change in pay scales and job availability, it is possible to overestimate the actual change in attitudes and values.

Only a generation ago there was the expectation that femininity was synonymous with submissiveness, that girls could not master "masculine" interests (science, mathematics). That expectation discouraged many girls from fully exploring their intellectual capacity. There seems to be an abundance of evidence that the social and scholastic world in the United States were, and probably still are, very different for girls and boys. Zelda's opportunities are not the same as Cranshaw's, even though they live in the same neighborhood and attend the same classes.

Sex differences are particularly evident in those areas that have traditionally been off limits to girls. Researchers find little difference in the arithmetic performance of preadolescent girls and boys. Yet, by age 17, boys have taken an enormous lead in tests of mathematical aptitude and performance (Hueftle, Rakow, & Welch, 1983; Benbow & Stanley, 1983).

Fox (1977) summarized these sex-related differences in mathematical aptitude:

> By the end of the secondary school years, young men are quite superior to young women with respect to mathematical reasoning ability. Among the very gifted seventh and eighth graders, the gap at the higher levels of mathematical reasoning ability is quite large. In three years of testing mathematically gifted students, the Study of Mathematically Precocious Youth

Attempts have been made to recruit girls for advanced placement in mathematics and science courses.
(© Herb Snitzer Photography)

(SMPY) found 167 boys, but only 19 girls, who as seventh and eighth graders scored 640 or above on the Scholastic Aptitude Test–Mathematics. (p. 115)

Some attempts have been made to group gifted girls together for special instruction in mathematics (Fox, Benbow, & Perkins, 1983). These studies use female role models and keep the intimidating element of male students out of the classroom, at least until the girls gain confidence in their own abilities. It is too early to judge the impact of segregation by sex on instruction of gifted girls.

Casserly (1979), looking for ways to encourage gifted girls in math and science, studied twelve American high schools that enrolled over twice the national percentage of girls in their advanced placement mathematics and science courses. These high-incidence schools shared several characteristics. Teachers of advanced placement math and science courses actively recruit girls. These teachers exhibit few signs of sex-role stereotyping in their thinking or in their classroom behavior. They expect high-level performance from the girls as well as the boys, and they demand it from both. Students were tracked as early as the fourth grade into homogeneously grouped, and sometimes accelerative, programs. Thus, the taking of advanced placement courses is a natural sequence in a special program for superior students.

These schools demonstrate the importance of creating a comfortable, encouraging environment for learning, particularly where other social and cultural barriers exist for the gifted student.

Of course, all gifted girls do not end up in the sciences. Sears and Barbee (1977) located 430 women who were in the original Terman sample. They found most of those women had college degrees, were satisfied with their lives, had fewer divorces, and were working outside the home. Sears and Barbee went on to point out an important fact about the group: "The lifestyle which brings happiness to one woman does not necessarily bring it to another woman with different experiential backgrounds" (p. 60).

The goal for gifted girls is that they have the education that will allow them to choose what they want to do, not what society believes they should do.

Gifted Underachievers

One of the many myths surrounding gifted children is the Cannonball Theory. The idea, simply put, is that these children can no more be stopped from achieving their potential than a cannonball once fired can be diverted from its path. Like most simplistic ideas about human beings, this one too is wrong.

The fact is that a substantial proportion of gifted children never achieve the level of performance that their scores on intelligence tests would seem to predict for them. The longitudinal study by Terman and Oden (1947) yielded information on these underachievers. The researchers identified a group of 150 men who had not achieved to the level of their apparent ability. Those men were compared with 150 other men who had done well. In their self-ratings and in ratings by their wives and by their parents, four major characteristics separated the underachievers from the achievers:

* Greater feelings of inferiority
* Less self-confidence
* Less perseverance
* Less of a sense of life goals

More striking was an examination of teacher ratings made on those men twenty years earlier, while they were in school. Even at that time, their teachers felt the underachievers lacked self-confidence, foresight, and the desire to excel.

Several other studies conducted on underachieving students have confirmed the close relationship between personality (attitude), and underachievement (Shaw & McCuen, 1960; Perkins, 1965).

Whitmore (1980) summed up the literature on the distinctive personality and behavioral traits that describe many underachievers:

> A negative self-concept, low self-esteem, expectations of academic and social failure, a sense of inability to control or determine outcomes of his efforts, and behaviors that serve as mechanisms for coping with the tension produced by conflict for the child in school. (p. 189)

Although the general unhappiness and social adjustment problems of gifted underachievers are clear, they do not directly implicate the family or necessarily point to a common pattern of *family* maladjustment. Butler-Por (1982) concluded that the evidence for such linkage in families of gifted underachievers is inconclusive.

Several educational strategies have been used to remediate high-ability students who are performing well below their potential. The first, personal counseling, assumes that if a student is having personality conflicts they should be confronted directly. Although the approach eases the anxiety and stress of underachievers (Butler-Por, 1982), there is little evidence that either short- or long-term counseling improves their academic status.

The second strategy is to create an educational environment more responsive to the special needs of underachieving students. This approach has generated some evidence of success when planning is careful and effort is intense. Casual or transitory attempts do not seem to yield measurable results.

Karnes et al. (1965) placed twenty-five fourth-grade gifted underachievers in homogeneous classes with gifted achievers, and another group of gifted underachievers in heterogeneous classes with students with a wide range of ability levels. They hoped that the achievers would model appropriate behavior, drawing the underachievers out of their negative patterns of behavior. The gifted underachievers in the homogeneous classes improved significantly in academic performance and made gains in relationships with their parents, but there were no differences in peer acceptance. The relative quality of the instruction in the homogeneous and heterogeneous settings was not noted and may have been a factor in the results.

Whitmore (1980) reported on a special program for gifted underachievers at the primary-grade level. One group of twenty-seven underachievers was placed in a special class that stressed a child-centered approach. The classroom climate encouraged freedom of expression without the threat of failure or rejection, and monthly meetings were held with parents, teacher, and child. After a year, twelve of the students had gained one and a half to three years in reading scores; only three failed to reach grade level in reading or arithmetic. Improved social behavior and work habits also were noted.

Whitmore pointed out that many of these children had shown signs of emotional disturbance. But the creation of a warm, accepting environment apparently dealt with the outward manifestations of those problems.

Butler-Por (1982) presented a third strategy. The key to the approach is encouraging students to take responsibility for their own behavior. A group of thirty-six underachievers of both gifted and average ability at the elementary school level held twelve weekly meetings with their teachers. At the first meeting, each student agreed on a goal (expected behavior) and a reward for reaching that goal (free time). The agreements were formalized in a written contract signed by each student and teacher. Every week, the progress of each child toward the individual goal was checked. In comparison with thirty-six underachievers who did not take part in the program, these students improved significantly in academic achievement and personal adjustment.

We know now that a carefully designed and implemented program within the classroom can help gifted underachievers. We also know that very few school systems offer these programs. Why? Because gifted underachievers seldom fail in school, which means they do not come to the attention of special educators.

Culturally Different Gifted Children

Each of the subcultures in this country has contributed children and adults of high intellectual and artistic ability to the benefit of the larger society. Because these subcultures have their own values and reward different kinds of behaviors, the children often show their gifts in ways not typical of the mainstream society. One of the tasks of the school is to discover and nurture their talents (Frasier, 1979).

Special educators use several approaches to identify culturally different gifted students. Each recognizes the limitations of those students who come from cultural groups in which emphasis is not placed on the verbal concepts that seem so central to traditional assessment of giftedness and to mastering of educational content.

Mercer and Lewis (1981) proposed the System of Multicultural Pluralistic Assessment (SOMPA), an identification technique that uses traditional measures of intelligence but weighs the results according to the social and familial characteristics of the child. A child with an IQ score of 111, when compared with children from similar sociocultural backgrounds, can obtain an estimated learning potential score of 134, placing the child in the top 1 percent of children in that sociocultural group. According to Mercer and Lewis, learning potential scores are indicators of ability that would have been demonstrated if the child had received equal opportunity.

Torrance (1976) uses another set of instruments, the Torrance Tests of Creative Thinking, to find gifted minority students. These tests require less past knowledge and reward divergent or original thinking patterns.

The Baldwin Identification Matrix takes a different approach to the search for hidden talent (Baldwin, 1978). The index is made up of standard IQ and achievement tests; teacher ratings on learning, motivation, creativity, and leadership; and peer nominations. Scores are accumulated into a weighted total to give an overall index of giftedness.

Wolf (1981) used a unique approach to qualify urban minority students for advanced work in the visual and performing arts. The identification process was in two stages. First, the top 15 or 20 percent of the student body was identified by performance on standard tests. That group was enrolled in a theater techniques program that emphasized expressive and communication skills. At the end of the program, the staff rated the students along a number of dimensions. Those who rated highly graduated to an independent study and seminar program of the Educational Center for the Arts, which provides training in music, dance, theater arts, and graphic arts.

Once culturally different gifted students are found, by whatever method, we must develop an educational plan for their special needs and circumstances. One objective for minority group youngsters is to encourage their understanding of and respect for their own cultural background. Biographies and the works of noted writers or leaders from the particular cultural group are often the basis of special programs. Because there are so many groups with such diverse backgrounds, these programs are usually unique (Frasier, 1979; Bernal, 1979).

At the same time, successful minority group students seem to have learned some of the characteristics of the mainstream middle class. Shade (1978), in a study of the families of gifted black children, found they demanded better-than-average school performance while providing a warm, supportive home environment. Close family ties, structured home life, moderate amounts of discipline, and help when needed, all mark the families of high-achieving black children.

As minority groups gradually assimilate into the larger community, educational programs carry the difficult task of encouraging their children to respect their cultural heritage, and, at the same time, to take on those characteristics of the larger society that will help them succeed within that society. The balance is a delicate one.

Gifted Children with Handicaps

Through the remainder of this book, we discuss children who have various disabilities. They may be unable to see or hear or walk, but that does not mean that they cannot be intellectually gifted. It only means that they stand a good chance of having their special talents overlooked.

Gearheart and Weishahn (1976) estimated that there are as many as 180,000 youngsters with handicaps who are also gifted. Whitmore (1981) described a child who not only went unrecognized as gifted, but who was actually considered mentally retarded:

> Kim. At seven years of age, this child with cerebral palsy had no speech and extremely limited motor control. In a public school for severely handicapped students, she was taught only self-help skills. Her parents, who were teachers, observed her use of her eyes to communicate and believed there was unstimulated intellect trapped in her severely handicapped body. Upon parent request, she was mainstreamed in her wheelchair into an open space elementary school. After two months of stimulation and the provision of a mechanical communicator, Kim began to develop rapidly. She learned the Morse code in less than two days and began communicating continuously to the teacher and peers through her communicator. Within four months she was reading on grade level (second), and subsequent testing indicated she possessed superior mental abilities—an exceptional capacity to learn. (p. 109)

It is not hard to imagine what Kim's world would have been like if she had not been given the opportunity to learn and communicate.

We know that children who are deaf can be encouraged to express themselves through drama. One outstanding example of talent development is the National Theatre of the Deaf. This touring company uses sign language while an interpreter narrates what is happening on the stage for the hearing audience (Maker, 1977).

Gifted children with learning disabilities can receive remedial work to correct their problem. If the problem lies in auditory memory (remembering what one has heard), exercises that require the use of visual memory to supplement auditory memory can help students gradually extend that memory (Fox, Brody, & Tobin, 1983).

The important thing to remember is that high intelligence and extraordinary talent can be found anywhere, even in children who have major problems in other areas of development.

FACTORS CONTRIBUTING TO GIFTEDNESS AND TALENT

Are gifted and talented children born or made? Will gifted children emerge whatever their opportunity or education? What role does heredity play in giftedness? How important is the social environment of gifted children?

Heredity

Over a hundred years ago, Francis Galton, in a study of outstanding English men concluded that extraordinary ability ran in families, that it was genetic in origin. Ever since, there's been a strong belief in the powerful role that genetics plays in producing high mental ability (Dennis & Dennis, 1976). Certainly studies of twins and the close relationship of the abilities of adoptive children to those of their natural parents demand that we recognize a hereditary element (Plomin, DeFries, & McClearn, 1980).

Twins have long been a source of evidence for hereditary influence. *Identical twins* come from the same fertilized egg and share an identical heredity. The performance of twins, then, should be evidence of the influence of heredity. Similarly, if heredity is a strong factor, we can expect a stronger relationship between identical twins than between fraternal twins, who come from two different fertilized eggs.

Nichols (1965) studied seven hundred identical twins and five hundred fraternal twins who participated in the National Merit Scholarship program. He found the following correlations on ability: for identical twins 0.87; for fraternal twins 0.63. He concluded that about 70 percent of performance is due to heredity, leaving 30 percent for the educator to challenge.

Krutetskii (1976), a distinguished mathematician in the Soviet Union, suggested that mathematically gifted individuals have a unique neurological organization—a hereditary condition—that he called a "mathematical cast of mind." He claimed that this cast of mind shows up by age 7 or 8 and later acquires broad transfer effects: "It is expressed in a striving to make the phenomenon of the environment mathematical, in a constant urge to pay attention to the mathematical aspect of phenomena . . . to see the world "through mathematical eyes" (p. 302).

What Krutetskii was suggesting, as have other scientists, is that extraordinary talent is shaped by heredity, but that its successful expression requires nurturing much as good seeds still need fertile ground for them to flower.

Family

We've talked about the role society plays in defining gifts and talents, and creating a reward system. If society shapes the gifted child, certainly the family, being closer, is also a powerful force, one that can be destructive or constructive. Our discussion of underachievers makes clear that family interrelationships can play inhibiting, as well as facilitative, roles.

One attempt to uncover the factors that are linked to extraordinary ability was carried out by Bloom (1982). He conducted a retrospective study of the early life of twenty-five world-class swimmers, pianists,

WALKING THE TIGHTROPE
BETWEEN "GIFTED" AND "NORMAL"

Kids,

First, I want to say I've been very lucky. Not lucky to be gifted or to have been born smart or anything like that; in fact, I still get angry when people talk about me that way. I've been lucky because good things happened to me, and because my family and many teachers helped a great deal.

Another lucky break: I wasn't alone. Starting in first grade, there was a whole group of bright kids in my class, good at a lot of different things—spelling, math, playing ball. And grade school is a good time to do different things: in high school, some kids work on the newspaper and some are on the math team, and by the time you get to college, a football player can spend four years without meeting a theater major. Generally, the more organized things are, the harder it is to do more than one of them.

Which I suppose is the most important thing I have to say: people are going to try to organize you. Most people see others in terms of categories—friend, enemy, athlete, egghead—and being gifted, more than anything else, means that you decide not to fit into anyone's pigeonhole. That's not easy.

It's not easy for other people to deal with *you*, either. Especially with "back to basics," they'll be tempted to lump you in with everyone else. I had a grouchy, tired, near-retirement-age fifth-grade teacher; he not only didn't spend extra time with bright kids, he made me and another student do his lesson plans for the others. (There are a few teachers or people in authority who just don't like kids, gifted or otherwise; these people are deadly.)

On the other hand, don't let society put a "gifted" label on you to the extent of shutting you out of everyday things. The only thing worse than being denied opportunities is being forced to take them. In fourth grade, a teacher tried to make me read only Newbery Award-winning books, taking only the best from the library instead of *Encyclopedia Brown* and race-car stories. He meant well, in that I *was* a good reader and that kids *should* read Newbery books (some of them are fantastic); but some of them are pretty boring, and there are a lot of other books that are in between prize-winners and mindwasting trash.

I'm making this sound like a tightrope walk between being "gifted" and being "normal." That's exactly how it is; that's exactly how it's going to be for much of your life. You can't deny your talents; you shouldn't waste yourself by loafing at half or two-thirds of your capacity. (My folks taught me to read at two, but I went through part of first grade pretending I was no better than the beginners, going slowly and stopping a lot during reading-aloud sessions.) But you can't put yourself on a pedestal, or ignore the people you share the world with. They're worth knowing.

I haven't mentioned getting along with other kids. I don't have any sage advice about that, except that it's very important—more so than the stuff you learn from books or the chalkboard. It'll affect your academic decisions, too:

continued

continued

I could have skipped sixth grade, for example, but my parents and I decided I wouldn't. For one thing, sixth grade was the big social year, with a week at camp and the end-of-school dinner; also, I was already up to a year younger than most of my classmates (my birthday's in September). I didn't particularly want to jump ahead to junior high. I wanted to avoid the image or reputation of not fitting in.

That's the problem. Some people don't look at you and see "better," they look at you and see "different." To minimize that, you have to work at it; you have to be friendly, be diplomatic, be honest without hurting people's feelings. It's better, when someone asks if you're smart, to say "in some things," which isn't lying. There's at least one thing that the person asking knows more about, or is better at, than you.

I'm 23 and I still think too much, take things too seriously, and envy people who I imagine don't even care that I do. It took me some time to learn that other people weren't having fun to spite me just as I wasn't being smart to spite them. (For a hot-shot gifted kid, I made a lot of mistakes and misunderstandings.) The truth is, you're not the only one who's smart, and there's nothing that says you can't have fun. In fact, you can have more than most people.

Good luck,
Eric Grevstad, 23, Connecticut

SOURCE: From *Gifted Children Speak Out* by James R. Delisle, Walker Publishing Company, New York, NY, 1984, pp. 116–117. Copyright © 1984 by James R. Delisle.

and research mathematicians. He identified the subjects through consultations with authorities in the fields and evidence of success (wins in national and international competitions, special prizes, fellowship awards). In interviews with the individuals, their parents, and their former teachers, he found that several general characteristics seem important regardless of the specific talent area:

* A willingness to do great amounts of work (practice, time, effort) to achieve a high level or standard
* Competitiveness with peers in the talent field and the determination to do the best at all costs
* An ability to rapidly learn new techniques, ideas, or processes in the talent field

Bloom suggested that the group's high motivation was stimulated in a powerful way by the early recognition of talent by parents and

The direction in which gifts and talents emerge depends to some extent on the areas in which interests and training are focused.
(Alan Carey/The Image Works)

friends, who went out of their way to obtain special instruction, and to encourage and nurture the talent. The enthusiasm and support within the family seemed to be a critical element in the emergence of those subjects into world-class performers.

If a child with special gifts or talents does not receive this support from family, it is the school's responsibility to offer the enthusiasm, encouragement, and recognition that appear to be so important for the full development of those gifts and talents.

IDENTIFICATION

Before we can place gifted children in special educational programs, we have to find them. And that is not an easy task. In every generation, many gifted children pass through school unidentified, their talents uncultivated. Who are they? Many come from low socioeconomic backgrounds or subcultures that place little stress on verbal ability. Others have dropped out of school for economic reasons. Still others have emotional problems that disguise their intellectual abilities.

There is a general expectation that teachers can spot these children and do something for them. But studies have shown that teachers do not always recognize gifted children, even those with academic talent. In fact, they fail to identify from 10 to 50 percent of their gifted students.

The first step in identifying gifted students is determining the reason for finding them. If we went to choose a group of students for an advanced mathematics class, our approach would be different than if we are looking for students with high aptitude for a creative-writing program. Specific program needs and requirements, then, shape the identification process.

Subjective evaluation—teacher judgment, parent referral—should be checked by standardized tests and other objective measures of ability. Any program for identifying gifted children in a school system should include both subjective and objective methods of evaluation. Classroom behavior, for example, can point up children's ability to organize and use materials, and reveal their potential for processing information better than can a test. Many aspects of creativity and verbal fluency are also best observed in a classroom or informal setting. But the classroom seldom challenges gifted children to the limits of their ability, as can a test situation.

When we are looking for children with special talent in creativity or the visual and performing arts or leadership, we must use different identification procedures than those used to find academically gifted children. A creativity test might ask: how many ways could a toy dog be improved, or what would happen if annual rainfall was reduced by half. Expert ratings on products (essays, poems, artwork) could also be used, along with teacher ratings, to find creative students.

The products of creative performance are a good guide for finding those who are already performing creatively. But what about those with just potential? Potential has largely been measured by extracting divergent thinking or other important elements from the creative process and using them to create an instrument.

The items in Figure 3.2 are a sample of questions that measure student potential. They focus on several abilities:

- *Fluency.* The ability to give many answers to a given question.
- *Flexibility.* The ability to give many different types of responses or to shift from one type of response to another.
- *Originality.* The ability to provide unique yet appropriate responses.

Suppose a question asks, "How many different ways can you use a brick?" A long list of answers focusing on the types of buildings in which bricks are used would receive credit for *fluency.* Answers that point out that bricks can be used as decorations, weapons, or weights, would receive credit for *flexibility.* And an answer that a brick can be

FIGURE 3.2
Sample items
measuring student
potential

Verbal Form

In the space below list all the uses you can think of for a brick. List as many interesting and unusual uses as you can think of. Do not limit yourself to any one size brick. You may use as many bricks as you like. Do not limit yourself to uses you have seen or heard about; think of as many possible new uses as you can.

1. _____

2. _____

3. _____

Figural Form

By adding lines to the incomplete figures on this page, you can sketch some interesting objects or pictures. Try to think of some picture or object no one else will think of. Try to make it tell as complete and interesting a story as you can by adding and building on your first idea. Make up an interesting title for your drawing and write it at the bottom of the block next to the number of the figure.

1. _____   3. _____

2. _____   4. _____

SOURCE: From *Developing Creativity in the Gifted and Talented* by C. Callahan, 1978, p. 10. Reston, VA: Council for Exceptional Children. Copyright 1978 by Council for Exceptional Children. Reprinted by permission.

crumbled up and used as a coloring agent would get credit for *originality.*

In the field of visual and performing arts, talent usually is determined by a consensus of expert judges, often in an audition setting. Experts in the arts are not enthusiastic about tests of artistic ability or musical aptitude. They trust their own judgment more, although their judgment is as susceptible to bias and limitation as is that of traditional teachers.

Table 3.3 lists several sample items from a teacher rating scale, a useful, convenient method for identifying gifted children. Later testing of intelligence shows that most children who have achieved high ratings on this type of scale are shown to be gifted. But a rating scale

Table 3.3

Sample Scale Items: Teacher Ratings for Behavioral
Characteristics of Superior Students

Learning characteristics	1. Has unusually advanced vocabulary for age or grade level; uses terms in a meaningful way; has verbal behavior characterized by "richness" of expression, elaboration, and fluency. 2. Is a keen and alert observer; usually "sees more" or "gets more out of" a story, film, poem, etc., than others.
Motivational characteristics	1. Strives toward perfection; is self-critical; is not easily satisfied with own speed or products. 2. Is quite concerned with right and wrong, good and bad; often evaluates and passes judgment on events, people, and things.
Creativity characteristics	1. Displays a great deal of curiosity about many things; is constantly asking questions about anything and everything. 2. Displays a keen sense of humor and sees humor in situations that may not appear to be humorous to others.
Leadership characteristics	1. Is self-confident with children his own age as well as adults; seems comfortable when asked to show work to the class. 2. Tends to dominate others when they are around; generally directs the activity in which he is involved.
Visual and performing arts characteristics	1. Incorporates a large number of elements into art work; varies the subject and content of art work. (Art) 2. Is adept at role playing, improvising acting out situations, "on the spot." (Dramatics) 3. Perceives fine differences in musical tone (pitch, loudness, timbre, duration).

SOURCE: From *Scales for Rating Behavioral Characteristics of Superior Students* by J. Renzulli, L. Smith, A. White, C. Callahan, & R. Hartman, 1976. Mansfield Center, CT: Creative Learning Products.

cannot protect against teacher bias. Substantial improvements can be made in teachers' ability to identify gifted students if the time is taken to provide specific training in this area (Gear, 1978).

Most schools have test scores available from group intelligence tests or group achievement tests. They can serve as a starting point in selecting candidates for a special program, but they have limitations:

- Group intelligence tests are not as reliable as individual tests.
- Group tests seldom differentiate abilities at the upper limits.
- Some children do not function well in a timed test situation.

Group intelligence tests are a practical means of screening large numbers of students. It is financially prohibitive to give all children individual examinations. Those children who are near the cutoff point or for whom a group test is not representative can be given individual examinations.

Achievement tests are even less discriminating. They detect only those children who are achieving well academically. Emotional disturbance, family problems, peer-group standards of mediocrity, poor study habits, a foreign-language background, and many other factors can affect a child's ability to perform academically. And, there are some children who, because of family pressures, good study habits, or intense motivation, achieve at a higher educational level than is consistent with their other abilities or their apparent mental level.

Another approach used to identify gifted students is to start with a particular program and find youngsters with the abilities that meet program requirements. Stanley (1979) used this method to initiate a talent search for mathematically precocious youngsters.

Aptitude tests in mathematics, like the Scholastic Aptitude Test, are used to screen students who are extraordinarily capable in mathematics. Other characterstics—motivation and academic efficiency—determine the type of special attention suitable for those who score at the highest level on these tests. Most special education programs for gifted students now use a combination of aptitude tests, teacher ratings, nominations, and scholastic records to help identify eligible students.

The reasons for going through the process of identifying gifted children are complex. Identification should be just the first step to a differentiated program. It can also be used to determine eligibility for financial aid from the state or to satisfy state or federal guidelines.

Sometimes it seems we spend more time designing identification procedures than designing the special programs the students are supposed to receive. Martinson (1972) put the activity in perspective:

> Identification per se does not improve learning. Children who are identified and placed in regular programs show no change. . . . Identification cannot reduce the impact of malnutrition, restricted learning opportunities, poor parent-child relationships, lack of interpersonal relationships, and other negative factors. But if a well-planned program reduces these or other defects, performance and achievement of a gifted child will considerably improve. (p. 135)

EDUCATIONAL ADAPTATIONS FOR GIFTED AND TALENTED CHILDREN

No one special program could meet the individual needs of all the children we've described. The diversity we find among gifted youngsters is reflected in the number and type of adaptations the schools are making to meet their special needs.

Educators, however, would agree on three general educational objectives for special programs for gifted and talented students:

- Gifted children should master important conceptual systems that are at the level of their abilities in various content fields.
- Gifted children should develop skills and strategies that enable them to become more independent, creative, and self-sufficient.
- Gifted children should develop a pleasure in and excitement about learning that will carry them through the drudgery and routine that are an inevitable part of the process.

Although the regular classroom teacher can, within the limits of class ability, help gifted children meet some of these goals, special programs are essential to achieving all of them.

We can modify the school program for any group of exceptional children in three major dimensions: learning environment, skills, and content. In this section we explore each of these areas, focusing on intellectually gifted children.

Learning Environment

There are many ways to change the learning environment. Most are designed to bring gifted children together for a period of time. Our reasons are threefold:

- To provide gifted students with an opportunity to interact with one another, to learn and be stimulated by their intellectual peers
- To reduce variance within the group on instructionally relevant dimensions (past achievement, for example) in order to make it easier for the teacher to provide instructionally relevant materials
- To place gifted students with an instructor who has special expertise in working with gifted students or in a relevant content area

Because changes in the learning environment affect the entire school system, they have received more attention at the school district level than have changes in skills or content, which remain primarily a classroom issue. Still, the three elements are closely related: Changes in the learning environment for gifted students are necessary to meet the instructional goals of special skills and differential content development.

Gallagher, Weiss, Oglesby, and Thomas (1983) described seven methods for changing the learning environment:

- *Enrichment classroom.* The classroom teacher conducts a differentiated program of study without the help of outside personnel.

- *Consultant teacher.*   A program of differentiated instruction is conducted in the regular classroom with the assistance of a specially trained consultant.
- *Resource room–pullout.*   Gifted students leave the classroom for a short period of time to receive instruction from a specially trained teacher.
- *Community mentor.*   Gifted students interact with an adult from the community who has special knowledge in the area of interest.
- *Independent study.*   Students select projects and work on them under the supervision of a qualified teacher.
- *Special class.*   Gifted students are grouped together during most of the class time and are instructed by a specially trained teacher.
- *Special schools.*   Gifted students receive differentiated instruction at a special school with a specially trained staff.

Figure 3.3 shows the relative popularity among teachers, administrators, and parents of these common strategies for changing the learning environment. Because there was substantial agreement among those questioned, the results were combined.

As the figure indicates, the preferred methods vary with grade level. The most popular choice at the elementary level is the resource room–pullout, which removes the student from the regular classroom for about an hour a day to work on special lessons with a specially trained teacher. The method appears to be popular because it combines two major goals of both parents and teachers: It provides a special education experience, and, at the same time, does not remove the child totally from his or her peers—an important social objective. Special schools are less popular precisely because they separate gifted children from their peers, even though they obviously offer those students more intense special instruction.

Enrichment in the regular classroom is also not a popular approach. Most teachers, administrators, and parents believe that a regular teacher cannot provide significant help without outside assistance. Neither mentors nor independent study is considered feasible for the majority of gifted students in elementary schools, although either might be used for the individual child with extraordinary abilities.

At the secondary level, the popular choice is the special class, often an advanced placement class that allows students to earn college credit while still in high school by taking college-level courses. Independent study, which allows students to pursue a topic of their own interest, under supervision, is also considered effective. The resource room concept is less popular here because it doesn't fit into the secondary school system of classes by subject (English, mathematics, history).

We should stress that all of these strategies can be useful in the right circumstances. If a school system is near a major computer company, the availability of knowledgeable mentors could lead local schools in that direction. If there are experienced master teachers available, the

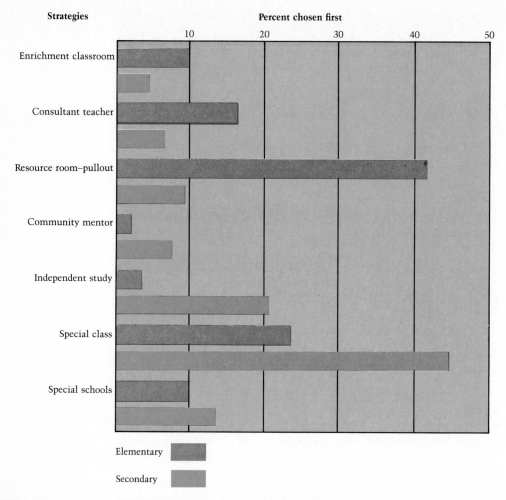

Elementary

Secondary

FIGURE 3.3
Choice of desired
learning environ-
ments by teachers,
administrators, and
parents ($N = 1,200$)

SOURCE: From *The Status of Gifted/Talented Education: United States Survey of
Needs, Practices, and Policies* by J. Gallagher, P. Weiss, K. Oglesby, & T. Thomas, 1983.
Los Angeles: National/State Leadership Training Institute on the Gifted and Talented.

consultant-teacher approach could work well. There is no one best
model, although certain methods clearly are more popular than others.

Student Acceleration

We can also create changes in the learning environment by varying
the length of the educational program. As more and more knowledge
and skills must be learned at the highest levels of the professions,
talented and gifted students can find themselves in school at age 30
and beyond. While skilled workers are earning a living and starting a
family, gifted students are often dependent for a good part of their
young adult life. The process of **acceleration**—passing students through

An adult who has special knowledge in a gifted student's area of interest may interact with the student as a mentor.
(© Jeff Albertson/Stock, Boston)

the educational system as quickly as possible—is a clear educational objective for gifted children. There are many different ways acceleration can be accomplished (Stanley, 1979):

- *Early school admission.*   The child, once shown to be intellectually and socially mature, is allowed to enter kindergarten at a younger-than-normal age.
- *Skipping grades.*   The child is accelerated by completely eliminating one semester or one grade in school. Skipping grades is an unpopular strategy because of its potential for creating temporary adjustment problems for the gifted student.

- *Telescoping grades.* The child covers the standard material, but in less time. For example, a three-year junior high program would be taught over two years.
- *Advanced placement.* The student takes courses for college credit while still in high school, shortening the college program.
- *Early college admission.* An extraordinarily advanced student may enter college at 13, 14, or 15 years of age.

Stanley (1979) found that acceleration, particularly early admission to college, is most effective for students who excel in mathematics. In a field like mathematics, in which the curriculum content can be organized in sequential fashion, it is possible for bright students to move quickly through the material. Stanley developed a program for accelerating students in mathematics courses and for awarding college credit to children 12 to 14 years of age. He described one such student:

> Sean, who at 12½ years of age, completed four and one-half years of precalculus mathematics in six 2-hour Saturday mornings compared with the 810 forty-five or fifty-minute periods usually required for Algebra I through III, plane geometry, trigonometry, and analytic geometry. . . . [D]uring the second semester of the eighth grade he was given released time to take the introduction to computer science course at Johns Hopkins and made a final grade of A. . . . While still 13 years old, Sean skipped the ninth and tenth grades. He became an eleventh grader at a large suburban public high school and took calculus with twelfth graders, won a letter on the wrestling team, was a science and math whiz on the school's television academic quiz team, tutored a brilliant seventh grader through two and one-half years of algebra and a year of plane geometry in eight months, played a good game of golf, and took some college courses on the side (set theory, economics, and political science). (p. 175)

All this work allowed Sean to enter Johns Hopkins University with 34 credits and sophomore status at the age of 14. And Sean was just one example. Stanley reported a number of cases in which the academic careers of youngsters with extraordinary talent in mathematics were shortened by accelerating either the content or the students.

The major objection to the strategy is the fear that acceleration can displace gifted children from their social and emotional peers, affecting their subsequent social adjustment. Weiss (1978) studied a group of 586 gifted adults who reflected on their experiences with acceleration and described how it affected them. The majority believed that acceleration helped them enter their careers earlier with no serious accompanying problems. But some did report social problems:

Skipping seemed desirable at the time, an honor; in retrospect, it was probably unwise to skip, as it led to feelings of insecurity due to physical and social immaturity.

In the long run, it was not worth it because I was too socially immature. (pp. 127–128)

The most positive responses were reserved for advanced placement programs. We can see some of the reasons in these comments:

Superb. A combination which did not isolate all the gifted from the rest.

It was a great joy and also intellectually stimulating to be exposed to peers and teachers who found the same excitement in learning that I did.

The class was one of the best I had in high school. I learned skills which were valuable to me in college and, in fact, from which I still benefit. (pp. 129–130)

From early admission to school to early admission to college, research studies invariably report that those children who have been accelerated have adjusted as well as or better than have children of similar ability who have not been accelerated. Despite these findings, some parents and teachers continue to have strong negative feelings about the practice, and some educational administrators do not want to deal with these special cases. The result is that many gifted students have been forced to spend the greater part of their first three decades of life in the educational system, often locked in a relatively unproductive role, to the detriment of themselves and society.

Skills

One educational objective that all educators who work with gifted and talented children would agree on is the necessity of increasing or enhancing those students' capability in productive thinking. The brain and central nervous system are able to add to stored information through the process of reasoning. The ability to generate new information through the internal processing of available information is perhaps the most valuable skill we have.

Practically all students at the elementary school level can solve this puzzle:

Mary is taller than Ruth.
Ruth is taller than Sally.
Sally is _____ than Mary.

Given the first two pieces of information, the students generate the third by themselves. Students who are gifted can use the reasoning process much more effectively than can average children, and are clearly superior in the tasks of problem solving, problem finding, and creativity.

- *Problem solving.*   The ability to reach a previously determined answer by organizing and processing the available information in a logical and systematic fashion.
- *Problem finding.*   The ability to review an area of study and to perceive those elements worthy of further analysis and study.
- *Creativity.*   A mental process by which an individual creates new ideas or products, or recombines existing ideas and products in a fashion that is novel to him or her. (Gallagher, 1985, pp. 268, 303)

Problem Solving and Problem Finding

The approach to enhancing problem-solving and problem-finding skills— an approach that can be taught in the regular classroom or a resource room or a special class—is to teach the students a set of strategies by which a problem can be attacked more efficiently. For example, Parnes, Noller, and Biondi (1977) developed a model for creative problem solving:

1. *Fact finding.*   Collecting data about the problem.
2. *Problem finding.*   Restating the problem in solvable form.
3. *Idea finding.*   Generating many possible solutions.
4. *Solution finding.*   Developing criteria for the evaluation of alternatives.
5. *Acceptance finding.*   Convincing the audience who must accept the plan that it can work.

This kind of a sequence can be used for any problem, from cleaning up the cafeteria to protecting a state's water resources.

Problem finding is the process of choosing a worthy problem. We can help students increase their problem-finding skills by having them ask themselves questions like these:

- How many people will be helped by the solution to this problem?
- What negative things will happen if the problem is not solved?
- What are the advantages (benefits) of solving this problem?

A computer can be a useful tool for teaching problem-solving and problem-finding skills. Computer programming demands the use of sequential logic: Each step must be specified in detail. If something is overlooked or out of sequence, the program does not work. Anything less than a perfect program (plan) must be corrected (Davis & Frothingham, 1981).

Creativity

There has probably been more attention paid to creativity than to any other single objective in the education of gifted and talented children. There is an expectation that superior intellectual development or talent gives students the ability to generate novel and better solutions for problems that no one has been able to solve.

Again, one instructional strategy is to enhance those elements of intellectual operation that seem particularly important to creative production. And, because creativity also seems to depend on a favorable emotional climate, some attempts are being made to improve that climate. Although it is possible to perform all of these activities in the regular classroom, it is much easier to work with a homogeneous group of gifted children.

Over the past decade, educators have been influenced by two theoretical models. Each provides a necessary structure that allows teachers to organize style and level of thinking processes as an objective for their classes. The first model is Bloom's Taxonomy of Educational Objectives (Bloom, 1956). It has six levels of thinking complexity through which teachers can shape questions or problems that stress those levels. Here are examples of those levels and educational triggers for the thinking process:

- *Knowledge.* List the major causes of World War I as stated in Jones's text.
- *Comprehension.* Explain the concept of détente and give an illustration of détente in action.
- *Application.* If the temperature rises and the amount of gas pressure increases, what would be the stress impact on [a] metal container?
- *Analysis.* What are the major components of a book? Compare and contrast their importance to the reader.
- *Synthesis.* Using the concepts of gerontology, describe an ideal pattern of behavior in old age.
- *Judgment.* Using standards of literary criticism, critique Jones's essay on modern education. (Feldhusen & Treffinger, 1977, p. 34)

Although all levels of thinking processes can be used to master a given topic, the dimensions of application, analysis, synthesis, and judgment would be expected to appear more often with gifted classes or resource groups.

By far the greatest amount of curricular effort has centered about the work of psychologist J. P. Guilford (1967), who developed a second theoretical model. He called that model of thinking processes the *structure of the intellect.* He divided human abilities into three major dimensions—*content, product,* and *operations*—and argued that productive thinking requires the use of many if not all of those abilities.

Guilford's model is too complex to deal with here. But we should recognize its importance to special educators. It focuses on two thinking processes not often measured in standard intelligence tests: *divergent thinking* and *evaluation.*

Divergent thinking (the ability to produce many different answers to a question) involves fluency, flexibility, and originality, three components often linked to creativity. To stimulate those elements, Treffinger (1980) proposed a series of tasks that can be applied by teachers to any content field:

1. *Just suppose that . . . (any unreal or "contrary to fact" situation).* What would be the results? What if it were against the law to smile? What if the Loyalists had won the Revolutionary War? What if a child from Mars enrolled in our class?

2. *Product improvement.* There are plenty of things it might be fun to make better. Our desks at school. The classroom. Our yard at home or the playground at school. Toys. Books. Tests. Chalkboards. Overhead projectors.

3. *Incomplete beginnings.* Create pictures, designs, or stories from incomplete beginnings. Here are some interesting shapes. What can you make from them? Here are some polygons. What can you do with them?

4. *New uses for common objects.* Usually, we use the ruler to measure things. What else might it be used for? How else might we use desks? Chairs? Calendars? Pencils? Books? Window shades? Bulletin boards?

5. *Alternate titles or endings.* For a story, a picture, or any situation, can you think of many possible titles? From a picture or the beginning of a story, think of (write down, act out, tell to others, etc.) many different endings. Can we all begin to make up a story, each person adding a line, or a character, or an event? (Each might finish it in his or her own way.) (p. 38)

Another accepted practice for extending intellectual fluency is **brainstorming** (Parnes, 1966). Using the technique, a group of people or a whole class discusses a particular problem (for example, how to improve local government), trying to suggest as many answers as possible. There are important ground rules:

1. *No criticism allowed.* Nothing stops the free flow of ideas like the criticism or scorn of a peer or teacher. The temptation to point

out faults in an answer is strong, but must be checked. Let students know in advance that evaluation comes later.

2. *The more the better.* The more ideas, the more likely a good one will be among them. Place a premium on unusual or unique solutions.

3. *Integration and combinations of ideas welcomed.* Be sure everyone understands that it's fine to combine with or add to previous ideas.

4. *Evaluation after all ideas have been presented.* Judge when the fluency or inventiveness of the class is lagging. At that point, encourage evaluative thinking on the part of students.

Notice that evaluation becomes an important part of the process after the divergent thinking takes place. Once the ideas are produced, the group can choose those that seem most likely to solve the problem. Brainstorming, then, requires divergent thinking; judgment is more evaluative.

An alternative approach to fostering creativity examines how creative people do their work (see, for example, MacKinnon, 1978). From that analysis, a pattern of personal style emerges, personality characteristics that set creative people apart. We find that most creative people have enormous self-confidence, are rarely swayed by the opinions of others, can tolerate ambiguity, and have a great fund of free energy (Gowan, Khatena, & Torrance, 1981).

These findings suggest that we can stimulate creativity by establishing a classroom climate that encourages self-confidence, self-expression, and individuality. A few suggestions by Callahan (1978) give the flavor of the approach:

- *Provide a nonthreatening atmosphere.* The classroom environment should be structured in such a way that students' ideas and opinions are respected and questions are encouraged.

- *Don't be the judge of the worth of all products in the classroom.* An open, nonjudgmental attitude on the part of the teacher allows more freedom for divergent thinking as well as for the evaluative skills necessary to complete the creative process. Encourage students to develop criteria to judge their own work and that of their peers.

- *Model creative thinking, or introduce others who can illustrate the creative-thinking process for the students.* It's important for the teacher to model creative problem-solving procedures as much as possible, not just during "creativity time."

- *Provide stimuli for as many of the senses as possible.* A variety of stimuli encourages students to view a problem from different perspectives. It also seems to enhance the sense of openness and psychological freedom.

Our explorations of how to allow the human spirit and imagination to soar in the classroom while achieving other educational objectives are only beginning. We know what *not* to do (lecture interminably, ridicule fresh ideas, discourage alternatives), but still have much to learn about the ways to stimulate productive thinking.

Content

Suppose you were told to learn the multiplication tables again and again, or to practice simple spelling over and over. You'd be bored. Boredom is a real problem for children like Cranshaw and Zelda, who are often forced to "learn" material they already know.

Renzulli, Smith, and Reis (1982) described a process called **curriculum compacting,** which allows gifted youngsters to move ahead. The process has three steps:

1. Find out what the students know before instruction.
2. Arrange to teach in a brief fashion the remaining concepts or skills.
3. Provide a different set of experiences to enrich or advance the students.

Renzulli and his colleagues used Bill, a sixth-grade student with a straight-A average in math, as a case in point:

> After two days in math class Bill explains to the teacher that he knows how to do the math. He describes his interest in working on logic problems and shows his teacher the beginning of a logic book that he is putting together for other students.
> Bill's teacher administers the chapter tests for units 1–3. . . . Bill scores 100 per unit. (p. 190)

The teacher responds to Bill's needs by arranging time for him to work on his logic book and to meet with people from a nearby computer center to develop his logic capabilities further.

What Bill's teacher is doing is creating a differentiated curriculum for him. Gallagher (1985) described four ways in which the gifted student's curriculum can be individualized: acceleration, enrichment, sophistication, and novelty.

Acceleration

The purpose of **content acceleration** is to move students through the traditional curriculum at a faster rate. The process allows students to master more complex sets of ideas. For example, by learning calculus in ninth grade, students have the foundation to begin physics and chemistry, subjects that require the skills of calculus.

Challenges to a gifted student's ability tend to lessen the chance of boredom and disinterest setting in.
(Courtesy The North Carolina School of Science and Mathematics)

Acceleration is a popular strategy in many schools because it requires no additional curriculum material.

Normal	Accelerated
Learning long-division facts and principles	Learning the nature of a variable Learn the operation of polynomials
Learning the early development of our country	Learning historical trends across the world.

Enrichment

Content enrichment gives students the opportunity for a greater appreciation of the topic under study by expanding the material for study (exploring additional examples, using specific illustrations). Having students read the diaries of Civil War soldiers on both sides, for example, enriches their perspective on the war. This form of differentiated content for gifted students is often used in the regular classroom because it requires no change in content, just additional assignments.

All students are expected to learn how history and culture emerge from past events and discoveries. A student like Zelda could take a single instance, say the invention of the chimney, and show how that simple discovery had far-reaching influence (Burke, 1978):

1. The chimney produced structural changes in houses. With a flue to conduct sparks, a fire no longer had to be in the center of a room and the chimney could be used as a spine against which to support more than one room, allowing the structure to be divided into a number of rooms, upstairs and downstairs.
2. The new house structure led to a separation of social classes: the privileged took the better, warmer rooms upstairs, leaving the workers downstairs. This may have been the beginning of the upstairs-downstairs separation of social classes in England.
3. The development of the chimney also had an effect on business. By providing enough warmth for paperwork to be continued in cold weather, it improved the commercial status of farms.
4. The chimney and fireplace improved personal hygiene by making bathing more comfortable.
5. Finally, romantic love was stimulated and encouraged by the fireplace. It introduced the concept of privacy, by dividing the hall into separate rooms. Lovemaking became a private, romantic activity.

As Burke (1978) pointed out, and as students can easily see for themselves, not all of the changes that take place through the introduction of technology are positive. The separation of social classes described above is a mixed benefit. Burke concludes: "The ties between the classes that had been expressed in the act of sleeping together before a common fire each night were broken. The tightly knit, agriculturally based, feudal world had gone up the chimney" (p. 161).

Sophistication

Content sophistication challenges gifted students to use higher levels of thinking to understand ideas that average students of the same age would find difficult or impossible. The objective is to encourage these children to understand important abstractions, scientific laws, or general principles that can be applied in many circumstances.

One example would be values, an area of interest for gifted students that is rarely explored in regular educational programs. The diversity in our society often causes us to overlook important common principles we share with one another. This can lead idealistic youngsters to believe they live in a valueless society, a society dominated by selfish people acting against the public interest.

How would we go about teaching values? We could assign students to look for those ethical standards held in common by classmates or neighbors, and then discuss how these common values hold the nation together. For example, Gardner (1978) pointed out several fundamental values held in common in our society:

- *Justice and the rule of law.*   The attempt to provide justice to all, while often falling short in practice, represents one of the most common themes of the American society.
- *Freedom of expression.*   The right to speak one's mind regardless of who it offends is another proud tradition. Without it, many of our other freedoms would likely vanish.
- *The dignity and worth of each person.*   Equality of opportunity for all—to give everyone a chance to reach their potential in a free society is a consistent theme. The insistence on special education for all handicapped children is a clear reflection of that value.
- *Individual moral responsibility.*   We are each responsible for the consequences of our actions. Even when we make allowances for differences in background and opportunities we, in the end, are the captains of our fate and will be judged as such by our friends, neighbors, and communities.
- *Our distaste for corruption.*   In this case, the larger purposes of the society may be betrayed by hatred, fear, envy, the smell of power or personal gain. Nevertheless, we agree that these things should not be, and we array our legal and social institutions to protect the larger society against personal frailty.

Novelty

Content novelty is the introduction of material that would not normally appear in the general curriculum because of time constraints or the abstract nature of the content. Its purpose is to help gifted students master important ideas.

Gifted students are able to draw relationships across content fields. This means a teacher could create one or two examples of an abstract nature and have the students work up others. Look at Table 3.4, which lists the impact of technology (automobiles, television) on society. The teacher could encourage gifted students to think about the consequences of other technological advances (air conditioning, computers) or to produce alternative sequences that yield more positive results (television gives us greater empathy for human suffering in faraway

Gifted students benefit from exposure to a series of activities in a variety of content fields.
(© Herb Snitzer, 1972 "Today Is for Children")

places). Because technology and science are central elements in modern society, it makes sense to teach their impact to youngsters, many of whom will be in positions to implement new discoveries when they are grown.

Computers are another tool that can be used to introduce content novelty into the curriculum. As Papert (1981) pointed out, computers allow children to be active, not passive, learners. Computers demand the use of systematic procedures. In the process of learning how computers think, children explore the ways they themselves think.

Davis and Frothingham (1981) reported on the use of microcomputers in the North Carolina School of Science and Mathematics, a secondary school for gifted and talented students. They identified three distinct uses for microcomputers:

- For classroom instruction in general subjects (history, foreign language, music), as well as in traditional subjects (mathematics, science).
- For independent study. By reducing computations, computers allow bright students to create projects and carry them out.

Table 3.4
Unintended Consequences of Technology

Automobile

First-order consequences: People have a means of traveling rapidly, easily, cheaply, privately door to door.

Second-order consequences: People patronize stores at greater distances from their homes. These are generally bigger stores with large clienteles.

Third-order consequences: Residents of a community do not meet each other so often and therefore do not get to know each other well.

Fourth-order consequences: Strangers to each other, community members find it difficult to unite to deal with common problems. Individuals find themselves increasingly isolated from their neighbors.

Fifth-order consequences: Isolated from their neighbors, members of a family depend more on one another for satisfaction of most of their psychological needs.

Sixth-order consequences: When spouses are unable to meet the heavy psychological demands that each makes on the other, frustration occurs. This can lead to divorce.

Television

First-order consequences: People have a new source of entertainment and enlightenment in their homes.

Second-order consequences: People stay home more, rather than going out to local clubs and bars where they would meet other people in their community.

Third-order consequences: Because they are home more, people do not get to know each other well. They are also less dependent on each other for entertainment.

Fourth-order consequences: Strangers to each other, community members find it difficult to unite to deal with common problems. Individuals find themselves increasingly isolated from their neighbors.

Fifth-order consequences: Isolated from their neighbors, members of a family depend more on one another for satisfaction of most of their psychological needs.

Sixth-order consequences: When spouses are unable to meet the heavy psychological demands that each makes on the other, frustration occurs. This

SOURCE: Adapted from *The Study of the Future* by E. Cornish, 1977. Washington, DC: World Future Society.

- As a topic of study (programming, languages, algorithms, applications, impact on society).

The authors found that gifted students are most excited about programming computers themselves, rather than responding to prescribed lessons, and argued that these children should have the opportunity to develop programming skills.

PROGRAM EVALUATION

Is there evidence that the program adjustments we've talked about in this chapter can help those students with high intelligence or special talents? There have been several attempts to determine the impact of programs for gifted children.

Gallagher, Weiss, Oglesby, and Thomas (1983) noted the following in their synthesis of program evaluation:

- Content acceleration has been implemented in many parts of the country. Students seem to be mastering the advanced ideas with few negative side effects.
- Intensive, specially designed programs to meet the needs of gifted underachievers are yielding positive results.
- The most popular method of accelerating gifted students is the advanced placement program. One reason for that popularity is the cost effectiveness of the program.
- Teachers can master new techniques for the stimulation of productive thinking.
- Programs that use mentors and independent study have received enthusiastic comments from participants.

There is also a growing body of knowledge that suggests that students with high intellectual or talent potential can profit measurably from the introduction of the educational strategies described in this chapter, and that these kinds of programs rarely if ever generate negative side effects.

LIFESPAN ISSUES FOR GIFTED AND TALENTED INDIVIDUALS

The economic and vocational futures for most gifted individuals are bright. The vocational opportunities awaiting them seem very diverse, including the fields of medicine, law, business, politics, and science. Only in the arts, where a limited number of opportunities exist to earn a comfortable income, do gifted people encounter barriers to their ambitions.

It is virtually certain that when most gifted students finish secondary school they go on to more school. They will often have eight or ten more years of training before they can expect to begin an independent life. This is especially true if they choose careers in medicine, law, or science.

The delay in becoming an independent wage earner creates personal and social problems for gifted people that are just beginning to be studied. Prolonged schooling means that they must receive continued financial support. The most common forms of financial support are assistance from one's own family and subsidies from private or public sources. If financial aid takes the form of bank or government loans, then the gifted individual will begin his or her career with a substantial debt. This period of extended schooling also tends to postpone marriage and raising a family for many gifted people.

The psychological problems of remaining essentially dependent on others for financial support for thirty years or so remain unexplored. They are surely issues we need to consider before we burden gifted students with more schooling requirements intended to meet the demands for more knowledge to keep apace in this rapidly changing world.

SUMMARY OF MAJOR IDEAS

1. Gifted children show outstanding abilities in a variety of areas, including intellect, academic aptitude, creative thinking, leadership, and the visual and performing arts.
2. Academically able children tend to show superior development in social and personality characteristics as well.
3. Gifted girls have shown less aptitude than boys in math and science, reflecting social attitudes about what is acceptable for girls to do.
4. The characteristics of gifted underachievers can be modified through careful, sustained educational programming.
5. The abilities of children who come from culturally different subgroups are often ignored or undiscovered, a substantial loss of talent to society.
6. Children with handicaps can be intellectually gifted, but often their talents are undiscovered because educators do not generally expect them to be gifted.
7. Heredity appears to play a significant role in intellectual giftedness, but environmental opportunities determine the level to which ability is developed.
8. The identification of gifted children has traditionally been accomplished through a combination of procedures, including intelligence testing, review of school records, and peer and teacher evaluation.
9. Of the common methods to change the learning environment, resource room–pullout programs are popular with educators and parents in elementary schools; advanced placement classes in specific content fields are favored at the secondary level.
10. There is an emphasis on stimulating productive-thinking skills as part of special education programs for gifted students. In particular, these programs focus on improving problem-solving, problem-finding, and creativity skills.

11. Differentiated content for gifted students can be developed through the process of curriculum compacting, which uncovers what students already know, allowing the teacher to present the rest of the material quickly, so that students can go on to other topics.

12. We can expand the content of course material for gifted students through acceleration, enrichment, sophistication, and novelty, all of which are appropriate in certain educational situations.

13. Evaluation of special programs for gifted students has yielded positive results for advanced placement programs and content acceleration. It has also confirmed the ability of teachers to use productive-thinking stimulation techniques.

UNRESOLVED ISSUES

1. *Love-hate relationships with gifted students.*   Many people who support special education for children with handicaps are reluctant to extend special programming to gifted students. These people define *exceptionality* in terms of deficits: Because gifted children are not lacking in ability, they warrant no special attention. It is critical that we accept responsibility for these students, a potential source of so many of tomorrow's leaders.

2. *Special teachers and classroom teachers.*   One problem facing special educators is the often difficult relationship between the classroom teacher and the special education teacher. Theoretically, they should work together as a team, but personal problems of professional status and authority often create a chasm between the two, ultimately hurting the gifted child. Both personal and administrative adjustments are needed to encourage greater cooperation among teaching professionals.

3. *Undiscovered and underutilized talent.*   For many reasons, including different cultural values, gifted and potentially gifted students are being overlooked in our public schools. Standard tests for identification are not helping the situation to any significant degree. We need more and better approaches to discover this hidden talent and, just as important, special programs to enhance it.

REFERENCES OF SPECIAL INTEREST

Bloom, B. (Ed.) (1985). *Developing talent in young people.* New York: Ballantine Books.

This book describes a major effort to identify factors that influence the development of significant talent in young people. The subjects in the study were 120 world-class performers, including concert pianists, sculptors, research mathematicians, research neurologists, olympic swimmers, and tennis champions. The book focuses on the long and intensive process of encouragement, nurturing, education, and training that these young people need in order to achieve the highest levels of capability in their chosen fields.

Feldhusen, J., & Treffinger, D. (1980). *Creative thinking and problem solving in gifted education* (2d ed.). Dubuque, IA: Kendall/Hunt.

A book for teachers that describes ways to instruct students in creative thinking and problem solving. Special features are reviews of other books and instructional materials for teaching creativity, and a chapter on the special needs of minority gifted students.

Gallagher, J. (1985). *Teaching the gifted child* (3d ed.). Boston: Allyn & Bacon.

This textbook presents a general review of the special problems faced by gifted students in the regular program. Program adjustments center on special learning environments, curriculum content, and the development of thinking skills.

Karnes, F., & Collins, E. (1980). *Handbook of instructional resources and references for teaching the gifted.* Boston: Allyn & Bacon.

A detailed guide for helping teachers find or adapt materials to enhance the learning experiences of gifted students. Includes check lists for evaluating materials, a comprehensive list of publishers, professional references, games and puzzles, and a general overview of the special needs of gifted children.

Maker, C. (1982). *Teaching models in education of the gifted.* Rockville, MD: Aspen Teaching System.

A fine examination of the major theoretical models that apply to the education of gifted children. The models of Guilford, Bloom, Renzulli, Taba, Kohlburg, and others are given fair, balanced treatment. The book allows the reader to compare various models and shows how each model can be applied in specific instances.

National Commission on Excellence in Education (1983). *A nation at risk: The imperatives for educational reform* (Report to the Nation and the Secretary of Education). Washington, DC: U.S. Government Printing Office.

This is the best known of the large number of commission reports on the state of American education. It stresses the need for excellence and higher standards in elementary and secondary schools. The recommendations would improve the situation for gifted students.

Whitmore, J. (1980). *Giftedness, conflict, and underachievement.* Boston: Allyn & Bacon.

The most comprehensive discussion of underachievement currently available. The author emphasizes the presence of emotional disturbance in most underachievers and describes in detail a program for modifying the classroom environment for gifted underachievers.

C·H·A·P·T·E·R Four

CHILDREN WITH MENTAL RETARDATION

Focusing Questions

What effect has the inclusion of adaptive behavior had on the current definition of mental retardation?

What are the factors that contribute to mental retardation in children?

What do information-processing models tell us about the thinking process?

What effect has preschool intervention had on the later academic performance of children who are mentally retarded?

What four areas of instruction generally make up the special education programs for students who are mildly or moderately retarded?

What are the roles of behavior modification, task analysis, and counseling in the instructional program for children who are mentally retarded?

How can we prepare youngsters who are retarded to function in the workplace?

*A*s we have always been aware that some children learn more quickly than others, so we have always known that some children learn more slowly than their agemates and, as a consequence, have difficulty adapting to the social demands placed on them. Organized attempts to help children who learn slowly began less than two hundred years ago, when Jean Itard, a French physician, tried to educate a young boy found wandering in the woods outside Aveyron. Although Itard failed, one of his students, Edward Seguin, later developed Itard's approaches and became an acknowledged leader of the movement to help mentally retarded children and adults. Political turmoil in Europe brought Seguin to the United States in 1848. His work had a marked effect on this country's efforts to provide education for mentally retarded children. Over the years, the care and education of children who are mentally retarded has moved gradually from large state institutions to special class provisions in the public schools to the current philosophy of integration as much as possible into society—into the least restrictive environment (Crissey, 1975).

Educators have identified three levels of mental retardation to indicate the educational implications of the condition: mild, moderate, and severe and profound. In this chapter we discuss children at the first two levels—mildly and moderately retarded. We examine those who are severely and profoundly retarded in Chapter 10.

DEFINITION

Each professional discipline that works with those who are mentally retarded offers definitions of the condition from its own perspective. So we have medical definitions and psychological definitions and behavioral definitions. We are interested in how educators describe mental retardation.

The most common of those definitions was devised by the American Association on Mental Deficiency (AAMD):

> **Mental retardation** refers to significantly subaverage general intellectual functioning existing concurrently with deficits in adaptive behavior and manifested during the developmental period. (Grossman, 1983, p. 1)

What does this mean? "Significantly subaverage general intellectual functioning" is a score on a standard intelligence test lower than that obtained by 97 to 98 percent of persons the same age. "Deficits in adaptive behavior" is the failure to meet standards of independence and social responsibility expected of the individual's age and cultural group. The "developmental period" is the time from birth to age 18. A child who is mentally retarded, then, would score in the bottom 2 or 3 percent on an intelligence test and would have problems learning basic academic skills or participating in appropriate group activities in the period from birth to age 18.

A key distinction between this definition and others is the emphasis on intellectual subnormality combined with adaptive behavior, an emphasis we discuss in the following paragraphs.

Intellectual Subnormality

No definition, no matter how comprehensive, is worth much unless we can translate its abstractions into some form of concrete action. Intellectual subnormality has traditionally been determined by performance on intelligence tests. One of the earliest of these tests was in fact developed by Alfred Binet for the express purpose of finding children who were not capable of responding to the traditional education program in France at the turn of the twentieth century. The performance of mentally retarded children on these tests is the mirror image of the performance of gifted students described in Chapter 3. Mentally retarded children are markedly slower than their agemates in using memory effectively, in associating and classifying information, in reasoning, and in making sound judgments.

Students who score between -2 standard deviations and -3 standard deviations on an intelligence scale are considered mildly mentally retarded if their social adaptation is also low. Students who score below -3 standard deviations but who are capable of responding to the test are considered moderately retarded. IQ scores can also be used as a rough indicator of level of retardation (Grossman, 1983):

Mild	IQ score of 50–55 to 70
Moderate	IQ score of 35–40 to 50–55
Severe and profound	IQ score below 35

Adaptive Behavior

The term *adaptive behavior* was added to the AAMD definition in recognition of the fact that some youngsters and adults perform acceptably in society despite low measured intelligence.

Grossman (1983) defined **adaptive behavior** as "the effectiveness or degree with which individuals meet the standards of personal independence and social responsibility expected for age and cultural group" (p. 1). Once again we can see the role played by society and the environment in defining a handicapping condition. In a farming community, where the demands on a child who is developing slowly intellectually are not great, a child who is mildly retarded may not be seen as exceptional. But in a technologically sophisticated society, where language and mathematics mastery is important, the same child would be in substantial trouble educationally and socially.

Despite the availability of a large number of adaptive behavior scales, the most common method for assessing adaptive behavior is the informal judgment of the teacher or others who have direct experience with the child. For the young child, most adaptive behavior scales focus on self-care skills (eating, dressing, toileting). As the child grows older and interacts with his or her surroundings, the scales have trouble assessing that interaction because that measurement depends, not only on the characteristics of the child, but on the expectations of the social group the child is encountering (see Mercer & Lewis, 1978). Are the expectations the same in rural Kansas and Detroit? Could the same youngster adapt satisfactorily in one place but not in another?

If mild retardation is determined by the expectations placed on the child, some puzzling things happen. A child can become "mentally retarded" by simply getting on a bus in a community where those expectations are low and getting off the bus in a community where they are high. More serious levels of retardation are obvious and permanent in any social setting; mild retardation is not. It can change with the expectations of the individual's community.

Not everyone agrees with a definition of mental retardation that includes social adaptation. Zigler, Balla, and Hodapp (1984) urged that the field return to a definition that focuses only on intellectual functioning: "The essence of mental retardation involves inefficient cognitive functioning; hence, mental retardation should be defined solely by subaverage performance on measures of intellectual abilities" (p. 227).

There is no question that using intelligence scores as the sole criterion of mental retardation would make diagnosis simpler. But complex criteria may be needed for complex situations. Some years ago the President's Committee on Mental Retardation (1970) published a report, *The Six-Hour Retarded Child*. It described mildly retarded children who were not adapting between 9 A.M. and 3 P.M. in school, where demands for effective reading and thinking were placed on them, but were adapting successfully in their neighborhoods and families at other hours of the day.

Edgerton (1984) followed many children and adolescents who had been diagnosed mentally retarded, into adulthood. He found that some of them were making a good adjustment in the community. Were they still mentally retarded? Not by the AAMD criterion of "poor social adaptation."

Despite the problems that the definition poses, most educators and psychologists see the wisdom of using the dual criteria—(1) poor social adaptation, (2) due to intellectual subnormality—as the key for identification of mild mental retardation.

Table 4.1
Levels of Mental Retardation

	Mild (Educable)	Moderate (Trainable)	Severe/Profound (Dependent)
Etiology	Considered a combination of genetic and socioeconomic conditions	A wide variety of relatively rare neurological, glandular, or metabolic defects or disorders	
Prevalence	About 10 out of every 1,000 people	About 3 out of every 1,000 people	About 1 out of every 1,000 people
School expectations	Will have difficulty in usual school program; needs special adaptations for appropriate education	Needs major adaptation in educational programs; focus is on self-care or social skills; may learn basic academic skills	Needs training in self-care skills (feeding, toileting, dressing)
Adult expectations	With special education can make productive adjustment at an unskilled or semiskilled level	Can make social and economic adaptation in a sheltered workshop or in a routine job under supervision	Will always be dependent on others for care

CLASSIFICATION

The term *mental retardation* covers a broad range of children and adults who differ from one another in the severity of developmental delay, in the causes of the condition, and in the special educational strategies that have been designed for them. It's important that we remember these differences. The *mild, moderate,* and *severe/profound* terms suggested by the AAMD are used here, although many special educators still use the terms *educable, trainable,* and *dependent* to describe the same basic categories (see Table 4.1).

Mild Mental Retardation

A child who is mildly retarded because of delayed mental development has the capacity to develop in three areas: (1) in academic subjects at the primary and advanced elementary grade levels, (2) in social adjustment to the point at which the child can eventually adapt independently in the community, and (3) the occupational potential to be partially or totally self-supporting as an adult.

Mild retardation often goes unidentified until a child reaches school age. Our expectations for the child are not heavily weighted with intellectual content during preschool years. But when learning ability becomes an important part of social expectations, the condition is then

Many mentally retarded people are capable of achieving some measure of self-supporting employment as adults. (© Jerry Howard/Positive Images)

noted. In most instances there are no obvious pathological conditions to account for mild retardation.

Moderate Mental Retardation

The child who is moderately retarded can (1) learn academic skills for functional purposes, (2) achieve some degree of social responsibility, and (3) attain partial vocational adjustment with assistance. This child is capable of acquiring self-help skills (dressing, undressing, toileting, eating); of protecting himself or herself from common dangers in the home, school, and neighborhood; of adjusting socially to the home or neighborhood (sharing, respecting property rights, cooperating); of learning basic academic skills (reading signs, counting); and of working in a sheltered environment or in a routine job under supervision. In most instances, children who are moderately retarded are identified during infancy and early childhood because of their marked developmental delays and sometimes by physical appearance.

Severe and Profound Mental Retardation

Most severely and profoundly retarded children have multiple handicaps that interfere with normal instructional procedures. For example, in addition to being mentally retarded, the child may have cerebral palsy and a hearing loss. The goal of training programs for these children is to establish some level of social adaptation in a controlled environment (see Chapter 10).

DEVELOPMENTAL PROFILES

Figure 4.1 shows the developmental patterns of a mildly retarded child and a moderately retarded child. The patterns revealed in the figure are not unusual for children of their intellectual development, although there are great individual differences from one child to another within each of these groups.

Bob is a mildly retarded ten-year-old. His physical profile (height, weight, motor coordination) does not differ markedly from others in his age group and would not set him apart from his peers. However, in academic areas—reading, arithmetic, and spelling—Bob is performing three and four grades below his age group. Depending on his classmates and the levels at which they are performing, Bob would fall at the bottom of the regular class group or be set apart in special classes. Bob's vision, hearing, and mobility are average, but he is having problems with interpersonal relationships. Although he is a likable boy under nonthreatening conditions, he is quick to take offense and fight on the playground. In the classroom he has a tendency to interrupt other children at their work and to wander aimlessly around the classroom when given an individual assignment. All of these characteristics add up to a situation in which Bob has only a few friends, although he is tolerated by his classmates. With special help he is able to maintain a marginal performance within the regular class.

Carol, the moderately retarded child, has a much more serious adaptive problem. In addition to attaining the developmental level of a four-year-old (her IQ score is in the 40s), Carol shows, as is typical of a Down syndrome child, poor motor coordination and some minor vision and hearing problems that complicate her educational remediation. Although Carol has a pleasant personality and is generally even-tempered, her physical appearance and her mental slowness have left her not well accepted by her agemates.

The developmental pattern in the figure shows that Carol's academic performance is well below first-grade level; indeed, at maturity Carol's reading and arithmetic skills are not likely to exceed a first- or second-grade level. She can learn important skills or concepts in an educational setting, but the standard academic program is clearly

FIGURE 4.1
Profiles of two
mentally retarded
children

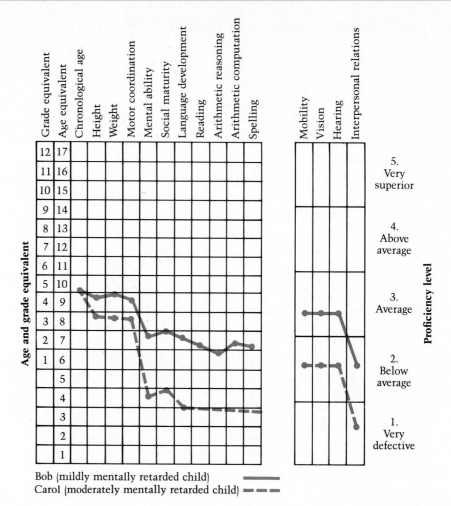

Bob (mildly mentally retarded child)
Carol (moderately mentally retarded child)

inappropriate for her. To develop her capabilities to their maximum potential, Carol is going to need some very special kinds of experiences with a trained teacher.

FACTORS CONTRIBUTING TO MENTAL RETARDATION

Is the human brain capable of understanding the human brain? The brain is more complex than the most advanced computer, and much of its function and development remains a mystery. Yet astonishing advances have been made during the past few decades. Those that have made the most difference in our understanding of the physical causes of mental retardation have been in genetics and biochemistry (Begab, 1981).

The AAMD has identified nine major groupings of causal agents for mental retardation (Grossman, 1983):

- Infection and intoxication
- Trauma or physical agents
- Metabolism or nutrition
- Gross brain disease
- Unknown prenatal influences
- Chromosomal abnormalities
- Gestational disorders
- Psychiatric disorders
- Environmental influences

We discuss a few of these categories here.

Genetic Disorders

Impressive advances in research in the field of genetics over the past decade have revealed much about the mechanisms by which chromosomes and genes influence or determine mental retardation.

> The genes are blueprints for the assembly and regulation of proteins, the building blocks of our bodies. Each gene is responsible for a code for a specific sequence of amino acids that the body assembles to form a protein. If even the smallest part of this chain is altered, the entire protein can malfunction. (Plomin, DeFries, & McClearn, 1980, p. 7)

Do certain patterns of genes predetermine certain types of behavior? Are we unwitting automatons moving through life driven by mysterious bursts of chemicals? Not really. No particular gene or protein forces a person to raise a whiskey glass to his or her lips, but some people have a genetic sensitivity to ethanol that may tip the scales in the direction of alcoholism if they drink frequently. The relationship between genes and behavior is very complex, and environmental influences are almost always an important factor.

The more we learn about the mechanisms of heredity, the more remarkable the transmission of genetic material becomes. It seems astonishing that a father and a mother each contributes twenty-three chromosomes with hundreds of genes resting in just the right location on each chromosome and performing just the right chemical process to produce a new human being. It's not surprising that in many cases the process goes awry. According to Plomin, DeFries, and McClearn (1980), human genetic abnormalities are common, involving as many as half of all human fertilizations. These are not noticed in the general population because most genetic abnormalities result in early spontaneous abortion. About 1 in 200 fetuses with genetic abnormalities survives until birth, but many of these babies die soon after they are born. The result is that though many deviations occur, most are never seen.

Over a hundred genetic disorders have been identified. Fortunately, most of these genetic abnormalities are relatively rare. Here we look at two of the more common ones.

Down Syndrome

One of the more common and easily recognized conditions is Down syndrome. This condition, once called mongolism because it creates a superficial resemblance to the Oriental race, was one of the first to be linked to a genetic abnormality (Lejeune, Gautier, & Turpin, 1959). People with this condition have forty-seven chromosomes instead of the normal forty-six. The condition leads to mild or moderate mental retardation, and a variety of hearing, skeletal, and heart problems. The presence of Down syndrome is related to maternal age, with the incidence increasing significantly in children born to mothers 35 or older. According to current figures, over 50 percent of Down syndrome children are born to mothers over 35. We do not know exactly why advancing age is related to the condition. We do know, however, that the mother is not the exclusive cause of the extra chromosome. The father contributes the extra chromosome in 20 to 25 percent of all cases (Abroms & Bennett, 1980).

Down syndrome can also be caused by a chromosomal abnormality translocation. The child has forty-six chromosomes, but a pair of one is broken and the broken part is fused to another chromosome. A third type is called mosaic Down syndrome. These two kinds of chromosomal abnormalities account for only 4 to 5 percent of Down syndrome in children (Lilienfield, 1969). The incidence of the condition is 1 to 2 births out of 1,000.

Phenylketonuria

Another condition caused by genetic irregularities is phenylketonuria (PKU), a single-gene defect that can produce severe retardation. Extensive biochemical studies have revealed that mental retardation in children with PKU is caused by the inability of the gene structure to break down a particular chemical, phenylalanine, which when accumulated at high levels in the blood results in severe damage to the developing brain. Although the condition is clearly the result of a genetic disorder, it's now possible to prevent mental retardation if the child is placed on a low-phenylalanine diet in the developing years. We have, here, the phenomenon of a genetic problem in which the most disastrous consequences of the condition can be prevented by an environmental intervention.

Some of the gains that have been made in the medical treatment of PKU themselves create problems. Girls who have been treated successfully are usually taken off the difficult diet by age 12. The resulting buildup of phenylalanine in the mature woman is not dangerous to her central nervous system, but it can damage the fetus if she becomes pregnant. This means the diet must be resumed if a woman finds herself pregnant. This fact combined with the greater likelihood of a treated woman marrying and having children (because she is intellectually normal instead of severely retarded) led Kirkman (1982) to predict a sharp rise in PKU children in the middle to late 1980s.

Toxic Agents and Infectious Diseases

Toxic agents ingested by the mother during pregnancy or by the child can disturb the internal biochemical balance. Viruses or germs in the form of infectious diseases can invade the body and cause long-lasting damage to the central nervous system beyond the course of the original disease.

Fetal Alcohol Syndrome

Heavy drinking by the mother during pregnancy has been identified as a possible cause of mental retardation in children. Although a precise threshold of safety has not been determined, as little as 3 ounces of pure alcohol can harm the fetus (Nitowsky, 1979). There is no doubt that alcohol crosses the placental barrier, remains in the fetus's bloodstream, and depresses central nervous system functioning in the fetus. Whether the actual damage is caused by the alcohol itself or the alcohol in combination with other risk factors (such as smoking) is not clear (Streissguth, Landesman-Dwyer, Martin, & Smith, 1980).

Lead Poisoning

The level of lead in the blood has turned out to be a significant factor in damage to the brain. Anything that increases that level to a significant point should be controlled if at all possible. Much of the lead comes through the atmosphere. The switch to unleaded gasoline is one specific attempt to control or reduce atmospheric lead levels (Graef, 1983). The ingestion of lead paint is another source of mental retardation in young children. Apparently the lead crosses from the blood into the brain, resulting in mental retardation.

Viruses

Rubella, or German measles, can cause mental retardation if the mother contracts the disease during the first three months of pregnancy. Encephalitis is caused by a virus that produces high fever and possible brain cell destruction with long-term effects. These are just two of a large number of conditions, fortunately rare, that have the potential to produce mental retardation.

Polygenic Inheritance

Although the single-gene effect has a dramatic impact on the development of individual children, many human traits (skin color, hair color, height, general body build) are controlled by the action of many genes operating together. The effects of that interaction are called **polygenic inherited characteristics**. Intellectual development is generally assumed to be the result of complex polygenic inheritance, which, when combined with certain environmental conditions, can result in mental retardation. Because environmental conditions are involved, many professionals have tried to change the environment to positively affect mental development, a subject we discuss later in this chapter.

CHARACTERISTICS OF MENTALLY RETARDED CHILDREN

The nature of special programming for mildly and moderately retarded children is shaped in part by the characteristics that distinguish these children from their agemates. We find marked differences in several dimensions: cognitive processes, language acquisition and use, physical and motor abilities, and personal and social characteristics.

Information Processing

The most obvious characteristic of children who are mildly or moderately retarded is their limited cognitive ability—a limitation that inevitably shows up in their academic work. These children, like Bob, lag by two to five grades, particularly in language-related subjects (reading, language arts).

Of course, it's not enough to know that children are not learning effectively. To help them, we must uncover the elements that are preventing them from learning. And to do this, we must understand how they think, how they process information.

How does information enter the human consciousness? How is that information acted on by individual experience? And how does behavior stem from that interaction? To answer these questions, psychologists

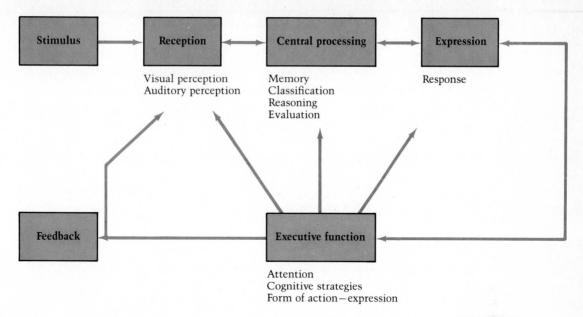

FIGURE 4.2
Information-
processing
components

have developed **information-processing models,** models of how people think that bear a close resemblance to our understanding of how computers function.

Information-processing models divide the thinking process into separate components that can be studied individually. They are interested, not only in what the child is able to do (as shown on IQ and achievement tests), but in how the child is able to do it—in the steps or processes that are activated between the time the child perceives a stimulus and the time the child responds to it.

Figure 4.2 shows a simple information-processing model. It is divided into three major steps:

1. *Reception.* The visual or auditory perception of a stimulus.
2. *Central processing.* Classification of the stimulus using the cognitive processes of memory, reasoning, and evaluation.
3. *Expression.* The choice of a single response from a repertoire of many possible responses.

Influencing and controlling these steps is **executive function**—the decision-making element that is central to all effective adaptive behavior. It controls what we pay attention to (reception), the problem-solving strategies we call into play (central processing), and our choice of action (expression).

Finally, **feedback** is the result of our response to the initial stimulus. It becomes a new stimulus, acted on by new experiences.

How does it work? Let's suppose a boy, playing outside, sees a big dog running toward him:

1. *Reception.*   The dog is the stimulus. The boy's awareness of the dog is the information that goes to central processing.
2. *Central processing.*   The boy remembers the dog is Spot, the neighbor's dog. He sees the dog's tail wagging and remembers that a wagging tail means a happy dog. Spot is not a threat. This information goes to expression.
3. *Expression.*   The boy has a number of responses he can call on. He can run away or cry or call for help or, in this case, say "Nice doggie" and pat the animal.

How is executive function operating here? It controls what the boy perceives as a stimulus (the dog, not a car passing by); it allows central-processing strategies to operate (the dog is not a threat); and it chooses the response (patting the animal). The dog's reaction to the response is feedback. It is also a new stimulus. If the dog sits quietly and licks the boy's hand, that information is fed into central processing, reinforcing the knowledge there that Spot is a friendly dog and that a wagging tail means a happy dog. If the dog moves back and begins to growl, the boy reacts with a different response.

We use the information-processing model to identify the processes that are most affected in exceptional children. Does the retarded child's inability to learn stem from an inability to perceive stimuli effectively? Does the difficulty lie with the child's problem-solving abilities? Does the child lack expressive skills? Is the child's executive function operating? Or does the child have problems in all of these dimensions?

Recent reviews of the literature cite executive function as one key factor in the poor performance of children who are mentally retarded (Baumeister & Brooks, 1981; Sternberg, 1982). It is not so much that these children cannot perceive a stimulus as it is that they cannot pay attention to the relevant aspects of a problem. It is not so much that they cannot reason as it is that they do not have the strategies to organize the information to a point where reasoning can take place. And it is not so much that they do not have a repertoire of responses as it is that they too often choose an inappropriate one. They lack "good judgment" their teachers often say.

Many children also have problems in central processing. **Classification**—the organization of information—seems to be a special problem for children who are mentally retarded. School-age children quickly learn to cluster events or things into useful classes: A chair, a table, and a sofa become "furniture"; an apple, a peach, and a pear become "fruit." Children who are retarded are less able to group things together. They can't tell us how a train and an automobile are alike.

Part of the difficulty these children have with classification stems from mediation. **Mediation** is the ability to apply past experiences to the current situation, to tie together apparently unrelated elements. Consider this task: "Fill in the blank: Monday, _____, Wednesday." For most of us, the answer is easy. But if we didn't know the days of the week or the sequence of those days or how to apply that knowledge, we couldn't possibly perform the task.

Memory is another central-processing function that is difficult for children who are retarded. Memory problems can stem from poor initial perception or poor judgment in applying what has been stored to the situation. Most children use rehearsal as a memory aid, saying a string of words or a poem to themselves until they remember it. Retarded children are less likely to rehearse information because their ability to use short-term memory for this purpose seems limited.

For children like Carol, problems are not limited to a specific function; instead, there is a substantial breakdown in the whole system. Most children whose IQ level is 50 or below suffer from biological damage to the brain and central nervous system that makes information processing very difficult.

Language Acquisition and Use

The ability of young children to use language to communicate would be considered phenomenal if it weren't so universal. The effective use of language is critical to success throughout life. Gallagher (1981) summarized what we know about language in general terms:

- Language acquisition and use [are] dependent on an internal system that is triggered by childhood experiences.
- Some relevant factors that influence the full development of language are: (1) the nature of adult stimulation, (2) the amount of stimulation, and (3) the timing of the stimulation (when in the development flow it occurs).
- A distinction can be made between *descriptive* language used for labeling and simple classification, and *interpretative* language used for delineating logical sequences, implication drawing, transformation of ideas, and so forth.
- The interpretative language usage depends on social modeling and extensive practice.
- Language development appears to influence the full growth of most of the other developmental channels (e.g., cognitive, social, adaptive).
- Language development in turn is affected by many factors in many different domains. Family, cultural values, and experience clearly have an impact on linguistic form and expression.

- Attempts to intervene to improve language performance can yield definable results. The programs that have clear and specific linguistic objectives appear to do better than those with a broad undifferentiated goal to "improve language." (pp. 388–389)

Children who are mentally retarded have a general language deficit and specific problems using interpretative language. These general and specific problems impede their development in cognitive, social, and adaptive areas.

We do not know how much of language delay is due to low cognitive abilities. Does the development of language in mentally retarded children follow the same sequence of development it does in normal children but at a slower rate? Or are there qualitative differences in the development of language in those who are mentally retarded? There appears to be evidence to support both positions in part.

One study revealed a rate difference in language development at early ages and a qualitative difference at later ages. Naremore and Dever (1975) collected 5-minute speech samples of normal and retarded children at each age level from 6 to 10. The retarded children were most deficient in using complex clauses and subject elaboration. These are important communication deficits because they limit the kind and amount of information the retarded child can communicate to others, particularly when sequences of activities are called for.

We can see the differences between the expressive language of normal children and that of mildly retarded children in the following samples, as two ten-year-olds describe the same television program (Naremore & Dever, 1975):

Normal ten-year-old

Every time he tried to start something they all started to play their instruments and wouldn't do anything so Lucy said that they needed a Christmas tree, a pink one, for the Christmas queen, but when Charlie Brown went out he found that there were lots of them that were pink and green and blue, but there was just one little one.

Mildly retarded ten-year-old

Charlie Brown didn't seem to have the Christmas spirit *and* so Linus said he should get involved *and* there's this little doctor place *and* Charlie Brown went over there *and* that's what Lucy told him to.

The retarded child's production not only is sparser than the normal child's, with limited content, but is also meager in structure. The retarded child depends heavily on *and* as a connective and lacks the ability to impose temporal or hierarchical structure on events.

Problems in language development for moderately retarded children are much more severe. In addition to slow development there are the problems that stem from the neurological or physiological cause of the retardation. Damage to the brain, for example, can have a devastating effect on a child's language development. **Aphasia** is the absence of language presumably due to injury to the language centers of the cerebral cortex. Few children are actually aphasic, but there are suspicions that partial damage to the brain can negatively influence the development of language skills in many cases.

Of course brain injury is not the only handicapping condition that can affect language development. Downs (1980) reported finding an unusually high percentage of Down syndrome children with mild hearing loss presumably associated with a susceptibility to otitis media, an infection of the middle ear. This kind of problem may well contribute to the poor language use of many Down syndrome children.

Physical and Motor Abilities

Only a few studies have been conducted on the physical development and motor proficiency of children who are mildly retarded (Francis & Rarick, 1960; Rarick & Widdop, 1970). They indicate that, in motor proficiency, the average scores on physical tests of these children are somewhat lower than the average scores of children of normal intelligence. In height and weight most mildly retarded children resemble their agemates. Of course we cannot generalize from group results to individual children. Some mentally retarded children are superior in height and weight to some average and gifted children.

Because mildly retarded children have a slightly higher incidence of vision, hearing, and neurological problems, we would expect some tendency to poorer physical and motor abilities. Still, individual youngsters can show outstanding physical and athletic skills.

The same cannot be said of moderately retarded children, however. Because the majority of children who fall within the moderate range of mental retardation show evidence of some form of central nervous system disorder or damage, we find problems involving coordination, gait, and fine motor skills (see Rie & Rie, 1980). A high prevalence of motor problems in children with various metabolic disorders has been noted as well. Even where a definitive neurological diagnosis of cerebral palsy is not possible, children who are moderately retarded appear to be awkward and clumsy and to walk with a stiff, robotlike gait (see Levine, Carey, Crocker, & Gross, 1983).

There are programs that focus on the physical abilities of retarded children. The Special Olympics, for example, encourages these youngsters to participate in sports, and demonstrates that even where children have identifiable physical and motor problems, practice and encouragement can significantly upgrade their skills in these areas (Shriver, 1980).

Programs like the Special Olympics help mentally retarded individuals improve their physical and motor skills.
(Alan Carey/The Image Works)

Personal and Social Characteristics

The school is interested in the personality and behavior of retarded children for two specific reasons. First, atypical behavior can create a barrier to learning within the classroom itself. Second, adult social adaptation depends heavily on social skills and behavior patterns. Retarded children often show special problems in personal and social characteristics. These problems relate in part to the reactions of others to their condition and to a history of failing to reach the level of performance expected by others. Certain characteristics—limited attention span, low frustration tolerance—can be attributed to a history of failure. Whether the intellectual limitations of those who are mentally retarded also limit their social adjustment is still uncertain, but the limitations in language development discussed earlier are almost surely a negative factor in social adaptation.

A recent addition to these behavioral factors is time-on-task or academic learning time (ALT). This is the total time the student is actually engaged in instruction or learning, as opposed to the amount of time in school. Studies show that retarded children spend much less time in ALT than do others. These students may be easily distracted or hyperactive or inattentive, or engaging in nonproductive activity (fighting, out-of-seat socializing) (Bloom, 1974). This is one reason why special education programs for mildly and moderately retarded children focus on socially approved classroom behavior. One instructional goal is to help these children into a proper learning set or posture so that they spend more time on task.

Polloway, Epstein, and Cullinan (1985) compared teacher ratings on behavior problems of 612 mildly retarded students with 1,116 nonhandicapped students. In addition to the teachers' judgment that the retarded students lacked self-confidence and felt inferior, the authors concluded:

> Mentally retarded pupils also exhibited more *attention deficit* problems than their [nonhandicapped] peers. They tended to be more distractible, inattentive and easily flustered, and to have a shorter attention span. In fact, well over half of the [mildly retarded] pupils were found to have problems indicative of an attention-deficit disorder. (p. 9)

One factor that influences memory is the ability to pay attention, to stay on task. Unless students maintain a focus on the task at hand, they are going to have trouble learning, retarded or not. Krupski (1979) compared the ability of mildly (educable) retarded students between the ages of 9 and 12 to stay on task with that of a group of nonhandicapped children matched for age and sex. The retarded children were in two special classes; the children of average ability, in the regular classroom. All the children were observed during periods when they were expected to work on their own. The results showed that the retarded students did spend more time off task, primarily through peer interaction and out-of-seat behavior. Many educators believe that such inattention may stem from a growing dislike of tasks the students cannot perform well.

These results, taken in the classroom setting, confirm laboratory findings on defects in the memory and attention of retarded children and indicate a special problem for teachers in getting mentally retarded students to focus on their lessons. They also implicate executive function (the source of attention) and central-processing mechanisms in this information-processing problem.

Moderately retarded children often have personal and social problems that stem from both the original cause of the retardation (brain injury) and the reaction of others to them. If a child has limited language capabilities and has consequently failed to meet expectations, his or her behavior is likely to be inflexible and repetitious, and at times passive. The damage to the central nervous system that created the retardation in the first place may explain a tendency toward hyperactivity and impulsiveness and regression to earlier, more childlike, behaviors in stressful situations (Rie & Rie, 1980).

Another major influence on the social behavior of moderately retarded children is the nature of the environment in which they find themselves. Many of these children live in institutions or group homes, environments that are powerful shapers of social behavior. Today many believe that some of the atypical behavior associated with the condition of mental retardation is caused by the special environment of the residential institution.

Suppose you were raised in a bedroom with a hundred other children, had a rotating list of adult caretakers (none of whom is present more than eight hours), and never had the experience of going to the store, exploring a neighborhood, or doing many of the things that young children do. You probably would have difficulty adapting to life outside the institution. It seems, then, that the inability of retarded youngsters to adjust to their community is in part a function of the environment, not just the condition of mental retardation.

If we can reduce the number of failure experiences, create novel experiences in which the child succeeds, and present successful models of behavior, we can improve the attitudes and behavior patterns that progressively prevent the mildly retarded child from making full use of his or her limited abilities.

FAMILIES OF MENTALLY RETARDED CHILDREN

The discovery that your child is mentally retarded is a stunning shock. It's proof of human resilience that most families recover from the shock and manage to cope, particularly with the help of professional assistance and programs.

Of course the relationship is not one-dimensional. In the same way that the child has an impact on the family, the family has an ongoing effect on the developing child. The families of mildly retarded children turn out to be quite different from those of moderately retarded youngsters. Mildly retarded children often come from lower socioeconomic backgrounds; moderately retarded children, whose condition usually stems from a genetic or metabolic accident, represent a full spectrum of family backgrounds.

The predominant role played by poverty and social disorganization in the families of children with mild retardation led Goddard and Terman and other psychologists in earlier days to view these circumstances as proof of genetic problems—that is, low-ability parents produce low-ability children. It is just as easy, however, to conclude that a disadvantaged home environment increases health risks and contributes to early and progressive language deficits and a variety of information-processing problems.

A typical finding about the families of mildly (educable) retarded children was reported by Richardson (1981). Not content to study only those retarded children found in local special education programs, Richardson and his colleagues gave group IQ tests to all youngsters ages 7 to 9 in a major city in Scotland. They followed up with an individual assessment of intelligence for those who scored low on group tests. In this way, the researchers were able to obtain a reasonable portrait of all mentally retarded children in one age group within the city. From that information Richardson tried to discern the unique characteristics of families with a mildly retarded child. They found these children were overrepresented in families

- with five or more children.
- who lived in the least desirable housing areas in the city.
- who lived in crowded homes (2 or more people per room).
- where the mother's occupation before marriage was a semiskilled or unskilled manual job.

Richardson also found, as did several earlier studies, that mildly retarded adults often are able to survive in the community with little or no special services.

Many of the well-educated parents of moderately and severely retarded children formed the vanguard of the parents' movement described in Chapter 1 (Turnbull & Turnbull, 1985). Over the past two decades more attention has been paid to providing different kinds of assistance to the families of retarded children, so that they in turn can help their children make an educational and social adjustment.

PREVENTING MENTAL RETARDATION

One of the best ways to cope with mental retardation is to keep it from happening in the first place. Prevention takes very different forms in the biomedical and psychosocial areas.

Biomedical Focus

In the biomedical area genuine progress has been made on specific, if rare, causes. Until the last decade the diagnosis of Down syndrome, as well as a number of other pathological conditions, was not made until the birth of a baby or later. The development of a new technique has made earlier diagnosis possible. **Amniocentesis** is a procedure for drawing some of the amniotic fluid from the pregnant woman. Fetal

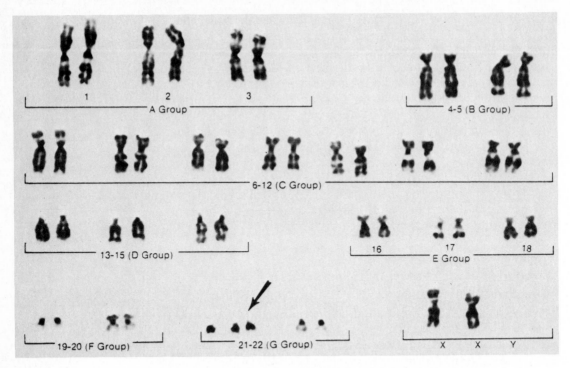

FIGURE 4.3
Chromosomal pattern of girl with Down syndrome, with extra chromosome in pair 21

SOURCE: From "The Child with Down Syndrome," by S. Pueschel, 1983, in *Developmental-Behavioral Pediatrics* by M. Levine, W. Carey, A. Crocker, and R. Gross (Eds.). Philadelphia: Saunders. Copyright 1983 by W. B. Saunders & Co. Reprinted by permission.

cells found in that fluid are then analyzed for chromosomal abnormality by **karyotyping,** a process by which a picture of chromosomal patterns is prepared (see Figure 4.3). The early diagnosis allows parents to decide whether the pregnancy should be terminated. That decision is not an easy one, and has generated questions about the right to life and genetic selection. The controversy over those issues has resulted in limited use of the amniocentesis procedure.

Several decades of concentrated work by an army of scientists have resulted in substantial gains in preventing mental retardation. Table 4.2 offers an overview of the progress. Certain conditions—rubella, phenylketonuria, galactosemia, and inborn errors of metabolism—seem to be under control; other infectious disorders—Tay-Sachs disease (a genetically influenced inborn error of metabolism), measles, and encephalitis—show a meaningful reduction.

Prevention methods (dietary restrictions, early vaccination, genetic counseling, blood replacement techniques) have had a significant impact on many of the factors that cause mental retardation. But their impact on the prevalence of the condition is limited. There are so many causes of mental retardation that even the total elimination of some of them cannot significantly reduce the total number of children

Table 4.2
Biomedical Prevention of Mental Retardation

Condition	Prevention Mode
Nearly total elimination	
Congential rubella	Early intervention and antibody screening
Phenylketonuria, galactosemia, and congenital hypothyroidism	Newborn screening followed by dietary management or blood replacement therapy
Major reduction	
Tay-Sachs disease	Prenatal diagnosis in persons at risk
Measles encephalitis	Early vaccination
Significant current efforts	
Neural tube defects	Maternal blood serum screening; prenatal diagnosis
Down syndrome	Counseling of older women; prenatal diagnosis
Lead intoxication	Screening of lead levels; environmental improvement
Fetal alcohol effects	Public education
Special assistance and relief	
Early identification and training for children with Down syndrome and multiple handicaps	
Support to families with handicapped children	
Genetic counseling when special risk is involved	

SOURCE: "Mental Retardation" by A. Crocker and R. Nelson, 1983, in *Developmental-Behavioral Pediatrics* (pp. 756–769) by M. Levine, W. Carey, A. Crocker, and R. Gross (Eds.). Philadelphia: Saunders.

who become mentally retarded each year. This is why early educational intervention and social supports for the families of retarded children are still so critical.

Psychosocial Focus

While biomedical scientists have been looking for the genetic and metabolic causes of moderate and severe retardation, social and behavioral scientists have concentrated on helping children with mild mental retardation. They reason that if family and environmental factors can have an unfavorable impact on the early development of children and lead to retardation, then reversing these conditions could prevent the intellectual subnormality and poor social adaptation that lead to a classification of mild (educable) mental retardation. Two generations of studies give us an idea of what can be done with existing educational methods.

Skeels and Dye (1939) moved thirteen youngsters identified as mentally retarded from an orphanage to an institution where they received much individual attention and care from older retarded women and attendants. These children's IQ scores went up an average of 27 points, while a comparison group of twelve children who remained in the unstimulating setting (the orphanage) lost an average of 26 points. Skeels (1966) reexamined the subjects some twenty years later and found observable differences. The experimental group (those who received attention) all had finished high school and were self-supporting; the comparison group had performed poorly, with five of the individuals ending up in an institution for the mentally retarded.

In a series of studies on young mentally retarded children, Kirk (1958, 1964) found similar results. In one study, fifteen institutionalized children who received special training were compared to twelve children in the institution who received no special training. The children who received the training improved substantially in mental and social maturity. During the same time, the control group showed decreases in rate of intellectual development and social adjustment.

In a similar experiment, twelve children from disadvantaged homes who attended a special community preschool for mentally retarded children were compared with their siblings living in the same homes but without the benefits of preschool education. While two-thirds of the children in the experimental group showed gains in their rate of mental development, the majority of children in the control group only maintained or dropped in their rate of social and mental growth. Compensatory education, then, increased the rate of social and cognitive development.

In another study, the Milwaukee Project (Heber & Garber, 1975; Heber, November 1977), the investigators chose families who lived in the most economically deprived neighborhoods and whose mothers had measured borderline intellectual ability. This time intervention began during the children's first year of life and the mothers also received some occupational training and strengthening of academic skills. Children in the program who had been predicted at risk for mental retardation were still performing at an average or above-average level at age 9 and substantially above the performance of the comparison group.

A similar project designed to provide stimulation for children considered at risk was conducted in North Carolina. The children were all from low-income families. They were randomly assigned to experimental and control groups. Both groups received nutritional supplements, but only the experimental group received systematic educational stimulation. Significant differences of about 8 to 10 points in IQ scores were found in measured intelligence at age 5 between the treated group and the control group (Ramey & Haskins, 1981).

How long do intervention effects last? A synthesis of the results of twelve major studies on preschool intervention with children from low-income families was carried out five years or more after the projects were completed (Lazar, Darlington, Murray, Royce, & Snipper, 1982).

A key factor in stimulating intellectual and social growth in mentally retarded children is to start working with them at an early age.
(© Alan Carey/The Image Works)

The majority of the children were 3 or 4 years old when first studied and were borderline or slow learners in ability. From their synthesis of follow-up results, the authors drew the following conclusions:

* Children from all types of preschool programs (home based, center based, and so on) surpassed their control groups for up to three years after the end of the program on measures of cognitive abilities. After that, the two groups no longer showed major differences.
* Fewer experimental than control children were assigned to special education classes at a later date.
* Fewer experimental children were held back a grade or more, compared to the control children.

Although cognitive gains are less visible over time, increased academic efficiency seems to remain.

Susan Gray, from the perspective of twenty years of experience, described the early overenthusiasm of educators and the realization of the role played by social environment (Gray, Klaus, & Ramsey, 1981):

> In 1962, when we began the study, we thought naively that it was possible to design a program that would be strong enough to offset the early handicaps that these children experienced. Our naivete was short-lived. It became readily apparent that the best we could hope to do was to provide a basis on which future schooling could build. . . . We could do little to help meet the pressing demands of living in poor housing with large families, low income, and all the associated ills. . . . Preschool is not an inoculation whereby the individual is rendered forever after immune to the effects of an adverse environment. (p. 216)

All of these projects approached the problem in the same way. They started with youngsters at an early age, and tried to sharpen their perceptual abilities, encourage the greater use of receptive and expressive language, and give practice in classification and reasoning. Some urged parents to continue and extend these activities at home. All attempted to strengthen the information-processing abilities of young children who were delayed in development, and all succeeded to a modest degree. But the message is clear. Projects with strong staff and valid objectives can make a difference in intellectual and social growth. Yet these programs are not a cure-all for children in the face of continuing poverty, hunger, and social disorganization.

EDUCATIONAL ADAPTATIONS FOR MENTALLY RETARDED CHILDREN

In previous sections we've talked about the developmental differences that can occur in children who are mentally retarded, and the differences in the social and family environments in which they find themselves. Here we focus on the strategies adopted by educators to cope with these differences.

Identification

In most school situations teachers identify the child who is mentally retarded through poor performance. Whenever a child is failing, alarm bells go off and various processes are set in motion to discover the cause of that failure.

Often the student is referred to a school psychologist for assessment, to determine why the child is failing. That assessment centers on the child's intellectual development and social adaptation, the two key elements in the AAMD definition of mental retardation.

The individual intelligence test remains the most common instrument used to determine intellectual subnormality, although some doubts have been raised about its appropriateness in all cases. A student whose scores fall below those of 98 percent of his or her agemates (2 standard deviations below the average) is considered intellectually subnormal (see Chapter 2).

The other dimension, social adaptation, is a much less definitive concept (although more and more attempts have been made to measure it). Two measures of adaptive behavior are currently in frequent use. Although similar in many respects, they have important differences. The first is the AAMD Adaptive Behavior Scale (Lambert et al., 1975). It is divided into two parts: The first contains ten competence domains, including independent functioning, physical development, language development, and vocational activities; the second contains twelve domains of maladaptive behavior, including antisocial behavior, untrustworthiness, withdrawal, inappropriate manners, unacceptable or eccentric habits, and hyperactivity. The scale is usually completed by a teacher and has been standardized on a sample of over twenty-six hundred children, including normal children as well as those identified as mildly mentally retarded, moderately mentally retarded, and educationally handicapped.

The second instrument, the Adaptive Behavior Inventory for Children (ABIC), is a subsection of the System of Multicultural Pluralistic Assessment (SOMPA) developed by Mercer and Lewis (1978). The instrument contains over two hundred items organized into six competence areas: family, community, peer relations, nonacademic school roles, earner/consumer, and self-maintenance. The scale has been standardized on a sample of over two thousand children divided among black, Hispanic, and white groups.

The difference between the two is that the AAMD scale focuses on behavior within the school setting; the ABIC, on behavior outside school. It is possible, therefore, that a child could get a reasonably average score on adaptive behavior outside of school on the ABIC and still receive a low adaptive behavior score on the AAMD scale because of inappropriate behavior within the school setting.

In many instances the assessment of social adaptation still depends on the judgment of teachers and other educational personnel who have had direct experiences with the child.

Many of the current methods for identifying retardation are based on the medical procedures for diagnosis, a cycle of identification, diagnosis, and treatment. Today many educators want to bypass much of the diagnostic and classification procedures and get right to work educating the child. As Forness and Kavale (1984) pointed out: "The essential diagnosis of a child's needs usually takes place only *after* the special education teacher or resource specialist has worked with the child in the special or regular classroom over a period of weeks" (p. 243).

It is important to differentiate diagnostic assessment (to which special education program should the child be referred?) and planning assessment (what elements should be included in designing an individual plan for the student?). In the opinion of many special educators, planning assessment is not necessary until the child has been in the classroom for a period of time.

Instructional Planning

Once a child is classified mentally retarded, we must identify the student's individual characteristics that will help shape a special educational program with specific priorities and objectives. We use the individualized education program (IEP) to generate this information. The IEP lists asessment data, long-range objectives, measurable goals, the personnel needed to carry out the program, and evaluation procedures to determine the success of the plan.

Figure 4.4 shows the summary of the individualized education program for Bob, the mildly retarded child described earlier in this chapter. (The program in its more detailed form would run five or six pages.) Bob, a fifth-grader, is performing at a second-grade level in reading and arithmetic. Although academic objectives are mentioned, the emphasis in the IEP is on Bob's attention and behavior problems, which school personnel and Bob's parents have identified as his key problems. Behavior control of unacceptable classroom activities form the short-range goals that should lead to better attention and greater self-control over the year.

Special services for Bob include systematic reinforcement when he stays in his seat and a set of procedures by which Bob will learn to control his own impulsive behavior.

The IEP specifies that Bob will stay in the regular classroom 75 percent of the time. He will spend the rest of the time in a resource room, where he will receive more individualized instruction.

Finally the dates for the beginning and ending of short-term goals are provided, allowing for later evaluation to see whether the goals are being met.

Learning Environment

Substantial attention in recent years has been given to where special education services are delivered. The strong emphasis on the least restrictive environment and mainstreaming has brought many retarded children in closer contact with their nonhandicapped peers. The four major types of placements for these students are the service-

Child's Name _Robert Carsen_				Summary of Present Levels of Performance	

Child's Name _Robert Carsen_
Date of Birth _6/11/74_
School _Jefferson Elementary_
Grade _5_
Date of Program Entry _9/29/83_

Summary of
Present Levels of Performance

WISC P 68 F 66
      P 42
CAT R 2.6
    A 2.2

Prioritized Long-Term Goals:
1. _Increase attention span_
2. _Better social skills_
3. _Self-monitoring of behavior_
4. _Improve academic skills_

Short-Term Objectives	Specific Educational and/or Support Services	Person(s) Responsible	Percent of Time	Beginning and Ending Date	Review Date
Reduce classroom wandering by half	Teacher aide	Teacher	75	9/84 - 1/85	2/85
Verbalize self-control statements	Resource teacher Psychologist	Resource teacher	25	9/84 - 12/84	2/85
Master addition + subtraction by 2 digits	Programmed learning text + materials	Teacher	75	9/84 - 11/84	2/85

Percent of Time in Regular Classroom

75%

Placement Recommendation

Continue in resource room

Committee Members Present

J. Johnstone
E. Martin
M. Well
W. Cullen

Dates of Meeting _____
9/20/84

FIGURE 4.4
Individualized education program: Summary

augmented regular classroom, the resource room, the special class, and the residential institution.

Regular Classroom

Many mildly retarded children and even some moderately retarded children now find themselves in the educational mainstream with their agemates. Of course placing these children in the regular classroom without additional help would be a step backwards. The regular program is supplemented with the special services (remedial reading, speech and communication therapy, psychological counseling) available in the school system.

One by-product of mainstream placements is the development of a noncategorical special education model. This model, an alternative to the standard classification system, merges mildly retarded children with those who have learning disabilities, mild behavior problems, and communication problems, on the assumption that these children share many educational problems and that those problems can be dealt with in a single educational setting (a resource room or the regular classroom). Classification and labeling obviously become less important, even irrelevant, in programs where the focus is on the educational needs of each child.

Resource Room

For mildly retarded children the resource room provides an opportunity to work with special education teachers and to focus on particular learning problems that are interfering with their performance in the regular classroom. These children leave the classroom for about an hour a day to take part in special lessons. The number of children in the resource room at any one time is usually much less than the number in the regular classroom, giving the resource room teacher an opportunity to work individually or in small groups with children who are retarded. In many schools, resource room programs combine other mildly handicapped children who are at a comparable developmental level with the mildly retarded children, allowing the teacher to plan for them in small groups.

Special Class

The greater the degree of handicap, the more likely the child needs a setting away from the regular classroom. The special class still provides the special educational services for most moderately retarded children in public schools. In the special class, a specially trained teacher provides a distinctive curriculum for a small group of children, typically no more than fifteen. The curriculum may include exercises in personal grooming, safety, preprimary reading skills, or any subject not appropriate for the normally developing child in the regular classroom but highly appropriate for the child like Carol, whose cognitive development is half or less of her normal age.

At the secondary school level special remedial classes or basic skills classes may enroll some mildly retarded children. Both mainstreaming and the resource room strategy appear better suited to the elementary school than they do to the secondary school, where the day is divided into separate classes by content field (English, history, math).

Residential Institution

Although the residential institution has shown a sharp drop in enrollment coincident with the strong movement toward deinstitutionalization in recent years (Scheerenberger, 1983), it is still a placement for many moderately retarded children and a few mildly retarded children whose conduct or behavior problems seem to require a more controlled environment or for whom no community placement is available. Many severe and profoundly retarded children are still living in residential institutions.

Although most residential institutions have active education and training programs, the environment limits their effectiveness. For example, Gunzberg (1974) questioned the usefulness of the institution as a training center for teaching social adaptation to mildly or moderately retarded children: How would they learn that houses are numbered odd and even on opposite sides of the street, that a round-trip ticket may save money, how to shop in a grocery store, or how to have comfortable relationships with the opposite sex?

And there are other problems. Institutions provide few opportunities for the modeling of appropriate behavior. In addition, chronic staff turnover often leads to an unwillingness on the part of the retarded individual to establish permanent social contacts or relationships. And, finally, many believe that institutions demand and enforce a conformity that fits the individual for institutional living but does not prepare him or her for life outside the institution.

Impact of the Learning Environment

Does the type of learning environment make a difference in the level of academic achievement, social adaptation, or cognitive development in mildly and moderately retarded children? To date research findings suggest learning environment by itself does not make a striking difference in any dimension.

Budoff and Gottlieb (1976) compared the achievement of mildly retarded pupils in a special class and those in a regular class who had resource room help. They found no differences in reading and arithmetic achievement between the groups after one year.

Does mainstreaming facilitate social acceptance for children who are mildly retarded? Early studies that showed relatively poor social acceptance of mentally retarded children in the regular class (Johnson & Kirk, 1950) seem confirmed by the mainstreaming literature. Generally, retarded students are not well accepted by nonretarded students, whether they are in special classes or the regular classroom (Gottlieb, Semmel, & Veldman, 1978).

Gottlieb, Rose, and Lessen (1983) in their review commented that

> a considerable amount of research has already indicated that merely placing retarded children in regular classes does not improve the social acceptance of them by nonretarded peers. . . . Retarded children in regular classes who misbehave or cannot conform to the standards of the classroom are apt to be

socially rejected, regardless of whether or not they are labeled as mentally retarded. (p. 197)

Project PRIME, a large-scale study of mainstreamed settings throughout the state of Texas, revealed that neither mainstream nor special settings influenced achievement test results. Mildly retarded children scored in the bottom 1 percent on reading and arithmetic regardless of setting (Gottlieb, Rose, & Lessen, 1983).

The impact of mainstreaming or special classes seems to depend on which handicapping condition is involved. A comprehensive review of available research revealed that children with mild learning disabilities and/or behavior disturbance problems seem to profit from special class programs, while mildly retarded children do less well in them (Kavale & Glass, 1982). The conclusion seems to be that by placing retarded children in a mainstream setting without changing their curriculum we are not likely to improve academic or social adaptation, although their self-concepts may be somewhat improved (Madden & Slavin, 1983). It becomes critical then to review the curriculum changes proposed for students who are retarded.

Content and Skills

Four major areas of instruction make up most programs for mildly retarded children:

- *Readiness and academic skills.* At elementary school age, basic reading and arithmetic skills are stressed. Later these skills are applied to practical work and community settings.
- *Communication and language development.* Practice in using language to communicate needs and ideas. Specific efforts to improve memory skills and problem-solving skills at the level of the student's ability.
- *Socialization.* Specific instruction in self-care and family living skills, gradually developing in secondary school into subjects like grooming, dancing, sex education, and drug abuse.
- *Prevocational and vocational skills.* Establishing the basis for vocational adjustment through good work habits (promptness, following through on instruction, working cooperatively on group projects). At the secondary level, this curriculum stream can focus on career education and include part-time job placement and field trips to possible job sites.

Basic Skills

The basic skills of reading and arithmetic are often presented to mildly retarded students using the unit approach. The teacher chooses a theme, say "community helpers," and weaves reading, arithmetic, writing, and spelling tasks into the general theme. The topics tend to be highly motivating because they are practical and within the direct experience of the child.

Mainstreamed children can be taught the basic skills of reading and arithmetic in the traditional fashion in the regular classroom, then again in the unit approach in the resource room.

An example of a more integrated set of concepts was part of a special curriculum program developed by the Biological Sciences Curriculum Study (BSCS) (Mayer, 1975). This team of biologists, teachers, and writers was originally organized to improve curricula for high school biology classes. The group scaled down information on important biological concepts to the reading and intellectual levels of mildly retarded junior and senior high school students. In this way, the retarded students were taught significant ideas at a level and in a format that they understood (see Table 4.3). Reports of field test evaluations confirmed that mildly retarded students can master relatively complex material if vocabulary and sentence structure are simplified and concrete illustrations and exercises are provided.

The teaching of reading to moderately retarded children focuses on functional reading (Snell, 1983). Although they are unlikely to ever read for comprehension or recreation, they should be able to identify key words in simple recipes, to develop a protective vocabulary (walk, don't walk, stop, men, women, in, out), and to recognize the skull and crossbones that denote poisonous substances. Traditionally, moderately retarded students are taught by the whole-word method, which helps them to recognize words in context and to act appropriately on them. Students may be asked to "read" television schedules or direc-

---

Table 4.3
Science Content of the BSCS Projects Designed for
Mildly Retarded Students

Me Now	Me and My Environment	Me in the Future
Digestion and circulation	Exploring the environment	Metrics
Respiration and body wastes	Self as an environment	Agribusiness
Movement, support, and sensory perception	Transfer and cycling of materials	Natural resources
Growth and development	Energy relationships	Construction
	Water and air	Manufacturing
		Personal services
		Public services
		Transportation
		Sports
		Nature

SOURCE: "Two Models for Developing Curriculum Materials" by W. Heiss, 1981, in *Curriculum Development for Exceptional Children* (p. 27) by H. Goldstein (Ed.). San Francisco: Jossey-Bass.

Arithmetic concepts taught to mentally retarded individuals should relate to everyday living, such as telling time and using money.
(Paul Conklin)

tions on food boxes, or to travel around their community learning to look for key words.

Moderately retarded children are not taught the formal arithmetic presented in the primary grades. They can learn quantitative concepts (more and less, big and little) and the elementary vocabulary of quantitative thinking. They can be taught to count to 10 and to identify quantity in small groupings. As they grow older, these children can learn to write numbers from 1 to 10, and time concepts, especially the sequence of activities during the day, telling time, and an elemental understanding of the calendar. Some can recognize and remember telephone numbers, their own ages, and simple money concepts. In general, the arithmetic they are taught is related to everyday living, as is the reading.

Language and Communication

There is a substantial effort in elementary schools to help moderately retarded children use language as a tool for communication. Students may be asked to describe a simple object, say a table. (It is round, it is hard, you place things on it, it is brown.) And they may learn to communicate feelings of joy, happiness, anger, or sadness using language.

An Israeli educator, Reuven Feuerstein, developed a training program called Instrumental Enrichment (Feuerstein, Rand, Hoffman, & Miller, 1980), which is designed to improve the problem-solving skills of children who are developmentally delayed. It includes a series of exercises to help youngsters identify the nature of the problem, draw conclusions, and understand relationships. For example:

> Draw a square next to the rectangle.   □
>
> Be sure that the square is not above the triangle.   △

This kind of exercise requires students to pay careful attention to directions and relationships.

Feuerstein successfully trained the intelligence or cognitive processes of adolescents, despite the fact that such training has primarily focused on preschool or primary grade children. The assumption was that this kind of training would have little effect on teenagers. Other educators have tried to apply Feuerstein's program in the United States with some encouraging results, although it is not possible to say at this point how permanent the effects are (Arbitman-Smith, Haywood, & Bransford, 1984).

Language exercises for moderately retarded children include the development of speech and the understanding and use of verbal concepts. It includes communication skills—listening to stories, discussing pictures, telling of recent experiences, and other activities familiar to the children in the classroom. One important area of study is the home and the community. Children learn about holidays, transportation, the months of the year and days of the week, and contributions to home life. Classes make use of dramatization, acting out a story or a song, playing make-believe, shadow play, and using gestures with songs, stories, and rhymes.

Socialization

Children who are retarded have difficulty transferring or applying ideas from one setting to another. Because of this, we teach needed social skills directly; we do not expect these skills to be automatically understood and applied from general experience.

The **social learning approach** was designed to develop critical thinking and independent action on the part of those who are mildly retarded. The approach builds lesson experiences around psychological needs (for self-respect, mastery), physical needs (for sensory stimulation), and physical maintenance and social aspects (dependence, mobility). For example, lesson experiences based on achieving economic security could include the following objectives: (1) choosing a job commensurate with skills and interests, (2) locating and acquiring a satisfactory job, (3) maintaining a job, and (4) effectively managing the financial resources earned from a job.

Goldstein (1974) has developed a comprehensive social learning curriculum that encompasses both behavioral and conceptual goals. The curriculum emphasizes the use of inductive questioning when presenting instructional activities—drawing forth from the children information about the event or situation they are studying. There is a five-stage process in the model:

1. *Labeling.* Questions that elicit the identities of what is being studied or explored. (What is in that picture? It is a big dog.)
2. *Detailing.* Questions that elicit the specific characteristics in the event. (What can you tell me about the dog? It is a big brown dog and it has a wagging tail.)
3. *Inferring.* Questions that elicit a conclusion based on available characteristics. (Why is the dog's tail wagging? Its owner is going to feed it.)
4. *Predicting.* Questions that elicit responses about the inference, given more information. (What would happen if the owner didn't give the dog the food? The dog would get mad and bark and bite him.)
5. *Generalizing.* Questions that elicit responses applying a general rule based on available information. (How should we treat dogs? We shouldn't tease them, especially if they are big.)

The social learning approach takes little for granted in the learning of retarded children. If we want them to learn a skill important for social adjustment, we must plan a series of experiences to develop that skill and allow for its practice under supervision.

Prevocational and Work/Study Skills

As the mildly retarded child reaches the secondary level, the objectives of the program turn to the development of work skills. The skills may be related to a specific occupation (assembling transistor radios) or to general work skills (cooperation, punctuality, persistence).

For the preadolescent retarded child, lessons often take the form of prevocational experience, focusing on the knowledge and skills that are the basis for vocational competence. For example:

- Given a road map, the student can demonstrate the route to be taken from one point to another.
- Given an assigned work task involving two or more students, they will work together until the task is completed.

- Given a newspaper, the student will demonstrate that he can find specific information when requested to do so. (Kolstoe, 1976)

These specific observable behaviors often are the crux of the IEP, giving teacher and student tangible attainable goals.

Vocational training focuses on a number of dimensions beyond the job itself: banking and using money, grooming, caring for a car and obtaining insurance, interviewing for jobs, and using leisure time. Adjustment to the work world involves adapting to the demands of life as well as to a specific job.

Some programs try to build a set of vocational skills progressively over time, drawing a variety of social agencies into the educational activities. Table 4.4 shows a career preparation profile for moderately retarded children stretching over the transition from school to work.

Table 4.4
Career Preparation Profile

Approximate Chronological Ages	Type of Program	Curriculum Emphasis	Participating Disciplines
5–12	Special class	Attitudes Behavior Career education Academics Self-care skills	Special education
12–15	Prevocational class	Career awareness Activities of daily living Social skills Work habits Academics	Special education Vocational education
15–18	Vocational training	Related academics Skill training Social skills Work habits Activities of daily living	Special education Vocational education Vocational rehabilitation
13–19	Competitive employment training	Core tasks On-the-job training Social skills Activities of daily living Work habits	Special education Vocational education Vocational rehabilitation
17–Adult	Sheltered facility	Support as needed (specified on IEP)	Vocational rehabilitation; (special education and vocational education for students aged 17–21)
17–Adult	Competitive employment	Same as for sheltered facility	Same as for sheltered facility

SOURCE: From "Competitive Employment Training for Moderately Retarded Adolescents" by G. Frith and R. Edwards, 1982, *Education and Training of the Mentally Retarded, 17*(2), 149–153. Printed with permission.

Fundamental activities and skills are taught in a special class setting. Then specific areas of prevocational and vocational training, including on-the-job training, are covered in the adolescent years. Finally, with the help of vocational rehabilitation, attempts are made to provide a useful work experience in either a sheltered workshop facility or a competitive employment setting.

This plan has the merit of establishing long-range goals that can be approached progressively in tasks at the developmental level of those who are moderately retarded.

The recent movement to mainstreaming for children who are mildly retarded has created a difficult conflict. As long as retarded children are in regular classrooms they are receiving the regular curriculum or some variation of that program. But the secondary school curriculum of content subjects (English, history, science) may not be the most appropriate for them. These students could profit more from a program emphasizing the practical and vocational skills needed for independent living (Childs, 1979).

Teaching Strategies

A major educational objective is to help mildly and moderately retarded children develop socially constructive skills and behaviors and to reduce the behaviors that impede learning and social acceptance. This is an objective whether children are in the regular classroom or in special programs, and can be applied by either regular classroom teachers or special personnel.

Special education draws heavily on learning theory to help children achieve constructive behavior. Many of the learning principles used to help retarded children to associate ideas or remember events have been used intuitively in classrooms and families for years. One popular approach, Premack's Principle (Premack, 1959), has actually been called "Grandma's Law": "First you eat your vegetables, then you get dessert."

The broader principle is to attach a desired but low-probability behavior to a high-probability behavior, which then becomes a positive reinforcer. In a practical sense, the teacher would say, "If you clean up your workplace on time, you can do a puzzle or listen to records." The difference between grandma and the special educator is the systematic way in which the principle is applied.

Behavior Modification

Behavior modification involves a variety of techniques designed to reduce or eliminate obnoxious or nonadaptive behaviors and to increase the use of socially constructive behaviors. It is based on the principles developed by Skinner (1953), who found that the systematic application of positive reinforcement (reward) following a behavior tends to increase the likelihood of that behavior occurring in the next similar situation. Negative reinforcement (punishment) causes unwanted behaviors to decrease. The absence of reinforcement, either positive or negative, causes a behavior to disappear or be extinguished. The quickest way to eliminate a behavior, then, is to ignore it while responding positively to a more acceptable form of the behavior.

The educational strategy here is to arrange the environment so that the particular behavior the teacher wants the child to repeat will occur. When the behavior does occur, it receives a positive reward (food, praise, a token, or some other symbol of recognition). If possible, the teacher should not respond to the undesirable or obnoxious behavior.

Gresham (1981) noted a variety of techniques that use these principles:

- *Differential reinforcement.* This approach follows the basic behavior modification procedures by rewarding those behaviors that are appropriate and ignoring the target behavior (for example, aggressive behavior). A variation provides rewards if the student can increase the time between displays of unacceptable behavior. If the child is showing a great deal of acting-out behavior, the teacher rewards a 10-minute period of acceptable behavior that reflects an increase in the elapsed time between periods of unacceptable behavior.

- *Time out.* Time out is the physical removal of a child from a reinforcing situation for a period of time, usually immediately following an unwanted response. If the child has shown unacceptable aggressive behavior in the classroom, the child may be asked to leave the classroom or be moved to a section of the classroom in which he or she is left alone with some reading or work materials, essentially isolated from the group for a period of time. The child is often asked to return when he or she feels in control of the unacceptable behavior. This procedure has proved effective in decreasing disruptive, aggressive, and inappropriate social behaviors.

- *Contingent social reinforcement.* A number of teachers who work with young handicapped children use a token system to teach appropriate social behavior. Tokens are handed out according to the appropriate use of certain social skills (greeting another child, borrowing a toy in an acceptable manner). If a child displays unacceptable behavior, tokens may be taken away. Tokens are saved and cashed in for toys or time to do a puzzle or play a game. This kind of reward program appears to be effective in controlling social behavior within groups of handicapped children and, to some extent, within the context of a mainstream class.

The use of behavior modification techniques with exceptional children has helped increase academic response rates and attendance, achievement, and grades, and has encouraged verbal interchange and following instructions (Sabatino, Miller, & Schmidt, 1981). Despite these positive results, however, the procedures are still controversial. They control the child's behavior without requiring or needing the participation of the child.

Cognitive Behavior Modification

A variation of behavior modification, cognitive behavior modification, uses reward techniques but focuses on the conscious feelings and attitudes of the child as well as on overt behaviors. For example, Meichenbaum and Goodman (1971) developed a system of self-instructional techniques to help a child control his or her own behavior by talking to himself or herself. First the child watches an adult model perform the behavior while talking to himself or herself. Then the child imitates the adult's behavior. Later the child may whisper the directions to himself or herself, and still later may use covert self-speech. The sequence is as follows:

Task	*Verbalization*
Problem definition	What is it I have to do?
Focusing attention	I have to concentrate, to think only of my work.
Planning and response	Be careful—look at one at a time.
Self-reinforcement	Good—I got it!
Self-evaluation	Am I following my plan?
Coping and error-correcting options	That's o.k. . . . Even if I make a mistake, I can back up and go slowly.

Task Analysis

Another approach in general use with both mildly and moderately retarded children is *task analysis*. Here we break down complex tasks into simple component parts and teach each of the components separately and then together. The method can be used to teach a simple self-help skill like tying a shoe or a more complex skill like assembling a bicycle. Tying a shoe may require fourteen or fifteen separate movements. The teacher can concentrate on the steps not mastered and then see to it that the child is able to move from one step to another in sequence, as shown in Figure 4.5.

Counseling

Classroom teachers cannot do everything. They often need the help of support personnel, of counselors and school psychologists. There are a number of indications, for example, that adolescence is a particularly

Model for developing instructional materials

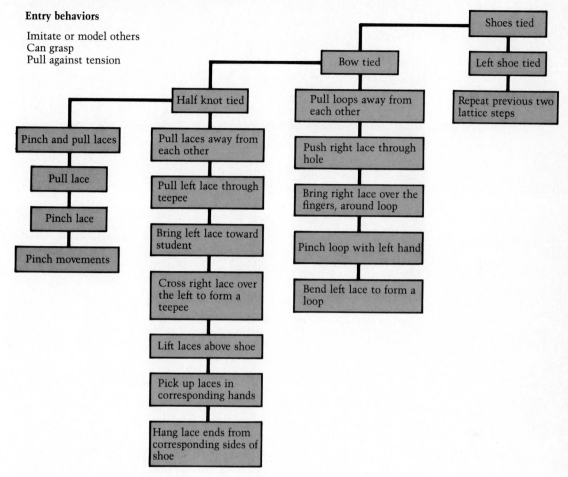

Entry behaviors

Imitate or model others
Can grasp
Pull against tension

SOURCE: From "Prototype Models for the Development of Instructional Material" by D. Smith, J. Smith, and E. Edgar, 1976, in *Teaching the Severely Handicapped* (Vol. 1, p. 167) by N. Haring and L. Brown (Eds.). New York: Grune & Stratton.

FIGURE 4.5
Lattice for "shoes tied"

difficult time for mildly retarded students. Zetlin and Turner (1985) conducted an eighteen-month study of twenty-five mentally retarded adults and their parents. The subjects, now 23 to 33 years old, were asked to reflect on the feelings, attitudes, and problems they had had during their adolescent years. They identified two major concerns— parent-child relationships and identity issues—concerns felt by many adolescents but sharpened and intensified by retardation.

The subjects had resented parental protectiveness, a reluctance to allow them to venture into new activities, and had become aware of their "differentness" and the effect it was having on their social life. They reported being teased by schoolmates and neighborhood children. At least 84 percent of the subjects had had some type of emotional or

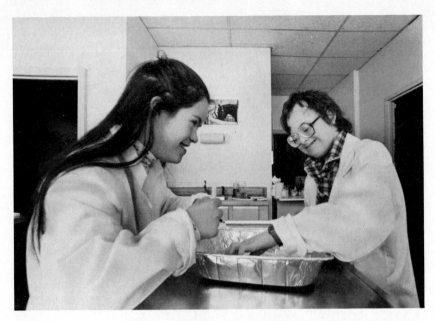

By obtaining successful employment, mentally retarded individuals not only become self-supporting members of the community but also experience feelings of accomplishment and a sense of independence.
(© Jerry Howard/Positive Images)

behavioral reaction in secondary school—drug or alcohol abuse, temper tantrums, destructive behavior, or withdrawal. Zetlin and Turner concluded: "A limited or unclear set of normative expectations by parents as well as the absence of a peer support network available to most nonretarded adolescents seem to have exacerbated adjustment disturbances" (p. 578).

Most schools now recognize that special programming for children who are retarded is a team responsibility, one that has classroom teachers, special teachers, and other professional personnel working together to help these children toward competence and social adaptation.

LIFESPAN ISSUES FOR MENTALLY RETARDED INDIVIDUALS

What happens to retarded children when they finish their schooling? Do they find employment? At what kinds of jobs? Where do they live? What kinds of support do they need to adapt to society? We know less than we would like to about these questions, but some interesting work has been done on some of them.

MANCHILD COMING OF AGE

My youngest son, Mark, has his suits and jackets fitted with extra care, because, 5 feet tall, he weighs more than 170 pounds and is built like a padded fire hydrant. He is dieting to fight that image, though, and has 27 Special Olympics awards on his wall to prove it, right beside life-size posters of Michael Jackson, Kenny Baker and Barbara Mandrell. Mark is a powerful swimmer, and five of the awards are for first place in the category.

For 31 years, Mark has been a central fact of our family life, knitting us together, trying our patience, helping us laugh, probably making us better people than we would have been without him.

I remember the night call, hours after he was born, and the doctor's trying to be gentle as the darkness around me grew suddenly deeper: "I regret having to tell you your new son may be mongoloid."

They don't say that anymore. They don't call leprosy leprosy, either. Now it's Hansen's disease. And mongolism is Down's syndrome, or trisomy 21, a chromosomal abnormality that hinders the development of the mind. The growing brain signals its imprisonment in the smaller skull by causing erratic gait, slower growth, vulnerability to infections, clubfeet, other anomalies.

Knowing I was a medical writer, the doctor shared with me the details that left little room for doubt: the epicanthal fold of the eyelids at either side of the nose, excessive bone-flex even for a newborn, deeper-than-normal post-natal jaundice, clubfeet, the simian line across the palm of each hand. Later, one of many specialists we consulted would say of Mark: "Let's leave a door open for me to back out of. There are people in Congress less bright than he may yet turn out to be."

Nobody's perfect, in other words. Even so: *mongoloid*. The word boomed in my soul like the tolling of a leaden gong. No more sleep for me. Next morning, I entered upon a conspiracy of one.

"Why can't I see the baby?" was my wife's first question after the kiss, the forced congratulatory smile. The lie. "They're getting him ready," came with clinical ease. "He'll be up to see you soon."

Then the quick maternal discovery of his clubfeet, and my too-swift assurance that the feet were "only an anomaly" which remedial measures would correct. Worst of all, her tearful puzzlement at learning we would have to leave him in the hospital "for a few more days" to make sure his casts "weren't on too tight"—or some such double talk.

Back home without him, I found myself unable to keep up the charade under mounting internal pressure. After a few miserable days, I blurted out the truth and endured her dry-eyed demand that we "Go bring him home, right away, so I can take care of him. Now. Today."

Caring for a baby with legs in plaster casts spread wide at the ankles by a rigid steel bar to straighten the growing feet can take its emotional toll. But from the start, Mark's older brothers, and especially his sisters, devoted them-

continued

continued

selves to helping us raise him. Under what I now look back on as a cascade of sunrises and sunsets "laden with happiness and tears," we overcame any misguided temptation we may have had to institutionalize him.

One undeniable result has been that he is much further along, and far better equipped to deal with life in spite of his limitations, than he would have been if we had done that to him. Today, as he stands poised to see whether he likes it in a group home, we take comfort in knowing we tried to do right by him. Another gain has been that he has done well by us; caring for him has matured us. Aged us too, no doubt, but that would have happened anyway.

The father of a retarded child wonders if in some unforeseeable way he may have contributed to the tragedy (in my case, possibly the case of mumps I had before Mark was conceived). Some men walk out on what they see as an impossible situation, a saddling of their marriage with an unending burden. Some come back. Each case is unique. No one outside it can judge.

Ironies abound. Long before Mark was born, I wrote an article on mental retardation. It helped, I'm told, get Federal funds for research into the causes. And when Hubert H. Humphrey's granddaughter was born retarded, he and I wrote pieces pleading with readers to recognize that mental retardation is a totally different affliction from mental illness. "It's not contagious, either!" Hubert would shout at me, as if I needed convincing. Yet in my own extended family some still think Mark is contagious.

Harder to take is watching him strive, in a family of writers, to produce copy. Pages of hand-scrawled and sometimes typed letters, all higgledy-piggledy, spill from his fevered efforts to "follow in your footsteps, Dad!" And almost nightly, lonely and eager for an audience, Mark interrupts our reading or television watching to rattle off plots from reruns of "M*A*S*H." We try to look attentive, even though it drives us nutty. Shouting matches help ease tension, and I have on occasion threatened to work Mark over. But sooner or later he forgives me. With a hug.

Indefatigable, Mark has handsawed his way through storm-toppled tree trunks without resting, mowed lawns, backstopped me on cement-laying jobs. I repay him with prodigious hero sandwiches, which he seldom fails to praise.

At 31, he still cannot read, but he does guess at numbers, at times embarrassingly well. When, here lately, he began to put a cash value on his toil and asked for pay, I offered him a dollar. He looked at me with a knowing grin and said, quite clearly despite his usual speech problems, "Five bucks, Dad, *five* bucks." I gave him five ones.

For signs like this that the manchild is coming of age, I am grateful. And for something else: I can't say we feel he's ready for Congress, but he has given us hope. Unlike the night he was born, in part because of Mark, I am no longer afraid of the dark.

Traditional wisdom on vocational placement is that many mildly retarded children and some moderately retarded children can be partially or fully self-sufficient in adulthood. Studies of employment of adults who are retarded have shown that

- Mildly retarded adults can learn to do unskilled and semiskilled work.
- Failure in unskilled occupational tasks is generally related to personal, social, or interpersonal characteristics rather than to an inability to execute the assigned task.
- Approximately 80 percent of mildly retarded adults eventually adjust to occupations of an unskilled or semiskilled nature and partially or totally support themselves.

But these studies are 20 to 50 years old (Channing, 1932; Kennedy, 1948; Charles, 1953; Baller, Charles & Miller, 1966). We need current information that is relevant to a rapidly changing and shrinking job market.

Brickey and Campbell (1981) reported on a major project to employ retarded teenagers and young adults in fast-food establishments. In a job-training program for the mentally retarded, seventeen retarded young adults were placed in McDonald's restaurants. Most were able to handle the necessary tasks, and the turnover rate was only 40 percent, compared to the 175 percent rate for regular employees and a 300 to 400 percent rate for high school and college students. According to Brickey and Campbell, the project demonstrated that McDonald's profited from hiring mentally retarded adults, and that the retarded employees experienced natural feelings of accomplishment and a sense of independence.

A review by Brickey, Brauning, and Campbell (1982) showed encouraging success in competitive job placements for mildly retarded students. They found that 48 percent of those who were in a Projects With Industry Program were subsequently placed in competitive jobs. One of the key elements to success in the program appeared to be the degree to which the job is sufficiently structured by the employer so that retarded students understand what is expected of them.

Sheltered Workshops

Sheltered workshops are a source of employment in larger communities for moderately retarded individuals who are unable to be regularly employed. The workshops enroll adolescents and adults, train them to do routine tasks, contract with industries for piecework, and develop and make salable products.

In well-established workshops, the retarded workers work a full day and are paid wages for their labor, which makes them partially self-supporting. Besides the remuneration received from contracts and the sale of products, sheltered workshops are also supported financially by parents' organizations, foundations, community funds, and donations. In some larger cities, the community center working with people at this level of mental retardation may include a diagnostic center, a preschool program, a sheltered workshop, and a recreation center.

Community Placement and Group Homes

Many mildly retarded individuals find jobs and places to live on their own. But there are increasing efforts by social agencies to provide a supervised living environment when that seems needed.

One alternative to the institution is the group home. In some communities small units have been established that operate much like a family, creating an environment in which the skills necessary for effective living can be mastered.

Other arrangements include foster family homes that provide retarded adolescents with care and support. There are also supervised apartment clusters for retarded adults. Some of these complexes also run training programs in social skills development or offer counseling to help residents through crisis periods.

The presence of these alternative living arrangements has allowed many retarded adults to remain in the community instead of having to be placed in residential institutions.

SUMMARY OF MAJOR IDEAS

1. The AAMD's current definition of mental retardation focuses on two major components: intelligence and adaptive behavior. An educational diagnosis of mental retardation, then, depends on the characteristics of the child and on the demands of the social environment.
2. Educators have identified three classifications of mental retardation: (a) mild (educable); (b) moderate (trainable); and (c) severe and profound (dependent).
3. Estimates on the prevalence of mental retardation vary widely. Conservative estimates indicate that approximately 0.50 to 1.50 percent are mildly retarded, and that approximately 0.25 to 0.50 percent are moderately or severely and profoundly retarded.
4. There are many causes of mental retardation. They include genetic disorders, toxic agents, infectious diseases, and polygenic inheritance. Numerous biomedical advances in genetics and an increased understanding of metabolic processes have led to the prevention of certain rare disorders that can result in mental retardation.
5. Retarded children have difficulty processing information. For many the problem lies in a poorly developed executive function. This

can affect their perception, problem-solving capabilities, and expression.

6. Developmental problems in language acquisition and use, physical abilities, and personal and social characteristics form the basis of special education plans for retarded youngsters.

7. The families of mildly retarded children usually are economically limited and have few resources to contribute to the total education program. The families of moderately retarded children come from all socioeconomic levels.

8. The importance of the early environment on young children has led to the expansion of preschool programs designed for prevention and remediation of mental retardation. These programs have contributed to academic performance but have not markedly increased intelligence.

9. The learning environments in which mildly retarded students are usually placed include mainstream regular classrooms, resource rooms, and part- or full-time special classes. Moderately retarded children are often found in special classes.

10. The particular educational environment in which the retarded child is placed is less important than the well-organized curriculum presented within the environment.

11. The curriculum for mildly retarded children who are in mainstream classes generally follows the regular program with supporting help in academic subjects.

12. In the special class or resource room, the program emphasizes socialization and prevocational skills, and teaches life experiences (the need for social cooperation) in addition to academic subjects.

13. Work/study programs for mildly retarded youngsters at the secondary level seem to help them prepare for independent or semi-independent community work.

14. Teachers use both operant conditioning and task analysis to teach basic skills to mildly and moderately retarded children.

15. Many mildly retarded individuals and some moderately retarded individuals are able to partially or totally support themselves in the community as adults. Their employment both increases their own self-respect and offers employers a source of reliable labor.

16. Sheltered workshops enroll retarded adolescents and adults, train them to do routine tasks, and sell the end product of their work.

17. A variety of living arrangements—group homes, foster homes, and supervised apartment clusters—have helped retarded citizens remain active particpants in the community.

UNRESOLVED ISSUES

1. *The culture of poverty.*   We are still not sure what factors within the culture of poverty are responsible for the slow development of mildly retarded children. Until we can determine the nature of

the problem (lack of motivation, poor language, inattention and hyperactivity, lack of effective adult models), it's impossible to design effective methods for preventing it.

2. *The changing job market.*   The future of mildly retarded students depends as much on the nature of the social envelope in which they live as on their education and training. The increasing complexity of modern society and the jobs it offers casts a shadow over the goal of independence for these youngsters. Is there a place in a shrinking job market for individuals who are mentally retarded? Or will they be part of a "surplus" population?

3. *The resilient family.*   Some families are able to adjust to the problem of having a child who is moderately to severely handicapped; others are shattered by it. Why? What gives some families the strength to adapt to this stress? There are two diametrically opposed approaches to the families of the handicapped: One wants them to be teachers of their handicapped children; the second approach stresses respite care to allow periodic relief from the daily burden of care. Which approach is more appropriate for which families?

4. *Continuum of services.*   Special education has brought additional resources to some of the children who need help in the educational setting. But there are many others (for instance, borderline retarded or slow learning students) who also need help within the framework of the traditional education program. Schools should offer a continuum of services to match the continuum of student needs instead of giving special help only to those with problems severe enough to qualify for special education programs.

5. *Secondary education.*   By mainstreaming mildly retarded youngsters at the secondary level we limit them to a standard curriculum. Yet these students need special instruction in prevocational and survival skills. How can we balance the benefits of mainstreaming against these special needs?

REFERENCES OF SPECIAL INTEREST

Brooks, P., Sperber, R., & McCauley, C. (Eds.). (1984). *Learning and cognition in the mentally retarded.* Hillsdale, NJ: Lawrence Erlbaum. Twenty-two chapters addressing the latest work on a topic of great interest in the field, the information-processing operations of retarded children. Much of this work comes from scientists in a national network of research centers devoted to the study of mental retardation. Included are chapters on attention, perception, generalization, and social understandings, and an update on where the field is in terms of cognitive processes of children and adults who are mentally retarded.

Edgerton, R. (Ed.). (1984). *Lives in progress: Mildly retarded adults in a large city* (AAMD Monograph No. 6). Washington, DC: American Association on Mental Deficiency.

A number of chapters, all dealing with the adjustment of mentally retarded adults in a large metropolitan area. Their employment experiences and social friendship patterns are documented along with the special problems of minority members in making adult adjustments. An important book for teachers, to see the end product of their efforts.

Feuerstein, R., Rand, Y., Hoffman, M., & Miller, R. (1980). *Instrumental enrichment.* Baltimore: University Park Press.

A detailed account of the techniques used by an Israeli team of psychologists and educators to train retarded children and youth in problem-solving activities. It assumes that once trained in basic problem-solving approaches, these children can adapt more easily to society.

Kirk, S., Kliebhan, J., & Lerner, J. (1978). *Teaching reading to slow and disabled learners.* Boston: Houghton Mifflin.

A comprehensive text detailing special procedures for reading instruction to meet the needs of children who are developmentally delayed. Both early and advanced stages of reading are given special attention. The book discusses formal and informal methods of student assessment and provides a detailed review of existing research on slow and disabled learners.

Mittler, P. (Ed.). (1981). *Frontiers of knowledge in mental retardation: Vol. 1. Social educational and behavioral apsects; Vol. 2. Biomedical aspects.* Baltimore: University Park Press.

An excellent compendium of chapters providing up-to-date information on advances in the social and biological sciences and dealing with mental retardation in professional fields extending from sociology to genetics. Volume 1 pays particular attention to educational and community issues.

Schumaker, J., Pederson, C., Hazel, J., & Meyon, E. (1983). Social skills curricula for mildly handicapped adolescents: A review. *Focus on Exceptional Children, 16*(4), 1–16.

A fine summary of one of the most active curriculum areas with special emphasis on the social skill needs of those who are mildly retarded. It reviews eight major curricula currently available on this topic, giving target populations, skills covered, general instructional approaches and teaching methodologies, and a set of criteria for selecting a specific curriculum.

C·H·A·P·T·E·R Five

CHILDREN WITH VISUAL IMPAIRMENTS

Focusing Questions

What is sensory compensation, and do we find evidence of it among children who are visually impaired?

How does their lack of vision impede the language development of children who are visually impaired?

How do we adapt the instructional program for youngsters who are visually impaired?

What special skills training is an essential part of the education program for students with visual impairments?

What effect are technological advances having on the vocational opportunities of those who are visually impaired?

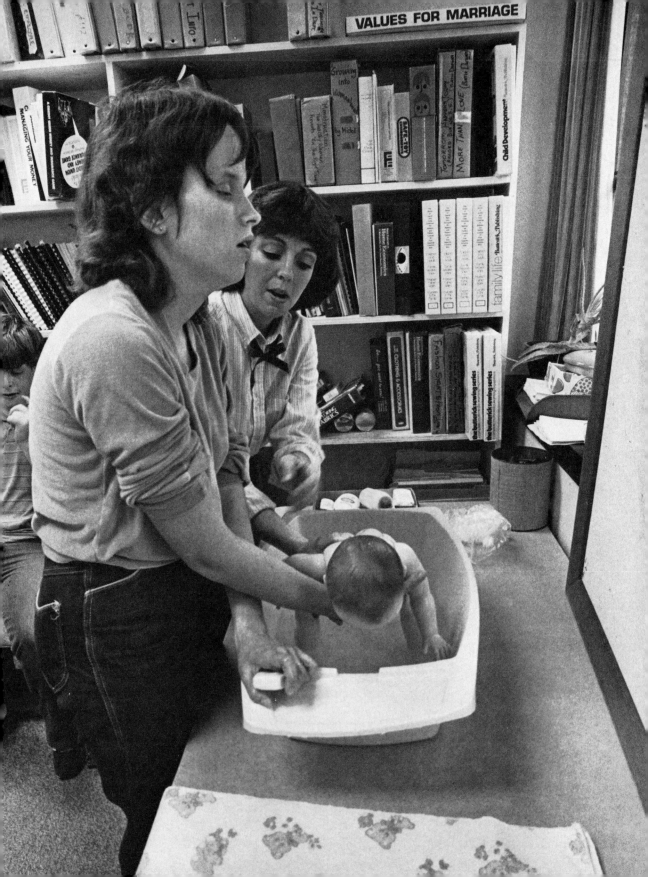

*A*bout one child in ten enters school with some degree of visual impairment. Fortunately, most of these problems can be corrected and have little or no effect on social or educational development. But for one out of a thousand children, visual impairments are so severe they cannot be corrected. These children are visually handicapped.

Here we discuss the special needs of children who are visually impaired and the educational adaptations that must be made for them.

DEFINITIONS

In general the term *visually handicapped* is used to describe all degrees of visual impairment—a continuum from severe visual impairment to total blindness. According to Barraga (1983), "a visually handicapped child is one whose visual impairment interferes with his optimal learning and achievement, unless adaptations are made in the methods of presenting learning experiences, the nature of the materials used, and/or in the learning environment" (p. 25).

Table 5.1
Classification of Children with Visual Impairments

Classification	Level of Vision	Level of Disability
Normal	Normal vision Near normal vision	Can perform tasks without special aids
	Moderate	Can perform tasks near normal with special aids
Low vision	Severe	Performs visual task at a reduced level of speed, endurance, and precision even with aids
	Profound	Has difficulty with gross visual tasks; cannot perform most detailed visual tasks
Blind	Near blind	Vision is unreliable—relies primarily on other senses
	Blind	Totally without sight—relies exclusively on other senses

SOURCE: From "Dimensions of Visual Performance" by A. Colenbrander, 1977, *Archives of American Academy of Ophthalmology, 83*, p. 333. Reprinted by permission.

There are several classifications of visual handicaps. Table 5.1 shows the system adopted by the World Health Organization (Colenbrander, 1977). The most common classification for educational purposes is blind and low vision.

Barraga (1983) described "a gradual trend to use blind and low vision to differentiate the population and to use visually handicapped as a generic term to refer to the entire population" (p. 21). She stated that people who are blind have light perception without projection (meaning they sense that light is present but are unable to project or identify the source of light), or have no light perception at all. Bateman (1967) defined the blind as those children who use braille. Low-vision children are severely visually impaired even with glasses but can use print. Faye (1976) stated that "the low vision person is one whose corrected vision is lower than normal but who does have significant usable vision" (p. 85).

VISUAL INTERPRETATION AND THE HUMAN EYE

Vision or visual interpretation is a function of the brain, experience, and the adequacy of the sense organ that receives stimuli from the outside world (the eye). Faulty visual interpretation can result from a defect in the brain, inadequate experience, or a defective eye. Figure 5.1 shows the process of visual interpretation. Light enters the eye, focuses on the retina, and is transmitted along the optic nerve to the brain, where visual information is interpreted. Two people with well-functioning sense organs can interpret a visual experience differently, depending on their training and experience.

Educators of children with visual impairments are concerned primarily with the adaptation of instruction to the impairment. To accomplish this, it is necessary to understand how healthy eyes operate and what problems can develop.

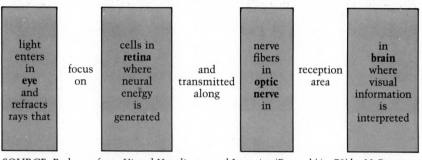

FIGURE 5.1
Process of visual interpretation

SOURCE: Redrawn from *Visual Handicaps and Learning* (Rev. ed.) (p. 78) by N. Barraga, 1983. Austin, TX: Exceptional Resources.

FIGURE 5.2
The human eye

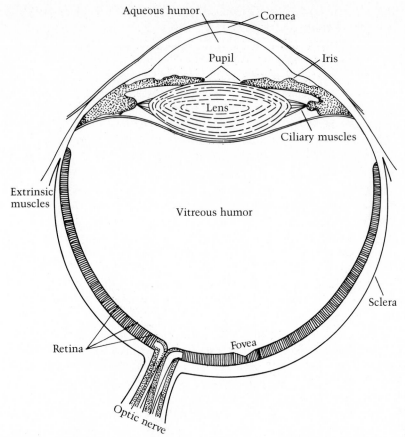

SOURCE: From *Human Information Processing* by P. Lindsay and D. Norman, 1972. New York: Academic Press, p. 154.

The Human Eye

The human eye is a complex system of interrelated parts (Figure 5.2). Any part can be defective or become nonfunctional through disease, accident, hereditary anomaly, or other causes.

The eye has been called a camera for the brain. Like a camera, the eye has a diaphragm, the **iris.** This is the colored muscular partition that expands and contracts to regulate the amount of light admitted through the central opening, or **pupil.** Behind the iris is the **lens,** an elastic biconvex body that focuses onto the **retina** the light reflected from objects in the line of vision. The **retina** is the light-sensitive innermost layer of tissue at the back of the eyeball. It contains neural receptors that translate the physical energy of light into the neural energy that results in the experience of seeing.

As Figure 5.2 shows, many other protective and structural elements in the eye can affect vision. The **cornea** is the transparent anterior portion of the tough outer coat of the eyeball. The **ciliary muscles** control changes in the shape of the lens so that the eye can focus on objects at varying distances. In the normal mature eye, no muscular effort is necessary to see clearly objects 20 feet or more away. When the eye looks at an object closer than 20 feet, the ciliary muscles increase the convex curvature of the lens so that the closer object is still focused on the retina. This changing of the shape of the lens is called **accommodation.**

There are also **extrinsic muscles** that control the movement of the eyeball in the socket. The changes made by these muscles are known as **convergence.**

Causes of Visual Impairments

There are many conditions and degrees of visual problems. The most common are refractive errors, defects of muscle function, and other anomalies. Some of these are described in Table 5.2.

The primary causes of blindness and visual impairments are infectious and general diseases (syphylis, diabetes), accidents and injuries, poisonings, tumors, and heredity. Hereditary factors remain a more frequent cause of blindness than do disease and accidents, both of which are increasingly less prevalent because of improved control measures and education.

Occasionally environmental conditions result in an unusual prevalence of children with visual handicaps. In the 1950s, a condition called *retrolental fibroplasia* (now called *retinopathy of prematurity*) reached epidemic proportions. Its cause was the administration of too much oxygen in the incubators of premature babies, and it accounted for over half of visually impaired infants at the time. Once the cause was discovered and corrected, prevalence dropped sharply. Still, there are times when a physician is faced with the difficult decision of increasing the oxygen supply in order to save an infant's life, knowingly placing the baby at risk of blindness (Hatfield, 1975). Tepin (1983) recently reported a slight worldwide increase in blindness from retrolental fibroplasia. He stated that the condition accounts for 1.8 to 4 percent of blindness.

Rubella (German measles) is another condition that seems to occur in epidemic form every seven to ten years. When mothers are affected in the early stages of pregnancy, their children can be born with a combination of visual defects, auditory defects, mental retardation, and other disabilities.

PREVALENCE

The number of children who are visually impaired is strikingly less than the number of children who are mentally retarded or learning disabled. Only one out of a thousand children is visually handicapped.

Table 5.2
Common Visual Disorders and Anomalies

Type of Disorder	Description
Refractive errors	
Hyperopia	Farsightedness; a condition in which rays of light focus behind the retina forming a blurred, unclear image; a convex lens before the eye increases bending of light rays and brings them into focus.
Myopia	Nearsightedness; a condition in which rays of light focus in front of the retina when the eye is at rest and is viewing an object 20 or more feet distant; a concave lens can refocus the image on the retina.
Astigmatism	A refractive error resulting from an irregularity in the curvature of the cornea or lens of the eye, causing light rays to be refracted unevenly at different planes so that horizontal and vertical rays are focused at two different points on the retina; usually correctable with lenses.
Defects of muscle function	
Strabismus	Crossed eyes caused by a lack of coordination of the extrinsic eye muscles; the two eyes do not simultaneously focus on the same object; can be constant or intermittent.
Heterophoria	Insufficient action of one or more muscles of the eye marked by a tendency for the eyes to deviate from the normal position for binocular fixation; creates difficulty in fusing the two images from the two eyes into one image; is not as apparent as strabismus and can sometimes be overcome by extra muscular effort.
Nystagmus	Quick, jerky movement of the eyeballs, resulting in marked visual inefficiency.
Other anomalies	
Albinism	A hereditary condition characterized by a relative absence of pigment from the skin, hair, choroid coat, and iris; often correlated with refractive errors and loss of visual acuity; lack of color in the iris allows too much light to reach the retina.
Cataract	A condition of the eye in which the lens or its capsule becomes opaque, with loss of visual acuity; treatment by surgery or other medical processes is usually possible; if the lens is surgically removed, artificial lenses are necessary and peripheral vision is affected.

(Remember, if an eye problem can be fully corrected by glasses, the defect is not considered a visual handicap in an educational sense.)

Statistics on the prevalence of visually impaired individuals are difficult to obtain. Different statistics are provided by the U.S. Office of Education, the Printing House for the Blind, and the American Foundation for the Blind. Kirchner (1983), for example, surveyed the reports from the U.S. Department of Education and the American Printing House for the Blind and concluded that the statistics underestimate prevalence of visual impairment because many visually impaired children and adults have not been reported. In summarizing the statistics, the American Foundation for the Blind (1983) reported:

Based on a national health interview survey, it is estimated that there are about 11.4 million persons in the United States with some kind of visual impairment: that is, persons who have trouble seeing even with corrective lenses. Of these, 1.4 million are severely impaired. This means that they are either "legally blind" or that they function as if they were "legally blind" even though their vision does not fall into that definition. According to the National Society to Prevent Blindness, only about 500,000 of the severely visually impaired are registered as legally blind.

Over one million persons—or about 70 percent of the severely visually impaired—are 65 years of age or older. This is because the diseases which are the major causes of blindness in this country are associated primarily with aging. They are the result of an increased life expectancy. Twenty-six percent of the severely visually impaired are in the 18-to-64-year-old age group. Approximately 37,000 are under age 18.

About 117,000 persons are in the labor force. According to the American Printing House for the Blind, there are approximately 32,000 legally blind children in kindergarten through twelfth grade and, as estimated by the Office for the Blind and Visually Impaired, about 6,000 legally blind college and university students in the United States.

DEVELOPMENTAL PROFILES

All of us with normal sight have wondered from time to time what it would be like to be blind. It's obvious that adapting to sensory loss has implications that are profoundly personal and social as well as educational. A comprehensive special education program must involve all areas of development and adjustment. The developmental profiles of two visually impaired youngsters are introduced here to highlight some of the adaptation problems of children with visual handicaps. Figure 5.3 shows the patterns of development of Ralph and Susan. Ralph, who has low vision, and Susan, who is blind, are both being educated in public schools where special provisions, personnel, and equipment have been made available for them.

Ralph is a tall, slim eleven-year-old who has a serious visual impairment for which maximum correction has been obtained with the aid of thick glasses. Ralph can read print material and, in the early grades, has been able to make a reasonable academic adjustment.

As the profile in Figure 5.3 shows, Ralph scored slightly above average in intelligence as measured by an adaptation of the Stanford-Binet and is currently doing average work as measured by achievement tests administered with no time limits. Yet this profile, though favorable, tends to disguise the future academic problems Ralph is likely to en-

FIGURE 5.3
Profiles of two children with differing degrees of visual impairment

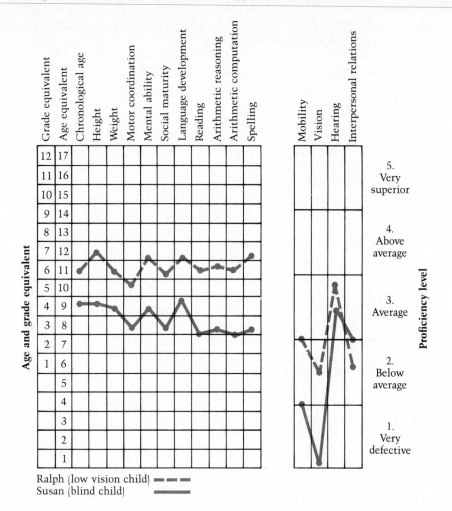

Ralph (low vision child) ▬ ▬ ▬
Susan (blind child) ▬▬▬

counter. He will be required to use higher thought processes as he progresses through the educational system, and is already beginning to experience the shift from concrete arithmetic to the more difficult (for him) abstractions of algebra and spatial concepts of geometry.

Ralph spends most of his time in school with a regular sixth-grade class, but leaves the program for about an hour a day to work with a specially trained resource teacher. Only three or four other youngsters at a time are in the resource room with Ralph, and the teacher can give him a good deal of tutoring in the academic areas in which he needs help.

Perhaps of more concern in school adaptation is how Ralph feels about himself. His visual handicap is serious enough so that he is sometimes unsure whether he belongs to the sighted community or to the blind community. He feels deeply about his awkwardness and inability to perform in athletics—a very important dimension in the life of an 11-year-old boy—but he does not discuss this with anyone.

Ralph also has some interpersonal problems. He reacts with a sharp tongue and a quick temper to any slights or negative comments, real or imagined, about his impairment. Consequently, many of the other youngsters ignore or avoid him except when class participation requires interaction. Above all, Ralph is beginning to wonder about his future: What is he going to do with his life when he grows up? How can he be independent? How will he establish friendships with girls? This is a topic of great importance to Brian, his older brother, who is in high school and whose life seems to revolve around girls. Brian's behavior is a source of amusement to Ralph now, but in a few years he will have to face interpersonal problems more seriously.

Susan's is the second profile shown in Figure 5.3. She is an average-looking nine-year-old who has been blind since birth. Like many blind children, she does have limited light perception that helps her mobility somewhat, but she cannot read print and has mastered the Grade 2 braille system that uses contractions, letter combinations, and shortened forms of words to save time and space in reading. In some respects, Susan is making a better adjustment than Ralph, despite her more severe handicap. Susan has a warm, understanding mother who has given her strong emotional support and a professional father who provides a comfortable income for the family. Her mother has tried to be a companion for Susan and has read to her extensively from the time Susan was 3 or 4. She has helped Susan through some difficult times, particularly when Susan was having trouble mastering the braille system. Susan's father is more distant, not seeming to know how to approach her.

In addition to her visual handicap, Susan shows some signs of mild neurological damage, which tends to make her physically awkward, but this condition is not serious enough to classify her as multiply handicapped. As the developmental profile shows, Susan's performance on tests of mental ability and her development in speech and language are average, perhaps testimony to the intensive work with her mother in early years, but in arithmetic her performance is somewhat below average.

Susan lives in an urban area with a large population where there are a number of children who are visually impaired. The school system buses these children from around the district to a school that provides a special program for them. Susan is well accepted by her classmates and has one or two close sighted friends. She has not yet had to face problems in relationships with boys or to deal with the often cruel behavior of young adolescents.

Susan has been affected in an important way by the educational trend of placing exceptional children in the least restrictive environment. She does not have to attend a large state school for the blind far from her home and family, as did many blind children of a generation or so ago. Sometime in the next three or four years, her mother and father will have to decide whether they want her to attend a residential school that provides advanced curriculum and educational facilities for the blind. But for now, they are happy that she is at home and able to get special help within the local school system.

CHARACTERISTICS

Children who are visually impaired have been studied extensively. By understanding their mental, physical, and social development, educators have been able to adapt instructional programs for them.

Intellectual Development

For many years, psychologists have tried to determine the intelligence of individuals who are blind by administering adapted psychometric tests. Hayes (1941) was one of the first (as far back as 1918) to adapt intelligence tests for the blind. In the Hayes-Binet Intelligence Test he deleted visual items, utilizing the nonvisual items of the Stanford-Binet. He examined 2,312 children in residential schools for the blind and found that their average IQ score was 98.8 on the adapted test. Later, performance tests in the Wechsler Intelligence Scale for Children (WISC) were used to examine children with visual impairments. Tillman (1967) and Tillman and Osborne (1969) compared educationally blind children with sighted children and found several differences:

- Blind children retain specific experiences as well as do seeing children, but these experiences are less integrated.
- Blind children score about the same as do seeing children on the subscales of Arithmetic, Information, Vocabulary, and Numerical Ability, but less well on Comprehension and Similarities.
- The vocabulary of blind children tends to be word definitions; sighted children use richer meanings.

Studies by Kephart, Kephart, and Schwartz (1974) also indicated that children with severe visual impairments tend to acquire the ability to communicate orally with others and are able to perform as well as seeing children on some standardized tests. On the other hand, their ability to process information often results in fragmented, distorted understandings of simple concepts.

The words used by children with severe visual impairments do not necessarily imply the same concepts as those used by seeing children. Sighted individuals often are startled to hear a blind person say "Look here" or "Now I see the problem," or to use phrases that require visual imagery ("pure as snow"). Does the visually impaired individual fully understand these words? Demott (1972) tested sighted and visually impaired children on their ability to meaningfully associate words and on their understanding of various words. He found that there were no marked differences between them in their understanding of ideas and concepts, and concluded that blind youngsters, like sighted ones, learn many words and their meanings, not from experience, but from their use in the language.

There have been few studies on the intellectual and cognitive development of children with severe visual handicaps in recent years. Educators have accepted that blindness does not necessarily result in inferior cognitive development, and that intellectual development is at least partly dependent on the experiences of the child, especially those at an early age. In reviewing the studies on the intellectual development of blind youngsters, Warren (1984) questioned the validity of conclusions that compare sighted and blind children. He claimed that the resulting IQ scores may reflect more on the limited experience and learning history of visually handicapped children than on their potential learning ability.

Sensory Perception and Compensation

Vision is a continuous source of information. We depend on our vision to orient ourselves, to identify people and objects, to regulate our motor and social behavior. People without sight have to rely on their other senses for information and all the other tasks our vision performs for us. How this is accomplished has been the focus of much speculation and research.

The doctrine of **sensory compensation** holds that if one sense avenue, say vision, is deficient, other senses are automatically strengthened, in part as a function of their greater use. Although this may be true in certain cases, research does not show that the hearing or touch sensitivity of blind children is superior to that of seeing children. Gottesman (1971) tested blind and sighted children ages 2 to 8 on the ability to identify by touch such things as a key, a comb, a pair of scissors, and geometric forms (triangle, cross). He found no difference between the groups. Samuelson (1981), on the other hand, found that proprioception (the sensation in the muscles, tendons, and joints resulting from internal stimuli) decreases with age in seeing children and increases with age in blind children. He explained that the proprioceptive movements sighted infants begin using are later replaced by visual sensations. At first, a baby crawls and reaches for a ball several times before he or she is able to grasp the ball. Later, using vision and space perception, the child crawls to the ball before reaching. A blind child cannot utilize vision to reach an object, so that child's proprioception increases with age.

Millar (1981) conducted a series of experiments on cross-modality to discover whether information received through one sense modality (hearing, touch) can contribute to that received by another. In other words, when a blind child feels an object—its texture, size, shape—is the child's mental image of the object similar to that of a sighted child who sees the object? She stated:

> The evidence suggests that vision, touch and movement contribute and emphasize different aspects of information about the world. . . . When vision is lacking, much of the information needed for spatial organization is reduced. But it can be gained through other senses. (p. 31)

Language Development

Seeing children acquire language by listening, reading, and watching movements and facial expressions. They express themselves first through babbling and later by vocally imitating their parents and siblings. Children with visual handicaps acquire language in much the same way, with the exception that their language concepts are not helped by reading or visual input. A seeing child develops the concept of a ball by seeing different balls; a blind child develops the same concept through tactile manipulation of different balls. Both are able to understand the word *ball*, and both are able to identify a ball.

Does their lack of vision impede the language development of children who are visually impaired? Cutsworth (1951), who was himself blind, tested congenitally blind children with a free-association test. He presented them with a noun and asked them to name its attributes. He found that they responded with words that were unrealistic to them. For the word *night*, they said, "dark," "black," "blue," and "yellow." Only one child out of twenty-six responded "coal." Cutsworth believed these responses were learned associative visual responses; they did not reflect the children's own tactile or hearing experiences. He explained that people who are visually impaired use **verbalisms** (words not verified by concrete experience) for social approval.

Other studies have compared children who are blind with seeing children to determine differences in language development and usage. Matsuda (1984) studied thirty-three blind and thirty-three sighted children and found no major differences in language usage. He concluded that blindness alone does not interfere with children's ability to communicate. Civelli (1983) demonstrated that intellectually normal blind children do not differ from their sighted peers in communication ability.

Anderson, Dunles, and Kekalis (1984) studied the development of language of six blind children for a period of three years. They concluded that on the surface the language of blind children seems like that of their sighted peers. But when examined for quality, the blind children have "less understanding of words as symbolic vehicles and are slower to form hypotheses about word meaning than sighted children" (p. 661).

Warren (1984), in a review of the literature on the language of those who are visually handicapped, arrived at these conclusions:

> For blind children without additional handicaps, there is little evidence of developmental differences from sighted children in some areas of language development. . . . The area where the question is still quite wide open is that of meaning (including "verbalism"). The new work of the past several years strongly suggests that, while blind children may use words with the same frequency count as sighted children, the meanings of the words for the blind are not as rich or as elaborated. It is not yet clear whether any such differences have implications for the adequacy of thought. (p. 278)

Personal and Social Adjustment

There are no inevitable personal or social problems that follow from being visually handicapped, nor does the impairment confer automatic nobility. However, the restricted mobility and consequent limited experiences of children who are visually handicapped appear to cause in many a state of passivity and dependency—a learned helplessness.

Tuttle (1984), in analyzing the self-esteem of children and adults who are blind, attributed lack of self-confidence and adjustment to lack of adequate interaction with sighted people and the attitude of sighted people about blindness. He maintained that the impact of blindness on self-esteem should be temporary and can be alleviated by the treatment those who are blind receive from other people. Children who are congenitally blind do not recognize that they are different until people begin to treat them differently or to point out that they cannot do things because they cannot see. Those who lose their sight after having experienced seeing tend to go through several stages: mourning, withdrawal, denial, reassessment, and reaffirmation. Finally, with training and interaction with sighted people comes self-acceptance and self-esteem.

The role of the teacher in this personal and social adjustment is critically important. Martin and Hoben (1977) offered the thoughts of some visually impaired students about how they are treated in school:

- Teachers should learn what "legally blind" really means. Lots of legally blind kids can do all sorts of things.
- Teachers should study handicapped people and learn about them—especially their feelings.
- If a teacher treats me different, the other kids think I'm a teacher's pet.

Self-esteem and self-acceptance in blind children are nurtured by positive interaction with sighted people. (© Betty Medsger 1981)

- I don't want to see an A on my report card when I know I earned a C.
- The worst thing for a handicapped person is for the teacher to pamper him.
- It's more fun, more challenge when you have to compete. You don't feel like you're an outsider.
- I appreciate the opportunity to get a better position in the classroom, but when the teacher asks me about it in front of the class it makes me feel like an idiot. I would tell teachers: if you want to tell me something that will help, don't make me feel like an idiot doing it.
- Just because I'm blind doesn't mean I'm handicapped in other areas. (p. 19)

Loosely translated, these students are saying, "Don't treat me like I'm helpless. Don't do me any special favors. Let me do it on my own." The reaction of many people who have not had experience with those who are handicapped is to lower their expectations. But these students don't want this kind of "favor."

The importance of emphasizing the social and behavioral side of visually handicapped adolescents was underscored in a study carried out by Meighan (1971). He gave the Tennessee Self-Concept Scale to 203 blind adolescents who were enrolled in three schools for the blind in the eastern part of the United States. The negative tone of the results was surprising. As Meighan pointed out, the sample "formed a very deviant and homogeneous group whose scores on the basic dimensions on self-concept were all found to be in an extremely negative dimension" (p. 35). The author believed that the youngsters' handicap was a dominant factor, overriding other influences and leading them to develop an uncertain self-identity.

Head (1979), in a later study using the same instruments, did not find negative self-concepts. Believing that Meighan's results were due to the sample of residential students, Head compared a residential sample with a resource room sample and an itinerant educational sample. There were no differences in self-concept scores in the three educational settings.

After surveying the literature on self-concepts of the blind, Warren (1984) stated that the studies have found no overall differences. He questioned the validity of Meighan's findings. He noted, however, that "to the extent that people expect of the child that he will not differ from a sighted child, the tendency for the blind child's self-concept to be different from that of the sighted child will be decreased" (p. 232).

IDENTIFICATION

School systems use many different approaches to detect children with visual impairments. Some schools refer children with suspected problems directly to an ophthalmologist or an optometrist. Others routinely screen youngsters to determine those who might have vision difficulties, and refer those who fail to pass that screening for more comprehensive assessment.

The standard school screening instrument is the **Snellen Chart,** which consists of rows of letters in gradually smaller sizes that children are asked to read at a distance of 20 feet. A variation consists of capital Es pointing in different directions. This is useful for screening young children and people who do not know letter names. The individual is asked to indicate the direction in which the arms of the E are pointing. Scores are based on how accurately the subject identifies the letters (or directions of the Es) using one eye at a time. A reading of 20/70 in either eye means the subject can see at 20 feet what a person with normal vision can see at 70 feet; a reading of 20/20 is normal. (Figure 5.4 shows the effect of vision impairment on visual acuity.)

The National Society for the Prevention of Blindness is the oldest voluntary health agency involved in the prevention of blindness. It has developed a number of screening tests for preschoolers and school-age children that utilize the Snellen Chart or modifications of it.

Hatfield (1979) advocated screening preschool children at two different age levels: at 6 months and between 3 and 5. For infants,

FIGURE 5.4
Contrasting visual
acuity

*Top: View as seen by person with 20/20 vision. Not only
can most of the letters be read, the person holding the
chart and the background objects are sharp and distinct. Bottom: View as seen by person with 20/200 vision. All the letters except the top one are indecipherable.
Although objects in the background are distinguishable,
much of the detail is lacking.*
From Who Is the Visually Impaired Child? *(Project MAVIS
Sourcebook 1) by M. Efron, 1979. Boulder: Social Science Education Consortium. Copyright 1980 by LINC Services. Reprinted by permission of the publisher.*

Table 5.3
Identifying Children in the Classroom with Vision Problems

Observe	Ask	Experiment
Can he/she read the chalkboard from the seat or does he/she need to walk up to it?	Read the cumulative record—any information about physical restrictions, medication, or the need for vision aids (magnifiers, lamps, etc.) should be noted on the eye report.	Try different lighting—is dim light or bright light better?
Does he/she squint when reading a book?		Try different seating—does he/she respond better if close or far away from the board or from you when you're talking to the class?
Does visual skill vary in different situations—on the playground, in reading group, at the desk?	Ask the parents—does the student like to watch T.V.? Where does he/she sit—close or far away?	Try different ideas—how does he/she do when lessons are taped?
	Ask the student what he/she sees outside the window, in the picture, in the book, on the board, etc.	

SOURCE: From *Visually Impaired Students in the Regular Classroom* (p. 30) by J. Todd (Ed.), 1979. Columbus, OH: Ohio Resource Center for the Visually Handicapped.

evaluation is based on observation of how the eyes are used; for three- to five-year-olds, both observation and the Snellen E chart are used. The consensus is that early diagnosis and treatment can prevent visual impairments in some children.

More extensive tests use elaborate equipment (Keystone Telebinocular, Bausch and Lomb Orthorater) to measure vision at far and near points and to test other characteristics (muscle balance, fusion, usable vision). The Titmus Vision Tester is the most widely used to screen vision in preschool children, school-age children, and adults.[1] Most of us who have taken a driver's license test have been screened for vision problems by the Titmus.

Once a vision problem is discovered, additional testing can be conducted to identify the extent of the problem using the Program to Develop Efficiency in Visual Functioning (Barraga, 1983). This scale was designed to assess the level of visual functioning through the presentation of a series of increasingly smaller words, sentences, and pictures. The purpose of the test is to determine the extent to which a child is able to use his or her vision even though that vision is impaired.

Just as the pediatrician is the first line of identification of handicapped children in preschool years, so the teacher is the prime source of identification of mild handicaps in school-age youngsters. Efforts have been made to sensitize classroom teachers to identify exceptional children. Table 5.3 lists some hints about what to look for and how to spot a child with visual problems.

---

1. The test is manufactured by Titmus, PO Box 191, Petersburg, VA 23804.

EDUCATIONAL ADAPTATIONS FOR VISUALLY IMPAIRED CHILDREN

Formal efforts in the United States to educate children with visual handicaps began in Boston in 1829, with the establishment of a residential school now called the Perkins School for the Blind. It was not until 1900 that the first public school class for blind children was organized in Chicago. The first class for children with low vision was established some thirteen years later.

Figure 5.5 shows the number of children with visual handicaps registered with the American Printing House for the Blind from 1949 to 1984. Notice that the large majority of children through 1955 were educated in residential institutions. Since then there has been a gradual shift from residential institutions to local schools. In 1955, only 20 percent of these children were educated in local school systems; in 1984, 71 percent were receiving their education in local schools and living at home. Also notice that the number of children with visual handicaps being educated in residential and local schools has gradually increased from year to year. In 1949, only 5,818 children were registered; in 1984, 44,313 were registered. This increase is due in part to the provisions of Public Law 94–142, which mandates the education of all handicapped children.

A number of adaptations in both materials and equipment are needed to fully utilize the visually handicapped person's senses of hearing, touch, smell, residual vision, even taste. Lowenfeld (1973) proposed three general principles that are important for adapting instruction to the educational needs of children who are visually impaired:

Concreteness.   Children who are educationally blind learn primarily through hearing and touch. For these children to understand the surrounding world, they must work with concrete objects that can be touched and manipulated. It is through tactile observation of real objects in natural settings (or models of dangerous objects) that students with visual handicaps come to understand shapes, sizes, weight, hardness, surface qualities, pliability, and temperatures.

Unifying experiences.   Visual experience tends to unify knowledge. A child who goes into a grocery store sees, not only shelves and objects, but also the relationships of shelves and objects in space. Visually impaired children cannot understand these relationships unless teachers present them with the experience of a grocery store or a post office or a farm. The teacher must bring the "whole" into perspective by giving students concrete experience and by explaining relationships.

Left on their own, educationally blind children live a relatively restricted life. To expand their horizons, to develop imagery, to orient them to a wider environment, it is necessary to develop experiences by systematic stimulation. We can lead children through space to help

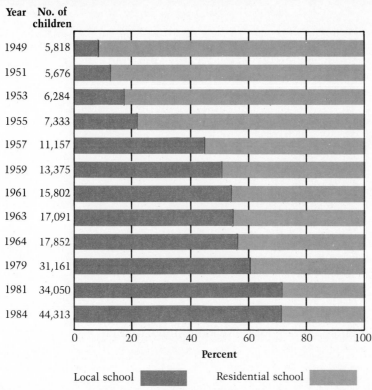

Year	No. of children
1949	5,818
1951	5,676
1953	6,284
1955	7,333
1957	11,157
1959	13,375
1961	15,802
1963	17,091
1964	17,852
1979	31,161
1981	34,050
1984	44,313

Percent

Local school   Residential school

SOURCE: Data for 1949 through 1964 from *Educational Programs for Visually Handicapped Children* (Bulletin No. 6, U.S. Office of Education) (p. 2) by J. Jones and A. Collins, 1966. Washington, DC: U.S. Government Printing Office. Data for 1979 through 1984 from American Printing House for the Blind.

FIGURE 5.5
Number and percentage of U.S. school children registered with the American Printing House for the Blind, by type of school, 1949–1984

them understand larger areas. We can expose them to different sizes, shapes, textures, and relationships to help them generalize the common qualities of different objects and note the differences. This verbalization of similarities and differences stimulates mental development.

Learning by doing.   For blind children to learn about the environment, we have to motivate them to explore that environment. A blind infant does not reach out for an object unless that object attracts the child through other senses (touch, smell, hearing). We have to stimulate the child to reach, to make contact, by introducing motivating toys or games (rattles, objects with interesting textures).

Visually handicapped children's ability to listen, relate, and remember must be developed to the fullest. They have to learn to use time efficiently because the process of acquiring information or performing a task can be cumbersome and time consuming. For the teacher, this means organizing material, giving specific directions, providing firsthand experiences, and utilizing sound principles of learning.

Infancy and Early Childhood

Experiences during the period from birth to age 5 are critical to subsequent development. It is especially important that the systematic education of visually impaired children begin as early as possible. Normal children absorb a tremendous amount of information and experience from their environment in the ordinary course of family events. Specially designed experiences that parallel those of normal children must be provided for visually impaired children. Table 5.4 lists four specific adaptations in the developmental areas of human attachment, object discovery, prehension (use of the hands in reaching and exploring), and locomotion.

The suggestions in the table would most likely be carried out by a child's parents, who may need careful instruction in the procedures to be followed.

In fact, much of the work with children at the preschool level in-

Table 5.4
Special Programming for Preschool Blind Children

Developmental Areas	Normal Child Expectation	Special Adaptation for Blind Children
Human attachment	Vision plays a crucial role in the establishment of human bonds.	Stress the importance of "learning to know" through tactile and auditory experience. Encourage holding and talking to the baby during feeding; create "social" times of holding, singing, and playing lap games as the baby's awake times increase.
Discovery of objects	Eye-hand coordination in the sighted child forms a nucleus from which many patterns of infant learning and development evolve.	Introduce some form of cradle gym or hanging apparatus over the crib. Lower the toy so that the baby's random movements will bring about touch and sound sensations.
Prehension	Prehension—the activity of the baby's hands, their organization, and progressive development—is intimately related to each of the other areas.	Play patty-cake games and other lap games that repeatedly bring the hands together at midline, encouraging their engagement. Let the baby's hands explore the mother's face, adding manual tactile experience to other sense impressions of the mother.
Locomotion	It is the reach for the out-of-range object that initiates the pattern for creeping.	When a baby demonstrates postural readiness for creeping and reach on a sound cue alone, initiate the pattern for creeping by providing a favorite sound toy just beyond reach.

SOURCE: Adapted from "An Educational Program for Blind Infants" by S. Fraiberg, M. Smith, and E. Adelson, 1969. *Journal of Special Education*, 3, pp. 121–153. Reprinted by permission.

Siblings as well as parents can be an important factor in the early development of a blind child.
(© Betty Medsger 1980)

volves the parents, with special educators teaching parents to interact more effectively with their handicapped child.

Educators have become increasingly sensitive to the importance of the early emotional life of blind children. Barraga (1983) provided a representative point of view: "With the visually handicapped infant, body play must replace eye play to communicate maternal concerns and love—the facilitators of developing a self-concept. More than the usual amount of time should be spent cuddling, holding, touching, stroking and moving the baby" (p. 31).

Learning Environment

As in other areas of exceptionality, there is a push to bring children who are visually impaired into the least restrictive environment. For some this means a mainstreamed regular classroom; for others, some form of special program. With the recognition of the many different needs of children who are visually handicapped has come a call for a continuum of services. Spungin (1981) described several of the essential services:

Preschool Program

Children aged 0–5 who have been identified as having a visual impairment will be provided with a qualified teacher and any necessary ancillary services designed to divert the educational and emotional ramifications resulting from such an impairment.

Such intervention will include strategies designed to provide sensory stimulation, body image, gross and fine motor skills, sensory-perceptual motor activities, and experientially based cognitive and language development for the child as well as parent education in the increasing awareness of expected growth and development of their child. (pp. 14–15)

Teacher Consultant

Visually handicapped pupils are enrolled in a regular classroom in the school building which they would attend if they were not visually handicapped and ordinarily require minimal support services. Such services are provided by a teacher consultant for the visually handicapped who spends less than 50% of his/her time in direct instruction to students. More than 50% of the teacher's time is in indirect services such as a consultation to parents, regular classroom teachers, and other appropriate school personnel; procurement of materials; assessment; coordination of related services; and other coordinating and supportive administrative activities. (p. 15)

Itinerant Teacher

Visually handicapped students are enrolled in a regular classroom in the school they would attend if they were not visually handicapped and require instruction in the development of special skills associated with the visual handicap. Such instruction is provided by an itinerant teacher of the visually handicapped who spends more than 50% of his/her time in direct instruction to students. (p. 15)

Resource Room

Students are enrolled in a regular class in a school which includes a special classroom for use by visually handicapped students who, ordinarily, require daily support services and specialized instruction. Such support services and direct instruction are provided and/or arranged by a teacher of the visually handicapped students according to the individual student's need. (p. 16)

Special Class

Students are enrolled in a special classroom and, ordinarily, require concentrated instruction for all or most of the school day. Instruction which emphasizes both subject matter skills and development of special skills is provided by a teacher of visually handicapped students in concert with other appropriate specialists. Such students may profit by participating in the regular school classes in special selected subject areas and/or other academic areas as appropriate to the changing needs of the student. (p. 16)

Special School Program

Students are enrolled in a special school which exclusively serves visually handicapped students and/or visually handicapped multiply-impaired students who require specialized instruction and support services beyond that which can reasonably be provided in the regular school programs. Such special school programs may be offered on a day or residential basis.

Students enrolled in special school programs should have access to the education programs in the local school district near the special school, either on a part-time or full-time basis. (p. 16)

Mainstreaming the Visually Handicapped Child

Mainstreaming in one form or another has been a part of the educational program for some visually impaired children since the early part of the twentieth century.

The greater the number of exceptional children who are placed in regular classrooms, the greater the need for support personnel who have practical experience in the area of exceptionality to be helpers and consultants. The following discussion is between Sarah, a classroom teacher, and Ellen, a specialist in visual impairment. Their conversation about Bruce, a child with low vision, illustrates the variety of adaptation problems Bruce and his teachers must face in order to make mainstreaming work.

Sarah: Come on in and sit down. Since things have slowed down a little bit this week, I thought we could take time for a cup of coffee.

Ellen: Thanks. These first few weeks really have been hectic. But I know we're both glad to have finished Bruce's IEP at the conference with his parents last week. How have things been going in class? Is the arrangement we designed working out?

Sarah: It's great except for one thing. Bruce still can't see the chalkboard from where he's sitting and he doesn't really like having a friend make a carbon copy of the board work for him, so he keeps jumping up and down to read what's on the chalkboard.

Ellen: Well, at least I'm glad he doesn't feel self-conscious about not being able to see the board. However, there are a couple of things we can do to alleviate the problem. First, you can be sure to read aloud whatever you write on the chalkboard. That way, Bruce can write important things down from the oral input and go up to the board later to copy longer lists. Most teachers find that oral input helps the other kids too. The other thing we can do is see if the janitor could help put wheels on Bruce's chair. He'd be able to get to the board without jumping up and down then. I'll check with Mr. Payne on my way out tonight.

Sarah: Those are both good ideas. Thanks, Ellen. But now let me tell you what's really got me concerned. It's the other kids. They were really excited about having Bruce in the class at first. Everybody wanted to take him around the school. I'll bet they showed him where the water fountain was at least fifty times! But lately the novelty seems to be wearing off. Today at recess Bruce just sat by the wall and listened to his portable radio while most of the others played softball.

Ellen: Lots of visually impaired youngsters do have a rough time being accepted. In fact, children with low vision, like Bruce, often find it harder to get along with sighted classmates than do children who are totally blind. I guess it's partly because the kids don't always know what Bruce can and can't see, what things he needs help with, and how they should act with him. But there are lots of other factors too, like how well Bruce does in his school work and how he handles group situations. It's hard to put your finger on a single cause.

Sarah: I know what you mean. The other day, Billy Turner—one of the real active tigers in my class—noticed that Bruce's handwriting was . . . well . . . kind of messy, and called the other kids over to look at it.

Ellen: Low vision students often write imperfectly because they see imperfectly. (Looking at Bruce's paper.) Hmm . . . it's certainly not beautiful handwriting, but this special boldline paper we ordered does seem to be helping. I'll plan to work with him on writing during the next few weeks. Another thing—

Bruce is about ready to learn to type. Although he can't type class notes because of the noise, he can type assignments and that should help. (Orlansky, 1980, pp. 9–10)

Discussions like this one are especially important for regular classroom teachers, most of whom have had limited experience in the special needs of children who are visually impaired. Itinerant (resource) teachers can help classroom teachers understand the problems these children face. For example, the classroom teacher of a boy with low vision got upset because he wanted to sit close to the closed-circuit television monitor and because he tended to hold books close to his eyes. The teacher was afraid that these practices would harm the boy's vision, a misconception dispelled by the expert advice of a special resource teacher. Another classroom teacher believed that a very bright light should always be available for visually handicapped children. In fact, dim light does not harm the eyes and, with certain conditions (cataracts, albinism), may be more comfortable for students.

A number of publications offer information to help teachers of visually impaired students. Corn and Martinez (1978), for example, described the use of special devices, ways in which visually handicapped children can work with printed material, and suggestions for helping these students manage other activities. Among their suggestions were the following:

Lamps and rheostats. With variable intensities and positioning, lamps can provide the additional or dimmed illumination that a visually handicapped child may require.

Large-type books. For comfort or for those children who cannot read regular print at close distance even with an optical aid, large-type is helpful. Its quality or typeface is as important to legibility as its size. Spacing between letters and lines is also important.

Raised line paper (writing paper, graph paper, etc.) Raised line paper allows a student to write script "on the line" or to maneuver a graph either by placing markers onto the graph paper or by punching holes to indicate specific points.

Cassette tape recorders. Children use the recorder to take notes, listen to recorded texts, or formulate compositions or writing assignments.

More time. Extra time will frequently be needed to complete assignments and exams. Allowing time and a half is usually considered acceptable. The child may complete his work in the resource room or school library. When you are certain that the child understands the work, it may be a good idea to shorten his assignments: for example, you may request that a student do only the odd-numbered problems in the math homework. (pp. 9–15)

Developing Special Skills

Using Braille

People who are visually handicapped must develop a series of special communication skills. For children who are blind, learning to use braille is a key skill for communicating with the sighted world.

Braille reading is a system of touch reading developed in 1829 by Louis Braille, a blind Frenchman. The system uses embossed characters in different combinations of six dots arranged in a cell two dots wide and three dots high (Figure 5.6). The symbols are embossed on heavy manila paper from left to right, and users usually "read" with both hands, one leading, the other following. Advanced readers may use the second hand to orient themselves to the next line while reading the line above, and may read as much as a third of the line with the second hand. Punctuation, music, and mathematical and scientific notations are based on the same system.

Although many others have been tried, Standard English braille was accepted in 1932 as the system for general use. It has been developed on several levels of difficulty.

Even the most efficient blind reader of braille shows an average rate of reading about two or three times slower than that of a print reader. In this area alone, we can understand how students who are blind fall progressively further and further behind sighted students.

FIGURE 5.6
Braille alphabet and numerals

The six dots of the braille cell are arranged and numbered thus:

1 ● ●4
2 ● ●5
3 ● ●6

The capital sign, dot 6, placed before a letter makes it a capital. The number sign, dots 3, 4, 5, 6, placed before a character, makes it a figure and not a letter.

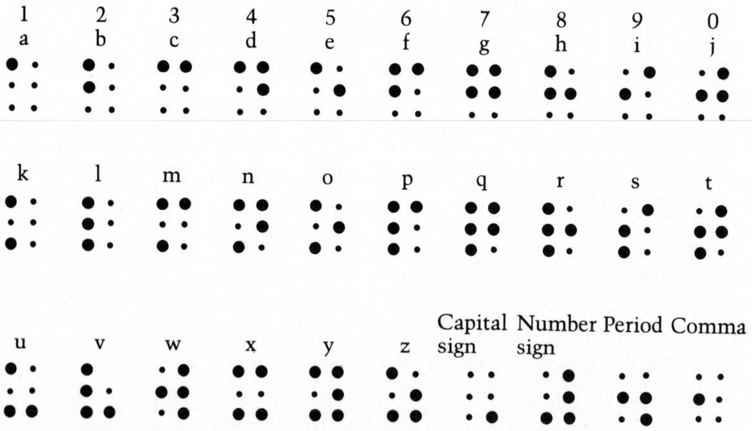

1 a	2 b	3 c	4 d	5 e	6 f	7 g	8 h	9 i	0 j

k	l	m	n	o	p	q	r	s	t

u	v	w	x	y	z	Capital sign	Number sign	Period	Comma

SOURCE: From the Division for the Blind and Physically Handicapped, Library of Congress, Washington, DC 20542.

KEVIN'S A TYPICAL CHILD ... AND BLIND

Kevin Minor attends a regular sixth grade in a central Colorado public school. Blind from birth, Kevin has been in a regular classroom since kindergarten.

"Kevin has succeeded," says his homeroom teacher, "because of his insistence on doing what other kids do, and because of his parents' support in his efforts to do so."

At first, Kevin's mother walked the few blocks with him to school. He wanted to go alone. After much practice, he convinced his parents that he could walk alone, although for several weeks he called home to announce his safe arrival.

Kevin was determined to learn to read in first grade, and he did. His itinerant Braille teacher explains, "Kevin learned Braille with the help of a Perkins Braillewriter and an Optacon. . . .

One of Kevin's biggest problems in kindergarten came from adults and peers at school trying to protect him. When he was not allowed to use the playground equipment, he made a special appeal, and with his parents' support the ban was lifted. "Now you could not tell him from any other child on the playground," reports his homeroom teacher.

Kevin has adjusted to the fact that his school has no special ramps or guideways. Some blind youngsters use a guide dog or cane, but Kevin does not. "If I've been someplace before," he says, "I usually remember. A few special things help, though, like the spot I have for my coat. A label with my name in Braille tells me where to put it and where to find it."

"Kevin usually remembers very well where things are located," agrees Kevin's reading teacher, who directed a recent play in which Kevin starred. "I only had to tell him once what direction to face for the audience."

Kevin explains, "Scenes in the play with other people were not too hard because I had their voices to guide me. What was hard was my grand entry when I had to jump onto the stage."

In the regular classroom, if information is put on the chalkboard, one of Kevin's classmates sitting nearby usually reads it for him. When Kevin's sixth-grade class began studying map skills. Kevin's teachers provided him with raised maps. They even created a map of his school to show where the rooms were, with Braille symbols and codes.

One unexpected problem arose for Kevin in fifth grade, when several new classmates expressed resentment at his excellent grades. They felt they should be doing better than someone who couldn't see and began to isolate Kevin from their activities. The teacher helped the class to realize how much time and effort goes into Kevin's achievements. With time and Kevin's positive attitude, the resentment disappeared.

Kevin's Braille teacher works with him on other social skills, too, such as looking at the person who's talking. "I can tell if you're tall or short by where your voice comes from," says Kevin.

continued

continued

"My Braille teacher helped me to write my name. She says there will be lots of times and places to use my signature. And, I've found one place already. I can check out my own Braille books." The school library maintains a rotating supply of Braille books for Kevin.

This leads to one of Kevin's favorite activities. "Something not many people do," Kevin claims. "I can read in bed in the dark. 'Lights out' time for me is when Mom takes the book away."

School personnel were taken aback when Kevin showed up for touch football tryouts. But they were surprised and proud when he made the team and completed a successful season as the team's offensive center. "It's his attitude," says the coach. "He really believes he can do things, and he's helped us learn that he's right."

Kevin's ability to develop successful routines at school began at home. He makes his own bed (a job he says he dislikes but which he is very proud he can do), takes out the trash, and has recently begun cooking and preparing weekend lunches for friends.

"At first I was sure the cooking was impossible," said Kevin's mother, "but we worked out ways of making it more safe, such as using a porcelain-topped stove, and wearing short-sleeved shirts while cooking. We cook together and we're quite a team!"

When asked to identify techniques that have contributed to Kevin's success in a mainstream situation, his parents and teachers pointed to these . . . factors.

• Kevin's personality causes him to try new things. Children who are afraid to try should be shown how to break big tasks into small ones and should be encouraged to attempt one of these small challenges each day.

• Parents and teachers "spot" for Kevin. They let him try new things, and stay close enough to him so they can help if needed. Kevin did not know, for example, that his mother followed him to school at a distance the first few times he tried it alone.

• Parents and teachers realize there are alternative ways to accomplish any given goal and help Kevin find them. Whereas many people think it impossible for a blind child to play football, Kevin's coach discovered that a child could play center by relying only on hearing and touch.

• In Kevin's school it's all right to be different. The staff works hard to stress the beauty of diversity and the importance of individual differences. Events are planned to emphasize this, such as the hall poster which read, "It's nice to be the same; it's nice to be different."

• Everyone realizes that Kevin is more like other kids than unlike them, and they treat him that way. Kevin himself does much to engender this feeling of normality. But since birth his parents have also reinforced Kevin's confidence in himself and his determination to be like everyone else.

continued

continued

- Kevin's positive outlook works miracles. He constantly thinks about what he can do, what he wants to accomplish, instead of what he can't do. He has an active sense of humor that puts people at ease and makes them concentrate on his strengths. Kevin's teacher declares, "This is the most important factor of all. Any teacher or parent who can give a child this sense of optimism has performed an invaluable service."

SOURCE: From "Kevin's a Typical Child . . . and Blind" by M. Perlman and V. Dubrovin, 1979. *Instructor, 88* (February), pp. 175–177. Reprinted from *Instructor*, February 1979. Copyright © 1979 by The Instructor Publications, Inc. Used by permission.

Umsted (1972) provided a training program for adolescent blind children to increase their skill in reading braille. He found that once a child had learned the system, little effort was made to improve efficiency. The assumption was that the code had been mastered effectively and would remain so. But Umsted discovered that almost 10 percent of the braille code was not correctly identified by blind students and that an intensive short-term training program designed specifically to help them use the code more effectively increased their reading level from 90 words a minute to 120 words a minute for a medium reading group, and to an average gain of 25 words a minute for a high reading group. Umsted suggested that continuing attention to the special skills that blind students must learn can improve their learning efficiency, that skills can atrophy unless practiced and reviewed.

Braille writing is another part of the curriculum of children who are blind. It is taught later than braille reading. There are various devices for writing the symbols, the easiest and fastest of which is the braille typewriter, or braillewriter. It has six keys corresponding to the six dots of the cell. A proficient user can type 40 to 60 words a minute. Braille can also be written by hand, using a special slate and stylus that allow the individual to make the raised dots in a standard braille cell.

Typing and Handwriting

Typing, seldom part of the elementary curriculum for sighted children, is very important for blind children. Only a small number of sighted people can read braille. For blind students to communicate with the

Blind children are taught to use a standard print typewriter to communicate in written form with the sighted world.
(© Betty Medsger 1981)

sighted world, then, they must learn to type. Instruction on the use of a standard print typewriter should begin as soon as possible, usually in the third or fourth grade.

For visually impaired students, handwriting is very difficult to learn. But most programs make an effort to teach these children to write their own signature. Not being able to write one's own name can be a source of embarrassment.

Mastering the Environment

Mastering their environment is of special importance to children who are blind, to their physical and social independence. The ease with which they move about, find objects and places, and orient themselves to new physical and social situations is crucial in determining their role in peer relationships, the types of vocations and avocations open to them as adults, and their own estimation of themselves as individuals.

How do we help blind children master their environment? From a very early age we have to teach them not to be afraid of new experiences or injury. Sighted children skin their knees, bump their shins, fall from trees, and step in holes. Blind children must have the same "privileges" if they are going to learn to control themselves and their environment.

Blind children should be taught to feel the difference in the weight of their forks when they have successfully cornered a few peas and when they haven't. They also should learn a system of marking and organizing clothes for both efficiency and good grooming.

Models—of a room, the World Trade Center, or the neighborhood—can help visually impaired children understand the relationship of one place or size to another. Of course models are not a substitute for experience. But they are an extension of experience, and a means of drawing perceptual relationships between areas too large to be included at one time in direct experience.

Orientation and Mobility

We cannot overemphasize the importance of training blind children and adults to move about in their environment. Two of the greatest limitations imposed by blindness are the problems of becoming oriented to one's environment and immobility. The situations that force dependence and can cause the greatest personality and social problems for visually impaired individuals usually involve mobility. Tools for improving mobility—long canes, seeing-eye dogs, sighted guides—are being used by adults. But children must also learn to move about their environment independently and safely. This is why orientation and mobility have become part of the curriculum in all schools for blind children.

One of the most important areas in helping those who are blind to move about their environment is learning how to avoid obstacles. We have long realized that many blind people seem to avoid obstacles very well: They make turns in hallways; they stop before they run into a door. How do they do it? Do they sense a change of air pressure on their faces? Do they use residual light and dark vision? Do they use their sense of hearing?

Over thirty years ago, in a classic study, Cotzin and Dallenbach (1950) carried out a series of experiments to find the answer. They asked blind people to walk down a path and stop when they sensed an obstacle. Then the researchers began to systematically eliminate various possibilities. They put a velvet hood over the face to eliminate cues from air pressure; they used blindfolds to rule out residual vision; they plugged the ears to eliminate hearing—each in turn. Out of these experiments came a single definitive answer: The subjects' judgment

*Developing orientation and mobility skills is crucial to
a blind person's independence.*
(© Bohdan Hrynewych/Southern Light)

suffered only when their ears were blocked. Clearly, they were using
sound much like bats do, to detect barriers in their path. The knowledge that hearing is an essential element in obstacle perception has
led educators to focus on enhancing (in natural and artificial ways) the
use of hearing to increase mobility.

In the decades since Cotzin and Dallenbach's study, Juurmaa (1970)
and other scientists have worked to devise electronic aids to mobility.
Two of these—the Sonicguide and the Laser Cane—are now being used
by people who are blind to move around more easily (see pp. 201–202).

Personal mobility and independence have particular significance for
adolescents, for children who are ready to break away from family
restraints and protection. The ability to control one's self and the environment is essential to developing independence and to gaining the
respect of peers. The schools are using physical education programs to

sharpen the orientation and mobility skills of these visually impaired youngsters.

In most cases, we increase the mobility of visually impaired individuals by teaching them ways to get around or to use available tools. But there is another way to ease the restrictions on those who are blind. Society has a responsibility to remove obstacles wherever possible. We have begun to see progress since 1968, when Congress passed the Architectural Barriers Act (Wardell, 1980). Advocates for those who are blind have convinced business and government to make public telephones accessible, to install wall fixtures that can be detected with a cane, to install handrails on staircases, and to affix braille symbols to button panels in elevators. All of these advances make moving around that much easier for those who are visually impaired, increasing their independence.

Map and Chart Reading

A favorite curriculum adaptation for children with visual handicaps are models or tactile maps representing spatial relationships that students can master through their sense of touch. Berla (1981) discovered that visually handicapped students, in particular younger pupils, can improve their ability to read maps if they are specifically taught systematic techniques for exploring a map. Teachers should not expect students to discover complex search techniques themselves. Just as sighted children need help in learning problem-solving techniques, visually handicapped children need instruction in specific search skills.

Special maps alone are not enough. Students must first have some understanding of what the maps represent. Napier (1973) described a careful comprehensive series of activities:

> Just as there must be readiness activities to prepare for the teaching of reading, there must be readiness activities prior to the teaching of map reading. Before the most rudimentary map can be read, children must experience a given area with all its details and cues. Therefore ... the classroom is the logical place to begin. In this setting, children learn that coats are hung in the closet left of the main door, that the teacher's desk is straight ahead from the door, that the wastebasket is immediately inside the door on the right, etc. (p. 239)

Listening

Sykes (1984) defined listening as "the ability to hear, understand, interpret, and critically evaluate what one hears" (p. 99). Listening is the foundation of all language arts. It is an even more important skill for those who are visually handicapped because much of the information they process is received through listening (to talking books, tapes,

verbal intercourse) and because of the importance of listening to obstacle perception.

With this knowledge, several teaching techniques have been developed to enhance listening skills. One is **compressed speech,** a process
that speeds speech electronically (by deleting nonessential sounds)
without losing clarity. With compressed speech, talking books and
tapes can be presented at the rate of 250 words a minute, about twice
as fast as normal. Increased speed does not seem to affect comprehension. In fact, Nolan and Morris (1967) reported that comprehension
improved beyond normal with students who were highly motivated.
High school and college students who are blind rely heavily on talking
books, tapes, and electronic aids, like the Versabraille, that read print
for them (see page 201).

Content

Most of the instructional material presented to visually handicapped
children is similar or identical to the material presented sighted children. This is particularly true when visually impaired students spend
the majority of their time in the regular classroom. However, some
modifications can be made to address specific areas of adaptive difficulty.

Science

Malone, DeLucchi, and Thier (1981) attempted to bring special content
in science to visually handicapped students. Their program, Science
Activities for the Visually Impaired (SAVI), was designed for upper
elementary school-age blind and low-vision children. The project stresses
hands-on activities that allow students to manipulate objects and conduct experiments. The tasks can be challenging for both sighted and
visually handicapped children who are working together, which makes
them appropriate for use in a mainstreamed educational setting.

Figure 5.7 shows a sample activity, part of a unit on kitchen interactions, that allows the students to measure the action of acids using
everyday objects plus a special plastic syringe with tactile notches.
Special braille recording sheets are also available to enable students to
quantify data. Through this kind of experience, students learn key
scientific procedures—observing, measuring, comparing, calculating,
and drawing conclusions.

Other units in the program cover scientific reasoning, communications, magnetism and electricity, and structures of life. Each module
has sets of activities, equipment, and detailed instructions for the
teacher, including special vocabulary terms and follow-up activities
that students can do at home or away from the classroom. Programs
like SAVI provide concrete systematic experiences that allow visually
impaired students to make full use of their intellectual abilities by
linking the physical environment to verbal interchange.

OVERVIEW

In *The Acid Test*, the students use baking soda to test for the presence of acid in common foods. They establish that when vinegar (an acid) is mixed with baking soda, a reaction occurs and a gas (carbon dioxide) is given off. When this reaction takes place in a bottle with a syringe stuck into the top, the carbon dioxide pushes the plunger out of the syringe barrel. The amount of acid in a measured sample of vinegar is the *standard* against which the amount of acid in other foods (orange juice, grapefruit juice, lemon juice) is compared.

Finally, the youngsters investigate the variables in the acid/soda reaction to help them "pop the top" (i.e. launch the plunger out of the syringe barrel).

BACKGROUND

How about a glass of acid with your peanut butter and jelly sandwich? Or how about tossing a little acid in the next batch of biscuits you bake? That sounds unappetizing to say the least, but acids are common in many of our favorite foods. The lemon juice that we use to make a tangy glass of lemonade, the buttermilk we use in biscuit dough, and the vinegar bath used to preserve pickles are all examples of acid ingredients in the foods we eat.

A simple technique for testing the acid content of foods involves using baking soda as an *indicator*. When an acid reacts with baking soda, two things happen. First, the acid is neutralized or converted into new substances that are not acidic; and second, a gas called carbon dioxide is liberated in the form of bubbles. The amount of gas produced by this *reaction* can be used to compare the strengths of

SOURCE: From *Science Activities for the Visually Impaired: SAVI Leadership Trainer's Manual* by L. Malone, L. DeLucchi, and H. Thier, 1981. Berkeley, CA: Center for Multisensory Learning, University of California.

FIGURE 5.7
Page from scientific experiment for visually impaired students

Mathematics

Another example of how specific content can be designed to help blind children master concepts was provided by Huff and Franks (1973) for teaching fractional parts. It is easy enough to understand fractions with a visual demonstration. But for blind students that understanding must be acquired through the sense of touch. Huff and Franks demonstrated that blind children in kindergarten through third grade can master fractions by working with three-dimensional circles of wood and placing them in a form board nest. Once they've placed a whole circle, the children can learn to assemble blocks representing a third of a circle and put them together in the nest to form the whole. This kind of tactile experience helps blind children, not only to master the idea of fractional parts, but to discriminate between the relative sizes of various fractional parts (halves versus quarters).

In the middle grades (fourth through eighth or ninth grades), visually impaired students work with supplementary materials to help them absorb the same information that sighted children learn. This is accomplished through talking books, recorded lessons, and remedial work when children require it.

The Uses of Technology

Advances in electronics and computers are having significant impact on the education of those who are visually impaired. These developments have given blind and low-vision people access to technology that expands their intellectual and physical worlds (Ashcroft, 1984).[2]

Most of the devices we discuss here share certain characteristics. First, they are complex. Their effective use requires careful, extensive instruction. Second, they are delicate. These devices can and do break down from time to time, which means users must be prepared to have them fixed or to make other adaptations. Third, they are expensive, a factor that limits their widespread use. And fourth, they can be awkward to use in normal settings, although ongoing advances in electronics are being applied to improve them.

Obtaining Written Information

The Optacon.   Developed at Stanford University, the Optacon scans and converts print into 144 tactile pins. These pins, when activated by print, produce a vibratory image of the letter on the finger. The machine is an optical-to-tactile converter, which makes available to

---

2. For detailed information on electronic aids, see the November 1984 issue of the *Journal of Visual Impairment and Blindness,* and the Winter 1984 issue of *Education of the Visually Handicapped.*

those who are visually impaired books that are not in braille. Bliss and Moore (1974) indicated that to learn to read with the Optacon, a child must be highly intelligent, spend long periods in training, and be highly motivated. Barraga (1983) stated that the Optacon is a worthwhile technological invention because it allows print material to be read without modification or transcription. At present, however, the cost of the machine and the difficulty in learning how to use it limit its widespread use by children who are blind.

Computer Automation.   At the Massachusetts Institute of Technology, a computer automation has been developed that translates ink-print into Grade 2 braille. The procedure is being used extensively at the American Printing House for the Blind. An expansion of the computer braille translator, the MIT Braille Emboss, is used with a tele-writer. When teachers of the blind want braille output for new materials, they request it by phone from a computer center, and it is returned in braille by means of a teletypewriter. Currently braille translations are performed by microcomputers that are usually available in schools for the blind.

The Versabraille System.   This system, which is manufactured by Telesensory Systems, stores braille on a cassette tape. Information sent from the tape through a microcomputer is displayed to the user either in print or in braille. The braille can be paper braille to be read later, or paperless braille to be read immediately as it is displayed line by line. Speed is regulated by the user. In addition, the user can send information to the computer. The advantage of electronic braille is that a 60-minute cassette tape can store the equivalent of 400 pages of paper braille (Ashcroft, 1984).

The Kurzweil Reading Machine.   The machine is an electronic device that automatically converts printed material into spoken English at normal speech rates. The user places the material to be read face down on the scanner of the desktop reading machine. The scanning mechanism locates the first line of text and begins scanning the page. Within seconds, an electronic voice is heard reading the material. In addition, the machine has the capability, when linked to a computer, of translating printed materials into full-page braille.

Increasing Mobility

Sonicguide.   This device resembles a pair of glasses. It emits high-frequency sounds (beyond the range of human hearing) that reflect back from objects in or near the travel path of a blind person and are fed back into the equipment and transformed into audible signals. It supplies three kinds of information about nearby objects: distance, direction, and some notion of surface characteristics. The Sonic Path-

The Kurzweil Reading Machine converts printed material into spoken English at normal speech rates.
(Courtesy Kurzweil Computer Products, Inc.)

finder is similar to the Sonicguide. It is mounted on a spectacle framework, and detects the direction of an object within an 8-foot radius (Heyes, 1984).

The Laser Cane. Used for traveling, the Laser Cane has three narrow beams of invisible infrared light. One beam detects objects 5 to 12 feet straight ahead; another detects obstacles at head height; and the third detects holes or drop-offs (stairs). Users move the cane as they travel and listen for the tone signaling an obstacle (Mellor, 1981).

Other Uses of Technology

The Speech Plus Talking Calculator is a hand-held calculator that announces (using a 24-word vocabulary) each entry and result. The speak key allows the user to hear the display contents without performing additional operations. The device costs between $35 and $50.

Telecommunication is the linking of computers via telephones. A modem or acoustic coupler translates electronic signals into auditory signals that are then transmitted over telephone lines. This allows two

Table 5.5
Jobs for Blind and Low-vision Computer Users

Applications programmer
Assistant director of a rehabilitation center for the blind
Assistant engineer
Attorney
Claims representative
Computer programmer
Customer engineer
Customer service representative
Dispatcher
Editor of a technical magazine
Engineer
Liquor store owner
Marketing secretary
Materials expediter in a purchasing department
Medical transcriber
Occupational technician
Physicist
Programmer analyst
Programmer trainee
Radio station assignment editor
Receptionist
Research specialist
Secretary
Senior software manager
Software specialist
Software support specialist
Staff engineer
Staff supervisor
Systems analyst
Systems programmer (trouble shooter)
Tax analyst
Word processing operator (trainee)
Word processor

NOTE: This is not an exhaustive listing of all jobs in which computers are used, but it shows the diversity of jobs held by visually impaired computer users.

SOURCE: From "Applications of Microcomputers by Visually Impaired Persons" by G. Goodrich, 1984. *Journal of Visual Impairment and Blindness,* 78 (November), pp. 408–414.

users hundreds of miles apart to exchange information. Although the system is used primarily by sighted individuals, it has applications for people who are visually impaired.

Advances in telecommunications, and in computer electronics generally, have opened a wide range of occupations for people who are visually impaired. Table 5.5 lists some of these computer-related jobs.

LIFESPAN ISSUES FOR INDIVIDUALS WITH VISUAL IMPAIRMENTS

Barraga (1983) outlined a plan for a state program for those who are visually handicapped. Table 5.6 shows program levels from infancy to adulthood, the personnel involved at different stages, and the nature and scope of services at each developmental level.

Table 5.6
State Plan for Services for Visually Impaired Children and Adults

Program Levels	Living Arrangements	Personnel Involved	Nature and Scope of Services
Preschool and early childhood (0–9 years)	Neonatal high-risk nurseries in hospitals Own homes, foster homes	Physicians and eye specialists, nurses, clinicians Screening teams Public health nurses, social workers Preschool counselors, teachers, diagnostic and placement team	Identification, assessment, reporting Public screening Case finding, referral Parent counseling, in-home teaching Preschool public school programs Local nurseries and kindergartens, programs in private agencies, preschool residential programs for multihandicapped
Elementary (6–14 years)	Own homes, foster homes, regional residential centers	Physicians, therapists, nurses Social workers, psychologists Special teachers and aides Mobility specialists Counselors Regular classroom teachers	Diagnostic and evaluation centers Local school programs, centers for multihandicapped, regional residential schools, screening and referral, parental counseling
Secondary (12–21 years)	Own homes, foster homes, halfway houses, regional residential settings	Vocational and/or career counselors Special teachers and aides Mobility specialists Psychologists and/or mental health counselors	Workshop training (sheltered workshops for multihandicapped), vocational or on-the-job training Academic programs in local schools or regional residential center
Adult (18 years to independent, tax-paying citizens)	With parents, halfway houses, independent settings	Vocational and/or career counselors Technical skills specialists Psychologists and/or mental health counselors Mobility specialists Placement specialists	Sheltered workshops Trade, technical, and/or vocational schools Business and professional schools Community colleges Senior colleges and/or universities

SOURCE: Adapted from *Visual Handicaps and Learning* (Rev. ed.) by N. Barraga, 1983. Austin, TX: Exceptional Resources.

Sex Education

One extremely important area of special instruction for visually impaired individuals is sex education—information on the physical and psychological aspects of sex. Barraga (1983) described the need:

> By the time visually impaired youth reach high school and begin to think about relationships (and marriage) with those of the opposite sex, they may have many erroneous ideas or be totally ignorant of the basic facts relating to body parts and sexual functioning. . . . Courses in sex education and preparation for marriage and family life are absolutely necessary for visually impaired children and youth. (p. 102)

A great deal of information has become available to help teachers of visually impaired children approach the topic of family life and interpersonal relations, a curriculum area often ignored in the past. Although the facts of sexual reproduction are not overlooked, attention focuses on how people live and work together:

Concept: A man and a woman who love each other marry and become husband and wife to each other and form a new family.

Learning Activities

1. Have children tell about weddings they have attended. Introduce terms such as bride, groom, wife, husband.
2. Note that when husband and wife have children they become father and mother also.
3. Invite children to tell about sister's, aunt's, neighbor's boy friends or girl friends.
4. Ask children "who can marry each other?" And who should not; i.e., sisters and brothers, and other close relatives.

Concept: A family is a group of people who live together and take care of each other.

Learning Activities

1. Discuss the different kinds of family groupings. Help the children to recognize that changes brought about by death, divorce, and separation do affect the composition of a family, but they are still families.
2. Ask children to identify members of their families and encourage them to bring in pictures.
3. Have children relate how their families have changed in size and discuss the effect on the family.
4. Ask children to name the "big people" within families and their relationships (grandmother, grandfather, aunt, uncle, cousin). (Dickman, 1975, p. 36)

Life Skills

Susan and Ralph, the youngsters whose developmental profiles appear earlier in this chapter, will soon reach adolescence and begin to think about where they are going to live and what they will do as adults. They both value and look forward to an independent, or at least semi-independent, living setting. They will think about going away to school or finding a job and an apartment.

In middle and late adolescence, children who are visually impaired must develop a whole series of orientation and mobility skills to cope with new settings. Sighted people can depend on their vision to become familiar with new surroundings. But visually impaired youngsters have to rely on their tactile and other senses to find the bathroom, the phone, or the cafeteria—to make a cognitive map of their environment.

Hatlen, LeDuc, and Canter (1975) described a systematic attempt to provide effective independent living skills for visually handicapped individuals. The Blind Adolescent Life Skills Center was made up of ten apartments in a seventy-five-unit complex. Twenty blind young adults lived in the center's apartments. The center provided services, including instruction on mobility as well as an orientation to the apartment, on an on-call (as needed) basis. Instruction included survival skills (shopping for groceries, preparing simple meals, managing finances, using the telephone for emergencies, dealing with roommates). In addition, it involved communication skills, recreational social skills, and prevocational training. Attempts were made to integrate these skills into daily living tasks. For instance, in order to get to a recreational activity, mobility skills were needed. One example of a relatively simple task for a sighted person, but a challenge for one who is visually handicapped, was described in the teaching notes:

> Pete asked me to help him make a grilled cheese sandwich. He felt he could do everything but turn the sandwiches in the skillet. I've helped him three or four times with this task. Painstaking, but steady improvement. By the time he had turned all six sandwiches he needed no help at all. However, getting the right amount of butter in the skillet, tipping the skillet to spread the butter evenly is not so easy. I'll bring in my pastry brush and help him paint some melted butter on the bread. Pete is eager for concentrated help on living skills and is getting better about asking for help. (Hatlen, LeDuc, & Canter, 1973, p. 112)

An item of special concern for blind and low-vision people is their personal appearance. Because they cannot see how others react to them, they cannot pick up visual cues to fix unruly hair, a crooked tie, or unbuttoned clothing. Sighted people know immediately when some-

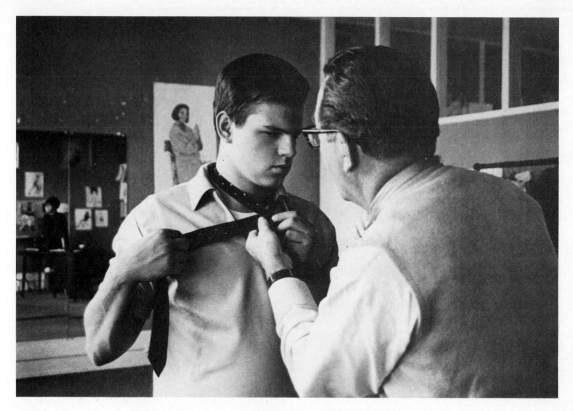

*People who are blind are taught to use their tactile sense
for personal grooming and for checking their appearance
before going out into the sighted world.*
(© B. Kliewe 1979/Jeroboam)

thing is wrong with their appearance by the looks they receive from
others. People who are blind must use their tactile sense to double-
check appearance before venturing out into the seeing world.

Many people who are blind have other handicaps. Some of these
individuals can function in a supervised environment, in a sheltered
or semisheltered workshop. We discuss the problems of multihandicapped individuals in Chapter 10.

SUMMARY OF MAJOR IDEAS

1. We use two basic classifications for students who are visually
   impaired: Those who are blind have light perception without
   projection or are totally without light perception, and must use
   braille to learn; those with low vision are severely impaired even
   with glasses but can read print.

2. The interpretation of the outside world by people who are visually impaired is a function of the brain, experience, and the adequacy of the eye.

3. Common types of visual disorders are refractive errors, defects of muscle function, and other anomalies.

4. Approximately one out of a thousand children is visually impaired.

5. Studies on the impact of visual impairment indicate that, in general, intellectual abilities are not markedly affected; the perception of other senses is not different from that of seeing persons; language development is affected only in those areas where the meanings of words are dependent on visual concepts; and self-esteem and self-confidence are not distorted except when a peer group has negatively influenced the individual's attitude.

6. Schools use the Snellen Chart as a means of identifying children with visual problems; then refer these students to an ophthalmologist or optometrist for further examination.

7. Before 1955 most visually impaired children (80 percent) were educated in residential schools; today the majority of these children (70 percent) are educated in local schools.

8. The educational program for visually impaired children is similar to that for sighted children, with special emphasis on concrete learning, unifying experiences, and self-activity.

9. A greater emphasis is now placed on education of visually impaired youngsters in infancy and early childhood. This emphasis has brought parents into the special education system as active participants in their children's development of skills and attitudes.

10. The many needs of visually impaired children demand a continuum of special services: preschool programs, teacher consultants, itinerant teachers, resource rooms, special classes, and special school programs.

11. Visually impaired students are now mainstreamed in regular classes whenever possible, using the services of resource rooms and itinerant teachers.

12. Orientation and mobility training, once directed just to adults, has become an important part of the curriculum for visually impaired children in elementary and secondary schools.

13. Technological advances have increased the availability of written material and improved the mobility of those who are visually impaired. In addition, the widespread use of computers has opened up new career opportunities for them.

UNRESOLVED ISSUES

1. *Multiple handicaps.* The growing number of children who have two or more handicaps presents a serious issue for special educators. Most youngsters with visual impairments are either mentally

retarded or deaf as well. We have to adapt our educational programs, then, to accommodate children with multiple handicaps, an adjustment that complicates an already serious challenge.

2. *Making technology accessible.* Technology is wonderful—when it is usable. The widespread use of technological developments for those who are visually handicapped has been impeded by the cost and size of equipment. We must find ways to subsidize costs or bring the costs down for devices like the Sonicguide and Sonic Pathfinder. In the same way, we have to increase accessibility to computers and word processors, which are transforming the academic and work worlds of those who are visually handicapped.

REFERENCES OF SPECIAL INTEREST

Barraga, N. (1983). *Visual handicaps and learning* (Rev. ed.). Austin, TX: Exceptional Resources.

A comprehensive readable introduction to the problems of schoolchildren who have visual handicaps. Good discussions of the impact of visual impairment on children, ways to conduct comprehensive assessments of individual children, and the nature of differential programming.

Dickman, I. (1975). *Sex education and family life for visually handicapped children and youth: A resource guide.* New York: American Foundation for the Blind.

A readable, much-needed examination of the key social adjustment problems of visually impaired children and adolescents. Provides teachers with practical guides to discussions on interpersonal relations, decision making, self-identity, and other pertinent topics. Provides teachers and students with a detailed list of books, films, and associations that deal with the topic of sex education.

Tuttle, D. (1984). *Self-esteem and adjusting with blindness.* Springfield, IL: Charles C Thomas.

This book, written by a professor who is himself severely visually impaired, is a major contribution to the literature on blindness. The book surveys the literature on the implications of blindness on personal development, includes sociological and psychological theory, and gives guidelines for the development of self-esteem. It offers an in-depth examination of factors that interfere with or help develop self-esteem, and describes how people adjust to congenital or adventitious blindness. The book ends with a section on fostering self-esteem and self-confidence.

Warren, D. (1984). *Blindness and early childhood development.* New York: American Foundation for the Blind.

A scholarly work that reviews the scientific studies on those who are blind. It includes discussions on infancy and early childhood, sensory integration and perception, intelligence, and cognitive abilities. A fine sourcebook for students and workers.

C·H·A·P·T·E·R
Six

CHILDREN WITH HEARING IMPAIRMENTS

Focusing Questions

What three factors are critical elements in the definition of hearing impairment?

Why is the concept of language so important to the cognitive and academic development of children who are deaf?

What causes the social and behavioral problems of youngsters who are hearing impaired?

What is the difference between American Sign Language and other manual methods of communication?

What do the individual limitations of the oral and manual methods mean for the future direction of education for children who are deaf?

What kinds of problems do deaf adults face in the workplace?

*D*eaf and hard of hearing children are not a homogeneous group. First they are children, with all the individual characteristics of children. And their impairments are individual too. Yes, they all suffer some hearing loss. But the degree of that loss, the age at which it was acquired, the type of loss, the cause of the loss—all combine to make each child's condition unique.

These differences along with other factors present special educators with a difficult and challenging problem. A hearing loss interferes with the reception and production of language. Because language influences practically every dimension of human development, the inability to hear or speak intelligibly is a critical handicap that can have enormous social and academic consequences.

DEFINITIONS

There are several factors involved in our definitions of hearing impairments: the degree of hearing loss, the time at which the loss occurs, and the type of loss.

Degree of Hearing Loss

Hearing is usually measured and reported in decibels (dB), a relative measure of the intensity of sound. Zero dB represents optimal hearing. A loss of up to 26 dB is within the normal range; a loss of between 27 and 70 dB is within the hard of hearing range; and a loss of 71 or more dB is within the deaf range.

Frisina (1974), in a definition of hearing impairment, described the physical and educational dimensions of the handicap:

> A deaf person is one whose hearing is disabled to an extent . . . that precludes the understanding of speech through the ear alone, with or without the use of a hearing aid.
>
> A hard-of-hearing person is one whose hearing is disabled to an extent . . . that makes difficult, but does not preclude, the understanding of speech through the ear alone, with or without a hearing aid. (p. 3)

Table 6.1 shows the common levels of hearing loss. The first three are in the hard of hearing range; the last two, in the deaf range. As the degree of hearing loss increases so does the need for special services.

To test hearing we measure two sound dimensions—frequency and intensity. Frequency is the number of vibrations (or cycles) per second

Table 6.1

Degree of Hearing Loss and Educational Significance

Level of Loss	Sound Intensity for Perception	Educational Implications
Mild	27–40 dB	May have difficulty with distant sounds. May need preferential seating and speech therapy.
Moderate	41–55 dB	Understands conversational speech. May miss class discussion. May require hearing aids and speech therapy.
Moderately severe	56–70 dB	Will require hearing aids, auditory training, speech and language training of an intensive nature.
Severe	71–90 dB	Can only hear loud sounds close up. Sometimes considered deaf. Needs intensive special education, hearing aids, speech and language training.
Profound	91 dB +	May be aware of loud sounds and vibrations. Relies on vision rather than hearing for information processing. Considered deaf.

SOURCE: "Abnormal Hearing and Deafness" by H. Davis in *Hearing and Deafness*, 3rd ed., by H. Davis and R. Silverman (Eds.). Copyright © 1970 by Holt, Rinehart & Winston. Reprinted by permission of CBS College Publishing.

of a given sound wave. The greater the frequency, the higher the pitch. A person may have difficulty hearing sounds of certain frequencies but not of others. Intensity is the relative loudness of a sound.

We can pinpoint an individual's level of hearing by determining the level of intensity at which the individual hears. To do this we use a pure-tone audiometer, an instrument that creates sounds of preset frequency or intensity. The individual responds (raises a hand, nods) when he or she hears a tone through the machine. The loss in each ear is plotted separately. The level of hearing is recorded on an audiogram that shows decibel loss at each relevant frequency.

Time of Hearing Loss

The second factor is the time at which the hearing loss occurs. Prelingual deafness is the loss of hearing before speech and language have developed. Postlingual deafness is the loss of hearing after spontaneous speech and language have developed. Prelingual deafness often leads to more serious educational problems. Deafness acquired after speech and language have begun to develop does not impede a child's making satisfactory progress in school to the extent that prelingual deafness does.

FIGURE 6.1
The human ear

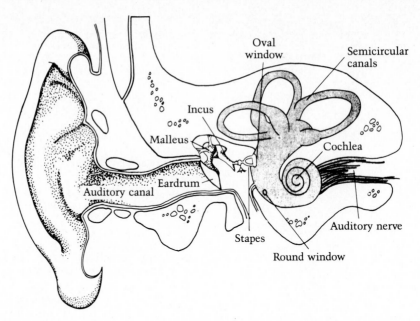

NOTE: The outer ear consists of the auditory canal. The middle ear consists of the eardrum, malleus (hammer), incus (anvil), and stapes (stirrup). The inner ear consists of the round window, the oval window, the semicircular canals, and the cochlea.

SOURCE: *Human Information Processing* (p. 221) by P. Lindsay and D. Norman, 1972. New York: Academic Press.

Types of Hearing Loss

The third factor is the type of hearing loss. The ear is a complicated structure (see Figure 6.1), and it functions in a complex way. Although there are many possible defects—in structure and function—we can classify them in two basic categories: conductive losses and sensorineural losses.

A **conductive hearing loss** reduces the intensity of sound reaching the inner ear, where the auditory nerve begins. Sound waves must pass through the auditory canal to the eardrum, where vibrations are picked up by a series of bonelike structures in the middle ear (malleus, incus, stapes) then passed on to the inner ear. The sequence of vibrations can be held up anywhere along the line. Wax or a malformation can block the external canal; the eardrum can be broken or punctured; the movement of the bones in the middle ear can be obstructed. Any condition that impedes the sequence of vibrations or prevents them from reaching the auditory nerve causes a loss in conduction. Conductive defects seldom cause hearing losses of more than 60 or 70 dB. And these losses can be effectively reduced through amplification.

Sensorineural hearing losses are caused by defects of the inner ear or of the auditory nerve, which transmits impulses to the brain.

Sensorineural hearing losses can be complete or partial, and can affect some frequencies (particularly high ones) more than others.

Tests with the audiometer can determine whether a hearing impairment is conductive or sensorineural. A bone conduction receiver measures the ability to pick up sound through bone conduction by masking sensorineural avenues. An air conduction receiver measures the effectiveness of sensorineural pathways.

Figure 6.2 shows the audiogram of a child with a conductive hearing loss. On the audiometer the child heard airborne sounds at about the 40-dB level at all frequencies in the better ear (the left). Using a bone conduction receiver, the child responded in the normal range. Notice that the hearing loss is fairly even at all frequencies. We see a very different pattern in Figure 6.3, the audiogram of a child with a sensorineural hearing loss. This youngster shows a profound loss at high frequencies (above 1,000 cycles) and a severe loss at lower frequencies. The bone conduction receiver in this case gave no better reception because the defect is in the auditory nerve, not in the middle ear structure that carries the sound vibrations to the nerve.

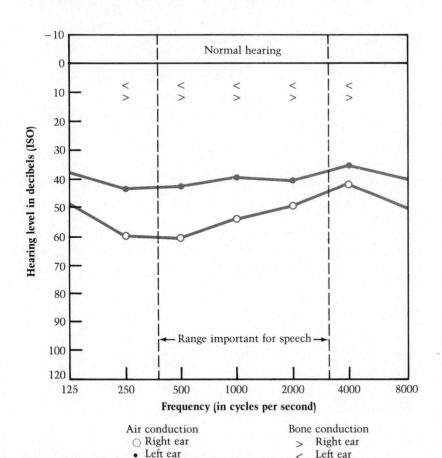

FIGURE 6.2
Audiogram of a child with a conductive hearing loss

FIGURE 6.3
Audiogram of a
child with a sensori-
neural hearing loss

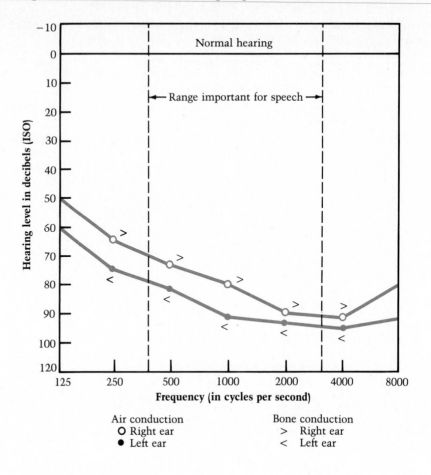

Air conduction
O Right ear
● Left ear

Bone conduction
> Right ear
< Left ear

CAUSES OF HEARING LOSS

Most of the available information about the causes of hearing impairments are concerned with deafness as opposed to mild hearing losses. Trybus (1985) listed six causes of childhood deafness in the United States today:

- Heredity
- Maternal rubella
- Complications during pregnancy and birth
- Meningitis
- Otitis media
- Childhood diseases, infections, and injuries

But these conditions cause just 60 percent of the cases of childhood deafness. Despite our sophisticated diagnostic tools, we just don't know the causes of the remaining 40 percent. Figure 6.4 shows the breakdown of causative conditions for 55,000 hearing impaired children. Maternal rubella (German mesles), heredity, and complications during pregnancy and birth are the most common reported causes.

Heredity

Many different genetic conditions can cause deafness. Transmissions have been attributed to dominant genes, recessive genes, and sex-linked genes. Although there is general agreement that heredity plays an important role, it's difficult to determine the exact percentage of children whose deafness is due to heredity. In Figure 6.4, 11.5 percent of the 50,000 students sampled had hearing loss attributed to heredity. Other estimates range from 30 to 60 percent (Moores, 1982).

Determining the hereditary influence is not simply a question of intellectual curiosity. Deaf adults tend to intermarry (Woodward, 1982). They need information about the probability of their children being born deaf. Genetic counseling, which tries to determine for couples the odds of their transmitting a condition to their children, can be an important resource for couples who are deaf or who have deafness in their families.

Maternal Rubella

The effects of rubella on the fetus during the first three months of pregnancy can be devastating. Hardy (1968) reported on 199 children whose mothers had the virus while pregnant during the 1964–1965

FIGURE 6.4
Causes of hearing loss

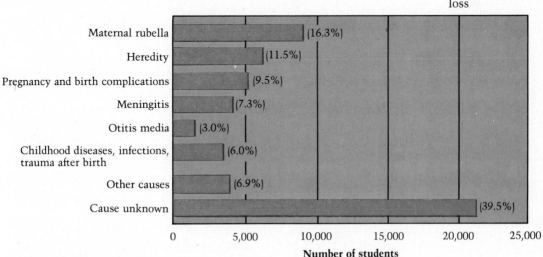

NOTE: Percentages given here reflect data on 55,000 students of an estimated total of 76,000 to 90,000 students. The data was compiled as part of the Gallaudet Research Institute's Annual Survey, 1982–83.

SOURCE: *Today's Hearing Impaired Children and Youth: A Demographic and Academic Profile* by R. Trybus, 1985. Washington, DC: Gallaudet Research Institute.

There is a great range of hearing impairment; those who are considered deaf may be aware only of loud sounds or vibrations while those who are moderately affected may, with the help of hearing aids, understand conversational speech.
(Courtesy of the Clarke School for the Deaf)

epidemic. Of these youngsters, 50 percent had auditory defects, 20 percent had visual defects, and 35 percent had cardiac defects (some of this last group also had auditory or visual problems or both). The National Communicable Disease Center reported that the epidemic caused deafness in 8,000 children (Hicks, 1970). Northern and Downs (1978) estimated that between 10,000 and 20,000 children were affected in the rubella epidemics of 1958 and 1964. Maternal rubella is the most common identifiable cause of deafness in children.

Pregnancy and Birth Complications

Rubella is not the only virus that can affect the fetus and cause deafness. Herpes simplex, when located in the genitalia, is a venereal disease that is transmitted sexually. It can sometimes cause deafness in the fetus and can be transmitted to the child in the passage through the birth canal if the virus is in the active state. The virus has reached epidemic proportions in the young adult population. It's estimated that between 20 and 25 percent of that population is infected with genital herpes in the active or inactive state (Vernon & Hicks, 1980).

We also find a higher-than-average incidence of deafness in premature infants, babies who weigh 5 pounds, 8 ounces or less at birth. Prematurity itself is generally not the cause of the problem but a symptom. The real cause—rubella, for example—may also stimulate an early birth. Or the real cause—a loss of oxygen or a brain injury—may be incurred during the premature birth process.

The Rh factor is another cause of deafness in newborns. Rh-positive and Rh-negative blood are incompatible. When a woman who is Rh-negative carries a child who is Rh-positive, the mother's system develops antibodies that can pass into the fetus and destroy the Rh-positive cells. The condition can be fatal. Those children who survive may have a variety of disorders, including deafness. If Rh incompatibility is diagnosed during pregnancy, it can be treated.

Meningitis

According to Vernon (1968), 8.1 percent of deaf children lose their hearing after birth as a result of meningitis, which involves a bacterial invasion that often occurs through the middle ear. Other estimates are lower: Ries (1973) reported a 4.9 percent statistic; Trybus (1985), 7.3 percent. Of the postnatal causes of deafness, meningitis is the most common. Although the incidence of deafness due to meningitis seemed to be decreasing in recent years—possibly due to greater use of antibiotics and chemotherapy—Trybus reported an upswing in the 1980s.

Otitis Media

Otitis media is an infection that causes fluid to accumulate in the middle ear, disturbing the conduction of sound. If the condition is chronic or untreated, it can create mild to moderate hearing losses. Otitis media is one of the most common childhood diseases—1 in 8 children is estimated to have six or more episodes before age 6. Children should have prompt treatment and careful preschool assessment for suspected hearing loss.

PREVALENCE

The number of children with hearing impairments is not large. Only 1 child in 1,000 is deaf, and only 3 to 4 children in 1,000 are severely hard of hearing (Office of Special Education, 1979). The Gallaudet Research Institute, which collects data on hearing impaired children, estimated in 1982–1983 that there were between 76,000 and 90,000 hearing impaired youngsters of school age in the United States (Trybus, 1985). These figures may understate the case slightly. Some children whose hearing losses are mild or correctable were not included in the data.

The vast majority of deaf students (92 percent) are in full- or part-time special education classes. About 45 percent of these youngsters are mainstreamed in regular classrooms for at least part of the day; about 55 percent are in self-contained classrooms.

These children come from different geographic areas and socioeconomic groups. In about 9 percent of their families, one or both parents are deaf (Rawlings & Jensema, 1977). Although the children of deaf parents more often than not have normal hearing, the incidence of deafness among them is significantly higher than that in the general population.

DEVELOPMENTAL PROFILES

Figure 6.5 shows the developmental profiles of three children: Sally, John, and Bill. All three children are 10 years old. Their profiles are similar in shape, but their intraindividual differences increase with the severity of hearing loss and age at the onset of deafness. Sally is hard of hearing; John is a postlingual deaf child; Bill is a prelingual deaf child.

The upper profile in the figure is Sally's, a child with a moderate hearing loss of 45 dB. Like John and Bill, Sally is of average height, weight, and motor coordination. She also shows average mental ability and social maturity for her age. Sally's speech development is slightly retarded: She has some difficulty in articulation and needs speech remediation. This language development problem has affected Sally's reading skills, but her achievement in arithmetic and spelling is at grade level. The only difference between Sally and her classmates is her slight difficulty in language development and reading.

When Sally was first fitted with a hearing aid, her special education program included instruction in its use. Now an itinerant speech-language pathologist gives her speech remediation, auditory training, and speech-reading lessons once a week.

Even though Sally's development and educational achievement are close to that of her peers, she does need some special attention from the classroom teacher. Her hearing aid makes her feel different from her friends, and this could become more of a problem when she is an adolescent. Also her hearing fluctuates somewhat when the weather changes or when she has a cold. Teachers who are not aware of this problem may think that she is deliberately ignoring them when in fact she simply cannot hear them.

The middle profile in Figure 6.5 shows the developmental pattern of John, who has a severe hearing loss. He was born with normal

FIGURE 6.5
Profiles of three
children with dif-
ferent degrees of
hearing loss

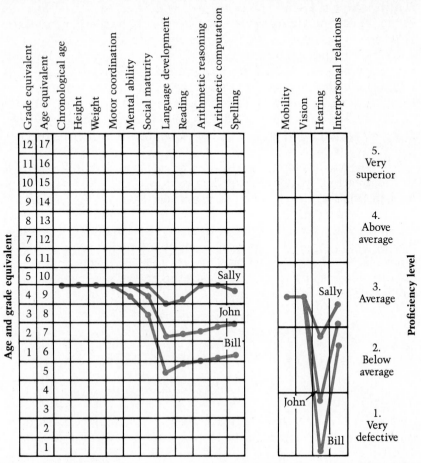

Sally = hard of hearing child; John = postlingual deaf child; Bill = prelingual deaf child

hearing but suffered a serious hearing loss in both ears at age 4. He is classified postlingually deaf. Although John is approximately normal in physical ability, intelligence, and social maturity, his speech and language have not developed normally. On an audiometer test he showed a hearing loss of 75 dB even after he was fitted with hearing aids. Fortunately, John learned to talk normally before his loss of hearing and had developed considerable language ability. This means he can learn through the auditory channel with the help of a hearing aid. Still his language development is at a second-grade level, as are his reading and other academic abilities. John's hearing loss has interfered considerably with his educational progress, but, with his hearing aids and speech habilitation and other special education services, he is moving ahead slowly.

John relies a good deal on his speech-reading skills. For this reason, and to utilize his hearing aids to best advantage, he sits in the front of the classroom, facing the teacher, not a window. John needs extra help in developing social skills and making friends.

The bottom profile in the figure is of a child with a profound hearing loss. Bill was born deaf. He has never heard a spoken word. A hearing aid might make him aware of environmental sounds but could not help him develop speech and language. Because of the severity of Bill's hearing loss—it tested at over 90 dB—he is in a self-contained special class. He would need intensive tutorial services if he were integrated in the regular classroom.

Bill's speech development is still very defective. Even though he has had instruction, he does not talk as well as a child of $2\frac{1}{2}$ years. His English language development is at a 5-year-old level. In reading and other academic subjects Bill is about four grades behind his agemates.

Because Bill's communication with his family and his peers is limited, so are his sources of information and his social experiences. He often reacts to social situations in ways that are characteristic of a much younger child. If he were placed in the regular classroom, he would need help making friends.

CHARACTERISTICS OF CHILDREN WITH HEARING IMPAIRMENTS

Cognitive Development

Because deaf children achieve significantly below grade level in school, particularly in the upper grades, there is a tendency to think of them as cognitively deficient. In fact their learning problems may actually stem from language difficulties, not cognitive disabilities (Rittenhouse, 1979, 1981).

There are two competing theories about the relationship between language and thought. One holds that language is more important than thought, that our ability to use language determines our level of cognitive development (Whorf, 1956). The other argues that cognition—the ability to form thoughts and have knowledge—is the more basic ability, that cognition provides the foundation for language (Piaget, 1970).

Because deaf children for many years were thought to have fundamental problems acquiring language skills, researchers studied them to prove one theory or the other. What they learned, however, is that deaf children are not necessarily deficient in language or in cognition. Although deaf children have difficulty acquiring, using, and reading the English language, they often are very skilled in the production and understanding of American Sign Language (ASL), a true language that meets the universal linguistic standards of spoken languages (Stokoe, 1960).

More important than the resolution of a theoretical argument is the understanding we've gained of the cognitive functioning of deaf children. Recent experimental studies have clarified the relationship between cognition in deaf children and the effects that language has on it. Rittenhouse (1981) found that deaf children are able to perform significantly better on cognitive tasks when language is specific and clear. In another experiment, Iran-Nejad, Ortony, and Rittenhouse (1981) found that deaf adolescents who were unable to understand figurative language at all did so with almost no difficulty once special instructions and task feedback were given them. In a third experiment, Rittenhouse, Morreau, and Iran-Nejad (1982) found that the ability to understand figurative language was strongly tied to the ability to solve cognitive problems. These findings suggest that deaf children do not have a special cognitive deficiency, that their poor cognitive and academic performance may actually stem from their difficulty with reading and writing the English language.

Language Development

For all children, cognition and language in dynamic interaction are probably the two most important factors in the learning process. The problems deaf children have with the English language, then, impede their learning across all subject areas.

We know that deaf adolescents have not mastered the grammatical properties or the syntax of the English language to the extent that much younger normal-hearing children have (Trybus, 1985; Quigley, Wilbur, Power, Montanelli, & Steinkamp, 1976). Why? Why do deaf youngsters have so much difficulty using language?

Many of these youngsters do not understand the concept of language. Brasel and Quigley (1977) highlighted the importance of that understanding in a study of deaf children. They found that children whose parents were also deaf did significantly better on standardized English tests than did children with normal-hearing parents. Why? Because the deaf parents used either ASL or manually coded English, not speech, to communicate with their children in their homes. Although sign language is grammatically and functionally different from English, it *is* a language system. And it offered these youngsters a foundation for later language learning.

Another problem is the complexity of syntax in the English language. In the early grades deaf children are exposed to simple syntactic structures (subject-verb, subject-verb-object) and concrete concept-familiar vocabulary. But beyond the third grade, educational materials become more complex. Sentences are longer and denote relationships; vocabulary is more abstract and often represents unfamiliar concepts. It is at this point that deaf and hard of hearing children begin to fall behind academically, losing more and more educational ground with each passing school year. The control these youngsters have over the linear syntax of the English language does not generalize or evolve into control over more complex structures. The result? These youngsters don't understand what they are reading and have difficulty translating what they want to communicate into writing.

Quigley (1978) showed how deaf children tend to apply a subject-verb-object pattern to sentences that seem to be linear in structure but that in fact demand a deeper or hierarchical search for the correct interpretation:

	Sentences	*Deaf interpretation*
Passive:	The boy was helped by the girl.	The boy helped the girl.
Relative:	The boy who kissed the girl ran away.	The girl ran away.
Complement:	The boy learned the ball broke the window.	The boy learned the ball.
Nominal:	The opening of the door surprised the cat.	The door surprised the cat.

The problems do not go away as these children get older. Look at these writing samples of two deaf youngsters, a ten-year-old and a fourteen-year-old:

> The boy see a dog. The woman more a basket. The will go to picnic. The family went to eat in the picnic. The boy see inside dog. The dog is sad. The boy is Love get dog. The family and see about a dog. The boy play a ball with dog. The woman work stove for meat. The girl help woman to picnic. The man is run. The man see airplane. The woman is drink. The boy go car. The girl give bread a dog. [10-year-old female, Performance IQ of 106, born deaf, Better Ear Average 100+ dB (ASA)]

> We will go to pinic, the woman package. A boy give to the dog eat the bread. The dog barked, the boy look at dog. the boy told a woman stop at car. He carried to the picnic dog sa. the mother told her sister put on the table. She park a car. He was fun. Her brothers played baskeball. the dog played with the boy. after with. He will go home at 6:45. his mother drive a car. [14-year-old male, Performance IQ of 104, born deaf, Better Ear Average of 90 dB (ASA)]. (Quigley & Kretschmer, 1982, p. 83)

Several recent studies found that once deaf children get their information by understanding complex sentences and figurative language or through inference, they begin to have academic problems (Locke, 1978; Lichtenstein, 1980). Even a knowledge of sign language—which helps these youngsters increase vocabulary and understand simple sen-

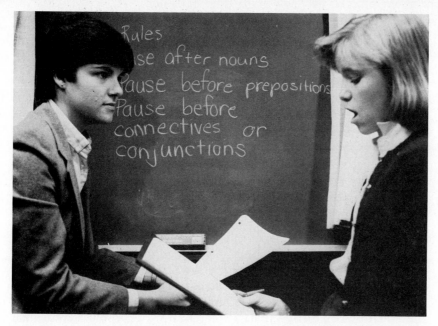

Deaf individuals have trouble understanding the concept of language, and many deaf adolescents have not mastered the grammar or syntax of the English language to the extent that much younger normal-hearing children have.
(Courtesy of the Clarke School for the Deaf)

tences—cannot help them read and write more complex English language. What they need to understand this more complex language code is an internalized speech code, something like the silent reading or repetition normal-hearing children use to learn new material.

Academic Achievement

With such serious problems with the English language, it's not surprising that deaf children, and to some extent hard of hearing children, have academic difficulties. The Center for Assessment and Demographic Studies at Gallaudet College annually administers the Stanford Achievement Test to hearing impaired children. Trybus (1985) reported the test results for thousands of deaf students enrolled in residential and day schools throughout the country. The eight-year-olds scored at a second-grade level in both reading and arithmetic computation. The seventeen-year-olds scored at a third-grade level in reading and a sixth-grade level in arithmetic. This difference in reading and arithmetic scores probably reflected the amount of language involved in each subject. And the underachievement in math probably stemmed from the more complex language necessary to read and solve complicated math problems.

Jensema (1975) analyzed achievement test scores of 6,873 children, ages 6 to 19, who had hearing handicaps severe enough to place them in special education programs. He found ten-year-olds doing arithmetic, and fourteen-year-olds reading, at a third-grade level. He noted:

> In a ten-year period from age 8 to age 18 the average hearing impaired student increases his vocabulary score only as much as the average normal hearing student does between the beginning of kindergarten and the latter part of the second grade. (p. 3)

Jensema also found that the age at which a hearing loss occurs and the degree of loss determine school achievement. Reading achievement was higher for those students who lost their hearing after age 3 than it was for those whose hearing loss happened earlier. And educational achievement suffered as the degree of loss increased.

Jensema's findings supported Quigley (1969), who had found a parallel relationship between degree of hearing loss and educational achievement among hard of hearing youngsters: The greater the loss, the worse the academic performance. But a straight-line relationship applied only to hard of hearing children. Once a loss measured in the severe or profound range (over 70 dB), academic performance dropped off markedly.

Trybus and Karchmer (1977) reported the progress in reading and arithmetic of 1,543 deaf students over a three-year period. They found nine-year-olds with reading comprehension at a second-grade level and twenty-year-olds testing at a fifth-grade level. This meant on average about a third of a year's progress every academic year in reading comprehension.

They also found a relationship between certain variables and the reading achievement of deaf students (Table 6.2). Girls and white students tended to do better than did boys and minority group members. The severity of reading problems increased with the degree of hearing loss and the presence of other handicapping conditions. Youngsters who started school at age 5 tended to do better than did those who started either earlier or later. And students whose parents were deaf showed better performance than did students with normal-hearing parents—a paradox we discuss on page 245.

Studies on the academic achievement of deaf students show little improvement in recent years. The vast majority of these youngsters perform significantly below grade level across all subject areas and ages. The reading skills of most deaf adults do not exceed a fourth- or fifth-grade level. Only about 10 percent of the deaf population has been able to achieve at grade level in academic subjects (including reading) throughout the school years.

Table 6.2

Relationships of Six Variables to Reading Achievement of
Deaf Students

Variable	Relationship with Reading Comprehension Level
Sex	Females score slightly higher than males.
Ethnic group	Whites score higher than Spanish-Americans or blacks.
Degree of hearing loss	Achievement level is inversely related to hearing loss.
Presence of additional handicapping conditions	Students with no additional handicaps score higher than those with one or more.
Age child began school	Children entering at age 5 score higher than those entering either earlier or later.
Parental deafness	Students with two deaf parents score higher than those with either one deaf parent or two normal-hearing parents.

SOURCE: "School Achievement Scores of Hearing Impaired Children: National Data on Achievement Status and Growth Patterns" by R. Trybus and M. Karchmer, 1977. *American Annals of the Deaf, 122,* p. 65.

Social and Personal Adjustment

Hearing impairment brings with it communication problems. And communication problems often lead to social and behavioral difficulties:

> Personality inventories have consistently shown that deaf children have more adjustment problems than hearing children. When deaf children without overt or serious problems have been studied, they have been found to exhibit characteristics of rigidity, egocentricity, absence of inner controls, impulsivity, and suggestibility. (Meadow, 1980, p. 97)

Think about the deaf boy on the playground who wants a turn on the swings. He can't simply say "I want my turn" or "It's my turn now." What does he do? He pulls another youngster out of the way. Obviously this kind of behavior is going to cause the child difficulties with interpersonal relationships. And when it's repeated over and over again, it can create serious social adaptation problems.

These problems intensify in adolescence. Davis (1981) reported the loneliness and rejection of children with hearing losses who were mainstreamed in a local school program. Most of the youngsters had

Good emotional and behavioral adjustment is one of the greatest challenges for deaf children who, along with their communication problems, often experience social difficulties.
(Freda Leinwand/Monkmeyer Press Photo Service)

just one or two close friends, and few were elected class officers or made cheerleaders or homecoming queens.

Of course adolescence is a difficult time for most young people. But for deaf youngsters it is especially so. They lack the communication skills so important for social functioning. Worse still, they are different:

> Hearing impairment, except in rare cases, affects the ease with which communication occurs, and communications form the basis for social interaction. The hearing impaired person's self-concept and confidence influence how rejection by others is perceived and handled. It is a rare hearing impaired child who does not perceive his social relations as inadequate and does not long for full acceptance by peers. If being different is the worst thing that can happen, then the next worst thing is associating with someone who is different. One cannot always

control the former, but one can control the latter. It is from this fact that the social problems encountered by hearing impaired adolescents often stem. (Davis, 1981, p. 73)

It's not surprising, then, that many deaf children want to be with children like themselves, with friends with whom they can feel socially accepted and comfortable. This wanting to cluster extends into adulthood. This is why in many large cities we find a culture of deaf people, a group of individuals who socialize with one another and intermarry.

The tendency to band together is not unusual. Most people—adults and children—feel most comfortable with people like themselves. This does not mean that deaf people do not want to be or cannot be integrated in society. But their access to hearing members of society is often limited by communication barriers. Nor does it mean that all deaf people are alike:

> In spite of consistencies in findings of personality studies, it would be a mistake to conclude that there is a single "deaf personality type." There is much diversity among deaf people, and it is related to education communication, and experience. (Meadow, 1980, p. 97)

IDENTIFICATION

The identification of deaf children or children who are severely hard of hearing is usually made before they enter school through public health screenings or pediatric examinations. Children with mild or moderate hearing impairments often go undiagnosed until academic performance indicates a problem. Even then an accurate diagnosis is not automatic. Many of the symptoms of a hearing loss are also indicative of other disorders. A child who stares blankly at the teacher may not be able to hear or may not understand what is being said or may be so emotionally disturbed that he or she blocks out communication.

Classroom Teacher's Role

How does the classroom teacher identify a child with a possible hearing loss so that he or she can be referred for comprehensive examination. Stephens, Blackhurst, and Magliocca (1982) suggested several things to watch for:

- *Does there appear to be a physical problem associated with the ears?* The student may complain of earaches, discomfort in the ear, or strange ringing or buzzing noises. You should note these complaints and so be alert for signs of discharge from the ears or excessively heavy waxy buildup in the ear canal. Frequent colds and sore throats are occasional indicators of infections that could impair the hearing.

- *Is there poor articulation of sounds, particularly omission of consonant sounds?* Students who articulate poorly may have a hearing problem that is preventing them from getting feedback about their vocal productions. Omission of consonant sounds from speech is often indicative of a high-frequency hearing loss.

- *When listening to radio, TV, or records, does the student run the volume up so high that others complain?* While it is much in vogue among young people today to turn up the amplification of rock music almost "to the threshold of pain," this determination will sometimes be difficult to make. Teachers can often get clues, however, by observing students listening to audio media that are not producing music, such as instructional records and sound-filmstrips.

- *Does the student cock the head or turn toward the speaker in an apparent effort to hear better?* Sometimes such movements are quite obvious and may even be accompanied by the "cupping" of the ear with the hand in an effort to direct the sound into the ear. In other cases, actions are much more subtle. Teachers often overlook such signs, interpreting them as symbols of increased inquisitiveness and interest.

- *Are there frequent requests to repeat what has just been said?* Although some students pick up the habit of saying, "Huh?" as a form of defense mechanism when they are unable to provide what they perceive as an acceptable response, such verbalizations may also indicate a hearing loss. When a particular student requests repeated instructions frequently, teachers should further investigate the possibility of hearing loss.

- *Is the student unresponsive or inattentive when spoken to in a normal voice?* Some students who do not follow directions or do not pay attention in class are frequently labeled as "trouble makers," which results in negative or punitive treatment. Often, however, these inappropriate school behaviors are actually caused by the inability of the student to hear. They can also be caused if the sounds that are heard appear to be "garbled."

- *Is the student reluctant to participate in oral activities?* Although reluctance to participate orally may be symptomatic of problems such as shyness, insecurity with respect to knowledge of subject matter, or fear of failure, it may also be due to a hearing loss. The child might not be able to hear the verbal interactions that occur in such activities. (pp. 43–44)

Audiological Testing

Measuring the extent of hearing loss and identifying the type of hearing impairment are important diagnostic steps. Although comprehensive audiological examinations are rarely done within public school systems, most schools do screen youngsters to find hearing problems, then refer them for comprehensive medical and audiological testing. Screening procedures in schools usually involve either individual or group tests of children in kindergarten through third grade and periodic examinations of older students.

A child's degree of hearing loss has major educational significance because it determines the type and amount of special training needed and the feasibility of hearing aids and amplifiers. Audiometric tests are one way to determine the level of hearing loss; other tests using carefully designed word lists also serve to estimate the ability of the child to hear spoken words (Brackett, 1981).

EDUCATIONAL ADAPTATIONS FOR CHILDREN WITH HEARING IMPAIRMENTS

Learning Environment

We know that 92 percent of hearing impaired children are receiving special education services (Trybus, 1985). Most youngsters with mild hearing losses are receiving these services in regular public schools—in regular classrooms, resource rooms, and special classes.

In the not-too-distant past, most children with severe and profound hearing losses were educated in state residential schools. Over the last two decades there has been a movement away from residential education. Although approximately 30 percent of deaf children are still learning in residential settings, most are in public or private day schools or classes (segregated classes held in regular public or private schools) (see Table 6.3). And of the 16,000 or so children who are in residential settings, more than 6,200 are day students. A large majority of deaf students in the United States today, then, are enrolled in programs that allow them to live at home.

Table 6.3
Enrollments in Schools and Classes for Hearing Impaired Students in the
United States, 1984

	Public Residential Schools	Private Residential Schools	Public Day Schools	Private Day Schools	Private Residential Classes	Public Day Classes (full-time)	(part-time &/or itin.)	Private Day Classes (full-time)	(part-time &/or itin.)	Facilities for Other Handicap(s)	TOTAL (793) Schs. & Classes
	70	8	39	20	1	435	161	3	3	53	
Total Enrollment	15,517	465	3,581	707	7	23,533	4,297	60	19	1,366	49,552
Male	8,749	258	1,943	379	2	12,363	2,344	22	9	795	26,864
Female	6,768	207	1,638	328	5	11,170	1,953	38	10	571	22,688
Residential	9,485	260	0	1	7	105	2	0	0	785	10,645
Day	6,032	205	3,581	706	0	23,428	4,295	60	19	581	38,907
Mainstreamed	299	24	321	101	7	6,637	2,046	11	0	211	9,657
Partially Mainstreamed	965	32	515	48	0	9,246	1,055	3	3	60	11,927

NOTE: Enrollments shown in this table do not include the more than 10,000 hearing impaired students who are multiply handicapped.

SOURCE: Excerpted from "Tabular Summary of Schools and Classes in the United States, October 1, 1984," April 1985, *American Annals of the Deaf, 130,* p. 132. Reprinted by permission of the American Annals of the Deaf.

Early Education

Although teachers of deaf students may disagree on methodology, they all agree on the importance of early education. Even a baby can learn about communication from the facial expressions, lip and head movements, gestures, touches, and vocal vibrations of those around. This is why it's so important for parents of deaf children to talk to them.

Many of the early education programs for deaf preschoolers focus on the parents. Some are counseling services, to help family members accept and adjust to the diagnosis of deafness and to understand the condition. Others train the parents to take an active role in teaching their children, carrying out developmental tasks in the home that are a part of the overall program. The extent of the parents' involvement is a function of their readiness to participate and the willingness of educators to include them.

Parent training and programs for very young deaf children are often provided in the home. They are also available in nursery schools and

Teachers of deaf students may disagree about methodology but they do all concur that early education is important and that parent training is a critical aspect of this education.
(Alan Carey/The Image Works)

day care centers and even some public schools. The primary objectives of these programs are

- to develop language and communication skills.
- to give deaf children opportunities to share, play, and take turns with other children.
- to help the children use their residual hearing (through auditory training or with hearing aids).
- to develop readiness in basic language, reading, and arithmetic.

   Intensive preschool training is a fundamental step in preparing deaf children for school. One very important part of that preparation for the children and their parents is learning to use sign language. Public Law 94–142 made preschool programs for hearing impaired youngsters mandatory at age 3. This means sign language interpreters are encouraged through this federal act to train these youngsters and their families in this critical communication skill.

Elementary School

The increasing popularity of mainstreaming, of integrating handicapped children in the regular classroom, has triggered controversy among teachers of deaf children. Obviously any academic program that attempts to mainstream children with hearing losses must provide trained supplementary personnel who are accessible to parents as well as children. The child's major responsibilities during the elementary years are to learn the basic skills: reading, arithmetic, and language. In most programs, despite best efforts, the deaf child seems to fall progressively behind the average child in achievement. The same is true of the hard of hearing child (Quigley, 1969), although with tutorial help, amplification, and preferential seating, the child's educational difficulty should be greatly reduced. It is difficult to totally mainstream severely handicapped deaf children because they are rarely able to compete at the same academic level as their peers. Many of these youngsters require time in resource rooms working individually or in small groups on auditory training, language, and speech training.

Secondary School

It is very difficult to mainstream deaf high school students successfully because they are often several grade levels behind their agemates in achievement. When they are mainstreamed, these students need sign language interpreters in the classroom as well as supplementary resource assistance.

Many school administrators in the field of deaf education believe state residential schools are the most viable setting in which to offer secondary education. With a much larger student enrollment than any single district could expect to have and with a greater degree of homogeneity among students, residential schools can design specialized programs that balance traditional academics and vocational and technical training. There are no available data on the placement of deaf high school students, but the rationale for centralized educational services makes sense. The average high school may have just a handful of deaf students. It's financially impossible for that school to maintain a teacher for every subject area. What happens? The special education teacher teaches everything, from language to biology. But English should be taught by an English specialist, and biology should be taught by a science specialist. This is feasible in special schools because of their enrollment.

Postsecondary Programs

In the mid-1960s, surveys of the vocational status of deaf adults revealed some disturbing facts. The unemployment rate among the population was four times greater than that of normal-hearing adults, and the level of employment was primarily fixed at unskilled or semi-skilled positions (for example, see Moores, 1969).

At about the same time, an effort to locate all hearing impaired individuals who had enrolled in or graduated from regular colleges and universities was under way. It yielded just 653 people, only 133 of them graduates who were prelingually deaf (Quigley, Jenne, & Phillips, 1968). Clearly one factor affecting the kinds of jobs deaf adults were finding was their limited educational opportunities.

Over the last twenty years things have begun to change. In that time we've developed an increasing number of vocational programs for young adults who are deaf. One major development was the establishment of the National Technical Institute for the Deaf in Rochester, New York, in 1967. The institute, which is supported by the federal government, was founded to provide technical and vocational training for deaf adolescents and adults.

In 1968 the federal government funded postsecondary vocational programs in three community colleges located in New Orleans, Seattle, and St. Paul. The schools offered training to a small group (sixty-five to a hundred) of hearing impaired young adults in the graphic arts, metal working, welding, automobile repair, food services, machine tool processing, and electronics (Craig, Craig, & Barrows, 1970). Moores, Fisher, and Harlow (1974), in an evaluation of the programs, found positive results. For example, three-quarters of the graduates were able to find positions in technical, trade, and commercial industries. But the study did not reveal any major breakthroughs into new job areas. Instead students tended to cluster in certain occupations: general office work for female students, printing for male students.

New job opportunities would come with educational opportunities. One academic alternative for deaf students is Gallaudet College in Washington, D.C., the only college in the world devoted to the liberal arts education of deaf students. The school was established by Congress in 1864 and is still supported by the federal government. It is an accredited four-year liberal arts college, and now includes a graduate school for both normal-hearing and deaf students. Gallaudet also operates the Kendall demonstration Elementary School and the Model Secondary School for the Deaf.

With the full implementation of Public Law 94–142, many state universities now have deaf and hard of hearing students on their campuses. They provide interpreting and note-taking services for these students. The impact of these new educational opportunities is yet to be determined. Much depends on the quality of earlier education:

It is doubtful that any postsecondary program, no matter how exemplary, can overcome the inadequate education most deaf individuals receive in the early intervention, elementary, and secondary years, despite improvements. Until education of the deaf, in general, begins to provide students with basic skills and helps them to develop to the limits of their potential, the economic position of deaf adults will continue to be below that which they are capable of obtaining. (Moores, 1982, p. 315)

Curriculum Content

We know that children with severe hearing impairments have serious academic problems. Special education programs for these youngsters have focused on communication and language skills in the hope that these skills would allow them to master the regular curriculum. For children with mild hearing handicaps, the expectation seems reasonable. With speech and language therapy these children are usually able to perform at grade level.

Over the past few years, however, it's become increasingly obvious that the more serious the hearing loss, the more likely that specific changes must be made in the academic content itself. Quigley and Kretschmer (1982) pointed out that the normal-hearing child learns to read by breaking the code of the word symbol system, by linking the symbols to already-learned language concepts that the child has mastered through speech. The deaf child has no speech-language base on which to build and has serious trouble with the syntactic structure of language. One of the major content adaptations for deaf children then, is teaching linguistic structure directly.

A popular structural linguistic system was developed at the Rhode Island School for the Deaf (Blackwell, Engen, Fischgrund, & Zarcadoolis, 1978). The system presents five basic sentence patterns:

- Noun phrase + verb (The baby cries.)
- Noun phrase + verb + noun phrase (The baby drinks milk.)
- Noun phrase + linking verb + adjective (The baby is cute.)
- Noun phrase + linking verb + noun phrase (The baby is a boy.)
- Noun phrase + linking verb + adverbial phrase (The baby is in the crib.)

All other syntactic patterns are taught as transformations of the five basic patterns.

Although the development of a linguistic-based instructional program for deaf children is a major step forward, problems remain. Because they start with a noun phrase, it's easy to see how deaf students can be baffled by a sentence like "Before the boy could turn around, the dog was upon him." They recognize all the individual words, but the way they go together makes the sentence incomprehensible.

FIGURE 6.6
Example from a
basal reading series
for deaf students

Mom   rolled   the dough.
The boys   looked for   the cookie pans.

21

The girl   helped   Mom   with the dough.
The boys   looked for   a jar of red jam.

22

The girl   poured   some red jam
on the cookies   with a spoon

23

Mom   waited   near the stove.
The boys   smelled   the cookies.
The girl   poured   some milk.

24

NOTE: *Reading Milestones* is used with deaf children in a manner consistent with traditional reading instructional practices. Key vocabulary words are pre-taught, often as part of a natural experience such as a simulation activity or field trip. Next, the story is read silently and then as a group in a "round-robin" fashion. In the group reading activity, the stories are signed by the children. As can be seen in this figure, longer sentences are introduced in a "chunking" or phrase format, and children are taught to group words as normal-hearing readers do in a natural way.

SOURCE: *Reading Milestones,* Level 3, DorMac Publishers, Beaverton, OR, pp. 21, 22, 23, 24. Reprinted by permission.

Mahoney and Weller (1980) described an ecological approach to language intervention in which language training is done in everyday social situations. Mealtime, bedtime, and bathing are opportunities for language interaction and communication. Cues the youngster picks up from the environmental context help the child master the language. The method redefines the role of language therapists and speech pathologists: They act, not as the primary deliverers of language instruction, but as consultants to those who are the primary language models—parents, teachers, and others who have close constant contact with the child.

Quigley and King (1981) developed a reading series for deaf students called *Reading Milestones*. They controlled the language of the readers by applying the results of research with deaf students (Quigley, 1976). There are eight levels of reading difficulty arranged in sequence. A child who has mastered them all should be able to begin reading traditional basal texts at a fourth-grade level. *Reading Milestones* is the most widely used reading series for deaf children (LaSasso, 1985). Figure 6.6 illustrates a page from this basal reading series.

Quigley and Rittenhouse are working on a second set of readers, modeled after *Reading Milestones*, that will control for figurative language and inferential meaning. The series, tentatively entitled *The Reading Bridge,* will give students the skill to read more difficult traditional texts. It is expected to be ready by the fall of 1987.

Communication Skills and Methods

Educators in this country agree that it is to the deaf child's advantage to learn to read and write the English language. But they hold sharply differing opinions on the form language instruction should take and the communication methods deaf children should use.

One group focuses on communicating with the normal-hearing society through speech and speech reading (lip reading). This method in its purest form is called the oral method because of its extensive use of auditory and speech-reading training.

The second group emphasizes the use of sign language. Its objective: early mastery of language and a usable communication system at least with other deaf individuals. The manual method includes the language of signs—a language system consisting of formalized movements of the hands or arms to express thoughts—and finger spelling, a kind of spelling in the air using the manual alphabet (see Figure 6.7). In communicating manually, deaf people generally use the two modes together, expressing some words through the language of signs and finger-spelling others.

This conflict between methods and objectives is over two centuries old and began in Europe with the establishment of two schools for deaf children, one in Scotland and one in France. The school in Scot-

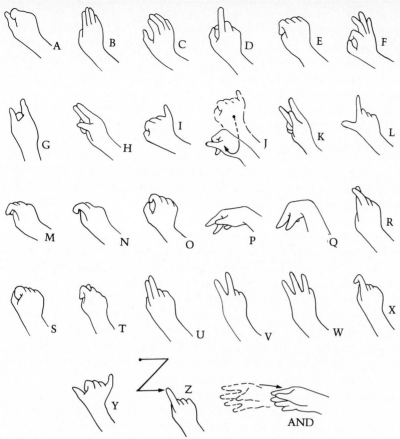

FIGURE 6.7
American Manual
Alphabet (as seen
by the finger
speller)

SOURCE: *Say It with Hands* (p. 1) by L. Fant, Jr., 1964. Washington, DC: Gallaudet College Centennial Fund Commission. Reproduced with permission.

land, which was founded by Thomas Braidwood, stressed the oral method; the school in France, established by the Abbé de l'Epée, stressed the manual method.

Thomas Gallaudet worked to start a program for deaf children in the United States. He visited the Braidwood school to find out more about the oral method, but the Braidwood family refused to share their methods with him. Disappointed and angry, Gallaudet went across the English Channel to visit Abbé Sicard, de l'Epée's successor, who was more forthcoming. Gallaudet came home to establish a school in Hartford, Connecticut, stressing manual communication. With him he brought Laurence Clerc, a deaf student of de l'Epée, who became America's first teacher of deaf children.

The early development of the oral method in the United States was fostered by a man who is generally known for his invention of the telephone but who actually spent most of his life working with deaf individuals. Alexander Graham Bell opened up new channels for teaching speech to deaf people. His method of visible speech helped children understand the placement of the speech organs in producing speech. His invention of the telephone led to the development and use of hearing aids and to the use of amplified sound to teach speech to children with severely defective hearing.

Bell and Gallaudet became bitter rivals, each aggressively and brilliantly defending his own method. And educators are still taking sides in the battle.

From the original oral and manual approaches have evolved several communication methods: the oral-aural method, the Rochester method, the auditory method, cued speech, sign languages, and the total communication method. Their effectiveness depends in part on the severity of the hearing impairment and the availability of early intervention.

Oral-Aural Method. The oral-aural approach uses residual hearing through amplified sound, speech reading, and speech to develop communication skills. Oral-aural programs do not use or encourage the use of sign languages or finger spelling, believing that manual communication inhibits the child's learning of language and oral skills and impedes the child's adjustment to the normal-hearing world.

One important skill in the oral-aural method is speech reading (lip reading)—the visual interpretation of spoken communication. It is the means by which deaf people receive communication from those who can hear. Because few normal-hearing people take the trouble to learn a complex system of manual communication, deaf individuals who want to keep in meaningful contact with the hearing world must learn to speech-read.

There are special problems in learning this unusual skill. Many sounds in the English language have a particular visual pattern on the face. For example, the *n* sound looks very different from the *k* sound. But other sounds are *homophones*—they are articulated in similar ways and look the same on the lips and face. Half of the words in the English language have some other word or words homophonous to them, which is one reason speech reading is so difficult.

A number of approaches are used to teach youngsters speech reading. When the child is young, the teacher or the parent talks to him or her in whole sentences. At first the child may not pick up any clues, but as the teacher or parent repeats the same expression over and over again in the same relationship to something that the child is experiencing—an object, an action, a feeling—the child begins to get an idea of what is being said. At a later stage these vague whole impressions are converted into lessons that emphasize details and exercises that help the child discriminate between different words and sounds. Eventually, the special education teacher uses speech reading as a method to present lessons in school.

We have little data to suggest how best to carry out the sequence of instruction on speech reading or to explain why some youngsters are

The manual method, which involves signing and finger spelling, is one of several major approaches developed for teaching hearing impaired individuals to communicate.
(© Betty Medsger 1977)

especially good at it while others are not. Intelligence and other factors often relevant to successful learning do not seem related to success in speech reading. We need careful research and evaluation to systematically improve instruction in this skill, a necessary bridge to the hearing world (Farwell, 1976).

Rochester Method.   The Rochester method was developed at the Rochester School in Rochester, New York, in 1878. It combines the oral method and finger spelling. Information is received through speech reading, amplification, and finger spelling; it is returned through finger spelling and speech. The teacher uses the manual alphabet to spell every word as it is spoken. The method encourages students to read and write the alphabet and words.

The Rochester method is similar to neo-oralism, an approach used in the Soviet Union to teach very young hearing impaired children.

Auditory Method.   The auditory method makes extensive use of sound amplification to develop listening and speech skills. It involves auditory training—teaching the child to listen to sounds and to discriminate between different sounds. Although the method is used widely with mildly and moderately impaired school-age youngsters, it's been most effective, particularly for children with a severe impairment, with preschoolers. Parents are an important part of the early training process, and one of the goals of hearing specialists is to instruct them and include them in the training.

The auditory method is also called the acoustic method, the acoupedic method, the unisensory method, and the aural method. Calvert and Silverman (1975), who labeled it the auditory global method, claimed the approach makes the maximum use of residual hearing. They also recommended that it be used with amplification as early as possible.

Cued Speech.   Cued speech was developed by Orin Cornett at Gallaudet College and introduced in 1967. It is a system of hand cues placed around the mouth and larynx that represent ambiguous phonetic elements of speech, with the hand shapes representing the consonant sounds and the hand positions representing the vowel sounds (see Figure 6.8). The hand cues help clarify the homophonous sounds that make speech reading so difficult.

Cued speech is a relatively new approach, and researchers have not yet compared its effectiveness to that of other teaching methods. Two studies of the speech-reading progress of deaf children who have been taught in the method, however, do show promise (Ling & Clarke, 1975; Clarke & Ling, 1976). With increased interest in an internalized speech-coding system for deaf children, cued speech may well become a component of speech and language instruction.

Sign Languages.   There are several manual methods of communication: American Sign Language, Pidgin Sign English, Seeing Essential English, and Signing Exact English. Of these, American Sign Language (ASL) is the only one considered to be a legitimate language (Bellugi & Klima, 1972).

Like all languages, ASL has its own grammar and syntax, both very different from English grammar and syntax.[1] It is this difference that has created a controversy over the use of ASL with deaf students. Many educators feel ASL inhibits the acquisition of English. Others, principally deaf teachers of deaf children and researchers, believe it is (or should be) the native language of deaf children, that it should be learned before English, a deaf child's second language.

We can see the grammatical differences between the two languages by looking at basic sentence structure:

English: The cow jumped over the moon.

ASL: Moon cow jump over.

---

1. Actually ASL is distinct from English in several dimensions. Space here limits our discussion, however.

Chart I: Cues for Vowel Sounds

	Side*	Throat	Chin	Mouth
Open	ah (father, got)	a (that)	aw (dog)	
Flattened-relaxed	u (but)	i (is)	e (get)	ee (see)
Rounded	oe (home)	oo (book)	ue (blue)	ur (her)

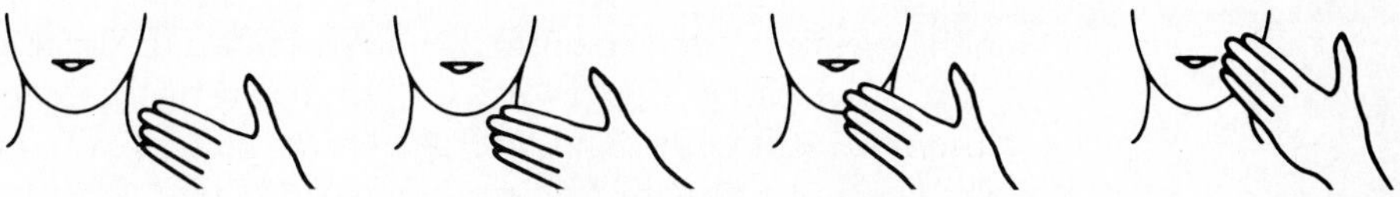

Chart II: Diphthongs

ie (my)	ou (cow)	ae (pay)	oi (boy)

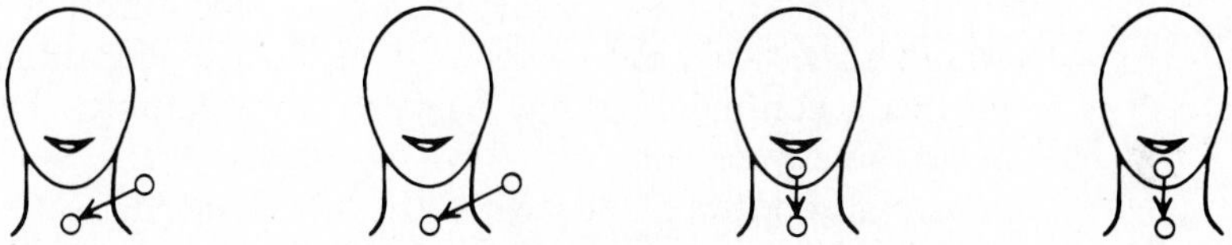

Chart III: Cues for Consonant Sounds

t†	h	d	ng	l	k	b	g
m	s	p	y	sh	v	n	j
f	r	zh	ch	w	dh‡	wh	th
					z		

* The side position is also used for a consonant without a following vowel.
†This hand shape is also used for a vowel without a preceding consonant.
‡dh was formerly written tH

FIGURE 6.8
Cued speech:
English

Notice that the object (*moon*) in the ASL sentence comes before the subject (*cow*), that the function words (the *the*s) are not used, and that the past tense inflection (-ed) is not added to the verb.

To communicate the ASL sentence, a signer would sign *moon* with one hand and leave the sign in space. *Cow* would be signed with the other hand. Then *jump* would be formed and would move over the *moon* sign. In the other manual systems, the sentence would be signed word by word (including the function words and the past tense inflective -ed) in the English syntactic pattern. Three signs are needed to produce the ASL sentence; seven signs are needed to produce the English sentence.

Pidgin Sign English (PSE), Seeing Essential English (SEE I), and Signing Exact English (SEE II) are manually coded systems that preserve the syntactic patterns of English. Of the three, PSE comes closest to ASL: It uses the same signs and occasionally omits English function words and inflections.

SEE I and SEE II are very much alike. Both systems maintain strict English structural patterns. Both systems use a one word–one sign format. And both systems use the "two out of three" rule to determine whether words should have the same or different signs.

The "two out of three" rule looks at three word elements: spelling, pronunciation, and meaning. If at least two of these elements are the same, the same sign is used; if at least two of these elements are different, different signs are used. For example, a *sock* is something you wear or a punch. The meanings are different but because the words are spelled and pronounced the same way, only one sign is used for both meanings. For the word *wind* (a gust of air, to rotate), both meanings and pronunciations are different, so two different signs are used. Although the "two out of three" rule reduces the number of signs, it can create confusion. What happens, for example, if someone signs "Please give me a sock"?

The major difference between the SEE I and SEE II systems is in the way each treats compound words (*babysit, cowboy*). SEE I borrows signs from ASL; SEE II treats each part of the word (*baby, sit*) separately.

Total Communication Method.   The total communication method, which is sometimes called the simultaneous or combined method, combines finger spelling, signs (one of the several signed English systems), speech reading, speech, and auditory amplification. The Conference of Executives of American Schools for the Deaf (1976) defined total communication as "a philosophy requiring the incorporation of appropriate aural, manual, and oral modes of communication in order to insure effective communication with and among hearing impaired persons" (p. 358).

Jordan, Gustason, and Rosen (1979) studied the number of classes that use the different methods of communication. They combined the oral and aural (auditory) methods and included cued speech. They found that total communication is the most common method and is used almost exclusively at the high school level, and that the oral-aural method is the next most common. The two procedures together were used by over 90 percent of the schools surveyed.

Research on Communication Approaches

Supporters of the oral method claim that children who are allowed to communicate with signs do not make the necessary effort to learn speech. Supporters of the manual method claim that language is retarded in children who are not allowed to sign or finger-spell and that the process of learning language through speech delays their language development. Both groups have been able to show individual examples of successful performance. But how do the systems compare? Do most hearing handicapped children do better using one or the other approach?

Studies over the last two decades have given us some very definite answers, answers that have surprised many special educators and forced them to rethink their methods for teaching deaf youngsters. For example, Goldin-Meadow and Feldman (1975) found that the oral method—the traditional model for teaching young deaf children throughout the 1950s and 1960s—had limited success. They studied the language development of five children from age 1½ who had had oral training with other deaf youngsters:

> By the end of the study, when the children ranged from thirty-two to fifty-four months, two produced no intelligible spoken words and one child produced fewer than five words. The other two children could speak and lip read single words in constrained settings such as pointing to correct items or naming items on flash cards. There was no transfer observed in speech and lip reading to general activities of daily living. (Moores & Moores, 1980, p. 54)

This was not the first study to raise questions about the effectiveness of the oral method. The discovery that the deaf children of deaf parents were adapting better academically and socially than were the deaf children of normal-hearing parents led many observers to conclude that the early intensive use of manual communication in the home has a positive impact on academic and social performance (Brasel & Quigley, 1977; Meadow, 1968; Vernon & Koh, 1971).

Other studies found a combination of methods effective. Quigley (1969) conducted a five-year study on the Rochester method (the combination of speech and finger spelling) and made several conclusions:

- Finger spelling and good oral techniques, together, improve language achievement.
- Learning finger spelling is not detrimental to the acquisition of oral skills.
- Finger spelling is more effective with younger rather than older children.
- Finger spelling is one of a number of useful tools for teaching deaf children.

In another study, Moores, Weiss, and Goodwin (1978) found that deaf children using the combined methods functioned in the normal range intellectually, had age-appropriate prereading skills, and were able to communicate effectively using speech and a manually coded English sign system.[2] They also found, however, that the youngsters' speech was difficult to understand and that the children had problems with grammatical structure. Still their data clearly showed that manual communication does not impede the development of speech and that communication need not be limited to one channel.

Moores and Moores (1980) summed up the various findings:

> Both in the classroom and in less formal settings, the trend seems to be toward the multisensory model; auditory training, manual communication, and speech training are being introduced at early ages and are used in coordination with one another. . . . The child is conceived of as a social being with complex patterns of active interactions relative to individuals and his environment. (pp. 59–60)

The Language Issue.   For most of this century the focus of educational research and practice with deaf children has been on language—its acquisition and use. For most of this time *language* was used synonymously for *English*. Only in the last fifteen years have researchers begun to clarify what we mean by "language in deaf children" (Quigley & Kretschmer, 1982).

Once again two competing theories have emerged. There are those who believe that English is the native language of America's deaf children. They feel that ASL is a limited system of communication, one that evolved in the homes of deaf parents with deaf children. Then there are those who believe that English is the second language of deaf children in this country, that ASL is actually their native language (Stokoe, 1960).

The first of these theoretical perspectives has guided the field of deaf education throughout most of its history. But in recent years its basic precepts have been called into question. Studies show us that deaf children schooled in traditional ways are having as much difficulty with the English language today as they were having in the early 1900s. It may be time, then, to make some changes.

One change that's been suggested is to teach deaf children English as a second language, in the same way that any second language is taught—in the child's native tongue. This would mean using ASL in the classroom for all subjects, in place of or with an English-based sign system. In fact that's exactly what's being done in some schools around the country. At the Pennsylvania School for the Deaf in Philadelphia, for example, elementary-age children are being taught in ASL and manually coded English.

This kind of change is not an easy one to implement. First, there are the practical considerations. Teachers cannot teach in a language

---

2. Because the teachers spoke in English, with English syntax, they signed with English syntactic patterns.

they do not know. Before any large-scale attempt to teach in ASL is made, then, we must train teachers in the use of the language—a process that takes both time and money. Second, there are strong philosophical arguments against the inclusion of ASL in the educational process. To counter them, there must be more research and data available to show that this change would benefit deaf students.

Directions for the Future.   Stokoe's (1960) examination of American Sign Language spurred hundreds of researchers to study all aspects of this manual language. They've analyzed and hypothesized about its grammar, its usage, even its psychology. In the process we've learned that sign language can help deaf youngsters remember words and concepts (Bellugi, Klima, & Siple, 1974). They use the three elements of the language—hand shape, location, and movement—as cognitive markers, much like hearing youngsters use "talking to themselves" to remember things.

Does this mean we've found an answer to the academic difficulties of deaf students? Unhappily no. Although sign language can help these youngsters remember words and process simple sentences, it is not a very effective way for processing complicated syntactic patterns (Lichtenstein, 1980; Locke, 1978). "The boy kissed the girl" is a simple sentence that can be processed efficiently through sign language. "The boy kissed the girl and ran" is more complex. We would have to freeze the subject (*boy*) in time until the verb acts on the direct object (*girl*).

What the students may need is an internalized speech-coding system like the system normal-hearing youngsters use (see page 236). Without it, it is almost impossible for deaf youngsters to read or write at or above levels of literacy.

The limitations of sign language may actually suggest an approach to teaching deaf children that is integrative. We would begin as early as possible with American Sign Language. Although structurally and grammatically different from English, ASL offers several plusses: It appears to be the easiest form of communication for deaf youngsters to learn; it has proved to give these youngsters an academic and social advantage when they reach school age; it is a language on which they can draw in learning English; and it shares certain syntactic structures with English. As children become more competent with this language, we would begin to introduce more complex structures, including English patterns. At the same time, we would teach the youngsters to use an internalized speech-coding system—say cued speech or one of the oral methods already used in programs for deaf children. The rate and level of instruction would depend on each child's readiness to learn.

We've learned so much about the education of deaf children in the last seventy-five years. We've used different methodologies, we've upgraded teaching standards, we've developed special materials, we've modified classrooms acoustically, we've conducted extensive research, we've refined amplification systems, and we've spent vast amounts of money to teach deaf youngsters to read and write the English language.

Yet these students still graduate from high school far behind grade level and their normal-hearing peers. Changes must be made so that every deaf child has the opportunity to achieve to his or her potential.

The Educational Team

The problems faced by a child with a significant hearing loss are so varied that no single professional can deal with them all. Instead the child's needs demand a team of professionals to produce a comprehensive program of education and therapy. A clinical audiologist must make a careful assessment of the hearing loss, its physical and functional dimensions; a speech therapist must help the child reach his or her potential in speech reading and production; and a special education teacher trained to work with deaf children must develop an individualized education program and a sequence of lessons to help regular educators understand the special needs of the child.

And this list is not exhaustive. The education of deaf children is changing. With the recognition that instruction must adapt to their needs, and that their needs appear to include some form of manual interpretation, we find interpreters in classrooms and teachers trained, not only in special education, but in subject areas as well.

One critical segment of the educational team is not professional at all. Over 50 percent of the families of deaf children use sign language in the home (Trybus, 1985). In over 80 percent of these families parents and siblings are normal-hearing (Rawlings & Jensema, 1977). In addition, family members are providing important reinforcement and even training throughout the critical preschool years.

USES OF TECHNOLOGY

Use of Hearing Aids

Perhaps the single most important development in this century to help hearing impaired individuals is the electronic hearing aid. Wier (1980) explained how a hearing aid works:

> All modern hearing aids have three basic components: a microphone, an amplifier, and a receiver. The microphone and receiver transduce energy from one point to another. Thus the tiny microphone on the hearing aid converts acoustic energy into electrical energy (like a telephone mouthpiece does), while the receiver performs the reverse conversion, transforming the electrical energy back into acoustical energy (like a telephone earpiece does).

Between these two components is the amplifier, a device that increases the signal level between the input and the output.

FIGURE 6.9
Contemporary
hearing aids

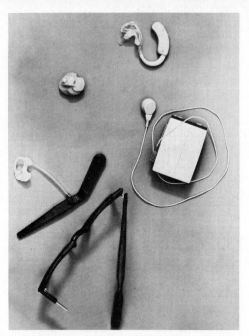

SOURCE: Courtesy of Dr. W. Wilson, University of Washington Child Development and Mental Retardation Center.

Figure 6.9 shows a number of hearing aids that are currently in use. They are inserted directly into the ear canal, worn in a shirt pocket, built into eyeglass frames, or placed on the bone directly behind the ear. An audiological analysis determines the type of aid best suited to an individual's needs. Also a factor is the wearer's concern about appearance.

The development of the transistor has transformed hearing aids from heavy, cumbersome units to more portable devices. And directional microphones have cut down on background noise, amplifying only those sounds coming from directly in front of the listener (Northern & Downs, 1978).

Despite the advantages of hearing aids, they have certain limitations. They are most effective for individuals with conductive hearing losses. And they can be tiring to use. Like all mechanical devices, hearing aids occasionally break down or misfunction. Just because a child is wearing a hearing aid does not mean that it is operating properly. Studies of hearing aids in school settings reveal that more than half of them operate poorly or not at all (Kemker, McConnell, Logan, & Green, 1979). Usually the problem is a weak battery, but other difficulties crop up too. This means the teacher should carefully monitor the child to be sure he or she is getting full use of the device.

Hearing aids are most effective when used in conjunction with an intense systematic education program taught by teachers who have been trained to work with deaf students. These teachers may have to combine their special knowledge with that of audiologists and speech-language pathologists to design individualized programs for their students (Martin, 1981).

Microcomputers

The microcomputer is now a common sight in classrooms for deaf students. Since a computer responds to manipulative touch and usually has no auditory requirements, hearing impaired students are not handicapped in working with this technology (Stepp, 1982). Although computers are basically visual, in order to interact effectively with the device a person must be able to read or at least to interpret symbols. Especially when appropriate software is utilized, this has not caused a problem for the majority of hearing impaired students, and students with varied skill levels have successfully been taught to use a microcomputer.

Some of the benefits of computer instruction for hearing impaired students include:

- Hearing impaired students (especially at the secondary level) are often overly dependent on individual instruction. This may place conflicting demands on the teacher who must continue to work with the rest of the class as well. Computer instruction provides a way for students to take more responsibility for their own learning and allows them greater independence.
- Computer usage and especially the learning of programming provide a way for hearing impaired students to demonstrate a commitment to learning and supply an incentive that has often been missing from other forms of instruction. This is especially true when programming—a form of "teaching the computer"—is involved. One study (Brady & Dickson, 1983) found that motivation for improving writing skills increased.
- The use of computer games as a behavior reinforcer has been found to be an effective way of helping hearing impaired students as well as other handicapped and non-handicapped students achieve academic goals.
- Computer usage requires active participation on the student's part and continuous use of an interactive communicative format.

Garvey (1982) describes a high school program for hearing impaired students that made extensive use of computer instruction. More than 300 programs were developed or adapted and keyed specifically to the language level of each learner, for math, science, health, home economics, English, social studies and career exploration instruction. This lesson development was a team effort between the classroom staff and a facilitator who provided ideas and expertise for computer applications.

An innovative program developed for junior and senior high school students (Brady & Dickson, 1983) focused on improving referential communication skills in a cooperative situation. One student (the sender) was given the task of describing one of a number of displayed visual foils that a second student was required to identify (a process similar to charades or a quiz game). In the study a hearing impaired student was paired with a nonhandicapped peer, which added an important social component to the experience. The program was tested on a heterogenous group of hearing impaired students with varied writing skills. In all but one case, the students were able to understand the task and were able to complete it. The interaction provided a longer period of communication than that which naturally occurred in the school environment, and students quickly improved their descriptions based on the peer feedback.

Rose and Waldron (1984) surveyed 224 programs for deaf youngsters about the use of instructional technology in the classroom. Over half (51 percent) reported the use of microcomputers. Although the data showed that most students had equipment available to them for between one and four hours a week, few of the programs had attempted to adapt the machinery to the students' needs:

- Very few programs had amplified their equipment for the students' use.
- Only 10 percent of the programs were using user-friendly languages.

A constant complaint among teachers of hearing impaired students is the scarcity of certain kinds of software. Although math programs are readily available, language and reading software is needed. DorMac, a company that publishes many materials designed specifically for deaf children, has begun to transfer these materials to software programs.[3] Interactive programs are also being developed to teach reading, language, and other subjects to deaf students.

Because the microcomputer is a highly visual medium for the presentation of information it holds special promise for deaf and severely hard of hearing students. But the effectiveness of the tool is going to depend on the software being developed. That material must be available at a level of language that deaf students can understand.

Other Technological Advances

A major advance in technology for deaf children and adults is the teletypewriter and printer (TTY), a device developed by a deaf orthodontist in 1964. The machine allows deaf individuals to communicate using a typewriter that transforms typed messages into electrical signals, then retranslates them into print at the other end of a phone

---

3. The company is located in Beaverton, Oregon.

connector. To make a TTY call, the individual places an ordinary telephone receiver on a coupler modem or interface between the typewriter and the telephone. The acoustic coupler transforms the electrical signals into two sounds at different frequencies that are then transmitted over the telephone and converted back into printed letters on the receiving end (Levitt, Pickett, & Houde, 1980). More sophisticated units that have computer capacity are now available, and research is under way to determine how the TTY can be used to improve social language skills (Rittenhouse, 1985). A series of similar systems have been generated over the last two decades. Generally they are called telecommunication devices for the deaf (TDD).

There are currently over 50,000 stations that send, receive, and print messages on TDD systems. Although costs are high—for the machines and the messages—the systems provide a very effective way for deaf people to communicate across long distances (Schein & Hamilton, 1980).

We are also seeing major technological advances in medicine. One exciting breakthrough is the cochlear implant. The implant is an electronic device that stimulates those nerves in the cochlea or inner ear that are not impaired. The implant system—a microphone, sound processor, transmitter, receiver, and one or more electrodes—converts sound into electrical signals.

Although the cochlear implant has helped some deaf children and adults to hear sounds, it has by no means made those sounds intelligible. According to Dr. William House (the physician who pioneered the cochlear implant), it "sounds like a radio that isn't quite tuned in." Users can make gross discriminations between sounds—distinguishing between a strange and a familiar voice, for example—but cannot understand what is being said.

The accessibility of films and television for deaf individuals has been increased through caption programs. Captioned Films for the Deaf is a federal program that began in 1958 to provide deaf students with a visual narration of educational films, to improve and enrich their curriculum. What began as a film loan service has expanded many times over. Today the program provides equipment for use in homes and schools, contracts for the development of educational media for deaf youngsters, and trains personnel in the use of educational technology. In addition, recent support from the U.S. Department of Education has allowed for extensive captioning and signing on selected television programs. This means deaf individuals can keep current with news or simply enjoy a drama or entertainment program.

MULTIPLY HANDICAPPED CHILDREN

About a fourth of children with hearing losses have other handicaps too. One estimate suggests that about 20 percent of deaf students are multiply handicapped; other estimates range as high as 30 to 50 percent (Craig & Craig, 1980). There are several reasons why these estimates vary so widely. First, the diagnosis of a second handicap is often informal. Second, hyperactivity and other behaviors attributed to a child's deafness often stem from a neurological injury or some other problem. Third, vague definitions of certain conditions mean variations in reporting procedures. Behavior that one school system recognizes as an emotional disturbance another school system may not. Craig and Craig (1980) found that the largest number of deaf youngsters who have other handicaps are either deaf and mentally retarded or deaf and learning disabled.

Vernon (1969) pointed out that several etiologies of hearing loss are linked to other disabling conditions. Significant among these is blood incompatibility between mother and child: An estimated 70 percent of these children have a major disability in addition to deafness. Maternal rubella during the early stages of pregnancy can cause cerebral palsy, mental retardation, blindness, heart defects, or an emotional disturbance in addition to a hearing loss. About a third of those children who lose their hearing because of meningitis also have an additional major handicap. In contrast, those children whose deafness is due to genetic transmission seldom have other handicapping conditions.

Any multiple handicapping condition severely complicates the educational program. Trybus and Karchmer (1977) found significantly lower academic achievement among youngsters with hearing losses who were identified as multiply handicapped.

Most observers predict a rise in the prevalence of multiply handicapped children. They cite two reasons: First, the diseases that cause hearing loss are not under complete control. Second, the medical profession is now able to save seriously damaged children from death but not from the consequences of the handicaps with which they are born. Chapter 10 discusses the problems of children with multiple handicaps in greater detail.

ADULTHOOD AND LIFESPAN ISSUES

Most deaf adults live in the normal-hearing society and adjust to the world around them (Woodward, 1982). But they face some very real problems. For the most part deaf people are significantly underemployed (Moores, 1982). Their poor skills in reading and writing put them at a disadvantage in a very competitive job market. Although postsecondary training is improving, it is still limited. Rawlings & Karchmer (1983) identified just a hundred postsecondary institutions with programs for deaf individuals. And of course deafness itself can significantly limit the ability to perform on a job—in fact or in the employer's thinking.

A number of studies have examined employers' attitudes toward handicapped workers (Jennings, 1951; Richard, Triandes, & Patterson,

*Two of the greatest hurdles facing hearing impaired youth
are getting an adequate postsecondary education (there
are only a hundred postsecondary institutions with appropriate programs) and finding rewarding employment.
(Courtesy of the Clarke School for the Deaf)*

1963; Furfey & Harte, 1968; Phillips, 1975). Generally they have found
an unwillingness to hire handicapped people, including deaf adults.
But these studies also report that prejudice is usually a function of
inexperience. Those employers who have hired handicapped workers
once are more than willing to hire them again (Furfey & Harte, 1968).

Finding a job is one problem; the nature of the job is often another.
Schein and Delk (1974) reported that 43 percent of deaf individuals
who had one or more years of higher education were working in jobs
below their level of preparation. Despite the general satisfaction of
employers with the performance of deaf workers and despite the stability of these workers, they are rarely promoted in their jobs (Altshuler & Baroff, 1963). It's not surprising, then, that the income of deaf
individuals is only about 74 percent of what it is for normal-hearing
workers.

On page 229 we talk about a deaf culture, a reality in many cities
across the country. Because their access to the normal-hearing world
is limited, deaf people tend to segregate themselves socially in clubs.
And most deaf adults marry other deaf adults (Woodward, 1982). This
does not mean that those who are deaf do not interact with normal-
hearing people. Baroff (1963) found that a significant number (45 percent) of deaf adults do socialize with normal-hearing individuals. But
it does mean that deaf people have developed a sense of community,

THE IMPACT OF A DEAF CHILD ON A FAMILY

Most families adjust adequately to the birth of the first child, and the family enters upon a new stage of functioning. The birth of additional children usually is not perceived as quite so traumatic as that of the first child. Since the birth of a child causes changes in role and function and by itself can be a catalyst of change, it is logical to assume that the strain is increased upon the birth of a deaf child or, more specifically, upon identification of the child as deaf. Effects of the strain, in turn, will have impact on the child. The deaf child presents the family—if it has not received adequate counseling—with specific problems in the form of shame, guilt, parental recriminations, and restricted communication.

The final identification of deafness might represent the culmination of a long, emotionally draining process. Typically, the mother has known for some time that something is wrong with the child, but she is not exactly sure what it is. Frequently, a pediatrician has offered assurances that the mother is over-concerned and that the child is merely a late bloomer. The final diagnosis may even be a relief—at least, the parents now know what is wrong—but the feeling of relief is quickly followed by overwhelming complications. Parents may wonder whose fault it is, the father's or mother's. Some interpret a child's deafness as God's way of punishing parents for past sins.

On a somewhat different plane, other practical considerations quickly emerge. Because of the parents' lack of knowledge about deafness, they may be uncertain about whether the child will ever be self-sufficient and eventually will assume a productive role in society or will be a lifelong burden, emotionally and financially draining family resources. The extent of the financial problem for families with young deaf children is immediate and extensive and should not be minimized. Medical care, consultation, and the almost-mandatory immediate fitting of the child with a hearing aid—which may cost hundreds of dollars—can quickly erode a young family's financial resources and plunge it into debt. Parents must react and cope with the shock immediately. The child needs their attention, and usually no professionals are available to help them work through their grief.

Finally, in their desire for the child to be an idealized extension of themselves, parents ask, "Will our child be normal? Above all, will speech be possible?" It is at this point that professionals first fail deaf children and their families. If parents receive inaccurate and misleading advice at this time, the negative effects may never be overcome. It is only natural for parents to think that the basic problem of the deaf child is an inability to speak, when, in reality, it is an inability to hear. Professionals have the responsibility to ensure that—as gently but as firmly as possible—parents are made to understand this.

Another fact of life that is difficult for parents to accept is the irreversibility of deafness. For most deaf children we deal with, there are no cures, and none

continued

continued

are projected for the foreseeable future. Parents, however, are not aware of this. Once the deafness is diagnosed, they expect remedial medical treatment. Raised in a society with a "disease" orientation toward difference, parents naturally assume that deafness can be treated in much the same way as appendicitis, tonsilitis, pneumonia, or the common cold. Surely there must be some medicine or surgical technique to help the child. It takes a great amount of adjustment for a parent to realize that the child, and the family, must be prepared for a lifetime of deafness.

Parents who never work through the trauma and grief to achieve a mature acceptance of the deafness are forced to assume a double burden of unacknowledged (and therefore unexpiated) grief and pretense. They may even deny the deafness. For some, the word *deafness* itself is anathema. Slogans such as "Happiness is a hearing world" and "Talk, Talk, Talk" proliferate. The term *deafness*, with all its harsh implications, is replaced by *auditorily handicapped, hearing handicapped*, and *soft of hearing*. Legitimate terms such as *hearing impaired* have been perverted in such a way as to constitute a denial of deafness.

The feelings of most parents include considerable ambivalence as they work through the outer and inner realities of what it means to have a deaf child. The establishment of family equilibrium cannot take place in a vacuum. Parents cannot plan for the needs of one member of the family without considering the total needs of the whole family. For example, should an entire family move to a place where there is a school or program for the deaf child? In a multichild family, it is disruptive to concentrate on one child alone. Research on families with retarded children suggests that normal sisters frequently are expected to assume responsibilities toward the handicapped sibling that they are not prepared to handle. This sometimes leads to personality problems for the nonhandicapped child. Although no comparable data exist for families with deaf children, it is possible that the presence of a deaf child in a family presents a potentially disruptive situation for a normally hearing sibling.

The effects of deafness, or the effects of communication limitations arising from deafness, have an early and profound impact on families and on parent-child communication. It is reported that, in comparison with mothers of young hearing children, mothers of young deaf children are rated as more controlling, more intrusive, more didactic, less flexible, and less approving or encouraging. Mothers of deaf children are less likely to show verbal antagonism. In one study, 40 percent of the behavior of mothers of preschool deaf children was reported "directing," and thirteen of sixteen mothers could communicate with their children only about things or events that were present in time and/or space. Mothers make more concessions to their deaf children than to hearing siblings and the siblings of deaf children report more feelings of jealousy than siblings of children with normal hearing.

In addition, parents of deaf children report a constant concern over whether they are being overprotective or underprotective. They use a more narrow

continued

continued

range of discipline techniques, with more reliance on spanking, and exhibit more frustration concerning deaf children. Some researchers have concluded that the protectiveness most families have for their deaf children probably retards social development.

Another report indicates that, because the deaf child's problem has been viewed as an educational problem, the mother is trained by educators to become a teacher. Thus, to the strain of communicative frustration is added the strain of extended demands on the mother's time and attention.

In conclusion, if the growth of a healthy personality and the maintenance of family integrity is dependent on complex action, reaction, and interaction among family members, what are the implications for a family with a deaf child? The combination of the strain on the parents with the pressure on deaf children to learn to communicate in a medium convenient to everyone but themselves produces extreme stress on the family. Instead of encouraging and enabling deaf individuals to develop to the limits of their potential, the world has been structured in such a way that they usually come to believe they are acceptable to society, to their families, and to themselves only when they are an imperfect copy of a hearing sibling. For the benefit of deaf individuals and their families, this destructive cycle must be broken.

SOURCE: Adapted from *Educating the Deaf: Psychology, Principles, and Practices*, Second Edition, by Donald F. Moores, Houghton Mifflin Company, Boston, MA, 1982, pp. 133–143. Reprinted by permission.

an awareness of their needs as a group. Over the last twenty years that awareness has been translated into political and social action to protect their individual and group rights (Gannon, 1981).

SUMMARY OF MAJOR IDEAS

1. Children with hearing losses fall into two major categories: hard of hearing and deaf. With sound amplification the hard of hearing child can understand speech; the deaf child cannot.
2. Prelingual deafness is the loss of hearing before speech and language develop; postlingual deafness is the loss of hearing after speech and language develop. The child who is prelingually deaf faces the most serious learning problems.
3. A conductive hearing loss reduces the intensity of sound reaching the inner ear. A sensorineural hearing loss is caused by a defect of the inner ear or auditory nerve. Conductive losses can be reduced through sound amplification; sensorineural losses cannot.

4. The most common causes of hearing impairments in children are heredity, maternal rubella, complications during pregnancy and birth, meningitis, otitis media, and other childhood diseases, infections, and injuries.

5. Only 1 child in 1,000 is deaf, and only 3 or 4 children in 1,000 are hard of hearing.

6. Recent studies show that deaf children are not cognitively deficient. Their poor cognitive and academic performance may actually stem from their difficulty reading and writing the English language.

7. Because deaf children do not understand the concept of language or complex syntactic structures, they have difficulty reading and writing the English language beyond elementary levels.

8. Most deaf children perform well below their age and grade level in academic subjects.

9. The social adjustment of deaf youngsters can be impeded by the difficulty of communication and the behaviors that evolve from their inability to communicate.

10. Although the identification of severe and profound hearing losses is usually made before a child enters school, a mild loss may go unnoticed. Teachers should be aware of certain behaviors that could indicate a child has a hearing impairment.

11. Early education programs for deaf youngsters are often provided in the home and include the parents. Most elementary and secondary programs bring deaf students into the public schools, either in regular or special classrooms. There are a limited number of postsecondary programs for young adults who are deaf. Most offer vocational training.

12. There are several communication methods being used to teach deaf students: the oral-aural method, the Rochester method, the auditory method, cued speech, sign languages, and the total communication method. The total communication method, which combines elements of both oral and manual approaches, is currently the most popular form.

13. Whether or not we accept the theory that American Sign Language is the native language of deaf youngsters in this country, we must accept that the use of sign language during the child's early developmental years has a positive effect on academic performance and adjustment. At the same time certain elements of auditory training seem to help deaf youngsters develop an internalized speech-coding system—a system that is essential to the comprehension of complex language forms. Our methods of teaching deaf students, then, must include both manual and oral instruction to allow these children to reach their potential.

14. Technology is having an impact on the deaf and hard of hearing population. Microcomputers are being used in over half the educational programs for deaf students; the electronic hearing aid

is employed extensively; cochlear implants offer the promise of increased hearing to some individuals; and captioned films and television programs are making visual channels more accessible.

15. Many of the problems facing deaf adults in our society are job related. Poor language skills, limited educational and vocational training, and employer prejudice make finding appropriate jobs very difficult. The underemployment and low-level employment of deaf adults gives them a financial handicap in addition to their physical disability.

UNRESOLVED ISSUES

1. *Educating the multiply handicapped child with a hearing impairment.* Approximately 1 out of every 4 deaf children has some other serious impairment. It's essential, then, to design educational programs for these youngsters. At present there are only a handful of pilot programs providing systematic education for deaf and emotionally disturbed children or deaf and learning disabled children. If we want to see a change here, we must begin training our teachers in the special needs of multiply handicapped deaf students.

2. *Stimulating language development.* The growing popularity of the total communication method reflects the importance of language to the deaf child's academic performance. Our teaching of the structural and conceptual aspects of language must be organized in sequence, so that the youngster can move from preschool to elementary to secondary programs that build on and reinforce earlier learning.

3. *Increasing occupational opportunities.* Although people with severe hearing losses are working, they are working at low-level, low-paying jobs. Even the availability of postsecondary vocational programs has not had substantial impact on their employment. In a world where communication and language have become increasingly important, how do we broaden the opportunities of deaf people so that they can communicate in the normal-hearing world? Most people who are deaf still find that interaction with the normal-hearing world is both painful and difficult. As a consequence, they segregate themselves as adolescents and adults. If we believe that integration is a valuable goal, then we must provide the means by which individuals with severe hearing problems can successfully be integrated—vocationally and socially.

4. *The factors that facilitate speech reading.* We must determine what factors are at work in the speech-reading process. "Speech reading, the hallmark of deaf education, remains an enigma. Even those deaf persons who are proficient lip readers are unable to

explain how they acquired the ability or what factors enable them to use this method of understanding speech" (Farwell, 1976, p. 27). Obviously it's impossible to teach a skill efficiently if we don't understand the factors that operate in helping the individual master the skill.

5. *Improving teacher-training programs.*   Most teacher-training programs reflect traditional philosophies and methodologies, not the innovative educational approaches suggested by research findings. All too often the preparation of teachers and the operation of research programs are mutually exclusive functions. Until teacher training programs begin to integrate preparation and research through faculty appointments and university emphases, the students who graduate from traditional programs may continue to use methods that are not working.

6. *Teaching reading and language to deaf children.*   Many deaf adolescents graduate from high school today with little control over the English language. Although significant changes in deaf education have occurred over the course of this century, deaf children and adolescents have as much difficulty reading and writing today as they did in 1900. With new findings in language and cognitive research and new materials, we may see some changes in the achievement of deaf youngsters. Of course this means new findings and materials must be assimilated directly into teacher-training programs if we want them to be implemented as soon as possible.

REFERENCES OF SPECIAL INTEREST

Birch, J. (1975). *Hearing impaired children in the mainstream.* Reston, VA: Council for Exceptional Children.
> Designed particularly to help teachers and administrators create a positive environment for the mainstreaming of mildly and moderately hearing impaired children. The text includes a statement of general principles for mainstreaming, guidelines for administrators, and descriptions of several programs using the mainstreaming principles.

Gannon, J. (1981). *Deaf heritage: A narrative history of deaf America.* Silver Spring, MD: National Association of the Deaf.
> A comprehensive history of deaf people in America. The text describes the educational, social, political, religious, and athletic achievements of deaf people and the contributions they have made to our society.

Moores, D. (1982). *Educating the deaf: Psychology, principles, and practices* (2nd ed.). Boston: Houghton Mifflin.
> The most comprehensive textbook on deaf children yet produced. It provides a rich historical background and up-to-date reports on

current research, educational trends, and preschool and postsecondary programs.

Quigley, S., & Kretschmer, R. (1982). *The education of deaf children.* Baltimore: University Park Press.

A comprehensive, readable report on the various issues and controversies surrounding the education of deaf and hard of hearing children. The book offers an especially good review of essential research over the past decade and presents the findings on the effectiveness of different communication systems in an even-handed way.

Quigley, S., & Paul, P. (1984). *Language and deafness.* San Diego: College Hill Press.

The newest, and perhaps the best, presentation of language in deaf children. The authors describe extensive research findings in an easy-to-read style, and present theories and issues that bear directly on the language development of deaf children.

Rittenhouse, R., & Myers, J. (1983). *Teaching sign language: The first vocabulary.* Beaverton, OR: C. C. Publications.

A book that offers a program for teaching vocabulary to severely and multiply handicapped deaf children. In addition to the program of instruction, the text presents 250 functional signs in a task-analysis format, evaluation methods, and IEP forms.

Ross, M., & Nober, L. (Eds.). (1981). *Special education in transition: Educating hard of hearing children.* Reston, VA: Council for Exceptional Children.

A series of chapters deal with different aspects of coping with the hard of hearing child in the public school system—from audiological and educational assessment to the development of individualized education programs. The text focuses on ways to help the hard of hearing child become a part of the normal-hearing world.

C·H·A·P·T·E·R
Seven

CHILDREN WITH COMMUNICATION DISORDERS

Focusing Questions

What parts do language and speech play in the communication process?

How has the field of communication disorders expanded over the last fifty years?

Why is an understanding of the normal stages of language acquisition so important to the remediation of language disorders?

How do the different dimensions of language appear in language disorders?

What are the three kinds of speech disorders?

Why do most speech and language remediation programs focus on children with mild or moderate articulation and voice problems?

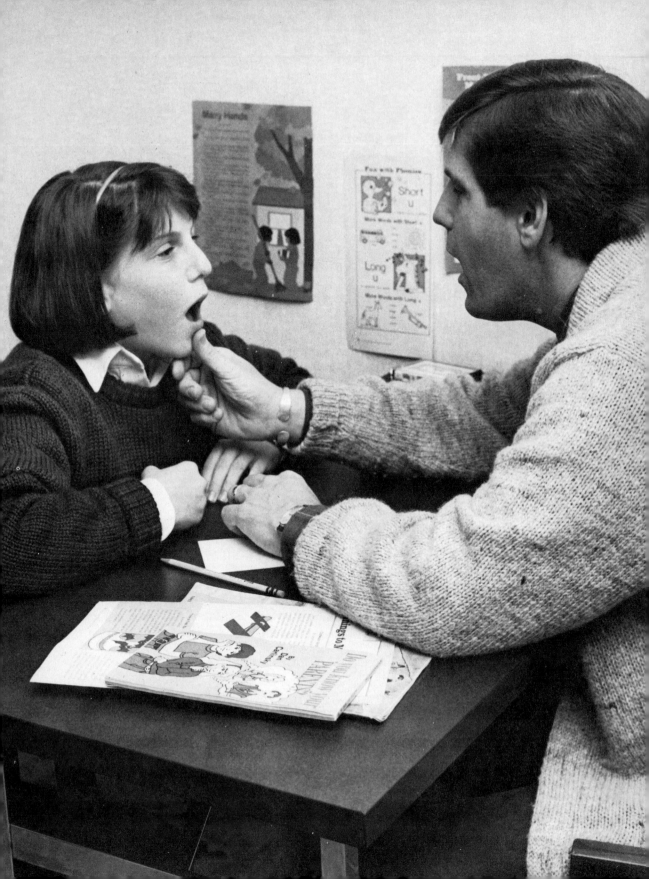

*T*n the increasingly interdependent modern world, the ability to communicate is a basic skill. Anything that interferes with communication can create serious problems for the developing child. These problems are not limited to education; they extend into every aspect of life. For example, one young woman described the social and psychological difficulties brought about by a speech disability:

> My friends tell me I'm attractive, but at 24 years of age I can count all the dates I've had on the fingers of one hand. Boys don't want to go out with girls who talk through their nose like I do. The doctors fixed my cleft lip so you can't hardly see the scar, but my voice is nasal and they say they can't help with that. In grade school the kids called me "honker" or "nosey" and mocked the way I talked. People don't do that now that I am grown-up, but they look at me funny or shy away. Or they are extra kind to me and that's worse. I don't want pity, I just want to live like everybody else. I wonder how many nights I've cried myself to sleep over these miserable years. (Van Riper, 1978, p. 5)

Before we discuss the factors that interfere with communication, we must understand the nature of communication, language, and speech, and the relationship of these three elements. *Communication* is a broad term that encompasses both language and speech (along with many other components). In a very general sense, communication is the transmission of information (Moerk, 1977). It can be verbal, nonverbal, or a combination of both. Whatever the mode, communication involves three components: a sender, a message, and a receiver (Irwin, 1982). Language enters the communication process at the point when the sender has a message that he or she wants to transmit. The sender formulates and sends the message according to the conventions of a particular language; that is, the sender translates the information into specific words and into a specific word order. When the message is transmitted verbally, the sender uses specific speech patterns to produce particular sounds. The receiver hears the sounds, decodes them, and translates them into the message. If there is no interference in encoding transmission, or decoding, the message the receiver receives should be the message the sender intended to send.

Figure 7.1 shows the communication process and the relationship among communication, language, and speech. Language is a factor in each phase of the process; speech is involved in the transmission when a message is being sent orally. Interference can occur at any point within the process.

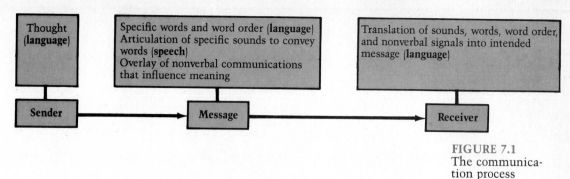

FIGURE 7.1
The communica-
tion process

DEFINITION

Over the last fifty years the types of services provided by specialists in the field of communication disorders have changed dramatically. An early emphasis on speech problems—articulation, voice disorders, and stuttering—expanded after World War II to include hearing problems and, later, language disorders.

These changes have been reflected in the titles we give speech specialists. Speech improvement teachers or speech specialists became speech therapists after World War II. And in the 1960s speech therapists became speech clinicians or speech pathologists, especially in clinics and hospitals. To emphasize the professional's role in language habilitation, the American Speech and Hearing Association (ASHA) adopted the title *speech-language pathologist* at its 1976 meeting.[1]

You should be familiar with speech and language disorders by now. Many children with other exceptionalities (mental retardation, learning disabilities, deafness) have communication problems. The definition of a speech problem includes the perception of the viewer as well as the objective character of the problem itself. Van Riper (1978) defined *speech disorders* as follows: "Speech is abnormal when it deviates so far from the speech of other people that it calls attention to itself, interferes with communication, or causes the speaker or his listener to be distressed" (p. 43). The key adjectives that characterize defective speech are *conspicuous, unintelligible,* and *unpleasant.*

When language disorders were included as an area of concern in the field, a definition of language impairment was formulated by a task force of ASHA. It defined *language impairment* as

> a state in which an individual does not display knowledge of the system of linguistic *needs* commensurate with the expected norm. Typically, a child is *called* language impaired

---

1. At the same time, the group changed its own name to the American Speech-Language-Hearing Association, although it has kept its familiar abbreviation (ASHA).

when his/her skills in the primary language are deficient relative to expectations for chronological age.

PREVALENCE

The estimated prevalence of speech and language disorders in the school-age population has been generally accepted for some time (National Institute of Neurological Diseases and Stroke, 1969). If the estimates of prevalence are correct, then there are many more children who need communication services but are not currently receiving them. As Table 7.1 indicates, less than half of the estimated children in need are actually being served.

Only an estimated 2.7 percent were being served instead of the 6 percent estimated. One possibility, of course, is that we have overestimated the true prevalence rate. Another is that the states and local school systems are not pressing to find all the children with communication problems who need special services. Was only one of every two children with communication problems receiving help?

McDermott (1981) pointed out a problem in determining the number of children with communication disorders. Some states count only those students whose primary problem is speech impairment and do not include those who have other problems in addition to a speech impairment. Unduplicated counts create the appearance that large numbers of children are not receiving services or that estimates of prevalence are much too high.

Several factors affect these prevalence figures. The vast majority of functional articulation cases are found in the earlier grades. Figure 7.2

Table 7.1
Estimated Prevalence of Speech and Language Disorders, 1984

Problem	Estimated Prevalence (Percent)	Number of Children Being Served
Functional articulation	3.0	565,000
Stuttering	0.7	131,840
Voice disorders	0.2	37,660
Cleft palate	0.1	18,780
Cerebral palsy	0.2	37,660
Retarded speech development	0.3	56,500
Impaired hearing	0.5	94,180
Language disorders	1.0	188,380
	Estimate 6.0	
Total	Actual 2.7	1,130,000

SOURCE: From *Seventh Annual Report to Congress on the Implementation of the Education of the Handicapped Act,* 1984. Washington, DC: U.S. Department of Education.

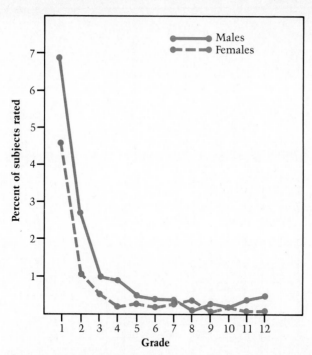

FIGURE 7.2
The effects of age
and sex on articula-
tory deviation

SOURCE: From *National Speech and Hearing Survey* (Project No. 50978, Bureau of
Education for the Handicapped, U.S. Office of Education, p. 37) by F. Hull, P. Mieike,
J. Willeford, and R. Timmons, 1976. Washington, DC: U.S. Government Printing Office.

shows the rapid decrease in prevalence of extreme articulation deviations for males and females from grades 1 to 12. According to the study
by Hull, Mieike, Willeford, and Timmons (1976), males had a prevalence rate of 7 percent in the first grade; females, a prevalence rate of
4.5 percent. This prevalence dropped to 1 percent for males and to 0.5
percent for females in the third grade, and to 0.5 percent and 0.2 percent in the twelfth grade. The study did not indicate whether the rapid
drop in rate between the first and third grades is due to remediation,
to maturation, or to both. The problem faced by speech-language pathologists is to predict whether a child will overcome articulatory,
voice, and stuttering problems through maturation or through intervention.

Articulation becomes much less of a problem as children mature
and their language and speech improve. In their report of research
conducted in a southern city, Gillespie and Cooper (1973) noted that
articulation problems accounted for 60 percent of the communication
difficulties reported in elementary schools but only 38 percent of the
problems in secondary schools. Stuttering, however, is reported as frequently as articulation as a problem at the secondary level. The number and type of communication problems, then, seem highly dependent
on the age of the children under consideration.

FIGURE 7.3
Profile of a speech
impaired child

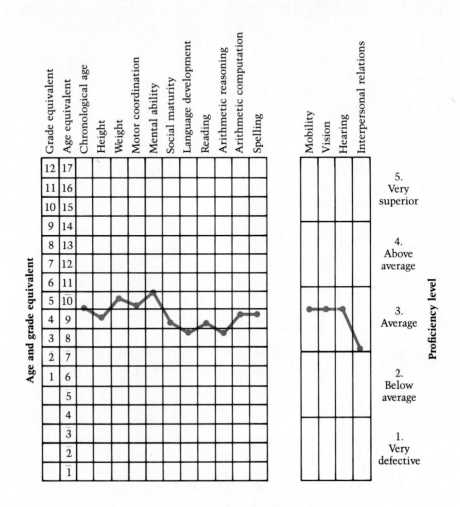

DEVELOPMENTAL PROFILE

Figure 7.3 shows the developmental profile of Betty, a 10-year-old child
with a mild speech impairment. Academically she is within the normal range except for her speech and, to a lesser extent, her language
development. Her sound substitutions and omissions are not so severe
that she cannot be understood but they do call attention to her speech.
A ten-year-old who says "wabbit" for *rabbit* can count on receiving
some negative attention from her peers. Betty is being affected by how
the other children react to her and sometimes mimic her speech. "She
talks funny" as one girl in her class noted.

Since her hearing has been checked and found to be normal and she
has no serious neurological problems, there is little doubt that Betty
will eventually speak within the normal range. Betty needs help for

her communication skills now because these minor problems can adversely affect her self-image and social interactions. Betty is in the regular classroom most of the time. An itinerant speech-language pathologist provides her with corrective lessons several times a week and gives the classroom teacher additional suggestions on how to help with Betty's speech. With this help, Betty's articulation difficulties will probably disappear or improve considerably.

The speech impaired child who is otherwise developing normally does not differ markedly from other children in educational performance. Betty does not have a special language difficulty except for the minor problem of denying herself practice in communication because she is sensitive about the reactions of others. She can and does profit from the regular education program.

As we discuss in Chapter 10, children with communication problems may have other handicaps. Children with multiple handicaps, among them a speech impairment, need an intensive special education program.

CLASSIFICATION

ASHA defined *communication disorders* as "impairments in articulation, language, voice, or fluency. Hearing impairment may be classified as a communication disorder when it impedes the development, performance, or maintenance of articulation, language, voice, or fluency" (*Comprehensive Assessment and Service (CASE) Information System*, 1976, p. 26).

- *Articulation.* Most communication problems in the public schools fall into this category. Children may substitute one phoneme (speech sound) for another, omit phonemes, or distort them.
- *Language disorders.*   There are two major language disorders: delayed language development and aphasia. Delayed language development shows up in vocabulary, in grammatical deficits, and in language use that prevent the child from expressing himself or herself as well as age peers. Aphasia is an impairment in comprehending or formulating messages, probably due to central nervous system damage or dysfunction.
- *Voice.* The human voice varies in pitch, quality, and loudness. The pitch can be too high or low, the quality can be hoarse or nasal, and the loudness can be too weak or strong.
- *Fluency.*   Stuttering occurs when the forward flow of speech is interrupted by repetitions or prolongation of a sound or syllable. Children who stutter also show avoidance behavior.

Communication problems also occur frequently in children with other handicapping conditions such as mental retardation, behavior disorders, or cerebral palsy. Since speech and language are among our most sophisticated and complex functions as human beings, they are easily disrupted by a wide range of neurological or developmental disabilities.

IDENTIFICATION AND DIAGNOSIS

In many school systems the procedure for establishing a communication disorders program follows three stages:

1. Screening procedures to identify children who require full diagnostic assessment
2. Diagnosing those selected through the initial screening and from other referrals
3. Selecting those children who require and can benefit from special speech and language intervention

Screening Procedures

Most school systems have established formal screening programs for vision and hearing. Similarly, a speech-language pathologist may conduct screening each year to locate those children suspected of having communication disorders. Children who show signs of articulatory, vocal, rhythmic, or linguistic impairment are then evaluated more thoroughly. In addition, children who are not detected by this formalized procedure are often referred to the speech-language pathologist by parents or by teachers in classrooms not included in the screening program when there is concern about performance in speech, language, or hearing.

Diagnostic Procedures

The diagnosis of a communication disorder involves five procedures:

- *Case history.* When a child is referred for a speech, hearing, or language examination, the speech-language pathologist obtains a history of the child to determine whether the problem is, or has been, recognized by other people (teachers, parents, physicians). This history furnishes background information on the developmental history of the child (the age at which the child walked or talked). It also can include a medical history, information about siblings and other family members with similar problems, a social history, school achievement records, and records of earlier examinations.
- *Intellectual assessment.* One of the first areas to be assessed in a child with a speech or language defect is intellectual development.

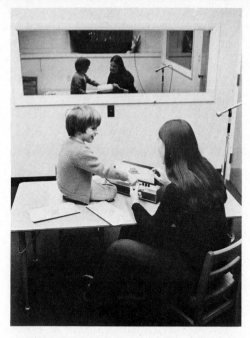

A child who is suspected of having a communication disorder may be referred to a speech-language pathologist who conducts a full diagnostic assessment.
(Hugh Rogers/Monkmeyer Press Photo Service)

In some cases psychological tests of nonverbal abilities are administered to determine whether a child's delay in speech or language is due to mental retardation.

- *Hearing assessment.* Because hearing loss is a common cause of speech and language problems, a careful audiometric examination is made of the child's ability to receive sound in each ear.

- *Assessment of defect.* A speech-language pathologist identifies the defect or defects by (1) obtaining spontaneous vocal responses from the child through response to pictures, (2) asking the child to repeat certain words that indicate an articulatory defect, (3) asking the child to repeat sounds in nonsense formation, and (4) obtaining samples of the child's habitual conversation. Each of these procedures—spontaneous speech, imitation, the nonsense syllable routine, and habitual conversation—has its place in helping the pathologist determine the type of speech defect.

- *Determining causal and correlated factors.* If a child has delayed language or a defect in articulation, voice, or rhythm, the next question is why. What factors are responsible for, or associated with, the difficulty? In the examination the speech-language pathologist evaluates lip movements and structure; dental alignment and tongue movements and structure; palatal structure and function; and pharyngeal adequacy. A judgment is made about any structural deviation that may contribute to the speech defect. Factors in the home environment are explored to see if they influence the speech problem. Some observed symptoms or problems may require the speech-language pathologist to refer the child to other specialists—an audiologist, an otolaryngologist, a plastic surgeon, a psychologist, or a neurologist.

Ordinarily the diagnosis suggests initial remedial procedures. Assessment, however, is an ongoing process: Many aspects of the child's difficulty will come to light during the remediation. The major purpose of the diagnosis, then, is to assess the special defects and so to lead to a program for remediation. The remediation sessions that follow depend heavily on ongoing assessment to find out what the child is able or unable to do.

In previous chapters we have discussed the likelihood of handicapping conditions appearing in clusters rather than singly. Is this also the case with children who have communication disorders? Baker, Cantwell, and Mattison (1980) carefully assessed one hundred children who had been referred to a community speech and hearing clinic. Fifty-three percent of the children were classified with at least one psychiatric diagnosis, indicating significant behavior problems in addition to the referring problem of speech or language difficulties. The most frequent diagnosis was attentional disorder with hyperactivity, followed by oppositional disorders (resistant children) and anxiety reactions.

In reviewing this problem Waller, Sollod, Sander, and Kunicki (1983) suggested that the accumulated evidence should alert clinicians to the high likelihood of behavior problems occurring in individuals with communication disorders and that the assessment of such children should include behavior ratings, tests of personality and self-concept, as well as traditional measures of speech and language.

THE ASPECTS OF LANGUAGE

Language involves five areas: phonology, morphology, syntax, semantics, and pragmatics. Children with delayed language development can have problems in one or in a combination of these areas.

- **Phonology** is the sound system of a language, the way sounds are combined into meaningful sequences. When we combine the sounds *k*, *a*, and *t* in that order, we create a meaningful word, *cat.*
- **Morphology** is the structure of words and the way affixes are added to words to change meaning or to add information. For example, by adding the prefix *un-* to the adjective *happy*, we change the meaning of the word. Or by adding the suffix *-ed* to a verb, we add specific information.

- **Syntax** is word order—the way in which words are organized in sentences—and the interrelationships of words within sentences. An understanding of syntax means an understanding of the parts of the sentence, knowing that the subject is the doer, the verb is the action, and the object is the recipient of the action.
- **Semantics** is the meaning of language, the relationships of individual words, groups of words, and sentences. It is an awareness of linguistic context, the knowledge that *pen* means "a writing instrument" in one sentence and "an enclosure" in another.
- **Pragmatics** is how the language is used in communication. It involves an awareness of the environment (home, school, playground) and the information that sender and receiver share. Whether we say "The pen is in my desk" or "It's in here" depends on the experience we share with the receiver. Pragmatics also refers to the ability to understand the implied meaning in language. "I'm chilly" can actually mean "Please close the window."

Bloom and Lahey (1978) called the dimensions of phonology, morphology, and syntax language form. Semantics is considered language content; pragmatics, language use.

NORMAL LANGUAGE DEVELOPMENT

The acquisition of language is a fascinating, complex process that we do not yet fully understand, despite the volume of research that has been produced over the last twenty years.

We do know that children acquire language through several sequential stages (Kretschmer & Kretschmer, 1978):

1. The preverbal stage
2. The single-word stage
3. The two-word stage
4. The three-word stage
5. The refinement stage
6. The complex-form stage

The research concerned with each of these stages attempts to explain form development (phonological, morphological, and syntactic development); semantic or content development; and, more recently, pragmatic development.

In the preverbal stage, even infants respond to communication and actively process the information they receive. They learn to discriminate among sounds and are aware of syllabic boundaries within words. They begin to learn the roles of intonation and stress, cues for some of the pragmatic aspects of language. They develop gestures that func-

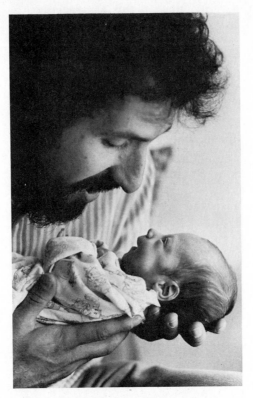

During the preverbal stage of language development, an infant learns to attach meaning to sounds in the environment and responds with gestures that function as language.
(Mark Antman/The Image Works)

tion as language, communicating needs or emotions. Gradually they begin to replace these gestures with symbolic speech.

In the single-word stage, children begin to communicate almost entirely with single words. The first spontaneous words are functional, related to people or objects in the child's immediate environment (*mommy, daddy, milk, ball*). During this stage, children seem to focus on the semantic and pragmatic aspects of language.

During the two-word stage, children express previously mastered semantic concepts while working to master new forms. At this point interindividual differences in pragmatic expression and comprehension are apparently related to the family's socioeconomic status and the child's sex. The different communication (and behavior) patterns mothers establish with their daughters and their sons are reflected in their children's pragmatic expression.

In the three-word stage, children begin to combine their two-word utterances. "No milk" and "want milk" become "no want milk." "Baby drink" and "drink milk" become "baby drink milk." Throughout this stage, children often adhere rigidly to the subject-verb-object word order.

In the refinement and complex-form stages, children begin to add morphological endings and to understand and use increasingly complex syntax. They also begin to acquire negation, question, and imperative forms. At the same time, they develop conversation skills and an understanding of how language is used.

Understanding the pattern of normal language acquisition is critically important for the speech-language pathologist and the classroom teacher. To determine whether a child has a language impairment we must know whether the child's difficulties are a function of age or of an actual disability. The normal pattern of language acquisition is also an important part of the remediation process. Intervention programs follow this pattern, working in sequence through the development process. Since language is so essential to effective communication, any unusual delay in progress from one stage to another becomes a matter of concern, and action in terms of diagnosis and treatment, if necessary, should begin early.

CHARACTERISTICS OF CHILDREN WITH COMMUNICATION DISORDERS

In the area of communication, just as in mental retardation, behavior problems, and learning disabilities, it is difficult to draw a line between mild problems worthy of some school attention and those serious enough to justify expenditures for major professional or special education services. Because each of the communication problems has a distinct cause and treatment, we examine them separately.

Language Disorders

A child who develops without language is deprived of a fundamental tool. This is why a serious discrepancy between expected and actual performance moves many different professionals into action.

Language disorders have been roughly classified into two related categories: delayed language development and developmental or congenital aphasia.

Delayed Language Development

Bangs (1968) defined *delayed language development* as orderly development that progresses at a slower rate than normal and that is significantly below the appropriate language performance for a child's chronological age. Children who have trouble understanding or speaking at the level of their peers may have difficulty in any one or more of a variety of functions.

Some of the causes of delayed speech and language are hearing loss, mental retardation, behavior problems, and environmental deprivation. To determine the cause of delayed speech and language can require the diagnostic services of a number of professionals in addition to a speech-language pathologist. The neurologist, for example, looks for evidence of cerebral dysfunction; the school psychologist attempts to rule out mental retardation; the audiologist is responsible for determining hearing abnormalities and level of acuity; the social worker, psychiatrist, or psychologist explores factors in the home or environment to throw light on emotional factors that might have a bearing on the language problem.

Delayed language development can mask other problems in some children. For example, a child who is mentally retarded is slow to master symbols. It is the inability to think and remember that is fundamental in this child. A child who is deaf, on the other hand, often does not develop language because of the inability to hear, but he or she may have nonverbal language. The child who is emotionally disturbed may not respond to language or use it, but may in fact have mastered it.

Children can experience difficulty with any of the five dimensions of language. Although we defined these dimensions as discrete categories, in reality they often overlap. Bloom and Lahey (1978) claimed that these aspects of language interact continually and that it is common for children to experience problems with several or all of them. The extent of a child's difficulties affect the remediation process: If a problem is limited to only one dimension of language, remediation can be handled in the classroom by the regular classroom teacher; if a problem extends to several dimensions, the speech-language pathologist may be involved in direct intervention.

Phonology Problems.   Some children's voice production can be unpleasant or grating to the listener because of *pitch, intensity,* or *resonation* problems. If the pitch is much higher or lower than expected, or if the child speaks in an unmodulated monotone, the listener may be negatively affected. If the intensity is so low that the child speaks in almost a whisper, then there may be strain on the vocal system, particularly if the child is expending a great deal of effort in trying to communicate. *Hypernasality,* which is a common resonance problem, occurs when too much air passes through the nose thereby distorting the vowels and the *m, n, ng,* sounds. *Hyponasality* occurs when too little air goes through the nasal cavity and the child sounds like he or she has a permanent cold in the nose.

Morphological Problems.   Some children are able to express age-appropriate ideas in correct sentence structures but are not able to use accepted rules of morphology. They have difficulty with pluralization, particularly irregular forms (*foot-feet*); with verb tenses (*run-ran, walk-walked*); with the third-person-singular form (*go-goes*); or with the use of prefixes (*un-, pre-*). In many instances these difficulties stem from impaired auditory perception and short-term memory (Wiig & Semel, 1980).

To determine whether a child has a language deficiency in the area of morphology, we must understand the stages and sequences of normal language acquisition. A five- or six-year-old who is following the normal pattern can still produce plural noun forms like *mouses* and *foots;* an eight-year-old should not. A first-grade teacher, then, who observes these forms being used in the classroom does not have to worry; a third-grade teacher, however, may have to initiate language assessment and implement specific intervention strategies. In planning these strategies the teacher or clinician should follow the sequence of morphological acquisition in normal language development.

Although morphological problems can occur in both spoken and written language, many children use word formation rules accurately when speaking but have problems applying the rules to reading and writing (Wiig & Semel, 1980). Intervention for these youngsters focuses on the transfer of rules from a verbal language code to a written one.

Syntactic Problems. Some children have difficulty with syntax, processing structurally complex sentences ("The car was hit by the truck") or syntactically compressed sentences ("The boy who hit the girl ran away") (Rosenthal, 1970). Semel and Wiig (1975) found that some children with language disorders have significant problems understanding and interpreting *wh-* questions; sentences with the demonstrative pronouns *this, that,* and *those;* passive sentences; sentences that express relationships between direct and indirect objects; and sentences with more than one clause.

Here too the intervention program should follow the normal language acquisition sequence. The choice of vocabulary is very important: We do not want the child to have to divide concentration between learning new words and new structures. Because children with language disorders tend to have problems recalling spoken sentences, phrases and clauses should be kept short. Wiig and Semel (1980) observed that children with language disorders are often limited in their use of imagery. Therefore intervention should use pictures whenever possible to illustrate the concepts of words, phrases, and clauses. They also suggest that intervention strategies should emphasize first recognition, then differentiation and interpretation, and finally the formulation of sentences.

Semantic Problems. Semantic difficulties can involve word meanings; word, phrase, and clause relationships; and figurative language. Specific problems can include

- delayed concept formation of some words or word classes (the child frequently uses indefinite designators like *this thing* or *that over there*).
- difficulty assigning appropriate alternative meanings to multiple-meaning words (the child is confused by words like *run* and *eye*).
- difficulty in interpreting word, phrase, and clause relationships when connective words (*before, after*) are used.
- difficulty in interpreting figurative language (*busy as a bee, run like a deer*).

Children with language disorders tend to assign a very narrow semantic context to words and word relationships. In planning intervention procedures, then, we should provide strategies that will broaden these conceptual contexts. For example, in the initial stages of intervention, we use best exemplars and typical situations—*flower-rose*, for example. Over time we extend the range of application to include less typical exemplars (say *hyacinth*) and finally atypical concepts (*Venus's-flytrap*) (Wiig & Semel, 1980). Usually we introduce general concepts before specific ones: *big* before *tall* or *wide* (Clark, 1973). Other considerations that affect our planning of intervention strategies include frequency of use of the concept in the child's environment, provisions for generalization of the concept, and functionality and impact of the concept on the student's present and future environments.

Pragmatic Problems.   Children with language problems in the area of pragmatics often have difficulty adapting their langauge and communication styles to fit the needs of the listener or the interpersonal context (Bryan, 1978). They tend to make more competitive and rejective statements and less helpful and considerate statements than do their peers in communicative interaction (Wiig, 1982). These youngsters may find it difficult to perceive implied meanings in a conversation and so respond inappropriately to conversational statements. For example, if someone says to them "Isn't it nice to have clean hands?" these children may respond with "yes" or "no." They don't interpret the statement as a request to wash their hands.

In planning an intervention program for a child with pragmatic deficits, we provide activities that will increase the child's pragmatic abilities and thus his or her communicative competence. Role playing is often used to enable the child to understand implied meanings in verbal messages. Another activity that can develop the child's abilities to use appropriate words and structures to communicate information is descriptive communication (Glucksberg, Krauss, & Weisberg, 1966). In one form of this activity, the child must communicate specific information about one of a series of objects or pictures; the listener must be able to identify the object or picture from the child's verbal communication. Other objectives are to strengthen role-taking abilities, to develop nonverbal social perception, and to increase the range of verbal and nonverbal communication styles available to the child (Wiig, 1982).

Developmental or Congenital Aphasia

The term *aphasia* has been used to describe the loss of speech and language in adults and older children as a result of a brain injury or trauma. It's been used also to describe children who fail to learn language possibly because of a congenital condition—hence the term *developmental* or *congenital aphasia*, or *childhood aphasia*.

Eisenson (1971, 1972) emphasized the difference between congenital aphasia and delayed speech and language development. He defined a child with delayed speech as "one whose competence (comprehension and/or performance production) is significantly below what we expect on the basis of age, sex, and intelligence" (1972, p. 194). According to Eisenson, congenital or developmental aphasia is "an identifiable syndrome that must be separately considered among the organic causes of language retardation" (1972, p. 197). He insisted on evidence of "atypical cerebral development" on a congenital basis before a diagnosis of aphasia is made.

The terms *developmental (congenital) aphasia* and *delayed speech* are often misapplied to children who show deviant language and speech behavior. The terms are difficult to differentiate in actual practice, and that differentiation may not even be necessary. Instead the evaluation of the child can deal with a learning disability related to *auditory* and *vocal disorders*. This method of attacking the problem of perception, speech, and language can lead to specific programs of remediation. The methods of remediation of language disorders in children are discussed in Chapter 9.

Researchers and clinicians are concerned with a differential diagnosis of delayed speech and developmental aphasia because remediation and prognosis in these areas are believed by some to be slightly different. If a child's delayed speech is due to mental retardation, we try to improve the child's vocabulary or semantics. However, if delayed speech is due to a severe hearing loss, our remedial or instructional emphasis is different. Following an initial emphasis on concept formation or cognition, we may give more time to proper syntactic and speech development. The language disorder of a child whose delay is due to environmental factors can be different from that of a child with a brain injury or developmental aphasia.

Remediation of Language Disorders

A number of exercises are available that allow children to strengthen specific language deficiencies. Eisenson and Ogilvie (1977) provided some examples that focus on the young child, but the level of difficulty can be adjusted as needed.

Linking Symbols to Reality

Do these make sense?
   The hot soup is in the refrigerator.
   The porch is inside the house.
   The rug is on the floor.

Language Rules

Here is one pencil, here are two _____.
Today for lunch, I am eating a hot dog.
Yesterday for lunch I _____ spaghetti.
Tomorrow I _____ hamburgers.

Auditory Perception

Which word does *goat* rhyme with?
cat   seek   coat

Visual Memory

Using flannel board patterns, the children arrange a series of pictures depicting a snowstorm in the right order—the snow falling, the men shoveling the snow, the snow melting.

Auditory Memory

A child is sick. After the doctor arrives, the mother must go to the store for aspirin, cold medicine, juices and ice cream. Make sure you remember all of them. (pp. 179–181)

In addition, several computer software packages are available. These programs help remediate language problems, particularly morphological, syntactic, and semantic difficulties, and motivate the student.

Speech Disorders

Before we discuss the causes and remediation of speech problems, it's helpful to understand the physical production of speech. Figure 7.4 illustrates the speech mechanism. There are four processes involved in the production of sound: respiration, phonation, resonation, and articulation.

- Respiration, or breathing, provides the source of energy for sound production.
- The breathstream activates the vocal cords, causing them to vibrate and produce sound, or to phonate.
- This sound is then transmitted to the cavities and bones of the head and neck where it is resonated—conserved and concentrated—to give a characteristic quality to each voice.

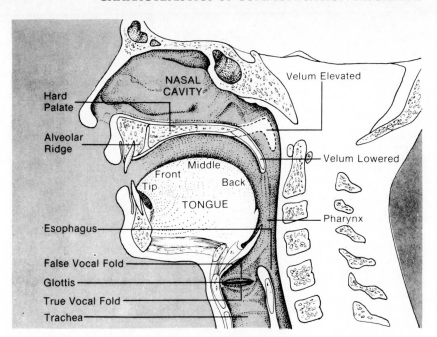

FIGURE 7.4
The speech mechanism

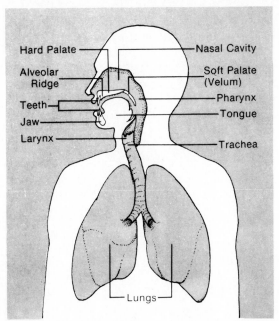

Source: C. Van Riper, *Speech correction: Principles and methods* (6th ed.). Englewood Cliffs, N.J.: Prentice-Hall, 1978, p. 77. Reproduced with permission.

• Finally, through movement of the parts of the mouth the sound is shaped into the phonemes of language and articulated with other sounds as speech. (Freeman, 1977, p. 10)

A breakdown in one or more of these systems interferes with speech sound production.

Articulation Disorders

Articulation disorders are speech deviations that involve substitutions, omissions, distortions, and additions of speech sounds (phonemes). These difficulties occur when the interaction of tongue, lips, teeth, jaws, and palate is faulty. The oral cavity is modified by the movements of jaw, lips, and tongue, which produce the various speech sounds. If the movements are faulty, improperly sequenced, or absent, speech is defective.

Organic factors, including deviations in the tongue, larynx, pharynx, lips, teeth, hard and soft palate, and the breathing mechanism, can cause speech difficulty. More often there are misarticulations with no apparent structural defect. These disorders of functional origin are attributed to several influences, including impoverished environment, infantile perseveration, bilingualism, emotional problems, and slow maturation.

Positioning of tongue and teeth, control of air stream, lip rounding, muscle tension—all play a role in proper sound production. Of course, we don't think about all of these motor changes when we speak anymore than we think about all of the separate movements that are part of walking. When speech and language are defective, diagnosticians approach the problem by analyzing the component parts of speech. Try, for example, to say *soup* with your tongue between your teeth. Where is your tongue when you say it properly? Tongue placement is important in helping children articulate.

Although speech problems obviously involve an incorrect expression of sound, the cause may well lie in a problem of auditory reception. If the child can't hear sounds, then he or she can't reproduce them accurately. This typical exchange between a speech-language pathologist and a young girl indicates that the child has trouble listening to her own words:

Therapist: Say *ssoup*, not "thoup."
Child: But I did thay *thoup!*

As Winitz (1979) pointed out:

> Whether learning a first or second language, auditory experience is a critical dimension. One must hear a new sound a certain number of times before all of its features are sampled. Equally compelling is the fact that the complex relation between discrimination and production is poorly understood. (p. 469)

Most articulation disorders are remediated by directly modifying the problem, *not* by eliminating its cause. In the case of hearing disorders, however, hearing aids and training in their use can substantially improve the child's ability to receive sounds and to hear his or her own sound production.

Nature of Articulatory Defects.   The most common articulatory defects are substitutions, omissions, and distortions.

Some typical substitutions are *w* for *r*, as in "wight" for *right*; *w* for *l*, as in "yewo" for *yellow*; and *th* for *s*, as in "yeth" for *yes*. This type of error is commonly found among young children with immature speech. Sometimes a sound like *p* is substituted for almost every plosive sound (*t* or *k*) or for the fricative *f*: "I peel punny." The substitution may not always be consistent. Sometimes a child substitutes for a sound that he or she is capable of pronouncing perfectly and using easily. Often the position of the letter in the word—at the beginning (initial position), in the middle (medial position), or at the end (final position)—determines whether the child substitutes.

Extensive omissions can make a child's speech unintelligible. The consonants are most likely to be dropped from the endings of words, though they may be dropped from the beginnings or the middles or from all three positions. Occasionally there is a stoppage of air (a glottal stop) between the vowels of successive syllables that substitutes for a consonant.

Distortions show an attempt to approximate the correct sound. Among older children they are relatively more frequent than omissions or substitutions. Where a younger child omits a sound or substitutes another, an older child tries to imitate the proper sound but produces a distortion. A distorted *s* sound can have many near approaches to the correct sound—the sibilant *s* (whistling), the lateral *s* (air emitted at side of tongue), and the dental *s* (tongue thrust against teeth)—all of which can be corrected by modification of the air stream and shift in oral pressures and positions.

In the broadest sense, articulatory difficulties can appear in every kind of speech deviation. Sometimes they exist alone or are associated with another dysfunction, like stuttering. Sometimes they occur as one of several speech-handicapping factors, as in cerebral palsy, in which vocal factors (timing, pitch, quality) merge into the articulatory defects. Table 7.2 is a summary of research on factors related to articulatory proficiency.

Identification of Articulation Problems.   There are several instruments used to identify articulation problems. Of these the Templin-Darley, the Laradon, and the Goldman-Fristoe tests are most popular. Each instrument uses pictures of common objects to encourage the child to articulate. The pictures are chosen to provide a variety of articulation sounds across the range of phonemes, so that a total por-

Table 7.2
Summary of Research on Selected Perceptual-motor and Psychosocial Factors and Articulatory Proficiency

Causal Factors	Relationship to Articulatory Proficiency
Perceptual-motor Factors	
Developmental and physical health	No relationship between such variables as height, weight, age of crawling or walking, childhood diseases, and articulation.
Intelligence	Within the normal range of intelligence, a slight positive relationship between intelligence and articulation.
Auditory discrimination	Considerable evidence that speech defective children score below nondefective children on tests of speech sound discrimination.
General motor skills	No relationship between such variables as speed or accuracy of eye-hand coordination, balance or rhythm, and articulation.
Oral area	
Oral structures	No difference between superior and inferior (adult) speakers on size or shape of lips, tongue, and hard palate.
Dentition	No sound-specific relationships between dental irregularities and articulation errors (excepting certain types of lisps).
Oral sensation	Some evidence that poor articulators score lower than normals on oral-form recognition tasks.
Oral motor	Some evidence that children with very poor articulation score lower than normals on tests of rapid speech movements.
Psychosocial Factors	
Socioeconomic level	Some evidence that proportionally more children from low socioeconomic homes (as indexed by parent occupation) have poor articulation.
Sex and sibling status	Some evidence that girls, first borns, and children with increased spacing between siblings have better articulation at some ages.
Personality and adjustment	Some evidence that children with severe articulation errors have a greater proportion of adjustment and behavioral problems than nondeviant children.

SOURCE: From "Developmental Phonological Disorders" by L. Shriberg, 1980, in *Introduction to Communication Disorders* (p. 281) by T. Hixon, L. Shriberg, and J. Saxman (Eds.). Reprinted by permission of Prentice-Hall, Inc., Englewood Cliffs, New Jersey.

Articulation exercises can be carried out in any number of ways, including the use of a multiple bubble maker to help the child shape the mouth.
(Meri Houtchens-Kitchens/The Picture Cube)

trait of the child's ability to communicate effectively can be determined. For example, a picture of a boat allows evaluation of the initial *b* sound and final *t* sound; a shoe elicits pronunciation of the initial *sh* sound and the *oo* vowel sound. The total examination identifies which consonants and vowels the child is misarticulating and how, enabling the speech-language pathologist to plan a remedial program that focuses on specific problems.

Speech Remediation for Articulation Disorders. Speech-language pathologists in schools find that more than half of the children they treat display articulatory deviations or defects. Misarticulations are particularly common in young children and often go unnoticed because they are expected. School personnel are not unduly concerned about the kindergarten child who is unable to make those sounds with which many children after age 5 have no difficulty (for example, *r*, *s*, or *th* sounds). When a child is developing normally, maturation usually takes care of speech development with a little help from a wise teacher or parent.

Because pathologists do not have the time to help every child, they must choose the children most in need of help. Unless a young child has an actual disorder and has difficulty communicating with others, pathologists usually give time and nature a chance to work. The problem is predicting which children will develop appropriate speech without remediation and which need help at an early age.

Children selected for speech remediation are scheduled for either individual or group lessons. The cooperation of classroom teachers and parents is necessary to transfer the practice in lessons to home and school situations. Individual speech remediation uses various approaches. There are differences of opinion as to whether it is best to have a child practice a sound in isolation and then integrate it into normal conversation or to use natural conversation as a basis for remedial work (Winitz, 1979). Both methods appear to work.

Another variation is noted by Van Riper (1978) who has reported on the process of *progressive approximation* in articulation therapy where the speech-language pathologist makes the same error the child makes and then makes some minor approximations toward the correct sound. Instead of going straight from "wabbit" to *rabbit* the child is led little by little to less of an error. This is similar to the "shaping" or operant conditioning described in the chapters on mental retardation and behavior problems.

Many speech-language pathologists utilize group remediation successfully. A developmental speech group offers students in the primary grades practice in listening to themselves and to others, practice in the production of new sounds and words, and practice in social interaction using speech.

In kindergarten and the first and second grades, speech improvement services from the classroom teacher can help every child toward more articulate speech without labeling or calling attention to those who appear to be different. The speech-language pathologist supervises this type of program, providing the teacher with material and routine procedures.

For mild problems, articulation cases uncomplicated by organic damage, the mainstream approach—keeping exceptional children in the regular classroom and providing supplementary professional services—is a pattern that has been followed for many years.

Stuttering

Problems of speech fluency have been reported back at least to Greek and Roman times. We know that the Greek orator Demosthenes stuttered, as did the Roman emperor Claudius. Yet we still are baffled by the causes of stuttering and continue to seek effective methods for long-term remediation.

Van Riper (1978) wrote that "stuttering occurs when the forward flow of speech is interrupted abnormally by repetitions or prolongation of a sound, syllable, or articulatory position, or by avoidance and struggle behaviors" (p. 257). This description of stuttering, however, does not include the fluency disturbances that many people experience. Normal disfluency can begin in the infant's early babbling, continuing into the jargon the child uses during the second year. The child may utter a stream of nonsense syllables using the inflections and stress of developed language. This can be a "fluency rehearsal," not a precursor to stuttering (Shames & Florence, 1982). Certain disfluencies in adult speech are acceptable, like the use of *um* and *uh* to give the speaker time to think or the excited repetition of sounds and words (Shames & Florence, 1982). These normal disfluencies should not be confused with true disorders, which are recognized by both the sender and receiver as deviant from expected speech.

There are many ironies in this problem, not the least of which is that the natural strategy that people adopt to cope with stuttering turns out to be the wrong thing to do. It's natural for people having difficulty with a task to invest more energy and effort to get it done, whether it's moving a heavy box or trying to loosen a screw that's rusted tight. The extra effort to speak well or fluently, however, tends to make the problem more severe. As the child who stutters tries harder and harder to force the sound to come out—the face contorts, muscles tense, the whole body seems to want to push the sound out— the block often becomes resistant.

Another irony is that in some kinds of speaking activities the child is perfectly fluent. Many children who stutter find that they can sing or recite poetry fluently. Yet if they try to speak the lyrics of a song they've just sung, they find themselves back into the speech blockage again.

A number of techniques can be used to create quick but temporary fluency. Motor movement while speaking—swinging one's arms or pounding one's fist into the thigh—works for a time. But once a distraction becomes a habit, it loses its power to control the block.

A final irony is that the fear of stuttering reinforces the problem. The fear creates the tension that creates the speech blocks, thereby creating more fear.

Webster and Brutten (1974), in describing the behavior profile of a child who stutters, pointed out several major characteristics:

- Fluency problems involve involuntary repetition or the prolongation of sounds and syllables.
- A large proportion of the repetitions and prolongations occur in the same words.
- Fluency failures are associated with emotional arousal.
- Voluntary efforts are used to deal with, or cover up, the involuntary occurrences of stuttering by verbal and nonverbal responses—repetition of words and phrases, changes in speaking rate and intensity, eye blinks, lip purses, and arm swings.

They explained that involuntary anxiety causes the stuttering, which motivates the individual who stutters to engage in avoidance behaviors. These behaviors can take the form of substituting certain sounds for others: The child does not say, "Get the ball" because the *g* sound develops a block but says "Hand me the ball." Many children who stutter become experts on synonyms in order to substitute for the sounds that they know cause a block.

Causes of Stuttering.   Many theories have been proposed to explain why children and adults stutter. Some argue that the problem is genetic; others insist it's physiological; still others claim it's environmental. Each group has fiercely defended its own proposition without considering an obvious answer—all of them may be true in part. Genetics appears to set up a predisposition that influences a neurological set that is triggered when the right type of environmental experiences are present.

> From every source we seem to learn the same lesson. Stuttering is caused by both heredity and environment. ... Nevertheless, it is true that as long as we remain ignorant of exactly what it is that some people carry in their genes that increases their chances of learning to stutter, and as long as we continue to disagree about precisely what they learn and how, what we do know about the origin of stuttering will seem to be comparatively little. (Bloodstein, 1979, p. 147)

Treatment for Stuttering.   Treatments for stuttering are as diverse as the theories about its cause. In one popular approach, sometimes called the Iowa therapy, the individual learns a rhythmic way to stutter. By using this form of therapy, the pathologist can remove one of the most serious fears of stutterers—blocking on a particular sound and being unable to get out of the block. Instead of worrying about their own reactions, they are given the task of watching how others respond to their speech. They make phone calls, go to stores, ask strangers for directions, anything to force them to face their problem rather than hide from it. As they become more comfortable with their stuttering behavior and more able to "stutter" themselves out of their blocks, they begin to improve and remain improved with only minor relapses (Bloodstein, 1979).

The other types of treatments are all behavior therapies that use elaborate programs to shape an approximation of normally fluent speech. The speech is then transferred to daily life and stabilized for permanence. Desensitization is used, for example, to have the student physically relax in the presence of the feared situation (say, speaking before the class). Relaxation can reduce the fear behavior, and good performance can be acknowledged with positive rewards (Perkins, 1980).

There are special concerns about the young child who stutters but does not yet show the tension, eye blinking, facial contortions, and other characteristics of the confirmed stutterer. Pathologists advise parents to be good speech models and not to call attention to the child's speech by saying "Slow down" or "Calm down" or "Speak more slowly." Reducing the pressure on the child and seeing that he or she is rested and healthy also help the child develop normal communication abilities. Parents must also be alert to their unwitting reinforcement of their child's stuttering.

> "Mommy, where does this go?" No reply. "Mommy, I can't make this work." No reply. "It won't fit!" Jerry's frustration mounted and his mother remained preoccupied. "M-m-mommy! Come here!" She came. "M——ommy, I can't make it fit." She kneeled beside him and gave him her full attention. Intentionally or not, Jerry's mother responded selectively to his stuttering. (Perkins, 1980, p. 472)

Parents should respond to their children when they are using fluent speech, ignoring their children's nonfluencies.

The erratic pace of treatment and the tendency for relapses make evaluation of competing treatments difficult. All of these techniques seem to work reasonably well in individual cases, but few quick cures last. And permanence—a lasting fluency—is the ultimate goal of the speech-language pathologist.

Voice Disorders

The child who talks in a voice that is too high or too soft or so harsh that it grates on the listener has both social and communication problems. Although relatively infrequent as a serious problem (about 2 in 1,000 children), voice disorders can create major adjustment difficulties.

One of the first steps in understanding voice disorders is to analyze the three basic components of voice: quality, pitch, and loudness. Voice is the production of sound in the larynx and the selective transmission of that sound including its resonance and loudness. The voice is produced by the outgoing air stream passing between the vocal folds in the larynx. From the larynx the sound travels upward through various cavities of the vocal tract (the throat, mouth, and nose) (see Figure 7.4). The normal voice should produce a clear tone (phonation) emitting from the vibrating vocal folds, and this tone should be appropriate in pitch (not too high or too low). The voice should be heard easily, and a person should be able to increase the loudness of it without undue strain. An inflectional speech pattern—rather than a monotone—is important to give meaning to what is said.

Vocal Quality The more common defects in vocal quality are found in phonation (the production of sounds) and in resonance (the direction of the sound in voice placement). The phonation, which originates in

the larynx, sometimes exhibits a breathiness, hoarseness, or huskiness. It may be caused by structural aberrations that result in failure
of the vocal cords to approximate properly in order to produce the
correct vibrations in the air flow. When vocalization is impeded by
paralysis of the vocal cords, the cords cannot meet to allow the proper
build-up of air pressure below them. The result is breathiness or
huskiness.

After an exciting basketball or football game, with lots of yelling
and tension, you may find yourself or your friends speaking with hoarse,
husky voices; with a whisper (aspirate quality); and sometimes with
no voice at all. The reason? Inflammation of the laryngeal tissue and
the vocal cords. If you continued to abuse your voice this way, over
time your voice quality would begin to change. Abuse of the voice can
lead to vocal nodules or growths on the vocal folds. Although small
nodules disappear completely with voice therapy, large nodes that have
been there a while can require surgical removal followed by voice
therapy to prevent their recurrence.

Resonance depends on the balance of amplification in the various
cavities—the oral cavity, the nasal cavity, the pharyngeal cavity (back
of the throat), and the laryngeal cavity (the phonation area). The balance of resonance is affected by the size of the cavities and one's ability
to direct the air-sound stream.

Two types of difficulty are common: hypernasal speech and denasal
speech. In hypernasal speech, sounds that should be emitted through
the mouth are emitted instead through the nasal cavity. This gives
consonants (other than /m/, /n/, and /ng/) and vowels a nasal twang.
This often occurs in partial or complete paralysis of the soft palate.
The same condition sometimes accompanies cerebral palsy when there
is a weakness in muscular coordination and control. An unrepaired
cleft palate provides an open passageway into the nasal cavity, which
can produce an almost unintelligible hypernasality. Often in children
with repaired clefts, tissue insufficiency or muscular incompetence
still create an abnormal misdirection of the air stream.

Denasality is an absence or inadequacy of nasal resonance. Some
children sound as if they have chronic head colds or enlarged adenoids
or as if they are pinching their noses. Insufficient air flows through
the nasal cavities and is evident not only on the nasal consonants but
also on sounds that are normally emitted through the oral cavity.

Vocal Pitch.   One of the most common problems of pitch occurs at
the time of adolescence and affects boys in particular. Some teenage
boys have a falsetto voice instead of the lower-pitched voice that usually accompanies the rapid growth of the larynx during puberty. During the transition in adolescence, the voice may break at times (to the
embarrassment of the boy who is not aware that these breaks are
perfectly normal). For boys who continue to speak in a high pitch,
there are often social problems.

Generally, pitch disturbances can be corrected when the child is older. Often the correction is natural as the voice changes, but there are instances of voice disorders that extend beyond the usual falsetto voice or breaks. Unusual or deviant adolescent voice characteristics can foster withdrawal behavior and embarrassment and may be symptoms of more serious physical problems. For those reasons, a medical examination should be a routine part of the voice examination.

Girls who manifest a pitch that is too low can have similar adaptation problems, and attention should be provided to bring the pitch back into the normal or acceptable range.

Loudness.   Persistent loud talking can be symptomatic of a hearing loss or a personality problem. Careful diagnosis is required. More frequently children do not speak loudly enough. In its most serious form this condition is called **aphonia**, a complete loss of voice. The failure to produce adequate breath pressure to generate speech is usually considered a psychological problem, not a physical one (Bloodstein, 1979).

Remediation of Voice Disorders.   Because a voice disorder can stem from anything from a serious health or psychological problem to temporary abuse, we cannot overstate the importance of a differential diagnosis before speech therapy begins. This diagnosis demands a diverse set of professional skills rarely, if ever, found in one person. This is why many speech clinics assemble the variety of professionals needed to conduct adequate diagnosis and treatment. It is also why many school systems depend on these clinics as sources of help; they cannot afford the range of professionals required to give comprehensive service.

For successful treatment of voice disorders, the child involved must be aware of and convinced that his or her voice needs to be changed. Once that is done, the child must be made aware of the problem itself. Often speech-language pathologists use tape recordings so that the child can hear the problem. Some use negative practice as a technique for awareness. The child is taught how to produce the abnormality to learn what not to do. Then he or she is rewarded for proper production (Eisenson & Ogilvie, 1977).

Often when a problem stems from abuse of the voice, the child can be kept away from the environments or settings that cause the abuse until the vocal apparatus has healed. The child's awareness of the problem and its causes is a major component of the therapy. The full restoration of normal voice is not always possible, but usually there are remedial techniques available that can help a person to more intelligible speech and to more normal vocal sound (Moore, 1982).

Various attempts have been made to bring preventive techniques into the schools so that children with voice disorders can receive early treatment. One of the problems is to sensitize classroom teachers to the existence of voice disorders in their students. Nilson and Schneiderman (1983) have developed a program of lessons for second and third graders that has proven successful in teaching children to understand and modify voice problems. One of the most effective ways to use such a program may be for the speech-language pathologist to alert the classroom teacher to the information that is being presented to the student.

Cleft Palate

The communication disorder that emerges in children with cleft palate and cleft lip is due not to cerebral dysfunction but to structural deficiencies caused by the failure of the bone and tissue of the palate to fuse.

Most of us do not realize that we all have a cleft palate at one point in time, usually three months or so after conception. As the embryo develops naturally, these tissues pull together to form the hard palate and the soft palate, which form a barrier to air rushing through the opening that otherwise would be there. If the fusion does not take place, the child is born with a cleft in the roof of the mouth and sometimes in the lip. Because the opening is not completely closed off, the air rushes through the vocal cords and through the nose as well as the mouth, creating a nasal tone in speech.

Youngsters with cleft palates and cleft lips present a clear example of how physical and congenital disorders cast long shadows on the educational and psychological development of the child. As Bzoch and Williams (1979) defined it, "Cleft palate is a congenital malformation of the speech and hearing mechanisms which frequently leads to severe and complex forms of communication disorders" (p. 18).

Cleft palate seems to be caused by a set of conditions: a genetic predisposition combined with an environmental problem while the mother is carrying the child, such as radiation or oxygen deprivation early in pregnancy.

There are two major ways in which the cleft or opening can be effectively closed. One is surgery to draw the available tissues together; the other is the use of an **obturator**, a false plate that is fitted into the empty space. The whole purpose of surgical repair or the use of an obturator is to shut off air flow to the nasal passage and produce a more normal voice quality. When surgical procedures are delayed too long, deemed inadvisable, or fail, all is not lost. Skillful fitting of an obturator can still improve speech. Any procedure for closing the physical opening must be accompanied by a sustained program of speech habilitation if the maximum use is to be made of these correction procedures.

Van Hattum (1974) described four stages in the remedial program for children who have cleft palates:

1. The parents provide stimulation for prelinguistic speech from birth until 18 months.

LEARNING TO TRY

When the doctors and their staffs were evaluating my month-old son to rec-ommend treatment programs for his cleft lip and palate, several of them re-marked with surprise at the extent of my cleft palate surgery and therapy and complimented my near perfect speech. It was a timely morale booster to be reassured that the series of operations and the years of speech therapy I had undergone had been worth all the effort. Hearing this from the professionals in this field, which has grown so much in the last twenty-five years, not only reaffirmed my successful struggle to achieve normal speech, but also left me with greater hopes that my son's ordeal would be easier than my own.

It is not difficult to recall the days of frequently being misunderstood when I spoke. As a young child I think this self-consciousness developed earlier than the concern that my appearance was "different." I was not aware of the dis-tinctions of tone and pitch; I just knew the words did not sound right. Sounds such as *s, z, l,* and *p* (and others) were distorted. I used to wish that my last name did not start with *s* (luckily it was a very common name) and that my birthday was not on the "sixth" of May, with its *s* and *x*. Naturally, time with family and friends was not threatening, but new people and school situations often were. Fortunately, I have mostly positive memories of teachers somehow conveying their understanding of my difficulties without singling me out as different.

Twenty-five years ago speech therapy was not available through the school system. My brother and I (my father and one brother also have cleft lip and palate) used to leave school early one day each week for speech therapy at a local rehabilitation center. We made a lot of progress in those early years with a wonderful speech therapist who filled our lessons with games, encourage-ment, and patience. The sessions ended when I achieved a level of passable communication skills and my motivation waned.

Adolescence brought all of the usual turmoil, including a renewed self-consciousness. Concern for my appearance was addressed through a series of cosmetic surgeries with results that did more for my self-confidence than I would admit at the time.

I also realized at this time that my speech was not good enough. When I was 15 a pharyngeal flap operation decreased the nasality of my voice, but I knew there was more work to be done on my part. There were probably many incidents that prompted me to reconsider speech therapy but one particular classroom scene highlights my predicament.

"Je m'appelle Lynn" was the way to begin any response in French class. "Je m'assie" was the closing before sitting down. I could only approximate this phrase because of the *s* sound in it. But the teacher kept having me repeat the phrase to correct my pronunciation. Didn't she know I could not pronounce it any more clearly? Finally, embarrassed, I said, "I can't say it." Then she let me sit down. Was she just insensitive to my difficulties, or was she pushing

continued

continued

me not to accept such imperfect speech? Either way, it helped me find new motivation to resume speech therapy.

My parents and I were pleased to find my former speech therapist still in private practice in our area. He was able to tailor the sessions to my needs as an adolescent as skillfully as he had when I was a child. He explained to me how the various sounds are made and what the surgery had accomplished.

Most importantly, I learned that motivation and desire are the keys to success. My progress was swift during those sessions. Because I could recognize what I did not like in my speech, I was able to direct and concentrate my efforts. My goal was clear to me—to have as normal speech as possible. As long as I could see progress toward that end, I looked forward to the lessons and practiced on my own. Within a few months, I could hear the difference. It was a while before I could begin to take for granted the mechanics of proper speech and could think of what I wanted to say without having to worry about how to say it.

Today I am encouraged that my son will achieve this level of speech at a much younger age. Earlier surgeries and refined techniques will minimize his needs for speech therapy. For my part, I hope he learns to try, and to listen.

SOURCE: "Learning to Try" was written expressly for this text by Lynn Smith Dennison, who lives in Brewster, New York, with her husband, Bob, and their son, Andrew.

2. From 18 months to 3 years the parents help a speech clinician in speech and language development and remediation.
3. From 3 to 5 years the emphasis in remediation is on correcting or minimizing aberrant speech.
4. From 5 years on, correction and follow-up continue.

Generally a child with a cleft palate continues to have speech therapy that focuses on velar (soft palate) and pharyngeal contraction, respiratory rhythms of speech, and articulation exercises for as long as needed to help the child achieve comprehensible, nonirritating speech.

Impairments Associated with Cerebral Palsy

Cerebral palsy is a disorder of motor functioning due to brain dysfunction that, in most cases, is present at or near the time of birth. Because speech is a motor function, children with cerebral palsy very often require sustained attention from a speech-language pathologist.

Those children also may have a variety of other problems with hearing and intellectual functioning and, consequently, social adaptation.

Speech Characteristics of Children with Cerebral Palsy. There are three different types of cerebral palsy and each has its own distinctive communication problems. The most common form is **spasticity,** a condition marked by excessively tense muscles, slow jerky movements, and a "scissors" gait. Whether walking or trying to speak, there is a sense of enormous effort being put forth by the child or adult to perform simple motor actions that most of us do automatically.

The speech of the spastic child often shows greater articulatory deviation than does the speech of children with the other types of cerebral palsy. Speech is labored and indistinct, and sounds—especially consonant blends like /sk/ or /sh/—are omitted, slurred, or distorted. Pitch changes are uncontrolled and abrupt rather than gradual and continuous. Vocal quality may be husky, guttural, and tense and may show hypernasality of vowels.

The **athetoid** form of cerebral palsy is marked by consistent tremors, involuntary writhing movements. The speech of the athetoid child is usually slurred in rhythm and constantly changes in pitch, inflection, effort, and emphasis, not unlike the postural balance characteristic of the athetoid type. Sounds are distorted inconsistently because of the continuous involuntary movements. The voice may lack force owing to respiratory disturbances and excessive movement. It may be unintelligible because of the irregular movements to which the speech masculature is subjected. If there is an effort at voluntary control of these muscle movements, the resulting coordination is much like that of the spastic child.

The **ataxic** child lacks balance in the coordination of muscles, usually the result of a lesion in the cerebellum. Errors in judgment seem to be common in the force or direction of the child's movements. Bloodstein (1979) noted that "ataxic speech is marked by a general inaccuracy of articulation in which errors tend to be inconsistent and unpredictable. Rather than specific distortions or substitution of sounds, there is an extreme lack of precision" (p. 269).

The causes of cerebral palsy are many, including maternal rubella, injuries, anoxia (lack of oxygen during the birth process), and early childhood infections (meningitis, encephalitis). The range of possible involvement of the nervous system is great in individual cases. It is wrong to assume that children with cerebral palsy are inevitably mentally retarded. Often their true ability is masked by their communication problems.

Speech Remediation for Children with Cerebral Palsy. Often the communication problems of the child with cerebral palsy are just one group of problems that need simultaneous attention. It is not unusual to find a child receiving occupational therapy, physiotherapy, speech training, and remedial reading instruction from a team of specialists.

The remediation of speech impairments in the child with cerebral palsy does not differ greatly from that for other children. Six major areas require attention:

- Because of the child's physical difficulties in walking, chewing, and swallowing, parents tend to overprotect or do too much for their child. Sometimes speech is delayed or inadequate partly because parents do not give their child the opportunity to exercise vocal masculature. If this is the case, it's necessary to solicit the cooperation of the parents and to motivate speech through experience and exercise.

- At times the speech-language pathologist must help alleviate the stigmata associated with cerebral palsy, including drooling and the protruding or hanging tongue. Efforts should be made to teach the child to swallow, and to close the mouth and enclose the tongue. Again the cooperation of the parents is required because they are in daily contact with the child.

- The use of mirrors depends on the speech-language pathologist's clinical judgment. Some argue that we increase muscle tension by showing the child his or her own reactions; others believe this an acceptable technique. For some children, becoming familiar with what they see in the mirror helps them learn to live with their handicap and to profit from using a mirror, which can prepare them to control speech and to make adjustments for social interactions.

- Language is aided by exploration, experience, and the need for verbal expression. The child with severe cerebral palsy is restricted in movement and does not have normal opportunities to move about and explore the environment. He or she needs experiences in motor activities. Because speech is a motor activity, it is necessary to use what speech-language pathologists call a multiple-sense modality approach: the use of auditory, visual, and kinesthetic senses in the production of speech.

- Children do not speak unless they are motivated to speak. One of the problems in working with children with cerebral palsy is creating a need for them to improve their speech. Their own efforts to correct inappropriate tongue and jaw movements and to breathe properly require concentrated attention. Motivating them to make those efforts is one of the primary responsibilities of the professional.

- The speech-language pathologist must help the child manage his or her tongue movements, control the synergetic movements of swallowing, control facial movements (grimaces, tics), and control breathing inflection and intonations of voice.

Remediation for these children, for all children who have neurological injuries, is painfully slow. And there is a tendency to overprotect them and oversympathize with their struggles that must be guarded against.

EDUCATIONAL ADAPTATIONS FOR CHILDREN WITH COMMUNICATION DISORDERS

Language, speech, and hearing services are offered by speech-language pathologists often in hospitals and clinics but also in public and private schools, in university speech clinics, and through private practice.

In many respects, the communication disorders treatment program exists outside or apart from the formal school program. Professionals who cope with children with communication disorders can form a clinical team that provides many different services but does not impinge on the regular school program. Mainstreaming fits well into the existing speech-language programs for the child with communication problems. These children typically respond to the regular education program with some additional help for their special communication problems.

Treatment Priorities

School systems must provide services of an appropriate nature to all students participating, but decisions can be made on who gets limited services and where the services are offered. A number of professionals have concerned themselves with the priorities in providing speech and language services within the educational program. Zemmol (1977) suggested the following:

1. *Communication disorders.* Severe articulation, voice, fluency, or language problems require intensive intervention. These disorders often interfere with academic achievement and social adjustment, and a variety of professionals may be needed to plan a treatment program. Children with severe stuttering, cerebral palsy, or cleft palate have communication disorders.
2. *Communication deviations.* These children have mild to moderate articulation or voice problems that may be causing school adaptation difficulties.
3. *Communication development.* This refers to efforts on the part of speech-language pathologists to improve the primary linguistic skills of all children. The goal is to prevent the development of mild speech problems.

In the past and still today, most of the attention of professionals has been focused on communication deviations, mild to moderate functional articulation cases. One reason is that many states or commu-

In today's schools most of the attention of speech-language pathologists is focused on children who have mild to moderate articulation or voice problems that may be causing school adaptation difficulties.
(© Frank Smith/Jeroboam, Inc./Herrick Hospital, Berkeley, CA)

nities establish case loads for the speech-language pathologist that may involve seventy-five to one hundred children. It would be impossible to cope with that many severe cases, which is why practitioners often ignore the urging of those not directly in the service delivery situation that they provide more service to severe cases.

Over the last decade, emphasis has shifted somewhat to the broader field of communication disorders in general. Many articulatory defects disappear without speech remediation as the child matures. Also it's been found that to be more effective, speech-language pathologists must work, not only with the child, but also with the classroom teacher and the parents. They have to broaden their operation, moving beyond speech problems to language development and language disorders. Consequently the training of speech-language pathologists has been broadened to include the study of language, linguistics, language disorders, and learning disabilities, in addition to the traditional areas of articulation, voice, and stuttering.

Van Hattum (1976) suggested that the remediation of children with articulatory disorders should continue but that visual aids and taped programs could be used for a majority of the children under the supervision of speech clinicians. This would free speech clinicians to become supervisors, administrators, master clinicians, consultants, or counselors. Van Hattum recommended that the duties of speech clinicians should emphasize the supervision of aides, "early case selection, . . . language (studies), more services to special groups, extension of services to new areas, . . . prevention, and improved methods of accountability" (p. 61).

The effectiveness of the various treatments for communication disorders over time is a much discussed but little researched topic. One study at the Kent State University Speech and Hearing Clinic that did pursue the question of treatment effectiveness was a fifteen-year follow-up of fifty children initially diagnosed as communicatively impaired (King, Jones, & Lasky, 1982). The investigators wanted to determine the educational level achieved by these children and whether their communication problems continued into adolescence and adulthood. The children had been seen at the clinic when they were between 3 and 6 years of age. There were thirty-six boys and fourteen girls in the final group, not an unusual sex ratio for communication problems.

In terms of educational functioning, eleven of the fifty children had been held back a grade at one time or another in their school career, and over half reported difficulty in one or more academic subjects. Still, most seemed to be progressing in an acceptable if not outstanding way in school subjects.

The research team found that the more serious the problems were in the early diagnosis, the more often they extended into adulthood. Of those who had been originally diagnosed as having no speech, 80 percent still reported communication difficulties. Of those who had been diagnosed as having a language disorder or delayed speech, 67 percent reported a continuing problem. However, of those who had been diagnosed as having only articulation problems, only 16 percent reported continuing difficulty.

On the positive side, several of the children took part later in their school careers in "activities which demand sophisticated levels of communication such as forensics, thespian activities, student council, and serving as officers of organizations. One subject won first prize in a national debate contest" (King, Jones, & Lasky, 1982, p. 31).

Implications for Classroom Teachers

Speech-language pathologists use many techniques to promote carryover of newly learned speech patterns into the classroom. These techniques include workbooks that are kept in the children's desks or cubbyholes for regular review by teachers, weekly conferences with teachers regarding specific speech objectives, and devices and props to remind the children to use their corrected speech pattern. A major task of the specialist is to help the classroom teacher use these tools effectively.

One shift in emphasis in the communication disorders field is the increasing attention paid by speech-language pathologists to language difficulties. There appears to be a much greater increase in cases that are identified primarily as language problems and a corresponding decrease in the proportion of cases of children with articulation disorders. This underscores the degree to which the professionals have expanded their earlier responsibilities as speech correctionists to include broader communication problems, both expressive and receptive (Taylor, 1980).

There seems to be a major difference between the type of program provided by the speech-language pathologist at the secondary level and that provided at the elementary level. A great deal of attention is placed on individualized work and the emotional status of the student at the secondary level. There are fewer standardized materials at this level, which means speech-language pathologists must design and develop their own materials both for children with impaired speech and for those with language problems (Neal, 1976).

Schiefelbusch (1980) identified several recent trends in language development and language instruction that increase the responsibilities of the speech-language pathologist:

1. *Developmental language.* The tracing of language from the birth cry to the development of adult roles. More attention has been paid to how earlier experiences result in later behavior.
2. *Functional language.* The emphasis on training children in language that can be put to direct use for social and affective communication, as opposed to learning to say . . . sounds in isolation from words or sentences.
3. *Infant intervention.* An emphasis on prelinguistic language (that is, gestures) and special training for children in danger of being derailed from the normal tract of acquiring skill in language use.
4. *Alternative modes of language.* The development of special non-speech strategies for seriously impaired children who are taught to use sign language, communication boards, and electronically presented symbol systems.
5. *Ecology of language.* The child is trained to use language in a variety of environmental contexts. Language learned in a special training lesson may not be carried over to other settings so the focus is on seeing to it that the child transfers skill in different settings. (pp. 9–10)

Service Delivery Options

The organization of programs for language, speech, and hearing disorders in the schools varies depending on the size of the district and other local factors. Here we discuss some of the common delivery services.

Itinerant Service

In the past, the most common delivery system has been the itinerant model, in which a speech-language pathologist travels from school to school to give direct service to children enrolled in the regular classrooms. This model is most applicable to areas with small schools and rural areas. In small schools and in sparsely settled areas, there may not be a sufficient number of children in one school to maintain the services of a speech-language pathologist on a full-time basis.

Resource Room

The resource room stations a speech-language pathologist in a room that accepts, individually or in small groups, children with language, speech, or hearing problems. In this model, the child is enrolled in a regular classroom, as in the itinerant model, but receives direct service in the resource room at scheduled periods. The model is applicable generally to large schools that have a sufficient number of children to warrant the full-time services of a speech-language pathologist.

Consultative Services

This model provides a school system with a speech-language pathologist who serves as a consultant to regular classroom teachers, special class teachers, aides, administrators, parents, and curriculum specialists in organizing a speech and language development program. The pathologist provides specialized materials and procedures, inservice education, demonstration sessions, and other activities designed to improve the communication skills of children in natural settings—the classroom and the home.

Self-contained Special Classroom

This type of delivery system is used for children with severe disabilities who cannot be managed in the regular classroom with supportive help. Children can be grouped for instruction in a small special class in which they receive individualized, as well as group, instruction. Only 5 percent of the children receiving services are in this type of setting; the remainder are in the regular classroom.

Special School

This is generally a private school entirely devoted to children with communication disorders. In the special school classes are small and the children are grouped according to developmental level or type of disorder. Less than 1 percent of children with communication problems would be found in this setting.

Residential School

For children with severe disorders and multiple handicaps who require residential care as well as educational services, there are residential schools. In these schools we find youngsters with severe cases of developmental aphasia and children with complex neurological problems.

Preschool Services

For young children who are actually or potentially language and speech handicapped, consultant help from a speech-language pathologist is given to parents and preschool teachers who are in a position to help the child. Although not common in the past, this model is becoming more popular as early childhood education for handicapped children increases. The growth of early childhood education has necessitated the recruitment of specialists for this work.

Diagnostic Centers

This model provides an interdisciplinary team for the diagnosis and temporary remediation of children assigned to these centers. The procedure allows for a thorough diagnosis of the problem and initial experimentation with effective procedures for remediation. These centers are sometimes found in hospitals and in university departments of speech and hearing sciences.

Role of the Speech-Language Pathologist

From the variety of settings and options for delivery of services to language, speech, and hearing handicapped children, it's obvious that a speech-language pathologist must be able to serve in more than one capacity. An itinerant or resource speech-language pathologist must be prepared to deal with a broad range of handicapping conditions— articulation problems, voice problems, stuttering, language disorders— as well as the problems found among children with hearing handicaps, cleft palate, and mental retardation.

Because speech-language pathologists must be competent in a number of areas, their training has been extended in the three hundred or so universities and colleges that prepare these specialists. Departments of education in most states have these same requirements for certification, based on the recommendations of ASHA, the professional organization representing the field.

The general responsibilities of speech-language pathologists in the schools were outlined by ASHA (Project Upgrade, 1973):

- *Supervision and administration of programs for children with communication disorders.*   For every ten to twenty-nine speech-language

Parents of young children who are potentially speech and language handicapped are encouraged to improve the communication skills of the child at home.
(Alan Carey/The Image Works)

pathologists in the school system, a supervisor is required to organize and supervise the program and personnel. This individual should be certified and should have broad experience with all communication disorders.

- *Identification and diagnosis.* In other areas of special education, the diagnostician may be a psychologist or a physician who refers the child to a teacher for education. In speech pathology, the diagnostician assesses the child and also provides the necessary remediation. This procedure may be the preferred one because diagnosis sometimes leads to classification but not remediation when the two functions are performed separately.

- *Consultation.* Speech-language pathologists can devote all their time to professional consultation: demonstrating procedures, providing inservice training of regular and special teachers to serve children with minor problems, training and supervising communication aides, disseminating information to teachers and administrators, and serving as a consultant to parents and preschool teachers.

- *Direct services.* The large majority of speech-language pathologists devote their time to identifying children with communication disorders and to directing remedial services for them. In this capacity they serve children who stutter; children who have voice problems, hearing handicaps, articulation defects, and language disabilities; and children with communication disorders associated with cerebral palsy, mental retardation, emotional disturbance, and developmental aphasia. They also serve preschool children and infants.

- *Recording and reporting.* Speech-language pathologists are required to keep records and reports on all children with communication handicaps. The report is part of the school record and is treated by the school as such. The case record includes a statement of the problem, the assessment, the remediation and assignment, and the termination.

Speech-language pathologists think of themselves, and are thought of by classroom teachers, as members of the staffs of their schools. They attend faculty meetings and in some instances maintain a regular place on the inservice agenda. They confer regularly with each classroom teacher in the school one or more times a week. Where it is a policy of the district for teachers to hold parent conferences following the first grading period of the year, speech-language pathologists attend these conferences so that both teachers and parents understand the children's speech and language goals and their relation to academic achievement.

Speech-language pathologists also play an integral part in the development of the individualized education program (IEP) for each student they work with in a special education program. They determine the long-term objectives and the short-term goals that help the students meet those objectives. Speech-language pathologists are also members of the interdisciplinary team that meets at least annually with parents and in some cases students to review the progress made and to formulate future educational plans. The interdisciplinary team brings together professionals who share a common goal: to create and implement the best educational program for the student. This means speech-language pathologists must interact and cooperate with classroom teachers, audiologists, health professionals, classroom aides, administrators, counselors, social workers, other support personnel, and parents. They must be able to communicate clearly with all of these people and to relate speech and language goals to the broader perspective of the child's entire education program.

A major continuing problem facing speech-language pathologists in the public schools is the heavy case load of children they must see. The burden can be eased somewhat without sacrificing service by establishing programs to train *communication assistants.* These paraprofessionals are required to have a high school diploma and acceptable basic skills in reading, writing, and arithmetic. They receive training in speech and language development, total communication skills, and classroom management (Shinn-Strieker, 1984). A number of model programs have been established to use the assistants. Reports indicate that they are particularly useful in helping with articulation therapy, language therapy, and the necessary clerical work related to treatment.

One conclusion appears certain. This dynamic field which has changed so much over the past few decades, is unlikely to remain at a standstill now. We can expect ongoing change as speech-language pathologists try to find their proper role among the large number of professionals serving exceptional children.

The Use of Microcomputers

Few things are more frustrating to children with communication problems than trying to produce assignments that are acceptable to their teachers and to themselves. The introduction of microcomputers in the classroom and their capabilities for word processing provide a way to avoid some aspects of this problem. Behrmann (1984) points out the major benefits of word-processing systems—benefits that are particularly, but not exclusively, relevant to children with communication disorders: "1) There is no penalty for revising. 2) It is easy for students to experiment with writing. 3) Interest in writing task is maintained. 4) Editing is simple: spelling, punctuation, and grammar can be changed or checked. 5) Writing and editing are less time consuming. 6) Frustration is minimized. 7) It is easy to produce perfect copy" (p. 96).

All of these advantages meant a lot to Marc whose problems with language and writing are described in the following excerpt:

> Before the introduction of word processing Marc hated writing anything. He always made mistakes. He would choose a wrong verb tense or make syntax errors, spelling errors, and so forth. Before he developed even one paragraph all desire to continue was gone. His only option was to erase and after six or seven corrections the paper was a mess. His papers always reflected the struggle, not the accomplishment—and that was if he finished it to begin with; most often he gave up long before completion.
>
> Marc's introduction to word processing was accidental. He had been watching me work each morning writing a book. One day he simply tapped me on the shoulder and said, "Mom, can I do that." I thought for a moment, got up from the computer and said, "Sure you can," and hurriedly wrote down five simple commands. . . .
>
> From that point on he was on his own. He sat there, and before my eyes a seventh grade science report was born. It had all the language errors common to his written attempts, but I let him go on and on. When he said, "Done," with a big smile on his face, I said, "Okay, let's print it."
>
> The first draft came off the printer and we proofread it together. I circled the errors, made some suggestions in the order of presentation, and then showed him how to bring his report back to the screen from disc storage. He was amazed when he

saw his work before him and immediately began to make the corrections.

Actually, it was at this point that the real learning took place. There was a question as to whether Marc had ever been asked to correct his errors in written language before. His errors had been pointed out because he had notebooks full of written language assignments covered with red circles and handwritten notes made by teachers, but nowhere did Marc actually recopy his work to produce errorless, correct written language. That is understandable, too, for few would have the heart to ask a language handicapped child to recopy again and again to the point of errorless copy.

Marc made all the corrections and again printed out the report. It was a moment always to remember, for there in front of us was the first perfect paper Marc had ever generated. It reflected the accomplishment, not the struggle. He was so very proud, and so was I. Together we had found a tool to help him with written language and one that instilled a new kind of motivation. This tool allowed Marc to generate written language in a way that made him feel good about his work and himself. (Behrmann, 1984, pp. 96–97)

LIFESPAN ISSUES FOR INDIVIDUALS WITH COMMUNICATION DISORDERS

What lies ahead in adulthood for the child who has a communication disorder? The answer to that question—and the available evidence is quite thin—depends on the nature of the disorder. Children who have articulation disorders and no additional complications would seem to have few special problems as adults, whereas children who have language disorders or who stutter may continue to have these problems as adults. They may need additional clinical services and rehabilitation as adults in order to make their best adjustment.

In an investigation by Winitz (1969), the results indicated that children with articulation problems either did not differ from nonimpaired children or they performed more poorly. Hall and Tomlin (1978) found in a retrospective study that the majority of parents of young adults who had articulation problems as children believed that their offspring exhibited no continuing communication problems. It was also found that the subjects with articulation disorders performed higher academically than the subjects with language disorders.

A review of the literature indicated that the onset of stuttering generally occurs during childhood sometime before nine years of age (Young, 1974). There is disagreement in the literature, however, on the recovery rate from stuttering. Some studies (Andrew & Harris, 1964; Sheehan & Martyn, 1970) indicated that the recovery rate might be as high as 80 percent; however, another study (Cooper, 1972) cited a recovery rate of approximately 45 percent. Wingate (1964) and Shearer and Williams (1965) reported that 50 percent and 64 percent of their respective subjects stated that they still stuttered occasionally.

The information in the literature appears to indicate a lack of consensus on exactly what the recovery rate from stuttering is. There seem to be several reasons for this problem. Most of the studies depended on retrospective data and the subjects' ability to recall speech problems with fluency. Another problem seems to be that some of the families might have identified periods of normal disfluency in the subject's early years as stuttering behavior. In addition, some young children experience short periods of time when they exhibit disfluency in communication that may cause a layperson to label the child as a stutterer when a speech-language pathologist would not. In summary, the lack of definitive terminology and the lack of empirical data make it difficult at this time to state precisely the recovery rate for stuttering.

There is a strong need for follow-up studies to trace children with communication disorders into adulthood before we can talk confidently about the long-term effect of our special education services.

SUMMARY OF MAJOR IDEAS

1. Communication can be verbal, nonverbal, or a combination of both. It involves three components: sender, message, and receiver. Language is a factor in every stage of the process; speech is a factor in verbal communication.
2. Over the last four decades, services in the field of communication disorders have been expanded to include hearing problems and language disorders as well as speech problems.
3. Impaired speech is characterized as being conspicuous, unintelligible, and unpleasant.
4. A child is language impaired when his or her skills in the primary language are markedly below those expected for the child's chronological age.
5. Approximately 6 percent of the schoolchildren in the United States have some form of speech or language impairment. In half the cases, the problem is one of articulation. In most instances, articulatory disorders disappear as children mature.
6. Communication disorders are impairments in articulation, language, voice, or fluency.
7. In many schools, establishment of a communication disorders program entails screening, diagnosis, and selection of the children who require and can benefit from speech and langauge intervention.
8. There are five dimensions in language: phonology (sound), morphology (word structure), syntax (sentence structure), semantics (word meaning), and pragmatics (function). A child can be impaired in any or all of these dimensions.

9. There is a six-stage sequence of language acquisition, from the preverbal stage to the complex-form stage. Understanding the pattern of language acquisition is an important part of identifying children with language disorders and developing remediation programs for them.

10. The physical processes needed to produce sound are respiration, phonation, resonation, and articulation. A breakdown in any of these processes can impair speech production.

11. Articulation disorders involve substitutions, omissions, and distortions. For young children, intervention in the regular classroom is the traditional method of remediation. Older children may require either individual or group sessions with a speech-language pathologist.

12. Fluency disorders (stuttering) can be alleviated temporarily through distraction and other devices. Permanent improvement is more difficult. Treatment involves the teaching of rhythmic stuttering and behavior therapy.

13. Voice disorders are the result of significant deviations in vocal quality, pitch, and loudness. Treatment involves careful diagnosis, removal of the cause where possible, and negative practice.

14. Most speech and language remediation programs focus on children with communication deviations—those with mild to moderate articulation or voice problems that are causing adaptation difficulties in school.

15. The most common models for the delivery of language and speech services are itinerant teachers, resource rooms, and consultative services—all of which fit well into the mainstream philosophy.

16. The role of the speech-language pathologist has expanded with the field, increasing the responsibilities of the profession. In the schools, the speech-language pathologist is a member of the interdisciplinary team that develops and monitors the child's individualized education program.

UNRESOLVED ISSUES

1. *Case load quotas.*   Over the last thirty or forty years, speech-language pathologists in the schools have traditionally spent 75 to 80 percent of their time on children with articulation problems, dividing the rest of their time among children with more serious problems (voice disorders, fluency problems, language difficulties). Is this the best division of time? Many believe that it is not, and that the reason the practice continues is to show a large case load in order to justify financial support for the professional within the school program. Meanwhile children with serious problems receive less remedial attention than they should. We must find a way to ease case load quotas without jeopardizing program funding so that professionals can devote more time to children with serious communication problems.

2. *Who "owns" the problems?* There is a growing dispute over who has responsibility for helping children who are learning disabled. Psychologists, learning disability teachers, remedial reading specialists, and speech-language pathologists, all have a legitimate professional claim to skills that can help these youngsters. The general public, however, is predictably unenthusiastic about nonproductive struggles among professionals. In the end, the group that appears to be doing the most good for the children will win. And that is where the focus of attention should be.

3. *Origins of communication problems.* Despite a long history of clinical work with a variety of communication problems, the causes of certain major disorders—stuttering and language disorders, for example—are still mysteries. This does not mean, of course, that we cannot help youngsters with these difficulties. Clinical practice and experience have led the way to a number of successful therapeutic approaches. Still, if we want to discuss prevention of a condition instead of remediation, knowing its cause becomes a central issue. We need major research to give us insight into the sources of these problems and to develop ways to stop their incidence in the next generation.

REFERENCES OF SPECIAL INTEREST

Hixon, T., Shriberg, L., & Saxman, J. (Eds.). (1980). *Introduction to communication disorders.* Englewood Cliffs, NJ: Prentice-Hall.
> A compilation of chapters, each written by recognized specialists in the field. In addition to coverage of the typical speech disorder areas, it includes several chapters on language problems and two chapters on hearing problems.

Shames, G., & Wiig, E. (Eds.). (1982). *Human communication disorders: An introduction.* Columbus, OH: Charles E. Merrill.
> A general textbook in which each chapter is written by a knowledgeable individual in the content area. Of special interest are the four chapters on language development and language disorders.

Swartz, A. (Ed.). (1984). *The handbook of microcomputer applications in communication disorders.* San Diego: College Hill Press.
> Organized into five sections, this handbook provides basic information on microcomputer systems, hardware, and software as well as consideration of current and future applications of microcomputer programs in the field of communication disorders.

Van Riper, C. (1978). *Speech correction: Principles and methods* (6th ed.). Englewood Cliffs, NJ: Prentice-Hall.
> Perhaps the most widely used text by one of the most respected professionals in the field. The author makes a comprehensive examination of all speech disorders and their treatment, with less emphasis on language problems than we find in later textbooks.

C·H·A·P·T·E·R
Eight

CHILDREN WITH
BEHAVIOR PROBLEMS

Focusing Questions

Why is there a wide range of estimates on the prevalence of youngsters with behavior problems in the school-age population?

What patterns are common among the families of children with behavior problems?

What is learned helplessness?

How is socialized aggression different from other forms of deviant behavior?

What are several potential causes of behavior problems?

How are drug therapy, behavior modification, and psychodynamic strategy used in educational adaptations for youngsters with behavior problems?

What techniques do we use to teach children to manage their own behavior?

*F*ew experiences are so disturbing to sensitive teachers as encountering children who are chronically unhappy or distressed, or driven to aggressive, antisocial behavior. These teachers feel helpless, knowing there's a problem but unable to do anything about it.

> I can't stop worrying about one little girl in my first grade. She behaves so peculiarly. She doesn't talk most of the time, though she can talk. She answers the other children and me with animal sounds. She hides under chairs like a dog and barks at people. . . . She has been on a clinic waiting list for six months, and I've had the child up for special service to test her for three months. In the meantime, the class all laugh at her, and she just gets worse, and I don't know what to do. (Long, Morse, & Newman, 1980, p. 212)

DEFINITION

It is not easy to define behavior problems in children. Most definitions assume that children with behavior problems reveal consistent age-inappropriate behavior leading to social conflict, personal unhappiness, and school failure. But almost all children reveal age-inappropriate behavior at one time or another. Our definition, then, depends on the dimensions of *intensity* and *duration* to distinguish between normal and exceptional behaviors. Because professionals in the field disagree on degree and persistence, we have widely varying estimates of prevalence.

Moreover, a child's behavior is not the only variable that determines classification in this category. The person who perceives the child's behavior as inappropriate plays a key role in the decision. Clearly, some kinds of behavior are unacceptable in any setting: physical attacks, constant weeping or unhappiness, extreme hyperactivity. But the acceptability of a wide range of other behaviors depends on the attitude of the perceiver.

Wood (1982) suggested that a definition of problem behavior, or a set of actions that follows from the definition, should include four elements:

- *The disturber element.* What or who is perceived to be the focus of the problem?
- *The problem behavior element.* How is the problem behavior described?

- *The setting element.*   In what setting does the problem behavior occur?
- *The disturbed element.*   Who regards the behavior as a problem? (pp. 7–8)

Public Law 94–142, the Education for All Handicapped Children Act, defines **behavior disabilities** as a condition in which one or more of the following are exhibited to a marked degree or over a long period of time:

- An inability to learn which cannot be explained by intellectual sensory or health factors.
- An inability to build or maintain satisfactory interpersonal relationships with peers or teachers.
- Inappropriate types of behaviors or feelings under normal circumstances.
- A general pervasive mood of unhappiness or depression.
- A tendency to develop physical symptoms or fears associated with personal or school problems. (Federal Register, p. 42478).

A somewhat less involved definition that captures what we've been discussing was provided by Kauffman (1977):

Children with behavior disorders are those who chronically and markedly respond to their environment in socially unacceptable and/or personally unsatisfying ways but also can be taught more socially acceptable and personally gratifying behavior. (p. 23)

It is possible to overdo confusion and disagreement about a definition. Many children would receive a unanimous vote on the question of whether they show problem behavior, and these are the children we are interested in studying and helping in special education.

DEVELOPMENTAL PROFILES

Figure 8.1 shows the profiles of two youngsters. Both have behavior problems, and both are experiencing academic difficulties. Each child, however, expresses these problems in very different ways.

Jim is an eleven-year-old who seems sullen and angry most of the time. He rarely smiles and has a history of terrifying temper outbursts. When he is frustrated, he sometimes blows up and attacks the nearest person with such frenzy that other children give him a wide berth and hesitate to interact with him.

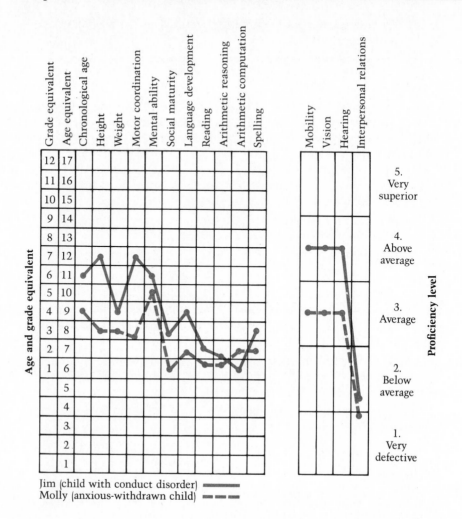

Jim (child with conduct disorder) ▬▬▬
Molly (anxious-withdrawn child) ▬ ▬ ▬

Stories in the neighborhood recount Jim's cruelty to animals, how he has tortured and killed cats and dogs. His language borders on profanity, and he has been known to challenge his teachers with the phrase "What are you going to do about it?" Jim is a threat, not only to his peers, but to his teachers' image of their own competence. His physical skills are advanced, even though his interpersonal skills are not, and this tends to complicate the situation. As he grows older, he will become less manageable physically. Although we can tolerate the temper tantrums of a five-year-old, the same outbursts from a fifteen-year-old are frightening.

School personnel are actively seeking alternative placement for Jim on the grounds that they are not capable, either physically or psychologically, of coping with his problems. Jim comes from a father-absent home; his mother is somewhat disorganized and seems to have given up trying to control her son. His social contacts are limited to a few other youngsters who have similar angry and acting-out propensities, and those who are close to Jim worry about his future.

Jim's performance in school, as shown in Figure 8.1, is two to five grades below his grade level, and his hostility and unwillingness to accept correction or help have caused his teachers much anxiety.

The second profile in Figure 8.1 shows Molly, a 9-year-old girl in the fourth grade who is having a difficult time at school. In contrast to Jim, who tends to externalize his problems, Molly internalizes hers. She is in tears and depressed much of the time. She is not able to make friends with the preadolescent girls who have formed the major social group in the classroom, and seems lonely and alone. Molly is so quiet that if it were not for the manifest unhappiness that shows in her face and physical demeanor, she would go unnoticed in school. She, like Jim, is seriously behind in her academic work.

Molly's middle-class parents are concerned about her and have tried many different routes, including therapy, to help her, but so far with few gains. She is a source of great frustration to her parents, who cannot understand why she is not like her older sister, who seems effortlessly successful in academic and social spheres. Molly is not the personal threat to teachers that Jim is because she does not challenge their ability to control the classroom. But she does challenge those teachers who want the children in their classes to be happy in school and who are upset by their inability to modify the sadness and low self-concept that are portrayed in Molly's behavior.

PREVALENCE

Any line we draw between normal children and children with behavior problems is obviously difficult to define. All children show aggressive, antisocial behavior or fearful behavior at one time or another. The difference for those children with special problems is in the frequency and intensity of their problem behavior and in the situations in which they act out.

Studies on prevalence show great disparity in the frequency of behavior problems in schoolchildren. Estimates vary from around 2 percent (Froomkin, 1972), to 8 percent (Ullmann, 1952), to 10.5 percent (Bower, 1960), to 20 to 24 percent (Kelly, Bullock, & Dykes, 1977; Salvia, Schultz, & Chapin, 1974).

What is the prevalence of behavior problems from the teachers' viewpoint? Rubin and Balow (1978) reported ratings of 1,586 children from kindergarten to sixth grade. Teachers were asked to identify those children who had behavior problems. The results of the survey were startling:

*Because practically all children exhibit inappropriate be-
havior from time to time, criteria for identifying problem
behavior depend largely on the frequency and intensity
of specific behaviors.*
(Mike Mazzaschi/Stock, Boston)

- More than half (60 percent) the children were classified as having
  a behavior problem at least once between kindergarten and sixth
  grade.
- Male students were identified three times more often than female
  students.
- Of all the students, 7 percent were identified in three or more years
  by different teachers as requiring special help.

How can we explain the high incidence of children with behavior
problems in elementary school? First, the structure of the survey may
have been faulty. Teachers were asked to identify those children who
were problems, not those who were "extremely difficult" problems.
And, of course, different teachers define *problem* differently. The re-

searchers left that definition to the individual teachers; they did not dictate a set of criteria.

Wood and Zabel (1978) offered another explanation. Most of the identification procedures require teachers to rate children in their classrooms *at that point in time* as having behavior problems. Apparently many children will manifest behavior problems at one time or another in the school program, and a one-time screening will identify them. Wood and Zabel believed that the low incidence figures of 2 to 3 percent generally refer to those students who have such serious, recurrent, or persistent problems in adjusting to school as to need special programming over an extended period of time.

In Chapter 1, (Figure 1.2) showed the number of behaviorally disturbed children who are actually receiving special education: just about 1 percent of the school population. Yet Public Law 94–142 requires treatment of all children who need help. Where have the rest of the children with behavior problems gone? Why haven't they been found?

One answer is that children, once identified, must be treated by law, often an expensive proposition. There is reason to believe that under these circumstances educators are identifying only the most serious cases, leaving large numbers of children with demonstrable problems officially unidentified and unfortunately untreated.

CLASSIFICATION AND CHARACTERISTICS OF CHILDREN WITH BEHAVIOR PROBLEMS

The purpose of any system of classification is to produce subgroups that either (1) improve our understanding of the origin or causes of a condition or (2) provide the basis for differential education and treatment. For example, both Jim and Molly can be classified "children with behavior disorders"; but they belong in different subcategories and would probably receive quite different educational programming.

In the past, category systems for children and adults with behavior problems emerged from psychiatry, to meet the needs of professionals in such fields as clinical psychology and psychiatric social work. Two major classifications systems were developed from that clinical perspective: the Diagnostic and Statistical Manual of Mental Disorders, third edition (DSM III) and the Classification System of Psychopathological Disorders in Children from the Group for the Advancement of Psychiatry (GAP). These systems contain subgroups like personality and developmental disorders, motor coordination disorders, and psychoneurotic disorders. As useful as these terms may be from a psychiatric standpoint, they hold little value for educators.

A somewhat different approach, made possible by the availability of computer facilities, involves the use of statistical techniques that isolate patterns of interrelated behaviors. By using check lists, rating scales, and similar measuring devices to evaluate large numbers of children, it is possible to sort out clusters of responses that separate one group of children from another. This approach has yielded four patterns of deviant behavior in children: conduct disorders, anxiety-withdrawal, immaturity, and socialized aggression (Quay, 1979).

Children who have a **conduct disorder** defy authority; are hostile toward authority figures (police officers, teachers); are cruel, malicious, and assaultive; and have few guilt feelings. This group includes children who are hyperactive, restless, and hyperkinetic. Jim clearly fits into this category.

Anxious-withdrawn children are shy, timid, seclusive, sensitive, and submissive. They are overdependent and easily depressed. According to Quay's study, these children come mostly from overprotective families in the higher socioeconomic levels. Molly tends to fit into this category.

The **immaturity** dimension refers to children who are inattentive, sluggish, uninterested in school, lazy, preoccupied, and reticent. They resemble children who are autistic or prepsychotic. They appear to be less able to function in the regular classroom than are children who are neurotic or who have conduct disorders.

Socialized-aggressive children have some of the same characteristics or behavior problems as those with conduct disorders but are socialized within their peer group, usually a gang. Common behaviors for these youngsters include stealing and truancy. Although these behaviors may not be considered maladaptive within the specific environment in which these children exist, they do present a clear danger to the larger society.

Conduct Disorders

The families in which children with conduct disorders are found follow certain predominant patterns. Frequently the father is aggressive and hostile, and uses physical force for discipline. In Jim's case, his father treated what he thought was Jim's misbehavior with spankings that verged on beatings. Apparently hostility breeds hostility, and Jim became even more of a problem when his father walked out on the family, leaving Jim's mother to cope with him. As is common in these families, the mother was inconsistent with discipline and preoccupied with financial survival. Hetherington and Martin (1979) described how the family system produces a child with a conduct disorder:

> It has been proposed that extremely restrictive, power assertive discipline, particularly in a hostile family environment, leads to a frustration of dependency needs and a heightened predisposition to respond aggressively. If the opportunity to express this aggression occurs through inconsistent discipline, laxity

in one parent, or active reinforcement for aggressive behavior outside the home, this may increase the probability of anti-social aggressive responses by the child. (p. 263)

One of the distressing aspects of conduct disorders is their stability over time (Wicks-Nelson & Israel, 1984). Gersten, Langner, Eisenberg, Simcha-Fagan, and McCarthy (1976) followed 732 New York families over five years and found that the patterns of behavior linked to conduct disorders in children (parental conflict, antisocial behavior, and fighting) increased or remained constant over the five years. Additional evidence for the stability of conduct disorders is provided in the follow-up study by Robins (1966) and a series of studies reported in the section on lifespan issues at the end of the chapter.

There are diverse opinions on the origins of conduct disorders but Patterson (1980) has provided a social learning explanation that is well accepted. He believes that the child's aggressive behaviors (often a boy) get him what he wants as the parent gives up. The child will use this response again in other situations and also learns that aggressive behavior stops others from annoying or bothering him. Parental punishment when it is used on the child is sporadic and ineffective and merely provides another model of aggressiveness for the child. In short, the child is rewarded for aggressive behavior and thus continues it.

Whatever the basic cause of the problem, there is little question that children with conduct disorders are a serious problem in a school setting. They show a marked inability to persist in a task, often disrupt class, are easily distracted, and present a constant irritation to teachers because of their inability to follow directions and maintain a learning set. As education has become more directly involved with these children, increasing concern has been expressed about their academic status.

The developmental history of hyperactive behavior, often associated with conduct disorder, reveals that the more manifest elements of the syndrome disappear over time. Douglas (1972) reported that hyperactivity decreased over preadolescence, but noted that impulsiveness and inattention remained serious problems. These youngsters are apparently unable to control their impulses in order to cope with situations in which care, concentrated attention, and organized planning are required. They tend to react to the first idea that occurs to them or to those aspects of the situation that are the most obvious or compelling. Douglas stated that they have a marked inability to "stop, look, and listen."

Obviously these children do not make ideal students. In most cases, serious academic problems go hand in hand with emotional or behavioral discrepancy. Glavin and Annesley (1971) compared a group of 130 behavior problem boys, identified by means of a behavior check list, with 90 normal boys of the same age and IQ level. Among the problem boys, 81 percent were underachieving in reading, 72 percent, in math.

Keogh (1977) noted that two of the characteristic responses of delinquent children are their impulsiveness and their inability to delay gratification.

Do conduct disorders disappear over time? Do children like Jim grow out of their problems? Some do, of course, but an important follow-up study by Robins (1966) suggested that many do not. Using a structured interview, she studied 524 adults who as children had received treatment in a child guidance clinic in a major metropolitan area. The elements used to diagnose adult sociopathic personality were work history, marital history, drug use, alcohol use, arrests, belligerence, unusual sexual behavior, suicide attempts, impulsiveness, truancy combined with other school problems, financial dependence, performance in the armed forces, vagrancy, somatic complaints, pathological lying, maintenance of social relationships, lack of guilt, and wild behavior in late adolescence. A control sample of 100 adults who had spent their childhood in the same neighborhood and school district was also interviewed.

Only 4 percent of the control subjects showed five or more antisocial symptoms as adults, compared with 45 percent of the clinic group. The problems experienced by the clinic group as adults were not attributed to the stigma of being a "problem child"; instead, they were linked to the nature and severity of the childhood behavior that occasioned referral in the first place. Those individuals who as children had been referred to the clinic because of antisocial behavior showed the most difficult adult adjustment. Those who had been referred for temper tantrums, learning problems, speech difficulties, and so forth did not show major antisocial tendencies in adulthood.

One hundred adults from both groups who were diagnosed by psychiatrists as having sociopathic personalities on the basis of written materials and structured interviews had chaotic, disturbed childhoods. Their histories showed juvenile theft, incorrigibility, running away from home, truancy, associating with bad companions, staying out late, and other problem behaviors. Most were discipline problems in school and had been held back at least one grade by the time they appeared in the clinic. Most never graduated from elementary school. Robins concluded that impulsive, antisocial behavior, not fearful, shy behavior, is the most ominous predictor of adult problems.

One of the most distressing elements in the development of behaviorally disturbed children is that their problems seem to carry over from one generation to another. In their own families, 78 percent of Robins's clinic group had already been divorced, with record-high rates of desertion and unfaithfulness in comparison with control samples. Perhaps more significant were the figures on the level of behavior problems in spouses of individuals from the clinic group. They showed a high incidence of neglect, alcoholism, and desertion relative to the control sample, suggesting that unstable, asocial adults tend to marry people like themselves. It was not surprising to see that the problems of the children born into these families were much greater than those found in the control group.

The problems of asocial and antisocial behavior, unless dealt with vigorously in childhood, can lead to antisocial behavior in adulthood, which in turn can create a new generation of antisocial children. And so the cycle continues.

Anxiety-Withdrawal and Immaturity

Anxious or withdrawn children are often a bigger threat to themselves than they are to others around them. Because they usually are not disruptive, they do not cause classroom management problems. But teachers often worry about children who are visibly unhappy, as these children are.

In contrast to children with conduct disorders, who show "too much behavior," anxious-withdrawn children show "too little" (Quay, 1979). Their problems are with ego control and ego resiliency (flexibility). Anxious-withdrawn children maintain firm control over their impulses, wishes, and desires in all settings. This leaves them rigid, unable to be spontaneous. Resilient children can delay gratification when the situation calls for it, but are able to respond spontaneously and enthusiastically when appropriate (Block & Block, 1980).

We find in children like Molly a **learned helplessness,** the belief that nothing they do can prevent negative things from happening. Learned helplessness results in severe deterioration in performance after failure, as though the children have said to themselves, "It's all happening again." These children have such low self-concepts that failure in a school task or a social setting only confirms for them their worthlessness and helplessness in the face of an unfriendly environment. Molly's poor performance in the classroom may be much worse than she is capable of doing simply because she is so pessimistic about herself and her ability. Low self-esteem seems to be at the heart of much of the underachievement of anxious-withdrawn children.

Where do fearful children come from? We know that many of these children have parents with similar problems. In addition, most professionals agree that chronic anxiety in children comes from being in a stressful situation, not being able to get out of the situation, and not being able to do anything to improve it. This inability to modify the situation adds to feelings of helplessness and reinforces low self-image. For college students, a crucial examination looming on the horizon can create chronic anxiety. For younger children, anxiety can stem from homes where they feel unwanted or are abused. Children are often too young to understand that their parents may be working out their own problems or that their parents' reactions have little to do with them. All they understand is that no matter what they do they are not getting praise or love from their parents.

One serious outcome of a prolonged, intense period of anxiety or depression are feelings of self-destruction. There is growing concern about the prevalence of suicide in schoolchildren. It has been estimated that suicides account for more than 4 percent of the adolescent mortality rate (Havighurst, 1972). And this figure may be low because many suicides are listed as accidental deaths. If a teenager has a one-car accident and runs into a tree or a bridge, it is difficult to know why. Was it an accident? Or was it deliberate? Even those accidents that are alcohol related may be a form of suicide if the use of alcohol was stimulated by depression.

The number of suicides and attempted suicides is much smaller among preadolescent children and young teens. Between 1976 and 1977, the suicide rate for this group rose slightly, from 1 per 100,000 to 1.6 per 100,000 (McGuire & Ely, 1984). In 1983, over 12,000 children between the ages of 5 and 14 were admitted to psychiatric hospitals (Matter & Matter, 1984). Interestingly enough, there does not seem to be any increase in suicide rates among children with handicapping conditions. As Bryan and Herjanic (1980) have commented, it takes both mental ability and physical strength to carry out suicide.

How do we identify youngsters who are having a depressive reaction? Birelson (1980) described four signals:

- Evidence of recently expressed unhappiness, sadness, misery, or weepiness.
- A history of behavioral change lasting at least two weeks, but less than one year.
- Evidence of recent impairment in social relationships and/or decline in school performance.
- The presence of two or more of the following symptoms: . . . Sleep disturbance, appetite disturbance, loss of usual energy or interest, reduction in activity, expression of self-deprecating ideas, suicidal threats or behavior, increased irritability, new somatic complaints, wandering behavior, and depressive delusions and hallucinations. (p. 76)

All of us have felt depressed at one time or another. Why do these feelings persist with some individuals and not with others? Schloss (1983) posed three separate theories:

- *Learned helplessness.* The children have used up all of their adaptive responses trying to cope with difficult situations, often in the family, and have failed. Their inability to cope becomes generalized, so that even when there are good adaptive behavior responses available to them, they do not use them. Schloss examined a number of research studies that show a pattern of learned helplessness among depressed individuals. They attribute their failures to factors

VIVIENNE: A TEACHER'S VIEWPOINT

In my teaching career, I have taught all ages. I have known children far more apparently injured than Vivienne, even abused. I have known adolescents with fewer successes and, to an observer, deeper feelings of worthlessness who nevertheless survived. Even Vivienne's preoccupation with death, had I known of it, would not have shocked me. The idea of personal death has impact at any age, but for adolescents it has particular force. Many young people struggle to incorporate their new awareness and even toy with death as a possible means of controlling their own destinies. . . .

. . . .Vivienne did not send signals to any Cambridge School adult and her pain was not visible. Her deepest injuries had occurred before we knew her and she had become clever about concealing them. But suppose we had seen some of her most dramatic writing? It takes an experienced eye to detect the difference between fatal despair and sensitive introspection. Adolescents are often dramatic in their writing. To an adult, young people sometimes seem to lack an emotional thermostat, so heated and volatile are their responses. They can be anguished at one moment, restored and vivacious the next. One must know a great deal about them to judge how serious their struggles are. . . .

All of this certainly crosses a teacher's mind when a student shares tragic thoughts. Empathetic teachers are aware of the pride and dignity, the sense of privacy young people feel so keenly. Here, indeed, is that puzzling line that teachers sometimes face between themselves and other professionals. When should a teacher report troubling news? When would it drive a wedge between him and the adolescent who trusts no one else? Can any sympathetic adult handle the situation?

Knowing what we know now, the answer seems simple. Vivienne tried to strangle herself. . . . The family should have been alerted. A therapist should have been called in.

But, in my experience, these are not easy decisions. We hesitate to cut lines of communication that may, in the end, help to heal. The strangulation description in Vivienne's letter is followed by "I have decided to stick this life of mine out," and she went on to report that she was writing poetry again.

These are reassuring communications and seem to put the suicidal impulse in the past. . . .

The issues are difficult ones. Adolescents don't seem to be the best candidates for therapy. They tend to see adult counselors as official parental representatives and consequently as a threat to their unsteady independence. They often lack, too, the deep and continuing discontent that informs the motivation of older people. It is hard for them to commit themselves seriously to regular appointments. They are inclined to flee when sessions come closest to the heart of their suffering. They would rather turn to trusted teachers or other adults when they need a listener. They prefer to remain in control of the time and the extent of their own confidences.

continued

continued

But this poses another problem. Teachers have their limitations. They may be frightened of emotional crises. They may mistake what they are hearing. They may lack the personal insight and training that illuminate for psychologists, not only the meaning of confidences young people offer, but, perhaps even more important, their own blind spots and denials. Teachers are not professional psychologists. They need to know when to turn to the experts. There is a distinct line between what the counseling profession offers and what educators can do to prevent suicide.

The distinction between the two is entirely proper. In some ways, teachers represent reality and daily partnership. A teacher may see as "lazy" what a psychiatrist would label "paralyzed." A teacher could respond to "hostility" where a psychologist would see "depression." Young people need to know both aspects of themselves: the effect of their behavior and, when it is troubling, the emotional logic that causes it. Perhaps these two functions cannot be blended in one person, but it is safe to say that the two viewpoints ought to come closer together and that teachers should make new relationships with counselors.

In our school we have a training group for teachers, now in its fourth year. We meet once a week for two hours under the supervision of an experienced psychologist. There we talk about ourselves, our students, relationships and events that puzzle us. The group serves to enlighten and inform us, deepen our personal insight and enrich our understanding of young people. We can better recognize and handle normal adolescent turmoil. It does not, however, make us psychologists, and we learn to be very respectful of that line between us. . . .

Vivienne died at fourteen. No one close to her was able to keep her from suicide. As Marianne Moore wrote, "What is our innocence, / what is our guilt? All are / naked, none is safe." Shaken and changed, we review Vivienne's suffering and reconsider the plight of adolescents everywhere. Her death reminds us again: all children are under our care.

SOURCE: From *Vivienne: The Life and Suicide of an Adolescent Girl* by John E. Mack and Holly Hickler, Little, Brown and Company, Inc., Boston, MA, 1981.

they cannot control; they do not respond well to social stimuli or events; they reduce their efforts after failure; and they verbalize their low self-concept following failure.

• *Social skills deficiency.* Depressed individuals seem less adept at obtaining positive reinforcement from social behavior, and are less able to reinforce others, which decreases their rate of positive social interaction.

- *Coercive consequences.* Chronic depression relies on coercive consequence patterns. When anxious-withdrawn children receive positive reactions from others (sympathy, support, reassurance), they fail to develop the personal behavior and social skills that lead to more effective behavior.

For each of these theories there is a predictable intervention technique. In the case of learned helplessness, we must convince those children that they are capable of influencing their own environment. In the case of social skill deficiency, we can teach and reinforce more effective interpersonal skills. In the case of coercive consequences, we can avoid reinforcing these children's dependency and helplessness, instead focusing on positive aspects of their personality and performance.

Cohen-Sandler, Berman, and King (1982) studied seventy-six children who had been admitted to an inpatient psychiatric unit of a children's hospital for being suicidal. They compared them with a group of children who were depressed and another group with a variety of psychiatric conditions not related to suicide. In explaining what separated the suicidal youngsters from the others, the authors concluded: "In a context of intensely stressful chaotic and unpredictable family events, children who otherwise were incapable of making an impact on these circumstances seem to use suicide as a means of interpersonal coercion or retaliation" (p. 184).

In short, suicide is often the means of expressing intense rage against more powerful adults, the only action that will have impact on those with whom the child is angry. The incidence of suicide increases dramatically in older children (ages 15 to 19), who have the physical ability and access to weapons and other devices to carry out their self-destructive patterns.

In less intense situations, withdrawn children often have limited or ineffectual social relationships. The reasons are twofold: most people are not comfortable with individuals who are continually self-destructive and unhappy. Then, too, withdrawn children have less practice socializing. If past social relationships have been unpleasant, there is a tendency to avoid the potential for similar relationships. If, for example, a girl's early experiences with her father have been bad, she may transfer her negative feelings to all men ("All men are alike!") and never be able to differentiate one from another. Because her tendency is to withdraw in social settings, she is not likely to try out new relationships that will help her discover that there can be important differences among individuals.

Extreme dependency is another manifestation of withdrawal. Maccoby and Masters (1970) reviewed a vast amount of literature on the relationship of parental behavior to child behavior. They concluded: "There is evidence that dependency is associated not with warmth but with its polar opposite, rejection or hostility" (p. 140). The parent who withdraws love and affection creates panic in the child; the child reacts in the way that has elicited affection in the past, becoming more babylike or dependent. This means the strategy of being cold and distant, which a parent might adopt in an attempt to "cure" the child of dependency, to force the child to grow up, may actually increase the likelihood that the dependent behavior will continue.

We know little about the special nature of immature children, but we can assume a similarity between these children and those who are anxious-withdrawn. The most serious of these disturbances, schizophrenia and autism, are discussed in Chapter 10.

Socialized Aggression

The patterns of behavior we've been talking about are maladaptive: They do not conform to the standards of any of our normal environments (family, friends, school, society). Socialized aggression, although disturbing to teachers, can be appropriate given the subcultures from which many children come. It is not the children's behavior that does not conform; it is the values of the subculture.

Bronfenbrenner (1979) focused on the family as a child-rearing system, on society's support or lack of support for that system, and on the effects of that support or lack of support on children. He maintained that the alienation of children reflects a breakdown in the interconnected segments of a child's life—family, peer group, school, neighborhood, work world. The question is not "What is wrong with socialized-aggressive children?" It is "What is wrong with the social system?"

Although most of these children do not have feelings of anxiety or guilt about their behavior, the conflict between the values of the mainstream society (and school) and those of their subculture can create tension. For example, what does a child do when he or she sees a friend cheating? Honesty—a valued societal ethic—demands that the child report the incident. But loyalty—a valued subcultural ethic—demands silence.

FACTORS RELATED TO BEHAVIOR PROBLEMS

Parents and professionals looking for the reasons why Molly and Jim are the way they are must examine an array of potential causes, from the individual's biological makeup, to the family, to the larger society.

Biophysical Factors

Over the past few decades, we've accepted that problem behavior stems from the interaction of children with their family, peer groups, neighborhood, and subculture. We've done this for two reasons: First, the effects of the family and social environments on these children are obvious. Second, we can do something about the environmental causes of behavior problems. But how do we trace the effects of heredity on behavior? And what can we do to correct problems if we find them?

These questions have not stopped researchers from tying maladaptive behavior to genetics. Schwartz (1979) pointed out credible evidence of the significant role heredity plays in shaping behavior and personality. For example, we find sex-linked differences in many behavioral conditions. Infantile autism, hyperactivity, and conduct disorders (alcoholism, antisocial behavior) occur in males four to eight times more often than they do in females. Depression and social phobias appear in postpubescent females two to three times more often than they do in males. Of course, we can tie these differences, at least in part, to the very different ways in which society treats boys and girls, men and women. But they also suggest that a sex-linked genetic factor is at work.

To what extent are deviant behaviors hereditary? To what extent are they environmental? We can probably say that there is no behavior that does not combine some elements of heredity and environment. The task of behavioral geneticists is to sort out the relative contribution of these forces in specific behavioral areas (Plomin, DeFries, & McClearn, 1980).

The evidence for the genetic influence on behavior has been traced through the study of identical twins (identical heredity), adoptive children (Is the child more like the biological parents or the adoptive parents?), and statistical analyses of the prevalence of conditions in certain families or populations over generations. Research indicates significant genetic influence in serious disturbances (schizophrenia, manic-depressive psychosis), but also shows genetic influence on the development of temperament characteristics that can create a favorable or unfavorable environment in which individuals must operate (Rosenthal, 1970).

Thomas and Chess (1977) followed several groups of children into adulthood, and identified three consistent temperament types over time:

- *The easy child.* Characterized by regularity, positive response to new stimuli, adaptability, and high tolerance for frustration (40 percent of the group).
- *The difficult child.* Characterized by irregular biological functions, negative withdrawal, poor adaptability, and frequent negativism (10 percent of the group).
- *The slow-to-warm-up child.* Characterized by a limited response to stimuli, a flatness of emotional response, and unsatisfactory adult-child interactions (15 percent of the group).

The rest of the sample (35 percent) was a mixture of the three basic types.

It is not hard to see that the "easy" child provides a base for favorable social interactions from infancy, or that the "difficult" or "slow-to-warm-up" child can frustrate those interactions. These basic temperamental differences, then, can set the tone for adult-child relationships throughout life.

Family Environment

The study of behavior problems or emotional disturbance has long focused on the family. Freud and his followers analyzed the relationships of child and parents, coining the phrases *Oedipus complex* and *Electra complex* to mark pathological mother-child and father-child relationships that cast long shadows into adulthood (White, 1963). Today, we no longer look automatically to the family as the source of behavior problems. We realize that the family too can be trapped in a larger ecological sphere that affects all family members negatively.

Still, we can identify certain familial conditions that can lead to emotional problems for children. For example, we know that children are not immune to family instability. Hetherington (1979) estimated that 40 percent of current marriages will end in divorce, and that 40 to 50 percent of the children born in the 1980s will spend some time living in a single-parent family. The stresses of the divorce situation have been carefully analyzed. Hetherington pointed out that "boys from divorced families, in contrast with girls and children from nuclear families, show a higher rate of behavior disorders and problems in interpersonal relationships in the home and in the school with teachers" (p. 853).

A number of reasons have been given to explain why boys are more influenced by divorce than are girls. Certain authorities believe that boys receive less positive support and nurturance from mothers and teachers in the period following divorce than do girls. Boys, then, may be exposed to stress and frustration greater throughout the divorce process.

Hetherington also concluded that a conflict-ridden intact family may be more harmful to family members than a stable home in which parents are divorced. Divorce can be a positive solution for a family that is functioning in a destructive manner. However, most children experience divorce as a difficult transition, and life in a single-parent family can be a high-risk situation for parent and child.

Social Environment

Are criminals bred by social conditions? Are bad neighborhoods the source of delinquency? The easy answer is yes, but we should be careful about oversimplifying here. We know that many youngsters emerge

Children who watch aggressive models who are rewarded for their aggressiveness tend to be more aggressive themselves.
(© Jack Prelutsky/Stock, Boston)

from what seem to be the most destructive social settings as effective adults. Individual patterns of development can overcome ecological forces, creating children who are invulnerable to their bad surroundings (Werner, 1979).

One dimension in the social environment that seems to be influential in shaping the behavioral patterns of children is the phenomenon of **modeling,** imitating the behavior of others. Bandura (1977) and his associates conducted a decade of research on the factors that cause children to imitate behavior they observe in person or on television or in movies. They made several relevant conclusions:

- Children who watch aggressive models who are rewarded for their aggressiveness tend to be more aggressive themselves.
- Children tend to identify with successful aggressors and find reasons for their aggressive behavior.
- Children who see models who set high standards and reward themselves sparingly behave in like manner. The behavior of models is influential in the development of self-control.
- There is no evidence that viewing violence dissipates aggressive drives and makes a person healthier (the catharsis hypothesis). Instead, a frustrated television viewer watching violence is more likely to act out violent impulses.

This work on aggression represents a significant component of social learning theory, which has stimulated a new set of treatment programs that focus on manipulating the social environment to create more rewarding interaction between child and setting.

One complication in the last two decades has been the increasing availability and use of illicit drugs. Does the presence of behavioral or emotional problems predispose an individual to use drugs? If you are anxious, depressed, or angry, are you more likely to take drugs? Common sense would answer yes, but research is not clear on the question.

Paton and Kandel (1978), for example, reported:

"For the most part these (drug use) studies reveal that the relationship between various psychological factors and drug use is nonsignificant" (p. 188). They surveyed over 8,000 adolescents in eighteen public secondary schools in New York state, asking them how many times in the last thirty days they had used any of eleven illegal substances. They also asked questions about their subjects' psychological condition at the time. Paton and Kandel found that boys are slightly more likely to take drugs than are girls; that older students are more likely to use drugs; and that there are ethnic differences in the choice of drugs. White adolescent girls are more likely to use drugs when depressed, but

> for black and Puerto Rican youths depressed mood bears little relation to illicit drug use, especially multiple drugs. For these groups the social context rather than intraindividual psychological state may be the most important determinant of drug usage. (p. 194)

The authors concluded that in no group do psychological factors seem to be a strong determinant of adolescent drug use. If their findings are true, the use of drugs may be a contributing factor to behavior problems but is not initiated by those problems. This means the real difficulty lies in the easy access to drugs.

IDENTIFICATION AND PLANNING

The first step in providing support for children with behavior problems is to find them. This is relatively easy in the case of aggressive youngsters; it is much more difficult with withdrawn children, who often escape notice.

Table 8.1 lists several methods used to identify children with behavior problems. The most common screening procedures are teacher ratings and self-reports, although parent and peer ratings are also used. Teachers can fill out a behavior check list (the Walker Problem Behavior Identification Check List, for example), which includes items like the following:

- Has temper tantrums
- Has no friends
- Refers to self as dumb, stupid, or incapable
- Must have approval for tasks attempted or completed

Teachers are asked to check an item if they believe a youngster exhibits any of the listed characteristics. Of course most children show these behaviors or traits at some time or other; therefore the criteria used to measure disturbance are how often, how intense, and how inappropriate is the behavior.

A major problem with screening lies in the errors produced by this quick sweep of all children in a class. There may be many **false positives;** that is, children identified as behavior problems who are eventually found not to be so. These false positives are a waste of time and money for school systems, which must conduct extensive diagnostic studies of all children identified with behavior problems, even those whose problems are mild (lacking intensity) or temporary (lacking persistence). **False negatives**—overlooked children who need special help—

Table 8.1
Methods of Identifying Behavior Problems

Method	Sample Instruments	Strengths and Weaknesses
Projective tests	Rorschach Ink Blot Thematic Apperception Test (TAT) Sentence Completion Tests	Gives testee opportunity to use ambiguous stimuli to reveal personal needs and perceptions. Often difficult to interpret; needs highly qualified clinician.
Objective tests	Coopersmith Self Esteem Inventory Piers-Harris Children's Self Concept Scale	Establishes patterns of answers of testee compared to answers of identified disturbed children or adults. Requires reading skills; depends on honest answers.
Behavior check lists	Quay-Peterson Behavior Problem Check List Walker Problem Behavior Identification Check List	Teachers or parents are asked to identify the presence of certain key behaviors. Depends on accuracy of observer; hard to measure intensity or frequency.
Behavior observation	McKinney SCAN	Child is observed in the classroom. No predetermined answers to which the child's responses are compared. Needs large samples of behaviors for adequate diagnosis.
Interviews	Vineland Social Maturity Scale	Information is collected from parents with predetermined set of questions. Usefulness depends on skill of interviewer.

can be a screening problem as well. Self-concept and self-esteem measures, like the Piers-Harris Children's Self Concept Scale (Piers & Harris, 1969), are used to find children who are depressed or feel badly about themselves.

A more expensive approach, but one that is possible where college students or volunteers are available, is classroom observation (Feagans & McKinney, 1981). The McKinney SCAN observation scale uses three major categories:

- *Constructive self-directed activity.* The child is performing appropriate classroom tasks on his or her own without direct teacher supervision or teacher participation in his or her group.
- *Off-task behavior.* The child's eyes are off the task, and he or she is inappropriately manipulating the task materials; or the child is physically wandering in the classroom; or the child is engaging in another inappropriate gross motor activity.
- *Dependency/aggression.* The child is engaged in excessive attention-seeking behavior directed toward peers or teacher, or the child is physically or verbally abusive to a peer or teacher.

These scales require extensive observation to produce reliable results.

Despite our more liberal definition of children with behavior problems—which includes the perceiver as well as the child—most diagnostic instruments now in use focus exclusively on the characteristics of the child and do not take into consideration the nature of the environment. Judgment on the role of the environment is still left to the discretion of the individual observer or clinician.

Once a child has been identified, the results of the educational assessment, which may include tests, interviews, and teacher ratings, can be used to develop an individualized education program (IEP). An IEP, when used properly, can be an effective guide for teachers who are trying to cope with children who show emotional or behavioral problems. Figure 8.2 shows a summary of the IEP developed for an eleventh-grade student. Robert has been having trouble controlling his temper, a problem complicated by substance abuse and specific academic difficulties in the area of writing (Kerr & Nelson, 1983).

The IEP includes several elements, among them

- a statement of long-term goals.
- a statement of short-term objectives that guide the student's day-to-day progress.
- a statement of educational and support services.

In Robert's case, the educational and support services include a contingency contract, which outlines his goals and the rewards or sanctions for meeting or failing to meet those goals. This contract, which

Child's Name _Robert Rimcover_

School _Washington High School_

Date of Program Entry ___9/14/81___

Prioritized Long-Term Goals:

1. _Control temper when corrected by adult_
2. _Eliminate drug intoxication at school_
3. _Increase writing skills_

Summary of
Present Levels of Performance

Achieving slightly above grade level in math, history, science & shop. Approx. 2 yrs. below in written composition. Refuses to engage in writing tasks.

Short-Term Objectives	Specific Educational and/or Support Services	Person(s) Responsible	Percent of Time	Beginning and Ending Date	Review Date
1.1 Given a direction, Rob will complete the required behavior within 10 seconds without committing a verbally or physically aggressive act.	Contingency contracting Time-out procedures Role playing	Reg. class & resource teacher	100	9/14/81 - 6/12/82	12/20/81 & 6/12/81
1.2 When asked to redo careless or inaccurate work, R will comply without committing a verbally or physically aggressive act.	Same as above plus immediate feedback on academic assignments.	Same as above plus peer tutors	100	Same as above	Same as above

Percent of Time in Regular Classroom

83%   (5 of 6 periods)

Placement Recommendation

Regular 11th grade (non-accelerated)

Committee Members Present

E. Dokes Principal
C. Dorsett, Counselor
Marrel Perez, Resource Teacher
F+R Rimcover, Parents

Dates of Meeting _8/17/81_

SOURCE: From *Strategies for Managing Behavior Problems in the Classroom* (p. 25) by M. Kerr and C. Nelson, 1983. Columbus, OH: Charles E. Merrill.

FIGURE 8.2
Individualized education program: Summary

is agreed to by student, parents, and teacher, gives Robert an opportunity to take greater responsibility for his own behavior.

What about Robert's writing skills? The teacher could assign him a series of compositions in graduated degrees of difficulty, which would give him the positive reinforcement of success, at least in the early stages. The teacher could also encourage Robert to use a typewriter or word processor to make self-correction easier, cutting down on the teacher-student confrontations that seem to lead to Robert's temper outbursts. Of course in addition to these specific remedial programs, Robert should receive positive reinforcement in the areas in which his work continues to be good.

The IEP is shaped not only by the student's specific problem, but also by available program resources. The presence of professional consultants in the psychiatric area or an active remedial program in the school gives both planning committee and parents more options to consider.

EDUCATIONAL ADAPTATIONS FOR CHILDREN WITH BEHAVIOR PROBLEMS

Three decades ago, the preferred treatment for children with behavior problems was psychiatric in nature. Since that time, emphasis and responsibility have shifted from mental health professionals to educational personnel. Several factors were at work. First only a small proportion of the children needing help could be treated by the limited number of psychiatrists, psychologists, or social workers available. Second, traditional mental health treatment, in which these children received one or two hours of counseling or therapy a week, generally was not successful in changing behavior. As a result, teachers are no longer supplementary; they are the responsible agents for treatment and receive supplementary help from psychiatrists, psychologists, and social workers.

Approaches

Although we talk about the various methods for coping with behavior problem children as distinct approaches, in actual practice, programmed intervention combines any or all of these strategies.

Drug Therapy

Most of the program interventions we discuss here are educational or psychological in nature. But there is also a biomedical form worth noting. In the past decade, a wide variety of psychoactive drugs has been used separately or in conjunction with educational treatments in an attempt to deal with the behavior problems of some children.

Conners and Werry (1979), in a review of the literature about the relative effectiveness of differing types of drugs with children who have learning and behavior problems, concluded that *stimulants*, in particular, have shown a positive effect when used in careful dosages and in conjunction with educational programs. There seems to be evidence that for some children the introduction of a proper dosage of stimulants improves both their behavior and mental functioning. The improvement in mental functioning, most researchers agree, is due, not to the direct stimulation of mental processes, but to the removal of barriers (that is, hyperactivity, limited attention) that have inhibited the child's full use of mental processes in the past.

Sprague and Sleator (1976), described a special problem. In studying the effect of drug management on older learning disabled children, they found that the optimum dosage for the influence of social behavior was different from the optimum required for cognitive behavior. This leaves us with a difficult educational, or even ethical, decision. Which dosage is appropriate? Do we concentrate on social behavior or cognitive ability? On the basis of a recent study on the use of drugs with hyperactive children, Charles, Schain, and Zelnicker (1981) advocated individual dosages relative to specific child responses.

Barkley (1979) claimed that the cooperation of parents and professionals is a critical factor in drug therapy. Barkley pointed out that the value of medication is to facilitate changes in the child so that certain responses become more likely (for example, attentiveness) or less likely (aggressive outbursts). However, whether these responses actually occur depends on other dimensions of the educational program.

Although psychostimulant medication has benefited many hyperactive children, O'Leary (1980) argued that these drugs do not necessarily improve students' academic performance or their long-term social behavior:

> It has been my experience that teachers often see little need for psychological or educational intervention after placing the child on psychostimulants. I would not initially use pharmacological interventions with most hyperactive children because the behaviors that characterized the hyperactive syndrome are so dramatically, although fleetingly, changed by psychostimulants that the parents, teachers, and children may view the medication as a panacea, and we know that such is very far from the truth. (p. 201)

The recent literature on the effectiveness of drugs on severe behavior disorders has been reviewed by Kavale and Nye (1984). In reviewing seventy studies that had adequate experimental and control subjects, they found a modest positive effect for drug intervention. These effects were manifested by improvements in attention span, learning rate, and scores on intelligence tests on the part of the experimental group receiving the drugs. Young adults between the ages of 16 and 25 responded best of all age groups, and those whose hyperactivity was a major problem improved significantly more than those with severe behavior disturbances or psychosis.

Behavior Modification

One of the most widely used techniques to encourage prosocial behavior and discourage antisocial behavior is behavior modification through operant conditioning and task analysis.

With **operant conditioning,** we control the stimulus that follows a response. For example, suppose a little boy sucks his thumb when watching television. If his parent turns the television off when his thumb is in his mouth and on when it is not, the child will soon learn that if he wants to keep the television on, he must not suck his thumb. In this situation, the operant (thumb sucking) is controlled by the stimulus (television off) that follows. Operant conditioning is based on the principle that behavior is a function of its consequence. The application of a positive stimulus (television on) immediately following a response is called **positive reinforcement;** the withdrawal of a positive stimulus (television off) is **punishment.**

One by-product of the increasing use of operant conditioning is a more precise definition of **target behaviors,** the characteristics we want to change or enhance. Kerr and Nelson (1983) described several of those behaviors:

General statement	*Target behavior*
1. Kim does not comply with teacher requests.	1. When asked to do something by the teacher, Kim will respond appropriately within 10 seconds without being asked again.
2. Andy is hyperactive.	2. Andy will remain at his desk, without moving and with all 4 legs on the floor, for 20 consecutive minutes.
3. Fred can't ride the school bus appropriately.	3. Fred will get on the bus, without pushing, hitting, or shoving, walk to his assigned seat, remain there without disturbing others throughout the ride, and exit from the bus without pushing, hitting, or shoving.
4. Betsy is aggressive.	4. Betsy will play with other children during recess without hitting, kicking, pushing, or calling them names during the entire period.
5. Billy is withdrawn.	5. Billy will initiate at least two peer interactions during any given 15-minute recess period. (p. 25)

To change a disruptive child's behavior, a teacher might use behavior modification to positively reinforce the child for doing lessons and staying seated during class time.
(© Elizabeth Hamlin, 1976/Stock, Boston)

Notice that the clear definition of a behavior allows greater precision in measuring its occurrence.

Another dimension of the process is the development of a reinforcement menu that permits a child to choose a reward (extra time at recess, free time, a field trip) (Paul & Epanchin, 1982). The process works effectively with groups as well as individuals.

The principles of operant conditioning have been applied extensively to children with acting-out behavior problems. The first step is to specify the behaviors that are to be changed (constant jumping up, bothering others, running around the classroom). The second is to provide material that requires the child to stay seated (step-by-step lessons). The third is to reinforce the acceptable behavior. Ordinarily, a teacher pays attention to children when they are out of their seats disrupting others and ignores them when they are working quietly. This actually can reinforce a child's disruptive behavior. To change the situation, the teacher must positively reinforce the child for doing lessons and staying seated.

Some object to the use of behavior modification techniques because they treat the child like a slot machine (insert a quarter, get good behavior) and have little impact on the child's basic personality. The criticism is not fair. The educational objective is to create a positive response in the child that can be expanded and used for better overall social adjustment.

·The usual procedure in behavior shaping in the classroom is to establish goals and organize tasks in small steps so that the child can experience continuous success. This procedure is called **task analysis.** The child receives positive reinforcement for each step or part of the total task as it is completed (arithmetic, reading, or spelling, for example). Assignments, then, are programmed in easy steps. After the child completes a task in a specified period of time, the teacher checks the work, praises the child (social reinforcement), and rewards the child with a mark, a grade, a token, or some other tangible reinforcement. In this way the child is able to work at assignments for longer and longer periods and to accept increasingly more difficult ones.

Figure 8.3 shows the type of record keeping that is an essential part of behavior modification (Kroth, Whelan, & Stables, 1972). The child's program was divided into *before, during,* and *after* intervention phases. The teacher first established a baseline, the performance of the child before treatment begins. In this case, the child completed only about four of twenty problems assigned over a ten-day period. The teacher, having noticed that the child likes to play with puppets in free time, made a contract with the child providing that if the problems were completed during the alloted time, the child would have twenty minutes of free time to play with a puppet. The figure shows the dramatic change in constructive behavior once the contract was established. On Day 23, the teacher decided to test the stability of the new pattern of behavior and collected seven days of data on what happened when a reward (puppet play) was no longer used. The results shown in the figure are fairly typical. The rate of performance decreased somewhat but did not fall back to the baseline performance. In other words, the treatment maintained much of its effect, probably strengthened by the child's improved self-concept, a function of improved performance. This technique can be utilized by regular or special classroom teachers with a little extra effort and planning, and can provide the tangible record of improvement so important to both student and teacher.

Axelrod (1971) reported on several studies using token reinforcement, marks or poker chips that can be exchanged for more tangible rewards (for example, more recreation time). The studies were almost unanimous in suggesting that token reinforcement produces favorable changes in the behavior of children in the classroom.

Psychodynamic Strategy

The primary objective of the psychodynamic approach is to help children become aware of their own needs, desires, and fears. Proponents of the model emphasize diagnosis, treatment, decision making, eval-

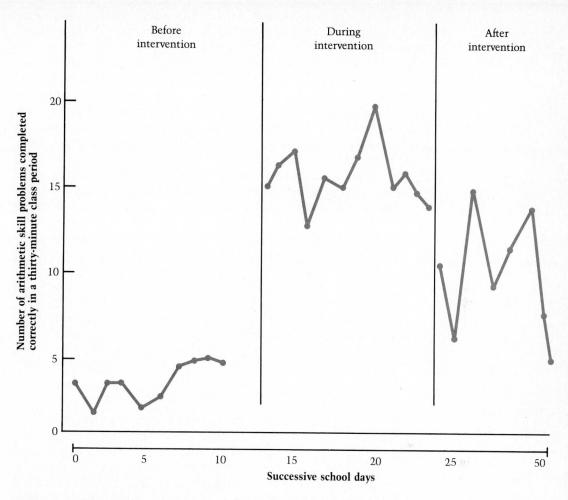

NOTE: Contract specified that child could earn time to play with a puppet if arithmetic problems were completed within thirty minutes.

SOURCE: From "Teacher Applications of Behavior Principles in Home and Classroom Environments" by R. Kroth, R. Whelan, and J. Stables. In *Strategies for Teaching Exceptional Children* by E. Meyen, G. Vergason, and R. Whelan (Eds.), 1972. Denver: Love.

FIGURE 8.3
Record of a child-teacher contract

uation, and other psychiatric procedures. They see maladaptive behavior as a symptom of intrapsychic conflict, and focus on removing the underlying cause of the conflict. They believe that removing a symptom (say aggressive behavior) without eliminating the cause results only in the substitution of another symptom.

Ecological Strategy

Supporters of the ecological model (Rhodes, 1967) maintain that behavior problems are a result of destructive interactions between the child and the environment (family, peers, teachers, cultural subgroups).

Treatment consists of modifying elements in the ecology, including the child (through counseling), to allow more constructive interactions between the child and the environment.

Hewett (1980), in a comparison of the ecological and psychodynamic models, used the following analogy to describe the problems with the psychodynamic model. Imagine that someone from another culture is trying to understand a baseball game. If that person focuses on the behavior of the first baseman (fielding, throwing, batting, running), he or she would not understand the nature of the game or the reasons behind the first baseman's behavior. The traditional clinical approach, Hewett claimed, has been to study one particular deviant member of the social system, which is what the psychodynamic model does. But if we study a child without examining the social system in which the child lives, we cannot fully understand the child or his or her behavior. Yes, we can describe the behavior, but we cannot interpret it effectively without an understanding of the social context in which it occurs.

Each method for treating behavior problems can work alone or in combination with another. Next, we examine how these approaches function in changing the learning environment, improving the skills, or adjusting the curriculum content for students with behavior problems.

Learning Environment

Students who are seriously disturbed often require a change in their learning environment in order to respond appropriately to educational programs. In the early part of this century, some of these children were expelled from school; others were placed in institutions for the mentally ill. Today we vary the educational setting in the spirit of the least restrictive environment, removing children from the normal classroom only for as long as necessary to allow them to gain the necessary skills and psychological stability to profit from the educational program.

The Re-Ed Program

Hobbs (1966, 1970, 1979) and his colleagues implemented the ecological strategy with programs for emotionally disturbed children that they called Project Re-Ed (reeducation). Remember, the ecological approach rejects reliance on psychotherapy. It assumes that the child is an inseparable part of a small social system, of an ecological unit made up of the child, family, school, neighborhood, and community.

Two residential schools in the Re-Ed program were organized to house approximately forty children each, ages 6 to 12. The plan was to reeducate these children for a short period of time (four to six months) and at the same time, through a liaison teacher, to modify the attitudes of the home, the school, and the community. The entire program was

Some children who are not able to cope with stressful situations can benefit from professional help.
(© Meri Houtchens-Kitchens, 1982)

oriented toward reestablishing the children as quickly as possible in their own homes, schools, and communities.

In general, a program of reeducation follows a number of principles:

- *Life is to be lived now.*   This is accomplished by occupying children every hour of the day in purposeful activities and in activities in which they can succeed.
- *Time is an ally.*   Some children improve with time. But children should not remain in a residential setting for long periods, which could estrange them from their families. Six months in the residential center is the stated goal of Project Re-Ed.
- *Trust is essential.*   Inspiring trust, according to Hobbs, cannot be learned in college courses. It is something that those working with emotionally disturbed children "know, without knowing they know."
- *Competence makes a difference.*   The arrangement of the environment and learning tasks must be structured so that children are able to obtain confidence and self-respect from their successes.
- *Symptoms can and should be controlled.*   The treatment of symptoms, causes, is emphasized.

The teacher-counselor is the key staff person in reeducation programs and is trained, not only in special education, but also in counseling methods designed for disturbed children. A liaison teacher-counselor works in the program to form effective alliances among home, school, and child. When a child is removed from a regular school and placed in a Re-Ed school, the liaison teacher-counselor keeps the school aware of his or her progress in the program and prepares the child and the school for his or her reentry into the public school when the time approaches.

A comprehensive follow-up evaluation was conducted on Project Re-Ed by Weinstein (1974). The progress of the children was compared with the progress of children who had comparable emotional problems but were not in the Re-Ed program as well as with a group of normal children of similar age and background. Comparisons of the three groups were made six months and eighteen months after the Re-Ed group had completed treatment. The results showed that the treated children had more positive self-concepts and greater confidence in their ability to control their own situations than did the untreated disturbed children. The Re-Ed children were judged by their teachers to be better adjusted than the untreated disturbed children both academically and socially. Although the Re-Ed students were doing better than the disturbed children who were not treated, the Re-Ed graduates continued to show more maladjustment on all measures than did the group of children designated normal. In other words, the reeducation program did not change the disturbed children into "normal" children, but it did reduce the level of their disturbance by a significant degree.

Open Education Program

Knoblock (1973) advocated an open education therapeutic setting for emotionally disturbed children. The open education program is both free and flexible, providing a setting in which children can act out feelings and trained teachers can immediately react to them. This allows children who have conflicts with authority and structured programs to work out their feelings in an environment that does not create a constant excuse for battles with authority.

Knoblock pointed out that the open education program requires decisions on the part of the child and also allows the child to exert a degree of control over the environment. Both features, in turn, provide constructive ego development because disturbed children often have negative self-concepts and feelings of inadequacy.

Knoblock appeared to be primarily addressing the problems of the withdrawn child, not the disruptive child, in recommending this particular setting. One general rule that might stand the test of application is that withdrawn, inhibited children need the opportunity to expand and express themselves and to try out new behavior styles.

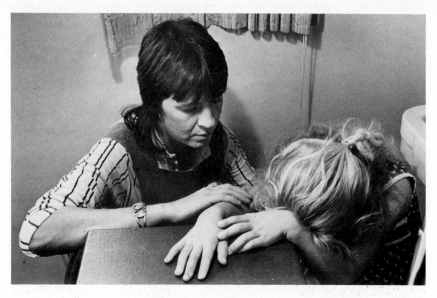

A helping teacher can be especially effective in assisting the classroom teacher by responding to a disturbed child in crisis while the regular teacher continues working with the rest of the class.
(Mitchell Payne/Jeroboam, Inc.)

Behaviorally disruptive children need to have environmental controls so that their own impulsive behavior does not carry them away and create a variety of secondary problems.

The Helping Teacher

One innovative suggestion for helping beleaguered classroom teachers is the helping teacher. Obviously a classroom teacher with twenty-five or thirty children cannot cope with all aspects of the classroom environment without help. Who can provide that help? Morse (1976), based on his work with disturbed or disturbing children, proposed the helping teacher. Morse explained his thinking this way:

1. Even the very disturbed child is not "disturbed all the time," meaning that there are only certain periods when the disturbed pupil cannot function in the larger group setting. These periods may be at certain regular times or in the press of a crisis. But most of the time, the disturbed child could benefit and fit into the regular class.
2. What is needed is direct assistance. Consultation is one thing, but real help is another. Psychologists and the like might offer advice, but they do not know what it is like

to try to administer a classroom with these kids in the room.

3. The direct service helping teacher should be omnipresent, not itinerant, and be trained as a teacher, but as a special teacher. The helping person should be able to respond to the disturbed child in crisis, but be able to help with both academic and emotional problems for all children. Many of the disturbed youngsters needed direct counseling help with their self-concept, but just as many could find growth through therapeutic tutoring.

4. There were times when the helping teacher could assist best by coming in and taking over the classroom while the regular teacher worked through a phase of a problem with a youngster.

5. Help should be based upon the reality of how the child was able to cope with the classroom and not on categories, labels, or diagnostic criteria. It was pointed out that many normal children need help during a crisis in the classroom or in their lives just as the chronically and severely variant youngster does. (pp. 1–2)

The helping teacher generally uses techniques that are an extension of regular education procedures, with an emphasis on support and encouragement. In addition, the helping teacher is able to provide important liaison services that are not within the capabilities of the heavily burdened classroom teacher. Children with behavior problems often need the help of a wide variety of professionals, pediatricians, psychologists, and paraprofessionals, and the helping teacher can coordinate these sources of assistance. Morse summed up the nature of the relationship as follows:

The plan envisions co-team teaching of the special and regular teacher. There is no intent to replace, only to supplement. The best staff education will come as a result of offering direct help; through service comes change. The job is overwhelming, all agree, but the direction has stood the test of time. (p. 8)

Mainstreaming

The goal of special education is to place behaviorally disturbed children in the regular education program whenever possible. The reasons are threefold: to give these students a chance to interact with children who are not handicapped, to have constructive models of behavior, and to keep in step academically.

It has become increasingly apparent that merely placing handicapped children in the same classroom with nonhandicapped children

Experiences that students have in working together to achieve mutual goals promote social relationships between handicapped and nonhandicapped children that carry over into other situations in the class.
(© Elizabeth Crews/Stock, Boston)

does not guarantee social integration. Newman and Simpson (1983) attempted to modify the attitudes of normal children at the first- and second-grade levels by talking with them about exceptionality, simulating blindness and deafness, pointing out similarities and differences between regular and special education students, and discussing famous people who have had to contend with a handicapping condition. After these lessons, the students were given the opportunity to interact with severely emotionally disturbed children, children who had been diagnosed autistic or schizophrenic from age 3. The researchers found that learning about handicaps was as effective, if not more effective, than direct experience with children who are handicapped. They also found that girls engaged in a significantly greater number of positive interactions with the disturbed pupils than did boys. Their evidence suggests that it is possible to create a more positive social environment through instruction, so that the nonhandicapped child, with a new understanding of and sympathy for handicapped children, reaches out to them in a positive way.

Can teachers take specific steps to arrange the learning environment or to change their own style to bring about healthy interaction? Johnson and Johnson (1981) addressed this question in a study of forty third-grade students, eight of whom were identified as having severe learning and behavior problems. Some of the exceptional students were provided cooperative learning experiences with nonhandicapped children in which group performance was important, and some were provided individualized learning activities. The researchers found that the experiences students had working together to achieve mutual goals promoted social relationships between handicapped and nonhandicapped students, and that those relationships carried over into other situations in the class. It seems, then, that by carefully arranging tasks and the learning environment, teachers can take an active role in facilitating the social integration of exceptional children in the regular program.

Another important question is whether the lack of social skills in delinquent youngsters is due to their unwillingness to perform appropriately or to their inability to recognize appropriate behavior. McFall (1976) suggested that some individuals behave maladaptively simply because they do not know proper social skills. He compared the responses of sixty adolescent boys—twenty who were in an institution for delinquents, twenty who came from the same basic socioeconomic background but were labeled "good citizens," and twenty who were identified as student leaders—to items on the Adolescent Personality Inventory. This inventory presents a series of social problem situations that have to be solved. For example:

1. The school principal threatens to suspend you for hassling a substitute teacher.
2. You want to ask the manager of McDonald's for a job.
3. Your father tells you to stay home on Saturday night.
4. Your friend is angry because you dated a girl he likes.

In answers to forty-four set situations, a clear difference in responses separated the delinquent boys from the others, with the delinquent boys showing significantly fewer social skills and more instances of inappropriate social behavior.

In a follow-up study, even when the items were provided to the students in a multiple-choice format that included socially appropriate behaviors, the delinquent youngsters still chose less socially acceptable behaviors. The lack of understanding of appropriate social skills can be one base for a specific curriculum or training program for youngsters identified as either socialized delinquents or children with conduct disorders.

One of the techniques that has emerged from the field of mental health and has been used successfully by teachers is the life space interview, which was designed by Redl (1959). Redl stressed the importance of a careful interview with the student directly following a particular crisis situation or event, so that the child is faced with the consequences of the behavior immediately instead of waiting a day or more for a regular counseling session, by which time the child has forgotten or has built sufficient defenses around the event for self-protection.

Let's look at how it works. Jim has been on the playground unmercifully teasing another youngster, Paul, who did something to irritate Jim in the classroom. Finally Paul, out of desperation, strikes out at Jim, giving Jim an excuse to hit back. The teacher immediately sits down with Jim quietly in a private setting and discusses the incident in detail. The teacher might ask Jim to describe what happened and his role in creating the event. Jim would have full opportunity to verbalize his own attitudes about the situation and to allow his feelings about Paul to be expressed.

Ideally, a life space interview ends with a plan for resolving the problem or for preventing similar problems in the future through specific steps. Some evidence supports life space intervention as a means of reducing maladapted behavior, not only by inhibiting undesirable behavior, but also by generating alternative solutions (DeMagistris & Imber, 1980).

Skills

The development of coping skills that enable children with behavior disturbances to develop positive work and social skills and to set aside negative characteristics is a major educational goal. There are a number of approaches designed to help children cope more effectively with their problems, among them self-management and overcoming learned helplessness.

Self-management

One way to teach coping skills is to enlist students in their own treatment program. Table 8.2 shows a series of steps that students can take to monitor their own behavior.

Suppose Jim has been having trouble staying in his seat. The first step is to teach him to recognize the behavior and, then, to record its frequency. Next, Jim negotiates a reward (perhaps some time to work a puzzle) for staying in his seat for a specified period. Once he has shown the ability to control that behavior, he can be given the opportunity to control his own schedule and make decisions about the content or skills he would like to work on in the time slot.

Table 8.2
Components of Self-management

---

1. *Self-assessment*	Student examination of his or her own behavior to decide whether he or she has performed a specific behavior.
2. *Self-recording*	The child *accurately* records the frequency of a specific behavior.
3. *Self-determination*	The child is taught to negotiate for a specific reward or activity that will be reinforcing.
4. *Self-administration of reinforcement*	The child is able to dispense the reinforcement (for example, use of free time) whenever it is appropriate.
5. *Self-selection of skills to be learned*	The child decides what he or she would like to learn in a given period of time.
6. *Self-selection of time to learn skills*	The student chooses when he or she wants to work on a particular skill (for example, reading).

SOURCE: Adapted from *Teaching Emotionally Disturbed Children* (pp. 118–119) by R. McDowell, G. Adamson, & F. Wood (Eds.), 1982. Boston: Little, Brown.

The entire procedure is designed to increase students' awareness and competence, and their commitment to the elimination of negative behaviors and the acquisition of constructive ones. For Jim this means that the teacher works with him to improve a series of self-awareness skills whereby he can increase his own control over his hyperactivity or distractibility.

Camp and Bash (1981) described a "think aloud" program that was designed to help teach self-control to impulsive, aggressive boys during the early elementary years. (Because problem behavior of this type appears most often in boys, many such programs focus on them.) Here, each child was asked to consider four specific questions:

1. What is my problem?
2. How can I control it?
3. Am I following my plan?
4. How did I do?

In a sense, the children were asked to stand outside themselves to gauge their own performance. By observing their own behavior, they were able to gain some control over it. Once boys like Jim understand the signals that trigger their aggressive behavior or hyperactivity, they are in a better position to control that behavior.

Camp and Bash reported that after thirty training sessions members of the experimental group in the study not only increased their scores in intelligence and reading tests, but also received higher teaching ratings on interpersonal behavior. Even more important, the study showed the generalized effect of the training program on such dimensions as reading and classroom social behavior. Apparently youngsters can be helped to see the signals in their environment that trigger their unacceptable behavior, to inhibit the impulse to respond immediately, and to develop a plan of action to meet situations. In many respects, the goal of learning these skills is as important to the education of these youngsters as are the more academic goals of reading and arithmetic. Furthermore, until these children are able to maintain their self-control or to achieve other social skills, they will be unlikely to learn more traditional academic skills.

Overcoming Learned Helplessness

While children like Jim are taught skills to control impulsive behavior, other techniques are used to help depressed children like Molly cope with their environment. Dweck (1975) reported an attempt to improve the status of elementary school children who evidenced extreme learned helplessness. One group of children received success-only treatments, in which the tasks were arranged so that the students succeeded in the vast majority of situations. Members of another group were allowed to fail, and were taught to understand the role they played in the failure. The performance of youngsters in the second group improved once they were shown how to avoid failure; those who had a heavy dose of success failed miserably when failure finally did come. Dweck concluded: "An instructional program for children who have difficulty dealing with failure would do well not to skirt the issue by trying to ensure success, or by glossing over failure" (p. 684).

Much of the work with fearful or withdrawn children is still done by mental health professionals outside the public school program. The limited budgets of school systems do not allow them to employ a battery of psychiatrists, psychologists, and social workers. The release of pent-up feelings and unspoken fears in a protected environment is one of the major goals of most child therapists. Classroom teachers often notice changes in children who have someone to talk to and relax with.

Content

For children with behavior disturbances, the path to academic success is often difficult and uncertain. Not only do they have poor relationships with many of their teachers, but their problems in personal and social spheres distract them from academic tasks. Consequently these children often find themselves far behind in their academic work and in need of remedial attention. The content of their curriculum is not different from that of other children but may have to be pegged at an earlier developmental level. The special education teacher in the resource room program where a child with behavior problems may come for an hour a day often spends much of his or her time in a combination of remedial reading and arithmetic combined with sympathetic counseling.

Mark is an 8-year-old boy who was referred to a special class for emotionally disturbed children because his mother was concerned about his immaturity and learning problems. After a thorough evaluation, the special services committee in his school agreed that Mark was excessively rigid, inhibited, and anxious. Even after the evaluation, however, it was not clear why he was having learning problems. Mark was placed in a special class for academic work. His teacher formulated an IEP that involved remedial work in reading and math. The teaching materials included stories about children and how they felt in various circumstances. In addition, the teacher tried whenever possible to give Mark psychological permission to express his feelings. For example, one day when the teacher was very late getting to him, she said, "I'm sorry I'm late. If I had to wait as long as you've had to wait, I'd be upset. Are you a little upset?" On another day, when a child ripped Mark's paper off the bulletin board, she said, "It's too bad about your paper. That upsets me!"

Gradually Mark began to express his feelings, and as he did it became increasingly evident that once he had vented his frustrations, he was learning and producing more efficiently. With this realization, the teacher began to teach Mark about himself—about how he behaved and how he could monitor himself.

Though Mark's problems were emotional in nature, they led to serious academic problems that could not be ignored. Even if, through some combination of drug treatment and psychotherapy, those emotional problems could have been "solved," Mark would still have been left with serious academic deficiencies that needed remediation.

One way to adapt program content for children with behavior problems is to design a self-awareness curriculum that provides students with an opportunity to learn more about their own feelings and those of other children. The teaching tools include carefully chosen literature, role playing, and class discussions in which the teacher stresses feelings and attitudes.

Kaplan (1971) recommended the use of curriculum units to teach mental health principles. These units can (1) be built around problems at various stages of child development, (2) become an integral part of courses already in the curriculum, and (3) provide consistent, systematic mental health interaction.

Other units focusing on principles of child development and behavioral self-control have been designed. Their objective is to increase the self-knowledge and understanding of children with behavior problems (Fagen, Long, & Stevens, 1975).

Using Microcomputers

The microcomputer may be an especially useful learning tool for a student with behavior problems because it provides an objective and neutral response to the child's sometimes provocative or challenging behavior. Children with a long history of social interaction problems may respond poorly to teacher feedback, particularly when criticism or correction is involved. The child who is adept at manipulating others can quickly change the focus of a discussion from his or her inadequate academic performance to the teacher's behavior. "Why are you always picking on me?" is a common theme.

With the microcomputer, however, the student must find a different approach. Obviously, the computer is unable to interact emotionally with the child. If the student has difficulty solving a problem, he or she must find out why and determine the right answer in order to proceed with the computer program. The student cannot resort to emotional manipulation or accusations of unfairness with a microcomputer.

Another common behavior problem can be helped by using computer programs in the classroom. Children who are hyperactive or who have problems with attention span are often quite scattered in their thinking and concentration. When working with a microcomputer, it is essential to pay some degree of attention to get results. The orderliness of the software programs can provide a systematic structure for students who have very little cognitive structure or self-discipline.

Given the extensive possibilities for the use of microcomputers with students who have behavior problems, it is surprising that little research on their impact has been published. Carman and Cosberg (1981) conducted a carefully designed study involving forty emotionally handicapped children, ranging in age from 7 to 14 years, who were of normal intelligence but more than two years behind in mathematics. The students were randomly sorted into treatment and nontreatment conditions in eight-week blocks. Students in the treatment group each received a Plato Computer-Managed Instructional Program in Mathematics. Those students under the special computer-managed program were able to show learning rate gains and also to pay significantly more attention to the tasks at hand, thereby confirming the potential of the microcomputer to help attentional difficulties while contributing to improvement in the content area.

LIFESPAN ISSUES FOR INDIVIDUALS WITH BEHAVIOR PROBLEMS

What does the future hold for children who are hyperactive or behaviorally disturbed? A growing body of research seems to yield consistent findings. Feldman, Denhoff, and Denhoff (1984) carried out a ten- to twelve-year follow-up study on forty-eight adults who had been diagnosed as hyperactive children. When these individuals were age 21, the researchers found that 91 percent were in school or working and seemed to be performing in a reasonably effective manner, although they had lower self-esteem and less educational achievement than their nonhyperactive siblings who made up the control group.

Hechtman and Weiss (1985) studied seventy-six youngsters originally seen in a psychiatric department of Montreal Children's Hospital where they were diagnosed as hyperactive at 6 to 12 years of age. These children were compared in young adulthood with forty-five control subjects, who were matched for sex, IQ, and socioeconomic status with the hyperactive subjects. The control subjects had no observable behavior or academic problems. Hechtman and Weiss found that the hyperactive subjects in young adulthood attained lower academic grades, had more car accidents, and received somewhat more court referrals. On self-report scales they indicated higher levels of anxiety, grandiosity, and hostility. The researchers concluded that few hyperactive children become grossly disturbed or chronic offenders of the law when they become adults, but they do have adjustment problems related to their impulsiveness and inability to concentrate, two characteristics that created problems in their school careers.

Chess and Thomas (1984) reported data on the New York Longitudinal Study that drew on an original group of 133 subjects from 87 middle and upper middle class families. These individuals were seen in infancy, preschool years, and early adult life. Chess and Thomas divided the subjects according to temperament—*easy, difficult,* and *slow to warm up.* (See discussion of Thomas and Chess, 1977, on p. 327.) Chess and Thomas found that factors in early childhood that create a high risk for overall adult maladjustment, or the presence of a psychiatric disorder in early adult life, were a difficult temperament, parental conflict, the presence of a behavioral disorder, and an overall poor adjustment by the age of 3. The behavior disorders exhibited by the sample of children in the study were mostly mild and often disappeared by adulthood.

Chess (1979) concluded that the emotionally traumatized child is not doomed, the parents' early mistakes are not irrevocable, and our preventative and therapeutic intervention can make a difference at all age levels.

What seems to emerge from these studies is that early problems such as a difficult temperament or hyperactivity increase the risk of poor adult adjustment but do not in any sense guarantee it. Our treatments can be effective, and favorable environmental circumstances can help a child cope more adequately with those characteristics of impulsiveness, lack of attentiveness, and feelings of hostility.

SUMMARY OF MAJOR IDEAS

1. Children with behavior problems exhibit impulsive, aggressive, anxious, or depressed behavior of such duration, intensity, and inappropriateness that schools feel compelled to take special action.

2. The difficulty in distinguishing between normal and abnormal behavior has created disagreement over the prevalence of behavior disorders among children. Estimates range from 2 to 24 percent. There is general agreement, however, that at least 2 to 3 percent of children have behavior problems that require intensive, prolonged treatment, although only 1 percent are now receiving special education services.

3. There are four major classifications of problem behavior: conduct disorders, anxiety-withdrawal, immaturity, and socialized aggression.

4. Genetic influences interact with environmental factors (family, society) to produce problem behavior in children.

5. Identification methods include teacher ratings, self-reports, parent and peer ratings, and behavior observations. Any and all of these methods can be used in school settings to develop a student's individualized education program.

6. There has been a shift in the responsibility for treatment of children with behavior problems, from mental health professionals to school personnel.

7. Approaches to modify the educational programs of children with behavior problems include drug therapy, behavior modification, psychodynamic strategy, and the ecological approach.

8. Drug therapy carefully administered under competent supervision can modify hyperactive behavior when combined with specially designed educational experiences.

9. Behavior modification techniques have yielded positive, consistent results in achieving specific objectives.

10. One strategy for helping children with behavior problems has been to focus on the ecological setting—the interaction of children and their environment. Treatment consists of direct counseling as well as efforts to change the surrounding environment, to make it more receptive to these children.

11. Several techniques that teach children to manage their own behavior seem to help children cope with acting-out behavior problems.

12. Treatment of withdrawn or depressed children generally focuses

on strategies that enable these youngsters to express fears and to improve, through developing competence, low self-concepts.

13. A difficult temperament that is observable in early childhood can increase the risk of later problems in adulthood but does not make such problems certain or inevitable.

UNRESOLVED ISSUES

1. *Increasing use of paraprofessionals.* One of the serious limiting conditions in delivering quality educational services to children with behavior problems is the current need for highly trained personnel. Unless a way can be found to use paraprofessional personnel, as has been done in behavior modification programs, it will not be possible to provide the help needed for the large number of youngsters identified as having behavior problems.

2. *Determining the mental health of society.* How do we judge the mental health or maturity of a society or subculture as opposed to the mental health of an individual? We have a wide variety of instruments designed to place the individual on a scale of mental illness or mental health, but nothing comparable for the larger culture. If we believe that some of the problems faced by individuals involve inappropriate demands by society, how do we judge the level or kind of inappropriateness?

3. *Understanding the causes of behavior problems.* Since World War II, the predominant thinking about causes of problem behavior has focused on psychological or sociological dimensions. Either the child was mentally ill because of unusual or bizarre psychic processes or was showing abnormal behavior as a result of some negative sociological or ecological condition. Now, with increasingly sophisticated analysis, the role of genetics in causing or influencing emotional behavior problems has been reintroduced. We need to sort out the relative role played by these various forces in creating unproductive behavior.

REFERENCES OF SPECIAL INTEREST

Kerr, M., & Nelson, C. (1983). *Strategies for managing behavior problems in the classroom.* Columbus, OH: Charles E. Merrill.

This text gives extensive examples of ways for teachers to deal with problem behaviors. The authors provide specific strategies for children showing aggressive behavior, social withdrawal, self-injurious behavior, drug abuse, and socially immature behavior. The text also includes discussion of a variety of strategies for working outside the classroom in the community.

Knoblock, P. (1983). *Teaching emotionally disturbed children*. Boston: Houghton Mifflin.

> A book specifically designed for teachers of emotionally disturbed children. It reviews current programs and practices, and presents a critical examination of the field. There is a special section devoted to severely handicapped children that focuses on autism.

Long, N., Morse, W., & Newman, R. (Eds.). (1980). *Conflict in the classroom: The education of emotionally disturbed children* (4th ed.). Belmont, CA: Wadsworth.

> A mix of short stories, sociological treatises, and a variety of educational and mental health articles, all dealing with disturbed or disturbing children. Most of the articles have appeared in journals elsewhere, but it is a great convenience to have them bound together. The editors have shown excellent judgment in their selections.

McDowell, R., Adamson, G., & Wood, F. (Eds.). (1982). *Teaching emotionally disturbed children*. Boston: Little, Brown.

> An excellent presentation of the major approaches to educational treatment—behavioral, psychoeducational, and ecological. Specific attention is paid to curriculum modifications made necessary by emotionally disturbed children. An excellent chapter provides a discussion of the parent's role in special education.

Paul, J., & Epanchin, B. (Eds.). (1982). *Emotional disturbance in children*. Columbus, OH: Charles E. Merrill.

> A collection of chapters on various aspects of educating disturbed children. The emphasis is on education, and a wide variety of new methods and procedures are included. This text probably reflects the best in current trends, even if these trends are not yet widely practiced. Evenhanded and eclectic.

Rhodes, W., & Head, S. (1974). *A study of child variance* (3 vols.). Ann Arbor: University of Michigan.

> This three-volume set provides the most comprehensive review to date of children at variance with society. It portrays the importance of social factors as they impinge on youngsters in trouble with authorities, and the roles, positive and negative, played by the various social institutions that try to modify these children's behavior or ecology.

C·H·A·P·T·E·R
Nine

CHILDREN WITH
LEARNING DISABILITIES

Focusing Questions

What is the difference between underachievement and learning
disabilities?

In what ways are developmental learning disabilities different from
academic learning disabilities?

What are the criteria used to identify children with learning
disabilities?

What are the four common strategies used to remediate learning
disabilities?

How does a child's age affect the remediation process?

Why are microcomputers so effective in the remediation of learning
disabilities?

*L*earning disabilities is the most recent exceptionality to be considered a specific classification. Since its recognition in the 1960s as a specific handicap, it has become the largest area of enrollment. In 1984 almost half (43 percent) of the children enrolled in special education programs were classified learning disabled.

One reason for the rapid expansion of programs for learning disabled children is the heterogeneous nature of these children. The group includes those who do not fit neatly into traditional categories of exceptional children. In any school system, a substantial number of children are slow in learning to talk or to acquire other communication skills, or to develop visual or auditory perception. Some have difficulty learning to read, to spell, to write, or to calculate. There are children who are not receptive to language but are not deaf; who are not able to perceive visually but are not blind; and who cannot learn by ordinary methods of instruction but are not mentally retarded. All of these children are learning disabled.

CASE ILLUSTRATIONS

Unlike deaf or blind children whose exceptionality involves one major disability, learning disabled children are a heterogeneous group. They have a range of different learning impairments. Here we describe five students, each with a different type of learning disability.

An Attention Deficit

Nancy performed poorly in first grade but was promoted. Her second-grade teacher immediately noticed that Nancy did not complete assignments and was constantly on the move, out of her seat talking to other children or looking for something else to do besides the assigned task. The teacher's continual admonitions ("Stay at your desk, Nancy," "Nancy, sit down," "Do your paper, Nancy") worked for a few minutes, but soon the child would be wandering about again. After many unsuccessful attempts to focus Nancy's attention, the teacher referred her for assessment. In the referral form, the teacher described Nancy as distractible, inattentive to tasks, and retarded in reading and arithmetic.

The child was examined by a multidisciplinary team. Its assessment showed an above-average intelligence—a finding based on Nancy's answers to questions, not an IQ test. The psychologist reported the child was difficult to test because of her extreme distractibility. Educational achievement tests placed her at the beginning–first grade level in reading and arithmetic. She was definitely behind her apparent mental development and grade placement. Although it was clear that the child was hyperactive, the team pediatrician decided that drugs were contraindicated at that time.

The IEP recommendation was that Nancy be assigned to a resource room for an hour a day, four days a week. The teacher there was to work with her individually, using praise and tangible reinforcement to gradually increase her time on task. The classroom teacher was asked to ignore Nancy's movements away from her desk, but to come to her desk and praise her when she stayed on task and completed an assignment. In other words, she was given positive reinforcement when she was on task and no attention when she was off task.

As she learned to read with the resource room teacher and applied her reading skill to on-task behavior in the classroom, Nancy's distractibility decreased. Her success gave added impetus to achieving. By the end of the year, she was functioning more like her classmates and was promoted to third grade. At that point individual instruction was discontinued. Although Nancy's third-grade teacher did notice some distractibility and periods of inattention, in general the child was progressing at a satisfactory rate academically.

An Oral Language Disability

Andy was a full-term baby, delivered without complications. He developed normally in motor abilities, crawling at an early age and walking at 1 year. But Andy was not speaking and appeared not to understand language at age 3. At age 4, his parents finally took him to a clinic and were told that Andy was mentally retarded, that he had a chromosomal translocation that is associated with Down syndrome. Because the boy could not talk or understand language, it was difficult to obtain an accurate intelligence rating. His IQ score was estimated at below 50, and he was placed in a private preschool for severely retarded children.

At that school, Andy was given a diagnostic test of abilities and disabilities. The results showed his ability to understand language was below that of a child of 2, but his ability to understand the meaning of pictures equaled that of a child of 6. On other instruments he scored at the 5- and 6-year levels on tests involving vision, and below age 2 on tests involving understanding or use of language. The child was diagnosed average or above average on visual and visual-motor tasks, and extremely retarded in auditory verbal abilities. It was obvious that Andy needed intensive instruction in listening and understanding oral language and in expressing himself in vocal terms. He was assigned to a university speech clinic, where he was systematically taught to listen and talk. With his mother's help at home—she had majored in speech pathology in college—he made substantial progress in verbal intercourse, and at age 5 was admitted to kindergarten. At the end of the year his verbal performance was only slightly below that of other children his age.

A Language Disability in a College Student

George's high school grades and low scores on achievement and aptitude tests limited his choice of colleges. He was accepted at only one school, where he spent two years before applying to the college of education at his state university. The admissions officer, a psychologist, noted that George had repeated freshman English three times, finally passing the course with a D. But he had earned Bs in math and science, and an A in an art course. In a series of tests, George showed superior ability in spatial relations and quantitative thinking, which helped explain his good grades in art and math. But he showed a marked deficiency in verbal fluency—the ability to think in words—that was clearly responsible for his difficulty with English and subjects like history.

After consultation, George was admitted to the art education department. A tutor helped him with required English courses, which he passed, with much effort, with Cs and Ds. In his art courses he continued to get As. When he graduated, he went on to graduate school and later became art director in a large city.

A Reading Disability

At age 9, Lane was not achieving academically. Although he did well in arithmetic and participated intelligently in class discussions, he was reading well below fourth-grade level.

A team examination found Lane was a well-adjusted boy of superior intelligence. But his test scores confirmed a problem. Although he scored at the fourth-grade level in arithmetic, his reading was at the beginning–first grade level. This meant a discrepancy of four to five years between his mental and reading abilities, and of three years between his arithmetic and reading levels. An analysis of Lane's performance showed he had no sound-blending ability and a problem with visual memory. When asked to reproduce an unknown word (say *horse*), it took him six trials to succeed.

Lane's ability to decode printed words apparently was blocked by two disabilities: blending sound into words and visualizing or learning words as a whole. In addition, the team ophthalmologist found an eye muscle imbalance that may have contributed to his visualization problem.

The team recommended treatment for Lane's eye muscle problem and tutoring in reading using the kinesthetic method (see page 391).

His mother, a former teacher, took on the job of helping Lane, reading lessons for him and working with him on courses that required extensive reading. Over the years, his reading skills improved. By the time he graduated from high school, he was reading at a fifth-grade level.

After he graduated, Lane spent two years in the army, then applied for admission to a university. He was not accepted. His reading skills were still at a fifth-grade level. Determined to go on to college, Lane hired a doctorate student who was majoring in special education to tutor him. Within six months, his reading had improved three grade levels and he was admitted to the university. He continued working with the tutor for another year, and went on to pass all but one of the courses required for a degree in animal science. The problem was a rhetoric test, a test he could not pass because of his poor spelling ability. (Apparently Lane's difficulty with visual memory had persisted.) Finally, after four tries, the test was waived and Lane was allowed to graduate.

A Disability in Arithmetic

Sampson was brought to a learning disabilities clinic at age 12. He was reading at grade level, but scored several grades lower in an arithmetic computation test. According to his father, Sampson's development was normal to age 8, when he suffered a concussion in a car accident. Since then, he had not been able to think quantitatively, to learn arithmetic beyond simple addition and subtraction. He had great difficulty understanding the significance of place values, a critical element in learning multiplication and division.

Sampson's teachers worked hard to improve his arithmetic achievement, as did the special tutors hired by his parents to improve his quantitative-thinking ability. Little progress was made. At age 14, Sampson began working part-time in his father's garage. Although his teachers gave him practical math problems related to his work in the garage, his quantitative-thinking ability did not improve appreciably. Despite his disability, Sampson tried to do his best in school and at work. He did not allow his problem to affect his cheerful personality.

DEFINING LEARNING DISABILITIES

It's been said that learning disabilities is like pornography: You recognize it when you see it, but it's difficult to define it. The problem, of course, (as illustrated by the diverse cases presented) is that *learning disabilities* is a catchall term used to describe many different learning problems.

The most widely accepted definition was introduced in 1968 by the National Advisory Committee on the Handicapped, and was subse-

As an exceptionality, learning disabilities is extremely heterogeneous: it includes students with perceptual problems and those with specific learning disorders in the different academic areas.
(Meri Houtchens-Kitchens)

quently used by Congress in 1975, with only a few changes, in Public Law 94–142, the Education for All Handicapped Children Act. It read:

The term "children with specific learning disabilities" means those children who have a disorder in one or more of the basic psychological processes involved in understanding or in using language, spoken or written, which disorder may manifest itself in imperfect ability to listen, think, speak, read, write, spell, or to do mathematical calculations. Such disorders include such conditions as perceptual handicaps, brain injury, minimal brain dysfunction, dyslexia, and developmental aphasia. Such term does not include children who have learning problems which are primarily the result of visual, hearing, or motor handicaps, of mental retardation, of emotional disturbance, or of environmental, cultural, or economic disadvantage.

This definition did not completely satisfy special educators. A number of professional associations separately and jointly formulated dif-

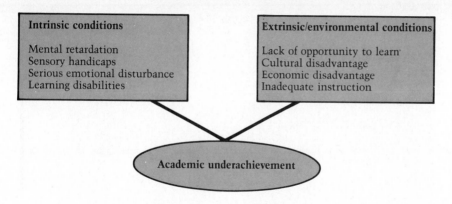

FIGURE 9.1
Conditions leading
to academic under-
achievement

ferent definitions. One repeated the general concepts in the federal definition but added that *learning disabilities* is a generic term and that the disorders are "intrinsic to the individual" (Hammill, Leigh, McNutt, & Larsen, 1981). That distinction—that an intrinsic psychological or neurological factor has inhibited or interfered with the normal development of the child in mental operations, language, or academic school programs—was implied or stated by every professional association. And most also excluded children who are mentally retarded or sensory handicapped or who lack the opportunity to learn.

Underachievement vs. Learning Disabilities

All children who are underachieving or who are markedly below grade level are not learning disabled. There are many factors that contribute to underachievement, and learning disabilities are just one of them. Figure 9.1 shows the major causes of underachievement in schoolchildren. On the left are the intrinsic conditions (elements within the child): mental retardation, sensory handicaps (blindness, deafness), serious emotional disturbance, and learning disabilities. Notice that learning disabilities are only one of the conditions that can lead to academic underachievement.

On the right side of the figure are the extrinsic or environmental factors (outside the child) that can lead to underachievement: lack of opportunity to learn, cultural disadvantage, economic disadvantage, and inadequate instruction. These underachieving children are not learning disabled because their problems stem from extrinsic sources and can be corrected by changing environment.

CLASSIFICATIONS AND CHARACTERISTICS

There are so many learning disabilities that it's almost impossible to classify them or even to draw up a specific list of the different types. After a year of study, the Bureau of Education for the Handicapped identified learning disabilities in the following areas (*Federal Register,* December 29, 1977):

- Listening comprehension
- Oral expression
- Basic reading skills
- Reading comprehension
- Written expression
- Mathematics calculation
- Mathematics reasoning

These classifications confined learning disabilities to three areas: (1) receptive and expressive language, (2) reading and writing, and (3) mathematics. Although no one would argue the inclusion of these areas, few educators would limit learning problems to this extent. In fact, researchers have identified disabilities in a wide range of skills and knowledge—motor development, attention, perception, memory, listening, speaking, reading, writing, written expression, arithmetic, self-concept, and social skills (Myers & Hammill, 1976; Brutten, Richardson, & Mangel, 1973; Lerner, 1985; Reid & Hresko, 1981; Kirk & Chalfant, 1984).

We can distinguish two broad categories of learning disabilities: developmental and academic. As Figure 9.2 shows, the major components of developmental learning disabilities are attention, memory, perception, and perceptual-motor disorders, and thinking and language disorders. Academic learning disabilities include disabilities in reading, spelling, writing, and arithmetic. These are the first problems to

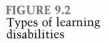

FIGURE 9.2
Types of learning disabilities

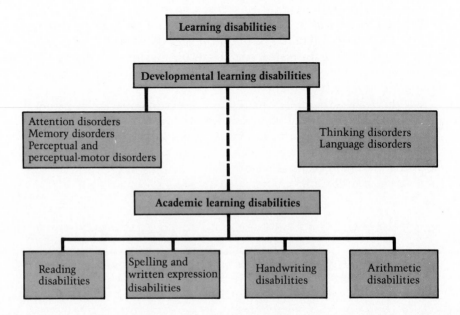

be noticed by teachers but require careful analysis to discover the underlying causes. Often academic disabilities are influenced by intrinsic or developmental conditions, a relationship we discuss on page 368.

Developmental Learning Disabilities

Developmental learning disabilities are deviations from the normal development of psychological or linguistic functions. These disabilities often, but not always, are associated with problems in academic achievement. Some children with perceptual-motor deficits cannot read; others with the same perceptual-motor difficulties do read. In some instances the association between developmental and academic difficulties reflects a lack of prerequisite skills. For example, before children can learn to write they must develop certain skills—eye-hand coordination, memory, and sequencing abilities. To learn to read, children need visual and auditory discrimination ability and memory, the ability to see relationships and to learn from the repetition, and the ability to concentrate their attention.

Attention Disorders

Attention is a necessary prerequisite for learning the task at hand. It is the ability to choose from the many competing stimuli that surround us at all times. Ross (1976) suggested that selective attention "helps us limit the number of stimuli that we process at any one time" (p. 60), and that an attention disability is "the result of delayed development in the capacity to employ and sustain selective attention" (p. 61). The child with an attention disorder is responding to too many stimuli. This kind of child is always on the move, is distractible, cannot sustain attention long enough to learn, and cannot direct attention purposefully. The discussion of Nancy at the beginning of this chapter presents a case in point.

Memory Disorders

A memory disorder is the inability to remember what has been seen or heard or experienced. Children with visual memory problems, like Lane, can have difficulty learning to read with a method that relies on recall of the visual appearance of words. In the same way, a disability in auditory memory can interfere with the development of oral language.

Visual Perception and Perceptual-motor Disorders

Children with learning disabilities in visual perception may not understand road signs, directional arrows, written words, or other visual symbols. They may not be able to grasp the meaning of pictures or numbers or to understand what they are. An extreme example was a boy who had adequate vision but could not recognize his classmates by sight. He could identify them only when he heard their voices or was told their names. He could not attach meaning to the things or people he saw. Other individuals cannot express concepts without words, cannot show how a spiral staircase goes up and around or how a person chops down a tree.

There are many factors in the environment with which perceptually disordered children cannot cope (Johnson & Myklebust, 1967; Kirk & Chalfant, 1984). These include, not only elements that signify deeper meaning, but an awareness of objects and their relationships to them. The disability, then, affects left-right orientation, body image, spatial orientation, motor learning, and visual closure (seeing the whole from presentation of a part)—all important abilities that do not involve the translation of symbols to gain meaning.

FIGURE 9.3
Profile of scaled scores on the ITPA of 237 children with severe oral language disorders

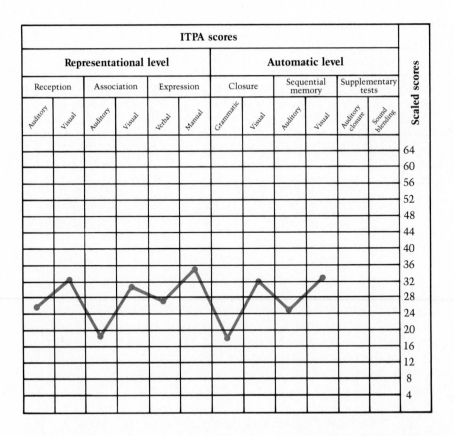

SOURCE: From "Profiles of Children with Severe Oral Language Disorders" by A. Luick, S. Kirk, A. Agranowitz, and R. Busby, 1982. *Journal of Speech and Hearing Disorders,* 47(February), p. 90.

Thinking Disorders

Thinking disabilities are difficulties in the cognitive operations of problem solving, concept formation, and association. **Problem solving,** a behavior that helps the individual respond or adapt to new situations, requires the analysis and synthesis of information. **Concept formation** is the ability to classify objects and events—for example, to recognize that a boat, a car, and a train are all used for transportation.

Thinking disorders are closely related to oral language disorders. In a study of 237 students with severe oral language disabilities, Luick, Kirk, Agranowitz, and Busby (1982) found a consistent profile on the Illinois Test of Psycholinguistic Abilities (ITPA). Notice in Figure 9.3 that the children showed normal ability on tests of visual and motor-expressive skills, but below-average ability on tests of auditory reception, verbal expression, and auditory sequential memory, and marked deficiencies on tests of auditory association ("Father is a man; mother is a _____.") and grammatic closure ("This is a bed; these are two _____."). Ninety-seven percent of the 237 children showed marked deficiencies in inner language (thinking abilities) as represented by the auditory association and grammatic closure tests. This same kind of thinking disorder was an underlying cause of Andy's oral language delay.

Language Disorders

Language disorders are the most common learning disability noted at the preschool level. Generally, the child does not talk, does not talk like older brothers or sisters did at a similar age, or does not respond adequately to directions or verbal statements. We discuss the diagnosis and remediation of language disorders in later sections and in Chapter 7.

Academic Learning Disabilities

Academic learning disabilities are conditions that significantly inhibit the process of learning to read, spell, write, or compute arithmetically. These disabilities show up when children are in school and performing well below their academic potential. Figure 9.4 shows a profile of a child with a significant disparity between his potential as measured by mental age, language age, and arithmetic computation age, and his performance on oral and silent reading tests. This child, a fifth-grader, has a mental age of 11 years, is able to understand fifth- and sixth-grade books when they are read to him (language age of 10 years), and scores at the fourth-grade level on arithmetic computation tests that do not require reading. His reading performance after five years in school is still at the beginning–second grade level. The disparity between his potential for reading and his actual reading grade is between

FIGURE 9.4
Profile of a child
with a significant
reading disability

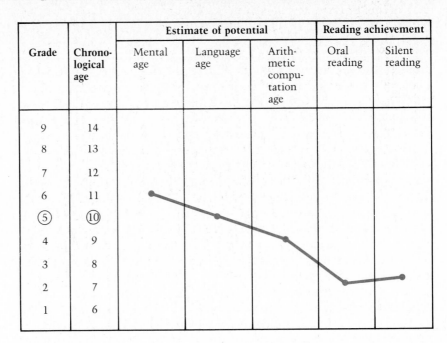

Grade	Chrono-logical age	Estimate of potential			Reading achievement	
		Mental age	Language age	Arith-metic compu-tation age	Oral reading	Silent reading
9	14					
8	13					
7	12					
6	11					
⑤	⑩					
4	9					
3	8					
2	7					
1	6					

two and three years. This boy is underachieving but not as a result of
mental retardation, serious emotional disturbance, or sensory handicap; and he is not environmentally deprived. He is learning disabled
in reading.

The Relationship of Developmental Learning Disabilities to Academic Learning Disabilities

In assessing academic disabilities, examiners always ask, "Why hasn't
this child learned to read (spell, write, do arithmetic) by the method
used for all children?" They then look for contributing factors, either
extrinsic or intrinsic to the child. If the lack of learning does not seem
to be related to environmental factors or to mental retardation or serious emotional disturbance, the clinicians look for problems in attention, memory, or language.

Research has not been able to pinpoint the exact relationship of
developmental learning disabilities to academic disabilities because
developmental problems do not always inhibit the ability to learn.
Fortunately people are flexible; we tend to adjust to different problems.
A child with a visual memory deficit (difficulty in learning words as
wholes) who is able to learn auditorially might be able to learn to read
using a phonic method. A child with an auditory perception problem
might compensate by learning to read through a visual channel. A
deficit in one developmental area, then, does not necessarily result in

an academic disability. In many instances multiple development learning disabilities are necessary to contribute to an academic disability. When both visual and auditory perceptions are deficient, as we saw in Lane's case, even superior intelligence cannot compensate for the disabilities.

PREVALENCE

How many children with learning disabilities are there in a given population? This is not an easy question to answer. Because of the difficulty of defining learning disabilities, most statements of prevalence are based on estimates derived from meager empirical information.

Most of the studies that have been made on the prevalence of learning disabled children include educationally retarded children as well as those who require special methods of instruction for their development. Myklebust and Boshes (1969) estimated that 15 percent of their subject population were slightly underachieving. When a stricter criterion was used, 7 percent were considered learning disabled. Likewise, Meier (1971), who studied the prevalence of educational retardation in 2,400 second-grade children, found that 15 percent were considered learning disabled. He stated that slow learners (IQ scores below 79) and children with learning disabilities were described by teachers in the same way. By using stricter methods of diagnosis and a stricter definition of learning disabilities, he concluded that only 4.7 percent were actually learning disabled.

The problem, then, is in the definition of learning disabilities. When underachievement is used as a criterion, prevalence figures are inflated. We believe, however, that students are learning disabled only when they have a developmental learning disability (attention, memory, perception, thinking, language) that manifests itself in educational retardation.

Table 9.1 lists the number and percentage of children who received special education and related services in programs for the learning disabled, speech impaired, and mentally retarded from 1978 to 1984. The percentages for the speech impaired and mentally retarded populations have remained relatively constant over the years. The percentage for learning disabled children, however, has increased from 1.79 percent in 1976–77 to over 4 percent in 1983–1984. As indicated in the table, the largest enrollment is in programs for the learning disabled. This population has grown from over 779,000 children in 1976–1977 to over 1.8 million students in 1983–1984.

One reason for this enormous increase is the referral of students with no learning disabilities. Shepard and Smith (1983) studied a thousand children assigned to programs for the learning disabled. They found that 57 percent of them were not really learning disabled. Among them were non–English speaking students (7 percent), children with other handicaps (10 percent), slow learners (11 percent), and students with minor behavior problems (4 percent).

Table 9.1

Number of Children Receiving Special Education and Related Services Under
PL 94–142 and PL 89–313 by Three Specific Handicapping Conditions, 1978–1984

	1976–1977		1980–1981		1983–1984	
	Total	% of Population	Total	% of Population	Total	% of Population
Learning disabled	797,213	1.79	1,455,135	3.01	1,811,489	4.57
Speech impaired	1,302,666	2.84	1,117,792	2.43	1,130,569	2.86
Mentally retarded	969,547	2.16	849,890	1.75	750,534	1.84

SOURCE: *National Enrollment Statistics, 1982–83* by the U.S. Department of Education, 1984. Washington, DC: U.S. Government Printing Office; and *Seventh Annual Report to Congress on the Implementation of the Education of the Handicapped Act* by the U.S. Department of Education, 1985. Washington, DC: U.S. Government Printing Office.

There are several other reasons for the rapid growth in enrollment of learning disabled youngsters:

- The concept of learning disabilities is becoming more accepted by parents, professionals, and schools.
- Children who were once misdiagnosed as mentally retarded are now being recognized as learning disabled.
- Remedial programs, formerly a provision of the federal government for the education of the disadvantaged, are receiving less support.
- Learning disability programs have been expanded to include preschool children and adolescents.

Also a factor is the inclusion of children whose academic problems stem from environmental conditions.

CAUSES OF AND FACTORS CONTRIBUTING TO LEARNING DISABILITIES

Causes of Learning Disabilities

From an educational point of view, the cause (etiology) of a condition rarely is relevant for remediation. To know that the etiology of a learning disability is brain injury or cerebral dysfunction does not change the educational program. Teachers use a developmental curriculum, starting where a child is and helping the child move up the developmental ladder step by step.

Still, a knowledge of etiology can be valuable. One teacher, for example, struggled for several months with a child's remedial reading problem, a problem later diagnosed as a brain tumor. Had the teacher recognized the medical cause, she would have been able to make a

Although discovering that the cause of a learning disability is brain injury or cerebral dysfunction does not change the educational program, it is nevertheless valuable for teachers to know something about etiology in order to aid in diagnosis.
(William Lupardo)

medical referral. It is important, then, for teachers of learning disabled children to know something about etiology in order to aid in diagnosis and remediation and to know if and when that knowledge is applicable (Gaddes, 1985).

Researchers have tried to identify the factors that inhibit the ability to learn. Some of the most common are brain dysfunctions, genetics, nutrition and other environmental factors, and biochemical factors.

Brain Dysfunctions

The brain is the control center of the body. When something goes wrong with the brain, something happens to any or all of the physical, emotional, and mental functions of the organism. Scientists have not yet been able to relate every behavior to a specific function of the central nervous system. What we have at present is only partial knowledge of the relationship of the central nervous system to behavior, and only partial knowledge of the relationship of behavior to special disabilities.

These relationships were the subject of a study by Alfred Strauss, a German neurologist who came to the United States in the late 1930s. His book *Psychopathology and Education of the Brain Injured Child* (Strauss & Lehtinen), published in 1947, explained the relationship of brain injuries to language, hyperactivity, and perceptual disorders.

Since that time, work on the brain and behavior has moved into neuropsychology. The most recent emphasis has been on hemispheric differences. According to Wittrock (1978) and Gordon (1983), the left hemisphere of the brain deals primarily with sequential linguistic or verbal tasks; the right side of the brain, with auditory tasks involving melodies and nonmeaningful human sounds, visual spatial tasks, and nonverbal activities.

The work of Harness, Epstein, and Gordon (1984) seemed to support these theories. They reported test results of children referred to a clinic for reading disabilities. They found that the children "performed, on the average, better than the norm by about 0.50 S.D. on tests usually attributed to the right cerebral hemisphere and poorer than the norm by the same amount on tests attributed to the left cerebral hemisphere" (p. 346).

The hemispheric theories may well influence special education in years to come. Today, however, there is simply not enough information to transfer our knowledge to strategies for teaching learning disabled persons (Kinsbourne, 1983).

Gaddes (1985), in a comprehensive book on learning disabilities and brain function, stated that half of the 15 percent of children who are underachieving academically "have some degree of central nervous system (CNS) dysfunction" (p. 25). The statement may be slightly exaggerated, but most agree that many learning disabled children have a neurological dysfunction.

Genetics

Many studies have focused on the role of genetics in reading, writing, and language disabilities. Hallgren (1950) conducted an extensive family study in Sweden, and found that the prevalence of reading, writing, and spelling disabilities among the relatives of those diagnosed as dyslexic provided strong evidence that these conditions are hereditary. Hermann (1959) contrasted identical twins, all of whom were dyslexic, with fraternal twins. Only a third of the fraternal twins showed both children of the pair to be dyslexic; among the rest, only one child of the pair was dyslexic. Because the identical twins had a greater frequency of reading disabilities (dyslexia) than did the fraternal twins, he concluded that reading, spelling, and writing disabilities are inherited.

DeFries and Decker (1981) conducted the most extensive family study of reading disabilities at the Institute of Behavioral Genetics at the University of Colorado. They administered a series of psychometric tests to 125 reading disabled children and their parents and siblings, and to 125 control families. The reading disabled children obtained lower scores on some cognitive tests (spatial reasoning, symbol processing speed). The researchers found that the data conclusively demonstrate "the familial nature of reading disability" (p. 24).

Environmental Deprivation and Malnutrition

The lack of early environmental stimulation and the effects of severe malnutrition at an early age are not always independent. In many cases, these factors are both operating on the same child. Cruickshank and Hallahan (1973) reviewed the studies on environmental deprivation and malnutrition. They found from studies conducted on both animals and children that, although a definite relationship between malnutrition and learning disabilities cannot be established, severe malnutrition at an early age can affect the central nervous system and hence the learning and development of the child.

Biochemical Factors

There are many children with learning disabilities who do not have neurologic or genetic problems or a history of environmental deprivation. One hypothesis is that they have some unknown biochemical imbalance comparable to the phenylketonuria found in those who are mentally retarded.

The use of drugs to ameliorate learning disabilities is still a largely untested area; scientific studies to determine the values and dangers have yet to be done. From time to time, reports that a certain drug can improve a learning disability appear, but these reports generally are not substantiated by further research. In an extensive review of studies on the use of drugs, Adelman and Comfers (1977) stated that stimulant drugs sometimes have a short-term effect in decreasing hyperactivity. But a few years later, Levy (1983) claimed that the use of stimulant medication does not have either short- or long-term effects on children.

Related to the biochemical question is the use of megavitamins and diets. One of the best known and most controversial diets is the Feingold Diet. According to Feingold (June 1974), an allergist, artificial food flavors and colorings cause hyperkinesis in children, which in turn can lead to learning disabilities. He recommended a diet that eliminates salicylates and artificial food additives. Many parents tried it with their children and reported positive results.

Research studies on the effects of the diet were less enthusiastic (Mattes, 1983; Kavale & Forness, 1983). According to Mattes, "based on the available studies, it seems fair to say that no single study has reported a consistent dietary effect on the symptoms of the hyperkinesis syndrome" (p. 321). But Rimland (1983) refused to accept the reviews or the results of these studies. He pointed out flaws in the experiments and stated that all of the critics had to agree that some children react unfavorably to artificial food additives.

Factors Contributing to Learning Disabilities

In the past, much emphasis was placed on finding the cause of a problem. But with learning disabled children the cause often cannot be found or corrected. Still, the behavior can be remediated.

Diagnosticians, then, look, not for causes, but for associated or contributing factors that interfere with learning. For example, a sound-blending disability can contribute to poor reading in children when certain methods of teaching reading (like the phonic method) are used. The disability is not a cause of poor reading (deaf children who do not have sound-blending ability can learn to read); it is a contributing factor.

The search for contributing factors within the child (physical or psychological) or in the environment focuses on those conditions that have been found to occur frequently with the disability and that need correction or amelioration. These factors may be physical, environmental (including instructional), motivational, or psychological.

The **physical conditions** that can inhibit a child's ability to learn include visual and hearing defects, confused laterality and spatial orientation, poor body image, hyperkinesis (hyperactivity), and undernourishment.

Environmental factors are conditions in the home, community, and school that adversely affect the child's normal development socially, psychologically, and academically. These include traumatic experiences, family pressures, instructional inadequacies, and lack of school experience. Although these conditions affect academic progress, a child is not considered learning disabled unless the environmental conditions have contributed to deficits in attention, memory, and other psychological processes.

Motivational and affective factors also contribute to learning disabilities. A child who has failed to learn for one reason or another tends to have low expectation of success, does not persist on tasks, and develops low self-esteem. These attitudes reduce motivation and create negative feelings about schoolwork. Torgesen (1982) called this "learned helplessness."

Psychological conditions (developmental learning disabilities) include attention disorders, auditory and visual memory disorders, perception disorders, cognitive disabilities, and language delay or disorders. These psychological conditions can be contributing factors to academic disabilities.

The Relationship Between Causes and Contributing Factors

There are several possible relationships between causes and contributing factors. Some authorities believe that abnormal behavior is caused by an abnormality in the biological organism—a brain dysfunction, a genetic condition, environmental deprivation or malnutrition, or a biochemical imbalance. Biological scientists hope that finding the cause will lead to prevention.

Of course certain physical conditions (defects in vision, hearing, and laterality) are not caused by brain damage or heredity, but by accidents or other factors. Unlike etiological factors, many of these difficulties can be overcome with medical or educational help. Vision can be corrected with glasses or improved by vision training. Hearing can be helped with hearing aids and auditory training. Physical and occupational therapy can correct problems of laterality or physical incoordination. When a condition can be corrected through a device or training, it is a contributing factor not a cause.

Some physical conditions may be associated with psychological deficits. A child who has a significant uncorrected eye muscle imbalance may have a fusion problem that may be contributing to a deficiency in visual memory. Sometimes a delay in one developmental function may delay another developmental ability. A deficit in selective attention and auditory memory may be related to a delay in language development.

We know, too, that developmental learning disabilities can be related to academic achievement. For example, a language disorder or a significant attention deficit can contribute to a learning problem in reading or arithmetic. Or a child with a severe spelling problem may be found to have a visual memory deficit.

In certain individual cases social and occupational maladjustment is related to significant educational retardation. We have known for some time that delinquent children are educationally retarded. This does not imply a cause-and-effect relationship. We do not know for sure whether delinquency influences educational retardation, or whether educational retardation contributes to delinquency, or whether each interacts with the other to produce problems.

The differences between causes and contributing factors are fundamental. We look for causes to prevent a condition; we look for contributing factors to remediate a condition. The objective of remedial education, then, is to ameliorate or remove physical and developmental contributing factors.

IDENTIFYING AND DIAGNOSING CHILDREN WITH LEARNING DISABILITIES

There is a major problem in identifying learning disabled individuals: differentiating the learning disability subset of educational underachievement from the other subsets of educational underachievement (mental retardation, sensory handicaps, serious emotional disturbance, environmental factors). How large a disparity must there be between potential and achievement for a child to be considered learning disabled? Must a child have an identifiable psychological (developmental) learning disability that has contributed to educational underachievement? Who makes the decision?

School systems, under the provisions of Public Law 94–142, are required to assemble a multidisciplinary team of professionals to examine the child psychologically, mentally, socially, and educationally, and, with the parents, to come to a decision on whether or not the child is eligible for special education. Most school systems follow a series of steps in the identification process:

1. A teacher, parent, or someone else refers a child for evaluation.
2. The referral is evaluated by a committee of teachers, including the special education teacher, to determine whether the child should be assessed by a multidisciplinary team.
3. Once an assessment is approved, parent permission is obtained.
4. The evaluation is conducted by a multidisciplinary team including psychologists, social workers, the classroom teacher, and the special education teacher.
5. Team members hold a conference and decide on eligibility.
6. If the child is eligible, an IEP is formulated and the child is placed in the appropriate service.

Criteria Used for Identification

In deciding whether a child has a learning disability, the evaluation team usually relies on three criteria: a discrepancy between potential and achievement, an exclusion factor, and a special education criterion.

The Discrepancy Criterion

Children with learning disabilities show marked intraindividual differences in either developmental or academic areas. Developmental learning disabilities are noticed first at the preschool level; academic disabilities, at school-age level.

A child with a developmental learning disability shows a wide disparity in linguistic, social, memory, or visual-motor abilities. Andy

Once an assessment is approved, the child's parents are consulted and their permission is obtained.
(© Sybil Shelton/Peter Arnold, Inc.)

(see page 359), a child who was not talking at age 4, but whose other perceptual, cognitive, and motor abilities were normal, had a developmental learning disability in oral language. Another child might have normal language skills but be extremely retarded in visual-motor activities (tying a shoe, for example).

Children with academic disabilities show wide discrepancies between potential and actual academic achievement. Children like Lane and Sampson, who have average intelligence but cannot learn to read or do arithmetic, have an academic learning disability.

The Exclusion Criterion

Most definitions exclude from the learning disability designation children whose difficulties in learning can be explained by mental retardation, auditory or visual impairment, emotional disturbance, or lack of opportunity to learn. The exclusion factor does not mean that children with hearing and vision impairments or children who are diagnosed as mentally retarded cannot *also* have learning disabilities. These children require multiple services.

The Special Education Criterion

Children with learning disabilities require special education for their development. Children who are retarded educationally because they have not had an opportunity to learn will learn by ordinary methods of instruction at their level of achievement. For example, a nine-year-old who has never been to school and learned to read and write, but who has normal cognitive and perceptual abilities, is not learning disabled despite the discrepancy between ability and achievement. This child will learn by developmental methods of instruction and does not need special education—an extraordinary or atypical program involving educational methods not ordinarily used with regular students.

The special education criterion is important, not only to identify learning disabled children, but to identify the ways to help them. Without this criterion, learning disability is just a label.

Using the three above-mentioned identifying criteria, then, we can describe learning disabilities as follows: *A learning disability is a psychological or neurological impediment to spoken or written language or perceptual, cognitive, or motor behavior. The impediment (1) is manifested by discrepancies among specific abilities and achievements or between evidenced ability and academic achievement; (2) is not primarily due to severe mental retardation, sensory handicaps, emotional problems, or lack of opportunity to learn; and (3) is of such nature and extent that the child does not learn by the instructional methods and materials appropriate for the majority of children and requires specialized procedures for development.*

Diagnosis of Children with Learning Disabilities

Diagnosing a learning disability means pinpointing the atypical behavior, explaining it, differentiating it from similar problems of other handicapped children (*differential diagnosis*), and determining the remedial program best suited to correcting or improving it. Our methods of identification and diagnosis are somewhat different for preschool children and school-age children. Preschoolers are identified through developmental disabilities; schoolchildren, through academic disabilities. For children of any age, however, there are general criteria for making a differential diagnosis. Is the atypical behavior a disability? If so, what is the nature of the disability that requires remediation? To answer these questions, special educators examine the sources and contributing factors to the problem, and each child's abilities.

Does the child have a learning disability or is the lack of achievement in language, reading, or other areas the result of some other handicap (impaired hearing, general mental retardation, lack of instruction, lack of opportunity to learn)? The reason for differential diagnosis is that the remediation of a child with a learning disability is different from the instructional program for children with other handicaps, even though the observable problem, say a language disorder, may be the same. For example, delayed speech and language can be the result of a marked hearing impairment, severe mental retardation, or an emotional problem. A deaf child is taught to compensate for hearing loss by developing communication through other sensory avenues; a child whose lack of auditory association skills impede understanding can be taught to process language through the sense of hearing.

How is the child's disability explained? If a child is mentally retarded or has a sensory handicap or has been environmentally deprived, the factors leading to the disability are clear. But there are times when the contributing or inhibiting factor in the child's information-processing system or personality is not obvious. Suppose a child does not understand oral language. Is the disability the result of a marked deficit in auditory discrimination? In vocabulary? In understanding syntax? Or are there other factors at work? Determining the exact nature of the problem is essential to organizing an appropriate remedial program.

What abilities does the learning disabled child have? Inherent in the concept of learning disabilities is the concept of intraindividual differences, of discrepancies among the child's areas of development. If a child has been in school under ordinary instruction for three years and has failed to learn to read, the diagnostician looks for areas in which the child *has* learned. Is the child's language average? Does he or she have adequate mental ability to learn to read? Has the child learned other school subjects (arithmetic)? If the child's other abilities and achievements are average or near average for the child's age, we can consider the child as having a learning disability in reading.

Diagnosis of Preschool Children

The identification of learning disabilities in preschool children is not based on failure in academic subjects; it is directly related to behavior observed by parents and preschool teachers on age-appropriate tasks. The most common disorders that show up in young children include (1) failure to understand or respond to meaningful expressions (oral language, visual symbols); (2) failure to be in tune with the environment or the child's own relationship to it (poor motor control, body image, visual and auditory discrimination); and (3) lack of attention and related disorders. In diagnosing preschool children, examiners rely on the observations of parents and teachers, rating scales, informal clinical diagnoses, and norm- and criterion-referenced testing. They function much like detectives, gathering clues and formulating and discarding hypotheses until they arrive at the solution that best fits the available evidence.

Language Disabilities.   The most common learning disabilities noted at the preschool level are language disabilities. To diagnose a language disability, psychoeducational examiners follow a series of steps:

1. Obtaining a description of the language behavior as observed by the parent, the preschool teacher, or both.
2. Reviewing the medical record to see whether there are possible explanations from a medical point of view.
3. Studying the family situation to determine whether there are factors in the home that contribute to the disability.
4. Examining the child, using formal and informal tests to determine abilities and disabilities in (a) understanding language, (b) relating things heard with past experiences, and (c) talking (What is the extent of the child's vocabulary and use of syntax?).
5. Determining what the child can and cannot do in a specific area. For example, if the child functions well in most areas but does not talk, the next step is to find out if he or she understands language. If the child does not understand oral language, the next step is to find out if he or she can discriminate between words, between phonemes, or between common sounds in the environment.
6. Organizing a remedial program that moves the child step by step into areas in which the child could not initially perform.

Perceptual-motor Disabilities.   In diagnosing perceptual-motor disabilities in preschool children, psychoeducational examiners ask the usual questions about medical and home background and through ratings, interviews, and formal and informal tests try to discover the contributing factors and significant difficulties of the child. In the process, examiners try to answer several questions:

- Can the child interpret the environment through the significance of what he or she sees (visual decoding or visual reception)?
- Can the child recognize the whole when only a part is seen (visual closure)?
- Can the child recognize visual objects and pictures rapidly (speed of perception)?
- Can a child recognize a specific object embedded in a picture (figure-ground perception)?
- Can the child express ideas in motor (nonverbal) terms through gestures, dramatics, and writing (motor expression)?

Attentional and Other Disabilities. Examiners use observation and formal and informal tests to diagnose attentional and other disorders. Here, examiners are trying to answer these kinds of questions:

- Can the child sustain attention to oral or visual stimuli?
- Is the child highly distractible?
- Does the child persevere in the face of difficulty or initial failure?
- Can the child discriminate between two pictures or objects (visual discrimination), between two words or sounds (auditory discrimination), or between two objects touched and felt (haptic discrimination)?
- Is the child oriented in space? Does he or she have right-left discrimination?
- Can the child remember immediately what was heard, seen, or felt?
- Can the child imitate the examiner orally or gesturally? Can the child mimic?
- Does the child have adequate visual-motor coordination? Is the child clumsy?

Diagnosis of Academic Disabilities

At the school-age level, teachers usually refer children for diagnosis because they are failing in basic subjects (reading, spelling, writing, and arithmetic). To assess a child's learning disability and to create an effective remedial program, we follow a systematic process of diagnosis, a process that generally proceeds in five stages or steps:

1. Determining whether the child's learning problem is specific, general, or spurious.
2. Discovering possible environmental, physical, or psychological contributing factors.
3. Analyzing the behavior descriptive of the specific problem.
4. Evolving a diagnostic inference (hypothesis) on the basis of the behavior and the contributing factors.
5. Organizing a systematic remedial program based on the diagnostic inference.

This process applies to the diagnosis of any academic disability. We can see how it works by looking at the evaluation of a reading disability.

Marie Sanchez, a third-grade teacher, had an 8-year-old boy in her class who was unable to read beyond the primer level. He was not learning readily and seemed to forget what he had learned from one day to the next. After working with Carl for four months, Sanchez referred him to a child-study clinic.

1. *The first step was to determine whether the learning problem was specific, general, or spurious.* The examiner administered a general intelligence test to find out if Carl had the mental capacity necessary to learn to read. If Carl showed an IQ score of 50, no one would have expected him to be able to read. In fact, he showed an IQ score of 104 on the Stanford-Binet. He also scored at the second-grade level on an arithmetic computation test, although, as Sanchez had predicted, he scored at a first-grade level (6 years, 3 months) on a series of reading tests. The psychologist now had the following information:

Chronological age	8–4
Mental age	8–10
Language age	8–2
Arithmetic computation age	7–8
Reading age	6–3

   There was a discrepancy between Carl's chronological age, mental age, language age, and arithmetic achievement age on the one hand, and his level of reading on the other. The child had attended school with fair regularity and had had adequate teaching for over two years, but still had not learned to read. It was clear that a problem did exist and that it was specific, not general. Carl could not read although the apparent capacity was there, as indicated by his other abilities and achievements.

2. *The second step was to discover the possible environmental, physical, or psychological factors contributing to the disability.* There are many reasons why children do not learn to read. Did Carl attend school regularly? Was his home background normal? Was he culturally deprived? An investigation of these factors proved negative, and a medical examination revealed no abnormalities. Carl's visual acuity was normal, and so was his hearing.

   There remained one handicap to investigate. Was Carl so emotionally disturbed that he was unable to learn? Sanchez had reported that he could not concentrate on the reading workbooks she gave him, that his attention to reading materials was very short, and that he resisted pressure to read. The psychiatric examination did not show emotional disturbance: Carl appeared normal in interpersonal relationships and was able to concentrate on tasks that did not involve reading or spelling. The clinic psychiatrist concluded that his inability to learn to read was not the result of an emotional condition.

   Finally, the clinic staff looked for physical or psychological correlates that were contributing to Carl's reading disability. Tests did show certain developmental problems that may have played a part in Carl's reading problem. Although functioning at or above his chronological age in most of the tests, Carl was very deficient in visual sequential memory (the ability to remember a sequence of figures or letters), auditory closure (the ability to recognize a word when only a portion is provided—"rabb" for *rabbit*), and auditory synthesis (sound blending)—all deficiencies commonly associated (together or in isolation) with poor reading.

3. *The third step was to analyze the behavior descriptive of the specific problem.*   At this point, the clinic staff began to delineate in detail exactly what Carl could and could not do in the reading process. They wanted to know more than his level of reading; they wanted to know how he was reading. What were his bad habits? How did he attack new words? What kinds of words did he confuse? What kinds of mistakes did he make? How fast did he try to read?

   A skilled diagnostician can answer some of these questions by watching a child read, but diagnostic tests are an important supplement to clinical judgment. In Carl's case, those tests revealed he was not using phonics. Although he could tell the sounds of different letters in isolation, he sounded only the first letter or two of a word. The tests also showed that the boy had difficulty reproducing short words from memory (his record described the problem Carl had had learning to write his name). He guessed at most words from context or by interpreting pictures. He knew a few sight words but often confused similar words—*that* and *what, the* and *ten, see* and *she.*

4. *The fourth step was to find a diagnostic hypothesis (inference) based on the errors in reading and the contributing factors.*   The diagnostic inference is one of the most important elements of a diagnosis. It involves specifying the relationship among symptoms and the contributing factors that have inhibited a child's learning to talk, read, write, or spell. It requires experienced clinicians who can use relevant tests and select relevant facts, and put the pieces together to explain the child's inability to learn. The diagnostic hypothesis must select the relevant variables in the case and pinpoint specific disabilities on which the remedial program can be organized.

   For Carl, two working hypotheses evolved from the information at hand. From the observation that the boy did not sound more than the first letter or two of a word although he knew the sounds of all of them in isolation, it was conjectured that he had not learned the skill of sound blending. That thinking was verified by the child's low score on a sound-blending test. A sound-blending disability would explain why Carl had so little success using phonics to decipher unknown words. The second inference stemmed from a low score on a visual sequential memory test coupled with the fact that the boy had learned very few sight words and was uncertain about many of the ones he thought he knew. The hy-

pothesis was that Carl's inability to remember a sequence of letters—to know what the complete word was supposed to look like—
made it difficult for him to identify sight words. This hypothesis
was corroborated by his difficulty in learning to reproduce short
words from memory and to write his name. The two handicaps,
the inability to use a phonic approach in identifying words and the
inability to use a sight-word approach, gave Carl no usable technique for decoding the printed page.

5. *The fifth step was to organize a systematic remedial program—
an individualized education program (IEP)—based on the diagnostic hypothesis.* The crux of a diagnosis is the effectiveness of
the remedial program it generates. The program should be based
on the inferences made in step 4 and should attempt to alleviate
the symptoms and, if possible, the contributing factors. This IEP,
which must be reviewed annually by a committee, includes

- a statement of the child's present level of educational performance.
- a statement of annual goals and short-term objectives.
- a statement of specific special education and related services to
be provided.
- a statement of other needed administrative services.

In Carl's case recommendations were given for improving visual
memory for words, in particular the use of a kinesthetic method
to learn new words, thereby training the use of visual imagery and
visual memory (writing words and phrases from memory) in the
process of reading. Likewise, specific suggestions were made for
developing his sound-blending ability. With the help of the program, Carl did learn to read.

EDUCATIONAL ADAPTATIONS FOR
CHILDREN WITH LEARNING DISABILITIES

Remediation Strategies

Children with learning disabilities are a diverse group. It isn't surprising, then, to find that the strategies and teaching approaches designed
to help these children are also diverse. Still, we can group the various
approaches into four broad categories: task training, in which the emphasis is on the sequencing and simplification of the task to be learned;
ability or process training, in which the focus is on the remediation
of a specific developmental disability; ability- or process-task training, in which the first two approaches are combined and integrated in
one remedial program; and behavioral and cognitive intervention
strategies.

The various remediation approaches can be grouped into four broad categories—task training; ability or process training; a combination method; or behavioral and cognitive intervention strategies.
(Teri Leigh Stratford/Monkmeyer)

Task or Skill Training

One fundamental strategy that teachers have always used with children who are having difficulty learning is to modify the nature of the task. In most instances, modification means simplification, breaking up the lessons into smaller, simpler units through task analysis (see Chapter 4). This allows the child to master elements of the task and then synthesize the components into the total task.

One remedial approach to swimming, for example, is to teach the child how to kick, how to tread water, and how to keep from breathing under water. The child is then asked to put each of these skills together through supervised practice. The same process is used to simplify reading and other academic subjects. The teacher breaks up the complex task of reading a paragraph into (1) learning syllables or phonetic elements in a word, (2) learning separate words in a sentence, and (3) learning a sentence. Eventually, by building up the child's skills, the student is reading a paragraph.

The task analysis approach does not assume any special learning problem or ability deficit within the child, just a lack of experience and practice with the task.

Some theorists do not find training in specific skills effective. They claim that a complex task like reading cannot be subdivided into a series of discrete skills and then reassembled, that reading is greater than the sum of its parts. And, they question whether children learn the sequence of skills in the order that adults who have analyzed the reading process have determined. Torgesen (1979) pointed out that it may be a mistake to ignore psychological process disorders when dealing with children who are learning disabled. The normal child, who has no neurological or psychological impediments to learning, profits from direct skill-instruction procedures. But the strategy may not be effective for the severely learning disabled child who also exhibits a developmental learning disability.

Ability or Process Training

In the second type of remedial strategy, the teacher or remedial specialist identifies a particular disability in the development of an individual child that, if not corrected, will continue to inhibit the learning processes regardless of how the teacher reconstructs the task. Here the teaching emphasis focuses on the particular disability that seems to be blocking progress.

If a child cannot swim because of weak upper-arm and shoulder muscles, the remediation strategy would focus on building up those muscles through exercises until the child had the minimum ability necessary to perform the task. Similarly, if a visual memory problem or a sound-blending difficulty is interfering with a child's reading ability, remediation would focus on the specific deficiency.

Process training, then, attempts to correct developmental deficiencies—in attention, memory, perception, thinking, and language—that can impede learning. And the curriculum in nursery schools and kindergartens is designed to develop these psychological processes, to give children the prerequisite skills for learning. If a child is inattentive, the teacher creates an environment to help the child develop selective attention. If a child does not understand directions, the teacher tries to improve the child's auditory reception skills. The developmental problem becomes the focus of the educational strategy. And the educational program generally uses life situations, not abstractions. Teachers do not train attention or memory per se; they train attention to a task or memory for words or letters or numbers.

Process (Ability)–Task Approach

Most specialists believe that for the ordinary child, whose problems stem from poor teaching or lack of opportunity, the task-training approach works effectively. Children with severe disabilities, however, require "child analysis" as well as task analysis. Remediation involves ability and task training; that is, teaching the child to use a particular process in accomplishing the task. We call this **process-task training** or **aptitude-task interaction.** It means we integrate the process and task in remediation. Instead of teaching visual discrimination of abstract, meaningless symbols like circles or squares, we train visual discrimination of letters and words. The approach integrates remediation of the process dysfunction with the task development as analyzed, and matches the instructional materials with the ability of the child to respond.

Let's look at an example of process-task training. Tom, who attended school regularly, was a nine-year-old who was not reading, despite an IQ score of 120. Analysis of the child's information-processing abilities showed a deficit in visual memory: He was unable to reproduce in writing and from memory words presented to him visually. He demonstrated his problem with visual memory on both informal and formal tests. The procedure for process-task remediation in Tom's case called for a program that would develop visual memory with the words and phrases to be taught. The procedure used was the Fernald Kinesthetic Method (Fernald, 1943), a system of training memory for words, not in the abstract—as is done in ability training of memory for digits or objects alone—but directly with the words and phrases needed by the child in learning to read. This method is described later in the chapter.

Behavioral and Cognitive Intervention Strategies

A learning disabled child has difficulty learning to read or spell or write or calculate. For more than a century, psychologists have studied learning and forgetting and have evolved different theories on how children learn. Here we look at two sets of theories: behavioral and cognitive.

Behavior analysis strategies utilize principles of learning. Smith (1981) described five stages of learning:

1. *The acquisition stage.* In this stage, the individual learns how to perform a task accurately. The teacher uses physical guidance, modeling, verbal directions, prompting, and reinforcement techniques.
2. *The proficiency stage.* During this stage, the student learns to perform the task quickly and automatically. The teacher uses

modeling, reinforcement for accuracy and speed of performance, and other techniques.

3. *The maintenance stage.*   This stage is reached when the student remembers what has been learned after a lapse of time. Praise and overlearning of a skill or knowledge help retention.

4. *The generalization stage.*   In this stage, the learner is able to transfer the skill or knowledge to a new situation. This transfer is not necessarily automatic; often the teacher must help with the generalization process.

5. *The adoption stage.*   At this point the skill or knowledge becomes part of the student's standard repertoire.

Cognitive intervention strategies focus more on the cognitive processes of learning than on behavior. Metacognition is an awareness of our own system of thinking or the ability to devise our own strategies for learning. Lerner (1985) identified several metacognitive strategies: advance organizers, search strategies, verbal rehearsal, self-monitoring, and self-questioning. These are explained on page 406.

Torgesen (1980, 1982) described two learning styles: reflective and impulsive. His studies and others showed that learning disabled children tend to have an impulsive learning style; they act before thinking. He attributed that impulsiveness to a deficiency in alternative cognitive strategies.

If this assumption is correct, it's important to teach children alternative strategies for learning. At the Kansas Institute for Research on Learning Disabilities, a research team concentrated on what Meichenbaum (1979) called "cognitive behavior modification." This meant creating intervention models using some of the technologies developed by behavior analysts. Schumaker, Deshler, Alley, and Warner (1983) found that learning-disabled adolescents who had learned the elements of basic skills were not achieving in content areas (social science, science) because they did not know how to study. The researchers had two choices: to tutor the students in secondary school subjects or to teach them how to learn. There's an old saying: "You can feed a fish to a hungry man and keep him alive for a day, or you can teach him to fish and keep him alive for a lifetime." The team opted to "keep the students alive for a lifetime." The cognitive strategies developed at Kansas are discussed on page 406.

We should point out that the distinctions among these remediation strategies are not always clear-cut. All remedial approaches are adequate in different situations, with different children. And each is valuable in the appropriate setting. Task training works well for minor academic problems. Process remediation is suitable for training an ability for its own sake, especially at the preschool level. The process-task approach is effective for severe cases involving a dual problem of a specific developmental disability and an academic disability. The cognitive approach, although applicable at all stages of development, has been utilized primarily with older children and adolescents.

Remediation Programs

The kind of remedial program used for a learning disabled individual depends on the age of the person and the severity of the disability. The lifespan program includes (1) preschool programs that attempt to remediate developmental disabilities, (2) elementary programs that deal primarily with the remediation of academic disabilities, and (3) secondary school programs that focus on remediating study skills in content areas.

The Preschool Program for Developmental Learning Disabilities

The preschool curriculum is set up to enhance developmental (cognitive) abilities. The process was clearly described by Lerner, Mardel-Czudnowski, and Goldenberg (1981). They defined cognitive skills as a series of mental activities that involve knowing and recognizing, organizing ideas, developing concepts, problem solving, remembering, understanding relationships, drawing inferences, generalizing, and evaluating—a list very similar to the developmental learning abilities described earlier.

Perceptual-motor Disabilities.

The work of Strauss and Lehtinen (1947) generated widespread interest in the problem of specific learning disabilities. Their thesis was that children with brain injuries incurred before, during, or after birth are subject to major disorders in perception, thinking, and behavior; and that these disorders affect the ability to read, spell, write, or calculate. They suggested instructional procedures and environmental changes to correct or ameliorate disturbances in perception, thinking, and behavior. They integrated these techniques with procedures for teaching reading, spelling, writing, and arithmetic. Their work stimulated subsequent developments in the study and remediation of learning disabilities. Among them were the perceptual-motor approaches of Cruickshank, Bentzen, Ratzeburg, and Tannhauser (1961), Kephart (1964), and Barsch (1967), and the visual-perceptual approaches of Getman (1965) and Frostig and Horne (1964).

Perceptual problems in young children are rare and can be unique. Each child's problem must be isolated, and sometimes a special method has to be created for that child. For example, Mary, age 5, was referred to a preschool for mildly and moderately mentally retarded children. She was diagnosed both mentally retarded and blind, the outcome of her mother's bout with rubella during pregnancy. The teachers noted that Mary had language ability above that of a child with an IQ below 50, and that she did have some residual sight. Her extreme nystagmus (eyes moving continuously), however, did not allow her to identify objects or pictures readily. After a period of observation, they decided that the child could learn to identify objects if given enough time. She had a "speed of perception" deficit, contributed by the nystagmus.

Pictures of objects were presented to her and labeled. She was asked to repeat the label. It was found that she could recognize the pictures if given enough time. A tachistoscope was then used with presentations of first 5 seconds, then 4 seconds, and so forth. In a three-month period, Mary was responding to pictures at 1/25 of a second. This training generalized to the classroom, where she was now able to identify pictures and even tell stories about action pictures in readers. This remediation of a specific developmental learning disability allowed Mary eventually to go to school and learn to read. Her IQ score at age 10 was around 90, and her reading and spelling tested at a third-grade level (Kirk, 1958).

Oral Language Disabilities.   Parents do not usually pick up on their children's perceptual, thinking, or memory problems. But they can and do recognize language delays and disorders.

Figure 9.3 (page 366) shows a profile of language-disordered children. Although this profile was derived from a sample of 6- to 8-year-old children, the same profile appears in preschoolers between ages 3 and 6. From the profile and from our own observation, we can identify three major oral language disabilities in young children: receptive language (understanding the spoken word); subvocal thinking (the inner process of manipulating verbal symbols); and expressive language (the ability to express ideas in verbal terms).

We discuss language disorders in detail in Chapter 7. But there are several principles of remediation—the work of Johnson and Myklebust (1967)—we should mention here:

1.   Begin language training early.
2.   Teach the child to understand oral language before training oral expression.
3.   Use simple words and simultaneously present an experience.
4.   Select the vocabulary to be taught based on the child's immediate experience.
5.   Teach concepts.
6.   Begin with the child's immediate concerns (food, body parts) and gradually progress to more-complex oral language.

Materials and Methods.   A number of programs to remediate developmental learning disabilities have been developed for preschool children. Most were generated from the model of the Illinois Test of Psycholinguistic Abilities (Kirk, McCarthy, & Kirk, 1968). This model included two channels of presentation (auditory and visual), and three processes (receptive, organizational, and expressive). It also included memory and closure. For expression, it utilized verbal and motor responses.

Karnes prepared a series of language training kits for parents and teachers. *You and Your Small Wonder* (1982b, 1982c) focuses on children from birth to age 3; *Language Development* (1982a) covers ages

3 to 6. These programs are the outcome of Karnes's research with normal and exceptional children, many from low-income families. Karnes, Zehrbach, and Teska (1974) reported on research showing the efficacy of early remediation for disadvantaged children. A follow-up study showed normal development through the third grade.

Using as a base a doctoral dissertation (Smith 1962) that showed mentally retarded children can profit from language lessons designed from the ITPA model, Dunn and Smith (1967) developed a series of instructional kits to be used for a whole class of children ages 2 to 8. Their emphasis is on the development of oral language through exercises, games, and lessons. Lessons are arranged in sequence and are designed to develop the psycholinguistic processes of auditory and visual reception, association, and verbal and manual expression. Directions for the teacher are explicit and follow a systematic, well-rounded approach.[1]

The MWM Program, developed by Minskoff, Wiseman, and Minskoff (1975), is also based on the ITPA model. It is presented on two levels, for ages 5 to 7 and 7 to 10. Each level includes three sets of material: record booklets, a series of manuals for teachers, and a series of workbooks for students. An inventory of observable language behavior is contained in a record book used by teachers to estimate each child's ability in the twelve subtests of the ITPA.[2]

Elementary-level Learning Disabilities

The most common learning disabilities at this age level are in the academic areas of reading, handwriting, spelling and written expression, and arithmetic. In addition, social perception has been recognized recently as a problem that requires remediation.

Reading. Failure to read is the most common indication of learning disabilities in school-age children. A large number of remedial reading methods have been prepared for children who are not reading at age level.[3] The **kinesthetic method** was developed by Grace Fernald and Helen Keller (1921). It teaches reading in four developmental stages:

* *Stage 1.* The child traces the form of a known word while saying it, then writes it from memory, comparing each trial with the original model.

---

1. These kits have been revised and extended by Dunn and others through 1982 by the American Guidance Service.
2. There are a number of other programs, some of them less formal. For a review, see Bush and Giles (1969), Lombardi and Lombardi (1977), and Kirk and Kirk (1971).
3. For an extensive discussion of these methods, see Kirk, Kliebhan, and Lerner (1978).

- *Stage 2.* The child looks at the word or phrase while saying it, then tries to write it from memory, comparing each trial with the model.
- *Stage 3.* The child glances at the word and says it once, then produces it from memory.
- *Stage 4.* The child begins to generalize, to read new words on the basis of experience with previously learned words.

Fernald's method has been subjected to considerable evaluation over the years, and experimental research has found that the kinesthetic approach aids retention (for example, Kirk, 1933; Berres, 1967; Hulme, 1981). In summarizing the research literature, Mather (1985b) concluded:

> The efficacy and benefits of the Fernald method appear to: (1) direct a student's attention to word learning, (2) provide a motor memory trace that improves retention of letters and words, (3) improve visual discrimination and visual recognition skills, (4) increase visual memory capacity for words, (5) assist in visual-verbal paired associative learning by helping the student associate the spoken and written word, and (6) improve verbal memory of visual forms. Tracing does not, however, appear to be effective or necessary for normal learners who can learn words efficiently using the visual and auditory modalities. (p. 34)

A second group of remedial reading programs uses phonics. The **phonic-grapho-vocal method** (Hegge, Kirk, & Kirk, 1936) was developed while the authors were working with educable mentally retarded children who were also classified as disabled readers. A revised version, the *Phonic Remedial Reading Program* (Kirk, Kirk, & Minskoff, 1985), is a programmed phonic system that emphasizes sound blending and incorporates kinesthetic experience. The lessons follow the principles of effective programmed learning:

- Minimal change (each lesson incorporating only one new sound)
- Overlearning through repetition of each new sound in a variety of settings and frequent review drills
- Promptings and confirmation
- Only one response taught for each symbol
- Self-reinforcement (the student's immediate knowledge of success) and social reinforcement (by the teacher)

The **visual-auditory-kinesthetic (VAK) method** of Gillingham and Stillman (1936, 1965) is a phonic system for the remediation of reading disabilities. Like Hegge, Kirk, and Kirk's remedial reading drills, it has been used successfully since its development, even during the period

One of the steps in the first stage of the Fernald kines-
thetic method requires the learning disabled child to
trace the form of a known word while saying it and then
to write it from memory.
(Alan Carey/The Image Works)

in which the use of phonics was severely criticized. In this method children learn both the names and the sounds of the letters. The names are used for spelling; the sounds, for reading. A systematic procedure is followed in which the child is told the name of a letter and then its sound. The child then says the sound and traces it or writes it from memory. After learning some consonants and vowels, the child is required to sound each letter and blend the sounds into a word. Once the child has learned to sound, write, and read three-letter words, the words are used in stories that the child reads silently and then aloud.

A variation on the VAK method, the **multisensory approach,** was designed by Slingerland (1974). The program includes a teacher's guide and a set of auxiliary materials. The child first hears the sound or letter or word, then sees it on a card, then traces it with large arm swings. The procedures were designed to teach writing, spelling, and reading to a small group of children in a classroom setting.

Handwriting.   Handwriting is a prerequisite skill for spelling and written expression. It begins when a young child first scribbles with pencils and crayons, imitating parents and siblings. Formal instruction in writing, however, does not begin until kindergarten or first grade.

Most schools teach two styles of handwriting: manuscript (printing) and cursive. Today, manuscript writing is taught in the first and second grades; cursive writing is taught later, if at all.

Several factors can contribute to writing difficulties. These include environmental factors (poor instruction, forced instruction, group teaching that allows children with handwriting disabilities to fall by the wayside, situations that allow a child to practice errors) and intrinsic factors (poor motor control, deficiencies of visual and spatial perception, deficient visual memory, left-handedness, ambidexterity, poor visual-motor coordination, reversals in writing).

The teacher's first task is to note the specific difficulty and uncover possible contributing factors. The remedial program should overcome or compensate for the contributing factors in teaching the child letter formation. For example, left-handedness in itself does not contribute to a writing disability; but lack of proper instruction for a left-handed child does. Otto, McMenemy, and Smith (1973) pointed out that right-handers pull the pen, while left-handers push the pen. They noted that

> some left-handers will show up in the upper grades needing remedial help in handwriting because they did not receive proper instruction earlier. They may have developed an extreme back slant, a hooked writing position, or other faulty characteristics. (p. 355)

Kirk and Chalfant (1984) suggested a series of steps be used in teaching a child to form letters:

1. Together with the child, establish a goal of learning to form letters legibly.
2. After obtaining the child's attention, form the letter to be taught while the child observes the movement and the shape of the letter.
3. Name the letter, "This is *a*," as you write it and ask the child to repeat the name. When the child repeats the name confirm it by saying, "Good, this is *a*."
4. Rewrite the letter and discuss the formation with the child. "See, we start here, then form the letter this way."
5. Ask the child to trace the letter with his or her index finger and name the letter. This should be repeated several times.
6. As the child traces the letter ask the child to describe the process as you did in the fourth step.
7. Write the letter in dots or short dashes (⟨a⟩) and ask the

child to trace it with chalk or a pencil to form the complete letter. Repeat several times.

8. Ask the child to copy the letter from a model. Repeat several times, being sure the child is copying legibly.
9. When the child is able to copy the letter legibly, ask him or her to write the letter from memory, without a model.
10. Help the child compare the written letter with the model.
11. When the child is able to write the letter legibly, introduce another letter, such as *b*, for learning. When *b* is learned, ask the child to "now write *a*." Then alternate *a* and *b*. This allows for overlearning and avoids overloading the child with too many partially learned letters in one session.
12. At all stages praise the child for adequate responses. (p. 209)

D'Nealian manuscript has proved to be an effective handwriting method for children with learning disabilities (Thurber, 1984). This multisensory method is based on the belief that handwriting is a progressively developed individualized skill (Thurber, 1970). The style combines manuscript and cursive letterforms. Letters are written with a consistent slant, using a continuous stroke that provides a natural progression into cursive writing. The form offers several advantages for learning disabled children:

- Visual and auditory clues to aid the memory process
- Fewer hand-eye coordination problems and reversals
- Presentation of handwriting as a visual-auditory-kinesthetic skill

Spelling and Written Expression.   Spelling is one of the language arts. Children normally learn to spell by reading. But reading and spelling are different. Some children who are reading will have great difficulty spelling. In reading we receive; in spelling we produce. We receive information by reading words; we express information by writing them.

Bradley and Bryant (1979) in a series of experiments found that most children can read more words than they can spell. On the other hand, 29 percent of backward readers spell more words than they can read. These findings show that spelling and reading do not necessarily develop at similar rates. Bradley and Bryant also found that in spelling children use phonological cues, cues they do not rely on for reading. Children learn to spell incidentally through reading and writing, directly by studying spelling lists, or through generalization (spelling new words based on their knowledge of similar words).[4] Good spellers

---

4. Henderson (1981) suggested creative writing as a method for learning spelling.

tend to use all three approaches; learning disabled children are deficient in one or more of these methods.

Children use the phonic elements of words to reproduce spelling. And, in fact, Bradley and Bryant found that backward readers tend to rely on phonemic cues. Of course this method limits the repertoire of words to those that are phonemic in structure. Words like *could* ("kood") and *night* ("nite") and *business* ("bizness") require more than phonetic cues.

Other children learn to spell by visualizing what a word looks like—creating the correct visual image of the word and reproducing it in writing. Children with severe visual memory problems find it difficult to remember how words look. For these children, Fernald (1943), Slingerland (1981), and others suggested seeing, hearing, tracing, and writing words from memory as a remedial method. Kirk and Chalfant (1984) described an effective remedial procedure:

1. Write an unknown word to be learned on the board or on paper and pronounce it.
2. Ask the child to look at it and to name it.
3. Then, while looking at the word, the child should trace each letter in the air as if copying the word. Let the child label each letter (either with the sound of the letter or with the letter name). This helps the child visualize the word more accurately.
4. Remove the word or cover it and ask the child to trace it in the air with a finger and say it while tracing it. The purpose of tracing in the air is to aid the child in visualizing the word.
5. Repeat Step 3 if necessary.
6. Repeat the tracing in the air and saying the word until the child is satisfied that he or she has perceived and remembered it correctly.
7. Ask the child to write the word from memory and say it. Then compare the reproduction to the original. Repeat if necessary.
8. Teach another word in the same way.
9. Now ask the child to trace the first word in the air and write it from memory. If the child fails, repeat steps 2 to 7.
10. When the child has learned to spell a word from memory and has learned other words, write the word in a progress notebook. This book of words learned can be both a progress record and a review program. It can also be used to record the number of words learned each day. Our experience indicates that the number of words learned each day will increase as the child improves in spelling skills.

> These improvements can be represented on a graph for motivational purposes.
> 11. Use the words learned in sentences and in homework wherever possible (p. 225)

Phonics and visualization alone cannot produce an efficient speller. Linguists claim that generalization is the most important factor in spelling ability. The teacher's role is to help the child generalize by presenting a group of words (*say, may, ray*) and then asking the child to spell rhyming words (*day, lay, hay*). With practice, the child will begin spelling new words that are similar to those he or she has learned.

The Education for All Handicapped Children Act includes written expression as a form of learning disability. In some instances, this classification has been used to include handwriting and spelling. Alley and Deshler (1979) and Deshler, Schumaker, and Lenz (1984) found that children with written expression difficulties show problems with listening, speaking, and writing. Johnson and Mylkebust (1967) linked auditory comprehension, oral expression, and reading to the development of written expression skills.

Remedial programs for written expression disabilities are similar in nature to those discussed for other content subjects. Alley and Deshler (1979) also suggested a group of cognitive strategies:

- Structuring paragraphs and themes
- Developing vocabulary
- Building sentences
- Writing questions
- Note taking
- Summarizing
- Monitoring written expression (p. 124)

Arithmetic.   Arithmetic disabilities of a severe nature show up less often than reading disabilities and receive less attention. With the availability of inexpensive electronic calculators, we have a temporary solution to the learning problem. But this does not eliminate the value of knowing fundamental arithmetic skills.

Arithmetic disabilities can be found in children of normal intelligence who perform adequately in reading and spelling. Just as children who are doing fifth- and sixth-grade work in arithmetic can be reading at the first-grade level, so children who are reading at the fifth- and sixth-grade level may be unable to add or subtract. This condition is called *dyscalculia* in the literature.

Like language and reading disorders, arithmetic disorders were observed originally in adults who had suffered cerebral injuries. Chalfant and Scheffelin (1969) cited the early works of Henschen on brain-

The developmental learning disabilities that appear to affect performance in math include problems in perception, discrimination, reversals, spatial relations, short- and long-term memory, sequential ability, closure, reasoning, and language.
(Alan Carey/The Image Works)

injured adults (who on autopsy were found to have lesions in one or more different areas of the brain) and Gertsmann and others (who found lesions in the parieto-occipital region in the dominant hemisphere). With children, it is difficult to determine the cause of an arithmetic disability. It could be the result of genetics or a cerebral dysfunction acquired before, during, or after birth; or it could be due to poor instruction, emotional factors, or lack of early exposure to quantitative thinking. Sampson's arithmetic disability, described on page 361, was caused by brain damage he suffered in an accident.

Bley and Thornton (1981) found that some students are enthusiastic about arithmetic until they fail; then their willingness to try decreases with age. They claimed that the biggest obstacle to learning math is the inability to perform independently, a problem that stems from several factors:

- The inability to think logically without help
- Visual-perception difficulties
- Poor retention
- Auditory-misperception problems with words

The developmental ·learning disabilities that appear to affect performance in math include problems in perception, discrimination, reversals, spatial relations, short- and long-term memory, sequential ability, closure, reasoning, and language.

Arithmetic disabilities are diagnosed in much the same way as other learning disabilities:

1. Determining whether a disability exists by comparing other skills to the level of performance in arithmetic
2. Studying the contributing factors
3. Analyzing the types of errors made in arithmetic
4. Evolving a diagnostic hypothesis
5. Organizing a remedial program

The most important part of the analysis is studying the kinds of errors made in calculations. The usual procedure is to test the child formally or informally on counting; reading and writing numerals; the four basic operations (addition, subtraction, multiplication, division); using fractions, decimals, and percentages; and a cognitive understanding of space, time, and quantity.

Effective remediation generally involves programmed instructional procedures, beginning at the level at which the child is performing and moving forward at a rate at which the child can learn successfully. Severe arithmetic disabilities require one-to-one tutoring to adapt to the student's rate of progress and to provide adequate reinforcement. If the disability is the result of poor motivation, poor instruction, or other environmental factors, the remediation of mechanical errors is generally adequate. If, however, the problem is the result of other factors—inadequate spatial relations, inadequate visual-motor integration, lack of verbal ability, deficiencies in inductive thinking—remediation must use the process-task approach. This means organizing the instruction to include the use of the disabled process in relation to the task requirement and developing an understanding of the errors observed during the operation of the task. Cognitive strategies—the students ask themselves questions, talk to themselves—are also effective (Deshler, Schumaker, & Lenz, 1984), as is the use of microcomputers, an increasingly popular tool for teaching arithmetic.

Kirk and Chalfant (1984) and others have suggested the following process-task approach:

1. Select the appropriate objective for the solution of the child's problem—what the child should learn next.
2. Break the objective down into operational skills. (Each instructional objective involves a number of subskills.)
3. Determine which developmental disability is involved in the task.
4. Consider the developmental disabilities in organizing instruction so that the disability is ameliorated in the arithmetic task.

There are a number of remedial and instructional programs that have been developed for arithmetic. Some are listed here for the interested reader:

- *The Computational Arithmetic Program* (Smith and Lovitt, 1982)
- *Structural Arithmetic* (Stern, 1965)
- *Distar* (Engelmann & Bruner, 1970, 1972, 1975)
- *Cuisinaire Rods* (Davidson, 1969)
- *Programmed Math* (Sullivan, 1968)
- *Project Math: Levels 1 & 2* (Cawley, Fitzmaurice, Goodstein, Lepore, Sedlack and Althouse, 1976a, 1976b)

Social Perception. A social perception disability is the inability to identify and recognize the meaning and significance of the behavior of others (Johnson & Myklebust, 1967). Those with social perception difficulties are insensitive to their peers and social situations; they lack empathy.

At the Chicago Institute for the Study of Learning Disabilities researchers spent five years studying the social competence of children with learning disabilities (Bryan, Pearl, Donahue, Bryan, & Pflaum, 1983). In general they found that learning disabled students do not deal successfully with people and tend to be rejected by their classmates. They also discovered "persistent personality and behavior differences between LD and normally achieving youngsters" (p. 17).

Another finding was that learning disabled children are pessimistic about their future. They assume that their failures in school and life are the result of their personal inadequacies. When they do succeed they usually do not attribute their success to their own efforts and abilities, but to luck or other people. As a result, they do not try as hard as children who are not learning disabled to improve their performance. This may explain why they are on task less than are other children. As Frieze (1963) explained: "Those who expect to do well will continue to have high expectations and those who have low expectations will maintain them regardless of how they actually perform" (p. 8).

At the Kansas Institute similar studies were conducted on the social characteristics of learning disabled adolescents. Deshler and Schumaker (1983) came to the same conclusion: Most learning disabled adolescents demonstrate social skill deficiencies. In fact, these adolescents scored lower than did a control group on seven of eight skills needed for social adjustment (Schumaker, Hazel, Sherman, & Sheldon, 1982).

Recognizing the seriousness of social perception problems in children with learning disabilities, Minskoff (1980a, 1980b) proposed a remedial program. To develop that program, she studied and task analyzed nonverbal communication, the language used to convey feelings

THE HANDICAP THAT HAD NO NAME

What was the problem? Why did I always wiggle in my chair? Why did my muscles have a mind of their own? And why did I write so slowly?

I thought of the story in one of our readers of Glenn Cunningham, the first American to run the four-minute mile. As a child, his legs had been burned in a fire and everyone told him he would never walk again. But he struggled and one day he took his first step. Everyone was amazed. . . . He practiced walking and then running. He practiced and practiced until he ran the four-minute mile. . . .

I studied my hands and legs. There was nothing wrong with them but they just did not do what I told them to. I had to practice and practice like Glenn Cunningham but my efforts received no recognition. As an adult I have words for my confused feelings then: I was jealous of Glenn Cunningham's handicap. It had a name: burned legs. Everyone admired him when he walked. My handicap had no name. . . .

Fifth grade, sixth, seventh, and eighth grade. Time went slowly then. Each second clicked by individually. I hated myself but I never gave up trying. During the summers, I learned how to swim. The Red Cross taught swimming in four two-week classes: Beginner, Intermediate, Junior, and Swimmer. It took me a full summer to complete each class.

I still had trouble in gym. In team games, I had to choose between doing nothing and infuriating my teachers or trying to participate and infuriating my peers. In gymnastics, I had to walk along a balance beam; I often fell off. My peers changed their methods of teasing me: They greeted me in an exaggerated manner or laughed at me behind my back. In eighth grade, my picture was crossed out of many yearbooks. . . .

In French class we had to memorize dialogues and recite them. I used to wait in dread for my turn because when I stood up all I could do was stutter. I was given a D in the course and the counselor called me in to discuss the grade.

"I can't memorize the dialogues," I explained. "I practiced every night; I read them over and over, but it does no good. The words fly out of my mind. It must be a mental block."

We spent an hour together, and got nowhere. Finally, she said, "Dale, can't you just pretend the dialogues are words to a song?"

"I can't memorize songs either. Every Christmas I try to learn the carols again. I listen, I look at the words, I have friends say the words and I repeat them, but it doesn't help."

We sat silently. How close we were to the core of my problems! However, at that time, the theory that would have explained me to myself did not exist. . . .

My vision was a problem. Things seemed to melt together so that it was hard for me to find the lock on my locker or a book on a shelf. I had no social

continued

continued

skills. In group projects, such as cooking or putting up a tent, I did not know how to help. And the flow of conversation was difficult for me to master. It took months of watching before I understood how people interrupted each other. Even so, I could not learn how to use the signals with ease. . . .

I applied to Antioch College because of their work-study program and their nontraditional approach to education. When I was accepted, I hoped once again to make a new start. . . .

Antioch College enabled me to socialize. Many students had been through encounter and sensitivity groups and they gave and received feedback freely. Group projects were common. I learned the things about myself that bothered people and I corrected them. I constantly reminded myself to blink and to move my eyes from person to person as each spoke. The movements confused me visually but they made other people more comfortable. I stopped jumping at the slightest sound and turned my eyes and head towards what I wanted to see. In fact, I became tense because of the constant awareness of my body. It was worth it because my peers avoided me less.

We went to school in four alternating quarters of work and study. Jobs could be taken anywhere in the world. . . . Things came to a head when I was employed as a factory worker at an electronics assembly company. . . . On my first day, . . . I was supposed to strip encasing rubber and insulation from three wires and then to twist the copper strands slightly. No matter how hard I tried, and despite [my supervisor] Marie's efforts to help me, I could not find the right amount of pressure to put on the blade. I cut my fingers again and again.

After four hours, Marie said, "Dale, you've caused too much scrap. You can try again tomorrow. Right now, I'm giving you another job—putting together probes." She took me to a winch. I took out my notebook and she objected because "it will take forever if you do."

She picked up a metal rod from the table. "Now you put this bar on the winch"—she turned the knob on the side of the winch—"then you screw this top on. . . ."

"How did you get the rod to fit in the winch?" I asked.

"I just explained that!"

"Well, I probably wasn't listening while you turned that knob because I needed to see how you did it."

Her face grew grim. She went through the procedure again with a running commentary. When the probe was assembled she stood aside and said, "Now you do it." I had no idea where to begin . . .

I decided to list my mistakes. . . . In my apartment I studied the error list. Over half my mistakes involved hearing. Hearing! I knew that my vision and touch were off. I knew I was clumsy and had no sense of direction. But I had assumed that my hearing was safe. I knew then that I could trust none of my senses. I was depressed for days. When my depression did not lift, I made an appointment at the college counseling center.

continued

continued

... I told [the counselor] everything that had happened and showed her my list of errors ... She asked me many questions. Finally, she said, "It sounds to me as if you might have perceptual problems. Your hearing difficulties sound like auditory sequencing problems."

"Auditory sequencing problems?" I questioned.

"Problems in hearing sounds in the right order. That's why you always have to write down what you hear.... Your visual and auditory problems and inability to tell right from left sound like perceptual problems, trouble taking in information through your senses. You really fit the constellation well. Why don't you read a textbook on learning disabilities? Most of them have a section on perception. I wish there was more I could suggest, but there are really no tests for people your age."

At the library the next day, I found that there was no catalogue category for learning disabilities, so I went to the special education stacks. I found plenty of material on physical and mental handicaps but nothing I could identify as my area of concern. After several hours of browsing, I came upon *Psychology of Exceptional Children and Youth* (Cruickshank, 1963). One chapter was called "Psychological Characteristics of Brain-Injured Children" ... The characteristics described by the authors appeared to be a problem-by-problem profile of myself. *Hyperactivity ... hyperdistractibility ... perseveration ... lability ... of affect* (emotional instability) *... motor dysfunction ... auditory problems* ... All my problems had been described in the 20 pages of the chapter. I was not crazy. I had an identifiable medical syndrome. I was not alone anymore....

I recommend that parents and teachers of learning disabled/minimal brain damaged children talk frankly about the handicap and its manifestations and express confidence that the children can handle it. It is important to recognize and reinforce the discipline it takes a person to overcome this handicap....

Learning about my problem changed me from a person who hated herself to someone who likes herself and knows that she is struggling with a real handicap. My problems have not changed but my attitude has.

SOURCE: From "The Handicap That Had No Name" by Dale Brown in *Reflections on Growing Up Disabled*, R. Jones (Ed.), 1983. Reston, VA: The Council for Exceptional Children.

and emotions. She identified four major nonverbal communication systems:

- *Kinesics.* Body language (facial expressions, gestures, postures).
- *Proxemics.* The use of space for communication (distance from people, spatial arrangements, territories belonging to a person).
- *Vocalic communication.* Voice pitch, loudness, tempo and pauses, giggling, whispering, and yawning.

- *Artifactual communication.* The use of clothing and cosmetics as a means of communication.

And she identified a training process for teaching those systems:

1. Discriminating critical visual and auditory social cues in one's own behavior and in the behavior of others
2. Developing an understanding of the meaning of those social cues
3. Expressing specific motor and oral cues as a specific social response
4. Discriminating negative nonverbal social cues in people with whom one is interacting

In applying the process to teaching facial expressions—part of the kinesic system—Minskoff suggested:

1. Discriminating facial expressions (happiness, surprise, fear)
2. Understanding the social meaning of facial expressions
3. Using facial expressions in a meaningful way
4. Applying facial expression cues to communication

She advocated using the same process—and role playing and verbal problem solving—in the programs for teaching proxemics, vocalic communication, and artifactual communication.

Adolescent Learning Disabilities

In junior and senior high schools we find students who have not yet mastered the basic skills sufficiently to cope with content subjects. English, mathematics, science, social science, history—all of these subjects require reading, and most of that reading is above the level of learning disabled youngsters.

These youngsters need the remedial programs in use with elementary children. And the schools are offering those programs in resource rooms and self-contained classrooms.

Characteristics of Adolescents with Learning Disabilities. The Kansas Institute for Research on Learning Disabilities has concentrated on the characteristics of learning disabled adolescents and on cognitive intervention strategies. Schumaker, Deshler, Alley, and Warner (1983) in a yearlong study of the characteristics of learning disabled adolescents found the following data:

- The learning disabled adolescents they studied had reached a plateau, making very little progress in academic skills. The tenth-grade students were reading and doing arithmetic at fifth- and sixth-grade levels.

An adolescent student who is learning disabled often faces heightened difficulties—for both the secondary school academic setting and the social or peer situation place increasingly complex demands on the individual. (Meri Houtchens-Kitchens)

- The learning disabled adolescents showed deficiencies in study skills. They were less efficient than were other students in note taking, listening comprehension, monitoring writing errors, test taking, and scanning.
- Many of the adolescents studied showed immature problem-solving skills. They were unable to create and apply strategies to new problems.
- The learning disabled adolescents demonstrated poor social skills.
- Secondary schools appeared to place complex demands on adolescents who were deficient in academic skills.

Learning Disabilities and Juvenile Delinquency. Commonly, juvenile delinquents' experience with schooling is marked by underachievement and the presence of learning disabilities. This fact has led to the belief that there is a causal link between learning disabilities and juvenile delinquency. However, it is not known whether deliquency causes learning disabilities or whether learning disabilities cause delinquency—or perhaps whether a common factor contributes to both in the same individual.

Two major studies have been reported on this issue. The first (Murray, 1976) was conducted under the auspices of the American Institutes for Research. Murray concluded that "the existence of a causal relationship between learning disabilities and delinquency has not been established; the evidence for a causal link is feeble." (p. 65)

The second study, conducted by the Association for Children with Learning Disabilities (ACLD) and the National Center for State Courts was reported by Dunivant (1982). Based on a sample of 1,943 adolescent males, this study found that learning disabilities and delinquency were definitely related. Most importantly this study demonstrated that "remedial instruction was effective in improving the academic skills and decreasing both the self-reported and official delinquency of learning disabled youths who had been officially adjudicated." (p. 46)

Recognizing that the results are not clear cut, Kirk and Chalfant nevertheless concluded from these studies that a learning disability may contribute to delinquency. "It is possible that a child who is predisposed to delinquency may become delinquent if untreated school failure leads to truancy and antisocial conduct." (p. 269)

Intervention Strategies.   The Kansas group concluded that learning disabled adolescents lack the academic skills required by secondary schools and the ability to cope with the demands placed on them. The intervention strategies, then, focused on the problems these students face in school. Their objective was to teach students how to study and how to learn, not to tutor them in content. For example, the program would not center on historical dates and events, but on ways to organize that material in preparation for a history test. A curriculum for learning strategies was just one intervention program. The researchers also developed a curriculum for learning social skills and modifications for instruction and material.

From the Kansas studies and other research (Conner, 1983), several cognitive and behavioral intervention strategies have evolved. Lerner (1985) summarized some of those strategies developed to improve reading comprehension:

- *Advance organizers.*   This technique is used to establish a mind set for the reader, relating new material to previously learned information before the material is read (Good & Brophy, 1978). Advance organizers could take several forms: introduction of general concepts, a linkage to previously learned materials, or a study of a complex introductory passage.

- *Search strategies training.*   In this strategy, students are taught how to scan the material before answering a question. They are taught to stop, listen, look, and think—to systematically consider alternative approaches and answers before responding to a problem. The aim is to reduce impulsive, thoughtless answers and to delay a response until a systematic search for the right one has been made.

- *Verbal rehearsal.* In this strategy, students learn to verbalize a problem encountered in reading comprehension. They state the problem to themselves as a planned approach for clarifying the problem. There are three stages for teaching this strategy: (1) the students observe the instructor's modeling of verbalization of the problem, (2) the students instruct themselves by verbalizing aloud or in a whisper, and (3) the students verbalize silently.

- *Self-monitoring.* In this strategy, students learn to monitor their own mistakes. Learning-disabled students need training in the strategy of checking their own responses and becoming conscious of errors or answers that do not make sense. To reach this stage requires active involvement in the learning process rather than passive learning, in which students are not conscious of incongruities.

- *Self-questioning.* In the *self-questioning* learning strategies approach, students develop their own comprehension questions. Through direct instruction learning-disabled students have been trained successfully to use self-questioning strategies while reading. They asked themselves such questions as what am I reading this passage for? what is the main idea? what is a good question about the main idea? The students learn to monitor their reading, and their comprehension improves significantly (Wong & Jones, 1982). (p. 393)

Microcomputers and Learning Disabled Individuals

Microcomputers have had an impact on the education of learning disabled children. They are an effective instructional tool for several reasons (Pommer, Mark, & Hayden, 1983; Schiffman, Tobin, & Buchanan, 1982):

- Microcomputers are nonjudgmental about mistakes.
- The machines have unlimited patience.
- Microcomputers provide immediate feedback and reinforcement.
- Graphics and game-playing situations make basic drill and practice more interesting.
- Microcomputers can be used to promote the discovery method of learning and the development of problem-solving skills.
- The machines allow students to work at their own pace, according to their own strengths and weaknesses.
- Branching capabilities ensure individualized instruction according to student needs.

Several authors have strongly recommended the use of word-processing programs with learning disabled students to help them overcome their resistance to writing and to alleviate written language problems (Hummell & Balcom, 1984; Mather, 1985a). Easy correction allows students to concentrate on content rather than form, and writing becomes a dynamic cyclic process of creating, reading, editing, evaluating, and revising. Data base management also has relevance for learning disabled students. The computer's electronic filing system allows students to sort, correct, and retrieve information quickly. Yet both word-processing and data base management involve students as active planners who must organize and input data to create a product (Hummell & Balcom, 1984).

Computer technology also allows multisensory instruction—the use of video tapes, video discs, graphic tablets, and voice synthesizers (Schiffman, Tobin, & Buchanan, 1982). Voice synthesizers have been instrumental in helping students who are visually impaired; they are also effective for learning disabled students. For example, by converting words typed on a keyboard into speech, speech reproduction can be paired with both reading decoding and spelling practice.

Pommer, Mark, and Hayden (1983) claimed that the actual use of computers reduces impulsiveness and improves memory for the task at hand. Computers are also equipped to provide the sustained drill and practice so essential to many learning disabled youngsters (Schiffman, Tobin, & Buchanan, 1982; Torgesen & Young, 1983).

Of course using computers demands certain skills. Students must be able to read quickly, for example (Torgesen & Young, 1983). And there are students for whom computer instruction is counterproductive. Although microcomputers can be an extremely effective learning tool (Bitter, 1984), they cannot take the place of careful remedial planning for each learning disabled child.

Learning Environment

Children with learning disabilities form a heterogeneous group. This means we cannot educate them all by the same method or with a single organizational procedure. The environments in which these children learn may be very different from one another, and certain organizational procedures work more effectively with certain kinds of learning disabilities.

There are many settings that can and do provide diagnosis and remediation: public schools, private schools, psychological clinics, university diagnostic centers, and private tutorial services. The choice of setting depends on many factors: the kinds of services available; the qualifications of available teachers; and the number of children who need help, their ages, their levels of attainment, their specific problems, and the severity of their disabilities.

Most essential services are available in the public schools, especially now that laws have made the education of all children mandatory. Within the schools we find five common forms of organization: self-contained classes, resource rooms, itinerant teachers, teacher consultants, and one-to-one tutorial services.

Self-contained classes usually consist of heterogeneous groups of children with different types of disabilities and different degrees of deficit. (In large school systems, more-homogeneous groupings can be made for part of the day.) Because these classes often include twelve to fifteen children with widely different needs, it is difficult for teachers to cover the regular curriculum and to provide each student with specific remediation. These limitations can make self-contained classes less effective than some of the other types of services. In fact, at times it is more productive to limit learning disabled children to just half a day in the self-contained class and mainstream them the rest of the time.

Resource rooms are used for small groups of children (one to three youngsters) for an hour at a time on a regular basis (two or three or five times a week). Although the organization offers less individual instruction time than does the self-contained class, the smaller number of children allows the teacher to focus on specific problem areas more easily.

Itinerant teachers usually serve in small communities where there are fewer learning disabled students and fewer severe problems. Most of these teachers are specialists who serve several schools, spending some time in each and guiding student programs in cooperation with classroom teachers. Itinerant teachers can give one-to-one tutoring when needed, or can work with several children together for special help two or three times a week.

Consultant teachers assess children referred by the classroom teacher, and advise the teacher on procedures that can be instituted in the classroom. The method helps the classroom teacher understand the student's problems and the ways to alleviate them. The organization is economical: One consulting teacher can serve a large number of children. But its effectiveness depends on the degree of deficiency. Consultant teachers can be very helpful for children who have minor learning disabilities; they are much less effective for children with severe problems.

One-to-one tutoring is the most effective type of service for children with severe developmental learning disabilities. In fact, for these children it is essential. The problem, of course, is cost. Most schools simply cannot afford to offer one-on-one instruction on a regular basis, although now and again a resource teacher may have the time to give individual help.

All of these services demand the cooperation of classroom teachers. It is the goal of special educators to develop performance so that learning disabled children can adapt to grade-level work and gradually eliminate the need for special services.

LEARNING DISABLED ADULTS

Many students with learning disabilities drop out of school, not because they aren't intelligent, but because they are failing academically. Of course some, with persistence and tutoring, get through high school and even graduate from college. Nelson Rockefeller considered himself a dyslexic, yet he graduated from law school and later ran for president (Lerner, 1985). But a large majority of learning disabled students become increasingly frustrated and discouraged as they grow older, and have difficulty adapting to life situations.

Lerner (1985) described Frank, an intelligent 36-year-old man with a reading disability:

> Frank is one example of a learning disabled adult. . . . Employed as a journeyman painter and supporting his wife and two children, he had learned to cope with many daily situations that required reading skills. Although he was unable to read the color labels on paint cans, could not decipher street and road signs, and could not find streets or addresses or use a city map to find the locations of his housepainting jobs, he had learned to manage by compensating for his inability to read. He visually memorized the color codes on the paint cans to determine the color; he tried to limit his work to a specific area of the city because he could not read street signs. When he was sent into an unfamiliar area, he would ask a fellow worker who could provide directions to accompany him, or he would request help from residents of the area to help him reach his destination. He watched television to keep abreast of current affairs and his wife read and answered correspondence for him. However, inevitably the day came when advancement was no longer possible if he did not learn to read. Moreover, his children were rapidly acquiring the reading skills that he did not possess. His handicap was a continual threat for him. (p. 257)

What's being done to help people like Frank? Legislation that once focused on children has begun to recognize the problems of learning disabled adults. The Rehabilitation Act of 1973 channeled funds to federal, state, and local agencies for educational and vocational programs. The U.S. Department of Education (1985) reported that many states have implemented transitional programs (bridging special education services and vocational training) and career-planning programs. Learning disabled adults in these states can continue their education or prepare for a specific career in work-study programs.

Learning disabled adults have also become more vocal about their own problems. They've formed committees and advocacy groups to educate high schools, universities, and vocational rehabilitation agencies about the difficulties of living life with a learning disability.[5]

SUMMARY OF MAJOR IDEAS

1. Learning disabilities afflict a heterogeneous group of children who are not developing or learning normally but who do not fit into the traditional categories of handicapped children.
2. The many definitions of *learning disabilities* agree on two major points: that an intrinsic psychological or neurological factor is inhibiting or interfering with normal development or academic achievement, and that the disability cannot be explained by mental retardation, a sensory handicap, emotional disturbance, or lack of opportunity to learn.
3. Underachievement and learning disabilities are not synonymous. Learning disabilities are just one cause of underachievement.
4. There are two kinds of learning disabilities: developmental learning disabilities in attention, memory, perception, thinking and language, and academic learning disabilities in reading, handwriting, spelling and written expression, and arithmetic.
5. The prevalence of learning disabilities in the general population ranges from 1 to 2 percent for children with severe problems to 5 to 7 percent for children with mild difficulties. In 1984 over 4 percent of children were obtaining services for mild and severe learning disabilities.
6. Several causes of learning disabilities have been identified: brain dysfunctions, genetics, environmental deprivation and malnutrition, and biochemical factors.
7. The factors that contribute to an academic learning disability are the conditions that inhibit or interfere with a child's academic progress in school. They include physical conditions, environmental factors, motivational and affective factors, and psychological conditions (developmental learning disabilities). Unlike causes, these contributing factors can usually be remediated.
8. Three criteria are used to identify learning disabled children: (a) discrepancy between abilities, or between potential and achievement; (b) the absence of mental retardation, a sensory handicap, serious emotional disturbance, or environmental disadvantage; and (c) the need for special education services to remediate their disability.
9. We diagnose learning disabilities in preschool children by as-

---

5. For information about these groups, contact the Learning Disabled Adult Committee of ACLD, 4156 Library Road, Pittsburgh, PA 15234.

sessing their developmental abilities and disabilities to determine discrepancies in growth. The diagnosis of school-age children requires an assessment of a significant discrepancy between potential (as measured by tests of intelligence and skills) and achievement in a specific subject; an analysis of contributing factors; an assessment of symptoms and correlates; a diagnostic hypothesis; and a remedial prescription (the IEP).

10.   There are four common strategies for remediation: (a) task or skill training, in which we simplify and sequence the components of the task or skill to be learned; (b) process training, in which we remediate a specific developmental disability or dysfunction; (c) process-task training, in which we integrate the first two approaches in one remedial program; and (d) behavioral and cognitive strategies, which are used for elementary and secondary students.

11.   Remedial programs for preschool children focus on the amelioration of developmental learning disabilities, including those affecting language, perception, memory, and so forth.

12.   Remedial programs at the elementary level concentrate on the tool subjects (reading, handwriting, spelling and written expression, arithmetic), and often on social perception problems.

13.   At the secondary level, remediation focuses on teaching the child how to learn independently.

14.   Microcomputers have had an impact on the education of learning disabled students. Although computers are an effective learning tool, they cannot take the place of careful remedial planning for each child.

15.   Special education services are delivered in a number of different ways: self-contained classes, resource rooms, itinerant teachers, consultant teachers, and one-to-one tutoring (the most effective and the most costly).

16.   Educational and vocational rehabilitation programs offer learning disabled adults the opportunity to adapt to life situations.

UNRESOLVED ISSUES

1.   *Potential and achievement discrepancy.*   Although federal regulations specify that a learning disabled child must have a discrepancy between potential and achievement, the degree of discrepancy has not been specified. As a result, learning disability programs are quite diverse. One school system may use a two-year discrepancy while another system uses half a year or one year as the criterion for eligibility for services. In one wealthy suburban area, 8 percent of schoolchildren were enrolled in services for the learning disabled; in a lower socioeconomic area of the same city, only 1 percent of children were receiving special education services. We

need an objective criterion for enrollment in programs and a system for differentiating mild, moderate, and severe disabilities.

2. *Environmental vs. constitutional factors.* It is important to differentiate between educational underachievement due to instructional, motivational, and other environmental conditions, and educational underachievement due to psychological or neurological factors. Children who are underachieving because of environmental influences can learn by the same methods used with all children; those with intrinsic problems require special education.

3. *Differentiating services.* The increase in enrollment in services for learning disabled children has been phenomenal, from less than 1 percent in the early 1970s to over 4 percent in 1984. Probably many children are now receiving learning disability services who could be better served through other programs or slight adaptations of regular school programs. The cost of these expanded services has made this an area of concern for state and federal authorities.

REFERENCES OF SPECIAL INTEREST

Alley, G., & Deshler, D. (1979). *Teaching the learning disabled adolescent: Strategies and methods.* Denver: Love.

One of the few comprehensive books that deal with adolescent learning disabilities. The text covers three broad areas: (1) remedial education for reading and mathematics, an extension of the elementary educational program; (2) a compensatory program stressing basic skills and using peer tutoring and other strategies; and (3) alternating curriculum including life-adjustment skills.

Bley, N., & Thornton, C. (1981). *Teaching mathematics to the learning disabled.* Rockville, MD: Aspen.

The authors present a developmental approach to teaching mathematics, beginning with some of the psychological problems.

Kirk, S., & Chalfant, J. (1984). *Academic and developmental learning disabilities.* Denver: Love.

The book is in four parts. Part I discusses the taxonomy of learning disabilities, historical perspectives, causes and contributing factors, and educational diagnosis. Part II devotes a chapter to each of the developmental disabilities. Part III focuses on academic disabilities. Part IV examines the major issues in the field. The book emphasizes teacher diagnosis by observation, and remediation.

Lerner, J. (1985). *Learning disabilities: Theories, diagnosis, and teaching strategies* (4th ed.). Boston: Houghton Mifflin.

A comprehensive book covering all aspects of learning disabilities: diagnosis, clinical teaching and delivery of services, theoretical perspectives, and teaching strategies.

C·H·A·P·T·E·R Ten

CHILDREN WITH MULTIPLE AND SEVERE HANDICAPS

Focusing Questions

How have advances in medical science actually increased the number of children with multiple handicaps?

What are several common combinations of handicapping conditions?

How have educational provisions for youngsters with multiple handicaps changed over the last century?

What kinds of programs are being implemented for multiply handicapped preschoolers?

How are the instructional programs for elementary-level students with multiple handicaps different from those for secondary-level students?

What kinds of living arrangements are available for adults with severe or multiple handicaps?

*T*hroughout this text, we've emphasized that handicapped children do not always fit into neat, well-defined categories. We find individual differences among children with hearing, visual, mental, and social impairments. We also find children who have more than one impairment and children who are severely handicapped. These youngsters are even more heterogeneous than other exceptional children. They require *very* special education.

A DEFINITION

Here too it is difficult to formulate an inclusive definition. The most widely used was adopted in 1974 by the U.S. Office of Education:

> Severely handicapped children are those who because of the intensity of their physical, mental, or emotional problems, need educational, social, psychological and medical services beyond those which are traditionally offered by regular and special education programs, in order to maximize participation in society and self-fulfillment. Such severely handicapped children may possess severe language or perceptual-cognitive deprivations and evidence a number of abnormal behaviors including failure to attend to even the most pronounced stimuli, self-mutilation, manifestations of durable and intense temper tantrums, and the absence of even the most rudimentary forms of verbal control. They may also have extremely fragile physiological conditions. (Sec. 121.2)

The federal definition describes, not only the severity of the problem, but also some of the characteristics that emphasize the severity of these handicaps. Fewell and Cone (1983) accepted this definition and elaborated on the kinds of children included:

> This definition would certainly include children often classified as deaf-blind, multiply handicapped, autistic, cerebral palsied, neurologically impaired, brain-damaged, schizophrenic, and mentally retarded, but in no way would it be limited to these groups. (p. 47)

Sontag, Smith, and Sailor (1977) offered a "basic skills" definition, stating essentially that multiply and severely handicapped children are those whose primary educational needs are the establishment and development of basic skills in social, self-help, and communication areas

Because severely handicapped children have physical, cognitive or emotional problems of an intense nature, they almost always require services beyond those which are traditionally offered by regular and special education programs.
(© Jerry Howard/Positive Images)

that represent the child's potential for survival in a supervised or protected world.

We should add that children with severe mental retardation generally have other handicaps and are considered multihandicapped. But some children are multihandicapped but not mentally retarded. Helen Keller, for example, was both deaf and blind but gifted intellectually.

PREVALENCE

Advances in medical science have produced an ironic situation. Today many children survive physical conditions from which they would have perished only a few years ago. But some of these children survive with serious and multiple handicaps.

Table 10.1 lists a number of conditions that can produce multiple handicaps. These are just a few of many such conditions. Fortunately they do not occur with high incidence. But statistics on the actual

Table 10.1
Sample Conditions Leading to Multiple Handicaps

Time of Injury	Affecting Agent	Agent Activity	Typical Result
Conception	Translocation of chromosome pairs at birth	Serious changes in embryo and fetus, often fatal	Down syndrome, mental retardation
	Inborn errors of metabolism (phenylketonuria)	Inability to carry out normal chemical and metabolic processes; injures fetal development	Severe retardation and other complications; can be reversed in part by early diagnosis and special diet
Prenatal	Drugs (thalidomide)	Drug used as a sedative for mother; can arrest normal development of embryo	Marked deformities; serious anomalies of heart, eyes, ears, and limbs
Natal	Anoxia (sustained lack of oxygen to fetus during birth process)	Prolonged lack of oxygen causing irreversible destruction of brain cells	Cerebral-palsied child who may or may not have mental retardation and other defects affecting vision and hearing
Postnatal	Encephalitis, meningitis	Infectious diseases (measles, whooping cough) leading to inflammation of brain and destruction of brain cells	Lack of attention, hyperactivity; can cause epilepsy, mental retardation, and behavior problems

incidence are difficult to obtain. Why? Because definitions of serious and multiple handicaps vary from place to place.

The most reliable estimates of prevalence come to us from the medical, social, and educational agencies that provide services for severely and multiply handicapped children. U.S. Department of Education (1985) figures for 1983–1984 reported an enrollment of 67,536 children. These figures do not include some groups of multihandicapped youngsters. For example, the number of deaf-blind children was reported separately, an enrollment of 2,512, as was the number of severely and profoundly retarded children.

CHARACTERISTICS OF CHILDREN WITH MULTIPLE HANDICAPS

Although any number of combinations of handicaps is possible, some combinations appear more often than others or are more difficult to cope with and so deserve special attention. The following sections focus on multiple handicapping conditions that have as their major dimension mental retardation, emotional disturbance, or deafness and blindness.

Major Dimension: Mental Retardation

In Chapter 4 we noted that one major problem for children who are mentally retarded is the slowness with which they learn or retain what they learn. When this problem is combined with other problems, the difficulties in teaching these children are compounded.

Mental Retardation and Cerebral Palsy

There is a tendency to assume that children with cerebral palsy are mentally retarded (see Chapter 7). A relationship does exist between the two conditions: Whatever genetic or environmental insult damages the central nervous system sufficiently to cause cerebral palsy—an injury to the motor system—can cause enough damage to the cerebral cortex to create retardation. But the relationship is not universal.

- Holman and Freedheim (1958) tested over a thousand cases in a medical clinic and found that only 59 percent of the cerebral-palsied children tested in the retarded range.
- Schonell (1956) found 45 percent of 354 cerebral-palsied children tested in the retarded range.
- Hopkins, Bice, and Colton (1954) tested 992 cerebral-palsied children and found 49 percent tested in the retarded range.
- A more recent review of the literature by Stephen and Hawks (1974) estimated that 40 to 60 percent of children with cerebral palsy are mentally retarded.

It is hard to justify making a diagnosis of mental retardation in cerebral-palsied children based on intelligence tests that are standardized on children with adequate speech, language, and motor abilities. Many cerebral-palsied children have expressive problems in both speech and psychomotor areas, which means their test results are often questionable. All we can conclude, then, is that when these children are tested with instruments standardized on other populations about half of them show IQ scores below 70 or 80. Statements that over half the cerebral-palsied population is mentally retarded may well overestimate actual prevalence, especially when one considers the current, broader definition of mental retardation which includes adaptability of behavior as well as intellectual performance.

Often the poor speech and uncontrolled spastic movements of cerebral-palsied children give the lay person the unwarranted impression that they are mentally retarded. Actually there is little direct relation between intelligence and degree of physical impairment in children with cerebral palsy. A child who is severely spastic may be intellectually gifted; another with mild physical involvement may be severely mentally retarded. The assessment of mental retardation in cerebral-palsied children is extremely difficult and may well take months to perform. If after prolonged appropriate instruction a child does not make relatively average progress in most areas, a diagnosis of mental retardation may be valid.

Mental Retardation and Hearing Impairment

Deafness brings with it language and communication problems; mental retardation, a slowness in learning. These problems are combined in children who are deaf and mentally retarded. In the past, most of these children were placed in public institutions for the mentally retarded.

In a review of this problem for the American Speech, Hearing, Language Association, Healey and Karp-Nortman (1975) reported that hearing impaired–mentally retarded individuals "have hearing impairments, subaverage general intellectual functioning, and deficits in adaptive behavior. The combination of these three factors requires services beyond those traditionally needed by persons with either mental retardation or hearing impairment" (p. 9). They estimated that 10 to 15 percent of children in residential institutions for mentally retarded individuals have hearing losses, and that a similar percentage of children in schools for the deaf are mentally retarded. Whatever the accuracy of these figures, it is still a fact that many of these youngsters require unique educational services and that placement in residential schools organized primarily for the mentally retarded or for the deaf is not meeting their needs.

Mental Retardation and Behavior Problems

We know there is a relationship between mental retardation and emotional disturbance. We also know that the more severe the retardation, the greater the probability of emotional disturbance. What we do not know is the exact frequency with which the two handicaps appear together. Estimates range from 24 to 87 percent (Matson & Barrett, 1982; Senatore, Matson, & Kazdin, 1985). Rutter, Tizard, Yule, Graham, and Whitmore (1974), in their classic study of children from the Isle of Wight, estimated a prevalence rate of psychiatric disorders 4 times greater for people who are retarded than for those who are not.

If the relationship between these two conditions is so prevalent, why has there been so little emphasis on the appearance of behavior problems in retarded individuals? The primary reason is a phenomenon called **diagnostic overshadowing**. The symptoms of mental retardation are so obvious and strong that accompanying emotional difficulties tend to be ignored or put aside. This means we do not offer the mentally retarded population many of the psychotherapeutic services and behavioral treatments needed (Reiss, Levitan, & Szyszko, 1982).

Another problem is that certain bizarre or stereotypic behaviors are symptoms of severe and profound retardation. Rhythmic repetitive behaviors like body rocking and head banging seem to have little to do with normal motivation and seem to occur independent of outside stimulation. Berkson (1983) believed that these behaviors are self-stimulatory, that the auditory, visual, or kinesthetic feedback the child receives apparently reinforces the behaviors. To prevent stereotypic behaviors, we must cut the link between the behaviors and the positive feedback, providing the child with rewards through other means.

Why do even mildly retarded children seem to have a higher incidence of emotional problems? Blacher and Myers (1983) theorized that the early attachment so essential to the development of a positive relationship between parent and child may be impeded by the mental retardation. Some evidence does suggest that the presence of a handicapping condition can delay or dull parent-child attachment. Richardson, Koller, and Katz (1985) found four possible reasons for the high prevalence of behavior problems in mildly retarded children:

- The damage to the central nervous system that may have caused the mental retardation may also cause behavior disturbances.
- Not infrequently stressful environmental or adverse socioeconomic conditions are present in the home of a mentally retarded child. In such situations, behavior problems also may develop for the retarded child.
- Factors intrinsic to mental retardation can cause behavioral disturbances. In other words, stresses that would not affect the normal child may disturb a retarded child.
- Mental retardation can create stress in the family, which can lead to bad interaction patterns, which eventually can lead to behavioral disturbances.

In their study of 143 pairs of children (matched for age, sex, and residential characteristics), Richardson and his colleagues found that the mildly retarded children showed more evidence of emotional disturbance. Although this was not linked to central nervous system disorders, it was clearly linked to the level of stability of family upbringing. The authors concluded that "the results provide the most support for the explanation that adverse conditions of upbringing contribute to later behavioral disturbance" (p. 6).

Whether a child is mildly, moderately, or severely and profoundly retarded, the issue of behavioral disturbance as an accompanying factor must be taken into account in the youngster's educational and vocational training programs.

Major Dimension: Behavior Disturbance

Children who respond to attempts at instruction in bizarre or unusual ways cause special problems for educators. The tried-and-true methods that work so well with other children seem to have little effect on these youngsters.

Autism

Autism is a term used to describe bizarre behavior and serious developmental delays in social and communication areas.

> Autism is a severely incapacitating life-long developmental disability which usually appears during the first three years of life. It occurs in approximately five out of 10,000 births and is four times more common in boys than in girls. It has been found throughout the world in families of all racial, ethnic, and social backgrounds. (National Society for Autistic Children, 1979)

Rutter (1978), a respected British educator, identified four criteria that distinguish autistic children from other exceptional children:

- Severe impairment in relating to parents, family members, and other people
- Delayed and deviant language development, characterized by inappropriate use of language when it does occur and including peculiar patterns of speech (echoing words or phrases)
- Stereotyped behavior ranging from repetitive body movements (finger flecking, twirling) to ritualistic behaviors (lining up toys or furniture in a particular order)
- Early onset of such behaviors, usually prior to 3 years of age

The total effect of these differences is extremely upsetting to parents and teachers alike. Consider the case of George, an eight-year-old. The child was difficult to understand because he made up and used his own words. He would often sit in the backyard holding a branch in his hand, rocking back and forth and talking gibberish to the branch. He would drag a moth-eaten stuffed animal—he called it "Toe Bunny"— around the house, and would not go to bed without it. Yet he scored above the retarded range on intelligence tests that did not require verbal responses.

BLUE-COLLARING IT IN ROCKVILLE

Only very infrequently do you read or hear news stories about people with autism. Rarer still are stories about adults who have this developmental disability, often mistaken for mental retardation or emotional illness. And autistic adults holding regular jobs in private industry? Unheard of, unless you are familiar with a vocational program in Rockville, Maryland.

"People laughed at us," recounts Doreen Coleman, Director of the Vocational Program at Community Services for Autistic Adults and Children, "when we told them three years ago what we intended for autistic adults in our community. Even today many professionals who work with autism cannot believe what we have achieved. They say it is impossible unless we are working only with very mild cases.

"But credibility in our program is building as people hear from different sources and channels that we are helping individuals with substantial degrees of autism to hold real production jobs. . . ."

The focus of the attention is a midsized town near the center of the state of Maryland, where two dozen adults with autism work in a variety of small manufacturing firms. The jobs include assembling machine parts, cutting and shaping copper tubing, welding, binding printed booklets and books, and recycling industrial materials.

In most other communities working-age persons with autism are not employed. Often they are kept at home or in institutions. Erratic behavior and even occasional anti-social behavior do not permit many employment opportunities—even in sheltered workshops. So isolated have people with autism been, the only images of them many professionals and the general public have are from the institutional experiences of autistic people: withdrawn, noncommunicative, screaming, banging on walls, and slow to respond to other people and nearby events.

Much different images of autism are available in Rockville, Maryland. There each morning of the work week adults with autism catch buses and travel to 14 different worksites. They maintain a high record of punctuality and have earned reputations for methodically working at their tasks with accuracy and high quality. . . .

Recognizing that autistic adults might have a unique value for small manufacturing firms helped to convince Patricia Juhrs (Director of Community Services, at which vocational placement is one of several programs for people with autism) that the vocational program could succeed. "We didn't tell employers," she asserts, "that we wanted them to be do-gooders and hire the handicapped. In fact, we usually didn't talk much about disability or autism. Instead we told them we had workers who could perform simple mechanical tasks effectively and would want to stay on the job.

"In addition, our program would provide the job training and place a full-time job site counselor to maintain the training and to take care of any problems related to the disability."

continued

continued

During the work day the Community Services job site counselor stays near the workers with autism, helping them to stay concentrated on their work and also helping them to adjust to changes in the work schedule or work pace. Job counselors also assist the workers to learn to use public transportation and, again, to learn how to adjust to changes in bus schedules and fares. Over the months the counselors have been intervening less and less, and Juhrs believes that some can eventually be withdrawn from the work sites altogether.

Of assistance in initially approaching employers was the Targeted Jobs Tax Credit available to employers who hire disabled employees. Some autistic workers could not commence employment at the standard production pace—that was something that they would achieve only with time and practice. In certain cases, the initial productivity was only 40–50 percent of the norm. But the federal tax law allowed firms to hire the disabled workers at standard wages and balance low productivity with a tax credit. After a few months or a few weeks, standard productivity was achieved and today most of the workers have earned raises up to $3.50, $4.00 and even $5.00 an hour.

Patricia Juhrs began the program with no idea of—and therefore no limitations on—what could be achieved, but even she has been pleasantly surprised.

- So far, only one placement has been a total failure; other placements have had problems, but adjustments were successfully made.
- Two autistic workers showed an interest in welding while working at production jobs. When they were temporarily laid off, they took welding courses at a community college and then were hired back at the same company— as welders. . . .

For Juhrs and the others at Community Services, a most gratifying sign of success is a request from the former owner of a firm at which the vocational program placed two autistic workers. The former owner now does similar manufacturing business in Baltimore, and he wants Juhrs to supply his company with good workers as she did when he did business in Rockville.

There have been many extra payoffs and side benefits from the work of Community Services in Rockville. For example, because of its good experience with autistic workers, one firm has decided to hire three hearing impaired workers.

Another benefit is the fact that the autistic workers are contributing from their wages to pay part of the cost of the job site counselors. This not only helps to perpetuate the program so that it can assist others, it also allows many of the workers to remain eligible for SSI and Medicaid benefits until they can truly be self-supporting. That part of the individual's wage going to pay for the job site counselor is considered a "work expense." . . .

continued

continued

Another benefit has a very personal focus. After a period of employment there have been marked changes in the behavior in some of the autistic adults. Some talk more than before, are less withdrawn; they socialize with other workers in the lunch room and throw a Frisbee around during a break. Others have learned new job tasks, of such sophistication that even Juhrs and other people at Community Services are surprised.

In the end, this must make one wonder about what are usually regarded as *symptoms* of autism. Perhaps some of them are not symptoms of autism, but reactions with which a person with autism defends him or herself from the responses of a society ignorant and fearful of severe developmental disability. If this is true, it is more evidence that mainstreaming employment solves human problems as well as economic ones.

SOURCE: From ''Blue-Collaring It in Rockville'' by R. Gorski, 1983–1984, *Disabled USA*, pp. 12–15.

A couple of decades ago, George's parents would have had an added burden to bear. At that time most professionals believed autism was the result of the mother's coolness and emotional problems in the home. But few accept that theory today. Schopler and Bristol (1980) summed up what we know about the causes of autism:

- For individual children, the specific causes are usually unknown.
- There is probably no single underlying cause to account for autism; instead there are multiple causes.
- Most likely the primary causes involve some form of brain abnormality or biochemical imbalance that impairs perception and understanding.

Can special educators help autistic children? Gallagher and Wiegerink (1976) insisted they can. They concluded that

- autistic children are educable.
- their unique learning characteristics are due to basic cognitive deficits in information processing.
- these deficits can be compensated for in part by carefully structured educational programs that use specific developmental learning sequences and reinforcing stimuli.
- structured educational programs should begin early in life, with a parent or parent surrogate as primary teacher.

Often unresponsive to the outer world, profoundly impaired in their relations with others, and severely delayed in language development, autistic children present a great challenge to educators.
(© Meri Houtchens-Kitchens)

- educational programs for these children are feasible and less costly in the long run than is institutional care.
- these children have a right to an appropriate education.

The educational approach for autistic children leans heavily on behavior analysis and operant conditioning to help these children overcome their speech and communication problems. Remediation is slow and erratic, but clear gains have been made using these methods in intensive treatment settings (Quay & Werry, 1979).

Behavior Disturbance and Hearing Impairment

Here too we have no accurate estimate of the number of emotionally disturbed–hearing impaired children. That number depends on the criteria for emotional disturbance and the degree of hearing loss. Altshuler (1975), a psychiatrist specializing in the treatment of emotionally disturbed–deaf children, reviewed the literature and concluded that "the 8 percent estimate [of deaf children who are emotionally disturbed] nationwide is a marked underrepresentation." He estimated that between 1 and 3 of every 10 deaf students have significant emotional problems that warrant attention.

Professionals who work with emotionally disturbed–deaf children tend to classify their condition as mild, moderate, or severe. Some severely involved children have been removed from schools for the deaf because their teachers were unable to cope with their bizarre behavior. About these children, Ranier (1975) wrote:

> It is my strong feeling on the basis of our two decades of experience in the psychiatric care of the deaf, as well as the reports of others, that there is a significant core of deaf children who cannot be educated or managed even in special classes without a total therapeutic milieu under psychiatric direction. Temporary separation of the child from his environment and placement in a controlled therapeutic setting is essential to help the child develop better control, better socialization, and better identification. Drug and behavior therapies as well as recreation, art, and occupational skills need to be furnished. At the same time, special teachers can provide continuing education on an individual basis. (p. 19)

Ranier indicated that following this type of program, a child could be returned to the special class and the home.

Mildly and moderately emotionally disturbed–deaf children are often enrolled in residential and day schools for the deaf. Here teachers work in structured programs, usually emphasizing pupil adjustment and success in assigned tasks. Education and cooperation of parents are also important elements in these programs.

As yet standard programs for emotionally disturbed–hearing impaired children have not been highly developed. The group is so heterogeneous that each child needs an individualized education program to fit his or her specific needs to an extent greater than that required for many other handicapped children.

Major Dimension: Deaf-Blind Impairments

When one of the two major systems that bring information to the child is impaired, the special education program emphasizes the unimpaired sense. For the child who is deaf, the visual channel is used to establish a communication system based on signing, finger spelling, or speech reading (lip reading). For the child who is visually handicapped, the program uses auditory aids to help compensate for the visual channel problem. But what do we do when both channels are impaired? How do we teach speech and language to a child who can neither hear nor see?

Whenever we think of deaf-blind people, we think of Helen Keller. She has become a symbol of what can be done against great odds. With the help of Anne Sullivan, her tutor and constant companion, and a

Attention has been increasingly focused on helping deaf-blind individuals make the transition from education to employment, and new emphasis has been given to vocational training and independent living skills.
(© Karen Preuss 1977/Jeroboam, Inc.)

keen mind, Keller learned to speak and communicate and achieved a high level of academic accomplishment. The popular play and movie *The Miracle Worker* is based on her discovery of the world around her with Sullivan's help. The challenge for educators is to make more Helen Kellers out of the twenty-five hundred deaf-blind children in the United States.

The deaf-blind child is

> a child who has both auditory and visual impairments, the combination of which cause . . . severe communication and other developmental educational problems that . . . cannot properly be accommodated in special education programs either for the hearing handicapped child or for the visually handicapped child. (Bureau of Education for the Handicapped, 1969, p. 1)

In the past the education of deaf-blind children was largely conducted in private residential schools for children whose parents could afford that education. To deal with the problem nationally, the federal government passed legislation in 1968 to establish eight model centers for deaf-blind children. Each center was given responsibility for a wide geographic area, enabling families of these multiply handicapped children to receive some degree of help wherever they lived in the United States. The program, which began in 1969, has provided a wide variety of family counseling services, medical and educational diagnoses, and itinerant home services, as well as teacher-training opportunities and full-time educational programs for deaf-blind children.

> These centers also conduct a program for helping state educational departments and other responsible agencies develop appropriate state plans assuring the provision of meaningful relevant and continuous services throughout the lifetime of the deaf-blind person; and each center collects and disseminates information about practices found effective in working with deaf-blind children and their families. (Dantona, 1976, p. 173)

Since 1969 there have been several changes of focus. In 1978, $16 million was appropriated for eight multistate centers and eight single-state centers. It was believed necessary to establish regional and state centers because of the low incidence in smaller, local areas of children who were both deaf and blind. Later, in 1983, the statutes were again revised, awarding state agencies the funds to develop their own programs for children and adolescents who are deaf and blind. The states are now responsible for both the appropriate education of deaf-blind youngsters and the transition of deaf-blind young adults (ages 22 and up) "from education to employment" including "vocational, independent living, and other post-secondary services" (U.S. Department of Education, September 3, 1985, pp. 2–3).

These programs have brought comprehensive diagnostic facilities and trained personnel in contact with children and adolescents who are deaf and blind, and have encouraged educators to think seriously about how to cope with this rare but difficult problem.

DEINSTITUTIONALIZATION AND NORMALIZATION

The first attempt to educate children with severe mental retardation in the United States was made in 1848, when Samuel Clifford Howe requested $2,500 from the Massachusetts legislature to establish a residential facility for what were called at that time "idiots." The legislature passed the appropriation, but the governor vetoed it. Howe wrote a stinging letter of objection to the governor. In that letter he enunciated the rights of the handicapped in a democratic society (reproduced in Kirk & Lord, 1974). On the basis of Howe's letter, the legislature overrode the governor's veto and an institution for people with severe mental retardation was created.

Since that time, state after state has had vast institutions built to house and educate individuals at all levels of mental retardation. By 1967 there were 167 public institutions serving 200,000 mentally retarded individuals in fifty states and the District of Columbia. Of the 200,000 residents, 57 percent were severely and profoundly retarded (Baumeister & Butterfield, 1970).

Until 1950 most youngsters with severe and multiple handicaps were either cared for at home or placed in institutions. By the end of World War II, most institutions were overcrowded and were refusing admission to new clients. At the same time, public schools were denying admission to severely and multiply handicapped children, presumably because they were considered ineducable. Parents began to protest. They were paying taxes for institutions and schools but were being denied services for their children at those facilities.

The overcrowded institutions and the parent movement sparked an interest in **normalization**—in keeping severely and multiply handicapped individuals in the community (Wolfensberger, 1972). Institutional populations began to decrease as community programs provided alternative services for those with multiple handicaps. These programs were offered in schools, at community centers, in sheltered workshops, and in boarding homes. Their objective was to allow individuals with severe and multiple handicaps to live as normal a life as possible.

New Jersey is one of many states that have begun removing children from residential facilities and normalizing them in local schools and communities. In 1977 the enrollment in New Jersey residential facilities was 7,932; by 1983 it had dropped to 5,942 (see Figure 10.1). In contrast, enrollment in community-based services rose from 705 in 1977 to 3,009 in 1983. Projections indicate that alternative placements will exceed institutional placements by about 25 percent in 1989. Although we will always have residential facilities for some individuals with severe and multiple handicaps, we expect that the large majority of these people will be served in a normalized environment.

EDUCATIONAL ADAPTATIONS

A Changing Learning Environment

In the past, many children with multiple and severe handicaps were excluded from public schools because they did not fit into ongoing special education programs or because they were not toilet trained.

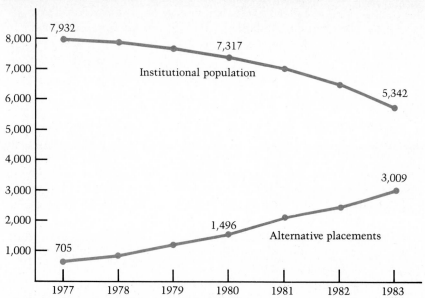

FIGURE 10.1
Decrease in institutional population and growth in alternative placements, New Jersey, 1977–1983

SOURCE: *New Directions.* National Association of State Mental Retardation Directors, Inc., 113 Oronoco St., Alexandria, VA, 22314. Vol. XIV, No. 4, April 1984.

Many of these youngsters were assigned to a residential institution for the more severe of their handicaps. For example, a child who was deaf and mentally retarded would be placed in a residential institution for the mentally retarded, often with neither the facilities nor the personnel to provide special education for hearing disabilities.

Things are different today. The Civil Rights Act and the Education for All Handicapped Children Act (Public Law 94–142) have made it mandatory for public schools to educate all children. This means the schools must now organize to meet the needs of multiply and severely handicapped youngsters.

Turnbull (1979) summed up the legislative and judicial actions culminating in PL 94–142 that have increased the educational attention paid children with multiple and severe handicaps:

- No handicapped child may be excluded from a free public education.
- Every handicapped child will be nondiscriminately evaluated so that his strengths and weaknesses may be identified, improved, or remedied.
- Every handicapped child is entitled to an appropriate and individualized education.
- Every handicapped child will be educated with nonhandicapped children to the extent possible.

- Every handicapped child has the right to procedural due process so he can challenge the actions of state and local educational authorities.
- The parents, guardians, or surrogates of each handicapped child have the right to share with educators the making of decisions that affect the child's education. (p. 1108)

Laski (1985) surveyed judicial decisions over the last decade or so. The first case was filed in 1972 by the Pennsylvania Association for Retarded Citizens (PARC). The decision struck down state laws that had allowed the exclusion from public schools of children with severe handicaps. In 1982, the Supreme Court in *Rowley* interpreted "appropriate education" to mean that a child must benefit from instruction. This decision allows the courts to supervise educational programs, to oversee what is taught, how it's being taught, and where the teaching takes place in the education of children who have multiple and severe handicaps. Laski concluded:

The extent to which the courts will exercise this oversight depends largely on whether the public schools, like the tugboat operator of 50 years past, "unduly lag in the adoption of new and available devices," and in doing so fail to effectively educate students with severe handicaps. (p. 48)

These judicial decisions and the passage of Public Law 94–142 ensured the development of community programs for many children who previously were institutionalized. Brown, Nietupski, and Hamre-Nietupski (1976) advocated very early that "severely handicapped students should be placed in self-contained classes in public schools. . . . They have the right to be visible functioning citizens integrated into everyday life of complex public communities" (p. 3).

A related but somewhat different approach was reported by Sailor and Guess (1983). They described an experimental program of instruction for students who are severely or multiply handicapped. The program assigns teachers to different work stations—sheltered work cites (hospital supply areas, industrial plants, fast-food franchises) or group homes. Students are rotated to these work stations and trained in work or domestic skills. As they move from site to site, communication therapists move with them, instructing them in speech and language.

Curriculum and Skills

Over the years a technology of teaching youngsters with severe handicaps has evolved. The strategies we talk about here are just examples of a large number of approaches.

The curricula that have been developed for severely and multiply handicapped students and the implementation of these programs draw on task analysis and operant conditioning. One is *The Teaching Research Curriculum for the Moderately and Severely Handicapped* by Fredericks and the staff at the Teaching Research Infant and Child Center (1980) in Oregon. This curriculum was developed by teachers of preschool handicapped children and includes task analysis of the behaviors to be taught and detailed steps for teaching target behaviors.

According to Fredericks, each behavior area has three possible subcomponents: skills, phases, and steps. A *skill* is a complex behavior requiring the acquisition of a number of subordinate behaviors; a *phase* is the breakdown of a skill into parts or units; a *step* is the breakdown of a phase. For example, consider self-help behavior. Undressing is a skill. One phase of undressing is removing pants. The eight phases in teaching a child to develop that aspect of dressing are described as:

Phase I	Student removes final leg of pants from foot.
Phase II	Student removes pants from one foot when both feet are in legs.
Phase III	Student sits down.
Phase IV	Student pushes pants down to ankles from the knees.
Phase V	Student pushes pants down to ankles from the thighs.
Phase VI	Student pushes pants all the way down to ankles.
Phase VII	Student grasps each side of pants at the waist.
Phase VIII	Student positions self in front of chair and completely removes pants. (Fredericks et al., 1980, p. 78)

Recent attempts have been made to produce a functional age-appropriate curriculum for severely handicapped students. This means that a 16-year-old boy who is severely handicapped is not asked to solve a four-piece puzzle of a dog—even if that task corresponds to his "mental" level. Instead, the task focuses on an activity the child can carry out to some degree like his nonhandicapped peers, say eating, communicating, or turning on a television set.

Brown, Branston-McClean, Baumgart, Vincent, Falvey, and Schroeder (1979) suggested that "since nonhandicapped adolescent and young adult students frequently make independent purchases at grocery stores, department stores, and drugstores, shopping skills should receive considerable attention in the curriculum for severely handicapped" youngsters (p. 86). They argued that the curriculum should focus on functional items as much as possible:

This	*Not This*
Placing coins in a vending machine	Placing pegs in a pegboard
Walking across bleachers at a sporting event	Walking a balance beam
Teaching students to zip their own jeans	Using a zipper on a zipper board
Learning to identify restrooms and exit signs	Learning the names of the primary colors

One goal in working with children who are severely and multiply handicapped is to have them interact with their environment and with the people around them. An example of a specific approach is shown in Table 10.2. This cued commands chart includes various requests for action on the part of the handicapped child. For most children, of course, responding to a parental request or command is an easy matter, hardly justifying a complex list and record keeping. For the multihandicapped child, these responses are made with great difficulty; therefore, a description of the situation and the criterion that designates success are useful to those who are helping the child. Once a list is constructed, it is not hard for a trained nonprofessional to follow through and give the child extensive practice responding appropriately.

Early Childhood and Preschool Level

In 1968 Congress passed the Handicapped Children's Early Education Program (HCEEP), which was designed to demonstrate the usefulness of preschool programs for all handicapped children. It assumed that the earlier a program is initiated, the more progress the child will make. Public Law 94–142 does not mandate an appropriate free public education for preschool children, but many states have passed legislation that provides services for preschoolers who are severely handicapped.

Children who are severely retarded or multihandicapped are usually identified at an early age. This means that both early examination and early intervention are possible. Various kinds of evaluation and intervention centers for young children who show early signs of a handicapping condition have been established. The specific intervention a community may use is dependent in part upon the nature of the environment: "Instructional precision and consistency may rest in the structure of the environment, including the use of the child's peers, as much as it does the actions of the teacher" (Vincent, Salisbury, Walter, Brown, Gruenewald, & Powers, 1980, p. 126).

To best describe the programs and curricula for severely and multiply handicapped children, we provide two examples: a community-based program and the Arizona Basic Assessment and Curriculum Utilization System (ABACUS).

Table 10.2
Cued Commands Chart

Uses: 1. To select functional commands to teach in following cued commands.
2. To suggest commands for aides and volunteers to use frequently.

Commands	Materials/ Situation	Suggested Criterion
"Sit (down)." (tap/point to place)	*S* is standing near chair, mat, toilet, swing.	*S* sits in the indicated place for at least 5 seconds.
"Stand (up)." (raise your arms/hands)	*S* is sitting on floor, in chair, in swing.	*S* stands up and remains up for at least 5 seconds.
"Let's go/Come on." (beckon and start walking)	*S* is sitting or standing next to you.	*S* walks with you at least 5 feet without stopping.
"Go over there." (point and nod your head toward place)	*S* is standing by you.	*S* walks to the indicated place (10 feet) and stops.
"Hold my hand." (stretch out your hand)	*S* is standing or sitting by you.	*S* places his hand in/ on yours for at least 5 seconds (while walking or balancing).
"Stop/No." (shake index finger)	*S* is engaging in undesirable behavior.	*S* stops the behavior for at least 5 seconds.
"Look." (point to place)	*S* is near a window or some stimulating target.	*S* turns his head in the indicated direction for at least 5 seconds.
"Give me _____." (hold out your hand and point to object)	*S* is holding an object.	*S* releases the indicated object in your hand.
"Take _____." (hold out object)	*S*'s hands are empty, but you are holding something.	*S* takes the indicated object and holds it for at least 5 seconds.
"Get _____." (point to object)	*S* is near an object: holding it; it is hanging on a hook or rack.	*S* goes to and picks up the indicated object.

SOURCE: *Programmed Environments Curriculum* by J. Tawney, D. Knapp, C. O'Reilly, and S. Pratt, 1979. Columbus, OH: Charles E. Merrill.

A Community-Based Program. One program for early intervention was organized by Fulton County, Georgia. The program is publicly funded, acting as a nonprofit community agency. It serves high-risk developmentally delayed or handicapped infants and preschoolers from birth to age 5 and their families. Some of the children in the center have severe and multiple handicaps.

Before a child is admitted, he or she is examined by physical therapists, speech and language pathologists, and other developmental specialists. After the child is evaluated in motor development, in speech and language, and in cognitive development, the staff discusses a program of intervention with the parents. An individualized program is then formulated. It includes physical therapy, speech and language, and cognitive development. The program is implemented by instructors in the center with continual consultation with the evaluation staff and parents.

Currently the center offers two programs. The first is a five-day-a-week classroom program from 9:00 A.M. to 3:00 P.M., in which children are given direct therapy by specialists. The second is an outreach program, where parents bring children to the center one morning a week and work with professionals, who teach them intervention procedures with their children.

The Arizona Basic Assessment and Curriculum Utilization System (ABACUS).

ABACUS (McCarthy, Lund, Bos, Glatke, & Vaughn, 1985) is a comprehensive system that screens, assesses, programs, and monitors the progress of preschool handicapped children. It focuses on children from ages 2 to 5½ who are mildly, moderately, severely, or multiply handicapped (except deaf and blind). It covers five basic developmental areas: body management, self-care, communication, preacademics, and socialization.

The system is composed of ten books that present the various components:

1. The System Manual
2. Assessment for Instruction
3. Monitoring Child Progress
4. Body Management—Individual and Group Programming
5. Self-Care—Individual and Group Programming
6. Communication—Individual and Group Programming
7. PreAcademics—Individual and Group Programming
8. Socialization—Individual and Group Programming
9. Parent Involvement and Home Teaching
10. Teaching Behavior Inventory

Book 1 is an overview of the system. Book 2 presents information relevant to assessment, including two screening instruments and a criterion-referenced assessment measure. Book 3 presents a system for monitoring individual child progress on a daily basis. Books 4 through 8 include instructional programs on how to teach skills and knowledge across the five developmental areas. Each offers appropriate programs for individual and group instruction. Book 9 discusses how to work with parents and how parents can teach a young handicapped child in the home. And Book 10 presents a means for evaluating teacher effectiveness. The system is coordinated so that each item on the assessment instrument has a curricular program designed to teach that skill,

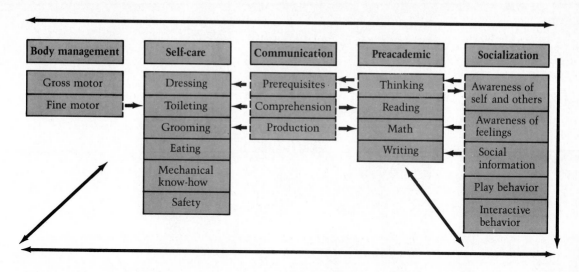

SOURCE: From *Body Management, Programming for Young Children with Special Needs* by J. McCarthy, K. Lund, and C. Bos, 1985. Denver: Love, p. 3.

FIGURE 10.2 Arizona Basic Assessment and Curriculum Utilization System crossover curriculum and developmental areas

and the curriculum is related across developmental areas, as shown in Figure 10.2. The arrows show interrelationships.

The ABACUS assessment process is in three parts. The first, PASS I, is a short screening check list of behavioral observations. It is made up of 10 items in each of the five developmental areas for each age level, and is scored by a parent or care giver. Children who rank in the lower quartile for their age group are evaluated further with PASS II, a 30-minute screening instrument consisting of 65 benchmark items taken from the criterion-referenced assessment measure. That measure contains 209 items across the five developmental areas.

McCarthy, Lund, and Bos (1983) briefly described these developmental areas:

- *Body management.* This incorporates gross motor skills involving large muscle development (such as sitting, walking, running, climbing, balancing, and throwing) and fine motor skills (grasping objects, stacking blocks, putting pegs in a pegboard, stringing beads, fitting pieces into puzzles, cutting, and the like).
- *Self-care.* The skills involved here are those that allow the child to function independently and to take care of personal needs (dressing, toileting, grooming, eating, mechanical know-how, and safety).
- *Communication.* Communication allows for the exchange of ideas or thoughts. The skills involved are divided, in the ABACUS, into prerequisite skills (attending, imitating vo-

One of the areas of importance for multiply and severely handicapped children is that of gross and fine motor skills; such skills can be improved through physical activities and training.
(© Gale Zucker)

calizations, etc.), comprehension (understanding gestures, words, and concepts), and production (expressing ideas either verbally or through the use of total communication).

- *Preacademics.*   Cognitive skills and knowledge labeled as readiness skills for school can be classified by thinking (e.g., matching objects and pictures, labeling the shape and color of objects), reading (print awareness, book handling, and reading basic words), mathematics (identifying numbers and numeral concepts 1 to 5), and writing (scribbling, making pre-writing strokes, copying first name, etc.).
- *Socialization.*   Skills that increase a child's ability to get along with other children and adults and to function and learn in school comprise socialization. (p. 8)

Assessment is not limited to the instruments in the system. For example, usually a speech-language pathologist performs an in-depth evaluation of language skills to arrive at an appropriate intervention program for language problems.

Another assessment used by the system is what the authors call an "ecological assessment":

> Ecological assessment is defined as a process to determine the physical, environmental, nutritional, and social correlates of the child's problem. It includes maternal perceptions, mother-child interactions, environmental variables, parental attitudes, nutrition, social support systems, and the like. The importance of parental input at this stage is obvious. And data supplied by the nurse or social worker might also be useful, with consideration given to specifics such as nutritional status, adequacy of diet, sleeping arrangements at home, and so on.
>
> Questions to be asked are not, "What is wrong with this child?" but, rather: "What does this child need to optimize his or her growth and development? What does the child need from each component of his or her ecosystem in order to survive and thrive?" (McCarthy et al., 1985, pp. 8–9)

This awareness of the ecological pressures on the child and of the child's support system is a critical element in the program. It allows the teacher to maximize the development of each child by matching the child's unique developmental characteristics with the demands of his or her environment.

The information derived from the assessment shapes the individualized education program and defines the child's curriculum. For example, let's assume a girl is having difficulty removing her shoes. Removing shoes becomes the target skill. Depending on the intensity of the teaching required for the student to learn the skill, the teacher would use either an individual or group program. With severely handicapped children, it's often necessary to begin working with students on a one-to-one basis, which would mean using an individual program, at least at the start. Figure 10.3 shows the individual program for teaching a child to remove shoes. Book 5 includes many similar individual and group programmed activities for all six areas of self-care. The other curriculum books follow the same pattern.

ABACUS is a comprehensive model for assessing, teaching, and monitoring the knowledge and skills of severely and multiply handicapped children. The assessment component leads to an individualized education program, which directs the teacher to specific programs in the curriculum. Daily monitoring not only indicates the child's ongoing progress, but gives a degree of accountability seldom found in a curriculum system.

FIGURE 10.3
ABACUS program
sheet for removing
shoes

Task: Undressing

*Program I: Removes shoes

Program objective: Child removes shoes when unfastened.

Prerequisite behaviors: Enough agility and strength to grasp and remove shoes

Program adaptation: Starting with a dressing doll may be helpful with some children

Step A

Step objective: Child removes shoes when heel is slipped out.

Materials: Child's shoes on his/her feet.

Teaching procedure: Untie/unbuckle shoes; loosen laces. Slip child's heels out of shoes. *Cue:* "Take off your shoes." Child should grasp and remove each shoe. Give manual assistance according to Unit directions.

Units: 1. Give manual assistance by placing hands over child's hands.
          2. Give no manual assistance.

Recording procedure: Code the Record Sheet as follows: (a) Record the program title and number. (b) In the "Step and Unit" column write "A" and the unit the child is on. Each shoe equals one opportunity.

Step B

Step objective: Child removes shoes when laces are loosened or buckles undone.

Materials: Same as Step A.

Teaching procedure: Same as Step A except do not slip child's heels out of shoes.

Units: Same as Step A.

Recording procedure: Same as Step A except in the "Step and Unit" column write "B" and the unit the child is on.

Step C*

Step objective: Child removes shoes when laces are untied.

Materials: Child's shoes with ties.

Teaching procedure: Same as Step A except do not slip child's heels out of shoes and do not loosen laces. To loosen laces, child should reach under top set(s) of crossed laces and pull.

Units: Same as Step A.

Recording procedure: Same as Step A except in the "Step and Unit" column write "C" and the unit the child is on.

---

*Optional. To be run for children who have tie shoes.
SOURCE: *ABACUS, Book Five: Self-care* (p. 17) by J. McCarthy, K. Lund, and C. Bos, 1985. Denver: Love.

Elementary Age Level

According to Tawney and Sniezek (1985), a standardized curriculum for elementary-age children with severe handicaps has not been developed. "The curricular status of elementary school programs may be described as 'that something that exists between infant intervention and vocational programming' " (p. 86). In other words, the curriculum for children with severe and multiple handicaps overlaps the programs for preschoolers and adolescents.

Because children with severe and multiple handicaps are a very heterogeneous group, the program must be adjusted to the child's age level, the kinds of disabilities (autism, severe mental retardation, deafness and blindness), and the qualifications of the teacher. Sailor and Guess (1983) identified three elements in the curriculum for elementary-age students: communication instruction, social development, and prevocational development.

Communication instruction, both verbal and nonverbal, is the area that has received most attention from linguists, psychologists, and others working with children who are severely handicapped. Ideally instruction focuses on speech. But if a child does not respond, nonverbal means such as manual signing and communication boards are used. Guess (1980) outlined in detail the methods of communication instruction for severely handicapped individuals.

Social development is another important ingredient in the curriculum. The integration of severely and multiply handicapped children with nonhandicapped youngsters is recommended whenever possible. Step-by-step instructional materials have been developed to foster the social development of this group of children. One social interaction curriculum developed at the San Francisco State University includes an environmental inventory completed by the parents (reported in Sailor & Guess, 1983). On the basis of this inventory, a social development program is outlined for the child. It consists of greetings, intercommunication between two people, and other social-interaction situations.

Sailor and Guess found that prevocational skills for children with severe handicaps are the least well developed. Although they recognized the difficulty of pinpointing a vocation at this age and developing the prerequisite skills for that vocation, they advocated that the curriculum include functional life skills appropriate to the elementary school special class. And, in writing about the future, they suggested the possibility of schools without walls, an organization that would allow us to integrate educational services with community resources, including the home.

Tawney and Sniezek (1985) tested a program for children who are severely and multiply handicapped. That program is shown in Figure 10.4. They recommended observing the child in each area of the curriculum and using only those areas in which the child shows ineffi-

Social/language		Cognitive	Profile motor		Eating	Self-help	
Receptive	Expressive	Cognitive	Fine motor	Gross motor	Eating	Dressing	Grooming
		Selecting a specified quantity; Counting rationally; Matching equal sets				Zipping jacket; Snapping; Unbuttoning; Hooking; Unbuckling	Brushing hair; Brushing teeth
		Selecting equivalent amounts			Eating with a fork	Zipping pants; Unzipping pants; Untying; Unhooking; Putting on T-shirt; Taking off T-shirt	Washing face; Washing hands
		Pairing equal sets				Putting on shirt; Putting on pants; Taking off shirt; Taking off pants; Putting socks on	Wiping nose
Identifying people		Sorting; Lining up objects; Putting objects in sequence			Eating with a spoon	Putting shoes on; Putting mittens on; Unzipping jacket; Putting hat on	Drying face; Using a napkin; Drying hands
Identifying body parts; Identifying objects	Naming objects; Naming actions	Identifying simple pictures; Matching					
Responding to signal words; Attending to own name	Shaping words; Producing sounds on request	Imitating actions; Finding source of sound	Placing in/on	Walking	Drinking from a cup	Unsnapping; Pulling off	
Following cued commands	Indicating preferences; Responding vocally to model	Finding hidden objects; Repeating teacher model; Responding to teacher model	Manipulating objects	Standing up; Crawling on hands and knees; Standing; Sitting up; Crawling on stomach	Eating finger foods; Chewing		
Attending to voice; Responding to social interaction	Making sounds	Attending to objects; Focusing attention	Grasping; Reaching for objects	Sitting; Controlling head movements			

FIGURE 10.4
Instructional profile from the Programmed Environment Curriculum

SOURCE: "Educational Programs for Severely Mentally Retarded Elementary-age Children: Progress, Problems, and Suggestions" by J. Tawney and K. Sniezek, 1985, in *Severe Mental Retardation: From Theory to Practice* [p. 83] by D. Bricker and J. Filler (Eds.). Reston, VA: Council for Exceptional Children.

cient performance. The curriculum is divided into four parts: social/language skills (reception, expression), cognitive functions, fine and gross motor skills, and self-help activities (eating, dressing, grooming).

Adolescents and Youth

The curricula of secondary and postsecondary programs for severely and multiply handicapped individuals stress functional age-appropriate skills. Brinker (1985), in an examination of curricula for those who are severely retarded, reported three approaches: the operant approach, the psychological model, and the ecological model. The objective of the ecological model is to move severely handicapped individuals toward *ultimate functioning*—the degree to which severely handicapped people are able to take a productive part in a variety of community situations appropriate to their chronological age (Brown, Nietupski, & Hamre-Nietupski, 1976).

Brinker's ecological model has the following features:

- A fundamental commitment to participation by severely handicapped students in the life and environments within the community
- An analysis of major environments within a community based upon an inventory of public places and their physical design
- An analysis of activities which generally occur within the various environments in the community
- Task analysis of the skills necessary to participate independently in selected activities in environments and a specification of the supports necessary for facilitating at least partial participation in the widest functional range of activities (p. 219)

Williams, Vogelsberg, and Schutz (1985) pointed out that educators should be familiar with the postschool environment in their community before they organize a secondary-age training program for students who are severely handicapped. The program should have three major goals: (1) to prevent institutionalization; (2) to prepare the students for different educational environments, independent living, and work; and (3) to provide for the transition of students into integrated, least-restrictive postschool environments and service delivery systems.

A large number of communities are using curricula for students who are severely or multiply handicapped. Many subscribe to the criterion of ultimate functioning advocated by Brown, Nietupski, and Hamre-Nietupski (1976). Sailor and Guess (1983) suggested a number of curricular components including teaching age-appropriate skills. Even

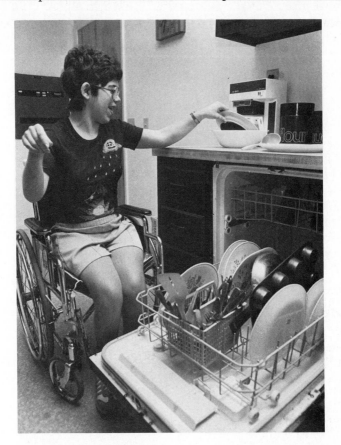

Age-appropriate activities and functional skills such as household chores, using a telephone, and shopping are stressed in many programs for multiply and severely handicapped teenagers and young adults.
(© Bohdan Hrynewych/Southern Light)

though they may not be able to add or subtract, by learning to count money students can shop in a store. They cited Brown, Hamre-Nietupski, Johnson, Wilcox, and Gruenewald (1978) and Brown and his colleagues (1979) as the source of a strategy for developing age-appropriate curricular content for adolescents and young adults. That strategy consists of six phases:

1. Delineating the four curricular domains: domestic skills, vocational training, use of leisure and recreational activities, and skills necessary for community living.
2. Identifying those environments in the community that require the use of domestic skills, vocational training, leisure time, and community living skills.

3. Identifying the smaller environments in which severely handi-capped students function or might function.
4. Making an inventory of the age-appropriate and age-related activ-ities that occur in the subenvironments. (The activities related to a bathroom, for example, would include toileting and cleaning the sink.)
5. Identifying the skills that must be taught to perform the tasks.
6. Using special teaching procedures to instruct severely handicapped students in the performance of the identified skills in a natural environment.

In addition to age-appropriate activities, the curriculum must ex-pand communication skills, a highly technical teaching procedure. That instruction should be carried out in the natural environment as much as possible. Studies show, for example, that a family-style meal pro-duces more communication than does a cafeteria-style meal (Sailor & Guess, 1983).

Children with severe and multiple handicaps must learn the life skills nonhandicapped children acquire incidentally. These include us-ing a telephone, exchanging money, shopping, and taking part in com-munity activities.

Program Development

Wetzel and Hoschouer (1984) described a system for developing pro-grams for individuals who are severely or multiply handicapped. The system was developed through their extensive work with both staff and residents in group home settings. It is equally applicable to public school programs and, in fact, is being used by many classroom teachers on a daily basis.

According to Wetzel and Hoschouer, residential and other commu-nity environments are teaching environments. Their approach to pro-gram development makes three basic assumptions:

All people, whatever their impairments or age, can learn through experience, and most people can learn more than they have so far.

Most behavior problems stem from defective teaching environ-ments, which are the result of unfortunate interactions between the environment and the developmental or physical disabilities of the individual.

The process of teaching appropriate behaviors can begin without eliminating maladaptive behaviors. In fact, many maladaptive be-haviors can be "crowded out" of an individual's behavioral reper-toire by designing environments that teach and maintain appropriate behaviors.

FIGURE 10.5
The relationship of
the six dimensions
of program develop-
ment

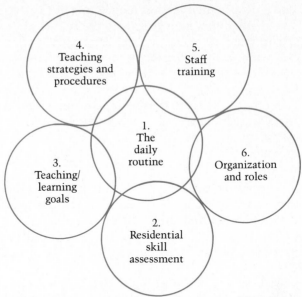

SOURCE: *Residential Teaching Communities: Program Development and Staff Training for Developmentally Disabled Persons* (p. 24) by R. Wetzel and R. Hoschouer, 1984.
Glenview, IL: Scott, Foresman.

Program development involves many different activities grouped into
six dimensions. These dimensions are illustrated in Figure 10.5 and
explained in the text that follows.

1. *The daily routine.* The first step in designing a teaching environment is to describe the behaviors the environment is supposed to
   teach and maintain. This requires the development and description of a daily routine, which in turn provides the basis for assessment and teaching activities. Teachers, staff, and others who
   work with those who are severely and multiply handicapped must
   be able to perform the daily routines as well as teach these behaviors to others.

2. *Skill assessment.* Target behaviors for instruction are provided
   by the detailed description of the individual's daily routine, regardless of whether that routine occurs in the classroom, the home,
   a group home, or the workplace. The purpose of assessment is to
   determine the individual's current functioning in the behaviors
   required by the routine. Assessment is accomplished by observing
   the individual as he or she follows the routine in various environments. This is why a routine must be established before competence can be assessed. Periodic observations provide a measure of
   the individual's progress and an index of the teacher and staff's
   effectiveness.

As a result of PL 94–142, schools have begun to organize for teaching and training multiply and severely handicapped youngsters within the framework of the public school system.
(© Meri Houtchens-Kitchens, 1982)

3. *Teaching/learning goals.* Once an individual's capabilities have been assessed, teaching objectives can be established. These objectives must be congruent with daily routines so that teaching procedures do not interfere with the normal flow of events in the classroom, the residence, or the workshop. In selecting objectives, the teacher must balance the individual's needs and the needs of the community as a whole. Also, the teacher must develop a way to monitor the individual's progress so that new objectives can be selected as they are needed.

4. *Teaching strategies and procedures.* Teachers and others who work with people who are severely and multiply handicapped look for teaching procedures that preserve appropriate routines in the various environments. Those strategies are often identified through a process of discovery. That is, through repeated experience, successful strategies emerge and are retained. This kind of activity concerns teacher and staff learning as much as student learning, and points to objectives for staff training.

5. *Staff training.* In a fully effective teaching environment, everyone learns. Teachers' aides, job supervisors, parents, and staff learn to teach, and teachers and program supervisors learn to train others to assume teaching roles. Much of this staff learning occurs just as it does for students—by exposure to the daily routine.

6. *Organization and roles.* Those who manage classrooms, group homes, and job sites for the severely and multiply handicapped are in every respect "environmental managers." They must design and oversee channels of communication among staff, parents, and others so that essential experiences are shared. They must design mechanisms for collective problem solving and decision making that support the goals of individual and community programs. They also must periodically redesign environments to support continued growth as those programs develop.

Adaptation for Nonvocal Students

Many children with serious physical and mental handicaps have major communication problems. Often they are unable or barely able to speak. This inability to communicate is one of the most fundamental problems children with severe handicaps face. It prevents them from interacting successfully with their environment and impedes their ability to learn from interactive experiences—something nonhandicapped children do so readily.

Several augmentive systems have been developed recently to help the nonvocal student (Yoder, 1980). These devices are designed, not to replace speech, but to add to and supplement available speech. They allow the nonvocal youngster to communicate basic needs and even ideas.

Yoder (1980) described three kinds of communication boards, one form of augmentive system (see Figure 10.6):

• *Direct selection.* The child is presented with a board on which a series of pictures or words appear. The child points to the picture or word that symbolizes his or her needs. For example, a youngster who is thirsty can point to the picture of a child drinking a glass of water. This is a fast, efficient system that effectively handles basic needs and routine requests. Even a child with severe cerebral palsy who is not able to point with his or her hands can hold a pointing stick in the teeth or look directly at the wanted object.

• *Scanning selection.* Message elements appear on the board in a prearranged sequence. The user responds to the correct message with a signal, nodding the head or moving the wrist to indicate assent. Electric scanning is also possible (see Figure 10.6). The user operates a moving light that systematically scans information until the wanted message is found.

Direction selection. Child simply points at
what he or she wants to say.

Scanning selection. Child operates a moving
light which makes a row and column scan to indicate
what he or she wants to say.

Encoding selection. Child somehow indicates
X and Y coordinates to designate the row and column
that indicate what he or she wants to say.

33 = Message of
selection

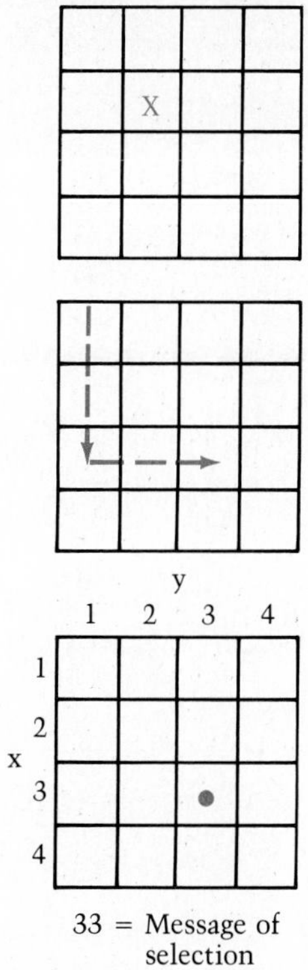

SOURCE: From "Systems and Devices for Nonoral Communication" by M. LeBlanc,
1982, in *Physically Handicapped Children: A Medical Atlas for Teachers* (p. 162) by
E. Bleck and D. Nagel (Eds.). New York: Grune & Stratton.

FIGURE 10.6
Communication
boards

- *Encoding selection.* The user communicates through a predeter-
  mined code (Morse code, finger spelling) that must be interpreted
  by the listener. The code can be memorized or displayed on a chart
  so that both people can use it. Encoding usually allows for a much
  larger vocabulary than does direct or scanning selection.

  The multiply or severely handicapped child can use any of these
methods either alone or in combination. They allow even the most
seriously impaired child to communicate, to be a part of society.
  The Touch Talker with Minspeak is a computerized language board
for individuals who are unable to speak. It is used by those who are
multiply or severely handicapped for the direct or scanning selection
of particular symbols, such as pictures, letters or words. Information
may be stored and retrieved at the word, phrase, or sentence level.
According to his or her level of cognitive functioning, an individual
can put together a very simple or complex message and communicate
this at a fast, fluent pace (see Figure 10.7).

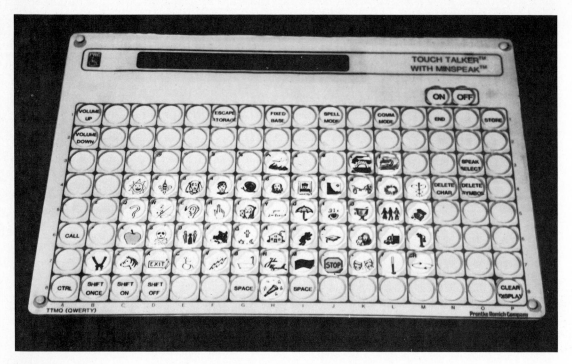

FIGURE 10.7
Computerized lan-
guage board: Touch
Talker with Min-
speak™

SOURCE: Photo courtesy of Prentke Romich Company.

ADULTHOOD AND LIFESPAN ISSUES

Attempts to normalize children with severe handicaps would be wasted if we did not provide for the normalization of adults in the community. Over the last twenty-five years, substantial efforts have been made to create community living arrangements to provide for adults who have been returned to the community from institutions and to prevent the institutionalization of youngsters who have been living in the community.

Programs for community living have been growing since 1961, when President Kennedy established the Presidential Committee on Mental Retardation (Rusch, Chadsey-Rusch, White, & Gifford, 1985). These programs include living facilities, vocational and rehabilitation workshops, and recreational activities (including the Special Olympics). All require a network of support systems from a number of community agencies.

The first step in the integration of adults with severe handicaps is the provision of adequate living arrangements. A number of options have been suggested, among them family and foster homes, group homes, apartments, and community residential institutions (Sailor & Guess, 1983).

Family and Foster Homes

Some parents of adults with severe handicaps choose and are able to keep their children at home. This allows the handicapped adult to participate in family life and to draw on the family for support in educational, vocational, and recreational activities.

A home living arrangement works well when parents and siblings accept and are willing to cope with the limitations of the handicapped individual and to include that individual in family activities; and when community agencies are available to support family members and to help them plan and carry out activities for the child or sibling who is severely handicapped. Unfortunately many severely handicapped adults who live at home do so without the care, protection, and social and vocational opportunities necessary for integration into the community. Some stay at home, taking part in chores around the house but rarely interacting with the outside world. Others do not receive the support they need from community agencies.

Foster homes offer a family-style living arrangement. Foster parents are paid from the individual's social security supplement or by state welfare or rehabilitation agencies. The success or failure of a foster home arrangement depends on several factors. The most important is the interest of the foster parents in the welfare of the severely handicapped adult. Some foster parents sincerely want to help the individual; others are in the business to make money. Then, too, foster parents need the day-to-day help of community agencies to provide the social, recreational, and vocational activities that are an integral part of the normalization process (Sailor & Guess, 1983).

Group Homes

An increasingly successful living arrangement for adults with severe handicaps is the group home. The form allows a small group of handicapped individuals, usually from six to twelve people, to live together under the supervision of house parents or a manager. Residents are integrated in social, recreational, and vocational activities outside the home. They also receive ongoing training in self-help, personal adjustment, and community living skills.

A major problem facing group homes is community acceptance. Some people do not want to see group homes established in their area. They don't object to the idea of group homes, but they don't want one in their neighborhood. In many communities the first step in creating group homes is educating the public about the human rights of individuals with severe handicaps.

Neighborhood support is just one factor in the success of a group home arrangement. Equally important are the managerial skills of the house parents and the support network of community agencies.

Apartments

For a small number of severely handicapped adults, semi-independent apartment living is possible. An apartment is rented for two or three individuals who are capable of caring for themselves and the apartment, and preparing their own meals. A supervisor visits the apartment two or three times a week, to help residents adjust to each other and to community activities. The supervisor also counsels residents about vocational workshops, competitive employment, and community recreational facilities.

There are several other semi-independent living arrangements for severely handicapped adults, among them boarding homes and clustered apartments. In each case, minimal supervision is a necessity, as is the availability of support through community agencies.

Community Residential Institutions

Many states have organized community residential institutions to house severely and multiply handicapped children and adults. These local facilities serve as way stations from state institutions to the family home, foster home, group home, or semi-independent living arrangement, or as residential centers for those who cannot adjust to integrative living arrangements. They are also training centers for community placement and coordinating facilities for other community agencies.

SUMMARY OF MAJOR IDEAS

1. The definition of severely handicapped youngsters adopted by the U.S. Office of Education in 1975 includes children who are severely and profoundly mentally retarded and who have multiple handicaps.
2. Between 60,000 and 70,000 children with severe and multiple handicaps are currently enrolled in special education programs.
3. Although many different combinations are possible, certain multihandicapping conditions are most familiar to educators. These include mental retardation and cerebral palsy, mental retardation and hearing impairment, mental retardation and severe behavior problems, autism, behavior disturbance and hearing impairment, and deaf-blind impairments.
4. Legislative and judicial actions over the last two decades have resulted in a movement to deinstitutionalize and normalize individuals with severe and multiple handicaps.
5. The teaching strategies for severely and multiply handicapped students have been influenced by task analysis and operant conditioning. These procedures break down a task into target behaviors and apply the principles of learning to instruction.

6. The early identification of multiple and severe handicaps in young children makes intervention programs for preschoolers feasible. These programs operate in the classroom or as outreach programs that involve parents in their child's education.

7. One program for preschool children with handicaps is the Arizona Basic Assessment and Curriculum Utilization System (ABACUS). The system assesses the level of functioning in five areas: body management, self-care, communication, preacademics, and socialization. The assessment results in an IEP for each child that targets specific skills or behaviors for instruction. The child's progress in acquiring these skills and behaviors is monitored daily.

8. The curriculum for elementary-age children who are severely and multiply handicapped should focus on communication, social development, and prevocational skills development.

9. The curriculum for severely and multiply handicapped adolescents focuses on their ultimate functioning, the degree to which these students are able to actively participate in community situations appropriate to their age level.

10. The development of educational programs for those who are severely or multiply handicapped requires an analysis of their daily routine, skill assessment, identification of teaching goals and strategies, staff training, and management of the many elements and participants in the program.

11. Augmentive systems have been developed to help nonvocal children communicate. Among these devices are communication boards.

12. Normalization is an ongoing process: It does not end as the severely handicapped child becomes an adult. One important element in the process is the creation of integrative living arrangements—in family or foster homes, group homes, apartments, or community residential institutions. In each of these living situations, the skills of the supervisor and available community support are critical factors.

UNRESOLVED ISSUES

1. *Preschool programs for handicapped children.* Extensive efforts have been made at state and federal levels to encourage local programs for handicapped children below the age of 5. Despite wide general agreement on the advantages of providing special services as early as possible, there are still many handicapped children who do not have the benefit of a preschool start to master basic social and adaptive skills.

2. *Integration of severely handicapped individuals.* Although much progress has been made in increasing the acceptance of children

and adults with severe and multiple handicaps, the negative reactions of many well-meaning people continue to cause adaptive problems. Integration in schools and communities is one solution to the problem; public education is another.

3. *The costs of intervention.* Some object to the cost of educating severely and multiply handicapped children. There is no question that special education programs are expensive. But is that expense justified? We must develop a system of accountability that will allow us to offer effective programs that are economically sound as well.

REFERENCES OF SPECIAL INTEREST

Bricker, D., & Filler, J. (Eds.). (1985). *Severe mental retardation: From theory to practice.* Reston, VA: Council for Exceptional Children.

Twenty-seven authors combined their talents to produce this book. They discuss the broad context of severe retardation, including policy and judicial opinions; programs for all age levels, from infancy to adulthood; and critical issues, including evaluation, curricula, behavior control, living arrangements, and methods of research.

Doyle, P., Goodman, J., Grotsky, J., & Mann, L. (1979). *Helping the severely handicapped child: A guide for parents and teachers.* New York: Crowell.

This book provides parents with very specific advice on how to help a handicapped child acquire a level of self-care at home (feeding, dressing, toileting). Other sections identify sources of help (community agencies, special equipment, even babysitting). The last section describes the legal rights of handicapped children, so that parents can protect the right of their child to receive a free appropriate education.

Fredericks, H., & Staff of the Teaching Research Infant and Child Center. (1980). *The Teaching Research curriculum for moderately and severely handicapped.* Springfield, IL: Charles C Thomas.

This two-volume publication provides eighty-five detailed task analyses of self-help, cognitive, and motor skills. The *self-help and cognitive* volume includes steps in teaching self-feeding, dressing, personal hygiene, personal information, reading, and number concepts. The *gross and fine motor* volume consists of twenty-five task analyses of motor skills. Most of the task analyses have been field tested extensively.

Sailor, W., & Guess, D. (1983). *Severely handicapped students: An instructional design.* Boston: Houghton Mifflin.

A comprehensive book covering the philosophy and rationale for educating students with severe and multiple handicaps. The authors present goals, objectives, and teaching strategies to maximize student progress toward independence in all different normal environments. The text describes legal imperatives, instructional designs, curriculum development and sequencing, education programs for all age levels, and postschool living arrangements.

Snell, M. (Ed.). (1983). *Systematic instruction of the moderately and severely handicapped* (2d ed.). Columbus, OH: Charles E. Merrill.

Seventeen chapters on teaching methods, written mostly by educators. Some address general issues: characteristics of educational services, parent-professional interactions, identification and placement, IEP development and implementation, and medical procedures. Others describe specific curriculum areas—motor, sensorimotor, conventional and nonspeech communication, social, self-care, daily living, functional reading, and vocational skills.

Wetzel, R., & Hoschouer, R. (1984). *Residential teaching communities: Program development and staff training for developmentally disabled persons.* Glenview, IL: Scott, Foresman.

This book describes a system of program development and staff training that the authors, two psychologists, developed through extensive work in institutional and group home settings. The system applies behavior analysis to the social integration of those who are developmentally disabled. Topics include deinstitutionalization, program development, daily routines, assessment, teaching goals, teaching strategies and procedures, staff training, and organization and roles.

C·H·A·P·T·E·R
Eleven

CHILDREN WITH PHYSICAL HANDICAPS

Focusing Questions

Is every physical or health impairment a handicapping condition?

How does the age at which a child becomes physically handicapped affect the child's adjustment to the condition?

What are the unique problems faced by children with handicapping conditions caused by disease?

What kinds of physical adaptations can the classroom teacher make to help a student with a physical handicap?

Why is it important for the classroom teacher to openly discuss a student's handicapping condition with the child's classmates?

How have judicial rulings and legislative action affected the education program of youngsters with physical handicaps?

How does the overprotectiveness of family and friends affect the adjustment of a child with a physical handicap?

*O*ne of the smallest but most diverse groups of exceptional children is the group classified as physically handicapped. Some physical handicaps are very obvious; others are subtle. Some are caused by disease; others are caused by injury. Most are permanent. Although many children with severe and multiple handicaps have physical handicaps, this chapter focuses on the children with physical handicaps that are not complicated by other learning problems. Some students with physical handicaps require modifications in the environment, content, or skills to benefit from education. Other students with physical handicaps may not require special education services, but may still need special understanding and support from their teachers. Here we describe some of the conditions that cause physical handicaps, as well as some of the ways teachers can increase the participation and success of students with physical handicaps in the educational environment.

DEFINITION

The population of children with physical handicaps is very heterogeneous because it includes youngsters with many different conditions. Most of these conditions are unrelated, but for convenience they are often grouped into two categories: physical disabilities or health impairments. A physical disability results from a condition like cerebral palsy or a spinal cord injury that interferes with the child's ability to use his or her body. Many, but not all, physical disabilities are considered orthopedic impairments. (The term *orthopedic impairment* generally refers to conditions of the muscular or skeletal system, and sometimes to physically disabling conditions of the nervous system.) A condition like cystic fibrosis or diabetes that requires ongoing medical attention is a health impairment.

According to Section 504 of the Rehabilitation Act of 1973, a person is "handicapped" if he or she has a mental or physical impairment that substantially limits participation in one or more life activities. When a physical or health condition interferes with a child's ability to take part in routine school or home activities, the child has a physical handicap.

By this definition, a student who takes medication to control a health impairment is not physically handicapped. Nor is the student with an artificial arm who successfully takes part in all school activities, including physical education. But when a physical condition leaves a student unable to hold a pencil, to walk from class to class, to use conventional toilets—when it interferes with the student's participa-

---

Note: This chapter was written by Dr. Beverly Rainforth, University of Connecticut, Storrs, Connecticut.

The relatively small number of physically handicapped students encountered by specialists, and certainly by regular teachers, means that school personnel often have very little experience understanding and adapting to these students' special needs.
(George Gardner/The Image Works)

tion in routine school activities—the child is physically handicapped. This does not mean the child cannot learn. But it does place a special responsibility on teachers and therapists to adapt materials and equipment to the student's needs, and to help the student learn to use these adaptations and to develop a strong self-concept.

PREVALENCE

How many children have physical handicaps? This question is difficult to answer both because of the way physical handicaps are defined and because of the way they are reported. Although we could determine the incidence of the conditions that can result in physical handicaps, these figures would greatly overestimate the number of children whose participation in routine activities is actually limited. For example, the Epilepsy Foundation of America (1982) reported that approximately 1 percent of the population has epilepsy. But medication can control seizures completely in half the cases and reduce the number of seizures in most other cases. With regular medication, then, most children with epilepsy can participate in the same activities as their friends and classmates. Less than half the total number of children with epilepsy would be considered physically handicapped.

Another possibility is for school personnel to report the number of children who require special education or related services because of physical handicaps. Sometimes, however, a diagnosis of a physical or health condition does not coincide with the teacher's recognition that a child's abilities have become limited. For example, a physician may diagnose a muscle disease in a child before the child begins to show the outward signs of the disease and requires special services at school. Although school personnel know about the student's condition and watch for symptoms, the child is not reported as physically handicapped for statistical purposes until special services are recommended or the student's activities become limited. Or a teacher may find that a child has difficulty with schoolwork. The teacher suspects a learning disability, but later an underlying medical condition (say, epilepsy) is diagnosed.

Local variations in how handicaps are classified further complicate the process of determining how many children have physical handicaps. For example, one state classifies a large number of students as other health impaired, while other states classify similar students as learning disabled. Or some states classify students as multihandicapped, while others classify similar students according to the primary handicapping condition (say orthopedically impaired) (U.S. Department of Education, 1984).

Finally, at the national level there is no specific educational category for children with physical handicaps. Table 11.1 lists the number and percentage of children receiving special education and related services during the 1983–1984 school year who were classified orthopedically impaired and other health impaired. Taken together, the figures probably provide the best estimate of how many school-age children have physical handicaps. These figures reveal that only about 2.5 percent of all the children receiving special education and related services (or .27% of the entire school population) are physically handicapped.

The low incidence of physically handicapped youngsters limits the exposure of educators to their special needs. Special education teachers might work with only a handful of students with physical handicaps in their careers, and these students might have very different handicapping conditions. Regular classroom teachers probably come in contact with even fewer of these children. This lack of experience can affect the education of youngsters with physical handicaps. When re-

Table 11.1
Handicapped Children Receiving Special Education and Related
Services Under Public Laws 94–142 and 89–313, 1983–1984

	Total	Percent of U.S. School-age Population
Orthopedically impaired	56,209	0.14
Other health impaired	54,621	0.13
All handicaps	4,341,399	10.89

SOURCE: Data adapted from *Seventh Annual Report to Congress on the Implementation of Public Law 94–142: The Education for All Handicapped Children Act* by the U.S. Department of Education, 1985. Washington, DC: U.S. Government Printing Office.

searchers studied thirty-five of these children, they found that most had difficulties in school (Hall & Porter, 1983). The majority of their problems were due to school personnel's failure to understanding the handicapping conditions and to adapt school tasks to those conditions; some children also had problems with access in school. The researchers claimed that teachers lacked both experience with children with physical handicaps and information about the specific conditions that affected their students.

DEVELOPMENTAL PROFILES

Erin and John are two children with physical handicaps. Their developmental profiles in Figure 11.1 show that Erin and John are like their agemates in many ways, but they also show some remarkable differences.

Erin is 8 years old. She has cystic fibrosis, a disease that affects many organs in the body, especially the lungs. The disease has left Erin pale, thin, and short for her age. Her breathing problems have caused her chest to become barrel shaped, which is typical for children with cystic fibrosis. Erin has had frequent bouts with pneumonia since she was 3 months old. She is a regular patient at the local hospital, where she has become a favorite with the nurses.

Erin is in the third grade. She is a good student, but frequent absences have made it hard for her to keep up. Even when her health is better, she has trouble breathing, and wheezes and coughs all day long at school. She is usually tired by lunch time, so she has a regular appointment with the school nurse. The nurse "claps" Erin's chest to loosen the secretions in her lungs, letting Erin breathe more easily for a while. During lunch recess she rests, reads, or works on assignments she has missed. Erin would like to play with her friends, but their activity exhausts her. She chooses to save her energy for the afternoon.

FIGURE 11.1
Profiles of two children with physical handicaps

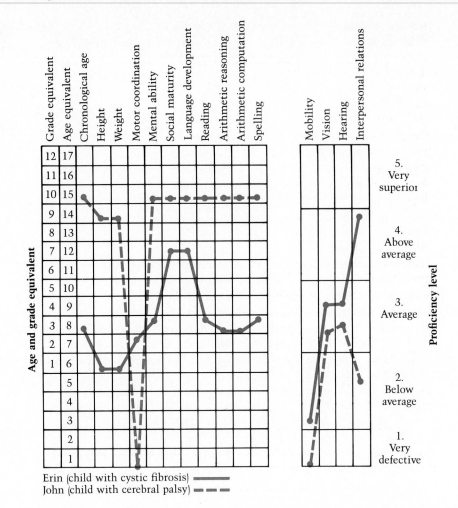

Erin (child with cystic fibrosis) ———
John (child with cerebral palsy) ━ ━ ━

Erin knows that cystic fibrosis is a progressive disease, that she may not live to adulthood. Her teacher has explained the condition to Erin's classmates and has always tried to answer their questions honestly. Whenever Erin is sick, the class sends letters to her. This gives the students another chance to ask questions or express concerns to the teacher, and reminds Erin that they are her friends and look forward to her return.

John was born with cerebral palsy, a condition that affects his nervous system and makes it hard for him to coordinate his muscles. Although he has average intelligence, he has never learned to sit by himself or walk. He cannot control the movements of his face and arms. And when he tries to speak, he makes grunts and groans instead of words.

For many years, his doctors and school personnel thought John was mentally retarded. When John was 8, he learned to use an electronic communication system. He has not stopped "talking" since. John now uses an Express 3 microprocessor that is programmed with the alphabet and about a hundred words and phrases.[1] By touching squares on the keyboard, John can construct sentences. Then he either prints out the sentences or "speaks" with the computer's voice synthesizer. John's communication system is mounted on his wheelchair, so he is never at a loss for words.

Now 15, John attends a regular tenth-grade class at a public high school. His schedule includes weekly occupational and physical therapy classes, which are focusing on the skills required for using the school bathrooms. These skills include maneuvering the electric wheelchair in and out of the bathroom, transferring to the toilet, and adjusting clothing. In other respects, John is fairly independent. He has several pieces of specially designed equipment, and his therapists are continually looking for new devices to improve his communication and self-care abilities.

After John was introduced to electronic communication systems, he developed a strong interest in computers, a subject he hopes to study in college. John's parents and sister are excited about his wanting to go to college and, as usual, will do what they can to help him achieve this goal. They have always been his greatest supporters and have helped him develop an optimistic outlook on life.

John sometimes regrets that he has cerebral palsy. Although he has a couple of close friends, he believes his outward appearance, his bulky equipment, and his inability to speak have limited his social relationships. John's friends agree that he has a wonderful personality but that it does take a while to get to know him. John looks forward to having girlfriends, getting married, and eventually having a family. He knows he will run into problems, but feels confident about overcoming them.

CHARACTERISTICS OF CHILDREN WITH PHYSICAL HANDICAPS

Children with physical handicaps have many different kinds of conditions. Although there are important differences among these conditions, there are also similarities. Each usually affects one system of the body in particular—the cardiopulmonary system (the heart, blood vessels, lungs), the musculoskeletal system (the muscles, bones, joints), or the neurological system (the brain, spinal cord, and nerves). Some conditions develop during pregnancy, birth, or infancy because of factors (known or unknown) affecting the fetus or newborn. Others develop later because of injury, disease, or factors that are not fully understood.

---

[1]The Express 3 is manufactured by the Prentke Romich Company, 1022 Heyl Road, Wooster, OH 44691.

Table 11.2
Conditions Resulting in Physical Handicaps

	Primary System Affected				Cause of Condition			
	Cardio-pulmonary	Musculo-skeletal	Neuro-logical	Other	Perinatal Factors	Injury	Disease	Other
Amputations		X			X	X	X	
Arthritis		X					X	
Arthrogryposis		X			X			
Asthma	X							X
Burns		X				X		
Cancer				X			X	
Cerebral palsy			X		X			
Cystic fibrosis	X						X	
Diabetes				X			X	
Epilepsy			X					X
Heart defects	X				X		X	
Myelomeningocele			X		X			
Muscular dystrophy		X					X	
Scoliosis		X						X
Spinal cord injury			X			X		
Traumatic brain injury			X			X		

Table 11.2 is a list of some conditions that cause physical handicaps, with information about the primary system of the body affected and the general cause of the condition. These categories offer a convenient framework for discussing the characteristics of children with physical handicaps.

Characteristics Related to the Primary System Affected

Children with physical handicaps may have impairments of the cardiopulmonary system, the musculoskeletal system, or the neurological system. Because these three systems of the body perform different functions, conditions affecting the different systems present children with different types of problems.

Children with Cardiopulmonary Conditions

The cardiopulmonary system includes the heart and lungs. The primary function of the lungs is to allow the blood supply to absorb oxygen and expel carbon dioxide. The heart pumps the oxygen-rich blood to all cells in the body, including cells in the brain, where oxygen is required for cell life.

When a handicapping condition affects the cardiopulmonary system, a child may have problems breathing (asthma, cystic fibrosis), or the heart may not pump blood properly (heart defects). Some children with these conditions cannot endure physical activities like running, climbing stairs, or even walking from one part of the school to another. Although it's possible to limit strenuous physical activity for these children, simply sitting in school all day takes more energy than some of them can produce. This inability to take part in normal activities with their agemates can create social problems for these youngsters. Adding to those problems is the fact that children with cardiopulmonary conditions are highly susceptible to illness. Frequent absences put them at an academic disadvantage, despite their normal intelligence.

Teachers can help students with cardiopulmonary conditions by adapting instruction and the learning environment to the child's needs. For example, they can schedule the most important learning activities during the child's period of greatest energy, allow the child to rest at certain intervals, give the child more time to complete assignments, arrange for locker space close to the classroom, or provide alternatives (and academic waivers) for physical education classes that exceed the child's capabilities.

Children with Musculoskeletal Conditions

The musculoskeletal system includes the muscles and their supporting framework, the skeleton. Conditions that affect the musculoskeletal system can result in progressive muscle weakness (muscular dystrophy), inflammation of the joints (arthritis), or loss of various parts of the body (amputation). Severe burns can lead to amputation, damage to muscles, or such severe scars that normal movement is prevented. Severe scoliosis (curvature of the spine) can limit movement of the trunk and cause back pain, and may eventually compress the lungs, heart, and other internal organs.

All children with musculoskeletal conditions have some limitations in their motor skills. For some children, these limitations are severe. They cannot walk or sit independently or use their hands. Their dependence on others for getting around, for eating, even for toileting, can both frustrate and embarrass them. Certain conditions affect appearance, which can increase these youngsters' social discomfort. Most children with musculoskeletal conditions have normal intellectual abilities, although mental retardation is associated with muscular dystrophy and other conditions (Batshaw & Perret, 1981). Children with musculoskeletal problems do not necessarily encounter academic difficulties, but their physical limitations and social and emotional adjustment can create educational problems.

Musculoskeletal conditions, which affect the muscles and their supporting framework, the skeleton, often severely limit a child's motor skills and can increase his or her social discomfort—but usually do not impair intellectual and academic abilities.
(Evan Johnson/Jeroboam, Inc.)

Teachers of children with musculoskeletal conditions can help their students by making adjustments for pain or poor endurance while encouraging as much physical activity as possible. They can arrange for a splint to hold a pencil or spoon, or a different faucet handle for a bathroom sink. They can be sensitive to the child's need for help with toileting, and make arrangements for someone to respond quickly and competently. And they can encourage classmates to volunteer to help the child with difficult activities.

Children with Neurological Conditions

The neurological system is made up of the brain, the spinal cord, and a network of nerves that reaches out to all parts of the body. The spinal cord and nerves transmit messages between the brain and the rest of the body. Among its other functions, the brain sends instructions about movement to the muscles, and the receptors in the muscles and joints send sensory feedback about speed, direction of movement, and body position to the brain.

With a neurological condition like cerebral palsy or a traumatic brain injury, the brain either sends improper instructions or interprets feedback incorrectly. In either case the result is poorly coordinated movement. With a spinal cord injury or myelomeningocele (a spinal cord deformity), pathways between the brain and muscles are interrupted, and messages are transmitted but never received. The result is muscle paralysis and loss of sensation beyond the point where the spinal cord (or other nerve) is damaged. Children with these neurological conditions have motor skill deficits that can range from mild incoordination to paralysis of the entire body. The most severely involved children are totally dependent on other people or sophisticated equipment to carry out academic and self-care tasks.

With epilepsy, the brain sometimes emits an uncontrolled burst of neural transmissions, which causes an epileptic seizure. Some children with epilepsy have only a momentary loss of attention (petit mal seizures); others may fall to the floor, then develop strong uncontrolled movements (grand mal seizures). Still other children may engage in what appear to be temper tantrums or purposeless activities (psychomotor seizures). The common feature in almost all types of seizures is a loss of consciousness. Epilepsy usually does not hurt the child physically. But uncontrolled movements or incontinence can frighten or embarrass the child, as well as onlookers. And the child may be confused and frustrated when teachers misinterpret undiagnosed seizures as daydreaming or intentional inappropriate behavior. Fortunately, once diagnosed, epilepsy usually can be controlled by medication and does not interfere with performance in school.

Most individuals with epilepsy and approximately 40% of those with cerebral palsy have normal intelligence (Batshaw & Perret, 1981). When the condition of cerebral palsy is as severely physically handicapping as it is for John, in the case presented earlier, fewer than 10% of those children affected would have normal intelligence.

Teachers can help students with neurological conditions by adapting the learning environment to their needs. But because neurological conditions often affect the brain, teachers must first determine which behaviors the child can and cannot control, and whether problems reflect a physical or a mental handicap.

They also have a responsibility to any exceptional child to create a supportive atmosphere, one that fosters the child's acceptance, by providing classmates with information about the student's condition.

Characteristics Related to Cause

Physically handicapping conditions can stem from factors affecting perinatal development, from later injury, or from disease. The cause of a condition and the age at which the condition develops influence the kinds of problems that children with physical handicaps experience.

Children with Conditions Caused by Perinatal Factors

Some children have congenital conditions: They are born with physically handicapping conditions or develop them soon after birth. These children do not have the same developmental experiences as do other children. The extent of the differences depends on the type and severity of the handicapping condition. At one extreme, youngsters like John never pass certain developmental milestones, like sitting and walking. At the other, children with congenital amputations who grow up using artificial limbs are sometimes so adept that their friends completely forget about the disability.

What are these children feeling? Naturally they feel badly that they have never experienced certain abilities. The expression of this unhappiness can range from wistfulness to bitterness or denial. Children with congenital physical handicaps talk about being disappointed, dissatisfied, and frustrated at times. This is healthy so long as there is balance with a sense of self-worth and achievement. How these children cope with handicapping conditions that developed at or around the time of birth certainly reflects the way others have accepted their handicaps and have supported them.

A teacher can help the child and the family understand the cause and implications of a particular condition. The teacher may be in the best position to refer the child or family members for genetic or personal counseling. The teacher also can see to it that the curriculum challenges the child mentally while individualized adaptations ensure optimal performance physically. And the teacher can help the child discover talents that may have been hidden by the handicapping condition.

Children with Conditions Caused by Injury

Some children progress through normal developmental sequences and experiences, then develop physically handicapping conditions because of injury. Some of these children are able to use their preinjury experiences during rehabilitation. For example, a child with traumatic brain injury may not be able to roll, sit, or stand up, but remembers how it was done and tries to imitate that process. Most children with physical handicaps resulting from injuries are motivated to regain or replace their former abilities. When a child loses an ability, however, he or she usually goes through a period of mourning. The ability to adjust to a physical handicap caused by injury depends on many factors, including the reactions of others, the importance of the lost abilities to the child's lifestyle, and the child's previously established style of coping (Heinemann & Shontz, 1984).

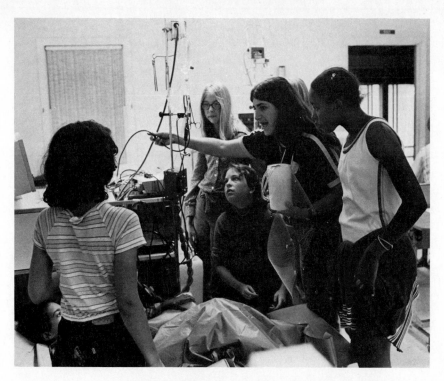

Chronic diseases involving long-term medical treatments usually mean that a student will miss school, sometimes for prolonged periods, and that the individual may experience pain and fatigue, which can interfere with learning.
(Alan Carey/The Image Works)

The teacher is generally the professional having the most consistent contact with the child. For this reason, the teacher's support and understanding is especially important during the adjustment period. The teacher can also teach other students and school personnel about the child's abilities and disabilities, and about ways in which the child can be supported and encouraged.

Children with Conditions Caused by Disease

Children whose conditions are caused by disease face special problems. Often the process of disease is poorly defined, and the extent of associated handicaps tends to change. Table 11.3 outlines the characteristics of some diseases that result in physical handicaps. Each of these diseases has acute or uncontrolled phases during which children are likely to miss school. Even when affected children return to school, pain and fatigue can interfere with learning. Although some diseases allow youngsters to live near-normal lives, others cause progressive

Table 11.3
Characteristics of Diseases Resulting in Physical Handicaps

	Description	Age at Diagnosis	Life Expectancy	Physical Effects
Arthritis	Inflammation of major joints	3 to 16 years	Normal	Joint pain, deformity, remissions
Cancer	Group of malignant disorders	Any	Varies; cure rates up to 90%	Damage to affected system, fatigue, treatment side effects
Cystic fibrosis	Exocrine gland disorder causing lung damage	Under 1 year	Uncertain, some survive into adulthood.	Respiratory problems, fatigue, poor growth, heart failure
Diabetes	Insulin deficiency causing irregular sugar metabolism	Any, most often at puberty	Reduced; influenced by proper diet and medication	Insulin reaction, circulatory problems, heart disease, blindness
Muscular dystrophy (Duchenne type)	Wasting of skeletal muscles	Under 5 years	18 years	Weakness, fatigue, respiratory problems, heart failure

SOURCE: Data from *Physical Disabilities and Health Impairments: An Introduction* by J. Umbreit (Ed.). Columbus, OH: Charles E. Merrill; and *Cancer Facts and Figures* by the American Cancer Society, 1985. New York: Author.

deterioration and eventually death. The prospect of impending death is frightening for children with health impairments, and for their classmates and teachers. Some children become withdrawn, passive, or bitter. The children who understand their conditions, who are encouraged to discuss them, and who are held to the same general expectations and limits as their peers tend to cope best with progressive diseases (Hutter & Farrell, 1983).

Chronic diseases often mean long-term medical treatments, which can create their own difficulties. Cancer radiation and chemotherapy treatments cause nausea and hair loss. These side effects and their emotional impact can lead children to try to avoid treatment. Or youngsters with diabetes, wanting to be like other children, may eat the wrong food or overexercise. These excesses can hasten the onset of irreversible problems associated with the disease.

What can teachers do for children with physical handicaps caused by disease? First, they can help monitor the effectiveness of and compliance with medical treatment. They can help the child understand the need for treatment or determine a way to manage treatment that better suits the child's routine and lifestyle. Teachers can also help the student adjust to the condition by setting reasonable expectations and limits. For a student with a progressive disease, teachers must come to terms with their own feelings about death and be ready to discuss the eventuality with the handicapped child and his or her classmates.

EDUCATIONAL ADAPTATIONS FOR CHILDREN WITH PHYSICAL HANDICAPS

Children with physical handicaps have such a variety of problems and needs that it would be difficult to discuss all the ways education could or should be adapted for these students. Instead, we focus on methods to meet general needs, the needs shared by many youngsters with physical handicaps.

Curricular and Instructional Adaptations

The academic curriculum and academic skills do not necessarily present problems to children with physical handicaps. Children who miss school frequently or for a long period because of illness or surgery may require special attention to catch up. Some children with health problems are unable to endure a full day in school, so the teacher must teach essentials over a shorter period of time or arrange for home instruction. Beyond these adjustments, the unique needs of children with physical handicaps require expansion of the traditional school curriculum into two areas: social-emotional adjustment and motor, health, and other self-care skills.

Social-Emotional Adjustment

Children with physical handicaps sometimes feel powerless, for reasons we can easily understand. Christie knows that she has leukemia and that she will probably live only a few more months. She is frequently absent from school. Although she misses her friends when she is away from school, when she returns she's afraid she is no longer part of the group. Besides being sick, she is lonely and is keeping to herself more and more. Josh faces an entirely different problem. He is recovering from a traumatic brain injury that has left him confined to a wheelchair. He is no longer able to do many things for himself, and has discovered that temper tantrums are an effective way to get people to respond to his needs immediately. It seems that the more people try to help Josh, the more aggressive he becomes.

Livneh and Evans (1984) identified twelve stages in adjusting to a physical handicap:

- Shock
- Anxiety

- Bargaining
- Denial
- Mourning
- Depression
- Withdrawal
- Internalized anger
- Externalized aggression
- Acknowledgments
- Acceptance
- Adjustment

Although withdrawal and aggression are normal stages in the process, children like Christie and Josh need support and help accepting and adjusting to their handicapping conditions. Christie's and Josh's behavior patterns are similar to those of children who face continuing academic or environmental problems. Much like the youngsters described in Chapter 8, Christie and Josh have lost control over certain aspects of their lives. Harvey and Greenway (1984) found that children with physical handicaps had "a lower sense of self-worth, greater anxiety, and a less integrated view of self" (p. 280) than did children without handicaps.

Research shows that people are more likely to accept their physical handicaps when the environment is supportive (Heinemann & Shontz, 1984), when they achieve some sense of control over the handicapping condition (Rosenbaum & Palmon, 1984), and when they begin to demonstrate new competence (Patrick, 1984). In addition to the methods described in Chapter 8, teachers can enhance the social-emotional adjustment of children with physical handicaps in several ways.

Increasing the understanding of the handicapping condition. The teacher of a student with a physical handicap should learn as much as possible about the condition—its cause, treatments, prognosis, and educational implications. Then, in cooperation with the child's parents, the teacher should help the child and other students understand relevant aspects of the condition. One of the major functions of organizations like the Epilepsy Foundation of America, the American Cancer Society, and United Cerebral Palsy is to provide information to the public. In addition, many of these organizations offer teaching kits or help in developing educational workshops to increase children's and adults' understanding of a particular condition. There are also commercial materials available, to help children learn about a variety of disabilities. One example is Kids on the Block,[2] a puppet show in

---

[2]Kids on the Block is produced by Barbara Aiello, Suite 510, The Washington Building, Washington, DC 20005.

which lifesize puppets with disabilities perform skits and answer questions from the audience.

When teaching children about handicapping conditions, teachers should help them understand that a physical handicap is an individual difference, not something to fear or ridicule or cause shame. One way to do this is to answer questions about a condition honestly. Another is to acknowledge and respect the way children (and adults) feel about handicapping conditions without condoning maladaptive behaviors (teasing, name-calling). A third way is to discuss the incidents that can occur at school—an epileptic seizure or an insulin reaction—and to have students decide how they could help or how they should behave during such an incident. One teacher saw the effectiveness of this method when, after the recess bell rang, a third-grader ran to her carrying an artificial limb. The girl reported, "Joanie broke her leg and it won't stay on!" In the distance another girl was carrying Joan piggyback toward the school. Only a few weeks before, these two girls had led efforts to exclude Joan from most activities.

Emphasizing the quality of life. Teachers can help students adjust to physical handicaps by helping them to see their handicaps as just one aspect of their lives and themselves. One elementary school approached this situation by offering a group counseling session, an hour each week, for children with physical handicaps (Williams & Baeker, 1983). One goal of the group was to develop a support system; another was to recognize individual limitations and strengths. Within the regular classroom a teacher might have students list what they like or admire about each of their classmates. This kind of exercise often gets surprising results, and is a good starting point for illustrating that children have different assets. Although children with physical handicaps must be allowed to talk about their limitations, they should also be encouraged to inventory their abilities, including the ability to help others. Although a physical handicap cannot be ignored, these children can learn to focus on the more positive aspects of their lives.

For a child like Christie, who faces a terminal illness, the process can be very difficult. Her teachers must first overcome their own feelings about death, especially the death of a child. According to Kübler-Ross (1969), who has worked extensively with children and adults with terminal illnesses, focusing on life and living helps people accept the process of death and dying. Hospice,[3] an organization founded on this philosophy, provides care and counseling services to people with terminal illnesses and their families. Hospice groups throughout the United States also offer training to teachers and other school personnel to help them deal with children who are terminally ill.

---

[3]The National Hospice Organization is located at 1901 North Fort Meyer Drive, Suite 402, Arlington, VA 22209.

Finally, teachers can improve the quality of life for a child like Christie by helping classmates show their interest and concern. When Christie is absent, her teacher has the other students send her letters, keeping her informed of the latest activities and reminding her that she is missed. When Christie returns to school, the teacher carefully avoids overprotecting and favoring the child, and keeps her involved in as many activities as her condition allows.

Increasing positive aspects of control.   Although Josh and Christie cannot control their physical handicaps, they can control many other aspects of their lives. It is very revealing to have children with physical handicaps list the aspects of their lives they believe they cannot control. Josh knew he could no longer move independently, but as a result he believed he was powerless. School personnel worked with Josh and his family to show the child that his temper tantrums were in fact one way to control people and events. They also helped Josh understand how he could achieve the same results in a more constructive way. Josh learned that his family and classmates were happy to help him when necessary and were interested in socializing with him when he took a more positive approach. He found that people understood his frustrations, and could help him find ways to express that frustration without damaging his relationships with others. Although he still has a severe physical handicap, Josh now believes he can control many aspects of his life.

Motor, Health, and Other Self-care Skills

Teachers can help a child adjust to a physical handicap by reducing the impact of the handicap. One child may be victimized by a condition because he or she does not really understand it. Another child may be dependent because he or she has not yet learned to be independent. We can deal with these problems by expanding the traditional curriculum in the areas of motor, health, and other self-care skills.

The special education team for most exceptional children includes teachers, a psychologist, and often a speech pathologist. For children with physical handicaps, the interdisciplinary team can also include a physical therapist, the school nurse, and an occupational therapist—individuals who can offer expertise in movement, health, and self-care.

Larry recently returned to high school after an accident that left him paralyzed from the waist down. His physical education teacher and physical therapist designed a weight-training program to increase the strength in Larry's upper trunk and arms. During gym class, he enjoys using the weight room with his friends, and they are amazed at how easily he now hoists himself in and out of his wheelchair. Rick, a student with cerebral palsy, has been working on a physical therapy program to improve coordination. He works with the physical therapist two times a week; on other days a friend helps him carry out a modified program that his teacher monitors. As a result he has learned

Professionals such as physical therapists, who often see students outside the school setting several times a week, have begun to increase their contact with teachers, and it is important that such cooperation be even further developed.
(George Bellerose/Stock, Boston)

to climb the steps of a bus and walk down the narrow aisle safely. Now Rick no longer needs to take the special education van but can ride to school on the regular bus with his friends. These are two examples of how programs can be adapted to increase the emphasis on motor skills, and thereby adjustment to a physical handicap.

Educational programs also must stress self-care skills, health and hygiene and independent living skills. At one time Pam had frequent diabetic insulin reactions because she did not balance her exercise, diet, and insulin injections. In her biology class this year, Pam studied metabolism, and the teacher stressed the relationships among diet, exercise, and sugar metabolism. At the same time, the home economics teacher presented information on nutrition and taught Pam's class to develop a balanced diet. In cooperation with Pam's family and physician, the school nurse had Pam test her urine for sugar each day before lunch and before basketball practice. Pam still has an occasional insulin reaction, but with a better understanding of her condition she realizes that she can control it.

Charlie has a myelomeningocele, which paralyzed his trunk, legs, and bladder. Last year he was absent frequently because of bladder infections. This year the school nurse and Charlie's teacher worked together to teach him to catheterize himself to empty his bladder. Now he can go to the bathroom whenever he needs to and has fewer bladder infections.

Bill was severely burned last year. Although he has recovered, he has many deformities and has lost most of his fingers. He's learned to use adaptations that allow him to write, feed himself, zip his jacket and pants, and put on his shoes and socks. Although an occupational therapist developed most of Bill's adaptations and was available for regular consultation, Bill's teacher provided most of the day-to-day instruction on how to use the adaptations.

As students like Charlie and Bill develop greater skill in motor, health, and other self-care activities, they also achieve greater control over their lives. This control is a critical element in accepting and finally adjusting to life with a physical handicap.

Related Educational Services. One adaptation for students with physical handicaps is the inclusion of related services in the educational program. Occupational and physical therapists have recently started working in educational settings, and school nurses have begun expanding their traditional roles. These professionals support the efforts of teachers in three primary ways:

- Providing direct services to students
- Developing IEPs and specific programs in cooperation with the classroom teacher
- Training the classroom teacher to carry out or follow through on specific interventions

The last two of these roles have been difficult for many therapists and nurses to assume because they are usually trained to provide direct services in medical settings (Chaston, 1983; Ottenbacher, 1982). The unfamiliarity of "medical" specialists with educational roles and the teacher's lack of knowledge about medical information and methods often deter these team members from working closely. Certainly it is easier for members of the educational team to confine themselves to their own areas of expertise, but students benefit more from consistent support and expectations. Consider the following example.

Martha goes to physical therapy three times a week to work on increasing her walking speed and endurance. The occupational therapist is teaching her to manage her clothing more independently. The therapists have reported Martha's achievements to her teacher, but they have never helped the teacher incorporate their methods into Martha's routine trips to the bathroom. As a result, Martha practices her walking and dressing skills only during therapy; she continues to need help going to the bathroom. Obviously Martha would benefit from greater cooperation between her teacher and her therapists.

Some teachers provide direct services generally associated with another discipline. For example, a teacher might dispense medication, teach a child to perform intermittent catheterization (inserting of a tube into the bladder to empty urine), or teach a child to use a wheelchair. The nurse or therapist assesses the child's needs, determines the proper method of intervention, then, with the educational team, decides who should carry out the intervention. The decision is based on several factors:

- Who can perform the function legally?
- Who has the expertise now?
- Who else could learn the necessary skills?
- Who is available consistently to teach the task?
- When and where does it make sense to teach the task?
- How quickly will the child learn to perform the task himself or herself?

If the classroom teacher is selected to carry out tasks outside of his or her expertise, a nurse or therapist provides the teacher with training and ongoing consultation to ensure that the student's needs are being met.

Just as it may not be appropriate for a teacher to carry out certain related services, it may not be appropriate to carry out all therapy or medical programs in a school setting. According to Public Law 94–142, related services are "required to assist a handicapped child to benefit from special education" (Section 121a.13). The courts have ruled that a health service like intermittent catheterization must be provided in school when without it, the student would be unable to receive an education in the least restrictive environment (Osborne, 1984; Stauffer, 1984). Similarly a child with cerebral palsy might need occupational therapy to achieve educational goals. In contrast, a child recovering from a broken leg would not be eligible to receive physical therapy in school because the child could remain in the least restrictive environment and make satisfactory educational progress without physical therapy services. Medical services that are not educationally relevant, then, remain the legal and financial responsibility of parents and health care providers.

Learning Environment

A variety of learning environments are being used to meet the many different needs of students with physical handicaps. Table 11.4 shows the percentage of students classified as orthopedically impaired and other health impaired who were educated in four types of learning environments in 1983–1984.

At one time educators believed that the social, educational, and medical needs of students with physical handicaps could best be met by placing them in classes for the orthopedically impaired or schools

Table 11.4

Learning Environments for Children with Physical Handicaps,
1983–1984

	Regular Class	Separate Class	Separate School	Other
Orthopedically impaired	35%	39%	17%	9%
Other health impaired	47%	20%	10%	23%

SOURCE: *Seventh Annual Report to Congress on the Implementation of Public Law 94–142: The Education for All Handicapped Children Act* by the U.S. Department of Education, 1985. Washington, DC: U.S. Government Printing Office.

for the physically handicapped. As public understanding and acceptance of people with physical handicaps has increased, so has support for the concept of integration. That change has not been without controversy, however. Gresham (1982) argued that children with handicaps do not benefit socially, and may even suffer, from placement in the mainstream. In response, Strain and Shores (1982) contended that these social problems reflect the failure of educators to give adequate instructional attention to social skills. Although Harvey and Greenway (1984) found that children with physical handicaps who attend special (segregated) schools had better self-concepts than did their counterparts in regular (integrated) schools, they also found support for the theory that children in special schools build up their self-concept because they are sheltered from normal expectations and interpersonal comparisons. In terms of preparing children to become well-adjusted contributing members of society, segregated environments may in fact interfere with the goals of education.

In keeping with these goals, Public Law 94–142 provides the incentive to educate students in the least restrictive environment and to offer the services necessary for students to succeed in that environment. Section 504 of the Rehabilitation Act of 1973 laid the groundwork for moving students with physical handicaps to less-restrictive environments by requiring that public buildings be accessible to all people. The figures in Table 11.4 show that most students with physical handicaps are being educated in public school environments. Although changes in reporting methods make it difficult to compare past and current figures, the U.S. Department of Education (1984) reported that the number of students with physical handicaps in public schools is increasing.

Individualization requires that the continuum of learning environments discussed in Chapter 2 be available to students with physical handicaps. This means we find these students in regular classrooms, resource rooms, special classes, special schools, perhaps at home and in hospitals—according to their needs.

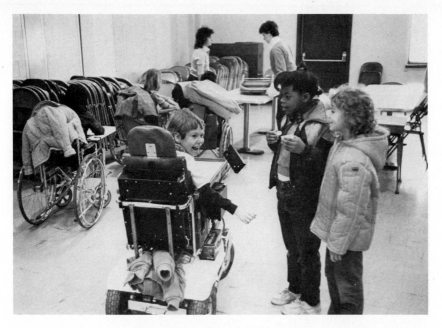

Often physically handicapped students who have no specific learning impairment require small but vital adjustments (such as additional time or space to maneuver a wheelchair) before they can be mainstreamed successfully into the regular school setting.
(Alan Carey/The Image Works)

Regular Classes

Students with physical handicaps who have no other learning impairments can achieve their greatest potential in the regular classroom. Here these children share the same learning opportunities and expectations of their nonhandicapped peers. If children with physical handicaps are going to learn to live in integrated environments as adults, they must attend regular schools and classes to the greatest extent possible. Often adjustments, like providing additional space to maneuver a wheelchair, extra time to change classes, or access to an elevator or a computer terminal, are the key to participation in a challenging curriculum and meaningful social interactions.

The classroom teacher is the source of important information about the need for and effectiveness of services for the child with a physical handicap. Because teachers have frequent intensive contact with their students, they are often the ones who notice physical problems, like the repeated staring spells associated with petit mal seizures. In fact teachers are the most reliable resource for determining the effects of medication on epilepsy, hyperactivity, and other conditions (Gadow, 1979). To help teachers make these observations, Dever and Knapczyk (1980) developed a screening tool for recognizing physical problems in educational settings. This nontraditional role is only one of the many roles classroom teachers have assumed for their students with physical handicaps. Although the prospect of new and extra responsibilities concerns regular classroom teachers, Frith and Edwards (1981) found that teachers who have already taught children with physical handicaps have far fewer concerns than those who have never taught this population.

Seven years ago Melanie entered the third grade at her neighborhood elementary school, where she already was friendly with some of her classmates. Because she used a wheelchair, the school built a ramp to the front door and put a larger bathroom stall with handrails into the girls' room. The teacher placed Melanie's desk near the classroom entrance and made wide aisles between her desk and the various learning areas in the room. In addition to the educational program shared with other third-graders, Melanie's educational team determined that she needed to become more independent in the bathroom, to build endurance and speed for wheeling her chair, and to become responsible for her own medication. Melanie's teacher believed she could address these needs in her daily and weekly routines, provided she had ongoing consultation with other team members. The team agreed that Melanie's teacher would coordinate and assume primary responsibility for implementing the child's individualized education program.

This year Melanie entered the tenth grade at the regional high school. Although her academic needs remain similar to those of her classmates, she continues to have unique motor, self-care, and health needs. She is still a popular student, but the emotional stresses felt by many teenagers are intensified for Melanie because of her physical handicaps. Like the elementary school, the high school has made environmental adaptations to improve Melanie's access to all program areas. Unlike the elementary school, Melanie now has eight different teachers, each seeing her for no more than an hour a day. A school counselor now coordinates Melanie's program and helps her with social adjustment problems. The high school physical education teacher continues to work on fitness with Melanie, and all of Melanie's teachers understand that she still has epileptic seizures. For a number of reasons, Melanie's educational team has agreed that her other unique needs can best be met with direct intermittent services from a physical therapist, a nurse, and an occupational therapist at school.

Resource Rooms and Special Classes

One student may need tutoring by a resource room teacher to catch up with a class after a long absence. Another may go to adapted physical education or physical therapy while classmates go to physical education. These services are most effective as integral supports to regular education rather than separate entities. But some students require such extensive adaptations that their needs can be met only in a separate class. For students without learning impairments, a special class should be a temporary placement, with instruction geared toward reducing barriers that currently prevent participation in regular classes. For example, school personnel determined that John had normal intelligence but could not communicate his needs or complete academic tasks because of severe cerebral palsy. It took approximately two years of intensive training to teach John to use an electronic communication system and to bring him up to grade level in essential reading, spelling, and arithmetic skills. During that time John was assigned to a special class. But it was understood that the assignment was temporary. The goal of John's education program was to integrate him in the normal classroom. John's special education teacher arranged for him to visit regular classes during a variety of activities and to have lunch with his agemates. When John was finally placed in the regular classroom, he knew his classmates and was prepared to enter the regular curriculum. Also, his classroom teacher understood his needs, and the special education teacher and related services continued to be resources.

Special Schools

With increasing societal acceptance and support, and with the legal requirements and incentives of Public Law 94–142 and Section 504, there remains little reason to educate students with physical handicaps in special schools. Unfortunately the figures in Table 11.4 indicate that many children with physical handicaps continue to receive their education in special schools. Although a family may have to place a child in a residential situation, this does not necessarily mean the child must be educated in a special school. Consider Chris, who has muscular dystrophy and must depend on others for most of his care and mobility. Chris attended public school programs in his home school district until about three years ago. At that time his parents found they could no longer manage Chris at home because of their own poor health. Reluctantly they placed him in a residential school in another community. This year Chris moved back to his hometown to live in a group home. Because an alternative (and less-restrictive) residential setting was available, Chris returned to the school system he once attended, where his educational needs are being met in the least restrictive environment. Good communications have been developed among Chris, his parents, his group home, and his school. Although Chris and his parents would prefer to live together again as a family, they are pleased that they live close to each other. And Chris enjoys going to school with friends he has known since childhood.

Homebound or Hospital Services

Children who are recovering from an acute illness, a serious accident, or surgery may have to continue their school programs at home or in the hospital. In some cases children's hospitals run their own schools to meet these needs. In other cases an itinerant teacher maintains contact between homebound or hospitalized students and their regular teachers. Schools have also begun to use microcomputers to maintain contact with homebound students.

When Julie was seriously injured in a fire, she was admitted to the burn unit at a large children's hospital. Once her burns healed she needed surgery to correct deformities caused by scarring, and intensive rehabilitation. She remained in the hospital for months. Because the hospital had many young patients undergoing long-term treatment, it had established a school program. The hospital school teacher contacted Julie's regular teacher for information about the curriculum and level at which Julie had been working. Julie was able to join a small group of children at her grade level for a reading class; her new teacher tutored her separately in arithmetic. In this way, Julie was able to keep up with her regular school program during her lengthy rehabilitation. When she was ready to go back to school, her hospital teacher informed the school about Julie's academic progress and her needs for social and emotional adjustment and self-care training.

Rob fractured a vertebra in his spine and was forced to stay home in traction for several weeks. His school provided an itinerant teacher for two hours a day to help him keep up with his class. It also loaned Rob a microcomputer and software that let him work at his own pace. A modem hook-up between school and home allowed Rob's teacher to send and receive assignments and tests over the computer. Rob and his classmates also discovered they could send messages back and forth and even play an occasional game of chess. Through the itinerant teacher and microcomputer, Rob was able to maintain both his academic performance and social contacts, which made his return to school easier.

LIFESPAN ISSUES

Limited Participation in Normal Life Activities

A child with asthma may be unable to play softball and basketball with youngsters in the neighborhood. In most cities a child in a wheelchair cannot take a city bus to the lake on a hot afternoon. A child with diabetes cannot eat ice cream sundaes with friends. Although these limitations seem relatively minor, they are the social indignities that create isolation, real or perceived, for children who are normal in all other respects. The day-to-day disappointments of children with handicaps is one source of controversy over whether these children should be clustered, or should be grouped in special environments. Some argue that integration is unkind because it forces children with handicaps to face daily disappointment. Others insist that society as a whole must come to accept all kinds of people, with all kinds of differences, and that segregation prevents people both with and without physical handicaps from facing issues of limited participation.

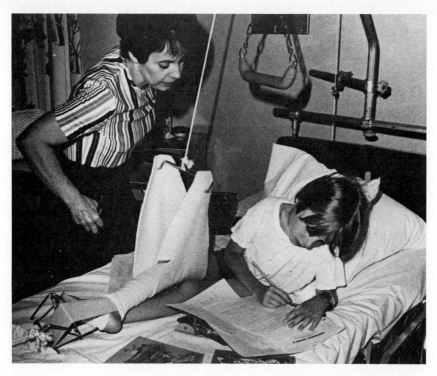

Children who are recovering from a serious accident or surgery may have to continue their school programs at home or in the hospital; in some cases an itinerant teacher maintains contact between such students and their regular teachers.
(© 1979 Laimute E. Druskis/Taurus Photos)

Limited Choices for Education, Career, and Lifestyle

As they reach adulthood, individuals with physical handicaps face restricted opportunities. Although many colleges and universities are working to implement the accessibility requirements of the Rehabilitation Act of 1973 (Marion & Iovacchini, 1983), higher education often remains inaccessible to or nonsupportive of students with physical handicaps. A premed student may be unable to complete required chemistry courses because the laboratory cannot be reached in a wheelchair. Campus transportation may be available weekdays but not nights or weekends, when other students use the library to study. A student with severe cerebral palsy may be forced to live in the infirmary because the university is unwilling or unable to find personal care attendants to help the student live in a dormitory.

When we limit opportunities for training, we limit career opportunities as well. And career opportunities are further limited by handicapping conditions themselves. A man with uncontrolled epilepsy cannot drive an automobile. This means he cannot get a job that requires driving or take a job that is inaccessible to public transportation.

It also means that he cannot work at a job in which an unexpected loss of consciousness could result in serious injury to himself, to others, or to the product (some factory and construction work, work handling expensive breakable items).

Both training and employment opportunities can be further limited for adults with physical handicaps by the need to stay near a reliable support system, family members or close friends. Every life decision— to change jobs, to move, get married, to raise a family—is complicated by the handicapping condition. Every life decision means an assessment: How will the disability affect the choice? And what impact will the choice have on the disability?

Length of Life

Children with health impairments like diabetes, cystic fibrosis, and cancer face shortened lives. These conditions follow different courses, however, which can present children with tremendous uncertainties. For youngsters with diabetes, even strict compliance with prescribed medication and diet does not guarantee good health or a normal lifespan, and violations often do not have immediate serious effects. Children with cystic fibrosis face a prognosis that is more certain but also more pessimistic: Few survive into adulthood. Children with advanced cancers face death daily.

Still, most children want to live as normally as possible. When a child with a terminal illness attempts to participate fully in life's activities, we may consider the child valiant. For a child with a condition like diabetes, which has a less certain course, efforts to live normally— such as eating the same foods as friends and family—may violate prescribed care. We may consider this child unaccepting, ambivalent, or noncompliant, but he or she may be experiencing a daily conflict between health needs and happiness. When we recognize the conflict, we can offer more effective support and guidance.

As a child with a terminal illness or progressive condition approaches the point where death becomes a certainty, he or she may face tremendous fear and grief—as may family members, classmates, and school personnel. Teachers must confront their own feelings about death and dying before they can offer support to children and their families.

Discrimination

People with physical handicaps face the intentional and unintentional discrimination of other people and the "system." Fear, ignorance, lack of experience, and inflexibility are the most common causes of discrimination. It is difficult to reconcile the fact that those limited by physical handicaps must also deal with limitations unnecessarily imposed on them by others.

BEYOND THE BARRIERS

While she was still a very young child, Rosemary Larking's parents were told in plain language that she would be "a vegetable" and would probably survive only a few years.

Instead, the 36-year-old Larking has fought osteoporosis, quadraplegia, and restrictive lung disease—as well as prejudice and physical barriers—to emerge as a leading advocate for the disabled in Massachusetts. And perhaps just as importantly, she defied the odds and the advice of experts to become a mother—her daughter Lorelei is now two years old, healthy and energetic.

"When I was born the doctor injured my spinal cord," recalls Larking matter-of-factly. "As a result, I wasn't sitting up and going through the correct stages of development. I didn't start walking until I was three." She underwent several operations "just to keep me standing on my feet," she says. Enduring operation upon operation, Larking, who grew up in the Springfield (Mass.) area and now lives in Newton, became frailer and frailer each year.

But instead of succumbing to the strain of "growing up different," Larking attended public school with her peers—the first severely disabled person in her school district to do so. It wasn't easy. "One year I missed three-quarters of the school year because I was in the hospital," Larking recalls.

At age 14 she developed scoliosis, a condition which results in the curvature of the spine, and was told she'd never walk again. "It seemed inevitable," says Larking. "It got progressively harder to walk. I had had so many operations."

She has been confined to a wheelchair ever since. But Larking has not only survived in a world that remains harsh and uninviting for those with disabilities; she has thrived. Her positive view of life is summed up simply but powerfully: "Never say no and never say I can't. Say I can do and can succeed."

In the Newton apartment which she shares with her husband Donald and their daughter, the phone rings constantly. Larking bought an answering machine the day after she appeared on a television program during which her home phone number was mistakenly flashed on the screen during a discussion on access for the disabled. She fielded calls from people seeking information all day and right through to midnight.

Officially, Larking calls herself "a self-employed consultant on issues of independent living and disabled persons." Unofficially, she is a one-woman crusade for the rights of disabled.

A slight woman with strawberry blonde hair, Larking is dressed in a pink sweatsuit and loafers as she greets a recent visitor in her apartment. She sits at the controls of a motorized wheelchair and leads a tour of the apartment, which has been specially designed for a disabled tenant. Still, Larking points out a number of design flaws, typical of the obstacles she and other disabled people face every day. A column which stands in the middle of a hallway blocks the passage of her wheelchair. There are no kitchen cabinets—"You're

continued

continued

expected to store all of your food on two boards above the sink, which is dangerous, especially if you have a small child," she says. The toilet is built between a sink and a wall which leaves no room to park the wheelchair. "For a new project, I don't understand (the problems)," laments Larking. "It means I have to be dependent on others." She is vigorously pursuing the matter with the management of the building.

But the barriers she faces are as much attitudinal as physical. "The medical profession always treats disabled persons as patients rather than persons," Larking says. "Patients are sick people. It's easier for society at large to deal with handicapped people as sick people."

Larking, who studied sociology, psychology and political science at the American International College in Springfield, is an expert at turning dissatisfaction into action. When a friend was prohibited from attending class at a state college while accompanied by a seeing-eye dog, Larking wrote and filed in the state legislature a bill to prohibit discrimination against blind people in admission to state colleges and universities. The bill is now law.

She has also authored three other bills which have been signed into law in the commonwealth: one creating a non-driver's I.D. card; another eliminating the requirement for verification of physical disability each time a permanently disabled person votes by absentee ballot; and a third which created a state commission to investigate the needs of the handicapped.

Larking has also found time to establish a group called Wheels Against Restrictions in western Massachusetts, to serve as an assistant staff psychologist at Belchertown State School in Belchertown, and to work for the Internal Revenue Service for three years. She was recently nominated by U.S. Secretary of Health and Human Services Margaret Heckler for the National Hall of Fame for Disabled Persons.

But the accomplishment she may be proudest of is the birth of her daughter. The delivery created problems, probably due to a lack of medical information on delivering babies of disabled mothers, according to Larking. "It wasn't until I was five months pregnant that I found a doctor to deliver the baby," she says. "The doctors recommended abortion. They didn't see how I could take care of her after she was born, and because of my size, they didn't think there would be room for the baby to grow. The attitude surrounding the pregnancy was condescending and reprimanding. People said I couldn't be a good mother because I couldn't do the physical things."

After giving birth, Larking was told she would be on an iron lung for the rest of her life. To add to the trouble, Larking says, "A social worker came every week to our apartment and suggested we give up my daughter for adoption. All (the social workers) did was play havoc with my mind. I got in a really depressed state, which is contrary to my whole philosophy."

Larking used the iron lung for awhile, then had it removed from her apartment and recovered on her own.

continued

continued

Larking and Lorelei expect to be competing (unofficially) in the Boston Marathon in two weeks. The mother designed a special chair which attaches to her wheelchair and allows Larking to carry Lorelei with her—a device which Larking says has already prompted interest from other disabled parents.

Thinking back, Larking says she cannot recall one disabled role model she had while growing up. "I always wanted to counsel the handicapped or the newly handicapped," she says now. "I thought I could serve as an inspiration to them, be a model to them."

SOURCE: Rhea Becker, "Beyond the Barriers," *The Tab*, March 26, 1985, p. 5.

Section 504 of the Rehabilitation Act of 1973 prohibits employers from discriminating against people with handicaps who are otherwise qualified for employment. This Rehabilitation Act further requires that all agencies receiving federal funds must make their programs and buildings accessible to those with handicaps. Although this legislation has substantially reduced some types of barriers, violations and other types of discrimination persist. Thus, public information and advocacy are still necessary to increase acceptance and access for individuals with physical handicaps.

Self-concept and Adjustment

Because their participation in activities and training and jobs is limited, because their life expectancy is often uncertain, because they face all kinds of discrimination, children with physical handicaps have problems with their self-concepts and social and emotional adjustment. Well-meaning family members and friends can make the situation worse by being overprotective or condescending. Children and adults with physical handicaps need empathy, support, and encouragement. To maintain their personal dignity and pride, they must be allowed and encouraged to do for themselves as much as possible. And they must also have opportunities to do for others.

SUMMARY OF MAJOR IDEAS

1. Children with physical handicaps need special education when their impairment requires that the learning environment or the curriculum be modified to meet their special needs.

2. A physical or health impairment is not a handicap unless it limits the individual's participation in routine activities.

3. It is difficult to determine the prevalence of physically handicapped children because of the way physical handicaps are defined and reported. Estimates place the proportion of children receiving special education services because of physical handicaps at 2.5 percent of the number of *all* students enrolled in special education programs—or at .27% of the general school population.

4. There are many conditions that cause physical handicaps. The primary system affected and the factors that give rise to the condition are ways of classifying the characteristics of children with physical handicaps.

5. Children with cardiopulmonary conditions have breathing or heart problems that limit their participation in physical activities. Children with musculoskeletal conditions have motor skill deficits that in severe cases prevent walking and sitting up. Children with neurological conditions suffer from a range of motor disabilities, from mild incoordination to total paralysis, and sometimes intellectual deficiencies that complicate their development.

6. Children with physical handicaps show a wide range of reactions to their condition. Those with congenital physical handicaps tend to make necessary adaptations to their conditions. Children whose handicaps are caused by injury generally go through a period of mourning before they finally accept and adjust to their conditions. Children whose conditions are caused by disease have the same adjustment problems of other physically handicapped youngsters but also face uncertainty and the academic pressure that stems from frequent absences.

7. Teachers can help students with physical handicaps by adapting the curriculum and the learning environment to individual needs. For example, by widening the aisles in the classroom to accommodate a wheelchair, the teacher can reduce the impact of the handicap on the student.

8. Curricular changes for children with physical handicaps who have normal intelligence focus on social and emotional adjustment, and motor, health, and other self-care skills.

9. Teachers can facilitate the social and emotional adjustment of their students in several ways: by increasing the understanding of the handicapping condition, by emphasizing the quality of life, and by increasing positive aspects of control.

10. The implementation of the educational program for children with physical handicaps often includes physical therapists, school nurses, and occupational therapists. These specialists should work in close cooperation with the classroom teacher, to reinforce skill learning.

11. Physically handicapped children, like other exceptional children,

should be taught in the *least restrictive environment.* For most of these children this means the regular classroom with extra attention in the resource room if needed. For children with normal intelligence, special classes are a means of bringing them up to grade level and equivalent capabilities, with the intention of integrating them as quickly as possible. For some children, however, special schools or homebound or hospital services are essential to their educational program.

12. The adult life that a child with physical handicaps will face may include limited participation in normal activities, limited educational and vocational choices, uncertain life expectancies, and intentional and unintentional discrimination. These problems create special difficulties in terms of self-concept and adjustment to the handicapping condition. Such children may need a variety of rehabilitation services following their special education programs in the schools.

UNRESOLVED ISSUES

1. *Participation in the mainstream.* Professionals and laypeople continue to disagree about the extent to which children with physical handicaps can or should participate in the mainstream. Much of the controversy stems from misconceptions and different experiences. In fact, there is no single "right" method. Decisions must be made case by case, based on individual needs, not a diagnosis or category of handicap. We must see to it that every child with a physical handicap remains in the mainstream until he or she demonstrates other needs. We cannot assume that certain children do not fit or cannot benefit from integration until they prove otherwise.

2. *Educational teamwork.* Students with physical handicaps often require an educational team comprised of members from diverse backgrounds. Professionals from traditional medical disciplines may have trouble adjusting to work in educational settings. Different terminology, methods, and philosophies further challenge the planning and implementation of coordinated educational programs. Unfortunately university training programs may not adequately prepare teachers and other personnel for their roles as effective educational team members. Individual school programs should work toward developing models of team service delivery that address the educational needs of individual students.

3. *Technology.* More than any other group of exceptional children, students with physical handicaps use adapted equipment. These devices range from specially designed spoons to customized electric wheelchairs to computerized communication systems. For many

people, adapted equipment means the difference between limited dependent existences and full independent lives. With technological advances have come new and better adaptations—but at a cost. School systems, insurance companies, and public assistance programs disagree about who should bear the cost of expensive adapted equipment.

REFERENCES OF SPECIAL INTEREST

Batshaw, M., & Perret, Y. (1981). *Children with handicaps: A medical primer*. Baltimore: Paul H. Brooks.

> The text explains how genetic abnormalities, problems during pregnancy and early infancy, and nutritional deficiencies can cause handicaps. It also describes how these problems affect the central nervous and musculoskeletal systems, and in turn child development. A small number of physically handicapping conditions are also discussed.

Bigge, J. (1982). *Teaching individuals with physical and multiple disabilities* (2nd ed.). Columbus, OH: Charles E. Merrill.

> A detailed examination of problems encountered by students with physical handicaps and important components of education for these students. Chapters focus on assessment, methods of instruction, and components of the curriculum. Throughout the book there are many examples of adaptations that minimize the impact of physical handicaps and help students benefit from the educational program.

Bleck, E., & Nagel, D. (Eds.) (1982). *Physically handicapped children: A medical atlas for teachers*. New York: Grune & Stratton.

> Written primarily by physicians in lay terms, the book has chapters on approximately thirty different handicapping conditions and on normal development, basic anatomy, nonoral communication, driving, counseling, and emergencies. There are also extensive lists of print and organizational resources.

Finnie, N. (1975). *Handling the young cerebral palsied child at home* (2nd ed.). New York: Dutton.

> Written for parents and others without medical background, the book explains how cerebral palsy affects the child's motor development and describes how to treat the condition, how to move the child, and adapted equipment.

Kübler-Ross, E. (1969). *On death and dying*. New York: Macmillan.

> The book presents a philosophy about dealing with terminal illnesses and death that focuses on life and living. The process of preparing for death described here is the basis for the Hospice organization in the United States.

Powell, T., & Ogle, P. (1985). *Brothers and sisters: A special part of exceptional families.* Baltimore: Paul H. Brooks.

> Information about many of the issues that families with an exceptional child must address. The informative text is complemented with vignettes of brothers and sisters of children with handicaps.

Stein, S. (1974). *About handicaps.* New York: Walter and Company.

> One of the many books about handicaps written for children. The book describes one child's fear when he first meets a boy with cerebral palsy and how the two become friends.

Umbreit, J. (Ed.). (1983). *Physical disabilities and health impairments: An introduction.* Columbus, OH: Charles E. Merrill.

> Information on the cause, treatment, prognosis, and educational implications of numerous handicapping conditions. The chapters are written in lay terms by physicians who specialize in treating the particular condition.

E·P·I·L·O·G·U·E

Consultant Teacher: Link Between the Regular Classroom and Special Education

In order to provide you with a greater understanding of what a real-life teaching situation might entail and in order to illustrate the importance of the collaborative effort between the regular classroom and special educators, we have interviewed Carol Long. Carol is currently working as a consultant teacher and as the Chairperson for the PL 94–142 process at the elementary level in the Hamilton-Wenham Regional School district, which is located just north of Boston in Massachusetts. She earned her B.S. degree in elementary education and her master's degree in special education. Before becoming a consultant teacher, Carol was the head teacher in a separate classroom for children with severe language impairments. Because she had previously taught in a regular classroom as well, she is able to bring a balanced perspective to her current position and to act judiciously as the critical link between elementary classroom teachers, specialists, and parents. In this interview you will learn how she helps to facilitate the pre-referral process for children who are called to her attention by the classroom teacher and then how she continues to work with the whole team of specialists, teachers, administrators, and parents in an effort to determine the best course possible for an individual child.

Interviewer: What is the mission of the consultant teacher?

Carol Long: In our district, and pretty much as set up by the state, the mission of the consultant teacher is to bridge the gap between special education and regular education. I help classroom teachers learn to look at a child's problem, to diagnose the problem. If a child does have a special need, I work with the regular classroom teacher and the special education staff to ensure that their curriculum, their efforts, and their communications are coordinated.

　　In the past, if a child had been "identified as having problems," the classroom teacher would write down the child's name, date of birth, and address on a piece of paper and give it to the Special Education Department. The child would then be given a full battery of tests. The teacher would then give a summary of the child's performance in the classroom, but the teacher wasn't given much information about how and what the child could learn. If a child was found to have any special need at all, he or she would be pulled out for special services. Whether those services were part-time or full-time depended on the severity of the difficulty. At that time, *special need* was defined as anything that was a little bit different—this has changed quite a bit. But the teacher never knew what the child's problem was. The process lacked any kind of component to train the regular education teachers in a) how to read an education plan, to become familiar with the lingo and jargon, and b) how to deal with a child who was going to be in the classroom for the five hours when he or she was not in the learning lab.

So, the mission of the consultant teacher is to address the needs of the regular classroom teacher and to coordinate services between special education and regular education.

Interviewer: Why was the position created in your district?

Carol Long: Massachusetts State Law (Chapter 766) recommends that a prereferral process be initiated prior to any referral of a child by a teacher. All efforts should be made in the regular classroom to provide for and accommodate a child. Those efforts need to be documented. They also need to be discussed prior to any referral. The prereferral process lays the foundation for special education personnel who need to know what kinds of efforts have been made before a child is formally referred.

When a new special education director was hired in our district, she found that there was no prereferral process in place, that every child who seemed to have a problem in school was referred for special services. Because of this some children who did not have a special learning problem were picked up for service. Some educational programs in the learning lab supplemented those in the regular classroom by using a tutorial approach and offering a low teacher-student ratio, but they did not truly modify or adapt regular classroom materials for children with special needs. In addition, there wasn't much communication between the special education teachers and the regular classroom teachers once a student was placed in the learning lab.

The director's goals were to study the caseloads, to make sure that any child receiving services had special needs, and to go by the letter of the law. The position of consultant teacher was created to carry out these goals in the school.

Interviewer: You mentioned that there was no prereferral process in place and that a primary goal in your district is more prereferral activity. Could you describe what prereferral activity is?

Carol Long: During the prereferral process, the consultant teacher and the classroom teacher act as a team, as a partnership, and make decisions together about the child's pro-

Acting as a team during the prereferral process, the consultant teacher and the classroom teacher meet frequently to map out a program for the child and to discuss what adjustments to make as the program is implemented.
(© Christopher Morrow/Stock, Boston)

gram. We first let everyone know there is a problem—principal, parents, other teachers who may be involved with the child. Background information about the child is then gathered by the classroom teacher—this might include talking with the parents on the phone to find out how things are going with the family. Then we define the problem, not by saying, "I have this feeling that this kid is not doing too well," but in specific behavioral terms. I help the classroom teacher learn to observe a problem and define it. We figure out tentative solutions and work out ways to accommodate the child. The teacher implements those modifications and both of us observe how they're working. The process is documented by the teacher and we meet again to talk about the results: how did the modifications work, can we change them, and so on.

Interviewer: Are there special tools that you give teachers to observe children? We all assume that we are observers, yet it seems that there is something special needed. How do you help teachers observe?

Carol Long: Once we have identified the child's difficulties, we talk about when they happened. I help the teacher devise different observational checklists, methods of anecdotal record keeping, or frequency checklists. For instance, when does the behavior occur, how often does it happen, how long does it last. The teacher keeps a daily record of the child's behavior and at the end of the week I count them up and analyze them.

Interviewer: So you analyze—they provide the data, you analyze it.

Carol Long: Pretty much so. I also try to work as a cognitive coach by prodding the teacher with questions: What do you mean by that? What do you think? When did it happen? Did it happen because of this? I think teachers have a lot of the answers anyway. They just didn't have somebody to bounce their ideas off of, someone really knowledgeable in specific learning difficulties who could help them target problems.

I've learned so much from teachers. I don't have all the answers, for sure. There is so much teachers pick up about kids.

I don't only observe, I do informal assessments as well. I take work samples of the child who is being observed. I make up tests of what has been covered in class or use an inventory to help develop a profile of the child's skills. If I see that there are huge discrepancies or gaps, I'm better able to clarify the type of difficulty the child may be having and to make more specific suggestions—for example, perhaps we're just not matching up to the child's learning style and the student is not learning as efficiently as he or she could.

Let me just add here that if there does appear to be a problem—whether it's behavioral or a language processing difficulty or whatever—I ask our specialists to come in and take a look. So, it's not only me; the entire team is involved. The consultant teacher facilitates the whole process.

Interviewer: You seem to be saying that prereferral activity is not a clear cut process, that it is a collaborative venture and that each child might require a different type of prereferral.

Carol Long: That's right. It really does change.

Interviewer: How often do situations end with prereferral, that the child didn't require a full referral because the modifications of the curriculum worked?

Carol Long: I don't have an exact figure but I would say about 50 percent of the cases ended with prereferral last year.

Interviewer: Could you give an example of a case in which your recommendations worked at the prereferral stage?

Carol Long: I received a prereferral form in which the description of the child's behavior was somewhat vague. The teacher, who was assigned to the third grade, said the child was very fidgety and just couldn't finish his work, he was all over the room and was just not there. In going in and observing the boy, I found that the teacher was right—he just wasn't there. He was all over the room and he was fidgeting around with his glasses and falling out of his seat. He wasn't finishing his work—he would lose it before he could finish it.

So, the teacher and I put our heads together. I think it is important to find out specifically what the teacher's perceptions of the situation are—every teacher is different. Some might think there is no problem at all, others find that such behavior grates on their nerves.

In doing a frequency analysis, I found out the boy was doing all the irritating behaviors a lot and doing them more after recess and after lunch when he was really hyped up. But I also noticed that when he was concentrating, he *was* concentrating; he was not that highly distractible. So we worked on reducing his fidgeting. He was given a little piece of clay that he could keep in a little box in his desk. He was so imaginative—he gave the clay a name and it had a family and he was the caretaker and he was really going to take good care of it. He was allowed to take the box out of his desk after he finished his work, so he now had a place to focus all that extra energy. This kid liked structure—after working on so many problems, he could feel that piece of clay.

We also worked out a checklist with the boy because he needed a little more responsibility for his own behavior. We talked about all the things that weren't acceptable in the classroom. Every day at the end of the school day he would check off the items on his list, like "Did I remember my pencil?" Forgetting pencils really irritated the teacher. When we had told the boy's parents about the difficulties he was having, forgetting pencils among them, they went out and bought piles of pencils. It's little, I know, but it helped his esteem and it prevented the teacher from going crazy trying to find this

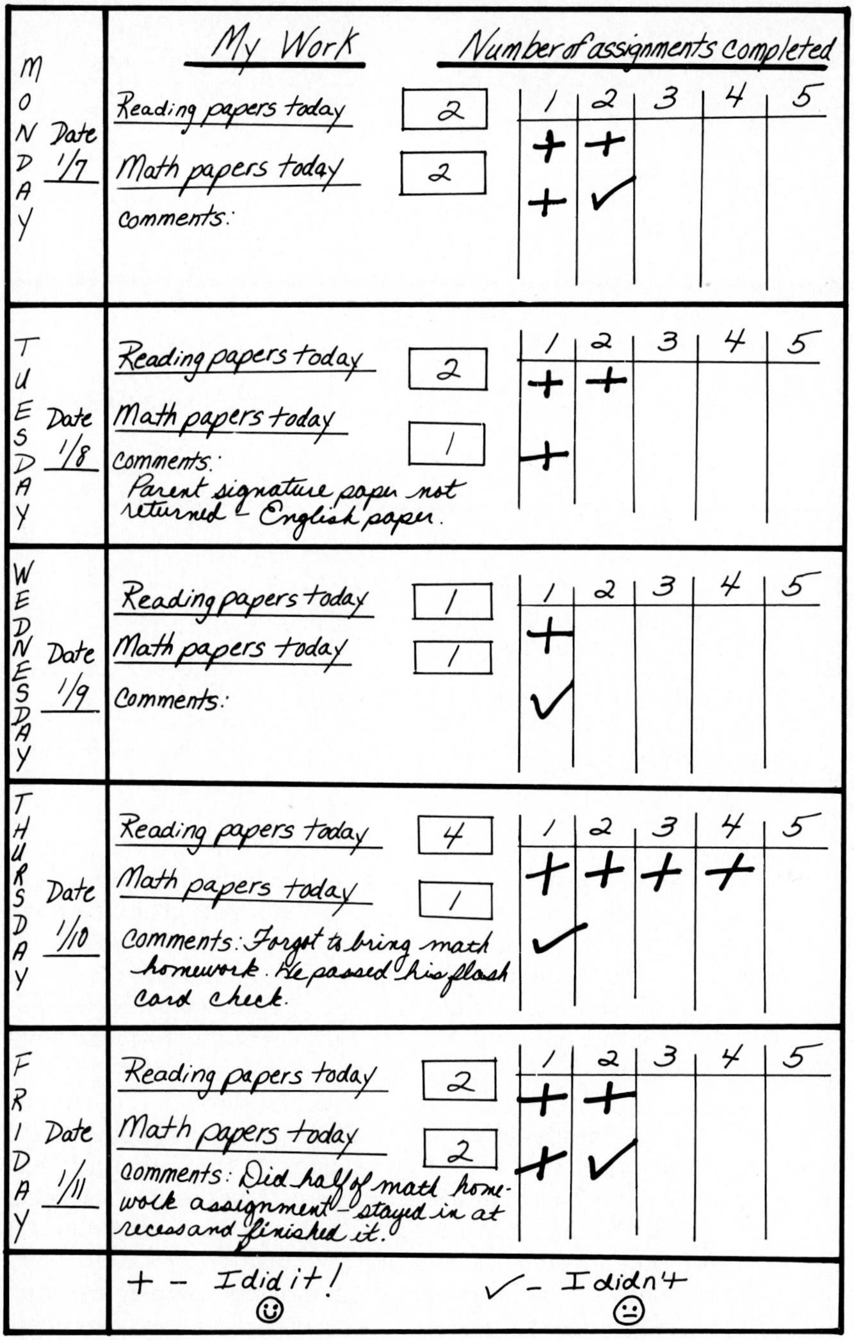

FIGURE 1
Work completion chart

NOTE: This chart is a sample of one type of checklist, drawn up by the teacher at the beginning of each week and filled in (in the righthand column) by the child himself or herself. Written comments are added by the teacher, and the checklist is taken home at the end of each week. This kind of informal checklist helps children monitor their own accomplishments and serves as a kind of weekly progress chart.

FIGURE 2
"Feelings barom-
eter" checklist

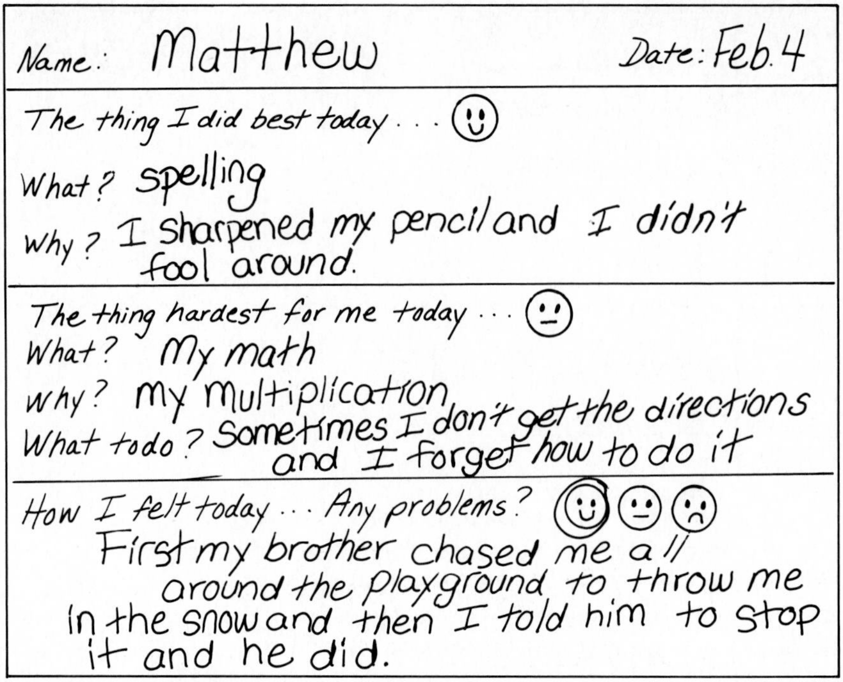

Name: Matthew　　　　Date: Feb. 4

The thing I did best today . . . 🙂

What? spelling

Why? I sharpened my pencil and I didn't
　　　fool around.

The thing hardest for me today . . . 😐
What? My math
Why? My multiplication
What to do? Sometimes I don't get the directions
　　　　　　and I forget how to do it

How I felt today . . . Any problems? 🙂😐☹️
　　First my brother chased me all
　　　around the playground to throw me
　in the snow and then I told him to stop
　it and he did.

NOTE: This informal device acts as a good jumping off point for communication between both parents and child and teacher and child. It is deliberately kept simple and
direct. Filled out each day, it helps children to become aware of their own emotional
fluctuations and attitudes.

kid a pencil. So, if he got so many checks in five days,
he and his friend could go to the library and pick out a
book.

He would take the checklist home for his parents to
sign and he would think he was just great. There was
lots of communication between the school and the boy's
home.

During my observations of the class, I thought the
teacher gave the kids too much seat work. I checked in
on the other third grade classes to see how much seat
work they had and discovered that the boy's teacher
gave more than anyone else. I approached her about it
and suggested she might try cutting the child's work
sheet in half. Let him do half at one sitting, give him
five minutes to do something else, then have him finish
the rest later. As it turned out, she cut down on the
paperwork for the whole class. She realized that this one
little boy's behavior was just a symptom of the problem—the other kids were suffering too. His anxiety sub-
sided after the work load was reduced. The teacher still

said he drove her crazy but the case didn't go to referral. He was one of the brightest little boys I had ever seen.

Interviewer: In the past he might have been identified as having a behavior problem. No one may have realized that the problem was not major. Did you talk with the parents?

Carol Long: I did, quite a bit. I also spent time with the child. He would come to see me before lunch for about ten or fifteen minutes. They had finished their work in class and were wrapping up some things. He needed somebody to help him regroup. It made him more aware of his behavior and it gave him the attention he needed. It also helped the teacher because then she had someone with whom to share her ideas and her frustration. So the suggestions helped and the child wasn't referred.

Interviewer: Do you feel that the teacher grew as a result of this experience, realizing that she had her own resources that she could use in a situation?

Carol Long: I think so. I do think she grew. She enjoyed the support and she learned more about a child.

Interviewer: Could we talk a bit about teachers and the resources that they have at their disposal?

Carol Long: Teachers are very much alone in a lot of situations when they are dealing with 27 kids. The demands on them from the community, the school committee are so great— you know, to cover certain curriculum in a specified period of time. I think teachers feel they don't have the resources of others with whom they can share ideas and brainstorm, like we do in special education. We have team meetings. We have many opportunities to meet and share ideas. I don't see that teachers have these resources. But now things are opening up. With the pre-referral process, teachers are starting to feel more comfortable about talking with specialists without being intimidated.

Interviewer: It sounds like the collaborative element is very important. But it's important for teachers to become aware of the resources they have; that is, their own experiences. How do you get teachers to recognize the value of their own experience?

Carol Long: I'm struggling with that because teachers often feel that we, the specialists, are very naive about large group management. In fact, maybe we are overly idealistic as far as what we think regular classroom teachers could

Because classroom teachers must work with large group management as well as with an individual child's specific needs, it is important for the specialist to be realistic in planning a program rather than to prescribe a "perfect method" that might be impossible to carry out.
(Meri Houtchens-Kitchens)

provide if they would only spend the time. However, I think specialists have come down the ladder some and we are now saying, "Let's see the kinds of things we can work out that aren't that big a deal, that are more simple. Okay, you can't change your reading methodology for this one kid because you have three reading groups—an hour and fifteen minutes every day for reading, and that's it." So we work with the teachers rather than impose our ideas upon them. We use more of our creative powers and juices, not for prescribing the perfect reading method for one particular child, but for helping that kid get along in the existing reading program with modifications. Teachers are realizing that we are listening to them and understand what they've been talking about.

Interviewer: What do you do when you're looking a third-grade teacher in the eye who is thinking that you don't know what it's really like to be a classroom teacher?

Carol Long: Well, I try to be totally sympathetic, to say, "You know, it's not that great for me either," to establish camaraderie. I guess all you can really say is, "The problem sounds bad; can I help?"

Interviewer: Do you ever feel that the classroom teachers don't know what it's like to be a special education teacher?

Carol Long: I think it's hard to understand. . . . When you look at your twenty-seven shining faces and then go into the learning lab and see only four or five kids with two teachers, well, the sheer number alone makes the regular teacher wonder, "What do these people do all day? It's so easy!" Some tend to forget the situation the special education teachers have, that these kids in special education have lots of problems. They couldn't read at all in the classroom, they had great difficulties learning. I'm sure many regular teachers do understand that and acknowledge the frustrations special education teachers must feel.

Interviewer: It sounds that if regular teachers can get over the initial barrier, if they stop a moment and really think, they can start to empathize with the special education teachers' situation.

Let's shift gears a bit. Parents are a large part of the child's world. How do you get them involved in the special education process?

Carol Long: In order to begin a prereferral process, the teacher has to call the child's parents and ask them to come in for a conference. The process opens up with contact, not with a form. So, the parents are told what's happening. There is then a 30-day period during which prereferral activities take place—observing, conducting informal assessments, implementing modifications, documenting results. At the end of that time, the parents come in and we talk about what went on, what worked and what didn't work. Then as a team—the principal, parents, teacher, and anyone else who is involved—we discuss whether to continue the modifications or to go on to a full referral. The parents decide if they want their child to be referred for evaluation; if the parents don't agree with a recommendation for referral, the child is not referred. It's important to note that we have a pre-

At the conclusion of the prereferral period, a team meeting—involving teachers, specialists, parents, administrators, and the consultant teacher—is held to determine whether a full referral is necessary.
(Sybil Shelton from Peter Arnold, Inc.)

referral only if a teacher requests it. If a parent comes in and asks to have the child evaluated, we skip prereferral and go right to the referral.

Also, we become interested in the family and the child's home life. It's amazing what you can find out and sometimes you say, *"That* explains it!"

Interviewer: So you really try to get the whole picture. What kind of information is available to parents to help them understand what you're all about?

Carol Long: Actually, the state publishes a simply written booklet that explains to the parents their rights—the right to an advocate, the right to appeal—and the whole timeline of the process. We give them as much information as we can.

Interviewer: Can you describe the overriding purpose of your job as a consultant teacher?

Carol Long: I think that the purpose of the job is to have somebody as a support service for the classroom teacher. A consultant teacher who is doing the job correctly would be training classroom teachers to be as independent as possible, to use their own creativity and imagination to make simple modifications. Classroom teachers should be encouraged to go ahead and start thinking about ways to accommodate a child who is different from the other kids. In my own district, we are focusing more on the idea that all children do not have to learn in the same way. Teachers are taking inservice courses in learning styles, evaluating their own teaching styles, and just learning that kids learn differently. My role is to bolster the teacher's growing awareness and to support the teacher.

GLOSSARY

Ability or process training A remediation strategy that attempts to correct developmental deficiencies—in attention, memory, perception, thinking, and language—that can impede learning.

Academic learning disabilities Conditions that significantly inhibit the process of learning to read, spell, write, or compute arithmetically.

Accommodation Changes in the shape of the lens of the eye in order to focus on objects closer than 20 feet.

Adaptive behavior The effectiveness or degree with which individuals meet the standards of personal independence and social responsibility expected for age and cultural group.

Adventitious Acquired accidentally in contrast to congenital or inherent causes.

Albinism Hereditary lack of pigment in the iris, skin, and hair.

American Sign Language (ASL) A manual language used by many deaf people that meets the universal linguistic standards of spoken languages.

Amniocentesis A procedure for analyzing the amniotic fluid (a watery liquid in which the embryo is suspended) to determine any genetic defects in the unborn child.

Anoxia Sustained lack of oxygen to the fetus during birth.

Anxiety-withdrawal A deviant behavior pattern in which children are shy, timid, reclusive, sensitive, submissive, overdependent, and easily depressed.

Aphasia The loss of speech and language as a result of a brain injury or trauma as well as the failure to learn language, possibly because of a congenital condition.

Aphonia A complete loss of voice.

Assessment A process for determining a child's strengths and weaknesses that involves five steps: screening; diagnosis, classification, and placement; instructional planning; pupil evaluation; and program evaluation.

Asthma A disease marked by recurrent attacks of wheezing coughs, labored breathing (particularly on expiration of air), and a sense of constriction due to spasmodic contraction of the bronchi.

Astigmatism A refractive error resulting from an irregularity in the curvature of the cornea or lens of the eye, causing light rays to be focused at two different points on the retina; usually correctable with lenses.

Ataxic cerebral palsy A form of cerebral palsy marked by a lack of balance in the coordination of muscles, usually the result of a lesion in the cerebellum.

Athetoid cerebral palsy A form of cerebral palsy that is marked by consistent tremors, involuntary writhing movements.

Attention disorder An inability to employ selective attention; that is, the inability to stop responding to too many stimuli.

Audiogram A graphic record of hearing acuity at selected intensities throughout the normal range of audibility, recorded from a pure-tone audiometer which creates sounds of preset frequency or intensity.

Audiometer An instrument for testing acuity of hearing.

Auditory association Ability to relate concepts presented orally.

Auditory discrimination The ability to discriminate between two words or sounds.

Auditory method A method of teaching deaf students that involves auditory training and makes extensive use of sound amplification to develop listening and speech skills. Also known as the *acoustic method, acoupedic method, unisensory method,* and *aural method.*

Auditory reception The ability to derive meaning from orally presented material.

Autism A severely incapacitating life-long developmental disability, characterized by bizarre behavior and serious developmental delays in social and communication areas, that usually appears before age 3.

Behavior modification A variety of techniques designed to change behaviors and to increase the use of socially constructive behaviors.

Blind Having light perception without projection, being totally without light perception, and needing to use braille.

Braille A system using embossed characters in different combinations of six dots arranged in a cell that allows blind persons to read by touch as well as to write using special aids.

Brain dysfunction Refers to a specific learning disability in mental functioning where the suspected cause is the physiological or neurological operation of the brain.

Brainstorming A technique in which a group of people discusses a particular problem, trying to come up with as many solutions as possible; often used with gifted children.

Cataract A condition in which the crystalline lens of the eye, its capsule, or both become opaque with a consequent dimming of vision.

Central nervous system (CNS) That part of the nervous system to which sensory impulses are transmitted and from which motor impulses originate; in vertebrates, the brain and spinal cord.

Central processing Classification of a stimulus through the use of memory, reasoning, and evaluation.

Cerebral palsy Any of a number of abnormal conditions, generally present at or near the time of birth, affecting control of the motor system due to brain dysfunction.

Chromosome One of the minute bodies in the nucleus of a cell that contains the genes or hereditary factors.

Ciliary muscles Muscles that control changes in the shape of the lens so that the eye can focus on objects at varying distances.

Class action suit Provides that legal action taken as part of a suit applies not only to the individual who brings the particular case to court but to all members of the class to which that individual belongs.

Classification The organization of information.

Cleft palate Failure of the bone and tissue of the palate (roof of the mouth) to fuse, often associated with cleft lip.

Cognitive behavior modification A variation of behavior modification that focuses on the conscious feelings and attitudes of the child.

Communication The transmission of information through verbal means, nonverbal means, or a combination of both, and involving three components: a sender, a message, and a receiver.

Communication assistants Paraprofessionals who receive training in speech and language development, total communication skills, and classroom management and who help the speech-language pathologist with articulation therapy, language therapy, and clerical tasks.

Communication disorders Impairments in articulation, language, voice, or fluency.

Compressed speech A recording and playback process that speeds speech electronically by deleting nonessential sounds.

Concept formation The ability to classify objects and events—for example, to recognize that a boat, a car, and a train are all used for transportation.

Conduct disorder A pattern of deviant behavior in which children defy authority; are hostile toward authority figures; are cruel, malicious, and assaultive; and have few guilt feelings. This group includes hyperactive, restless, and hyperkinetic children.

Conductive hearing loss A condition that reduces the intensity of the sound vibrations reaching the auditory nerve in the inner ear.

Congenital Present in an individual at birth.

Consultant teachers Specially trained teachers who are available to regular teachers to answer questions about a child, materials, or methods of instruction, and to provide supplementary teaching aids and materials.

Content acceleration A process that moves students through the traditional curriculum at a faster rate.

Content enrichment Gives students the opportunity for a greater appreciation of the topic under study by expanding the material for study.

Content novelty The introduction of material that would not normally appear in the general curriculum in order to help gifted students master important ideas.

Content sophistication Challenges gifted students to use higher levels of thinking to understand ideas that average students of the same age would find difficult or impossible.

Contingent social reinforcement A behavior modification technique using a token system to teach appropriate social behavior.

Cornea The transparent anterior portion of the tough outer coat of the eyeball.

Creativity Mental process by which an individual creates new ideas or products, or recombines existing ideas and products in a fashion that is novel to him or her.

Criterion-referenced test A test designed to measure a child's development in terms of absolute levels of mastery, as opposed to the child's status relative to other children.

Cued speech A system of hand cues placed around the mouth and larynx that represent ambiguous phonetic elements of speech. Hand shapes represent the consonant sounds, and the hand positions represent the vowel sounds.

Curriculum compacting A process for allowing gifted youngsters to move ahead that consists of three steps: finding out what the students know, arranging to teach the remaining concepts or skills, and providing a different set of experiences to enrich or advance the students.

Cystic fibrosis A hereditary disease that affects many organs in the body, especially the lungs, as a result of a generalized dysfunction of the pancreas.

Deaf Having such poor hearing that understanding speech through the ear alone, with or without the use of a hearing aid, is impossible.

Decibel (dB) A measure of the intensity of sound.

Deinstitutionalization The process of releasing as many exceptional children and adults as possible from the confinement of residential institutions into their local communities.

Delayed language development Orderly development that progresses at a slower rate than normal and that is significantly below the appropriate language performance for a child's chronological age.

Developmental (congenital) aphasia The failure to learn language, possibly as a result of a congenital condition.

Developmental learning disabilities Slow or absent development of psychological or linguistic functions; these include attention deficits, memory disorders, thinking disorders, and language disorders. If not remediated, these disabilities make learning difficult or impossible.

Diabetes mellitus A disorder of carbohydrate metabolism, characterized by insulin deficiency and an excessive amount of glucose (sugar) in the urine and in the blood.

Diagnostic overshadowing A phenomenon that occurs when one set of symptoms is so strong and obvious that accompanying symptoms are ignored or put aside.

Diagnostic prescriptive teaching An educational strategy of delineating a child's strengths and weaknesses and then designing a specific program for teaching on the basis of those findings.

Differential diagnosis Pinpointing atypical behavior, explaining it, and distinguishing it from similar problems of other handicapped children.

Differential reinforcement A behavior modification technique that provides rewards if the student can increase the time between displays of unacceptable behavior.

Divergent thinking The ability to produce many different answers to a question.

Down syndrome A chromosomal abnormality that leads to mild or moderate mental retardation and a variety of hearing, skeletal, and heart problems.

Drug therapy The use of psychoactive drugs separately or in conjunction with educational treatments to deal with the behavior problems of some children.

Due process A set of legal procedures designed to ensure that an individual's constitutional rights are protected.

Dyscalculia The inability to perform mathematical functions.

Dysgraphia Inability to produce the motor movements required for handwriting.

Dyslexia Impairment of the ability to read.

Ecological assessment A process for determining the physical, environmental, nutritional, and/or social factors that accompany or contribute to a child's problems.

Ecological model A view of exceptionality that examines the child in complex interaction with environmental forces and believes that behavior problems should be treated by modifying elements in the ecology to allow more constructive interactions between the child and the environment.

Embryo The human organism from conception up to the third month of pregnancy.

Encephalitis A disease accompanied by high fever and inflammation of the brain that can produce mental retardation.

Epilepsy A group of nervous diseases marked primarily by convulsions of varying forms and degrees.

Etiology The study of causes or origins of a disease or condition.

Exceptional child A child who differs from the norm in mental characteristics, sensory abilities, communication abilities, social behavior, or physical characteristics to the extent that a modification of school practices, or special educational services, is required for the child to develop to maximum capacity.

Executive function The decision-making element that is central to all effective adaptive behavior.

Extrinsic muscles Muscles that control the movement of the eyeball in the socket.

Feedback The result of a response to a stimulus.

Fetal alcohol syndrome A possible cause of mental retardation related to heavy drinking during pregnancy by the mother.

Fetus The unborn child from the third month of pregnancy until birth.

Finger spelling Spelling in the air using a manual alphabet.

Fluency The ability to give many answers to a given question.

Fluency disorders Stuttering.

Frequency The number of vibrations (or cycles) per second of a given sound wave.

Galactosemia An inherited condition of mental retardation caused by an error in the metabolism of the galactose in milk.

Haptic Pertaining to the sense of touch and kinesthesis.

Haptic discrimination The ability to discriminate between two objects touched and felt.

Hard of hearing Having a hearing disability sufficient to make it difficult to, but not impossible, to understand speech through the ear alone, with or without a hearing aid.

Helping teacher A direct service special teacher, working in the classroom with the regular teacher to provide support, encouragement, and therapeutic tutoring.

Heterophoria Insufficient action of one or more muscles of the eye that makes it difficult to fuse the two images from the two eyes into one image.

Hyperactivity Excessive movement or motor restlessness, generally accompanied by impulsiveness and inattention.

Hyperkinesis Pathologically excessive motion.

Hypernasality A common resonance problem that occurs when too much air passes through the nose.

Hyperopia Farsightedness.

Hyponasality (or denasality) A common resonance problem that occurs when too little air goes through the nasal cavity.

Immaturity A deviant behavior pattern in which children are inattentive, sluggish, uninterested in school, lazy, preoccupied, and reticent.

Incidence The number of new classes occurring in a population during a specific interval of time.

Incus The central one of the three small bones in the middle ear that transmit sound to the inner ear.

Individualized education program (IEP) A program written for every handicapped student receiving special education that describes the child's current performance and goals for the school year, the particular special education services to be delivered, and the procedures by which the outcome will be evaluated.

Information-processing models Models of how people think.

Instructional planning The use of diagnostic information to design an individualized education program based on the child's needs.

Intelligence quotient A score on an intelligence test that compares a child's performance with that of other children of the same age.

Intelligence test A test measuring the development of memory, association, reasoning, and classification—mental operations that are important to school performance.

Intensity The relative loudness of a sound.

Interindividual differences Substantial differences between people along key dimensions of development.

Intraindividual differences Major variations in the abilities or development of a single child.

Iris The colored muscular partition in the eye that expands and contracts to regulate the amount of light admitted.

Itinerant teachers Teachers who serve several schools, visiting exceptional children and their teachers at regular intervals or whenever necessary.

Karyotyping A process by which a picture of chromosomal patterns is prepared to identify chromosomal abnormality.

Kinesics Body language (facial expressions, gestures, postures).

Kinesthesis Sensations from nerve endings in the muscles, joints, and tendons that are stimulated by bodily movements and tensions.

Kinesthetic method A remedial reading method in which children trace the form of a known word before writing it from memory.

Labeling Assigning a name for a category of exceptionality to a child; used to identify children who are eligible for special education services.

Language impairment A condition in which a child's primary language is significantly below what would be expected for that person's chronological age.

Laterality Awareness of the two sides of the body and the ability to identify left and right. Often used to mean preferential use of one side of the body.

Learned helplessness The belief that nothing one does can prevent negative things from happening.

Least-restrictive environment The educational setting in which a child with special needs can learn that is as close as possible to the regular classroom.

Lens The elastic biconvex body that focuses light on the retina of the eye.

Life space interview A careful interview with a student, directly following a crisis situation or event, in which the student discusses the event with the teacher and generates alternative solutions to the problem.

Low vision A condition in which one has difficulty performing visual tasks even with glasses but has significant usable vision.

Mainstreaming The process of bringing exceptional children into daily contact with nonexceptional children in an educational setting; the placement of exceptional children in the regular education program whenever possible.

Malleus The largest and outermost of the three small bones in the middle ear that carry sound to the inner ear.

Manual method A method of educating deaf students that uses sign language and finger spelling.

Mediation The ability to apply past experience to the current situation.

Medical model A view of exceptionality that implies a physical condition or disease within the patient.

Memory disorder The inability to remember what has been seen, heard, or experienced.

Meningitis Inflammation of the meninges (the membranes covering the brain and spinal cord), sometimes affecting vision, hearing, and/or intelligence.

Metacognition An awareness of one's own system of thinking or the ability to devise one's own strategies for learning.

Modeling Imitating the behavior of others.

Morphology The structure of words and the way affixes are added to words to change meaning or to add information.

Muscular dystrophy One of the more common primary diseases of muscle. It is characterized by weakness and atrophy of the skeletal muscles with increasing disability and deformity as the disease progresses.

Myelomeningocele A spinal cord deformity that results in paralysis and loss of sensation beyond the point of damage.

Myopia Nearsightedness.

Neurologic Pertaining to the normal and abnormal functions of the nervous system.

Nondiscriminatory evaluation A full individual examination appropriate to a student's cultural and linguistic background.

Normalization The creation of as normal as possible a learning and social environment for the exceptional person.

Nystagmus Quick, jerky movement of the eyeballs, resulting in marked visual inefficiency.

Obturator Any organic structure (e.g., the soft palate) or prosthetic device that closes or stops an opening in the body.

Operant conditioning A technique of behavior modification that works by controlling the stimulus that follows a response.

Oral-aural method An approach to teaching deaf students that uses residual hearing through amplified sound, speech reading, and speech to develop communication skills.

Otitis media An infection or inflammation of the middle ear.

Perceptual-motor disorders Difficulties in responding to the meaning of pictures or numbers or to understand what they are.

Pharynx That part of the throat that leads from the mouth and nose to the larynx.

Phenylketonuria (PKU) A single-gene defect that can produce severe retardation because of the body's inability to break down phenylalanine, which when accumulated at high levels in the blood results in severe damage to the developing brain.

Phonation The production of speech sounds.

Phonology The sound system of a language; the way sounds are combined into meaningful sequences.

Polygenic inherited characteristics Human traits controlled by the action of many genes operating together.

Positive reinforcement The application of a positive stimulus (reward) immediately following a response.

Postlingual After spontaneous speech and language have developed.

Postnatal After birth.

Pragmatics The understanding of how language is used in communication and the ability to understand implied meaning.

Prelingual Before speech and language have developed.

Prenatal Before birth.

Prevalence The number of people in a given category in a population group during a specified interval of time.

Process-task training A remediation strategy in which the child is taught to use a particular process to accomplish a task. Also known as *aptitude-task interaction.*

Program evaluation Determining the effectiveness of a special program through tests and observation.

Proprioception The sensation in the muscles, tendons, and joints resulting from internal stimuli, which gives information concerning the position and movement of the body and its members.

Proxemics The use of space for communication (distance from people, spatial arrangements, territories belonging to a person).

Psychodynamic strategy A treatment approach designed to help children become aware of their own needs, desires, and fears.

Psychopathology The study of the causes and nature of mental disease.

Psychotropic drug A medication used primarily for its behavioral effects; used with children particularly for its influence on attention and hyperactivity.

Punishment The withdrawal of a positive stimulus immediately following a response.

Pupil The central opening of the eye through which light enters.

Reinforcement A procedure to strengthen a response by the administration of immediate rewards (positive reinforcement).

Reinforcement menu A variety of rewards that a child may select as part of a behavior modification program.

Resonance The vibrating quality of a sound.

Resource room Any instructional setting to which an exceptional child comes for specific periods of time, usually on a regularly scheduled basis.

Respite care A program that provides child care services for a handicapped youngster while parents take time for themselves.

Response The activity of an organism or an organ, or the inhibition of a previous activity, resulting from stimulation.

Retina The light-sensitive innermost layer of tissue at the back of the eyeball.

Retinopathy of prematurity (also called **retrolental fibroplasia**) A disease of the retina in which a mass of scar tissue forms in back of the lens of the eye. Both eyes are usually affected, and it occurs chiefly in infants born prematurely who received excessive oxygen.

Retrolental fibroplasia See *retinopathy of prematurity.*

Rh incompatibility When a mother who is Rh-negative carries an Rh-positive child, the mother's system can develop antibodies that can cause deafness and other serious consequences for the fetus unless the condition is identified and treated.

Rochester method A method of teaching deaf students that combines the oral method and finger spelling.

Rubella German measles, which in the first three months of pregnancy can cause visual impairment, hearing impairment, mental retardation, and birth defects in the fetus.

Screening Procedure for quickly and economically finding high-risk children who may need a more thorough examination.

Self-contained special class A separate class in which a special education teacher assumes primary responsibility for the educational program of handicapped students.

Semantics The meaning of language; the relationships of individual words, groups of words, and sentences.

Sensorimotor Referring to an act whose nature is primarily dependent on the combined or integrated functioning of sense organs and motor mechanisms.

Sensorineural hearing loss A defect of the inner ear or the auditory nerve in transmitting impulses to the brain.

Sensory compensation The theory that if one sense avenue is deficient, other senses are automatically strengthened. This theory is not supported by research.

Skill A complex behavior requiring the acquisition of a number of subordinate behaviors.

Snellen Chart A chart, consisting of rows of letters in graduated sizes, that is used to determine visual acuity, or ability to see clearly at a specified distance. A variation used with younger children and people who do not know the letter names consists of capital *E*s pointing in different directions.

Socialized aggression A deviant behavior pattern displayed by children who are hostile, aggressive, and have few guilt feelings but who are socialized within their group, usually a gang.

Social learning approach A curriculum designed to develop critical thinking and independent action on the part of mildly retarded individuals by building lesson experiences around psychological, physical, and social needs.

Social perception disability The inability to identify and recognize the meaning and significance of the behavior of others; insensitivity to peers and social situations; lack of empathy.

Sound blending Ability to synthesize the separate parts of a word and produce an integrated whole.

Spasticity A condition marked by excessively tense muscles that resist flexion and extension, slow jerky movements, and a "scissors" gait; a type of cerebral palsy.

Speech disorder Speech that is so different from the speech of other people that it is conspicuous, unintelligible, or very unpleasant.

Speech-language pathologist A trained professional who provides supervision and administration, diagnosis, consultation, and direct services for children who have communication disorders.

Stapes A small stirrup-shaped bone, the innermost of a chain of three bones in the middle ear transmitting sound to the inner ear.

Stereotypic behaviors Rhythmic repetitive behaviors like body rocking and head banging.

Stimulus The physical, chemical, biological, or social event that acts on the individual.

Strabismus Crossed eyes caused by lack of coordination of the muscles that control the movement of the eyeball in the socket.

Student acceleration Passing students through the educational system as quickly as possible; generally achieved through early school admission, skipping grades, telescoping grades, advanced placement, or early college admission.

Syntax That part of the grammar system that deals with the arrangement of word forms to show their mutual relations in a sentence.

Synthesis Process of putting together to form a whole.

Tactile (tactual) Having to do with the sense of touch.

Task analysis A method that breaks down complex tasks into simpler component parts, teaches each of the components separately, and then teaches them together. A procedure under which a child receives positive reinforcement for each step or part of the total task as it is completed.

Task training A remediation strategy that emphasizes the sequencing and simplification of the task to be learned, using task analysis, and teaching one skill at a time.

Taxonomy The science of classification of objects or events into natural or related groups based on some factor common to each.

Time out The physical removal of a child from a reinforcing situation for a period of time, usually immediately following an unwanted response.

Token reinforcement A behavior modification technique using marks or poker chips that can be exchanged for more-tangible rewards.

Total communication method A method of teaching deaf students that combines finger spelling, signs, speech reading, speech, and auditory amplification. Also called *simultaneous* or *combined method.*

Trauma Any experience that inflicts serious damage on the organism. It may be a psychological as well as a physiological insult.

Ultimate functioning The degree to which severely handicapped people are able to take a productive part in a variety of community situations appropriate to their chronological age.

Verbalisms Words not verified by concrete experience.

Visual acuity The ability to see details clearly or identify forms at a specified distance.

Visual-auditory-kinesthetic (VAK) method A phonic system for the remediation of reading disabilities.

Visual discrimination The ability to discriminate between two pictures or objects.

Visual sequential memory The ability to remember a sequence of figures or letters.

Zero reject principle The principle that all children with handicaps are to be provided a free and appropriate public education and that local school systems cannot decide not to provide needed services.

REFERENCES

Abeson, A., & Zettel, J. (1977). The end of the quiet revolution: The Education for All Handicapped Children Act of 1975. *Exceptional Children, 44*, 114–128.

Abroms, K., & Bennett, J. (1980). Current genetic demographic findings in Down's syndrome. How are they presented in college textbooks on exceptionality? *Mental Retardation, 18*, 101–107.

Adelman, H., & Comfers, B. (1977). Stimulant drugs and learning problems. *Journal of Special Education, 11*(4), 377–415.

Adler, M. (1967). Reported incidence of giftedness among ethnic groups. *Exceptional Children, 34*, 101–105.

Alley, G., & Deshler, D. (1979). *Teaching the learning disabled adolescent: Strategies and methods.* Denver: Love.

Altshuler, K. (1975). Identifying and programming for the emotionally handicapped deaf child. In D. Naiman (Ed.), *Needs of emotionally disturbed hearing impaired children.* New York: New York University School of Education.

Altshuler, K., & Baroff, G. (1963). Educational background and vocational adjustment. In J. Rainer, K. Altshuler, & F. Kallman (Eds.), *Family and mental health problems in a deaf population.* New York: New York State Psychiatric Institute.

American Foundation for the Blind. (1983). *Facts about blindness and visual impairment.* New York: American Foundation for the Blind.

Anderson, E., Dunlea, A., & Kekalis, L. (1984). Blind children's language: Resolving some differences. *Journal of Child Language, 11*(3), 645–664.

Arbitman-Smith, R., Haywood, J., & Bransford, J. (1984). Assessing cognitive change. In P. Brooks, R. Sperber, & C. McCauley (Eds.), *Learning and cognition in the mentally retarded* (pp. 433–472). Hillsdale, NJ: Lawrence Erlbaum.

Ashcroft, S. (1984). Research on multimedia access to microcomputers for visually impaired youth. *Education of the Visually Handicapped, 15*(4), 108–118.

Astin, H. (1974). Sex differences in mathematical and scientific precocity. In J. Stanley, D. Keating, & L. Fox (Eds.), *Mathematical talent: Discovery, description, and development.* Baltimore: Johns Hopkins University Press.

Axelrod, S. (1971). Token reinforcement programs in special classes. *Exceptional Children, 37*, 371–379.

Bailey, D., & Harbin, G. (1980). Nondiscriminatory evaluation. *Exceptional Children, 47*, 590–596.

Baker, L., Cantwell, D., & Mattison, R. (1980). Behavior problems in children with pure speech disorders and in children with combined speech and language disorders. *Journal of Abnormal Child Psychology, 8,* 245–256.

Baller, W., Charles, O., & Miller, E. (1966). Mid-life attainment of the mentally retarded: A longitudinal study. *Genetic Psychology Monographs, 75,* 235–239.

Balthazar, E., & Stevens, H. (1975). *The emotionally disturbed, mentally retarded.* Englewood Cliffs, NJ: Prentice-Hall.

Bandura, A. (1977). *Characteristics of children's behavior disorders.* Columbus, OH: Charles E. Merrill.

Bangs, T. (1968). *Language and learning disorders of the pre-academic child with curriculum guide.* New York: Appleton-Century-Crofts.

Bank-Mikkelsen, N. (1969). A metropolitan area in Denmark: Copenhagen. In R. Kugel & W. Wolfensberger (Eds.), *Changing patterns in residential services for the mentally retarded.* Washington, DC: President's Committee on Mental Retardation.

Barkley, R. (1979). Using stimulant drugs in the classroom. *School Psychology Digest, 8,* 412–425.

Barraga, N. (1983). *Visual handicaps and learning* (Rev. ed.). Austin, TX: Exceptional Resources.

Barsch, R. (1965). *A movigenic curriculum.* Madison: Wisconsin State Department of Public Instruction.

Barsch, R. (1967). *Achieving perceptual motor efficiency: A space-oriented approach to learning.* Seattle: Special Child Publications.

Bateman, B. (1967). Visually handicapped children. In N. Haring & R. Schiefelbusch (Eds.), *Methods in special education.* New York: McGraw-Hill.

Baumeister, A., & Brooks, P. (1981). Cognitive deficits in mental retardation. In J. Kauffman & D. Hallahan (Eds.), *Handbook of special education.* Englewood Cliffs, NJ: Prentice-Hall.

Baumeister, A., & Butterfield, E. (1970). *Residential facilities for the mentally retarded.* Chicago: Aldine.

Begab, M. (1981). Frontiers of knowledge in mental retardation. In P. Mittler (Ed.), *Frontiers of knowledge in mental retardation: Vol. 2. Biomedical aspects.* Baltimore: University Park Press.

Behrmann, M. (1984). *Handbook of microcomputers in special education.* San Diego, CA: College-Hill Press, Inc.

Bell, R. (1979). Parent, child and reciprocal influences. *American Psychologist, 34,* 830–931.

Bellugi, V., & Klima, E. (1972). The roots of language in the sign talk of the deaf. *Psychology Today, 6,* 61–76.

Bellugi, V., Klima, E., & Siple, P. (1974). Remembering in signs. *Cognition, 3,* 93–125.

Benbow, C., & Stanley, J. (Eds.). (1983). *Academic precocity.* Baltimore: Johns Hopkins University Press.

Berkson, G. (1983). Repetitive stereotyped behaviors. *American Journal of Mental Deficiency, 88*(3), 239–246.

Berla, E. (1981). Tactile scanning and memory for a spatial display by blind students. *Journal of Special Education, 15,* 341–350.

Bernal, E. (1979). The education of the culturally different gifted. In A. Passow (Ed.), *The gifted and the talented: Their education and development* (Seventy-eighth Yearbook of the National Society for the Study of Education, Part 1). Chicago: The University of Chicago Press.

Berres, F. (1967). *The effect of varying amounts of motoric involvement on the learning of nonsense dissyllables by male culturally disadvantaged retarded readers.* Unpublished doctoral dissertation, University of California, Los Angeles.

Birelson, P. (1980). The validity of depressive disorder in childhood and the development of self-rating scale: A research report. *Journal of Child Psychology and Psychiatry, 22,* 73–88.

Bitter, G. (1984). Hardware and software selection and evaluation. *Computers in the Schools, 1,* 13–28.

Blacher, J., & Myers, C. (1983). A review of attachment formation and disorder of handicapped children. *American Journal of Mental Deficiency, 87*(4), 359–371.

Blackwell, P., Engen, E., Fischgrund, J., & Zarcadoolis, C. (1978). *Sentences and other systems.* Washington, DC: Alexander Graham Bell Association.

Bley, N., & Thornton, C. (1981). *Teaching mathematics to the learning disabled.* Rockville, MD: Aspen.

Bliss, J., & Moore, M. (1974). The Optacon reading system. *Education of the Visually Handicapped, 6,* 98–102.

Block, J., & Block, J. (1980). The role of ego-control and ego-resiliency in the organization of behavior. In W. Collins (Ed.), *Minnesota symposia on child psychology* (Vol. 13). New York: Erlbaum.

Bloodstein, O. (1979). *Speech pathology: An introduction.* Boston: Houghton Mifflin.

Bloom, B. (Ed.). (1956). *Taxonomy of educational objectives: The classification of educational goals.* New York: McKay.

Bloom, B. (1974). Time and learning. *American Psychologist, 29,* 682–683.

Bloom, B. (1982). The role of gifts and markers in the development of talent. *Exceptional Children, 48,* 510–522.

Bloom, L., & Lahey, M. (1978). *Language development and language disorders.* New York: Wiley.

Bower, E. (1960). *Early identification of emotionally handicapped children in school.* Springfield, IL: Charles C. Thomas.

Brackett, D. (1981). Assessment: Adaptations, interpretations, and implications. In M. Ross & L. Nober (Eds.), *Special education in transition: Educating hard of hearing children.* Reston, VA: Council for Exceptional Children.

Bradley, L., & Bryant, D. (1979). Independence of reading and spelling in backward and normal readers. *Developmental Medicine and Child Neurology, 21,* 504–514.

Brady, M., & Dickson, P. (1983). Microcomputer communication game for hearing-impaired students. *American Annals of the Deaf, 128,* 835–841.

Brasel, K., & Quigley, S. (1977). The influence of certain language and communication environments in early childhood on the development of language in deaf individuals. *Journal of Speech and Hearing Research, 20,* 95–107.

Brickey, M., Brauning, L., & Campbell, K. (1982). Vocational histories of sheltered workshop employees placed in projects with industry and competitive jobs. *Mental Retardation, 20,* 52–57.

Brickey, M., & Campbell, K. (1981). Fast food employment for moderately and mildly mentally retarded adults: The McDonald's project. *Mental Retardation, 19,* 113–116.

Brinker, R. (1985). Curricula without recipes: A challenge to teachers and a promise to severely mentally retarded students. In D. Bricker & J. Filler (Eds.), *Severe mental retardation: From theory to practice.* Reston, VA: Council for Exceptional Children.

Bronfenbrenner, U. (1979). Content of child rearing: Problems and prospects. *American Psychologist, 34,* 844-850.

Brown, L., Branston, M., Hamre-Nietupski, S., Johnson, F., Wilcox, B., & Gruenewald, L. (1978). A strategy for developing chronological age-appropriate and functional curricular content for severely handicapped adolescents and young adults. *The Journal of Special Education, 13,* 81–90.

Brown, L., Branston-McClean, M., Baumgart, D., Vincent, L., Falvey, M., & Schroeder, J. (1979). Utilizing the characteristics of current and subsequent least restrictive environments in the development of curricular content for severely handicapped students. *AAESPH Review, 4,* 407–424.

Brown, L., Nietupski, J., & Hamre-Nietupski, S. (1976). Criterion of ultimate functioning. In M. Thomas (Ed.), *Hey, don't forget about me.* Reston, VA: Council for Exceptional Children.

Brown, N. (1982). Computer-assisted management of educational objectives. *Exceptional Children, 49,* 151–153.

Brutten, M., Richardson, S., & Mangel, C. (1973). *Something's wrong with my child.* New York: Harcourt Brace Jovanovich.

Bryan, D., & Herjanic, B. (1980). Depression and suicide among adolescents and young adults with selective handicapping conditions. *Exceptional Education Quarterly, 1*(2), 57–65.

Bryan, T. (1978). Social relationships and verbal interactions of learning disabled children. *Journal of Learning Disabilities, 11,* 107–115.

Bryan, T., Pearl, R., Donahue, M., Bryan, J., & Pflaum, S. (1983). The Chicago Institute for the Study of Learning Disabilities, research in learning disabilities: Summary of the institutes. *Exceptional Education Quarterly, 4*(1), 1-22.

Budoff, M., & Gottlieb, J. (1976). Special class students mainstreamed: A study of an aptitude (learning potential) X treatment interaction. *American Journal of Mental Deficiency, 81,* 11.

Burke, J. (1978). *Connections.* Boston: Little, Brown.

Bush, W., & Giles, M. (1969). *Aids to psycholinguistic teaching.* Columbus, OH: Charles E. Merrill.

Butler-Por, N. (1982). Giftedness across cultures. In B. Shore, F. Gagne, S. Larivee, R. Tali, & R. Tremblay (Eds.), *Face to face with giftedness* (pp. 250-270). New York: Trillium.

Bzoch, K., & Williams, W. (1979). Introducing rationale, principles, and related basic embryology and anatomy. In K. Bzoch (Ed.), *Communicative disorders related to cleft lip and palate* (2nd ed.). Boston: Little, Brown.

Cain, L. (1976). Parent groups: Their role in a better life for the handicapped. *Exceptional Children, 42,* 432–437.

Callahan, C. (1978). *Developing creativity in the gifted and talented.* Reston, VA: Council for Exceptional Children.

Calvert, D., & Silverman, R. (1975). *Speech and deafness.* Washington, DC: Alexander Graham Bell Association.

Camp, B., & Bash, M. (1981). *Think aloud: Increasing social and cognitive skills: A problem solving program for children.* Champaign, Il: Research Press.

Carman, G., & Kosberg, B. (1981). Educational technology research: Computer technology and the education of emotionally handicapped children. *Educational Technology, 22,* 26–30.

Casserly, P. (1979). Helping able young women take math and science seriously in school. In N. Colangelo & R. Zaffrann (Eds.), *New voices in counseling the gifted.* Dubuque, IA: Kendall/Hunt.

Cawley, J., Fitzmaurice, A., Goodstein, H., Lepore, A., Sedlack, R., & Althouse, V. (1976b). *Project math (level 1).* Tulsa: Educational Development.

Cawley, J., Fitzmaurice, A., Goodstein, H., Lepore, A., Sedlack, R., & Althouse, V. (1976b). *Project math (level 2).* Tulsa: Educational Development.

Cawley, J., & Goodstein, H. (1972). *A developmental program of quantitative behavior for handicapped children* (Research report to Bureau of Education for the Handicapped). Washington, DC: U.S. Office of Education.

Cawley, J., & Vitello, S. (1972). A model for arithmetic programming for handicapped children. *Exceptional Children, 39* (October), 101–110.

Chalfant, J., & Scheffelin, M. (1969). *Central processing dysfunctions in children. A review of research.* Washington, DC: U.S. Department of Health, Education, and Welfare.

Channing, A. (1932). *Employment of mentally deficient boys and girls* (Department of Labor, Bureau Publication No. 210). Washington, DC: U.S. Government Printing Office.

Charles, D. (1953). Ability and accomplishment of persons earlier judged mentally deficient. *Genetic Psychology Monographs, 47,* 3–71.

Charles, L., Schain, R., & Zelnicker, T. (1981). Optimal dosages of methylphenidate for improving the learning and behavior of hyperactive children. *Developmental and Behavioral Pediatrics, 2,* 78–81.

Chaston, M. (1983). School nurses' learning experiences related to providing services to mainstreamed orthopedically impaired children. *Journal of School Health, 53,* 621–623.

Chess, S., & Thomas, A. (1984). *Origins and evolution of behavior disorders.* New York: Brunner/Mazel.

Childs, R. (1979). A drastic change in curriculum for the educable mentally retarded child. *Mental Retardation, 17,* 299–301.

Civelli, E. (1983). Verbalism in young children. *Journal of Visual Impairment and Blindness, 77*(3), 61–63.

Clarizio, H., & McCoy, G. (1983). *Behavior disorders in children* (3rd ed.). New York: Harper & Row.

Clark, E. (1973). What's in a word? In T. Moore (Ed.), *Cognitive development and the acquisition of language.* New York: Academic Press.

Clarke, B., & Ling, D. (1976). The effects of using cued speech: A follow-up study. *The Volta Review, 78,* 23–34.

Cohen-Sandler, R., Berman, A., & King, R. (1982). Life stress and symptomatology: Determinants of suicidal behavior in children. *Journal of Child Psychiatry, 21,* 178–186.

Colenbrander, A. (1977). Dimensions of visual performance. *Archives of American Academy of Ophthalmology, 83,* 332–337.

Comprehensive assessment and service (CASE) information system. (1976). Washington, DC: American Speech-Language-Hearing Association.

Conference of Executives of American Schools for the Deaf. (1976). *American Annals of the Deaf, 121,* 4.

Conner, F. (1983). Improving school instruction for learning disabled children: The Teachers College Institute. *Exceptional Education Quarterly, 4*(1), 23–44.

Conners, C., & Werry, J. (1979). Pharmacotherapy. In H. Quay & J. Werry (Eds.), *Psychopathological disorders of childhood* (2nd ed.). New York: Wiley.

Corn, A., & Martinez, I. (1978). *When you have a visually handicapped child in your classroom: Suggestions for teachers.* New York: American Foundation for the Blind.

Cornish, E. (1977). *The study of the future.* Washington, DC: World Future Society.

Cotzin, M., & Dallenbach, K. (1950). "Facial vision": The role of pitch and loudness in the perception of obstacles by the blind. *American Journal of Psychology, 63,* 485–515.

Craig, W., & Craig, H. (1980). Directory of services for the deaf. *American Annals of the Deaf, 125,* 179.

Crissey, M. (1975). Mental retardation: Past, present, and future. *American Psychologist, 30,* 800–808.

Crocker, A., & Nelson, R. (1983). Mental retardation. In M. Levine, W. Carey, A. Crocker, & R. Gross (Eds.), *Developmental-behavioral pediatrics* (pp. 756–769). Philadelphia: Saunders.

Cruickshank, W., Bentzen, F., Ratzeburg, F., & Tannhauser, M. (1961). *A teaching method for brain-injured and hyperactive children.* Syracuse: Syracuse University Press.

Cruickshank, W., & Hallahan, D. (1973). *Psychoeducational foundations of learning disabilities.* Englewood Cliffs, NJ: Prentice-Hall.

Cutsworth, T. (1951). *The blind in school and society* (2nd ed.). New York: American Foundation for the Blind.

Dantona, R. (1976). Services for deaf-blind children. *Exceptional Children, 43,* 172–174.

Davidson, J. (1969). *Using the Cuisenaire rods.* New Rochelle, NY: Cuisenaire of America.

Davis, S., & Frothingham, P. (1981). Computing at a new public high school for gifted students. In J. Nazzaro (Ed.), *Computer connections for gifted children and youth.* Reston, VA: Council for Exceptional Children.

Dearman, N., & Plisko, V. (1981). *The condition of education.* Washington, DC: National Center for Education Statistics.

DeFries, F., & Decker, S. (1981). Genetic aspects of reading disability. In P. Aaron & M. Halatesha (Eds.), *Neuropsychological and neuropsycholinguistic aspects of reading disabilities.* New York: Academic Press.

DeMagistris, R., & Imber, S. (1980). The effects of life space interviewing on academic and social performance of behaviorally disordered children. *Behavior Disorders, 6,* 12–25.

DeMott, R. (1972). Verbalism and affective meaning for blind, severely visually impaired, and normally sighted children. *New Outlook for the Blind, 66,* 1–25.

Dennis, W., & Dennis, M. (Eds.). (1976). *The intellectually gifted.* New York: Grune & Stratton.

Deshler, D., & Schumaker, J. (1983). Social skills of learning disabled adolescents: A review of characteristics and intervention. *Topics in Learning and Learning Disabilities, 3,* 15–32.

Deshler, D., Schumaker, J., & Lenz, B. (1984). Academic and cognitive intervention for LD adolescents, Part I. *Journal of Learning Disabilities, 17*(2), 108–117.

Dever, R., & Knapczyk, D. (1980). Screening for physical problems in classrooms for severely handicapped students. *The Journal of the Association for the Severely Handicapped, 5,* 194–204.

DeWeerd, J. (1983). Introduction. In D. Assael (Ed.), *1983–84 Handicapped children's early education program directory.* Chapel Hill, NC: The University of North Carolina at Chapel Hill, Technical Assistance Development System (TADS), Frank Porter Graham Child Development Center.

Dickman, I. (1975). *Sex education and family life for visually handicapped children and youth: A resource guide.* New York: American Foundation for the Blind.

Douglas, V. (1972). Stop, look, and listen: The problem of sustained attention and impulse control in hyperactive and normal children.

Canadian Journal of Behavioral Science, 4, 259–282.

Downs, M. (1980). The hearing of Down's individuals. *Seminars in Speech, Language, and Hearing, 1,* 25–28.

Dunivant, N. (1982). *The relationship between learning disabilities and juvenile delinquency.* (Executive Summary.) Williamsburg, VA: National Center for State Courts.

Dunn, L., & Smith, J. (1967). *Peabody language development kits.* Circle Pines, MN: American Guidance Service.

Dweck, C. (1975). The role of expectations and attributions in the alleviation of learned helplessness. *Journal of Personality and Social Psychology, 31,* 674–685.

Edgerton, R. (1967). *The cloak of competence.* Berkeley: University of California Press.

Edgerton, R. (Ed.). (1984). *Lives in progress: Mildly retarded adults in a large city* (AAMD Monograph No. 6). Washington, DC: American Association on Mental Deficiency.

Education for All Handicapped Children Act. (1975). Public Law 94–142. Ninety-fourth Congress, November 29.

Eisenson, J. (1971). The nature of defective speech. In W. Cruickshank (Ed.), *Psychology of exceptional children and youth* (3rd ed.). Englewood Cliffs, NJ: Prentice-Hall.

Eisenson, J. (1972). *Aphasia in children.* New York: Harper & Row.

Eisenson, J., & Ogilvie, M. (1977). *Speech correction in the schools* (4th ed.). New York: Macmillan.

Embry, L. (1980). Family support for handicapped preschool children at risk for abuse. In J. Gallagher (Ed.), *New directions for exceptional children* (Vol. 4). San Francisco: Jossey-Bass.

Englemann, S., & Bruner, E. (1975). *Distar: An instructional system.* Chicago: Science Research Associates.

Epilepsy Foundation of America. (1982). *Questions and answers about epilepsy.* Landover, MD: Author.

Fagen, S., Long, N., & Stevens, D. (1975). *Teaching children self-control: Preventing emotional and learning problems in the elementary school.* Columbus, OH: Charles E. Merrill.

Farber, B. (1976). Family adaptations to severely mentally retarded children. In M. Begab & S. Richardson (Eds.), *Mentally retarded in society.* Baltimore: University Park Press.

Farwell, R. (1976). Speech reading: A research review. *American Annals of the Deaf, 121,* 19–30.

Faye, E. (1976). *Clinical low vision.* Boston: Little, Brown.

Feagans, L., & McKinney, J. (1981). The pattern of exceptionality across domains in learning disabled children. *Journal of Applied Developmental Psychology, 1,* 313–328.

Federal Register. (1977, August 23). [42(163), 42478]. Washington, DC: U.S. Office of Education.

Federal Register. (1977, December 29). Procedures for evaluating specific learning disabilities [42(250), Section 121a.541]. Washington, DC: U.S. Office of Education.

Feingold, B. (1974, June). *Hyperkinesis and learning difficulties (H-LD) linked to the ingestion of artificial colors and flavors.* Paper presented at the annual meeting of the American Medical Association, Chicago.

Feldhusen, J., Thurston, J., & Benning, J. (1966). Sentence completion responses and classroom social behavior. *Personnel and Guidance Journal.*

Feldhusen, J., & Treffinger, D. (1977). *Teaching creative thinking and problem solving.* Dubuque, IA: Kendall/Hunt.

Feldman, D. (1979). The mysterious case of extreme giftedness. In A. Passow (Ed.), *The gifted and the talented: Their education and development* (Seventy-eighth Yearbook of the National Society for the Study of Education, Part 1). Chicago: The University of Chicago Press.

Fernald, G. (1943). *Remedial techniques in basic school subjects.* New York: McGraw-Hill.

Fernald, G., & Keller, H. (1921). The effect of kinesthetic factors in the development of word recognition in the case of non-readers. *Journal of Educational Research, 4*(December), 355–377.

Feuerstein, R., Rand, Y., Hoffman, M., & Miller, R. (1980). *Instrumental enrichment.* Baltimore: University Park Press.

Fewell, D., & Cone, J. (1983). Identification and placement of severely handicapped children. In M. Snell (Ed.), *Systematic instruction of the moderately and severely handicapped* (2nd ed.). Columbus, OH: Charles E. Merrill.

Forness, S., & Kavale, K. (1984). Education of the mentally retarded: A note on policy. *Education and Training of the Mentally Retarded, 19*(4), 239–245.

Fox, L. (1977). Sex differences: Implications for program planning for the academically gifted. In J. Stanley, W. George, & C. Solano (Eds.), *The gifted and the creative: A fifty year perspective.* Baltimore: Johns Hopkins University Press.

Fox, L. (1983). Gifted students with reading problems: An empirical study. In L. Fox, L. Brody, & D. Tobin (Eds.), *Learning disabled/gifted children: Identification and programming.* Baltimore: University Park Press.

Fox. L., Benbow, C., & Perkins, S. (1983). An accelerated mathematics program for girls: A longitudinal evaluation. In C. Benbow & J. Stanley (Eds.), *Academic precocity* (pp. 113–138). Baltimore: Johns Hopkins University Press.

Francis, R., & Rarick, L. (1960). *Motor characteristics of the mentally retarded* (Cooperative Research Monograph No. 1). Washington, DC: Department of Health, Education, and Welfare, U.S. Office of Education.

Frankenberg, W. (1977). Considerations for screening. In N. Ellis & L. Cross (Eds.), *Planning programs for early education for the handicapped.* New York: Walker and Company.

Frasier, M. (1979). Counseling the culturally diverse gifted. In N. Colangelo & R. Zaffrann (Eds.), *New voices in counseling the gifted* (pp. 304–311). Dubuque, IA: Kendall/Hunt.

Fredericks, H., & Staff of the Teaching Research Infant and Child Center. (1980). *The Teaching Research curriculum for the moderately and severely handicapped.* Springfield, IL: Charles C. Thomas.

Freeman, G. (1977). *Speech and language services and the classroom teacher.* Reston, VA: Council for Exceptional Children.

Frieze, C. (1963). *Linguistics and reading.* New York: Holt, Rinehart & Winston.

Frisina, R. (1974). *Report of the Committee to Redefine Deaf and Hard of Hearing for Educational Purposes.* Mimeo.

Frith, G., & Edwards, R. (1981). Misconceptions of regular classroom teachers about physically handicapped students. *Exceptional Children, 48,* 182–184.

Froomkin, J. (1972). *Estimates and projections of special target group populations in elementary and secondary schools* (Report prepared for the President's Commission on School Finance). Washington, DC: U.S. Government Printing Office.

Frostig, M., & Horne, D. (1964). *The Frostig program for the development of visual perception.* Chicago: Follett.

Furfey, P., & Harte, T. (1968). *Interaction of deaf and hearing in Baltimore City, Maryland.* Washington, DC: Catholic University of American.

Gaddes, W. (1985). *Learning disabilities and brain function: Neuropsychological approach* (2nd ed.). New York: Springer-Verlag.

Gadow, K. (1979). *Children on medication: A primer for school personnel.* Reston, VA: Council for Exceptional Children.

Galbraith, G. (1978). An interactive computer system for teaching language skills to deaf children. *American Annals of the Deaf, 123,* 706–711.

Gallagher, J. (1976). The sacred and profane uses of labeling. *Mental Retardation, 141*(6), 3–7.

Gallagher, J. (1981). Transforming research to policy in the field of language studies. In P. Mittler (Ed.), *Frontiers of knowledge in mental retardation: Vol. 1. Social, educational, and behavioral aspects.* Baltimore: University Park Press.

Gallagher, J. (1985). *Teaching the gifted child* (3rd ed.). Boston: Allyn & Bacon.

Gallagher, J., Aschner, M., & Jenne, W. (1967). *Productive thinking of gifted children in classroom interaction* [CEC Research Monograph Series B, No. B-5]. Reston, VA: Council for Exceptional Children.

Gallagher, J., & Bristol, M. (in press). Families of young handicapped children. *Research integration of selected issues in the education of handicapped children.* Pittsburgh, PA: University of Pittsburgh, Learning Research and Development Center.

Gallagher, J., Forsythe, P., Ringelheim, D., & Weintraub, F. (1975). Federal and state funding patterns for programs for the handicapped. In N. Hobbs (Ed.), *Issues in the classification of children* (Vol. 2). San Francisco: Jossey-Bass.

Gallagher, J., Weiss, P., Oglesby, K., & Thomas, T. (1983). *The status of gifted/talented education: United States survey needs, practices, and policies.* Los Angeles: National/State Leadership Training Institute on the Gifted and Talented.

Gallagher, J., & Wiegerink, R. (1976). Educational strategies for the autistic child. *Journal of Autism and Childhood Schizophrenia, 6,* 1.

Gannon, J. (1981). Deaf heritage: A narrative history of deaf America. Silver Spring, MD: National Association of the Deaf.

Gardner, J. (1978). *Morale.* New York: Norton.

Garvey, M. (1982). CAI as a supplement in a mainstreamed hearing-impaired program. *American Annals of the Deaf, 127,* 613-616.

Gearhart, B. (1976). *Teaching the learning disabled: A combined task-process approach.* St. Louis: Mosby.

Gearhart, B., & Weishahn, M. (1976). *The handicapped child in the regular classroom.* St. Louis: Mosby.

Gersten, J., Langner, T., Eisenberg, J., Simcha-Fagan, O., & McCarthy, E. (1976). Stability and change in types of behavioral disturbance of children and adolescents. *Journal of Abnormal Child Psychology, 4,* 111–127.

Getman, G. (1965). The visuo-motor complex in the acquisition of learning skills. In B. Straub & J. Hellmuth (Eds.), *Learning disorders* (Vol. 1). Seattle: Special Child Publications.

Getzels, J., & Jackson, P. (1962). *Creativity and intelligence: Exploration with gifted children.* New York: Wiley.

Gillespie, S., & Cooper, E. (1973). Prevalence of speech problems in junior and senior high schools. *Journal of Speech and Hearing Research, 16,* 739–743.

Gillingham, A., & Stillman, B. (1936). *Remedial work for reading, spelling, and penmanship.* New York: Hackett and Wilhelms.

Gillingham, A., & Stillman, B. (1965). *Remedial training for children with specific disability in reading, spelling, and penmanship* (5th ed.). Cambridge: Educators Publishing Service.

Glavin, J., & Annesley, F. (1971). Reading and arithmetic correlates of conduct-problem and withdrawn children. *Journal of Special Education, 5,* 213–219.

Glucksberg, S., Krauss, R., & Weisburg, R. (1966). Referential communication in nursery school children: Method and some preliminary findings. *Journal of Experimental Child Psychology, 3,* 333-342.

Goldin-Meadow, S., & Feldman, H. (1975). The creation of a communication system: A study of deaf children of hearing parents. *Sign Language Studies, 8,* 225–234.

Goldstein, H. (1974). *The social learning curriculum.* Columbus, OH: Charles E. Merrill.

Good, T., & Brophy, J. (1978). *Looking in classrooms.* New York: Harper & Row.

Gordon, H. (1983). The learning disabled are cognitively right. *Topics in Learning Disabilities, 3*(1), 29–39.

Gottesman, M. (1971, June). A comparative study of Piaget's developmental schema of sighted children with that of a group of blind children. *Child Development,* pp. 573–580.

Gottlieb, J., Rose, T., & Lessen, E. (1983). Mainstreaming. In K. Kernau, M. Begab, & R. Edgerton (Eds.), *Environments and behavior: The adaptation of mentally retarded persons* (pp. 195–212). Baltimore: University Park Press.

Gottlieb, J., Semmel, M., & Veldman, D. (1978). Correlates of social status among mainstreamed mentally retarded children. *Journal of Educational Psychology, 70,* 396–405.

Gowan, J., & Groth, N. (1972). The development of vocational choice in gifted children. In J. Gowan (Ed.), *The guidance and measurement of intelligence development and creativity.* Northridge, CA: San Fernando Valley State State College.

Gowan, J., Khatena, J., & Torrance, E. (1981). *Creativity: Its educational implications* (2nd ed.). Dubuque, IA: Kendall/Hunt.

Graef, J. (1983). Environmental toxins. In M. Levine, W. Carey, A. Crocker, & R. Cross (Eds.), *Developmental-behavioral pediatrics* (pp. 427–439). Philadelphia: Saunders.

Graubard, P. (1964). The extent of academic retardation in a residential treatment center. *Journal of Educational Research, 58,* 78–80.

Gray, S., Klaus, R., & Ramsey, B. (1981). Participants in the early training projects: 1962–77. In M. Begab, C. Haywood, & H. Garber (Eds.),

Psychosocial influences in retarded performance (Vol. 2). Baltimore: University Park Press.

Gresham, F. (1981). Social skills training with handicapped children: A review. *Review of Educational Research, 51*(1), 139–176.

Gersham, F. (1982). Misguided mainstreaming: The case for social skills training with handicapped children. *Exceptional Children, 48,* 422–433.

Grimes, L. (1981). Computers are for kids: Designing software programs to avoid problems of learning. *Teaching Exceptional Children, 14*(2), 49–53.

Grossman, H. (Ed.). (1983). *Manual on terminology and classification in mental retardation.* Washington, DC: American Association on Mental Deficiency.

Guess, D. (1980). Methods in communication instruction for severely handicapped persons. In W. Sailor, B. Wilcox, L. Brown (Eds.), *Methods of instruction for severely handicapped students* (pp. 105–225). Baltimore: Paul H. Brooks.

Guilford, J. (1967). *The nature of human intelligence.* New York: McGraw-Hill.

Gunzberg, H. (1974). The education of the mentally handicapped child. In A. Clarke & A. Clarke (Eds.), *Mental deficiency: The changing outlook.* London: Methuen.

Hall, C., & Porter, P. (1983). School intervention for the neuromuscularly handicapped child. *Journal of Pediatrics, 102,* 210–214.

Hallgren, B. (1950). Specific dyslexia (congenital word-blindness): A clinical and genetic study. *Acta Psychiatrica et Neurologica, 65,* 1–287.

Hammill, D., Leigh, L., McNutt, G., & Larsen, S. (1981). A new definition of learning disabilities. *Learning Disability Quarterly, 4*(Fall), 336–342.

Hardy, J. (1968). The whole child: A plea for a global approach to the child with auditory problems. In *Education of the deaf: The challenge and the charge.* Washington, DC: U.S. Government Printing Office.

Harness, B., Epstein, R., & Gordon, H. (1984). Cognitive profile of children referred to a clinic for reading disabilities. *Journal of Learning Disabilities, 17*(5), 346.

Harvey, D., & Greenway, A. (1984). The self-concept of physically handicapped children and their non-handicapped siblings: An empirical investigation. *Journal of Child Psychology and Psychiatry, 25,* 273–284.

Hatfield, E. (1975). Why are they blind? *Sight Saving Review,* Spring, 1–22.

Hatfield, E. (1979). Methods and standards for screening preschool children. *Sight Saving Review, 49*(2).

Hatlen, P., LeDuc, P., & Canter, P. (1975). The Blind Adolescent Life Skills Center. *New Outlook for the Blind, 69,* 109–115.

Havinghurst, R. (1972). *Developmental tasks and education* (3rd ed.). New York: David McKay.

Hayes, S. (1941). *Contributions to a psychology of blindness.* New York: American Foundation for the Blind.

Head, D. (1979). A comparison of self-concept scores for visually impaired adolescents in several class settings. *Education of the Visually Handicapped, 10,* 51–55.

Healey, W., & Karp-Nortman, D. (1975). *The hearing impaired, mentally retarded: Recommendations for action.* Washington, DC: American Speech and Hearing Association.

Heber, R. (1977, November). *Research on the prevention of socio-cultural retardation through early prevention.* Paper presented to the extraordinary session of the International Union for Child Welfare Advisory Group on Social Problems of Children and Youth, Ostend, Belgium.

Heber, R., & Garber, H. (1975). The Milwaukee Project: A study of the use of family intervention to prevent cultural-familial mental retardation. In B. Friedlander, G. Sterritt, & S. Kirk (Eds.), *Exceptional infant* (Vol. 1). New York: Brunner/Mazel.

Hechtman, L., & Weiss, G. (1985). Long-term outcome of hyperactive children. In S. Chess & A. Thomas (Eds.), *Annual progress in child psychiatry and child development—1984.* New York: Brunner/Mazel.

Hegge, T., Kirk, S., & Kirk, W. (1936). *Remedial reading drills.* Ann Arbor, MI: George Wahr.

Heinemann, A., & Shontz, F. (1984). Adjustment following disability: Representative case studies. *Rehabilitation Counseling Bulletin, 28*(1), 3–14.

Heller, K., Holtzman, W., & Messick, S. (Eds.).

(1982). *Placing children in special education: A strategy for equity.* Washington, DC: National Academy Press.

Henderson, E. (1981). *Learning to read and spell: The child's knowledge of words.* DeKalb: Northern Illinois University Press.

Hermann, K. (1959). *Reading disability: A medical study of word-blindness and related handicaps.* Springfield, IL: Charles C. Thomas.

Hetherington, E. (1979). Divorce: A child's perspective. *American Psychologist, 34,* 851–858.

Hetherington, E., & Martin, B. (1979). Family interaction. In H. Quay & J. Werry (Eds.), *Psychopathological disorders of childhood* (2nd ed.). New York: Wiley.

Heuftle, S., Rakow, S., & Welch, W. (1983). *Images of science.* Minneapolis: University of Minnesota, Minnesota Research and Evaluation Center.

Hewett, F. (1980). Behavioral ecology: A unifying strategy for the 80s. In R. Rutherford, A. Prieto, & J. McGlothlin (Eds.), *Severe behavior disorders of children and youth.* Phoenix: Arizona State University.

Heyes, A. (1984). The Sonic Pathfinder: A new electronic travel aid. *Journal of Visual Impairment and Blindness, 78*(May), 200–202.

Hicks, D. (1970). Comparison profiles of rubella and non-rubella deaf children. *American Annals of the Deaf, 115,* 65–74.

Hobbs, N. (1966). Helping disturbed children: Psychological and ecological strategies. *American Psychologist, 21,* 1105–1115.

Hobbs, N. (1970). Project Re-Ed: New ways of helping emotionally disturbed children. In Joint Commission on Mental Health of Children, *Crisis in child mental health: Challenge for the 1970's.* New York: Harper & Row.

Hobbs, N. (1979). *Helping disturbed children: Psychological and ecological strategies, II. Project Re-Ed, twenty years later.* Nashville: Vanderbilt University, Center for the Study of Families and Children.

Hollingworth, L. (1942). *Children above 180 IQ.* Yonkers, NY: World Book.

Holman, L., & Freedheim, D. (1958). Further studies on intelligence levels in cerebral palsied children. *American Journal of Physical Medicine, 37,* 90–97.

Hopkins, T., Bice, H., & Colton, K. (1954). *Evaluation and education of the cerebral palsied child.* Arlington, VA: International Council for Exceptional Children.

Horner, M. (1970). Femininity and successful achievement: A basic inconsistency. In J. Bardwick, E. Douvan, M. Horner, & D. Gutmann (Eds.), *Feminine personality and conflict* (pp. 45–76). Belmont, CA: Brooks/Cole.

Huff, R., & Franks, F. (1973). Educational materials development in primary mathmatics: Fractional parts of wholes. *Education of the Visually Handicapped, 5,* 46–54.

Hull, F., Mieike, P., Willeford, J., & Timmons, R. (1976). *National speech and hearing survey* (Project No. 50978, Bureau of Education for the Handicapped, U.S. Office of Education). Washington, DC: U.S. Government Printing Office.

Hulme, C. (1981). *Reading retardation and multisensory teaching.* London: Routledge & Kegan Paul.

Hummell, J., & Balcom, F. (1984). Microcomputers: Not just a place for practice. *Journal of Learning Disabilities, 17,* 432–434.

Hutter, J., & Farrell, F. (1983). Cancer in children. In J. Umbreit (Ed.), *Physical disabilities and health impairments: An introduction.* Columbus, OH: Charles E. Merrill.

Iran-Nejad, A., Ortony, A., & Rittenhouse, R. (1981). The comprehension of figurative uses of English by deaf children. *Journal of Speech and Hearing Research, 24,* 551–556.

Irwin, J. (1982). Human language and communication. In G. Shames & E. Wiig (Eds.), *Human communication disorders: An introduction.* Columbus, OH: Charles E. Merrill.

Jennings, H. (1951). Twice handicapped. *Occupational Psychology, 30,* 176–181.

Jensema, C. (1975). *The relationship between academic achievement and the demographic characteristics of hearing impaired children and youth.* Washington, DC: Gallaudet College, Office of Demographic Studies.

Johnson, D., & Myklebust, H. (1967). *Learning disabilities: Educational principles and practices.* New York: Grune & Stratton.

Johnson, G., & Kirk, S. (1950). Are mentally handicapped children segregated in the regular grades? *Exceptional Children, 17,* 65–68.

Johnson, R., & Johnson, D. (1981). Building friendships between handicapped and nonhandicapped students: Effects of cooperative individualistic instruction. *American Educational Research Journal, 18,* 415–423.

Jones, R. (1972). Labels and stigma in special education. *Exceptional Children, 38,* 553–564.

Jordan, I., Gustason, G., & Rosen, R. (1979). An update on communication trends in programs for the deaf. *American Annals of the Deaf, 124,* 350–357.

Juurmaa, J. (1970). On the accuracy of obstacle detection by the blind. *New Outlook for the Blind, 64,* 104–117.

Kaplan, L. (1971). *Mental health and human relations in education* (2nd ed.). New York: Harper & Row.

Karnes, M. (1982a). *Language development (ages 3 to 6 years)* (Rev. ed.). Springfield, MA: Milton Bradley.

Karnes, M. (1982b). *You and your small wonder (ages birth to 18 months).* Circle Pines, MN: American Guidance Service.

Karnes, M. (1982c). *You and your small wonder (ages 18–36 months).* Circle Pines, MN: American Guidance Service.

Karnes, M., Zehrbach, R., & Teska, J. (1974). The Karnes preschool program: Rational curricular offerings and follow-up data. In S. Ryan (Ed.), *A report on longitudinal evaluations of preschool programs* (Vol. 1) [DHEW Publication No. (OHD) 77–24]. Washington, DC: Office of Child Development.

Kauffman, J. (1977). *Characteristics of children's behavior disorders.* Columbus, OH: Charles E. Merrill.

Kavale, K., & Forness, S. (1983). Hyperactivity and diet treatment: A meta analysis of the Feingold Diet. *Journal of Learning Disabilities, 16*(June-July), 324–330.

Kavale, K., & Glass, G. (1982). The efficacy of special education interventions and practices: A compendium of meta-analysis findings. *Focus on Exceptional Children, 15*(4), 1–14.

Kavale, K., & Nye, C. (1984). The effectiveness of drug treatment for severe behavior disorders: A meta-analysis. *Behavior Disorders, 9*(2), 117–130.

Keating, D. (1974). The study of mathematically precocious youth. In J. Stanley, D. Keating, & L. Fox (Eds.), *Mathematical talent: Discovery, description, and development.* Baltimore: Johns Hopkins University Press.

Kelly, T., Bullock, L., & Dykes, M. (1977). Behavioral disorders: Teachers' perceptions. *Exceptional Children, 43,* 316–318.

Kemker, F., McConnell, F., Logan, S., & Green, B. (1979). A field study of children's hearing aids in a school environment. *Language, Speech, and Hearing Services in the Schools, 10,* 47–53.

Kennedy, R. (1948). *The social adjustment of morons in a Connecticut city.* Hartford: Social Service Department, Mansfield-Southbury Training Schools.

Keogh, B. (1977). Current issues in educational methods. In J. Millichap (Ed.), *Learning disabilities and related disorders.* Chicago: Yearbook Medical Publishers.

Kephart, J., Kephart, C., & Schwartz, G. (1974). A journey into the world of the blind child. *Exceptional Children, 40,* 421–429.

Kephart, N. (1964). Perceptual-motor aspects of learning disabilities. *Exceptional Children, 31,*(December), 201–206.

Kerr, M., & Nelson, C. (1983). *Strategies for managing behavior problems in the classroom.* Columbus, OH: Charles E. Merrill.

King, R., Jones, C., & Lasky, E. (1982). In retrospect: A fifteen year follow-up report of speech-language disordered children. *Language, Speech, and Hearing Services in the Schools, 13,* 24–36.

Kinsbourne, M. (1983). Models of learning disabilities. *Topics in Learning Disabilities, 3*(1), 1–13.

Kirchner, C. (1983). Statistical Brief No. 23. Special education for visually handicapped children: A critique of numbers and costs. *Journal of Visual Impairment and Blindness, 77*(1), 219–223.

Kirk, S. (1933). The influence of manual tracing on the learning of simple words in the case of subnormal boys. *Journal of Educational Psychology, 24*(October), 525–535.

Kirk, S. (1958). *The early education of the mentally retarded.* Urbana, IL: University of Illinois Press.

Kirk, S. (1964). *Research in education of the mentally retarded.* Urbana, IL: University of Illinois Press.

Kirk, S., & Chalfant, J. (1984). *Academic and developmental learning disabilities.* Denver: Love.

Kirk, S., & Kirk, W. (1971). *Psycholinguistic learning disabilities: Diagnosis and remediation.* Urbana, IL: University of Illinois Press.

Kirk, S., Kirk, W., & Minskoff, E. (1985). *The Phonic Remedial Reading Program.* San Rafael, CA: Academic Therapy Publications.

Kirk, S., Kliebhan, J., & Lerner, J. (1978). *Teaching reading to slow and disabled learners.* Boston: Houghton Mifflin.

Kirk, S., & Lord, F. (1974). *Exceptional children: Resources and perspectives.* Boston: Houghton Mifflin.

Kirk, S., McCarthy, J., & Kirk, W. (1968). *The Illinois Test of Psycholinguistic Abilities* (Rev. ed.). Urbana, IL: University of Illinois Press.

Kirkman, H. (1982). Projections of a rebound in frequency of mental retardation from phenylketonuria. *Applied Research in Mental Retardation, 3,* 319–328.

Knoblock, P. (1973). Open education for emotionally disturbed children. *Exceptional Children, 39,* 358–365.

Kolstoe, O. (1976). *Teaching educably mentally retarded children* (2nd ed.). New York: Holt, Rinehart & Winston.

Kramer, M. (1975). Diagnosis and classification in epidemiological and health services research. In N. Hobbs (Ed.), *Issues in the classification of children* (Vol. 1). San Francisco: Jossey-Bass.

Kretschmer, R., & Kretschmer, L. (1978). *Language development and intervention with the hearing impaired.* Baltimore: University Park Press.

Kroth, R., Whelan, R., & Stables, J. (1972). Teacher applications of behavior principles in home and classroom environments. In E. Meyen, G. Vergason, & R. Whelan (Eds.), *Strategies for teaching exceptional children.* Denver: Love.

Krueger, M. (Ed.). (1978). *On being gifted.* New York: Walker.

Krupski, A. (1979). Are retarded children more distractible? Observational analysis of retarded and nonretarded children's classroom behavior. *American Journal of Mental Deficiency, 84,* 1–10.

Krutetskii, V. (1976). *The psychology of mathematical abilities in school children* (J. Teller, Trans.). Chicago: University of Chicago Press.

Kubler-Ross, E. (1969). *On death and dying.* New York: Macmillan.

Lambert, N., Windmiller, M., Cole, L., & Figueroa, R. (1975). Standardization of a public school version of the American Association on Mental Deficiency Adaptive Behavior Scale. *Mentgal Retardation, 13,* 3–7.

LaSasso, C. (1985). *The reading and language teaching practices of United States teachers of deaf students.* Paper presented at the Council on Education of the Deaf convention, St. Augustine, FL.

Laski, F. (1985). Judicial address of education for students with severe mental retardation: From access to school to state-of-the-art. In D. Bricker & J. Filler (Eds.), *Severe mental retardation: From theory to practice.* Reston, VA: Council for Exceptional Children.

Lazar, I., Darlington, R., Murray, H., Royce, J., & Snipper, A. (1982). Lasting effects of early education: A report from the Consortium for Longitudinal Studies. *Monographs of the Society for Research in Child Development, 47,* 1–151.

Lejeune, J., Gautier, M., & Turpin, R. (1959). Etudes des chromosomes somatiques de neuf enfants. *C.R. Academie Sci., 248,* 1721–1722.

Lerner, J. (1985). *Learning disabilities: Theories, diagnosis, and teaching strategies* (4th ed.). Boston: Houghton Mifflin.

Lerner, J., Mardel-Czudnowski, C., & Goldenberg, D. (1981). *Special education for the early childhood years.* Englewood Cliffs, NJ: Prentice-Hall.

Levine, M., Carey, W., Crocker, A., & Gross, R. (Eds.). (1983). *Developmental-behavioral pediatrics.* Philadelphia: Saunders.

Levitt, H., Pickett, J., & Houde, R. (1980). *Sensory aids for the hearing impaired.* New York: Institute for Electrical and Electronics Engineering Press.

Levy, H. (1983). Developmental dyslexia: A pediatrician's perspective. *Schumpert Medical Quarterly, 1,* 200–207.

Lichtenstein, E. (1980). *A proposal for the experimental investigation of recording strategies used by deaf readers during reading* comprehension. Urbana, IL: University of Illinois, Center for the Study of Reading.

Lilienfield, A. (1969). Epidemiology of mongolism. Baltimore: Johns Hopkins University Press.

Ling, D., & Clarke, B. (1975). Cued speech: An evaluative study. American Annals of the Deaf, 120, 480–488.

Livneh, H., & Evans, J. (1984). Adjusting to disability: Behavioral correlates and intervention strategies. Personnel and Guidance Journal, 62, 363–365.

Locke, J. (1978). Phenomic effects in the silent reading of hearing and deaf children. Cognition, 6, 175–187.

Lombardi, T., & Lombardi, E. (1977). ITPA: Clinical interpretation and remediation. Seattle: Special Child Publications.

Long, N., Morse, W., & Newman, R. (Eds.). (1980). Conflict in the classroom: The education of emotionally disturbed children (4th ed.). Belmont, CA: Wadsworth.

Lowenfeld, B. (Ed.). (1973). The visually handicapped child in school. New York: John Day.

Luick, A., Kirk, S., Agranowitz, A., & Busby, R. (1982). Profiles of children with severe oral language disorders. Journal of Speech and Hearing Disorders, 47(February), 88–92.

McAndrew, I. (1976). Children with a handicap and their families. Child Care, Health, and Development, 2, 213–237.

McCarthy, J., Lund, K., & Bos, C. (1983). Assessment of young children with special needs. Focus on exceptional children. Denver: Love.

McCarthy, J., Lund, K., Bos, C., Glatke, J., & Vaughn, S. (1985). Arizona Basic Assessment and Curriculum Utilization System for young handicapped children. Denver: Love.

Maccoby, E., & Masters, J. (1970). Attachment and dependency. In P. Mussen (Ed.), Carmichael manual of child psychology (Vol. 2). New York: Wiley.

McConnell, B. (1982). The Handicapple: A low cost braille printer. Creative Computer, 8(10), 186–188.

McDermott, L. (1981). The effect of duplicated and unduplicated child count on prevalence of speech-impaired children. Language, Speech, and Hearing Services in the Schools, 12, 115–119.

McDowell, R., Adamson, G., & Wood, F. (Eds.). (1982). Teaching emotionally disturbed children. Boston: Little, Brown.

McFall, R. (1976). Behavioral training: A skill-acquisition approach to clinical problems. Morristown, NJ: General Learning Press.

McGuire, D., & Ely, M. (1984). Childhood suicide. Child Welfare, 63(1).

MacKinnon, D. (1978). In search of human effectiveness. Buffalo: Creative Education Foundation.

Madden, N., & Slavin, R. (1983). Mainstreaming students with mild handicaps: Academic and social outcomes. Review of Educational Research, 53(4), 519–569.

Mahoney, A. (1980). Gifted delinquents: What do we know about them? Children and Youth Services Review, 2(3), 315–330.

Mahoney, G., & Weller, E. (1980). An ecological approach to language intervention. In D. Bricker (Ed.), Language intervention with children (Vol. 2). San Francisco: Jossey-Bass.

Maker, C. (1977). Providing programs for the gifted handicapped. Reston, VA: Council for Exceptional Children.

Malone, L., DeLucchi, L., & Thier, H. (1981). Science activities for the visually impaired: SAVI leadership trainer's manual. Berkeley, CA: Center for Multisensory Learning, University of California.

Mansfield, R., Busse, T., & Krepelka, E. (1978). The effectiveness of creativity training. Review of Educational Research, 48(4), 517–536.

Marion, P., & Iovacchini, E. (1983). Services for handicapped students in higher education: An analysis of national trends. Journal of College Student Personnel, 24, 131–138.

Marland, S. (1972). Education of the gifted and talented (Report to the Congress of the United States by the U.S. Commissioner of Education). Washington, DC: U.S. Government Printing Office.

Martin, G., & Hoben, M. (1977). Supporting visually impaired students in the mainstream. Reston, VA: Council for Exceptional Children.

Martinson, R. (1972). An analysis of problems and priorities: Advocate survey and statistics sources. In S. Marland (Ed.), *Education of the gifted and talented* (Report to the Congress of the United States by the U.S. Commissioner of Education). Washington, DC: U.S. Government Printing Office.

Mather, N. (1985a). The Bank Street Writer, Screenwriter II. In J. Hummell, N. Mather, & G. Senf (Eds.), *Microcomputers in the classroom: Courseware reviews.* New York: Professional Press.

Mather, N. (1985b). *The Fernald Kinesthetic Method revisited.* Unpublished manuscript, University of Arizona, Tucson.

Matson, J., & Barrett, R. (1982). *Psychopathology in the mentally retarded.* New York: Grune & Stratton.

Matsuda, M. (1984). A comparative analysis of blind and sighted children's communication skills. *Journal of Visual Impairment and Blindness, 78*(1), 1–4.

Matter, D., & Matter, R. (1984). Suicide among elementary school children: A serious concern for counselors. *Elementary School Guidance and Counseling, 18,* 260–267.

Mattes, J. (1983). The Feingold Diet: A current reappraisal. *Journal of Learning Disabilities, 16*(June-July), 319–323.

Mayer, W. (Ed.). (1975). *Planning curriculum development.* Boulder: Biological Sciences Curriculum Study.

Meadow, K. (1968). Early communication in relation to the deaf child's intellectual, social, and communicative functioning. *American Annals of the Deaf, 113,* 29–41.

Meadow, K. (1980). *Deafness and child development.* Berkeley: University of California Press.

Meichenbaum, D. (1979). *Cognitive behavior modification.* New York: Plenum.

Meichenbaum, D., & Goodman, J. (1971). Teaching impulsive children to talk to themselves: A means of developing self-control. *Journal of Abnormal Psychology, 77,* 115–126.

Meier, J. (1971). Prevalence and characteristics of learning disabilities found in second grade children. *Journal of Learning Disabilities, 4*(January), 6–19.

Meighan, T. (1971). *An investigation of the self-concept of blind and visually handicapped adolescents.* New York: American Foundation for the Blind.

Melcher, J. (1976). Law, litigation, and handi-

capped children. *Exceptional Children, 43,* 126–130.

Mellor, C. (1981). *Aids for the 80s.* New York: American Foundation for the Blind.

Mercer, J. (1975). Psychological assessment and the rights of children. In N. Hobbs (Ed.), *Issues in the classification of children* (Vol. 1). San Francisco: Jossey-Bass.

Mercer, J., & Lewis, J. (1978). *System of multicultural pluralistic assessment.* New York: Psychological Corporation.

Mercer, J., & Lewis, J. (1981). Using the system of multicultural pluralistic assessment to identify the gifted minority child. In I. Sato (Ed.), *Balancing the scale for the disadvantaged gifted* (pp. 59–66). Los Angeles: National/State Leadership Training Institute on the Gifted and Talented.

Millar, S. (1981). Crossmodal and intersensory perception and the blind. In R. Walk & H. Pick, Jr. (Eds.), *Intersensory perception and sensory integration.* New York: Plenum.

Minskoff, E. (1980a). Teaching approach for developing nonverbal communication skills in students with social perception deficits: Part 1. *Journal of Learning Disabilities, 13*(3), 118–123.

Minskoff E. (1980b). Teaching approach for developing nonverbal communication skills in students with social perception deficits: Part 2. Proxemic, vocalic, and artifactual clues. *Journal of Learning Disabilities, 13*(4), 203–208.

Minskoff, E., Wiseman, D., & Minskoff, J. (1975). *The MWM Program for developing language abilities.* Ridgefield, NJ: Educational Performance Associates.

Moerk, E. (1977). Processes and products of imitation: Additional evidence that imitation is progressive. *Journal of Psycholinguistic Research, 6.*

Montour, K. (1977). William James Sidis, the broken twig. *American Psychologist, 32,* 265–279.

Montour, K. (1978). Charles Louis Fefferman: Youngest American full professor. In J. Stanley, W. George, & C. Solano (Eds.), *Educational programs and intellectual prodigies* (pp. 59–60). Baltimore: Johns Hopkins University Press.

Moore, P. (1982). Voice disorders. In G. Shames & E. Wiig (Eds.), *Human communication dis-*

orders: An introduction. Columbus, OH: Charles E. Merrill.

Moores, D. (1969). The vocational status of young deaf adults in New England. Journal of Rehabilitation of the Deaf, 2, 29–41.

Moores, D. (1982). Educating the deaf: Psychology, principles, and practices (2nd ed.). Boston: Houghton Mifflin.

Moores, D., Fisher, S., & Harlow, M. (1974). Post secondary programs for the deaf: Monograph VI. Summary and guidelines (Research Report No. 80). Minneapolis: University of Minnesota, Research, Development and Demonstration Center in Education of Handicapped Children.

Moores, D., Weiss, K., & Goodwin, M. (1978). Early education programs for hearing impaired children: Major findings. American Annals of the Deaf, 123, 925–936.

Moores, J., & Moores, D. (1980). Language training with the young deaf child. In D. Bricker (Ed.), Language intervention with children (Vol. 2). San Francisco: Jossey-Bass.

Morse, W. (1976). The helping teacher/crisis teacher concept. Focus on Exceptional Children, 8, 1–11.

Murray, C. (1976). The link between learning disabilities and juvenile delinquency. (Prepared for the National Institute for Juvenile Justice and Delinquency Prevention.) Washington, DC: Office of Juvenile Justice and Delinquency Prevention, Law Enforcement Assistance Administration.

Myers, P., & Hammill, D. (1976). Methods for learning disorders (2nd ed.). New York: Wiley.

Myklebust, H., & Boshes, B. (1969). Minimal brain damage in children (Final Report, Contract 108-65-142, Neurological and Sensory Disease Control Program). Washington, DC: Department of Health, Education, and Welfare.

Napier, G. (1973). Special subject adjustments and skills. In B. Lowenfeld (Ed.), The visually handicapped child in school. New York: John Day.

Naremore, R., & Dever, R. (1975). Language performance of educable mentally retarded and normal children at five age levels. Journal of Speech and Hearing Research, 18, 82–95.

National Advisory Committee on the Handicapped. (1968). First annual report, Subcommittee on Education of the Committee on Labor and Public Welfare, U.S. Senate. Washington, DC: U.S. Government Printing Office.

National Advisory Committee on the Handicapped. (1976). The unfinished revolution: Education for the handicapped, 1976 annual report. Washington, DC: U.S. Government Printing Office.

National Institute of Neurological Disease and Stroke. (1969). Human communication and its disorders: An overview. Bethesda, MD: Public Health Service.

Nave, G., Browning, P., & Carter, J. (1983). Computer technology for the handicapped in special education and rehabilitation: A resource guide. Eugene, OR: International Council for Computers in Education.

Neal, W. (1976). Speech pathology services in the secondary schools. Language, Speech, and Hearing Services in the Schools, 7, 6–16.

Newman, R., & Simpson, R. (1983). Modifying the least restrictive environment to facilitate the integration of severely emotionally disturbed children and youth. Behavior Disorders, 8(2), 102–112.

Nichols, R. (1965). The National Merit twin study. In S. Vanderberg (Ed.), Methods and goals in human behavior genetics. New York: Academic Press.

Nilson, H., & Schneiderman, C. (1983). Classroom program for the prevention of vocal abuse and hoarseness in elementary school children. Language, Speech, and Hearing Services in Schools, 14, 121–126.

Nitowsky, H. (1979, Winter). Alcohol syndrome. Rose F. Kennedy Center Notes. Bronx: Albert Einstein College of Medicine.

Nolan, C., & Morris, J. (1969). Learning of blind students through active and passive listening. Exceptional Children, 36(November), 173–187.

Northern, J., & Downs, M. (1978). Hearing in Children (2nd ed.). Baltimore: Williams & Wilkins.

Oden, M. (1968). The fulfillment of promise: Forty-year follow-up of the Terman gifted group. Genetic Psychology Monographs, 77, 3–93.

O'Leary, K. (1980). Pills or skills for hyperactive children? Journal of Applied Behavior Analysis, 13, 191–204.

Olsen, J. (1982). Do I have to go to recess? Electronic supplements in language instruction. *American Annals of the Deaf, 127,* 602–606.

Orlansky, M. (1980). *Encouraging successful mainstreaming of the visually impaired child* (MAVIS Sourcebook No. 2). Boulder: Social Science Education Consortium.

Osborne, A. (1984). How the courts have interpreted the related services mandate. *Exceptional Children, 51,* 249–252.

Ottenbacher, K. (1982). Occupational therapy and special education: Some issues and concerns related to Public Law 94-142. *American Journal of Occupational Therapy, 36,* 81–84.

Otto, W., McMenemy, R., & Smith, R. (1973). *Corrective and remedial teaching* (2nd ed.). Boston: Houghton Mifflin.

Pannbacker M. (1984). Classification systems of voice disorders: A review of the literature. *Language, Speech, and Hearing Services in Schools, 15,* 169–174.

Papert, S. (1980). *Mindstorms.* New York: Basic Books.

Papert, S. (1981). Computers and computer cultures. In J. Nazzaro (Ed.), *Computer connections for gifted children and youth.* Reston, VA: Council for Exceptional Children.

Parnes, S. (1966). *Programming creative behavior.* Buffalo: State University of New York.

Parnes, S., Noller, R., & Biondi, A. (1977). *Guide to creative action.* New York: Scribner's.

Passow, A. (1982). Differentiated curricula for the gifted/talented. *Proceedings of the First National Conference on Curricula for the Gifted/Talented* (pp. 1–20). Los Angeles: National/State Leadership Training Institute on the Gifted and Talented.

Paton, S., & Kandel, D. (1978). Psychological factors and adolescent illicit drug use: Ethnicity and sex differences. *Adolescence, 13,* 186–200.

Patrick, G. (1984). Comparison of novice and veteran wheelchair athletes' self-concept and acceptance of disability. *Rehabilitation Counseling Bulletin, 27,* 186–188.

Patterson, G. (1980). Mothers: The unacknowledged victims. *Monographs of the Society for Research in Child Development, 45* (Serial No. 186).

Paul, J. (in press). Where are we in the education of emotionally disturbed children? *Behavior Disorders.*

Paul, J., & Epanchin, B. (Eds.). (1982). *Emotional disturbance in children.* Columbus, OH: Charles E. Merrill.

Perkins, H. (1965). Classroom behavior and underachievement. *American Educational Research Journal, 2,* 1–12.

Perkins, W. (1980). Disorders of speech flow. In T. Hixon, L. Shriberg, & J. Saxman (Eds.), *Introduction to communication disorders.* Englewood Cliffs, NJ: Prentice-Hall.

Phillips, J. (1975). An exploration of employer attitudes concerning employment opportunities for deaf people. *Journal of Rehabilitation of the Deaf, 9,* 1–9.

Piaget, J. (1970). Piaget's theory. In P. Mussen (Ed.), *Carmichael's manual of child psychology.* New York: Wiley.

Piers, E., & Harris, D. (1969). *The Piers-Harris Self Concept Scale.* Nashville: Counselor Recordings and Tests.

Pittman, J. (1963, November 1). *The future of the teaching of reading.* Paper presented at the educational conference of the Educational Records Bureau, New York.

Plomin, R., DeFries, J., & McClearn, G. (1980). *Behavioral genetics: A primer.* San Francisco: Freeman.

Polloway, E., Epstein, M., & Cullinan, D. (1985). Prevalence of behavior problems among educable mentally retarded students. *Education and Training of the Mentally Retarded, 20,* 3–13.

Pommer, L., Mark, D., & Hayden, D. (1983). Using computer software to instruct learning-disabled students. *Learning Disabilities, 2*(8), 99–110.

Premack, D. (1959). Toward empirical behavior laws: I. Positive reinforcement. *Psychological Review, 66,* 291–333.

Project Upgrade. (1973). *Model regulations for school language, speech, and hearing programs and services.* Washington, DC: American Speech and Hearing Association.

Propp, G., Nugent, G., & Stone, C. (1980). Videodisc update. *American Annals of the Deaf, 125,* 679–684.

Quay, H. (1979). Classification. In H. Quay & J. Werry (Eds.), *Psychopathological disorders of childhood* (2nd ed.). New York: Wiley.

Quay, H., & Werry, J. (Eds.). (1979). *Psychopathological disorders of childhood* (2nd ed.). New York: Wiley.

Quigley, S. (1969). *The effect of small hearing losses on the educational performance of hard of hearing students.* Springfield, IL: Office of the Superintendent of Public Instruction.

Quigley, S. (1969). *The influence of finger spelling on the development of language, communication, and educative achievement in deaf children.* Urbana, IL: Institute for Research on Exceptional Children.

Quigley, S. (1976). *Syntactic structures in the language of deaf children.* Urbana, IL: University of Illinois.

Quigley, S. (1978). *Test of syntactic abilities.* Beaverton, OR: DorMac.

Quigley, S., Jenne, W., & Phillips, S. (1968). *Deaf students in colleges and universities.* Washington, DC: Alexander Graham Bell Association.

Quigley, S., & King, C. (1981). *Reading milestones.* Beaverton, OR: DorMac.

Quigley, S., & Kretschmer, R. (1982). *The education of deaf children.* Baltimore: University Park Press.

Quigley, S., Wilbur, R., Power, D., Montanelli, D., & Steinkamp, M. (1976). *Syntactic structures in the language of deaf children.* Urbana, IL: University of Illinois, Institute for Child Behavior and Development.

Rahimi, M. (1981). Intelligent prosthetic devices. *Computer, 14*(1), 19–23.

Ramey, C., & Haskins, R. (1981). The modification of intelligence through early experience. *Intelligence, 5,* 5–19.

Ranier, J. (1975). Severely emotionally handicapped hearing impaired children. In D. Naiman (Ed.), *Needs of emotionally disturbed hearing impaired children.* New York: New York University School of Education.

Rarick, L., & Widdop, J. (1970). The physical fitness and motor performance of educable mentally retarded children. *Exceptional Children, 36,* 509–520.

Rawlings, B., & Jensema, C. (1977). *Two studies of the families of hearing impaired children* (Office of Demographic Studies, Series R, No. 5). Washington, DC: Gallaudet College.

Rawlings, B., & Karchmer, M. (1983). *College and career: Programs for deaf students.* Washington, DC, and Rochester, NY: Gallaudet College and the National Technical Institute for the Deaf.

Redl, F. (1959). *Mental hygiene and teaching.* New York: Harcourt Brace Jovanovich.

Reid, D., & Hresko, W. (1981). *A cognitive approach to learning disabilities.* New York: McGraw-Hill.

Reiss, S., Levitan, G., & Szyszko, J. (1982). Emotional disturbance and mental retardation: Diagnostic overshadowing. *American Journal of Mental Deficiency, 86*(6), 567–574.

Renzulli, J., Smith, L., & Reis, S. (1982). Curriculum compacting: An essential strategy for working with gifted students. *Elementary School Journal, 82,* 185–194.

Renzulli, J., Smith, L., White, A., Callahan, C., & Hartman, R. (1976). *Scales for rating the behavioral characteristics of superior students.* Mansfield Center, CT: Creative Learning Press.

Rhodes, W. (1967). The disturbing child: A problem of ecological management. *Exceptional Children, 33*(March), 449–455.

Richard, T., Triandes, H., & Patterson, C. (1963). Indices of employer prejudice toward disabled applicants. *Journal of Applied Psychology, 47,* 52–55.

Richardson, S. (1981). Family characteristics associated with mild mental retardation. In M. Begab, C. Haywood, & H. Garber (Eds.), *Psychosocial influences in retarded performance* (Vol. 2). Baltimore: University Park Press.

Richardson, S., Koller, H., & Katz, M. (1985). Relationship of upbringing to later behavior disturbance of mildly mentally retarded young people. *American Journal of Mental Deficiency, 90*(1), 1–8.

Rie, H., & Rie, E. (Eds.). (1980). *Handbook of minimal brain dysfunctions: A critical view.* New York: Wiley.

Ries, P. (1973). *Reported causes of hearing loss for hearing impaired students: 1970–1971* (Annual Survey of Hearing Impaired Children and Youth, Series D. No. 12). Washington, DC: Gallaudet College.

Riesz, E. (1984). *First years of a Down's syn-*

drome child. Iowa City: University of Iowa Publications.

Rimland, B. (1983). The Feingold Diet: An assessment of the reviews by Mattes, by Kavale & Forness. *Journal of Learning Disabilities, 16*(June-July), 331–334.

Rittenhouse, R. (1979). Conservation interrogation of deaf and normal hearing children. *Journal of Childhood Communication Disorders, 3*(2), 120–127.

Rittenhouse, R. (1981). The effect of instructional manipulation on the cognitive performance of normal-hearing and deaf children. *Journal of Childhood Communication Diseases, 5*(1), 14–22.

Rittenhouse, R. (1985). *TTY language in deaf adolescents: A research report.* Normal, IL: Illinois State University.

Rittenhouse, R., Morreau, L., & Iran-Nejad, A. (1982). Metaphor and conservation in deaf and hard of hearing children. *American Annals of the Deaf, 126*(4), 450–453.

Robins, L. (1966). *Deviant children grow up.* Baltimore: Williams & Wilkins.

Robinson, N. (1978). Mild mental retardation: Does it exist in the People's Republic of China? *Mental Retardation, 16,* 295–298.

Rose, S., & Waldron, M. (1984). Microcomputer use in programs for hearing-impaired children: A national survey. *American Annals of the Deaf, 129,* 338–342.

Rosenbaum, M., & Palmon, N. (1984). Helplessness and resourcefulness in coping with epilepsy. *Journal of Consulting and Clinical Psychology, 52,* 244–253.

Rosenthal, D. (1970). *Genetic theory and abnormal behavior.* New York: McGraw-Hill.

Rosenthal, J. (1970). A preliminary psycholinguistic study of children with learning disabilities. *Journal of Learning Disabilities, 3,* 391–395.

Ross, A. (1976). *Psychological aspects of learning disabilities and reading disorders.* New York: McGraw-Hill.

Rubin, R., & Balow, B. (1978). Prevalence of teacher identified behavior problems: A longitudinal study. *Exceptional Children, 45,* 102–111.

Rusch, F., Chadsey-Rusch, J., White, D., & Gifford, J. (1985). Programs for severely mentally retarded adults: Perspectives and methodology.

In D. Bricker & J. Filler (Eds.), *Severe mental retardation: From theory to practice* (pp. 118–140). Reston, VA: Council for Exceptional Children.

Rutter, M. (1978). Diagnosis and definition. In M. Rutter & E. Schopler (Eds.), *Autism: A reappraisal of concepts and treatment.* New York: Plenum.

Rutter, M., Tizard, J., Yule, P., Graham, P., & Whitmore, K. (1974). Isle of Wight studies. *Psychological Medicine, 6,* 313–332.

Ryan, W. (1971). *Blaming the victim.* New York: Random House.

Sabatino, D., Miller, P., & Schmidt, C. (1981). Can intelligence be altered through cognitive training? *Journal of Special Education, 15,* 125–144.

Sailor, W., & Guess, D. (1983). *Severely handicapped students: An instructional design.* Boston: Houghton Mifflin.

Salvia, J., Schultz, E., & Chapin, N. (1974). Reliability of Bower Scale for screening of children with emotional handicaps. *Exceptional Children, 41,* 117–118.

Samuels, J. (1981). Individual differences in the interaction of vision and proprioception. In R. Walk & H. Pick (Eds.), *Intersensory perception and integration.* New York: Plenum.

Scheerenberger, R. (1978). Public residential services for the retarded. In N. Ellis (Ed.), *International review of research in mental retardation* (Vol. 9). New York: Academic Press.

Scheerenberger, R. (1983). A study of public residential facilities. *Mental Retardation, 14,* 32–35.

Schein, J., & Delk, R. (1974). *The deaf population of the United States.* Silver Spring, MD: National Association of the Deaf.

Schiefelbusch, R. (1980). Synthesis of trends of language intervention. In D. Bricker (Ed.), *New directions for exceptional children: Vol. 2, Language intervention with children.* San Francisco: Jossey-Bass.

Schiffman, G., Tobin, D., & Buchanan, B. (1982). Microcomputer instruction for the learning disabled. *Journal of Learning Disabilities, 15,* 557–559.

Schloss, P. (1983). Classroom-based intervention for students exhibiting depressive reactions. *Behavioral Disorders, 8,* 231–236.

Schonell, F. (1956). *Educating spastic children.* Edinburgh: Oliver and Boyd.

Schopler, E., & Bristol, M: (1980). *Autistic children in public school* (ERIC Exceptional Children Education Report, Division TEACCH). Chapel Hill, NC: University of North Carolina.

Schumaker, J., Deshler, D., Alley, G., & Warner, M. (1983). Toward the development of an intervention model for learning disabled adolescents. The University of Kansas Institute. *Exceptional Education Quarterly, 4*(1), 45–74.

Schumaker, J., Hazel, J., Sherman, J., & Sheldon, J. (1982). Social skill performance of learning disabled, non learning disabled, and delinquent adolescents. *Learning Disability Quarterly, 5,* 388–397.

Schwartz, J. (1979). Childhood origins of psychopathology. *American Psychologist, 34,* 879–885.

Sears, P., & Barbee, A. (1977). Career and life satisfaction among Terman's gifted women. In J. Stanley, W. George, & C. Solano (Eds.), *The gifted and the creative: A fifty-year perspective.* Baltimore: Johns Hopkins University Press.

Seeley, K. (1984). Giftedness and juvenile delinquency in perspective. *Journal for the Education of the Gifted, 8,* 59–72.

Semel, E., & Wiig, E. (1975). Comprehension of syntactic structures and critical verbal elements by children with learning disabilities. *Journal of Learning Disabilities, 8,* 53–58.

Senatore, V., Matson, J., & Kazdin, A. (1985). An inventory to assess psychopathology of mentally retarded adults. *American Journal of Mental Deficiency, 89*(5), 459–466.

Shade, B. (1978). Socio-psychological characteristics of achieving black children. In R. Clasen & B. Robinson (Eds.), *Simple gifts* (pp. 229–242). Madison, WI: University of Wisconsin Extension.

Shames, G., & Florence, C. (1982). Disorders of fluency. In G. Shames & E. Wiig (Eds.), *Human communication disorders: An introduction.* Columbus, OH: Charles E. Merrill.

Shaw, M., & McCuen, J. (1960). The onset of academic underachievement in bright children. *Journal of Education Psychology, 51,* 103–108.

Shepard, L., & Smith, M. (1983). An evaluation of the identification of learning disabled students in Colorado. *Learning Disability Quarterly, 6*(2), 115–127.

Shinn-Strieker, T. (1984). Trained communication assistants in the public schools. *Language, Speech, and Hearing Services in Schools, 15,* 169–174.

Shriver, E. (1980). *Facts on Special Olympics.* Washington, DC: Special Olympics.

Skeels, H. (1966). *Adult status of children from contrasting early life experiences* (Monographs of the Society for Research in Child Development, No. 31). Chicago: University of Chicago Press.

Skeels, H., & Dye, H. (1939). A study of the effects of differential stimulation on mentally retarded children. *Proceedings of the American Association on Mental Deficiency, 44,* 114–136.

Skinner, B. (1953). *Science and human behavior.* New York: Free Press.

Slingerland, B. (1974). *A multisensory approach to language arts for specific language disabled children.* Cambridge: Educators Publishing Service.

Smith, B., & Barresi, J. (1982). Interpreting the rights of exceptional citizens through judicial action. In J. Ballard, B. Ramirez, & F. Weintraub (Eds.), *Special education in America: Its legal and governmental foundations* (pp. 65–81). Reston, VA: Council for Exceptional Children.

Smith, D. (1981). *Teaching the learning disabled.* Englewood Cliffs, NJ: Prentice-Hall.

Smith, D., & Lovitt, T. (1982). *The Computational Arithmetic Program (CAP).* Austin, TX: Pro-Ed.

Smith, J. (1962). Effects of a group language development program upon psycholinguistic abilities of educable mentally retarded children. *Special Education Monograph.* Nashville, TN: George Peabody College for Teachers.

Snell, M. (Ed.). (1983). *Systematic instruction of the moderately and severely handicapped* (2nd ed.). Columbus, OH: Charles E. Merrill.

Sontag, E., Smith, J., & Sailor, W. (1977). The severely/profoundly handicapped: Who are they? Where are we? *Journal of Special Education, 11*(1), 5–11.

Spalding, R., & Spalding, W. (1957). *The writing road to reading.* New York: Morrow.

Sprague, R., & Sleator, E. (1976). Drugs and dosages: Implications for learning disabilities. In R. Knights & K. Bakker (Eds.), *The neuropsychology of learning disorders.* Baltimore: University Park Press.

Spungin, S. (Ed.). (1981). *Guidelines for public school programs serving visually handicapped children* (2nd ed.). New York: American Foundation for the Blind.

Stanley, J. (1979). Identifying and nurturing the intellectually gifted. In W. George, S. Cohn, & J. Stanley (Eds.), *Educating the gifted: Acceleration and enrichment.* Baltimore: Johns Hopkins University Press.

Stauffer, D. (1984). Catheterization: A health procedure schools must be prepared to provide. *Journal of School Health, 54,* 37–38.

Stephen, E., & Hawks, G. (1974). Cerebral palsy and mental subnormality. In A. Clarke & D. Clarke (Eds.), *Mental deficiency: The changing outlook* (3rd ed.). New York: Free Press.

Stephens, T., Blackhurst, A., & Magliocca, L. (1982). *Teaching mainstreamed students.* New York: Wiley.

Stepp, R. (1982). Microcomputers: Macro-learning for the hearing impaired. *American Annals of the Deaf, 127,* 472–475.

Stern, C. (1965). *Structural arithmetic.* Boston: Houghton Mifflin.

Sternberg, R. (Ed.). (1982). *Handbook of human intelligence.* Cambridge: Cambridge University Press.

Stokoe, W. (1960). *Sign language structure: An outline of the visual communication systems of the American deaf* (Studies in Linguistics, Occasional Paper No. 6, Reissued). Washington DC: Gallaudet Research Institute.

Strain, P., & Shores, R. (1982). A reply to "Misguided Mainstreaming." *Exceptional Children, 50,* 271–273.

Strauss, A., & Lehtinen, L. (1947). *Psychopathology and education of the brain-injured child.* New York: Grune & Stratton.

Streissguth, A., Landesman-Dwyer, S., Martin, J., & Smith, D. (1980). Teratogenic effects of alcohol in humans and animals. *Science, 209,* 353–361.

Sullivan, M. (1968). *Programmed math.* New York: McGraw-Hill.

Sykes, K. (1984). *The curriculum for children with visual handicaps.* Unpublished manuscript, University of Arizona, Tucson.

Tawney, J., & Sniezek, K. (1985). Educational programs for severely mentally retarded elementary-age children: Progress, problems, and suggestions. In D. Bricker & J. Filler (Eds.), *Severe mental retardation: From theory to practice* (pp. 76–96). Reston, VA: Council for Exceptional Children.

Taylor, J. (1980). Public school speech-language certification standards: Are they standard? *ASHA, 22,* 159–165.

Tepin, S. (1983). Development of blind infants and children with retrolenal fibroplasia: Implications for physicians. *Pediatrics, 71,* 6–12.

Terman, L. (Ed.). (1925-1959). *Genetic studies of genius* (Vols. 1-5). Stanford, CA: Stanford University Press.

Terman, L., & Oden, M. (1947). *Genetic studies of genius* (Vol. 4). Stanford, CA: Stanford University Press.

Thomas, A., & Chess, S. (1977). *Temperament and development.* New York: Brunner/Mazel.

Thompson, J. (1985). *Information and referral services for parents of the disabled.* Chapel Hill, NC: The University of North Carolina at Chapel Hill: Bush Institute for Child and Family Policy.

Thurber, D. (1970). *D'Nealian manuscript: A continuous stroke print* (ERIC Document Reproduction Service No. ED 169 533). Redwood City, CA: San Mateo County.

Thurber, D. (1984). *D'Nealian manuscript: A continuous stroke approach to handwriting.* Novato, CA: Academic Therapy Publications.

Tillman, M. (1967). The performance of blind and sighted children on the Wechsler Intelligence Scale for Children. *International Journal for the Education of the Blind, 16,* 65–74, 106–172.

Tillman, M., & Osborne, R. (1969). The performance of blind and sighted children on the Wechsler Intelligence Scale for Children: Interaction effects. *Education of the Visually Handicapped, 1,* 1–4.

Torgesen, J. (1979). What should we do with psychological processes? *Journal of Learning Disabilities, 12*(October), 514–521.

Torgesen, J. (1980). Conceptional and educational implications of the use of efficient task strategies by learning disabled children. *Journal of Learning Disabilities, 13,* 364–371.

Torgesen, J. (1982). The learning disabled child

as an inactive learner. *Topics in Learning and Learning Disabilities, 2,* 45–52.

Torgesen, J., & Young, K. (1983). Priorities for the use of microcomputers with learning disabled children. *Journal of Learning Disabilities, 16,* 234–237.

Torrence, E. (1976). *Torrance Tests of Creative Thinking* (Rev. ed.). Princeton: Personnel Press.

Treffinger, D. (1980). *Encouraging creative learning for the gifted and talented.* Los Angeles: National/State Leadership Training Institute on the Gifted and Talented.

Trybus, R. (1985). *Today's hearing impaired children and youth: A demographic and academic profile.* Washington, DC: Gallaudet Research Institute.

Trybus, R., & Karchmer, M. (1977). School achievement scores of hearing impaired children: National data on achievement status and growth patterns. *American Annals of the Deaf, 122,* 35–53.

Turnbull, A., Strickland, B., & Brantley, J. (1982). *Developing and implementing individualized education programs* (2nd ed.). Columbus, OH: Charles E. Merrill.

Turnbull, H. (1979). Law and the mentally retarded citizen: American responses to the declarations of rights of the United Nations and International League of Societies for the Mentally Handicapped—Where we have been, are, and are headed. *Syracuse Law Review, 30,* 1093–1143.

Turnbull, H., & Turnbull, A. (Eds.). (1985). *Parents speak out: Then and now* (2nd ed.). Columbus, OH: Charles E. Merrill.

Tuttle, D. (1984). *Self-esteem and adjusting with blindness.* Springfield, IL: Charles C. Thomas.

Ullmann, C. (1952). *Identification of maladjusted school children* (Public Health Monograph No. 7). Washington, DC: U.S. Government Printing Office.

Umsted, R. (1972). Improving braille reading. *New Outlook for the Blind, 66,* 169–177.

U.S. Department of Education. (1984). *Sixth annual report to Congress on the implementation of Public Law 94-142: The Education for All Handicapped Children Act.* Washington, DC: U.S. Government Printing Office.

U.S. Department of Education. (1985, September 3). *New services for deaf-blind children program* (SEP Memorandum). Washington, DC: U.S. Government Printing Office.

U.S. Department of Education. (1985). *Seventh annual report to Congress on the implementation of the Education of the Handicapped Act.* Washington, DC: U.S. Government Printing Office.

U.S. Department of Education. (1985). *Seventh annual report to Congress, to assure free appropriate public education of all handicapped children.* Washington, DC: U.S. Government Printing Office.

U.S. Office of Education. (1974). Definition of severely handicapped children. *Code of federal regulations,* Title 45, Section 121.2. Washington, DC: Bureau of Education for the Handicapped.

Vanderheiden, G. (1982). Computers can play a dual role for disabled individuals. *BYTE, 7,* 136–162.

Van Hattum, R. (1974). Communication problems associated with cleft palate. In S. Dickinson (Ed.), *Communication disorders, remedial principles and practices.* Glenview, IL: Scott, Foresman.

Van Riper, C. (1978). *Speech correction: Principles and methods* (6th ed.). Englewood Cliffs, NJ: Prentice-Hall.

Vernon, M. (1968). Current etiological factors in deafness. *American Annals of the Deaf, 113,* 106–115.

Vernon, M. (1969). *Multiply handicapped deaf children* (Research Monograph). Reston, VA: Council for Exceptional Children.

Vernon, M., & Hicks, D. (1980). Relationship of rubella, herpes simplex, cytomegalovirus, and certain other viral disabilities. *American Annals of the Deaf, 125*(5), 529–534.

Vernon, M., & Koh, S. (1971). Effects of oral preschool compared to early manual communication on education and communication in deaf children. *American Annals of the Deaf, 116,* 569–574.

Vincent, J., Salisbury, C., Walter, G., Brown, P., Gruenewald, L., & Powers, M. (1980). Program evaluation and curriculum development in early childhood/special education: Criteria of the next environment. In W. Sailor, B. Wilcox, & L. Brown (Eds.), *Methods of instruction for severely handicapped students* (pp. 303–328). Baltimore: Paul H. Brooks.

Walberg, H. (1969). Physics, femininity, and creativity. *Developmental Psychology, 1,* 47–54.

Walberg, H. (1984). Improving the productivity of America's schools. *Educational Leadership, 41*(8), 19–30.

Waller, M., Sollod, R., Souder, E., & Kunicki, E. (1983). Psychological assessment of speech and language-disordered children. *Language, Speech, and Hearing Services in Schools, 14,* 92–97.

Wardell, K. (1980). Environmental modifications. In R. Welsh & B. Blasch (Eds.), *Foundations of orientation and mobility* (pp. 427–524). New York: American Foundation for the Blind.

Warren, D. (1984). *Blindness and early childhood development.* New York: American Foundation for the Blind.

Warren, F. (1985). Call them liars who would say all is well. In H. Turnbull & A. Turnbull (Eds.), *Parents speak out: Then and now* (2nd ed.). Columbus, OH: Charles E. Merrill.

Webster, L., & Brutten, G. (1974). The modification of stuttering and associated behaviors. In S. Dickinson (Ed.), *Communication disorders, remedial principles and practices.* Glenview, IL: Scott, Foresman.

Weinstein, L. (1974). *Evaluation of a program for re-educating disturbed children: A follow-up comparison with untreated children.* Washington, DC: U.S. Department of Health, Education, and Welfare. (Available through ERIC Document Reproduction Service, ED-141-966.)

Weiss, P. (1978). *Attitudes towards gifted education.* Unpublished doctoral dissertation, University of North Carolina, Chapel Hill.

Werner, E. (1979). *Cross-cultural child development.* Monterey, CA: Brooks/Cole.

Werry, J. (1968). The diagnosis, etiology, and treatment of hyperactivity in children. In J. Hellmuth (Ed.), *Learning disorders* (Vol. 3). Seattle: Special Child Publications.

Wetzel, R., & Hoschouer, R. (1984). *Residential teaching communities: Program development and staff training for developmentally disabled persons.* Glenview, IL: Scott, Foresman.

White, R. (1963). Ego and reality in psychoanalytic theory. *Psychological Issues, 3*(11).

Whitmore, J. (1980). *Giftedness, conflict, and underachievement.* Boston: Allyn & Bacon.

Whitmore, J. (1981). Gifted children with handicapping conditions: A new frontier. *Exceptional Children, 48*(2), 106–114.

Whorf, B. (1956). *Language, thought, and reality.* Cambridge: MIT Press.

Wicks-Nelson, R., & Israel, A. (1984). *Behavior disorders of childhood.* Englewood Cliffs, NJ: Prentice-Hall.

Wiederholt, J., Hammill, D., & Brown, V. (1978). *The resource teacher: A guide to effective practices.* Boston: Allyn & Bacon.

Wier, C. (1980). Habilitation and rehabilitation of the hearing impaired. In T. Hixon & J. Saxon (Eds.), *Introduction to communication disorders.* Englewood Cliffs, NJ: Prentice-Hall.

Wiig, E. (1982). Language disabilities in the school-age child. In G. Shames & E. Wiig (Eds.), *Human communication disorders: An introduction.* Columbus, OH: Charles E. Merrill.

Wiig, E., & Semel, E. (1980). *Language assessment and intervention for the learning disabled.* Columbus, OH: Charles E. Merrill.

Williams, K., & Baeker, M. (1983). Use of small group with chronically ill children. *Journal of School Health, 53,* 205–208.

Williams, W., Vogelsberg, R., & Schutz, R. (1985). Programs for secondary-age handicapped youth. In D. Bricker & J. Filler (Eds.), *Severe mental retardation: From theory to practice* (pp. 97–118). Reston, VA: Council for Exceptional Children.

Winitz, H. (1979). Articulation disorders: From prescription to description. In E. Meyen (Ed.), *Basic readings in the study of exceptional children and youth.* Denver: Love.

Wittrock, M. (1978). Education and the cognitive processes of the brain. In J. Chall & A. Mirsky (Eds.), *Education and the brain: The seventy-seventh yearbook of the National Society of the Study of Education (Part II)* (pp. 61-102). Chicago: University of Chicago Press.

Wolf, M. (1981). Talent search and development in the visual and performing arts. In I. Sato (Ed.), *Balancing the scale for the disadvan-*

taged gifted (pp. 103-116). Los Angeles: National/State Leadership Training Institute on the Gifted and Talented.

Wolfensberger, W. (1972). *The principle of normalization in human services.* Toronto: National Institute on Mental Retardation.

Wong, B., & Jones, W. (1982). Increasing metacomprehension in learning disabled and normally achieving students through self-questioning training. *Learning Disability Quarterly, 5*(3), 228–240.

Wood, F. (1982). Defining disturbing, disordered, and disturbed behavior. In F. Wood & K. Laken (Eds.), *Disturbing, disordered, or disturbed?* Reston, VA: Council for Exceptional Children.

Wood, F., & Zabel, R. (1978). Making sense of reports on the incidence of behavior disorders/emotional disturbances in school-aged children. *Psychology in the Schools, 15*, 45–51.

Woodcock, R., Clark, C., & Davies, C. (1967). *The Peabody Rebus Reading Program.* Circle Pines, MN: American Guidance Service.

Woodward, J. (1982). *How you gonna get to heaven if you can't talk to Jesus.* Silver Spring, MD: T. J. Publishers.

Worlery, M., & Bailey, D. (1985). *Early childhood education of the handicapped: Review of the literature.* Charleston, W VA: West Virginia State Department of Education.

Yin, R., & White, L. (1984). *Microcomputer implementation in schools.* Washington, DC: Cosmos Corporation.

Yoder, D. (1980). Communication systems for nonspeech children. In D. Bricker (Ed.), *Language intervention with children: Vol. 2. New directions for exceptional children.* San Francisco: Jossey-Bass.

Zangwell, W. (1983). An evaluation of a parent training program. *Child and Family Behavior Therapy, 5*(4), 1–16.

Zemmol, C. (1977). A priority system of case load selection. *Language, Speech, and Hearing Services in the Schools, 8*, 85–98.

Zetlin, A., & Turner, J. (1985). Transition from adolescence to adulthood: Perspectives of mentally retarded individuals and their families. *American Journal of Mental Deficiency, 89*, 570–579.

Zigler, E., Balla, D., & Hodapp, R. (1984). On the definition and classification of mental retardation. *American Journal of Mental Deficiency, 89*, 215–230.

Author/Source Index

SUBJECT INDEX

AN INVITATION TO RESPOND

We would like to find out a little about your background and about your reactions to the Fifth Edition of *Educating Exceptional Children*. Your evaluation of the book will help us to meet the interests and needs of students in future editions. We invite you to share your reactions by completing the questionnaire below and returning it to: *College Marketing; Houghton Mifflin Company; One Beacon Street; Boston, MA 02108.*

1. How do you rate this textbook in the following areas?

	Excellent	*Good*	*Adequate*	*Poor*
a. Understandable style of writing	——	——	——	——
b. Physical appearance/ readability	——	——	——	——
c. Fair coverage of topics	——	——	——	——
d. Comprehensiveness (covered major issues and topics)	——	——	——	——
e. Organization of book around content, skills, and learning environment adaptations for each exceptionality	——	——	——	——
f. *Of Special Interest* boxed articles	——	——	——	——
g. Material on lifespan issues that go beyond the classroom	——	——	——	——
h. *Epilogue* as a real-life illustration of text discussions	——	——	——	——

2. Can you comment on or illustrate your above ratings? ————

————————————————————

————————————————————

————————————————————

3. What chapters or features did you particularly like? _____

_____

_____

_____

4. What chapters or features did you dislike or think should be changed? _____

_____

_____

5. What material would you suggest adding or deleting? _____

_____

_____

_____

6. What was the title of the course in which you used this book?

_____

_____

7. Are you an undergraduate student? _____ If so, what year? ___

_____

8. Are you a graduate student? _____ If so, have you taught before? _____

9. Have you taken any other courses in special education? If so, which courses? _____

_____

10. Will you be teaching in a regular classroom or in a special classroom? _____

11. Do you intend to keep this book for use during your teaching career? _____

12. Did you use the *Study Guide* that accompanies this textbook?
_____ Yes _____ No

13. We would appreciate any other comments or reactions you are willing to share. _____

_____

_____